Kierkegaard and Political Theology

Kierkegaard and Political Theology

EDITED BY
Roberto Sirvent
AND
Silas Morgan

FOREWORD BY
Gordon Marino

☙PICKWICK *Publications* • Eugene, Oregon

KIERKEGAARD AND POLITICAL THEOLOGY

Copyright © 2018 Wipf and Stock Publishers. All rights reserved. Except for brief quotations in critical publications or reviews, no part of this book may be reproduced in any manner without prior written permission from the publisher. Write: Permissions, Wipf and Stock Publishers, 199 W. 8th Ave., Suite 3, Eugene, OR 97401.

Pickwick Publications
An Imprint of Wipf and Stock Publishers
199 W. 8th Ave., Suite 3
Eugene, OR 97401

www.wipfandstock.com

PAPERBACK ISBN: 978-1-4982-2482-6
HARDCOVER ISBN: 978-1-4982-2484-0
EBOOK ISBN: 978-1-4982-2483-3

Cataloguing-in-Publication data:

Names: Sirvent, Roberto, editor. | Morgan, Silas, editor. | Marino, Gordon Daniel, 1952–, foreword.

Title: Kierkegaard and political theology / edited by Roberto Sirvent and Silas Morgan ; foreword by Gordon Marino.

Description: Eugene, OR : Pickwick Publications, 2018 | Includes bibliographical references.

Identifiers: ISBN 978-1-4982-2482-6 (paperback) | ISBN 978-1-4982-2484-0 (hardcover) | ISBN 978-1-4982-2483-3 (ebook)

Subjects: LCSH: Kierkegaard, Søren, 1813–1855. | Political theology.

Classification: B4377 .K54 2018 (print) | B4377 .K54 (ebook)

Manufactured in the U.S.A.   02/16/18

For Amy Laura Hall and Kyle Roberts,
who first taught us to read Kierkegaard

> The most one person can do for another is to unsettle him.
>
> —Søren Kierkegaard,
> *Concluding Unscientific Postscript*

> I believe in making a difference by thinking little thoughts and sharing them widely. I seek to provoke, annoy, bother, irritate, and amuse; I am chasing small projects, micropolitics, hunches, whims, fancies.
>
> —Jack Halberstam, *The Queer Art of Failure*

> And this way, which is Christ, this narrow way, as it goes on, becomes narrower and narrower to the end, to death.
>
> —Søren Kierkegaard, *For Self-Examination*

Contents

List of Contributors | xi
Foreword by Gordon Marino | xiii
Acknowledgments | xvi
List of Abbreviations | xvii
Introduction by Silas Morgan and Roberto Sirvent | xix

Part 1: Kierkegaard and Political Theology

1 Destitution of Sovereignty: The Political Theology of Søren Kierkegaard | 3
 —Saitya Brata Das

2 Kierkegaard and the Critique of Political Theology | 17
 —Anthony Rudd

3 Johannes Climacus and the Two Kierkegaards: Strategies for Theology and Social Engagement | 30
 —David Lappano

4 Politics as Indirect Communication in *The Moment* and the *Attack upon "Christendom"* | 43
 —Stephen Backhouse

Part 2: Kierkegaard and the Politics of Faith, Hope, and Love

5 Downward Bound: The Knight of Faith and the Politics of Grace | 65
 —Heather C. Ohaneson

6 Searching for a Secular God: A Prolegomena to a Political Theory of Love | 81
 —Jamie Aroosi

7 Equality: A Proposal Rooted in Kierkegaard's Theological Anthropology and Theology of Love | 94
—Natalia Marandiuc

8 Loving the Ones We See: Kierkegaard's Neighbor-Love and the Politics of Pluralism | 105
—Jennifer Elisa Veninga

9 Kierkegaard, Badiou, and Christian Hope | 127
—Vincent Lloyd

Part 3: Kierkegaard and the Politics of Philosophy

10 The Time Is Out of Joint: On Social Ontology and Criticism in Kierkegaard and Heidegger | 141
—James D. Reid and Rick Anthony Furtak

11 Kierkegaard's "Single Individual" and Hardt and Negri's "Multitude": Theological Resources for a Post-imperial Political Subjectivity | 163
—Silas Morgan and Kyle Roberts

12 Tagore and Kierkegaard as Resources for Political Theology | 180
—Abrahim H. Khan

13 Theater, Theology, and Empowerment: Kierkegaard and Boal | 198
—Helene Russell

14 Politicizing Kierkegaardian Repetition: On Schmitt and Kierkegaard | 213
—Dana Lloyd

15 Lost Expectations: On Derrida's Abraham | 226
—Mary-Jane Rubenstein

Part 4: Kierkegaard and the Politics of Theology

16 On Whose Authority? Søren Kierkegaard and Ada María Isasi-Díaz on Christian Truth-Witnessing | 247
—Mariana Alessandri

17 Politics of the Church, Hidden and Revealed, in Søren Kierkegaard and John Howard Yoder | 262
—Jason A. Mahn

18 How (Not) to Write a Kierkegaardian Political Theology: Between Niebuhr and Levinas on Anxiety, Faith, and Love | 274
—Howard Pickett

19 The Spotlight and the "Courage to Be an Absolute Nobody": Toward a Kierkegaardian-Chestertonian Political Theology of Ego | 288
—Roberto Sirvent and Duncan Reyburn

Part 5: Kierkegaard and the Politics of Communication

20 Kierkegaard's *Dagdriver*: Loafing as a Means of Resistance to the Technological, Media, and Consumer System | 307
—Bartholomew Ryan

21 Søren Kierkegaard, Indirect Communication, and the Strength of Weak Authority: A Reflection on Parliamentary Democracy | 327
—Burkhard Conrad, OPL

22 Sociological Categories and the Journey to Selfhood: From the Crowd to Community | 341
—Matthew D. Kirkpatrick

23 Kierkegaard and the Politics of Time | 358
—Kara N. Slade

Contributors

Editors

Roberto Sirvent, Associate Professor of Political and Social Ethics at Hope International University in Fullerton, CA, USA.

Silas Morgan, Hamline University, St. Paul, MN, USA.

Contributors
(in order of appearance)

Gordon Marino, Professor of Philosophy, Director of the Hong Kierkegaard Library at St. Olaf College, Northfield, MN, USA.

Saitya Brata Das, Assistant Professor at the Centre for English Studies, School of Language, Literature and Culture Studies at Jawaharlal Nehru University, India.

Anthony Rudd, Associate Professor of Philosophy, St. Olaf College, MN, USA.

David Lappano, Centre for Christian Studies, Winnipeg, Canada

Stephen Backhouse, Lecturer in Social and Political Theology, St Mellitus College, London, UK.

Heather C. Ohaneson, Assistant Professor of Philosophy and Religious Studies, Faculty Fellow in the William Penn Honors Program, George Fox University, USA.

Jamie Aroosi, Visiting Assistant Professor, Yeshiva University, New York, NY, USA.

Natalia Marandiuc, Assistant Professor of Christian Theology, Perkins School of Theology, Southern Methodist University, Dallas, TX, USA.

Jennifer Elisa Veninga, Associate Professor of Religious and Theological Studies at St. Edward's University in Austin, TX, USA.

Vincent Lloyd, Associate Professor of Theology and Religious Studies at Villanova University, Villanova, PA, USA.

CONTRIBUTORS

James D. Reid, Associate Professor of Philosophy, the Metropolitan State University of Denver, Colorado, USA.

Rick Anthony Furtak, Associate Professor of Philosophy at Colorado College, Colorado, USA.

Kyle Roberts, Schilling Professor of Public Theology and Church and Economic Life, United Theological Seminary of the Twin Cities, New Brighton, MN, USA.

Abrahim H. Khan, Professor in Faculty of Theology, Trinity College, University of Toronto, Toronto, CA.

Helene Russell, Associate Professor of Theology, Christian Theological Seminary, Indianapolis, IN, USA.

Dana Lloyd, Ph.D. candidate, the Department of Religion, Syracuse University, Syracuse, NY, USA.

Mary-Jane Rubenstein, Professor of Religion and Feminist, Gender and Sexuality Studies, Wesleyan University, Middletown, CT, USA.

Mariana Alessandri, Assistant Professor of Philosophy at the University of Texas Rio Grande Valley, Edinburg, Texas, USA.

Jason A. Mahn, Associate Professor of Religion and Director of the Presidential Center for Faith and Learning at Augustana College, Rock Island, IL, USA.

Howard Pickett, Assistant Professor of Ethics and Poverty Studies, and Director of the Shepherd Program for the Interdisciplinary Study of Poverty and Human Capability at Washington and Lee University, Lexington, VA, USA.

Duncan Reyburn, Senior Lecturer, Faculty of the Humanities, University of Pretoria, South Africa.

Bartholomew Ryan, Researcher and Coordinator of CultureLab, Nova Institute of Philosophy (IFILNOVA), New University of Lisbon, Portugal.

Burkhard Conrad, OPL, Diocesan Liaison Officer for Universities, University Chaplaincies, and Adult Education, Archdiocese of Hamburg, Hamburg, Germany.

Matthew D. Kirkpatrick, Lecturer in Ethics and Doctrine at Wycliffe Hall, University of Oxford, UK.

Kara N. Slade, Theologian in Residence and Associate Chaplain at the Episcopal Church in Princeton, Associate Rector for Formation, Trinity Parish, Princeton, NJ, USA.

Foreword

GORDON MARINO

I USED TO COMPLAIN that those of us who became enamored of Kierkegaard were wrongly inclined to try and find everything in him. Back then, I would even jab, why not a Kierkegaardian physics or economics or political theory? After all, there is little that Kierkegaard does not touch upon in his sprawling authorship. You can find almost everything and also almost anything you want in him. For me, it has always been a matter of where the accents fall and I think the major emphasis in his writings is clearly on the question of what it means to have faith.

Although he lived during a period of volcanic political upheaval, Kierkegaard was all but indifferent to the political sphere, and what he did have to say did not exactly invite a political theology. Recently, the Kierkegaard scholar Matías Tapia reminded me of a letter Kierkegaard wrote to his walking partner, Conferentsraad Kolderup-Rosenvinge. The letter was penned in August of 1848, the very year in which there was a peaceful transition to a constitutional monarchy in Denmark. Kierkegaard's friend complains that on a recent promenade they "did not get around to talking about politics." Kierkegaard responds:

> No, politics is not for me. To follow politics, even if only domestic politics, is now days an impossibility, for me, at any rate. Whenever anything happens very quickly—well, then one attempts to follow it; whenever anything goes very slowly—well then one attempts to put up with the boredom of following it. But whenever something fluctuates back and forth, up and down and down and up, and then comes to a halt, and around and up and down and back again, then I am incapable of voluntarily following.... That is why I keep away from politics.[1]

During the same month, in another missive to the Conferentsraad, Kierkegaard commented, "Any purely political movement ... is a vortex," a vortex that "cannot be

---

1. Kierkegaard, *Letters and Documents*, 253.

stopped except by religion."[2] Much of the turbulence that Kierkegaard slammed his window on, had to do with the struggle for equality. Clearly, Kierkegaard believed that there is only one true form of equality—equality before God. "But is it not then," asks Kierkegaard, "like an obsession, that worldliness has gotten the idea of wanting to force perfect equality, likeness and to force it in a worldly way. . . . Ultimately only the essentially religious can with the help of eternity effect human equality."[3]

For Kierkegaard, politics was basically synonymous with the theme of equality. As we know, the Danish firebrand was able to live very comfortably off of his large inheritance. He worked tirelessly, perhaps even to the point of death; but save for a very brief interval as a Latin instructor, he never had to bear the strain of having to work for someone else. Even though he recognizes and in his *Journals* wrestles with himself about the frisson between his understanding of a Christian existence and his highly privileged life, I have to confess that I have been inclined to hold his inborn wealth against him. Imagine, in his *Works of Love*, he offers the loving counsel that the poor and hungry should be merciful to the fat cats by not making them feel guilty at their feasts! Perhaps it is an instance of the causal fallacy, but it is no wonder our well-heeled magister did not experience any urgency about the necessity of implementing a more equal distribution of wealth, rights, and opportunities.

Those who pull faces and take offense at Kierkegaard's pietistic Christianity can try to secularize Kierkegaard to their hearts' content; nevertheless, it is clear that from near the beginning to the end of his life, he believed that the only truly decisive either/or was whether or not you were faithful to the Lord and the idea that you are a self, a spirit with an eternal element.

Maybe he was wrong. I suspect he was. It seems to me that circumstances can choke our spiritual breath. But on Kierkegaard's reckoning, neither your position in life nor the size of your bank account have anything to do with making the movements of faith. In that sense, Kierkegaard's "ho-hum" attitude toward the hubbub of politics seemed consistent to me and so I supposed that scouring Kierkegaard for his position on politics was akin to studying Karl Popper's works for his views on theology.

The wide, rich, and diverse chorus of voices herein orchestrated by Roberto Sirvent and Silas Morgan has, however, convinced me that I was mistaken. It is a proof positive that Kierkegaard had a political theology. After all, Kierkegaard certainly had it within him to critique the politics of the Danish State Lutheran Church. Why not political arrangements in general?

In the preface to the *Philosophical Fragments*, Johannes Climacus insists that he has no opinions. Still, the author behind that author certainly held opinions about what it means to be human and because we humans are relational creatures, there is a powerful warrant for pondering Kierkegaard's position, or, perhaps it would be better

---

2. Ibid., 262.
3. Kierkegaard, *Point of View*, 104.

to say, his "positions" on the kind of social and political structures that his anthropology enjoined.

In his *Point of View*, Kierkegaard points to the politician (for whom he seldom has a kind word) and bids him or her to be patient for, says Kierkegaard, "I am convinced that he, too, will become aware . . . that the religious is the transfigured rendition of what a politician, provided he actually loves being a human being and loves humankind has thought in his most blissful moments, even if he will find the religious too lofty and too ideal to be practical."[4] How exactly can the religious inform and infuse the political realm? And are those who see "the religious" as a null set, excluded from garnering any sociopolitical insights from Kierkegaard?

Or again, Kierkegaard expresses nothing but repugnance about political parties and movements. Dr. Martin Luther King Jr. read and took notes on Kierkegaard. But, how would Kierkegaard have responded to the civil rights movement that was born of American churches? My dissertation supervisor, Stephen Toulmin, used to instruct, "Abuse is no argument against use." Again and again, Kierkegaard reminds us that the tree shall be known by its fruits. Were the fascists who found substance in the fruits of Kierkegaard's authorship misreading him, or is there something in Kierkegaard that lent itself to such interpretations?

This collection responds to these questions and just about every other that might float to mind concerning the connection between Kierkegaard's Christianity and his views, implicit and otherwise, on the ideal sociopolitical structures.

Bibliography

Kierkegaard, Søren. *Letters and Documents*. Edited and translated by Henrich Rosenmeier. Princeton: Princeton University Press, 1978.

———. *The Point of View*. Edited and translated by Howard V. Hong and Edna H. Hong. Princeton: Princeton University Press, 1998.

4. Ibid., 103.

Acknowledgments

NO ONE WRITES A book alone. In this case it took twenty-nine people. It is our editorial privilege to thank a few of those who have been especially helpful in bringing this work to the surface. Together, we want to sincerely thank all our contributors to this volume for their careful work and collaborative spirit, but mostly for their patience. We both always knew we wanted to dedicate this volume in part to Amy Laura Hall at Duke Divinity School, whose kindness, patience, and care has taught us both more than how to read *Works of Love* or *Fear and Trembling*—though that, too. Roberto would like to thank Donna Potts and M. Craig Barnes at Princeton Theological Seminary, Gordon Marino at the Hong Kierkegaard Library at St. Olaf College, and Jon Stewart at the Søren Kierkegaard Research Center at the University of Copenhagen for being such generous hosts as he conducted research for this volume. He would also like to thank his wife, Krista, for being the best study partner anyone could ever ask for. Silas would like to thank Kyle Roberts at United Theological Seminary of the Twin Cities. First a teacher, then a mentor, and now a close friend, every page of this book was edited with their many testy conversations about Kierkegaard in mind. Memories of that first seminar on Kierkegaard and postmodern theology still ring fresh—and true. This volume is also dedicated to him in the hope that it leads to further disagreements. Kierkegaard was terribly unlucky in love, perhaps by choice and disillusioned stubbornness, but thankfully Silas has been more fortunate. He will be forever grateful for his little family.

Abbreviations

CA   *The Concept of Anxiety*. Edited and translated by Howard V. Hong and Reidar Thomte. Princeton: Princeton University Press, 1980.

CD   *Christian Discourses* and *The Crisis and a Crisis in the Life of an Actress*. Edited and translated by Howard V. Hong and Edna H. Hong. Princeton: Princeton University Press, 1997.

CUP *Concluding Unscientific Postscript to "Philosophical Fragments."* 2 vols. Edited and translated by Howard V. Hong and Edna H. Hong. Princeton: Princeton University Press, 1992.

EO1 *Either/Or*. Vol. 1. Edited and translated by Howard V. Hong and Edna H. Hong. Princeton: Princeton University Press, 1987.

EO2 *Either/Or*. Vol. 2. Edited and translated by Howard V. Hong and Edna H. Hong. Princeton: Princeton University Press, 1987.

EPW *Early Polemical Writings*. Translated by Julia Watkin. Princeton: Princeton University Press, 1990.

EUD *Eighteen Upbuilding Discourses*. Edited and translated by Howard V. Hong and Edna H. Hong. Princeton: Princeton University Press, 1990.

FSE *For Self-Examination* (published with *Judge for Yourself!*). Edited and translated by Howard V. Hong and Edna H. Hong. Princeton: Princeton University Press, 1990.

FT   *Fear and Trembling; Repetition*. Edited and translated by Howard V. Hong and Edna H. Hong. Princeton: Princeton University Press, 1983.

JFY *Judge for Yourself!* (published with *For Self-Examination*). Edited and translated by Howard V. Hong and Edna H. Hong. Princeton: Princeton University Press, 1990.

JP   *Søren Kierkegaard's Journals and Papers*. Edited and translated by Howard V. Hong and Edna H. Hong. Princeton: Princeton University Press, 1967–78.

ABBREVIATIONS

LD   *Letters and Documents*. Edited and translated by Henrich Rosenmeier. Princeton: Princeton University Press, 1979.

LR   *A Literary Review*. Translated by Alastair Hannay. London: Penguin, 2001.

Pap.   *Søren Kierkegaard's Papirer* [Søren Kierkegaard's papers]. 2nd ed. Edited by Niels Thulstrup. 16 vols., with index vols. 14–16 by Niels Jørgen Cappelørn. Copenhagen: Gyldendal, 1968–1978.

PC   *Practice in Christianity*. Edited and translated by Howard V. Hong and Edna H. Hong. Princeton: Princeton University Press, 1991.

PF   *Philosophical Fragments*. Edited and translated by Howard V. Hong and Edna H. Hong. Princeton: Princeton University Press, 1985.

POV   *The Point of View*. Edited and translated by Howard V. Hong and Edna H. Hong. Princeton: Princeton University Press, 2009.

SKS   Danish edition of the Collected Works of Kierkegaard (*Søren Kierkegaard Skrifter*). 28 vols.

SLW   *Stages on Life's Way*. Edited and translated by Howard V. Hong and Edna H. Hong. Princeton: Princeton University Press, 1988.

SUD   *The Sickness Unto Death*. Edited and translated by Howard V. Hong and Edna H. Hong. Princeton: Princeton University Press, 1988.

TA   *Two Ages: The Age of Revolution and the Present Age; A Literary Review*. Edited and translated by Howard V. Hong and Edna H. Hong. Princeton: Princeton University Press, 1978.

TDIO   *Three Discourses on Imagined Occasions*. Edited and translated by Howard V. Hong and Edna H. Hong. Princeton: Princeton University Press, 1993.

TM   *The Moment and Late Writings*. Edited and translated by Howard V. Hong and Edna H. Hong. Princeton: Princeton University Press, 1985.

UDVS   *Upbuilding Discourses in Various Spirits*. Edited and translated by Howard V. Hong and Edna H. Hong. Princeton: Princeton University Press, 2005.

WA   *Without Authority*. Edited and translated by Howard V. Hong and Edna H. Hong. Princeton: Princeton University Press, 1997.

WL   *Works of Love*. Edited and translated by Howard V. Hong and Edna H. Hong. Princeton: Princeton University Press, 1995.

Introduction

SILAS MORGAN AND
ROBERTO SIRVENT

AS ITS TITLE SUGGESTS, this book is about Søren Kierkegaard and political theology. With help from our collaborating authors, we have tried to bring the writings and ideas of Søren Kierkegaard into conversation with major trajectories of thought within contemporary political theology as they wrestle with questions of truth, human dignity, the future of democracy, the return of religion, sovereignty, resistance, and the politics of love—to name a few of the issues and questions confronting the growing (and diversifying) field.

Our primary objective in this volume is to convene a kind of symposium between Kierkegaard studies and contemporary political theology. All this sounds innocuous enough—standard boilerplate stuff. But what kind of engagement is this, exactly? Is this a dialogue or a confrontation? Usually, the dialogical metaphor denotes a pleasantry, a congenial encounter between a multiplicity of viewpoints or subjectivities, but one that ultimately moves toward mutual agreement, confluence, and the claiming of common ground. The goal, it seems, is to bring all parties and views to a new, progressive place, ostensibly drawn closer together as a result of the dialogue. Dialogues are different than arguments in that they are distinct from interventions or confrontations; they are more productive in that progress is made, the achieved objective is one of commonality and agreement—any chasm between them is closed, not open or reaffirmed. We will ultimately leave it to our readers to make the final judgment about what engagement these chapters provoke between Kierkegaard's writings and political theology today, but the product of this book is not a research agenda or a set of future questions, but rather a resetting of the questions about the use of Kierkegaard in our time: does Kierkegaard resonate with current political struggle and the ongoing debate about the role of religion and theology in that work?

The volume developed out of a paper session on Kierkegaard and political theology at the annual meeting of the Pacific Division of the American Philosophical Association in Vancouver in April 2013. The papers and responses presented during the session became the seed for what this project is now and the result is certainly far from straightforward. Indeed, the volume before you does not speak with one voice and certainly cannot be used to set in place a cohesive set of principles or ideas that characterize the current place that Kierkegaard has in political theology—or should have in the future of the discipline.

This is the case for at least three major reasons. First, there are still well-established fault lines in Kierkegaard studies that have been in place since the beginning of the Anglophone reception and they have yet to be resolved in a meaningful way. These fault lines correspond in complicated ways to disagreements in political theology today, especially in terms of what is meant by the term and what one thinks one is doing when one is doing political theology. Second, the very nature of the Kierkegaardian authorships (the pseudonymous nature of parts of the authorship, the contested character of the religious writings—the "edifying discourses" and the second authorship—the strategy of "indirect communication," and the slipperiness of his irony) resists any kind of systemic reading or reception. Anything that can be said about Kierkegaard requires at least ten qualifications (if not a thousand!), meaning that all his ideas resist being *used* in any way—even if they are nevertheless quite useful. Often, the most one can confidently say about Kierkegaard is that he *seems* to say *this* in *that* text in *this* context. This makes any application of Kierkegaard's theology or philosophy in our context (much less understanding how it functioned in its own) quite difficult and prone to error. Finally, the reception of Kierkegaard in the English-speaking academy gives us reason to pause out of concern for the dangers of "appropriation," itself an often-misunderstood Kierkegaardian theme. History tells us that there has often been quite a bit of daylight between Kierkegaard's original intentions and the Kierkegaardian spirit which gets taken up into various and differing systems and sorts of thinking. Only with the benefit of history are we able to see afterward that such systems and sorts do strange injustice to the works and words of the man himself—and the irony of his authorial intent (if we can even speak of such a thing in an ordered and structured way).

Take for example the influence that Kierkegaard had on major European intellectuals of National Socialism—Martin Heidegger and Carl Schmitt, mostly notably. The use of Kierkegaard's work for fascist and authoritarian ideas is a dark part of the history of his reception in Europe, and casts a long shadow over any attempt to read Kierkegaard politically in our own time. Bartholomew Ryan has argued that the world as it is now—full once again of authoritarian claims to racial supremacy and ethno-nationalist fervor—makes it all the more important that we name the role that Kierkegaard played in the work of Nazi thinkers.[5] Ryan contends that while it is important to name this influence and understand its provenance, it is equally important to contest the readings themselves. Neither the influence nor the readings can be completely discounted and so the resultant irreducible tension between them remains.[6]

5. Ryan, *Indirect Politics*, xx–xxi.
6. Ibid.

INTRODUCTION

One need not choose between overlooking this influence or abandoning Kierkegaard because of it. Refusing this false choice illustrates well what we think it means to read Kierkegaard and political theology together—namely, that it is a matter of immanent critique, of a formally negative hermeneutics whereby the detection of contradictions and gaps between Kierkegaard and political theology are precisely the mechanism through which they can and should be thought together productively; that is, whether they are able to suggest possibilities for human freedom and happiness.

The Book in Its Context

In *The Point of View*, Kierkegaard moaned: "In these times everything is politics."[7] This book and its chapters came together amid extraordinary global political challenges. Civil wars, religious violence, economic inequality, disaster capitalism, food scarcity, the rise of right-wing authoritarian governments, rising temperatures (and the resultant melting ice caps) are but a few of the social and political struggles we must urgently confront as a global community. Indeed, the high stakes here have led to many important social and intellectual shifts, most notably within academic and culture circles, the return of religion, or as some prefer, its new visibility. This concerns not only the power of religion in the public sphere, but also its role in official political decision-making. Some consider this an affront to "the Great Separation" afforded by secularism and required by liberal democracy (Mark Lilla), while others recognize that a post-secular society acknowledges that religion continues to matter in the lived experience of people and as such, shapes their practical reasoning. An auxiliary effect of the resurgence of interest in religion has been a reassessment of political theology, albeit understood in very different ways.

Søren Kierkegaard is an odd person to turn to in such a context. Kierkegaard himself made it quite clear how little interest he had in politics, no matter how one might parse such a project. In numerous places and contexts (as many of our authors rightly point out), Kierkegaard sets up numerous roadblocks to anything like a political theology, which he assumed could only result in the alliances inherent to the "cultured Christianity" of the Danish state church. He rejected the political (and politics), insisted on the priority of singularity over the collective, conflated politics with the state and roundly rejects them both. Kierkegaard seems ill-suited to the task we gave to ourselves and our authors.

Furthermore, there are a set of presuppositions about Kierkegaard's work which are well-fixed in time and that, if true, certainly justify the long-held view that one cannot wring a political project out of Kierkegaard, most certainly not one connected to his theological views or religious writings. He infamously rejected the political, and his penchant for radical singularity and distaste for the public sphere, the "crowd,"

---

7. Kierkegaard, *Point of View*, 104.

left his ideas empty of useable concepts or insights for sociopolitical struggles. He has long been dismissed by political philosophers and critical theorists for his radical individualist sensibilities and his fideistic religious positions, both of which leave Kierkegaard disconnected from social reality, and susceptible to readings friendly to authoritarian and totalitarian politics. Examples abound, but most notable is Theodor Adorno's *Kierkegaard: Konstruktion des Ästhetischen* (published in 1933 in German, 1989 in English). While rejecting Kierkegaard in part because his sideways association with Nazis and other proto-fascist writers, Adorno's political goal is to reach intellectuals in Germany at the dawn of Hitler's regime who were still opposed to the emerging fascist Nazi state. Marcia Morgan argues that this internal burden leads Adorno to misread Kierkegaard: "His claims have less to do with Kierkegaard than with a desire to read something else into and against Kierkegaard."[8] Morgan makes the case that there is more to Kierkegaard than Adorno thought, and this is borne out in later generations of critical theory who find him helpful for the politics of a post-nationalist and post-secular society.[9]

The other presupposition with which this book wrestles is that Kierkegaard was a religious author and specifically a Christian theologian with traditional ideas about the nature of God, the human person, salvation, and "life after death." Steven Shakespeare recently challenged this by charting out the two stories told about Kierkegaard, arguing that the first story overlooks the centrality of paradox and contradiction in Kierkegaard's writings and method of communication. The first story Shakespeare tells is that Kierkegaard is often "enlisted to serve an existentially inflected Christian orthodoxy."[10] What appears at first to be a deliberate set of techniques and strategies meant to excoriate Christianity—irony, direct communication, apophasis—are merely devices through which to inject Christianity back into the aesthetic and ethical culture of Danish Christendom—an authentic social "faith" based more on convention and habit than conviction and decision.[11] What is left is a traditional Lutheran Christianity, based on confessional accounts of biblical writings, all of which present and protect doctrinal formulations of divine transcendence, the objectivity of the risen Christ, and the role of faith in overcoming the limits of human reason. The theological Kierkegaard takes on various positions against immanence, paradox, and the like, positioning itself with orthodox Christianity in ways that resist many of the sensibilities inherent to political theologies.

The "second story" (as told by Shakespeare) is that Kierkegaard's concept of God comes out of his analysis of abyss and despair as the conditions that shape human existence. Human freedom and authenticity are possible only after such conditions are dialectically overcome and are borne out of "relating absolutely to the absolute."

8. Morgan, *Kierkegaard and Critical Theory*, 20.
9. Ibid., 65–94.
10. Shakespeare, *Kierkegaard and the Refusal of Transcendence*, 1.
11. Ibid., 2.

Michael O'Neill Burns turns to David Wood and others to make the point that God is not a thing that the subject believes in, an object of faith, but rather is identified *by religion* as the infinite potency of human freedom itself when that freedom is lived out in the liminal spaces of paradox.[12] This redirects Kierkegaard away from the traditional religious conception of God as transcendent being that belongs more to ontology than to politics, and toward an understanding of God as an ethics of immanence: "the possibility of creating a variety of different realities in our own world."[13]

As we have gathered and put these chapters together, we have often asked ourselves (and each other): how does this book take on these presuppositions? Does it challenge or reinforce them? While we will leave the final judgment to the reader, the book raises hard questions about Kierkegaard's usefulness—whether he fits well into this time and this place. Why not let Søren be as the Melancholy Dane of the nineteenth century? Why not let him be that of which he seemed quite fond: negative, apolitical, inscrutable, and unusable? Why do we keep dragging him back into our crazy little business, trying to get him to speak to contexts and matters about which he could not fathom in his time?

Kierkegaard may not have cared much for politics and may not have been a Christian theologian. But he also did not think highly of readers who always thought they knew exactly what he was saying and what he meant by it. Maybe he was a Christian (the good sort). Maybe he wasn't. The dialectics in the authorship(s) make both claims certainly plausible—and we hope this book adds to the debate. But our editorial hand has been guided by the belief that the enduring productivity of Kierkegaard's thought is generated in the liminal space between these arguments, and so celebrate the fact that our authors represent the diversity of views on the subject. The book does not speak with one voice on these matters. The cumulative effect of the book, however, does solicit something of a dramatic choice—a passionate decision about how best to understand what Kierkegaard means for our time—and if he means anything at all for political theology today.

The Book's Chapters

This project understands "political theology" as a multivalent term that addresses a number of varying and differing projects, disciplines, and agendas. The spaces between these understandings leads to an instability or at worst, an aporia that may be less of a bug and more of a feature in terms of understanding the role of Kierkegaard's work in these discourses. We subdivided the book into five parts that all feature analysis of the relationship of Kierkegaard to political theology, understood in various ways. We leave it to the authors to make themselves—and their understanding of political theology—clear.

12. O'Neill Burns, *Kierkegaard and the Matter of the Philosophy*, 103.
13. Ibid.

INTRODUCTION

Part 1

Part 1, "Kierkegaard and Political Theology," features incisive chapters that are both broad and deep and set the stage for what is to come. Saitya Brata Das takes us back to the dubious beginnings of contemporary political theology—Carl Schmitt and the exceptional decision—and argues that Kierkegaard's Christian passion incubates an exceptional reasoning that brings the end of sovereignty. Anthony Rudd insists that if political theology is a project in which the content of theology is converted into political ideas through a process that summarily suspends all essential normative claims about God, the human, or the good, Kierkegaard would have nothing to do with it. Misreadings of the teleological suspension of ethics as a kind of "decisionism" occur because they fail to see that for Kierkegaard, faith (for example, as laid out in *Fear and Trembling*) is a thoroughly religious concept. However, lest we forget that there is no single voice in Kierkegaard, David Lappano offers a sketch of three approaches to social engagement within "Kierkegaard's" authorship that range from Climacus's admonition to listen to others and the late Kierkegaard's direct activism and disobedience to state power in the "attack" writings in 1855. Stephen Backhouse directly links the political in Kierkegaard with the attack on Christendom in his late writings, which Backhouse sees as emblematic of the "indirect communication" of his earlier writings. Rather than an aberration from his earlier allergy to the political, Kierkegaard's attack illustrates what "indirect communication" was about the whole time.

Part 2

Much of the political-theologically relevant material in Kierkegaard's work itself lies in his analysis of faith and subjectivity, shaped by his Christian ethics of love. Part 2, "Kierkegaard and the Politics of Faith, Hope, and Love," explores these ideas in conversation with major theological voices and philosophical movements over the last century, including Alain Badiou, Jürgen Habermas, Emmanuel Levinas, and others. Heather Ohaneson links the politics of faith in *Fear and Trembling* to theories of dance that see rhythm as a political mode of graceful resistance. In their respective chapters, Jamie Aroosi and Jennifer Elisa Veninga speak to constructive opportunities in Kierkegaard to help political thought recapture the power of love in the context of pluralism and systemic oppression.

Kierkegaard's theory of Christian love is often seen as opposed to the preferences inherent to poetic love. While it is common to read Kierkegaard as saying that neighbor-love calls the subject to suspend desire, inclination, and attachment in lieu of the higher demand of universal love, Natalia Marandiuc argues that neighbor love is "a ground which holds firm the root of preferential loves," and as such, Kierkegaard does not disregard particular attachments in route to neighbor-love. Neighbor-love is the political-theological mechanism through which those attachments and inclinations write equality into structural practices of recognition whereby the particularity of persons and groups is essential to democratic solidarity.

With all the focus on faith and love in Kierkegaard, Vincent Lloyd redirects our attention to hope's political relevance. Lloyd charts the fertile relationship between despair and hope; it is not that hope leads us out of despair, but rather teaches how to despair more skillfully.

Part 3

Political theology is not solely a theological matter—in fact much of political theology today is a feature of the "return of religion" to philosophy—or as some prefer, its "new visibility." Part 3, "Kierkegaard and the Politics of Philosophy," explores the intersections and tension between Kierkegaard and philosophical voices in political theology today. Kierkegaard and Heidegger are brought closer together by James D. Reid and Rick Anthony Furtak's essay on social ontology, where they are shown to have common cause on the issue of whether philosophy ought to carry out "temporally specific" social criticism. One such example of this may be evinced by how Silas Morgan and Kyle Roberts reinterpret Kierkegaard's single individual in light of Michael Hardt and Antonio Negri's postmodern Empire, and so calls upon the revolutionary potential of the multitude in contradistinction to the Crowd or the People. Singularity is read as a multitudinal state of existence, a concretized way of being that is about intensity, not "individuation." Abrahim Khan offers a compelling piece about Rabindranath Tagore, a poet and social reformer in colonial India. He argues that both writers offer warnings about the dangerous alliances formed between modern liberal democracies and religious ideas in this post-secular age, particularly in relation to the social character of the moral self in relation to the nation-state.

The rise of protest and resistance politics—not only in the United States but around the world—has led to an interest in thinking of performance as a helpful metaphor for why public political acts of dissent work—and how they can be made more effective. Augusto Boal's liberation philosophy of the theatre decentralizes power and responsibility in political spaces, and this, Helene Russell notes, resonates with Kierkegaard's critique of ecclesial authority. Russell highlights the latter's resourcefulness for rethinking Christian worship as a theatrical exercise or social justice meeting.

Many of the writers in this volume have identified "sovereignty" as a theme that ties otherwise disparate political-theological discourses together. This reflects the multiple ways that political theology must—in one way or another—go through Carl Schmitt, for whom "sovereignty" was the paradigmatic illustration of his infamous thesis that "all significant concepts of the modern theory of the state are secularized theological concepts."[14] Dana Lloyd treats sovereignty both in Schmitt and Kierkegaard

---

14. Schmitt, *Political Theology*, 36.

as an element of the self, constituted in and through repetition. Kierkegaard was convinced that the political was ineffectual because it lacked the stability of passionate decision for the truth inherent to religious belief. *Repetition* ontologized that pattern, which explains why Kierkegaard was so attractive to Schmitt and his theory of the political as exceptional reasoning.

Mary-Jane Rubenstein celebrates Jacques Derrida's "faithful betrayal" of de Silentio's *Fear and Trembling*, but not for the reasons one might think. Taking exception to the trendy postmodern readings of the last decades, she insists that Derrida's faith in the justice-to-come cannot be thought of as a politics because it cannot be thought of at all. It exists only as a specter of a still and chastened hopelessness in the impossible—the "otherwise" that will never come.

Part 4

Whatever else it may be, political theology is most certainly an analysis of the politics inherent to theological claims made by religious traditions about God, the human being, and their relation within the social world. For Kierkegaard, this relationship was fraught with crisis and danger—it was too easy for the social world to see itself in God, to tell its own heroic story in ways that ignore the more material anxieties that make our existence properly *human*. A troublemaking writer who often flirted with being a churchman, had it not been for the Corsair affair and his seemingly endless list of rivalries with leading church officials, Kierkegaard would likely have retreated to a country church to live out his days in the banality of the Christian ministry in rural Denmark. Essays from Mariana Alessandri and Jason A. Mahn, respectively, clarify Kierkegaard's relationship to the politics of the church—and how that politics shaped important theological voices in the last century, including Reinhold Niebuhr and John Howard Yoder.

Howard Pickett charts a course between Levinas and Niebuhr on the question of the relationship between love and justice. Kierkegaard politicizes anxiety through faith; when the subject is called upon to redress one's anxiety through an absolute relation to God, it is dialectically reshaped into a "revolutionary love" for others that cannot escape its own demand to be political. Roberto Sirvent and Duncan Reyburn celebrate Kierkegaard's penchant for despair and anxiety because it offers a critique of ego in a time when so much of our social relations are full-scale marketing and branding strategies. It is not just our relationships but also our identities that are for sale, and Sirvent and Reyburn sense an opportunity—with the help of G. K. Chesterton—to give up both hero narratives and spotlights in favor of the nobodies. The giving up of the ego is illustrated in Kierkegaard's narrative theology of the incarnation where God hides Godself, and thus gives human persons the freedom to choose God for themselves out of their own desire, not as a result of being overwhelmed by the shock and awe of divine power.

INTRODUCTION

Part 5

One of the problems in Kierkegaard studies has always been that there are many Kierkegaards, one for each differing reader. If Kierkegaard is really interested in communicating, why is he so hard to understand? What are the implications for the dynamics between resistance and authority, selfhood and the crowd, time and death that haunt the political-theological hyphen? This book ends where it began—the politics of communication. The most programmatic part of the book, part 5, "Kierkegaard and the Politics of Communication," carefully parses out the political-theological valences of this theory, essentially arguing that communication is a problem for political theology, namely that it makes it a problem for human existence, it unsettles it, knocks it out of orbit, which of course would be music to Kierkegaard's ears.

In a world marked by the culture industry of speed, purpose, and efficiency, Bartholomew Ryan celebrates Kierkegaard's loafer (*Dagdriver*) as a model of resistance. Burkhard Conrad, OPL, examines the link between parliamentary democracy and indirect communication, arguing that the latter helps commend the former as an exemplary model for large-scale collective decision-making. Arguments about Kierkegaard's complicated relationship to the political usually revolve around his preference for the radical singularity over the "crowd." But Matthew D. Kirkpatrick makes the point that Kierkegaard's perspective on the community differs from that of the crowd or the people, and while not a religious idea, it stymies all-too-quick accounts of Kierkegaard as an antisocial individualist. For Kara N. Slade, communication is a political maneuver because it is about time, or rather, it is about how time is arranged to give or deny meaning to certain human experiences. We cannot escape time, but for Slade, Kierkegaard helps explains how and why the figure of Jesus exchanges time for contemporaneity, repositioning all of us as responsible for the other.

Bibliography

Kierkegaard, Søren. *The Point of View*. Translated by Howard V. Hong and Edna H. Hong. Princeton: Princeton University Press, 1998.

Morgan, Marcia. *Kierkegaard and Critical Theory*. Lanham, MD.: Lexington, 2012.

O'Neill Burns, Michael. *Kierkegaard and the Matter of the Philosophy: A Fractured Dialectic*. Lanham, MD.: Rowman and Littlefield, 2015.

Ryan, Bartholomew. *Kierkegaard's Indirect Politics: Interludes with Lukacs, Schmitt, Benjamin and Adorno*. New York: Rodopi, 2014.

Schmitt, Carl. *Political Theology: Four Chapters on the Concept of Sovereignty*. Translated by George Schwab. Chicago: University of Chicago Press, 2005.

Shakespeare, Steven. *Kierkegaard and the Refusal of Transcendence*. New York: Palgrave Macmillan, 2015.

PART 1

Kierkegaard and Political Theology

1

Destitution of Sovereignty

The Political Theology of Søren Kierkegaard

SAITYA BRATA DAS

And at midnight there was a cry made.

—MATTHEW 25:6

The Event

IN HIS 1922 *POLITICAL Theology*, Carl Schmitt famously says:

> A Protestant theologian who demonstrated the vital intensity possible in theological reflection in the nineteenth century stated: "the exception explains the general and itself. And if one wants to study the general correctly, one only needs to look around for a true exception. It reveals everything more clearly than does the general. If they cannot be explained, then the general also cannot be explained. The difficulty is usually not noticed because the general is not thought with passion but with a comfortable superficiality. The exception, on the other hand, thinks the general with intense passion.[1]

The citation is from a text entitled *Repetition*. At stake here is the question of "the event": Schmitt is here thinking, with the help of the Protestant thinker called Søren Kierkegaard (who is the thinker of the event par excellence), the event of "the political" which in its verbal resonance rests on the exceptionality of "a decision and not on a norm."[2] What Schmitt here thinks as "the political" is the advent, apocalyptic in its resonance, which is inaccessible to and unattainable in the purely constituted order of the normative. It is as though, for the event to be possible, the constituted-normative order must be suspended: the event, then, cannot be said to belong to the positive order

---

1. Schmitt, *Political Theology*, 15.
2. Ibid., 10.

of the norm, for the intensity of the event is each time exceptional to what is given and normatively valid. The exceptional decision, taken at the limit of all situations (it is verbal, since "all law is 'situational law'"), the event is, for Schmitt, each time irreducible to "the everyday frame of life":[3] this is so because the "homogenous medium," like this "everyday frame of mind," "must exist" in order for the norm to be applicable at all. This normative state of affairs (the idea that there is no space, within the concrete order of the state, which is not occupied by the law) does not explain the event of the political itself (that is, the possibility of decision and the possibility of the norm itself); it does not explain the agonal *topos* where the decision between enmity and friendship may erupt, the intensity of which alone accounts the very possibility of the political. The passion for the exception and the intensity of decision that *break through* the immanent-normative order (which is "the general"): it is this passion and intensity that is, according to Schmitt's own claims, supposed to bring the apocalyptic Kierkegaard in proximity to his own "political theology." By citing Kierkegaard here, Schmitt claims that even for the "Protestant" thinker (why Schmitt mentions Kierkegaard as "Protestant" is revealing as well as concealing), as much as for himself, this "passion" or "intensity" would essentially be the theological (Kierkegaard would rather say "religious") passion (thus passion par excellence): it interrupts and tears *apart* the fabric of the normative constitution of existence, opening the constituted order to certain transcendence (to the absolutely heterogeneous, that which is radically asymmetrical to the "homogeneous medium" of the "everyday frame of life"). The event is the opening up of the abyss of a dissymmetry that cannot be understood on the basis of the positivistic totality of the already existing norm. The "theological" here for Schmitt has an institutional history: it has a history of institutions (that Schmitt would then go on to display), for what—at the last moment—interests Schmitt is none other than the "institutional" possibility of *nomos* through exception and by exception.

It is true that what Kierkegaard would call "faith" is indeed this exposing of ourselves to the event *breaking through* the immanent regime of the law: the event suspends the closure of immanence by tearing it from normative validity and opening it to the incalculability of decision with "utmost passion." But, precisely for that matter—and this is important—the event refuses to be embodied in "history" (of institutions): the absolute event of Christ dying on the cross, which alone opens up the *eschaton* to come, is a wholly otherwise event; it cannot be understood as the historical event in the name of which "the *nomos* of the earth" can seek legitimacy. To understand this, it will be necessary for us to understand Kierkegaard's decisive eschatological critique of historical Reason.

For Søren Kierkegaard, the Hegelian pantheistic immanent metaphysics of history—which is the most consummate form of "theodicy" in Occidental metaphysics—cannot address the question of faith whose *distance* or *heterogeneity* (dissymmetry or disjunction) is essentially nourished by that absolutely singular, exceptional and

3. Ibid., 13.

decisive event of Christ's humiliation on the cross. Kierkegaard's eschatological passion, then, lies in this self-given task that seeks to release the singularity of decision and of the exceptional event of opening to "the wholly other" (which is essentially tied up with "religion," namely, "Christianity") that Hegel attempts to subsume under the "general" or "the universal" (totality) by a dialectical "cunning of reason" through "mediation."[4] One can, thus, say that Hegel's theodicy of history is none other than "the nomothetic operation"[5] at the service of worldly sovereignties. Kierkegaard names the worldly kingdom (*saeculum*), whose legitimacy rests in eliciting from us "normative obligations"[6] from a theological foundation (which nevertheless it liquidifies), as "Christendom": when Christianity is seduced by history, it becomes "Christendom." It thereby forgets completely (there is no more "Christian" left in Christianity) the true Christian *passion*, that is, to be *contemporaneous* to that absolute event of divine foolishness, to that absolute event of *kenosis*. What, then, becomes obscure to Christendom is this paradox: how *kenosis* is inseparable from the event of the Lord's glory: God dying the most ignoble death on the cross, the event in relation to which the eighteen hundred years of "Christendom" appears as a history of tragic betrayal. By forcibly separating these two moments (Christ's humiliation [*kenosis*] and his exaltation [glory])—this is the metaphysical violence of Christendom—and by merely taking up the moment of glory as the only Christian example, Christendom has obfuscated the decisive event of Christianity on the stage of history, the decisive event being that of bringing about (or at least bringing about an anticipation of) a conflagration (of what the Origenist eschatology calls *Apokatastasis*) that is paradoxical to the utmost degree, for it consists of bearing the unbearable experience of suffering unto death and thereby the opening of that chasm or the abyss, of that radical heterogeneity in respect to any worldly sovereignty in the profane order. Christendom has not only violently substituted—by a force or power alien to its original eschatological spirit—the event *Kenosis* with glory, but what is even worse, it has further substituted glory of the Lord with worldly pomp and splendor, repressing thereby the abyss that the event invokes: "abyssus abyssum invocat" (Ps 42:7).

This is, then, what "the event" is for Kierkegaard: "abyssus abyssum invocat," exemplified only in one individual, who himself is paradoxical to the utmost, who has appeared only once on the stage of history to undo "the truth of the world" ("I am the truth": John 14:6)[7] and un-figures the *figura*[8] of the world: *the event of truth (this is the truth of the event: that is, dying on the cross) invokes the abyss, for it undoes* the truth of the world ("scandal for the Jews and foolishness for the Gentiles": 1 Cor 1:23) and *un-figures* the sovereign figures who rule, not by *pistis* but by *nomos*. But

---

4. Kierkegaard, *Concept of Dread*, 9–21.
5. Schürmann, *Broken Hegemonies*, 11.
6. Ibid.
7. See Henry, *I Am the Truth*.
8. Balthasar, *Glory of the Lord*, 619–27.

the truth, the event of truth that alone is *pneumatic*, the glorious truth of exception, is the absolute paradox, for it is inaccessible and invisible to the glories of the world, for the truth of this glory is at the same time none other than the eternal passing away of all worldly glories.

Such event, then, eschatologically burns the existence of the Christian in his inwardness and it still burns, after eighteen hundred years, in Kierkegaard's very existence ("whose very existence interests him infinitely"): for here is involved an existential faith, since faith by definition has to be *existential*. Faith is, then, worklessness: it is the impossible, impossible because of its absolute *distance* from all possibility or capacity; impossible because its inwardness is more radically exterior than any exteriority; impossible because of its absolute *heterogeneity* in relation to any *potentia* that emanates from a sovereign *auctoritus*. Here existence must be understood, if one goes with Kierkegaard, as an infinite *ex-sistence*, that is, existence being set *apart* (for faith means "setting apart" or being "set apart" from "the foundation of the world") from the worldly being, even though that mode of being may be aesthetically pleasing or ethically ennobling: "Beware of those who go about in long robes" (Luke 20:46). Kierkegaard, being neither a preacher nor an apostle, is without authority: he is this *ex-sistence* as an open wound, torn open by faith to the transcendence without *potentia*. Existence, then, can never be thought on the basis of the force of the law or by the sovereign power of the worldly *nomos*. Only *existentially* may Kierkegaard still hope (for hope is without *auctoritus*), by virtue of having to bear, in the inwardness of passion, a messianic abyss, to be contemporaneous with the one whose manifestation on the stage of history means, paradoxically, to be *incognito* to all those who are on this earth. Almost in one-sided manner, Kierkegaard intensifies the moment of the absolute abandonment ("My God, My God, why hast thou abandoned me?": Matt 27:46), of absolute poverty over against the splendor of the worldly glory in order to reintroduce the spirit of that absolute event which has been done away by the eighteen-centuries-old Christendom: "the measuring rod of the unconditional" is *the* paradox, for it is the immeasurable itself, that is, an unconditional sacrifice."[9] Here the religious passion is so radically heterogeneous[10] to all worldly *potentia* that it can only be a scandal, a "danger" or an "offence" that sets the world on fire: "Christianity is incendiarism, Christ himself say, 'I am come to set fire on the earth' and it is already burning, yea, and it is doubtless becoming a

---

9. Kierkegaard, *Training in Christianity*, 55.

10. Kierkegaard, *Attack upon "Christendom,"* 11: "The term 'witness to the truth' stands in relation to the fact that Christianity is heterogeneous to this world, by renunciation, by suffering, and this is the reason why such a mode of being is of so little capable of being something else at the same time. But to want to have all worldly goods and advantages (the witness to the truth being what he is precisely by renunciation and suffering), and then at the same time to be a witness to the truth—one might Christianly say, 'the dance of a witness that is! Such a witness to the truth is not merely a monster but an impossibility, like a bird which is at the same time a fish, or like an iron tool which has the remarkable peculiarity of being made of wood.'"

consuming conflagration, best likened to a forest fire, for it is 'Christendom' that is set on fire."[11] The faith anticipates the arrival of the holy conflagration (the conflagration of the holy), that is—as Taubes describes it:

> separation (*Aussonderung*) and setting apart (*Absonderung*); being holy means being apart. The holy is the terror that shakes the foundations of the world. The shock caused by the holy bursts asunder the foundations of the world for salvation [das *Heil*]. It is the holy that passes judgment in the court of history. History exists only when truth is separated from error, when truth is illuminated from mystery. History is elucidated from the mystery of error to the revelation of truth.[12]

Is the event that Schmitt is concerned with the same as this arrival of the holy, the latter being that event (as it is for Kierkegaard) which delegitimates ("sets fire on the earth") any political theology that justifies the rule of sovereign power by constitutional (a mere human book of the law, which is to be distinguished from the divine commandment) means (while worldly *nomos* is a "means and end" relation, commandment is that where this is annulled), even though it implies suspending the normative order guaranteed by the constitution? Is the (Schmittean) "paradox" here (suspending the constitutional order of worldly *nomos* in order to reinstitute the sovereign figure precisely by constitutional means [Article 48 of Weimer Republic]) the same as the Kierkegaardian *paradox* of faith that affirms the unthinkable and incalculable event of the "monstrous copulation"[13] (as the tragic Hölderlin affirms in his own way), this joining together of the divine and mortal (in Christ) that *sets apart* the true exception (that never becomes rule in turn) from worldly hegemonies anchored on the nomothetic figure of the sovereign? Here is an impossible affirmation, affirmed eschatologically (that is, as the judgment upon history and not merely a historical judgment), affirmation of an unthinkable and incalculable *distance* (that "yawning abyss," that vertigo of thought) that uncouples in advance ("always already") any possible "analogia entis" between the *eschatological event* (which is a secret, a monstration, radically invisible in the light of world-historical politics) of conflagration ("I am come to set fire on the earth") and world-hegemonies on the immanent plane of profane history. It is as though Kierkegaardian eschatological faith must, in advance and monstrously (a "scandal," a "danger," a "thorn in the flesh"), undo any political-theological justification of a political situation: for what is earthly is the order of utter transiency which, as such, must pass away in the blazing landscape of apocalypse; for the divine affirms the world only by throwing an immense question mark, an absolute No to the world; for it is an affirmation from which the

---

11. Ibid., 41.
12. Taubes, *Occidental Eschatology*, 194.
13. Hölderlin, "Becoming in Dissolution," 96–100. Elsewhere he writes: "King Oedipus has an eye many perhaps.... Life is death and death is a kind of life." Hölderlin, *Poems and Fragments*, 604–5.

eschatological judgment is immediately tied up, for it is not a mere dialectical, that means, a "mediated" affirmation (an affirmation is not affirmation if it has to be "mediated": therefore Hegel's philosophy is only negative philosophy, a conceptual maneuvering); for the divine refuses "at any price [to] be a kingdom of this world; on the contrary, it would be that the Christian might venture life and blood to prevent it from becoming a kingdom of this world."[14]

Therefore, the state, and for that matter, the visible church, cannot be the "figure of the absolute," unlike what Hegel saw in the dialectical mirror of the concept: the true measure of the unconditional, which is the immeasurable, is such that it does not figure itself into the kingdom of the worldly, for Christianity is essentially a "polemical concept."[15] Christianity is *stasis* or "militant" or an infinite "opposition" against powers of the world. This is the Kierkegaardian either/or: "only either/or is the embrace which grasps the unconditional."[16] But here the either/or, where what is to be opposed (the enemy) is not dialectically mediated, is not a political concept. It is inaccessible to the Schmittean friend/enemy "either/or" of the worldly hegemonic regimes which are founded upon the power of earthly *nomos*. Rather as the purely Christian event, it has only a religious meaning, which is the meaning of *covenant* held fast in the language of love: "the terrible language of the Law is so terrifying because it seems as if it were left to man to hold fast to Christ by his own power, whereas in the language of love it is Christ that holds him fast."[17] Who can miss here the Pauline messianic paradox of faith? As soon as this opposition is taken away[18] and the thorn in the flesh is taken out, only then do we all become "Christians" in "Christendom" and the absolute becomes dialectically embodied in the figure of the state. The intensification of the political passion with which sovereign powers of worldly hegemonies may decide on the "friend-enemy" either/or is not the Kierkegaardian existential passion of either/or: "All religion has to do with passion, with having passion. It will be true therefore of every religion, especially in ages of rationalism or common sense, that it has only very few adherents."[19] This demands a radical separation, pursued with the most intense passion, which the seriousness of the event of religion itself demands from us:

> It is necessary to practice separation, discrimination, between the infinite and the finite, between a striving for the infinite and for the finite, between living for something and living by something, which our age—most indecently!—has put together in the closet, got them to curdle together or coalesce into one, which Christianity on the contrary, with the passion of eternity, with the

---

14. Kierkegaard, *Attack upon "Christendom,"* 132.
15. Ibid., 127.
16. Ibid., 82.
17. Kierkegaard, *Training in Christianity*, 61.
18. Kierkegaard, *Attack upon "Christendom,"* 127.
19. Ibid., 185.

most dreadful either/or, holds apart from one another, separating them by a yawning abyss.[20]

It is this passionate exception without sovereignty, this immeasurable measure which is vertigo of thought (because it is *the* paradox) which demands from us the decision with an absolute either/or: it is this non-sovereign exception (which as love and as gift is so excessive and outpouring that it arrives to us only by our unconditional sacrifice of worldly glories) which, for Kierkegaard, "thinks the general with the utmost passion."

Delegitimation

The idea of "political theology" prophetically announces the decisive crisis of the self-legitimizing project of modernity which, as we know from Karl Löwith is none other than the secularization of the Judeo-Christian "'eschatological pattern' of history."[21] In contrast to the Greek conception of history, whose fundamental principle is "verification of prognostications concerning historiconatural event,"[22] the philosophy of history opens up "the temporal horizon for a final goal," "an eschatological future" which "exists for us only by expectation and hope."[23] In Hegel's philosophy of history, the secularization of the "eschatological pattern" assumes the form and movement of pantheistic metaphysics. Here again the eruption of Christ on the stage of history is the paradigm, but it is now invested with speculative meaning:[24] through Christ's death, there takes places the "reconciliation" or "mediation" (the dialectical "synthesis": this dialectical concept of mediation is precisely the target of Kierkegaard's eschatological critique) of the infinite (God) and the finite (the world) in a movement of the self-cancellation of negativity (*Aufhebung*), in a purely immanent manner, needing no

---

20. Ibid., 144.
21. Löwith, *Meaning in History*, 2.
22. Ibid., 9.
23. Ibid., 6. "The Christian and post-Christian outlook on history is futuristic, perverting the classical meaning of *historein*, which is related to present and past events. In the Greek and Roman mythologies and genealogies the past is re-presented as an everlasting foundation. In the Hebrew and Christian view of history the past is a promise to the future; consequently, the interpretation of the past becomes a prophecy in reverse, demonstrating the past as a meaningful 'preparation' for the future. Greek philosophers and historian were convinced that whatever is to happen will be on the same pattern and character as past and present events; they never indulged in the prospective possibilities of the future." Löwith goes on to say further: "The Greek historians wrote pragmatic history centred around a great political event; the Church Fathers developed from Hebrew prophecy and Christian eschatology a theology of history focused on the supra-historical events of creation, incarnation, and consummation; the moderns elaborate a philosophy of history by secularizing theological principles and applying them to an ever increasing number of empirical facts. It seems as if the two great conceptions of antiquity and Christianity, cyclic motion and eschatological direction, have exhausted the basic approaches to the understanding of history." Ibid., 19.
24. Löwith, *From Hegel to Nietzsche*, 17–50.

outside as "foundation" and "ground." In the Hegelian "philosophy of history" (Löwith reminds us that this term is derived from Voltaire) follows the eschatological pattern of biblical thought, but attempts to realize the kingdom of God on the immanent plane of "universal world history," the self-legitimizing task of modernity (which is the meaning of *saeculum*) needs no "outside," for the order of *saeculum* bears within itself the prerogative of the eschatological judgment, now grasped as the *telos* of a triumphal march of the universal world-historical politics.[25]

Paradoxically, the self-legitimizing task of modernity, precisely in its mere taking up of the eschatological pattern, neutralizes or liquidifies the apocalyptic thorn, the poisonous sting of eschatological judgment that, in biblical discourses, judges the course of the worldly regimes and puts earthly sovereignties into question. It is not for nothing that Kierkegaard in his *Concept of Dread* speaks of the speculative-dialectical idea of mediation as intolerable and at best as "equivocal."[26] This purely conceptual category (which nevertheless pretends to grasp "reality," "actuality," "event" or "existence") liquidifies or neutralizes the apocalyptic intensity of decision. There is, as Kierkegaard would say, no longer any radical distance or heterogeneity between the foolishness of Christ and the wisdom of the world; there is, as Schmitt will say, no longer any radical distance between the exception and the norm. Kierkegaard sees in Hegelian dialectical "cunning of Reason"—where the principle (*arché*) of Reason serves as the "hegemonic fantasm" or as the "sovereign referent" of this epochal condition of modernity[27]—an apotheosis of the worldly order of sovereignty:

> That the established order has become something divine or is regarded as divine constitutes a falsehood which is made possible only by ignoring its origin. When a bourgeois has become a nobleman he is eager to make every effort to have his *vita ante acta* forgotten. So it is with the established order. It began with the God-relationship of the individual; but now this must be forgotten, the bridge hewn down, the established order deified.[28]

The Hegelian concepts are like money:[29] the economic logic that governs the equivalences of values is the same logic which converts Real to Reason and vice versa, which has led to his (Hegel's) announcement that the Prussian state of Hegel's own time is

---

25. We know that Friedrich Nietzsche writes one of his *Untimely Meditations*, namely, "On the Uses and Disadvantages of History for Life," where he criticizes the Hegelian theodicy (the Hegelian "justification of the ways of God" [Hegel, *Lectures on the Philosophy of History*, 16]): "Such a point of view has accustomed the Germans to talk of a 'world process' and to justify their own age as the necessary result of this world-process; such a point of view has set history, insofar as history is 'the concept that realizes itself,' 'the dialectics of the spirit of the peoples,' and the 'world-tribunal,' in place of the other spiritual powers, art and religion, as the sole sovereign power." Nietzsche, *Untimely Meditations*, 104.

26. Kierkegaard, *Concept of Dread*, 11.

27. Schürmann, *Broken Hegemonies*, 12, 21.

28. Kierkegaard, *Training in Christianity*, 74.

29. Kierkegaard, *Attack upon "Christendom,"* 238.

the objective expression of the Absolute (we know Marx's critique of Hegel begins precisely here).[30] In the epochal condition of modernity which gives itself the self-legitimizing and immanent task of secularizing of the eschatological (and yet neutralizing the eschatological sting of judgment), political theology—if it is possible—must think, with the apocalyptic intensity of passion, the possibility of transcendence anew as the event of *breaking* through the *nomos* of the profane order. That means for Kierkegaard the task of introducing the radical disjunction between the eschatologically oriented secrets of salvation history (*Heilsgeschichte*) and the profane order of the world-historical politics (*Weltgeschichte*): Christendom "reduces sacred history to profane history."[31] Justice is the reason for the birth and the death of Christ—who, being this paradox, cannot be understood historically as a "historical" figure but must be understood eschatologically—this justice puts into question, and judges by "an immeasurable rod," the immense march of eighteen-century-old Christendom: this intimate relation between judgment and justice, as much as the two instances of Christ's humiliation and glory, cannot be grasped by the empty form of dialectical (Hegelian) time (which is the vulgar temporality of Christendom). This demands the time of faith which is the Now-time of being contemporaneous with that absolute event of *Kenosis*, which occurred some eighteen hundred years before; this demands an eternity in the midst of time as Now-time, the Now-time as "an atom of eternity,"[32] the Now-time that, by virtue of the eschatological faith, de-formalizes the empty form of successive, qualitatively undifferentiated instances and thereby bringing into proximity what lies in the remote, some hundred years back:

> For in relation to the absolute there is only one tense: the present. For him who is not contemporary with the absolute—for him it has no existence. And as Christ is the absolute, it is easy to see that with respect to Him there is only one situation: that of contemporaneousness. The five, the seven, the fifteen, the eighteen hundred years are neither here nor there; they do not change Him, neither do they in any wise reveal who He was, for who He is, is revealed only to faith.[33]

Here is an eschatological critique of the historical Reason of modernity: the historical Reason of modernity, in the name of secularism, deifies worldly hegemonies and replaces the possibility of the justice, which in the profane order can only be stern

---

30. Commenting on this point Löwith writes: "Hegel believes that, as a Christian philosopher, he can answer this question by secularizing the Christian doctrine of providence and converting the salvation story of Christianity into a secular theodicy, for which the divine spirit is immanent in the world, the state is an earthly god and all history is divine." Löwith, *From Hegel to Nietzsche*, 216.
31. Kierkegaard, *Training in Christianity*, 28.
32. Kierkegaard, *Concept of Dread*, 79.
33. Kierkegaard, *Training in Christianity*, 58.

judgment, with a totalitarian celebration: "the religion of suffering has become the religion of mirth, but it retains the name unchanged."[34]

> The deification of the established order is the secularization of everything. The established order may be quite right in affirming that, so far as worldly things are concerned, one must attach oneself to the established order, be content with the relativity, etc. But in the end one secularizes also the God relationship, insists that this shall be congruous with a certain relativity, not essentially different from one's station in life, etc.—instead of which it must be for every individual man the absolute, and it is precisely this God-relationship of the individual which must put every established order in suspense, so that God, at any instance He will, by pressure upon the individual has immediately this God-relationship a witness, a reporter, a spy, or whatever you prefer to call it, one who in unconditional obedience, or by unconditional obedience, by persecution, suffering and death, puts the established order in suspense.[35]

This suspension has nothing much to do with Schmittean suspension of the normative order of constitution by constitutional means (Article 48 of Weimer Republic): the former is the *kenosis* of the worldly sovereignties; the latter is focused on the *Katechon* figure of the worldly sovereign who restrains from chaos rising from below and thereby legitimates itself as the sovereign power.

Political Theologies

Schmitt's political theology traces back all the evils of the contemporary society (the technology of politics in today's secular-liberal world of mass consumption, the neutralization of politics in the name of "objective," "value free" truth, the totalization of administrative rationality) to the secularizing project of modernity whose most consummate expression is to be found in Hegelian pantheistic metaphysics of history:

> Conceptions of transcendence will no longer be credible to most educated people, who will settle for either a more or less clear immanence-pantheism or a positivist indifference toward any metaphysics. Insofar as it retains the concept of God, the immanence philosophy, which found its greatest systematic architect in Hegel, draws God into the world and permits law and the state to emanate from the immanence of the object.[36]

Schmitt goes on:

> If viewed from this perspective of the history of ideas, the development of the nineteenth-century theory of the state displays two characteristic moments:

---

34. Kierkegaard, *Attack upon "Christendom,"* 142.
35. Kierkegaard, *Training in Christianity*, 77–78.
36. Schmitt, *Political Theology*, 50.

the elimination of all theistic and transcendental conceptions and the formation of a new concept of legitimacy. The traditional principle of legitimacy obviously lost all validity. Neither the version of the Restoration based on private law and patrimony nor the one founded on a sentimental and reverent attachment was able to resist this development. Since 1848 the theory of public law has become "positive," and behind this word is usually hidden its dilemma; or the theory has propounded in different paraphrases the idea that all power resides in the *pouvoir constituant* of the people, which means that the democratic notion of legitimacy has replaced the monarchical.[37]

At stake here is the question of legitimacy: with the loss of authority (as a result of the liquidification of the established order of religion in modernity), legitimation of the sovereign power is in crisis which Schmitt laments. Against such state of affairs, Schmitt constructs a political theology of apocalypticism that has nothing to do with suspension of the worldly hegemonies but everything to do with securing a place for the sovereign power who, being *Katechon*, restrains chaos rising from below. Against such political theology of legitimation of the (earthly) sovereign power, Jacob Taubes evokes a "negative political theology," political theology "from below."[38] Against the apocalyptic counterrevolutionary political theology[39] of Schmitt, which is inspired by counterrevolutionary philosophers of the state such as de Maistre, Bonald and Donoso Cortes, Taubes invokes the political theology of exception without sovereignty, taking seriously into account the Pauline paradoxical messianic logic of *Verbund* ("covenant") which is free not only from ethnic ties. But also from the earthly *nomos* of the Roman empire.[40]

Coming back to Carl Schmitt, it is important to explain his citation of Kierkegaard. Despite being "Protestant" (Schmitt, as we know, is "Catholic"), Kierkegaard is, for him, the apocalyptic thinker of decision and exception who offers, at the epochal closure of modernity, the decisive critique of the secularizing project of historical Reason. Schmitt, then, finds in this Protestant critique of the secularizing liquidification and neutralization of political elements of his own political theology, based upon the notion of sovereignty. Schmitt's notion of sovereignty ("Sovereign is he who decides on the exception")[41] is based on the (Catholic) theological concept of *analogia entis*.[42]

---

37. Ibid., 51.

38. Taubes, *To Carl Schmitt*, 13: "Carl Schmitt thinks apocalyptically, but from above, from the powers that be; I think from the bottom up."

39. Ibid., 1–18.

40. Taubes, *Political Theology of Paul*, 65–66.

41. Schmitt, *Political Theology*, 5.

42. Schmitt writes: "All significant concepts of the modern theory of the state are secularized theological concepts not only because of their historical development—in which they were transferred from theology to the theory of the state, whereby, for example, the omnipotent God became the omnipotent lawgiver—but also because of their systematic structure, the recognition of which is necessary for a sociological consideration of these concepts. The exception in jurisprudence is analogous to

The apocalyptic intensity of decision is the prerogative of the sovereign figure who, as the power "to suspend valid law," is true *auctoritus* ("Because the authority to suspend valid law . . . is so much the actual mark of sovereignty").[43] For Schmitt, this possibility of *auctoritus* ("to suspend valid law"), must invoke the very power of the myth ("to great politics belongs the 'arcanum'").[44] The apocalyptic intensity of exception and decision, in Schmitt's counterrevolutionary political theology, turns into the figure of the sovereign who is the very locus of *auctoritus*, who alone can suspend the general order of legality to bring forth an entire new order of *nomos*: exception here, as Benjamin reminds us, turns demonic by becoming the rule[45] against which Benjamin thinks of a messianic exception without sovereignty, exception that suspends the *nomos* of the worldly without founding a new earthly hegemonic order in turn.[46] It is, thus, not surprising that, for Schmitt, the dictator has remained the paradigmatic example of the sovereign figure who, as the true *Katechon*, restrains the chaos rising from below that threatens to destroy the state:[47] in this manner, Schmittean *Katechon* becomes the real *raison d'état*, the ultimate *arché* of earthly hegemonies, the principle of justification and legitimation of worldly sovereignties eliciting from us "normative obligations."[48] The task left to us today, then, is to think of a political theology of exception that weakens sovereignties and destitutes worldly hegemonies. This demands that we put forward an infinite critique of historical Reason (which assumes, in the philosophical discourse of modernity, the name of "philosophy of history")—which is provided in such a powerful way by Søren Kierkegaard—along with a tireless deconstruction of the politico-theological principle of *analogia entis*. Thus Kierkegaard writes:

> "Then give to the Emperor what belongs to the Emperor, and to God what is God's." Infinite difference! Whether the Emperor be called Herod or Shalmanezar, whether he be Roman or Japanese, is to Him the most indifferent of all things. But, on the other hand—the infinite yawning difference which He posits between God and Emperor: "Give unto God what is God's!" For they with worldly wisdom would make it a question of religion, of duty to God, whether it was lawful to pay tribute to the Emperor. Worldliness is eager to embellish itself as Godliness, and in this case God and Emperor are blended together in the question, as if these two had obviously and directly something to do with each other, as if perhaps they were rivals one of the other and as if

---

the miracle in theology. Only by being aware of this analogy can we appreciate the manner in which the philosophical ideas of the state developed in the last centuries." Ibid., 36.

43. Ibid., 9.
44. Schmitt, *Roman Catholicism and Political Form*, 34.
45. Benjamin, "Theses on the Philosophy of History," 255.
46. Benjamin, "Theologico-Political Fragment," 312–13.
47. Schmitt, *Nomos of the Earth*, 59–61.
48. Schürmann, *Broken Hegemonies*, 514.

God were a sort of Emperor—that is to say, the question takes God in vain and secularizes Him. But Christ draws the distinction, the infinite distinction.[49]

I conclude here with another citation from Kierkegaard, this time with a comment from Jacob Taubes:

> And so Kierkegaard has the presumption to prophesy the Antichrist: like mushrooms after rain, demonically infected figures will appear, "who will boldly make themselves apostles, on the level with the apostles, some having the task of fulfilling Christianity, and soon even becoming founders of a religion themselves, founders of a new religion, which is alleged to meet temporal and worldly demands in a different way from the asceticism of Christianity." The most dangerous thing is when the demonic figures themselves become apostles—like thieves masquerading as policemen—the founders of religion that will find disastrous support in such a critical time because, viewed from the perspective of eternity, it is true to say about this time that religiousness is needed, true religiousness; whereas viewed from the demonic perspective, the same age says of itself that religiousness is needed, but demonic religiousness.[50]

Bibliography

Balthasar, Hans Urs von. *The Glory of the Lord: A Theological Aesthetics*. Vol. 1. Translated by Erasmo Leiva-Merikasis. Edinburgh: T. & T. Clark, 1982.

Benjamin, Walter. "Theologico-Political Fragment." In *Reflections*, edited by Peter Demetz, 312–13. New York: Schocken, 1986.

———. "Theses on the Philosophy of History." In *Illuminations*, edited by Hannah Arendt, translated by Harry Zohn, 245–55. New York: Schocken, 1985.

Hegel, G. W. F. *Lectures on the Philosophy of History*. Translated by J. Sibree. London: Bells, 1900.

Henry, Michel. *I am the Truth: Toward a Philosophy of Christianity*. Translated by Susan Emanuel. Stanford: Stanford University Press, 2002.

Hölderlin, Friedrich. "Becoming in Dissolution." In *Essays and Letters on Theory*. Translated by Thomas Pfau, 96–100. Albany: State University of New York Press, 1988.

———. *Poems and Fragments*. Translated by Michael Hamburger. London: Routledge and Kegan Paul, 1966.

Kierkegaard, Søren. *Attack upon "Christendom."* Translated by Walter Lowrie. Princeton: Princeton University Press, 1968.

———. *The Concept of Dread*. Translated by Walter Lowrie. Princeton: Princeton University Press, 1957.

———. *Training in Christianity*. Translated by Walter Lowrie. New York: Vintage, 2004.

Löwith, Karl. *From Hegel to Nietzsche: The Revolution in Nineteenth-Century Thought*. Translated by David E. Green. New York: Columbia University Press, 1991.

---

49. Kierkegaard, *Training in Christianity*, 153.

50. Taubes, *Occidental Eschatology*, 190–91. Taubes's citation of Kierkegaard gives the following reference: Kierkegaard, *Das Eine Was Nottut*, 7.

———. *The Meaning in History: The Theological Implication of the Philosophy of History*. Chicago: Chicago University Press, 1957.

Nietzsche, Friedrich. "The Uses and Disadvantages of History for Life." In *Untimely Meditations*, translated by R. J. Hollingdale, 57–124. Cambridge: Cambridge University Press, 1997.

Schmitt, Carl. *The Nomos of the Earth: In the International Law of the* Jus Publicum Europaeum. Translated by G. L. Ulmen. New York: Telos, 2006.

———. *Political Theology: Four Chapters on the Concept of Sovereignty*. Translated by George Schwab. Chicago: University of Chicago Press, 2005.

———. *Roman Catholicism and Political Form*. Translated by G. L. Ulmen. New York: Greenwood, 1996.

Schürmann, Reiner. *Broken Hegemonies*. Translated by Reginald Lilly. Bloomington: Indiana University Press, 2003.

Taubes, Jacob. *To Carl Schmitt: Letters and Reflections*. Translated by Keith Tribe. New York: Columbia University Press, 2013.

———. *The Political Theology of Paul*. Translated by Dana Hollander. Stanford: Stanford University Press, 2003.

2

Kierkegaard and the Critique of Political Theology

Anthony Rudd

Was Kierkegaard a "political theologian"?[1] Or—perhaps a better question—what, if anything, is there of interest or value in Kierkegaard's work for those who do think of themselves as practitioners of political theology? The answer will of course, depend on what is meant by "political theology"—a richly suggestive but ambiguous term. It seems to have two main kinds of meaning. First, it can refer to the enterprise of drawing political conclusions from theological premises—trying to work out what political actions are suggested or required by certain religious commitments. This is a project that has been pursued by religiously committed thinkers across the centuries and across the political spectrum, from Joseph de Maistre to Liberation Theology.

In the second sense, "political theology" has a less straightforward meaning; it refers to the project, undertaken by atheist thinkers, of taking theological ideas and turning them into political ones. Or, showing that what had been confusedly thought in theological terms can be better expressed in political terms. This should not be confused with the more straightforward secularism which takes theology to be simply mistaken and argues that we should turn away from it to unrelated but more useful topics such as politics. Atheist political theologians do think that something important will be lost if we simply ignore or dismiss the theological tradition(s), but they also suppose that this something needs to be de-theologized and made into politics. The pioneer of this project was of course Feuerbach, whose analysis was in large measure taken up—though also transformed—by Marx and his followers. As Habermas puts it: "Rather than save religion in thought, they want to realize its profanized contents in a political effort of solidarity praxis. This pathos of a desublimated earthly

---

1. I should say that this paper developed out of my responses to the papers by Vincent Lloyd, Silas Morgan, Jamie Aroosi, and Tom Miles at the session on "Kierkegaard and Political Theology" at the American Philosophical Association (Pacific Division) meeting on April 2, 2015. I am very grateful to all the speakers at the session—and to our chair, Roberto Sirvent—for stimulating me to think more about these issues.

realization of the Kingdom of God is the driving force behind the critique of religion from Feuerbach and Marx to Bloch, Benjamin and Adorno."[2] And, perhaps a little surprisingly, this project is still continued in some ways by contemporary Marxist thinkers like Žižek and Badiou.

How is Kierkegaard relevant to all this? Some interpreters have found in him a positive political theology of the first sort.[3] I do not think they are simply wrong to suppose that Kierkegaard's religious views might have application to political life, though I do not think there is any such thing as a Kierkegaardian political program to be extracted from his writings. As for the second kind of project, a number of practitioners of atheist "political theology" were significantly influenced by Kierkegaard, and, among our contemporaries, Žižek and Badiou both engage critically, but quite sympathetically, with him.[4] I think it is clear, nevertheless, that Kierkegaard would be deeply opposed to the whole project. That is not by itself a reason to reject it, but in this paper I will try to at least sketch a Kierkegaardian argument against "political theology" of this second kind. This will go roughly as follows: Some political thinkers try to take certain ideas from Kierkegaard while rejecting his metaphysical, theological, or substantive normative claims. The idea most often extracted in this way is that of radical choice, which stresses the autonomy of the self over against any framework of norms or principles that it might or might not choose. (This is often connected with the "teleological suspension of the ethical," as discussed in *Fear and Trembling*—which has been taken by some thinkers as a model for the idea that ethical prohibitions on violence can be suspended for the sake of a political goal.)

Some other political thinkers have, on the contrary, looked to Kierkegaard primarily for an understanding of the self as fundamentally intersubjective, dependent on an other, and therefore limited in its autonomy. For Kierkegaard, these aspects of selfhood—its autonomy and dependence, or, as I shall say, its transcendence and immanence—can hold together only if the self as a whole is properly oriented to a transcendent Good (God). Without such an overriding teleological orientation, choice collapses into an arbitrary decisionism, and intersubjectivity into social conformism. I will argue that Kierkegaard is right about this; or, at the least, that there is good reason to take his concerns on this score very seriously. If I am right, the attempts to de-theologize Kierkegaard give us little that is either intellectually plausible or politically helpful; while the real Kierkegaard, with his substantive metaphysical commitments, has much more to offer us. I will conclude with some reflections on *Fear and Trembling*—the Kierkegaardian work most often invoked by "political theologians"—and

---

2. Habermas, *Future of Human Nature*, 112.

3. See Kirmmse, *Kierkegaard in Golden Age Denmark*, and Westphal, *Kierkegaard's Critique*.

4. Badiou's only significant discussion of Kierkegaard is in his *Logics of Worlds*, 425–35. Žižek discusses Kierkegaard in various writings; see, e.g., Žižek, *Enjoy Your Symptom!*, 78–86, 92–96; Žižek, *Parallax View*, 75–80, 85–90, 104–5.

the question of whether it suggests a justification for political violence, whether or not religiously motivated.

I.

Historically, it does seem that Kierkegaard has been invoked politically primarily as a theorist of decisionism. This appropriation of him is based on the familiar existentialist picture of Kierkegaard as the advocate of a "leap of faith" which takes us beyond reason and may call on us to "suspend" our normal ethical codes and responsibilities. This popular, though simplistic, reading of Kierkegaard was given a political twist by Georg Lukacs who seems to have quite consciously opted to support Bolshevism and join the Hungarian Communist party in 1918 as a political equivalent of Kierkegaard's leap of faith.[5] He did so despite unresolved intellectual doubts about Marxist theory, and serious ethical concerns about the Bolsheviks' use of terror. His willingness to not only condone the latter but, as a member of the short-lived Hungarian revolutionary government in 1919 to actively practice it,[6] was seen by him as equivalent to Abraham's "teleological suspension of the ethical."[7] There was no objectively valid philosophy of history that could demonstrate the necessity of such political terror for the creation of a just society; but one faced the existential choice between standing aloof, or being willing to dirty one's hands in the hope—or faith—that good would come of such violence. But, of course, having committed himself not only to revolutionary Marxism in general, but to the Communist Party and the Soviet Union as its authoritative embodiments, Lukacs could not continue to admit—even, in the end, to himself—the Kierkegaardian nature of his commitment. Eventually he seems to have resolved this cognitive dissonance by persuading himself of the objective truth of Stalinist historical determinism.

Such political decisionist readings of Kierkegaard were not confined to the Left. Carl Schmitt in his *Political Theology* refers to Kierkegaard's notion of "the exception" and uses it as a model for his theory that sovereignty is defined by the power to suspend the normal operations of the law.[8] Such suspension needs to be a matter of personal will—if there had to be a law to determine when the law can be suspended we would get into an infinite regress. And, although such a decision to suspend need not be irrational—reasons can be given—only the will of the sovereign can determine whether these reasons are compelling enough: "The exception is more interesting than the rule. The rule proves nothing, the exception proves everything: it confirms not only the rule but also its existence, which derives only from the exception. In the exception, the power of real life breaks through the crust of a mechanism that has

---

5. Kadarkay, *Georg Lukacs*, 193–206; Nagy, "Abraham, the Communist," 206–7.
6. Kadarkay, *Georg Lukacs*, 213–14, 222–24.
7. Nagy, "Abraham, the Communist," 207–8.
8. Schmitt, *Political Theology*, chs. 1 and 2.

become torpid by repetition."⁹ Schmitt went on to use this conception to justify the Nazis' rule by emergency decree. For Schmitt, the Sovereign becomes like the God of Abraham, who is significant precisely because he does *not*, *pace* Kant and Hegel, vanish into the universal, the purely ethical, and thus become "an invisible vanishing point, an impotent thought."¹⁰ God's power to suspend the ethical demonstrates his superiority over it and thus becomes the model for the Sovereign's power over the law. And so those who accept the Sovereign's "exceptional" authority and do not require it to be backed up by law, would, it seems, become analogous to Abraham. This is really not so far from Lukacs, of course, for whom the God-like Sovereign is the Party, which demands the suspension of the ethical prohibition against murder; its loyal follower, who accepts that demand, is "Abraham—the Communist."¹¹

Versions of this supposedly Kierkegaard-derived decisionism are still in vogue. Alain Badiou has invoked Kierkegaard in the course of his discussion of "worlds," "truths" and "points." A "world" is defined as a structure of more or less settled meanings. "Truths" are "events" which challenge or disrupt these normally unquestioned assumptions. A "point" is the appearance to a subject of the choice between embracing a truth or turning away from it. One can certainly see some parallels with Kierkegaard's account of the stages of life—which are normative frameworks—and the ways that one may choose to beak with them or move between them.¹² And Badiou makes the parallels explicit, describing the point as "Kierkegaard's 'either/or,' through which the confused totality of the elements of the world is re-evaluated."¹³ However, Badiou goes on to claim that "Kierkegaard sees perfectly well that the theory of the point is a formal or transcendental theory. That is because the apparent content of the alternative is of little import, it is the capacity to treat the point that matters, what I have called the existence of an organ for the point."¹⁴ Elaborating on this, Benjamin Noys comments, "The importance [*sic*] is not the content of choice but the fact of choice itself."¹⁵ But here Badiou seems to be following Sartre, rather

---

9. Schmitt, *Political Theology*, 15.

10. Kierkegaard, *Fear and Trembling*, 68. Schmitt's only explicit reference to Kierkegaard in *Political Theology* is, however, to *Repetition*, not to *Fear and Trembling* (Schmitt, *Political Theology*, 15). For more on Kierkegaard and Schmitt, see Dana Lloyd's essay in this volume.

11. Nagy, "Abraham, the Communist," 207–8. For further discussion of Kierkegaard's relations to Lukacs and Schmitt, see Ryan, *Kierkegaard's Indirect Politics*, chs. 2 and 3.

12. Although one substantial difference is that, for Badiou, "the subject is always a formal body, or a collection of individuals . . . one cannot be a subject until that moment at which they join the collective body" (O'Neill Burns, "Alain Badiou," 48). This seems obviously paradoxical. (Who was it then who made the decision to join the body?) A partial parallel is offered by Kierkegaard's Judge William, who says that the ethical self "has not existed before because it came into existence through the choice." But the Judge is careful to immediately qualify the claim: "and yet it has existed, for it was indeed 'himself.'" Kierkegaard, *Either/Or* II, 215.

13. Badiou, *Logics of Worlds*, 406.

14. Ibid., 432–33.

15. Noys, "Either/Or: Badiou/Kierkegaard," 6.

than Kierkegaard. For Sartre, choice reveals the existence of a subject who has the power to transcend the "world" of meanings it had inhabited and to negate it; but this subject has no content of its own and no criteria to justify its decisions to either negate or accept the existing order, or to try to replace it with one rather than another alternative. The ultra-Leftism of Sartre's politics after the late 1940s thus rested on an arbitrary decision to take that side rather than another.[16] It is not clear to me that Badiou's own ultra-Leftism rests on anything more substantial or less arbitrary than this.[17] (I am inclined to think that much the same could be said about Žižek, though I do not have the space to go into that here.)[18]

The idea that Kierkegaardian choice is absolute (in the sense of being guided by no criteria) and formal (in that anything—Bolshevism, Nazism, Maoism—could be the object of a Kierkegaardian choice) is widespread. Alasdair MacIntyre expounded this decisionist interpretation of Kierkegaard in his *After Virtue*, writing: "Suppose that someone confronts the choice between them [the aesthetic and the ethical] having as yet embraced neither. He can be offered no *reason* for preferring one to the other"[19]—because the choice he has yet to make is the choice of what will count for him as a reason for doing something. But this is not Kierkegaard's claim. No one, for him, exists outside one or other of the spheres of existence. If you think you are an autonomous outsider in that way, you are thereby showing that you are in fact an aesthete of a particular kind. No existing individual can be an unsituated "pure thinker" contemplating the possibilities of existence from a neutral, detached distance.[20] And yet, it can be said that someone who chooses to leave one sphere—or someone who chooses consciously to remain in one, while aware of doing so under conditions of "objective uncertainty"—is clearly recognizing that things could be otherwise, that *I could choose otherwise*; and is thus in a sense transcending that sphere. This is true, and this power of transcendence is indeed essential to who we are, according to Kierkegaard. In *Sickness Unto Death*, he explains selfhood as a "synthesis of the infinite

---

16. Though, like Lukacs, Sartre did eventually come to accept Marxism as objective doctrine—at least to the point where he could claim that, for now, Marxism had become "the horizon for all culture" and that there was no "going beyond" it until the historical moment it represented had passed (see Sartre, *Search for a Method*, 7). This surrender to the alleged requirements of the *zeitgeist* is a paradigm example of what Sartre would once have considered "Bad Faith."

17. According to O'Neill Burns, on Badiou's account, "an individual (or more often a group of individuals) experience an event . . . they subsequently make a wager on the truth contained within this event; there is never a guarantee, and so the subject must make a leap of faith." O'Neill Burns, "Alain Badiou," 42.

18. I have been encouraged in this supposition by the accounts of Žižek in the papers by Jamie Aroosi and Vincent Lloyd to which I responded at the APA session mentioned earlier, although they were both much more sympathetic to Žižek than I am.

19. MacIntyre, *After Virtue*, 40. It should be said that MacIntyre firmly rejects the decisionism he ascribes to Kierkegaard. He is wrong in the ascription, but right in the rejection.

20. For a number of critiques of MacIntyre's interpretation of Kierkegaard as a decisionist and irrationalist, see Davenport and Rudd, *Kierkegaard After MacIntyre*.

and the finite, of the temporal and the eternal, of freedom and necessity."[21] Thus he sees a human person as existing in—or better, existing *as*—a tension between poles of transcendence and immanence; a tension that is ideally creative (though usually in fact destructive). But although our transcendence *is* essential to us, it is not that of the "pure thinker," lacking the ballast of necessity, finitude and temporality, and nor is it that of the decisionist, choosing or even creating values from an initial point that stands outside of them.

I think we can best see Kierkegaard's account of the progression from the aesthetic, through the ethical to the religious, not as a series of blind leaps, choices that might have had any content at all; but as a version of the Platonic Ascent.[22] Our transcendence allows us to recognize that a particular world of meanings is not adequate; that a life spent in the pursuit of pleasure, or power, or wealth, or "the interesting"; even one spent deepening committed relationships, advancing the good of society, or struggling for justice, leave us unfulfilled. There are needs in us, which we may repress but cannot simply ignore, which keep us searching for a world of meaning which will wholly satisfy us; one that we *cannot* transcend. That we can transcend a world doesn't mean that we have created it, or that it depends on us; but that its meaning is not full or rich enough to satisfy us. It is true, though, that for Kierkegaard our freedom does allow us to turn away even from what for him is the ultimate Good—God. But this is the despair of defiance; a kind of pathological self-hatred, dressing itself up as hubristic self-assertion. (And, indeed, even the "lower" forms of despair, which keep us from transcending the limited worlds of meaning which we *should* transcend, are really forms of defiance, of refusal to really attend to the limitations and defects of the world around us, because we don't want to see them.) Kierkegaard's view, of course, presupposes that there is an objective Good (God) that we are striving toward, and that human nature has a *telos*—to "rest transparently in the power that established it."[23] And this presupposes what can fairly be called an essentialist view of human nature—though a subtle one. (For Kierkegaard, our power of transcendence is part of our essence, though not—as it is for Sartre—the whole of it.) Kierkegaard is often seen (as by Habermas) as a "post-metaphysical" thinker.[24] On some interpretations of that almost infinitely ambiguous word, "metaphysical," no doubt he is. But this shouldn't blind us to the fact that he is also in many ways a very traditional thinker.

---

21. Kierkegaard, *Sickness Unto Death*, 13.

22. This is classically articulated in the speech of Diotima in Plato's *Symposium* and also in the Myth of the Cave in the *Republic*.

23. Kierkegaard, *Sickness Unto Death*, 14.

24. Habermas, *Future of Human Nature*, 5–6.

II.

Decisionism is, I think, unacceptable, either in politics or outside it. And it remains unacceptable even when the political principles arrived at by acts of arbitrary choice are themselves more benign than Lukacs's, Schmitt's or Badiou's. This is something Habermas worries about. He accepts the Rawlsian notion of a pluralistic society which is not regulated by any substantive notion of the good, but only by a "thin" procedural notion of justice, designed to give maximum freedom for individuals to work out their own richer notions of what makes for a well-lived life. But he is nevertheless uncomfortable about this, noting that "deontological theories after Kant may be very good at explaining how to ground and apply moral norms but they are still unable to answer the question of why we should be moral *at all*"[25]—even in a limited Rawlsian sense. Rawlsian liberalism thus hangs in the air—and this seems to force us back into decisionism. If we accept Rawlsian procedural justice, it is because we have made an ungrounded choice to do so.[26] But there can be no more *reason* to make that choice than to make an opposite one. Furthermore, Habermas fears that, even if we can motivate people to be "moral" in the sense of obeying essentially negative, procedural rules of justice; still, such a purely Rawlsian society may be unable to inspire any sense of solidarity among its members, such that they will actively care about one another's well-being.[27] If such a solidarity does arise, it seems that either it would have to come from an arbitrary decisionist choice or from the residual influence of non-Rawlsian ways of thinking, ones that the Rawlsian state cannot promote or even recognize.

It is for help with these problems that Habermas turns to Kierkegaard. This is very interesting, for Habermas is trying to use Kierkegaard, not to bolster decisionism, but to find a way out of it. He looks, not to Kierkegaard's account of choice, but to his view of the subject as constituted by its relation to another: "The hopeless failure of . . . the stubborn wanting to be oneself entirely on the basis of ones' own resources—pushes finite spirit to transcend itself and recognize its dependence on an Other as the ground of its own freedom."[28] However, Habermas's "post-metaphysical" commitments lead him to reject Kierkegaard's specifically theological conception of the self: "The power beyond us—on which we as subjects capable of speech and action depend in our concern not to fail to lead worthwhile lives—cannot be identified with 'God in time.'"[29] Rather, he gives "a deflationary interpretation of the 'wholly Other'"

---

25. Ibid., 4.

26. Or it is because we have just gone along with what is, as a matter of contingent fact, the established form of our societies without caring about their lack of ultimate justification for their principles. Rorty, for one, has argued that we should not be bothered by this: see Rorty, *Contingency, Irony and Solidarity*, ch. 3. Kierkegaard would see decisionism as over-stressing our transcendence, Rortian conformism as overstressing our immanence.

27. Habermas, *Future of Human Nature*, 4.

28. Ibid., 9.

29. Ibid., 10.

in terms of human intersubjectivity—the "power" we depend on is the human linguistic community, which is the condition for the framing of the normative judgments in which we can express our freedom.[30]

So, just as Badiou tries to take Kierkegaard's views about choice in a purely formal way, Habermas takes Kierkegaard's insights into selfhood purely formally—to relate properly to ourselves, we must relate to (some) other, but this need not (or even cannot) be The Other (God). Again, Kierkegaard is taken to be making a general, formal point—this time about intersubjectivity; and so his own theological concerns are set aside. Now it is certainly true that Kierkegaard *is* concerned with our relations to specific human others in concrete social situations. But he is also convinced that it is only through wholeheartedly willing the transcendent Good (i.e., God) that we can distinguish between what is good and bad in such relationships. Habermas refers to the ways in which we are dependent for our development as autonomous reasoners on the linguistic communities in which we are raised; and this might serve as the basis for a local, communitarian social morality. Habermas himself thinks we can go beyond that to a universal "discourse ethics." I am very skeptical about this proposal, as I am about related contractualist and constructivist moves in recent analytic moral philosophy.[31] For Kierkegaard it is only if there is a source of values beyond the merely humanly intersubjective that we can gain the distance from particular social circumstances that we need to take up a properly critical stance to them (which does not, incidentally, mean an indiscriminately negative one). In other words, we need the religious, as transcending the ethical, to prevent the ethical from collapsing into uncritical social conformism.[32] As Johannes de Silentio says in *Fear and Trembling*, the person of faith "determines his relation to the universal by his relation to the absolute, not his relation to the absolute by his relation to the universal."[33] But if there is no absolute, from what perspective are we to take a critical stance on the "universal"—i.e., Hegelian social morality, *Sittlichkeit*? Perhaps there can be a rational, nonreligious basis for a morality that will go beyond merely communal values, but I think we have good reason to doubt this—and, as I noted above, Habermas himself worries that secular deontological theories have failed to provide a rational answer to the question of why we should be moral at all. If they have failed to do that, and if there is no absolute to give the individual a higher perspective on the universal, then how can the individual mount a critique of social ethics that does not simply collapse back into an arbitrary decisionism? Without the religious, can we be left with anything more than a merely aesthetic critique of the ethical?

30. Ibid.

31. See, e.g., Korsgaard, *Sources of Normativity*; Scanlon, *What We Owe*.

32. Note by the way that the group to which we uncritically conform may be a marginalized and oppressed one. Uncritical social conformism may as easily be revolutionary as conservative.

33. Kierkegaard, *Fear and Trembling*, 70.

On Kierkegaard's view, we can transcend—"teleologically suspend"—the (socially) ethical only if there is really is a *telos* beyond the (socially) ethical. And this is an important challenge—to put it a bit sloganistically, it is the claim that politics can only be properly critical if it is grounded in theology. As it stands, that is a bit too simple—I do not think Kierkegaard himself supposed that "the absolute" which gives us perspective on the universal need be the God described in specifically Christian theology.[34] But he is committed to the view that we need to think of the Good as radically transcendent; *not* in any way a product of human intersubjectivity. He is, in short, a Platonic Realist about the Good, and it is this Platonic Realism that is the basic content of the generic "Religiousness A" discussed in the *Postscript*.[35] That this Platonism will meet a lot of resistance in the contemporary intellectual and cultural *milieu* goes without saying, and this is not the place to attempt a detailed defense of it.[36] But it is precisely because it goes against the grain of contemporary thought that it is important that this challenge be clearly heard and carefully responded to. And to reduce Kierkegaard's theological or metaphysical claims to generic ethico-political ones, as Habermas does, is to occlude this challenge.

III.

Fear and Trembling does open a space for critical reflection on the socially established ethical world, but to many that space has seemed a strange and frightening one. For the book has often been read as endorsing, or at least opening up the possibility for, a religious justification for political terror. And, as we have seen, nonreligious "political theologians" have also taken inspiration from *Fear and Trembling*, and have found ways to take its "teleological suspension of the ethical" to justify or excuse the use of political violence in the service of secular ideologies. Nor is this clearly just a thing of the past. Žižek has invoked Kierkegaard in the course of what seem to be admiring comments about the terrorists of the German Red Army Faction[37] and elsewhere he claims that "'Left' is defined by this readiness to suspend the abstract moral frame, or, to paraphrase Kierkegaard, to accomplish a *political suspension of*

---

34. His enthusiasm for Socrates makes that clear.

35. See Kierkegaard, *Concluding Unscientific Postscript*, 387–555. I am not suggesting that the distinctive features of Christianity are unimportant to Kierkegaard. Christianity for him is what offers us salvation when the generic ethico-religious consciousness has suffered "shipwreck" on the fact of our sinfulness, our (culpable) inability to do as we should. But it presupposes and in a sense, rescues the generic religious consciousness, rather than negating it. It is important to notice that even in some of his signed works, Kierkegaard restricts himself to the level of generic, Platonic religiousness—the long discourse usually known as "Purity of Heart" in Kierkegaard, *Upbuilding Discourses in Various Spirits*, is a good example.

36. I have tried to do so elsewhere; see my *Self, Value and Narrative*.

37. Žižek, *Enjoy Your Symptom!*, 77–78.

the Ethical."³⁸ It is, I think, important to see that the book has been badly misread by those who have seen in it a justification for political violence, whether religious or secular. In arguing this case, I will focus on two important notions from *Fear and Trembling*—those of tragic heroism and the distinction between the Knight of Faith and the Knight of Infinite Resignation.

In Johannes de Silentio's examples of tragic heroism, fathers kill their children for ethical reasons. The clearest example for our purposes is Junius Brutus, who, in his position as consul of the Roman Republic ordered the execution of his sons for plotting to restore the monarchy.³⁹ He sets aside what would normally be both his wish and his ethical duty—to protect and support his children—in obedience to his higher ethical duty to the state and the good of the people as a whole. However painful this is for him, we can perfectly well understand what he is doing and why he does it; he can give a public justification for his action and we can (so Johannes assumes) see that he is right to do what he does. Abraham, though, steps out of the sphere of ethics altogether and his action is incapable of being publically defended or justified. However, the "religiously motivated terrorist"—let us assume a member of Al Qaeda or ISIS—would rarely even reach the level of tragic heroism, let alone that of infinite resignation, let alone that of faith. Indeed, the "religiously motivated" label is a bit of a red herring in this context. Modern political terrorism, as it has existed since the late nineteenth century, was until recently an almost entirely secular matter, terror tactics being used to advance purely secular ideologies—anarchism, nationalism, communism, fascism. Al Qaeda's or ISIS's political ideologies are derived from their religious commitments—in that sense they are indeed "political theologies"—but in the structure of their self-justification these groups are indistinguishable from their secular equivalents. All these terrorists, secular or religious, consider their cause to be a just one and their killings in support of it to be justified killings. Their victims are either people who explicitly oppose their (supposedly just) cause; or people deemed by their ideology unfit to live in any case (whether racial inferiors, class enemies, apostates or infidels); or they are people who are admittedly innocent, but whose killing is justified on consequentialist grounds as necessary to put pressure on unjust governments, publicize the cause, etc. So far there is nothing in this that parallels anything in Johannes's analysis of Abraham, even if the principles underlying the terrorists' political ideology happen to be derived from theology rather than a secular philosophy.

Terrorists of this sort might get as far as being tragic heroes, if they hate what they are doing and do it only with deep reluctance, as required by the higher ethical demand they feel. Some of the pre-1917 Russian terrorists seem to have been of this

---

38. Žižek, *Universal Exception*, 177, italics original. As my comments on Schmitt above will have suggested, I think this willingness to take the political as trumping the ethical is as characteristic of the radical right as of the radical left (Žižek's attempts to differentiate between them are notably feeble). It is, indeed, characteristic of Machiavellian *realpolitik* through the ages.

39. Kierkegaard, *Fear and Trembling*, 58.

sort—some deliberately allowed themselves to be arrested after their attacks and were willing to be executed to atone for the evil they had done, even while continuing to believe that evil to be justified as a tragic necessity. (These people fascinated Camus, who wrote about them in *The Rebel* and put them on stage in his play *The Just*.)[40] But most terrorists are not, I suspect, like that. They either hate their victims or are callously indifferent to their fate. The tragic hero goes against his or her inclinations as well as "lower" ethical duties in order to obey a higher ethical demand; but most terrorists are acting in accord with their inclinations as well as what they believe to be just. Even if they are "religiously motivated," they have nothing to do with the sort of case that concerned Kierkegaard. Furthermore, their supposed justification comes from a publically accessible tradition, from Scripture, from theology, not from the purely personal relationship to God that drove Abraham; and they act as members of a group, not as individuals. Even in the rare cases of a genuine tragic hero with such a public or collective religious motivation—a "church-related hero" as Johannes de Silentio calls him—Johannes is very clear that this case is radically different from that of a Knight of Faith.[41]

Moreover, the Knight of Faith needs to be distinguished not only from the Tragic Hero, but also from the Knight of Resignation. For what makes Abraham a Knight of *Faith* is not just his willingness to "resign" Isaac—and, with him, all that makes his own life meaningful—to God. Abraham's faith consists in his confidence that he will "get Isaac back," that Isaac will not be demanded of him, or will, even if killed, be returned to life. "He climbed the mountain, and even in the moment when the knife gleamed, he had faith—that God would not require Isaac."[42] Abraham is willing to carry out God's command, not because he is simply terrified of God (that would not be faith) nor because he thinks that God arbitrarily determines standards of right and wrong by sheer *fiat*; but because he trusts God. Since God has commanded this, it must be good—not because God decides what counts as "good" but because he believes that God will only command what is in fact good. This is not even the consequentialist reasoning sometimes used by terrorists—that most people will benefit in the long run. (Kierkegaard himself certainly distained that sort of utilitarianism.) Rather, Abraham's faith is that somehow this will conduce to the good of those concerned—Abraham himself, and Isaac, and Sarah, too. And will do so in this world—not only in the hereafter. This is on the face of it "absurd"—but it is the willingness to trust, even when all the circumstances seem to ensure that what is trusted in is impossible, that constitutes faith for Johannes.[43] It seems hard to imagine any kind of political terrorism that could offer a parallel. A terrorist who goes off to kill, but has faith that his victims will not in fact die? Someone may hope desperately, and even

40. See Camus, *The Rebel*, 164–73, and Camus, *The Just*.
41. Kierkegaard, *Fear and Trembling*, 74.
42. Ibid., 65.
43. Davenport, "Faith as Eschatological Trust," 229–31.

believe, that the government will make concessions, so that planting the bomb will not be necessary; but to believe this, not as a rational calculation of probabilities, nor as a pathetic self-delusion, but knowingly, trustingly, despite all the evidence, on "the strength of the absurd"? Abraham trusts in God to ensure that "all will be well." But without a God to trust in, it seems that such an attitude would be, not the "absurdity" of faith, but just plain craziness.

So is a nonreligious analogue of Kierkegaardian faith wholly impossible? Perhaps there could be a real analogy as far as the element of personal trust goes: the absolute trust of one human individual in another, based on personal love, maintained even when all the objective evidence seems to show that the beloved has been unfaithful, or is guilty of some terrible crime. One might consider whether this could be transposed onto the political sphere; for instance, the belief that, contrary to all the evidence, Comrade Stalin is really acting for the best. But such "believers" are not acting on the basis of any personal, individual relation to the Leader; and there is no "getting back" either—the children they offer up really are slaughtered.[44] It does seem that the stance of faith as described in *Fear and Trembling* can only be a religious one—and if Lukacs or Schmitt thought that they were in some way following in the footsteps of Abraham, they were deeply mistaken. And so I will conclude, first, that the "faith" considered in *Fear and Trembling* is an essentially religious concept, not a generic one that might have secular as well as religious instances; and second, that, although *Fear and Trembling* does not rule out an Abraham-like case, its twin requirements of an absolutely personal, incommunicable relationship to God and a faith in "getting Isaac back" mean that it offers no justification for religiously inspired *political* terror.

Bibliography

Badiou, Alain. *Logics of Worlds*. Translated by A. Toscano: London: Continuum, 2009.
Camus, Albert. "The Just." In *Caligula and Other Plays*. Translated by H. Jones. London: Penguin, 1984.
———. *The Rebel*. Translated by A. Bower. New York: Vintage, 1991.
Davenport, John. "Faith as Eschatological Trust in *Fear and Trembling*." In *Ethics, Love, and Faith in Kierkegaard: Philosophical Engagements*, edited by Edward Mooney, 196–233. Bloomington: Indiana University Press, 2008.
Davenport, John, and Anthony Rudd, eds. *Kierkegaard After MacIntyre*. Chicago: Open Court, 2001.
Habermas, Jurgen. *The Future of Human Nature*. Translated by W. Rehg. Cambridge: Polity, 2003.
Kadarkay, Arpad. *Georg Lukacs: Life, Thought and Politics*. Oxford: Blackwell, 1991.
Kierkegaard, Søren. *Either/Or*. Vol. 2. Translated by Howard V. Hong and Edna H. Hong. Princeton: Princeton University Press, 1987.
———. *Fear and Trembling; Repetition*. Edited and translated by Howard V. Hong and Edna H. Hong. Princeton: Princeton University Press, 1983.

44. Nagy, "Abraham the Communist," 208–9.

———. *The Sickness Unto Death*. Edited and translated by Howard V. Hong and Edna H. Hong. Princeton: Princeton University Press, 1988.

Kirmmse, Bruce. *Kierkegaard in Golden Age Denmark*. Bloomington: Indiana University Press, 1990.

Korsgaard, Christine. *The Sources of Normativity*. Cambridge: Cambridge University Press, 1996.

MacIntyre, Alasdair. *After Virtue*. 3rd ed. South Bend: University of Notre Dame Press, 2007.

Nagy, Andras. "Abraham, the Communist." In *Kierkegaard: The Self in Society*, edited by George Pattison and Steven Shakespeare, 196–222. New York: Macmillan, 1998.

Noys, Benjamin. "Either/Or: Badiou/Kierkegaard." Unpublished paper. No date. https://www.academia.edu/620004/_Either_Or_Badiou_Kierkegaard.

O'Neill Burns, Michael. "Alain Badiou: Thinking the Subject after the Death of God." *Kierkegaard's Influence on Social-Political Thought*, edited by Jon Stewart, 41–52. London: Ashgate, 2011.

Rorty, Richard. *Contingency, Irony and Solidarity*. Cambridge: Cambridge University Press, 1989.

Rudd, Anthony. *Self, Value and Narrative: A Kierkegaardian Approach*. Oxford: Oxford University Press, 2012.

Ryan, Bartholomew. *Kierkegaard's Indirect Politics*. Amsterdam: Brill, 2014.

Sartre, Jean-Paul. *Search for a Method*. Translated by H. Barnes. New York: Vintage, 1968.

Scanlon, Thomas. *What We Owe to One Another*. Cambridge: Belknap, of Harvard University Press, 2000.

Schmitt, Carl. *Political Theology*. Translated by G. Schwab. Cambridge: MIT Press, 1985.

Westphal, Merold. *Kierkegaard's Critique of Reason and Society*. University Park: Pennsylvania State University Press, 1991.

Zizek, Slavoj. *Enjoy Your Symptom!* London: Routledge, 2001.

———. *The Parallax View*. Cambridge: MIT Press, 2006.

———. *The Universal Exception*. Edited by Rex Butler and Scott Stephens. London: Continuum, 2006.

3

Johannes Climacus and Two Kierkegaards

Strategies for Theology and Social Engagement

DAVID LAPPANO

WHEN KIERKEGAARD CLAIMS, ON numerous occasions and in various voices, that he is really engaged in a kind of poetic communication, that the *single individual* is the sole audience and goal of his writing, that he speaks without authority, and that he is absolutely not interested in politics, I believe we ought to take him seriously. But taking Kierkegaard seriously means not taking his rejection of politics *directly*. Why not? Kierkegaard has indicated, through what he calls his "maieutic carefulness," that not only does he care about sociality, but that his authorship is nothing if not an invitation to venture into existence with others as an *active*, fully *engaged* ethical-religious subject. This engagement comprises what we can call Kierkegaard's *politics* in the soft sense of the term. Certainly, for Kierkegaard this requires deep psychological reckoning with the spiritual or theological dimensions of our human experience. Hence, we can speak of a "political *theology*."

My intention here is not to settle a debate about Kierkegaard's politics. I am not going to argue for the *true* Kierkegaard, or that Kierkegaard properly *belongs* to any particular faction recognizable to twenty-first-century political allegiances.[1] I do acknowledge that Kierkegaard's anti-political and anti-democratic direct statements make him susceptible to a conservative and reactionary politics. But I believe that his indirect communication and the long-view of his authorial project seriously undermine the "conservative" reading of Kierkegaard's more direct statements. Admittedly, then, I will rely on the elasticity of Kierkegaard's thought to stretch him perhaps beyond his own acknowledged positions, but I am confident that the configuration here remains faithful to Climacus and the two "Kierkegaards" I will highlight.

Søren Kierkegaard's deliberate use of pseudonyms and genres are often explained in terms of a strategy he deploys for presenting his three spheres, or "stages"

---

1. For an overview and critical analysis of Kierkegaard's contribution to a "politics of action" in the twentieth century, see Pattison, *Kierkegaard and the Quest for Unambiguous Life*, 86–114.

of existence.² In the conventional reading, those differing authorial voices present the inner psychological dynamics of the aesthetic, ethical, and religious life-views. But what I want to develop here is their outward social-political application. Let us assume that we have taken Kierkegaard's dialectic of inwardness seriously and we are in the process of becoming ethical-religious individuals, then from this perspective those same pseudonyms and genres perform another function. Rather than simply being devices for self-assessment, they address certain social domains, offering strategies for social engagement, social critique, and activism that aim for a diverse society of existential integrity.

Just as Kierkegaard recognized that subjectivity is complex and differentiated, so too does he recognize the need for a complex and differentiated approach to our social communication, engagement, and activism.³ Therefore, I identify four approaches to social engagement that incorporate his religious imperative to work for edification *and* to provide for polemical critique. Each approach is associated with a particular voice or "Kierkegaard" and each voice presents a strategy for social engagement. (1) Johannes Climacus communicates a pedagogy of becoming from the point of view of a philosopher, or otherwise ethically committed individual who understands the religious life-view. (2) Søren Kierkegaard (1847), in *Works of Love*, invites us to direct personal engagement with our fellow humans, but also demands vigilance against closed structures of belonging. (3) Søren Kierkegaard (1855) presents us with the direct-action option of provocation and disobedience toward a church triumphant or a divinized political order.

Johannes Climacus (*Concluding Unscientific Postscript to Philosophical Fragments*, 1846)⁴

Climacus speaks to philosophers and those who are engaged in historical cultural criticism. If one of the tasks of the theologian is to participate in scholarly and theoretical conversations about the *good* and the *true*, then Climacus is a model for this kind of engagement for two simple reasons. First, the presumed task of a "scientific scholarly" academic is the immediate target of his critique.⁵ Second, he appreciates how scholars

2. Taylor, *Journeys to Selfhood*, 92.

3. See Mooney, "Pseudonyms," 191–210. Mooney's essay speaks to the intricacies, possibilities, and dilemmas arising from Kierkegaard's pseudonymity without really breaching its wider sociological opportunities.

4. Citations to Kierkegaard's *Concluding Unscientific Postscript* will be indicated in the text by (*CUP*).

5. Edward F. Mooney opts for "Unscholarly Postscript" rather than the more common translation, "Unscientific Postscript" (Mooney, "Pseudonyms," 199). In both cases, the point is to demonstrate how systematic philosophy is ultimately incapable of working through the ethical-religious predicament of existing human beings. But what Mooney fails to acknowledge here is that Climacus employs scholarly technique and language—albeit as a jazz musician reverentially undermines musical convention.

and cultural critics are socially influential. When theologians shift their mode of communication, this impacts how a society approaches its significant questions because they are also educators and cultural producers (for the time being, anyway).

Another important facet to Climacus's discourse is his *public* relationship to theology. Although he speaks comfortably and knowledgably about Christianity, Climacus does not speak publically from a confessional point of view. He neither assumes Christianity as a starting point nor does he expect a person to arrive at Christianity necessarily as a result of his discourse. Climacus merely explores the question of the meaning of Christianity from the point of view of an interested outsider (*CUP*, 36–39). This may seem odd to some readers since Christology is central to *Philosophical Fragments*, and since the matter of becoming a Christian is the stated task of Climacus in the *Postscript*.

Certainly Climacus is challenging the speculative understanding of history and consciousness, which regards religious faith as a preliminary stage followed by scientific-philosophical comprehension as advanced consciousness. Against this historical-developmental understanding, he argues that faith is not immediacy but the highest passion, that faith is a possibility only after or through understanding—not before or without understanding. However, for reasons I will outline below, according to Climacus the highest social goal is to become ethical-religious subjects (in a secular/immanent sense), and it is this that ought to be the universally human aim of any concrete philosophy. Becoming religious (in the Christian sense) is a further particular qualification taken in inwardness. For Climacus, then, the existential question is really how to become and remain ethically and spiritually interested individuals in a society that lures us toward abstractions and ambivalence, and as it turns out, this is also the live question of political theology. Below I identify, and merely outline, three strategies in the direction of developing ethical-religious personalities, and which lure away from abstraction.

First Climacean Strategy: Commitment to Process and Communication, or Keeping the "Wound of Negativity Open"

Climacus's philosophical environment comprised of positive thinkers and negative thinkers. Positive thinkers adhere to a scientific-scholarly outlook. They seek to understand existence objectively-empirically, historically, and speculatively. However, Climacus insists these categories cannot be existentially inhabited, and therefore they are ethically and socially secondary to the task of subjectivity (*CUP*, 197–98). Furthermore, he reminds us that every science is an approximation process and, as far as truth is concerned, objectively uncertain (*CUP*, 81). And since scientific thinking (positive thinking) "fails to express the state of the knowing subject in existence," since it is indifferent to subjectivity, it actually describes a "fictive objective subject" (*CUP*, 81). What worries Climacus is how knowledge systems dissociate from concrete existence.

Through the positive approach, Climacus notices, a person "comes to know much about the world, nothing about himself" (*CUP*, 81). But Climacus is not dismissing scientific and historical knowledge outright. Rather, he is suggesting that insofar as this knowledge is not, or cannot be, appropriated by individuals into their developing worldview then the knowledge is meaningless (*CUP*, 193).

And yet, to exist purely negatively is also impossible; after all, every person is an existing *thing* in a *world*. Therefore a person is just as positive as negative and vice versa (*CUP*, 85), which means that a person *is* the tension between the finite and the infinite, is bound by necessities and is open to possibilities. As long as a person exists these tensions cannot be resolved in speculative or positive results because that would mean both existence and the individuals are complete, which they obviously are not (*CUP*, 192). Therefore, in order to maintain the integrity of the tension, which, for Climacus, is the structure of existence, the subjective existing thinker "always keeps open the wound of negativity" (*CUP*, 85). But this is not some theoretical operation; it is precisely the passion for existence, and more specifically, the passion for the infinite which keeps the person striving. Politically, it means resisting final solutions or the belief that existing structures of power and belonging are optimal.

The most important question for a person, then, is how to relate to one's existential situation, or how we relate to our changing knowledge and how we develop in relation to what we are coming-to-understand. "The passion of the infinite, not its content, is the deciding factor, for its content is precisely itself. In this way the subjective 'how' and subjectivity are the truth" (*CUP*, 203). What is at issue is nurturing in oneself and others a passionate relationship to existence, and in Climacus's language this carries the ethical-religious significance of relating to an absolute idea, or the infinite (*CUP*, 203, 406–7).

For those who choose subjectivity as the ultimate task, then what it means to teach and to learn becomes intertwined in a very deliberate and artful way with expressing the process of subjectivity. "Whenever the subjective is of importance in knowledge and appropriation is therefore the main point, communication is a work of art" (*CUP*, 79).

Second Climacean Strategy: Teaching Capability or "Existence-Communication"

What is the art of communication that Climacus challenges the learned educators to emulate? What makes Climacus's indirect communication an art is that it must stir passion in the other person's own subjectivity. And the communicator must do this in such a way that demonstrates how communicator and addressee are both in a process of becoming. Climacus offers this analogy:

> To stop a man on the street and to stand still in order to speak with him is not as difficult as having to say something to a passerby in passing, without standing still oneself or delaying the other, without wanting to induce him to go the same way, but just urging him to go his own way—and such is the relation between an existing person and an existing person when the communication pertains to the truth as existence-inwardness. (*CUP*, 277)

Beyond movement we notice that communication ought to avoid controlling or determining the direction of another person's understanding or appropriation. The communicator urges the others to go their own way. Where subjectivity is concerned the communicative task combines ethics with pedagogy—that is its art. In fact Climacus even indicates that "the secret of communication specifically hinges on setting the other free" (*CUP*, 74). Sometimes this can involve calculated deception, which, Climacus insists, is particularly necessary when communicating with the scholarly and academically educated who believe they are "in the know."

The particular danger that besets this category of thinker is a confidence that they have made easy what is genuinely difficult (*CUP*, 275). For Climacus, this represents a movement from striving to rest, from interestedness to indifference, from passion to ambivalence. And therefore the task of the communicator is to reframe a person's knowledge in order to reintroduce the difficulty and get the striving apparatus of existence in motion again (*CUP*, 275–76).

Third Climacean Strategy: Acknowledging Allies

Finally, I would like us to consider the extent to which Climacus makes room for strategic ecumenical and inter-convictional alliances. While Climacus himself explores how an individual strives toward the highest pathos of Christian faith, and while he believes that such faith is indeed the "highest," he is under no illusion that such a life-view is objectively valid or objectively communicable—to insist otherwise is irreligious and fanaticism. And from a purely psychological and ethical point of view, inwardness itself is the task, regardless of various external expressions. Recall Climacus's comment about relating to truth subjectively: "If only the *how* of this relation is in truth, the individual is in truth, even if he in this way were to relate himself to untruth" (*CUP*, 199). Speaking more inter-culturally about relating to an absolute he writes,

> If someone who lives in the midst of Christianity enters . . . the house of God . . . and prays, but prays in untruth, and if someone lives in an idolatrous land but prays with all the passion of infinity, although his eyes are resting on the image of an idol—where, then, is there more truth? The one prays in truth to God although he is worshiping an idol; the other prays in untruth to the true God and is therefore in truth worshiping an idol. (*CUP*, 201)

And in an often-overlooked passage near the end of *Postscript*, Climacus disparages the Christian propensity for wanting to defend its doctrine against other doctrines. This propensity reveals two illusions: the illusion that one possesses and relates to sound doctrine, and the illusions held about the doctrines of another. "The most dangerous illusion of all is to become so sure of being [a Christian] that all Christendom must be defended against the Turk—instead of defending the faith within oneself against the *illusion about the Turk*" (*CUP*, 608). These passages not only warn against judging the inwardness of other deeply held worldviews, they also invite us to consider the profound affinity between all people who are existentially committed to ethical-religious deepening.

What distinguishes an ethical-religious worldview from an aesthetic worldview is a person's relation to an absolute *telos*. Ethical-religious worldviews (whether they adhere to immanent or transcendent cosmologies) are marked by this: that they relate *absolutely* to an *absolute*. Aesthetic individuals either relate *relatively* to an *absolute* or relate *absolutely* to what is *relative* (*CUP*, 407).

Ethical-religiousness knows that it cannot base its eternal happiness on anything historical and therefore relates itself absolutely to an ideal, a god, or gods. *Christian-religiousness* follows Ethical-religiousness and understands it to be true, subjectively and objectively, but then it chooses another possibility, against the understanding, to base its eternal happiness on something historical (this is the first paradox)—the Christ event (this is the second paradox, that the so-called historical object it relates to claims to be the eternal in temporality).

However, what is important for our purposes here is what takes place at the level of social and ethical action. And in fact at the level of outward ethical and existential activity there is no discernable difference between the *ethical-religious* and *Christian-religious*. Their difference, which is an essential difference of subjectivity, is hidden in inwardness. At the level of social action there are tremendous opportunities for collaboration in the areas of cultural critique and civil emancipation. Both remain committed to nurturing the existential capability in others. They also need each other to be vigilant against the temptation to "succumb to the positive and go roaring into the world in order to recommend, urge, and offer their beautifying negative wisdom for sale" (*CUP*, 84). Where they work to keep the wound of negativity open and exist in that tension between the infinite and the finite they are allies; where they work indirectly to communicate an absolute relation to an absolute and nurture ethical commitment to existence they are allies.

Finally, we cannot help but notice that Climacean strategies for social engagement are more pedagogical than plans or programs, precisely because what is at stake is everyone's subjectivity rather than a predetermined objective result. This may irritate the practitioner of *realpolitik*, but for the theologian who is interested in a substantive deepening of social and ethical life Climacus's indirect method provides a workable guide.

PART 1: KIERKEGAARD AND POLITICAL THEOLOGY

The Two Kierkegaards (*Works of Love*, 1847, and *The Moment*, 1855)

We begin with Kierkegaard and his 1847 *Works of Love*.[6] This form of communication is more directly related to homiletics and devotional material,[7] offering inspirational (but challenging) reflections on Scripture. It is intended to spur the reader toward action. As spiritual inspirational material, it is addressed to every religious individual regardless of cognitive or physical capabilities, regardless of social rank or education, and regardless of party-political preferences. The task of love is not easier for some and harder for others, rather it is equally rigorous and equally uplifting for all who undertake it.

However, despite its pleasant title and its edifying purpose *Works of Love* has received ambivalent reception with respect to its social-political significance. Foremost among the criticisms is Theodor Adorno's fierce essay.[8] Peter George has also warned against using *Works of Love* as a source for Kierkegaard's sociality, claiming that other texts do a better job where *Works of Love* unfortunately fails.[9] Recently, however, a number of studies have chosen to highlight the significance of *Works of Love* in Kierkegaard's authorship as a counterpoint to the view that his philosophy espouses only a solitary self-sufficient individual.[10]

Although theologians have given much thought to Augustine's question (What do I love when I love my God?), Kierkegaard's question in 1847 could be restated as, "*How* should I love if I love God?" There are two responses in particular that I will highlight here as the strategies offered by this Kierkegaard. The first is personal attentiveness to people and a real consideration of their actual particular needs and qualities. The second is to maintain vigilant opposition to domineering and exclusive structures of belonging.

First Kierkegaardian Strategy: Being Present *To* and *For* Others

How, then, are we to love if we say we love God? Kierkegaard's discourse is a reflection on 1 John 4:20, which reads, "If anyone says, 'I love God,' and hates his brother, he is a liar; for how can he who does not love his brother, whom he has seen, love God, whom he has not seen?" What is not possible is to love God by neglecting the people we see.

---

6. Citations for Kierkegaard's *Works of Love* will be indicated in the text by (*WL*).

7. While Kierkegaard utilized this genre earlier in the authorship, 1847 marks renewed attention to the genre and it coincides with his reading of Luther and Thomas à Kempis. See Hinkson, "Luther and Kierkegaard," 27–45; Podmore, "Lightning," 562–78; Rasmussen, "Thomas à Kempis," 289–98.

8. Adorno, "On Kierkegaard's Doctrine of Love," 413–29.

9. George, "Something Anti-Social," 70–81.

10. Formidable examples of this kind of defense can be found in Evans, *Kierkegaard's Ethic of Love* (2004); Ferreira, *Love's Grateful Striving* (2001); Hall, *Kierkegaard and the Treachery of Love* (2002).

Kierkegaard dismisses the notion that God is envious and selfishly demands our devotion to the exclusion of the world. This is to change God into "an unreal something, a delusion" (*WL*, 160). Instead, we are told,

> God does not have a share in existence in such a way that he asks for his share for himself; he asks for everything, but as you bring it to him you immediately receive, if I may put it this way, a notice designating where it should be delivered further. (*WL*, 161)

We must really turn our attention to people because it is "our duty to love the people we see" (*WL*, 154). Kierkegaard is helping his reader to make sense of the separation that typically exists between the object of love and the love itself. When it is a duty to love the people we see we cannot be distracted by a meticulous quest for the loveable object. Rather, "the task is to find the once given or chosen object—loveable, and to be able to continue to find him loveable no matter how he has changed" (*WL*, 159). Kierkegaard is offering a variation on the error of loving the unseen. Not only is it a misunderstanding to love the unseen God at the expense of people, but it is also a misunderstanding of love to love some unseen perfections or values at the expense of the actual qualities that exist in specific individuals. In other words, loving the people we see requires that we give up our fanciful illusions about what we think the objects of our regard must be and look like. When we bind ourselves to the duty to love the neighbor, to love the people we see, "*then in loving the actual individual person it is important that one does not substitute an imaginary idea of how we think or could wish that this person should be. The one who does this does not love the person he sees but again something unseen, his own idea or something similar*" (*WL*, 164). The warning here is not to make an idol of ourselves. That is, we ought not to make our own image or ideal the ideal that people must conform to if they are to enjoy our association.

When loving the actual people I see, I am inwardly being asked, "Do I hear their story, or am I listening only to a story being told about them, a story I am creating about them?" Kierkegaard is mining as much as he can from the verb, to see, but it seems impossible to follow through on what Kierkegaard is developing here unless there are also sincere interactions involving attentive listening and the space for development, which indirect communication provides. But in everything, avoid controlling another person's story. And this means incorporating the complexity of others into how we love the actual people we see.

Second Kierkegaardian Strategy: Opposing Domineering and Closed Structures of Belonging and Power

Kierkegaard is typically not regarded as someone who addresses structural questions in society, except to reject those questions as subjectively diminishing. For those who believe this is a narrow interpretation of Kierkegaard, *Two Ages* is often used as the basis for a Kierkegaardian social critique.[11] However, within the mostly direct communication of *Works of Love*, I notice an indirect warning and opposition to socially segregated, closed, and domineering social formations. This is most evident in the discourse titled "Love Does Not Seek Its Own."

In this discourse, Kierkegaard contrasts what he calls "small-mindedness" with a genuinely loving approach. Elsewhere we read, "Love is not a being-for-itself quality but a quality by which or in which you are for others" (*WL*, 223). Now we are shown a little more of what that looks like. Love, we are told, does not seek its own. Instead, "the truly loving one . . . loves every human being according to his distinctiveness; but 'his distinctiveness' is what for him is *his own* that is, the loving one does not seek his own; quite the opposite, he loves what is the other's own" (*WL*, 269). What Kierkegaard means by "one's own" is distinctiveness, and what he says about distinctiveness in this discourse involves a rather mystical explanation of "God's gift by which he gives being to me . . . gives being to all" (*WL*, 271). But what he means more precisely by distinctiveness is a person's way through their existential process. Or, it is their ethical-religious self-expression. In Climacus's terminology distinctiveness is their existence-communication. By contrast, "the small-minded person has clung to a very specific shape and form that he calls his own; he seeks only that, can love only that" (*WL*, 272).

The loving way, which is our guide for social life, looks for diversity and open associations in the hope of nurturing distinctiveness. For those who are committed to seeking the others' own good, "no strange distinctiveness is a refutation but rather a confirmation or one more demonstration" of God's gift of distinctiveness" (*WL*, 272). Alternatively, the small-minded view looks for similarity of *one's own* and forms closed associations or domineering associations in the hope of designing a comfortable homogeneity. For small-mindedness, "every distinctiveness is a refutation [of itself, of its *own*]; therefore it feels a clammy, uncomfortable anxiety upon seeing an unfamiliar distinctiveness, and nothing is more important for it than to get rid of it" (*WL*, 272). This anxiety is characteristic of every prejudice we are familiar with including racism, sexism, ableism, heterosexism, nationalism, or any combination.

What is important here is how Kierkegaard depicts small-mindedness as a social pathology and not simply a personal psychological expression. He notices that "small-mindedness holds together with small-mindedness," and this "alliance is then praised as the highest love, as true friendship, as true, loyal, honest harmony" (*WL*, 272). We can infer from the tone of this discourse that the behavior of a domineering and small-minded individual is interchangeable with the behavior of alliances in small-mindedness. Kierkegaard goes on to list ways this small-mindedness attempts to transform or extinguish any alien distinctiveness: it claims God's support for its own vision, it claims that its demand for conformity is an altruistic attempt to include

---

11. See Marsh, "Marx and Kierkegaard," 155–74; Westphal, *Kierkegaard's Critique of Reason and Society*, 43–59; Tilley, "Kierkegaard's Social Theory," 944–59.

people in *the truth*, and it keeps a lookout for the slightest infraction in order to demonstrate the deficiency of an alien distinctiveness (*WL*, 272–73).

Based on this discourse, structures of belonging that demand conformity to the dominant or even majority identity are rejected as universalized forms of selfish self-love. In fact, this assessment of small-mindedness stands as a critique of any identity politics that demands association or dissociation based on likeness to a definite, recognizable, and authorized pattern. Populist-nationalist movements are exposed as small-mindedness, and so are race, class, and gender prejudices. This is not to say that these identities don't exist or don't bear on our distinctiveness, but those identities do not constitute the horizon of our belonging and they cannot shield us from our responsibility to each other.[12] Therefore, rather than affirming a politics of identity Kierkegaard encourages us toward a more open politics of encounter and interaction and risk.

Understandably, for some readers this is a fragile interpretation given that *Works of Love* also contains the direct statements that "Christianity turns our attention completely away from the external" (*WL*, 376), that "Christianity does not want to make changes in externals" (*WL*, 139). And what is more devastating is how this last passage is used by Kierkegaard to dismiss societal shifts toward the political and legal emancipation of women. But in those and other similar cases Kierkegaard contravenes the spirit of his own reflections and the Scriptures he bases them on.

Kierkegaard-1847's ethic of love, while certainly personalistic, also implies unavoidable sociological demands: (a) it demands an egalitarian ethic, (b) the pursuit of a common good that recognizes diversity rather than sameness as essential to the good, (c) a personal and social rejection of self-serving or domineering power, and (d) replacing the master/slave dynamic with a lover/beloved (or seducer/seduced) relationship.

If Climacus's strategy is to direct the academic's thinking toward the concrete, to think existence and communicate existence, then Kierkegaard-1847's strategy is to show what it looks like to *do* the concrete task religiously assigned to one. This is what Merold Westphal has termed *Religiousness C*—the mode of existence that would follow Climacus's analysis into Christian social praxis.[13] Strategically the task is to uphold diversity *and* to pay attention to its intricacies, particularly the distinctiveness of individuals.

---

12. It is worth thinking about how "responsibility" may be very different depending on one's societal "distinctiveness." The responsibility of someone from a historically dispossessed or oppressed group may involve embodied resistance to dominant power and critique of those from a historically oppressing group. And the responsibility of those from a historically domineering group may involve difficult words of repentance, genuine acts of abdication, or reparations.

13. Westphal, "Kierkegaard's Religiousness C," 535–48.

PART 1: KIERKEGAARD AND POLITICAL THEOLOGY

Third Kierkegaardian Strategy: Public Activism and Disobedience[14]

"When the castle door of inwardness has long been shut and finally is opened, it does not move noiselessly like an apartment door which swings on hinges" (KAUC, 81). This is how Kierkegaard explained to a friend why he was embarking on such an outspoken and radical attack on nineteenth-century Christendom. Here, he expresses the need for a communicative strategy that is not only outwardly active, but which also must be loud and disruptive. The articles published in *Fedrelandet*, and his self-published pamphlet *The Moment* (*Øieblikket*), reveals an activist Kierkegaard whose aim, it appears, is to arouse public opposition to the state and ecclesiastical authority of Denmark. But the strategy of this Kierkegaard also reveals an essential flaw that we can avoid, partly because Climacus and Kierkegaard-1847 have warned us.

There is widespread and ongoing debate about the motives, aims, and outcomes of Kierkegaard's "Attack" campaign against Danish Christendom in 1855. Placing Kierkegaard's action within the contemporary politics of his age is fraught with complications, but it was a decisively political form of activism. He knew that his audience was the entire Danish public and that his targets were the political class, consisting of bourgeois liberal officials (legal, economic, and legislative), Danish nationalists, and most importantly, the clergy of the Danish People's Church. As George Pattison puts it, for Kierkegaard-1855, "the Church is simply a hypocritical front" because "it sought to combine being an institution serving bourgeois and national self-satisfaction whilst claiming also to be the Church of Jesus Christ."[15] In Christendom, existential and spiritual struggle in Christianity is replaced by a kind of religious cultural custom, propriety, and good taste. And the Christian association with the oppressed (Kierkegaard uses "lowly") and marginalized had been replaced by wealth, high cultural esteem, and state power.

Others have taken Kierkegaard's attack on the bourgeois character of Christendom (church and state) more seriously as what makes Kierkegaard's particular action more broadly applicable to twentieth- and twenty-first-century political theology.[16] Pattison is also sympathetic to these readings, with the proviso of some important cautions and questions.[17] I am convinced that Kierkegaard-1855's attack on the church absolutely includes an equal attack on bourgeois ethics, politics, and religiosity. The question remains, what alternative ideology are we left with if we follow Kierkegaard's critique? I will not venture an answer here.

---

14. Citations to Kierkegaard's *Attack upon "Christendom"* will be indicated in the text by (KAUC).

15. Pattison, *Kierkegaard and the Quest for Unambiguous Life*, 111–12.

16. M. J. Matuštík (1993); Michael Plekon (1983); Bartholomew Ryan (2014); Merold Westphal (1991).

17. Pattison, *Kierkegaard and the Quest for Unambiguous Life*, 109.

What is important here is not the content of his attack (which contains unnecessary vitriol and hyperbole) but the form. Kierkegaard-1855's actions demonstrate his conviction that living Christianly or Socratically necessarily collides with an established order. He also understood that direct action means being prepared to risk reputation and position, and even face real danger.[18] Tactically, Kierkegaard-1855 utilizes both popular newspapers and self-published pamphlets for public distribution in order to foment public anger at the state-church arrangement. Second, he called for a complete public boycott of the Danish People's Church, which included for him refusing to receive communion from a priest when he was dying.

From Kierkegaard-1855 we learn that there is indeed a "moment" (Øieblikket) when our words and technique must align with actions in the world, and that one must be prepared to face the consequences of opposition.[19] But Kierkegaard-1855 is also a case study in "what not to do." The problem for me is not that his aims are too radical or his claims unjustified. None of that scandalizes me. Neither is the content of his campaign inconsistent with the critiques of earlier Kierkegaards and pseudonyms. The error is not even in the directness of the message or the public medium of pamphleteering. The error, as I read it, was simply that Kierkegaard-1855 believed he was without any allies. Even more disappointing is that this Kierkegaard seemed to believe having an ally would undermine his truth and conviction. This solitary battle can therefore just as easily be interpreted as the tantrum of an eccentric rather than an important political and spiritual challenge to the existing social order. It also calls into question whether he actually believed that another social-spiritual reality was possible, because when people form communities of opposition and emancipation they demonstrate their ideals even if their revolutions fail. The ideal that Kierkegaard-1855 remains true to is the ideal of the Socratic citizen, the gadfly.[20] As it stands, it is no wonder that he became the hero of twentieth-century reactionary and fascist theorists—he appears a singular soul who dares to oppose bourgeois-liberal authority.

However, had the attack campaign been waged in association with Climacean allies and in the spirit of forging loving, open, associations of neighbors, then he could have allowed himself to be part of something, a movement, that demonstrates those ideals. In the end, Keirkegaard-1855 failed to be a good reader of Kierkegaards and pseudonyms prior to 1850. But we are able, with imagination and courage, to bring these strategies together.

---

18. Kierkegaard himself never faced the violence of state power, but he noticed and deplored how the church did employ the power of the police (Kierkegaard, *Attack upon "Christendom,"* 140).

19. Being willing to face consequences is not the same as accepting them.

20. Pattison, *Kierkegaard and the Quest for Unambiguous Life*, 110.

Bibliography

Adorno, Theodor. "On Kierkegaard's Doctrine of Love." *Studies in Philosophy and Social Sciences* 8 (1939) 413–29.

Evans, C. Stephen. *Kierkegaard's Ethic of Love*. Oxford: Oxford University Press, 2004.

Ferreira, M. Jamie. *Love's Grateful Striving: A Commentary on Kierkegaard's Works of Love*. Oxford: Oxford University Press, 2001.

George, Peter. "Something Anti-Social about *Works of Love*." In *Kierkegaard: The Self in Society*, edited by George Pattison and Steven Shakespeare, 70–81. London: Macmillan, 1998.

Hall, Amy Laura. *Kierkegaard and the Treachery of Love*. Cambridge: Cambridge University Press, 2002.

Hinkson, Craig. "Luther and Kierkegaard: Theologians of the Cross." *International Journal of Systematic Theology* 3 (2001) 27–45.

Kierkegaard, Søren. *Concluding Unscientific Postscript to Philosophical Fragments*. Translated by Howard V. Hong and Edna H. Hong. Vols. 1–2. Princeton: Princeton University Press, 1992.

———. *Kierkegaard's Attack upon "Christendom."* Translated by Walter Lowrie. New Jersey: Princeton University Press, 1946.

———. *Works of Love*. Translated by Howard V. Hong and Edna H. Hong. Princeton: Princeton University Press, 1995.

Marsh, James L. "Marx and Kierkegaard on Alienation." In *International Kierkegaard Commentary: Two Ages*, edited by Robert Perkins, 155–74. Macon, GA: Mercer University Press, 1984.

Mooney, Edward F. "Pseudonyms and 'Style.'" In *The Oxford Handbook of Kierkegaard*, edited by John Lippitt and George Pattison, 191–210. Oxford: Oxford University Press, 2013.

Pattison, George. *Kierkegaard and the Quest for Unambiguous Life: Between Romanticism and Modernism*. Oxford: Oxford University Press, 2013.

Plekon, Michael. "Prophetic Criticism, Incarnational Optimism: On Recovering the Late Kierkegaard." *Religion* 13 (1983) 137–53.

Podmore, Simon D. "The Lightning and the Earthquake: Kierkegaard on the *Anfechtung* of Luther." *Heythrop Journal* 47 (2006) 562–78.

Rasmussen, Joel D. S. "Thomas à Kempis: *Devotio Moderna* and Kierkegaard's Critique of 'Bourgeois-Philistinism.'" In *Kierkegaard and the Patristic and Medieval Traditions*, edited by Jon Stewart, 289–98. Kierkegaard Research: Sources, Reception and Resources 4. Aldershot, UK: Ashgate, 2008.

Taylor, Mark C. *Journeys to Selfhood: Hegel & Kierkegaard*. New York: Fordham University Press, 2000.

Tilley, J. Michael. "Kierkegaard's Social Theory." *Heythrop Journal* 55 (2014) 944–59.

Westphal, Merold. *Kierkegaard's Critique of Reason and Society*. University Park: Pennsylvania State University Press, 1991.

———. "Kierkegaard's Religiousness C: A Defense." *International Philosophical Quarterly* 44 (2004) 535–48.

4

Politics as Indirect Communication in *The Moment* and the *Attack upon "Christendom"*

STEPHEN BACKHOUSE

I PROPOSE FIRST THAT Kierkegaard is a political actor and thinker, second that his politics is embodied by his attack upon Christianized culture, and third that this attack is itself an example of indirect communication. Hence the claim of the title: politics as indirect communication in *The Moment* and the *Attack upon "Christendom."*

Any examination of the political dimension to Kierkegaard's project will have to consider the literature and events which together comprise the final phase of his life where he openly courted controversy with the Danish establishment. Kierkegaard famously eschewed most forms of party politics, however, this does not render him apolitical by any means. His engagement with "Christendom" encompassed a swirl of nationalism, civic identity, language rights, individual freedom, tribal allegiance, religious conscience, monarchy, bishops, revolution, reformation, bourgeois economic aspirations, and the plight of the common man. When *The Fatherland* published the first article attacking Mynster and Martensen in February 1854, Kierkegaard took a confident stride into the very heart of a perfect storm of politics.

Yet it is a common assumption that this final phase of Kierkegaard's life is a deviation from the method of indirect communication the earlier Kierkegaard had carefully cultivated. Kierkegaard's attack, so the feeling runs, is not really *Kierkegaardian*. Our examination of Kierkegaard's attack will thus consider the relationship of this latter phase of his career with the earlier: is the pseudonymous, public, and accessible nature of *The Moment* and other late writings an aberration from the pseudonymous, personal and cryptic authorship? By speaking out loudly in his own name, did Kierkegaard abandon indirect communication? In answer to these questions I argue that Kierkegaard does not abandon indirect communication in his attack. Furthermore, I suggest that a proper recognition of the indirect form that his attack takes is crucial for understanding not only Kierkegaard as a political agent but also a Kierkegaardian political posture applicable today.

To be sure, "indirect communication" as a concept develops throughout the authorship to the point where it looks different in the attack than it does in the works of key pseudonyms such as Johannes de Silentio, Johannes Climacus, and Anti-Climacus, and yet, it remains "indirect'" all the same. Subsequent pseudonyms bring Kierkegaard to the point where he is able to make his public attack on Christendom without also abandoning his precious category of indirect communication. Indeed, by the time indirect communication reaches its full development, *public expression is seen to be a necessary component of indirect communication*. The communication of *The Moment* and other late writings is more than mere printed words directly stating Kierkegaard's case. The communication adopts an intentionally unbalanced polemic designed to be a corrective. It openly courts the possibility of offense by inviting the readers to look at the incongruous life of the author in order to elicit an emotional and personal choice not based on emulation or objective arguments. It is existential, subjective, and offensive, creating the catalyst for a personal decision regarding one's allegiance and love, rather than demanding intellectual assent to a set of logical propositions. In other words, it is *indirect*. Its target is the relationship one has to one's social context, group affiliation, and the rights and responsibilities that a Christ follower has toward an inherited civic identity and moral order which has become "Christianized." In other words, it is *political*. Thus, it is precisely this mode of indirect communication which he adopts at the end of his life that constitutes Kierkegaard's politics.

A Brief Overview of "Indirect Communication" in the Key Pseudonyms

The literature divides communication into two categories, *direct* and *indirect*.[1] Johannes de Silentio does not specifically dwell on the definitions, but both Johannes Climacus and Anti-Climacus understand *direct communication* as the imparting of knowledge by a legitimate authority, and *indirect communication* as the communication of capability, in other words, the bringing of each individual to the point where they can make a decision for themselves and in themselves.[2] For Johannes de Silentio, true to his name, indirect communication happens through "silence,"[3] for Climacus through "double reflection"[4] and for Anti-Climacus through "reduplication."[5] With his attack upon Christendom, the possibility of indirect communication as reduplication is extended from a unique mode available only to Christ, to a form

---

1. For examples, see the story of the king who tries to communicate his love to a peasant girl in Kierkegaard, *Philosophical Fragments*, 26–32; Kierkegaard, *Concluding Unscientific Postscript*, 72–80, 242–50; Kierkegaard, *Practice in Christianity*, 127–36.
2. Kierkegaard, *Concluding Unscientific Postscript*, 75; Kierkegaard, *Practice in Christianity*, 142.
3. Kierkegaard, *Fear and Trembling*, 14, 23, 38–41, 53, 82–120.
4. Kierkegaard, *Concluding Unscientific Postscript*, 72–118, 251–300.
5. Kierkegaard, *Practice in Christianity*, 123–27, 131–32, 133–36.

of communication embodied by Kierkegaard when he becomes an offensive sign of contradiction to his native culture.[6]

Communication, to be indirect, must repel the listener to some extent. Johannes de Silentio's silence repelled would-be followers, forcing them to face God on their own. Climacus's double reflection repelled followers by forcing them away from the communicator, separating the message from the one giving it. With reduplication, Anti-Climacus presents a new level of indirect communication that also repels listeners, but in a very different way than the previous, non-Christian pseudonyms were repelled. For the religious-ethical Johannes de Silentio, and the religious-intellectual Climacus, what was repelling was not intrinsic to the communicator. The ideal figures of Abraham and Lessing were not men who were fundamentally repellent *in themselves*. At all times, the otherwise attractive men had to use either silence or double reflection to divert would-be disciples. What repels listeners in the books by Johannes de Silentio and Climacus is not Abraham or Lessing, but the radically individual demands of faith and the incomprehensible and intellectually offensive claims of Christianity. But Anti-Climacus is not concerned with "faith," or even so much with the religious system that is labeled "Christianity." Rather, Anti-Climacus is overwhelmingly concerned with the person and life of Jesus Christ. In *Practice in Christianity*, Anti-Climacus complains (against Climacus?) that the God-Man has been made into "speculative unity" or turned into "that no-where-to-be-found medium of pure being" instead of seeing that "the God-Man is the unity of God and an individual human being in a historically accurate situation."[7]

Anti-Climacus defines reduplication as the teacher existing in the teaching,[8] and what is more:

> Wherever it is the case that the teacher is an essential component, there is reduplication, the communication is not completely direct paragraph-communication or professor communication. . . . And now, when the teacher, who is inseparable from and more essential than the teaching, is a paradox, then all direct communication is impossible . . . [and] Christ is infinitely more important than his teaching.[9]

What is potentially repellent for Anti-Climacus is not any idea or demand that Christ communicates. It is Christ himself who "repels" because he exists as a *sign of contradiction*.[10] A sign of contradiction "is a sign that intrinsically contains a qualitative contradiction in itself."[11]

6. Kierkegaard, *The Moment*, 15, 20–25, 38, 42, 46, 60, 74, 78, 83–84, 135, 180–82, 197, 213, 290, 311–12, 316, 321, 324, 333, 329–54.
7. Kierkegaard, *Practice in Christianity*, 123.
8. Ibid.
9. Ibid., 123–24.
10. Ibid., 124–28, 132, 134–36, 141.
11. Ibid., 124.

The God-Man repels not by avoiding disciples—but by calling them to himself. The incarnation "draws attention to itself and then represents a contradiction."[12] For such a figure, direct communication is shown to be an impossibility.[13] This is because even straightforward invitations like "believe in me,"[14] are obscured by the intrinsic contradiction inherent in who it is who is doing the speaking. For Jesus Christ there can only be indirect communication, because direct expression involves directly recognizing what the communicator essentially *is*, an act impossible with the God-Man who is profoundly *incognito*.[15]

Jesus Christ is reduplication because he exists as his message. In effect, that message is "I am God," taking the discrepancy between message and messenger to its extreme:

> If someone says directly: "I am God, the Father and I are one," this is direct communication. But if the person who says it, the communicator, is this individual human being, an individual human being just like others, then this communication is not quite entirely direct. . . . Because of the communicator, the communication contains a contradiction, it becomes indirect communication.[16]

Christ, precisely because of what he is, simply cannot give a direct communication:

> The single direct statement, like the miracle, can serve only to make aware in order that the person who has been made aware, facing the offence of the contradiction, can choose whether he will believe or not.[17]

Anti-Climacus hints at, but does not develop, the idea that normal humans can embody messages the way that Christ embodies his.[18] The reduplication that Kierkegaard will extend to himself and others in his polemic against Christendom is yet to be fully developed in the Anti-Climacean literature. The *imitatio Christi* (the move from human witness to reduplication) does not occur with any pseudonym, but only with Kierkegaard himself. However, it is by maintaining Anti-Climacus's vision of reduplication, that Kierkegaard can preserve the precious indirect communication necessary for Christianity, even while descending to a direct war with the established order.

---

12. Ibid., 126.
13. Ibid., 127, 133–39.
14. Ibid., 135, quoting John 14:1.
15. Ibid., 131–32.
16. Ibid., 134.
17. Ibid., 136.
18. Ibid., 129–31.

The *Attack upon "Christendom"* as Indirect Communication

It is false to assume that it is pseudonyms alone that constitute the whole of what it means for Kierkegaard to communicate "indirectly." Of course, many commentators do hold that when Kierkegaard is writing or speaking out in his own name, the communication is automatically "direct." This assumption is widespread in popular, accessible research sources[19] but also in the secondary academic literature, apparently without there being seen a need to craft an argument to back up this belief. Instead it is simply taken for granted that if Kierkegaard is using his own name, then of course he must be communicating directly.[20] The Hongs speak for many when they write: "Whereas the pseudonymous works from *Either/Or* through *Concluding Unscientific Postscript* are indirect communication, the signed discourses from first to last are direct."[21]

The assumption that writing under Kierkegaard's own name equals direct communication colors the interpretation of much of Kierkegaard's private journals and later literature. In opposition to this type of approach, I propose that Kierkegaard's attack is not an example of direct communication. By drawing attention to his own life and his own inadequacies as an ideal Christian, and by the very polemical and corrective tone of the writings which make up the attack, Kierkegaard shows us that he is not offering up a wholesale version of his views, as if he were a serving boy presenting "Christianity" on a silver platter. Instead, *The Moment* continues from the precedent set by the previous pseudonymous authors, indirectly communicating an awareness of the responsibility of the listeners to personally appropriate the message.

---

19. See, e.g., the entries on Kierkegaard in the peer-reviewed *IEP* (*Internet Encyclopaedia of Philosophy*) and the *Stanford Encyclopaedia of Philosophy*. A notable exception is the online resources provided by D. Anthony Storm.

20. Examples are legion, including but not confined to the early days of English Kierkegaardian scholarship. Sample commentators include: Arbaugh and Arbaugh, *Authorship*; Blanchot, *Faux Pas*; Brookfield, "What Was Kierkegaard's Task," 23–35; Damgaard, "Biblical Variations"; Dunning, "Who Sets the Task?," 18–33; Elrod, *Kierkegaard and Christendom*; McCombs *Paradoxical*; McCracken, *Scandal*; Pojman, *Logic*; Sponheim, *Kierkegaard on Christ and Christian Coherence*; Stocker, *Kierkegaard on Politics*. Two notable recent exceptions include Mooney, "Pseudonyms and 'Style,'" and Westfall, *Kierkegaardian Author*.

21. These sentiments have been widely influential in the reception history of Kierkegaard. Cf. Kierkegaard, *Eighteen Upbuilding Discourses*, xi. The Hongs also include the Anti-Climacus works *Sickness Unto Death* and *Practice in Christianity* among the number of self-penned, and therefore in their opinion, directly communicated, works. In the translator's introduction to *Fear and Trembling*, the Hongs equate "indirection" with pseudonymity (Kierkegaard, *Fear and Trembling*, x). In this the Hongs do not substantially depart from the earlier translator, Walter Lowrie. Lowrie says that Kierkegaard's final period "amounts to a retraction of the pseudonyms and the whole elaborate apparatus of 'indirect communication.'" Lowrie, *Short Life*, 187, but also 172, 175, 176, and 198. On Kierkegaard's frankness of speech as his supposed aversion to indirect communication, see the translator's introductions to *Attack upon "Christendom,"* xv; *Sickness Unto Death*, 138; *Point of View*, xxiv. See also Kierkegaard, 1:271–80, esp. 277, and 286–90; Kierkegaard, 2:467.

> If you imagine that I am a waiter, then you have never been my reader; if you actually are my reader, then you will understand that I can even regard it as my duty to you that you will be strained a little.[22]

There are three reasons why the final works should not be interpreted as an abandonment of indirect communication. First, the critique is indirect because it is a *corrective*, and does not represent a point of view that is independent of other views.[23] Direct communication does not require the cooperation of the listener, nor an interaction with any other messages in the public domain, in order to be true.[24] This is not the case with the attack, which intentionally adopts an extreme polemic in order to counterbalance the opposite extreme of comfortable Christendom, and whose truth emerges only in conjunction with the faulty message to which the attack is a dialectical partner. Second, the attack is indirect because Kierkegaard eschews followers, actively working to repel would-be pupils.[25] Instead, he seeks to *make people aware* of the choice that is facing them and impress upon them the responsibility that they have to make an honest decision for themselves. The communication is not delivered with complete disregard for the individual (i.e., "objectively"),[26] but instead the ultimate fulfillment of the message is found only in the individual's new awareness of the stark difference between authentic Christianity and Christendom, and the decision that they must make as result of this awareness. Third, and most importantly, the attack is indirect for in his writing and in his life, Kierkegaard himself *reduplicates* his message, adopting for himself the Christ-mode as the sign of contradiction.[27] Jesus Christ's existence as God and man is the message that contains the possibility of offense, his invitation prompting a choice that can only be either faith or disobedience.[28] As such, Kierkegaard calls attention to his life and his own inadequacies in relation to his message. He himself cannot be the model of ideal Christianity that he espouses in his writings. For this reason, Kierkegaard's message is not "follow me," but "make a decision," and his very existence as an offensive, ridiculous and potentially hypocritical fool forces the reader to have to make an honest choice about Christianity that is not based on any direct proof of Kierkegaard's life.

> Very simply—I want honesty. I am not, as some well-intentioned people—I cannot pay attention to the opinions of me held in bitterness and rage and impotence and blather—have wanted to represent me, I am not Christian

---

22. Kierkegaard, *The Moment*, 106.
23. Ibid., 12, 24, 34, 40–41, 51, 67, 99–100, 106–7, 130, 143, 211, 217–20, 226, 335.
24. Kierkegaard, *Concluding Unscientific Postscript*, 73–76.
25. Kierkegaard, *The Moment*, 13, 29, 33–34, 40, 46, 48–49, 73–74, 76, 97, 101, 110, 130, 197, 212, 236, 336–37, 340–47.
26. Kierkegaard, *Concluding Unscientific Postscript*, 75.
27. Kierkegaard, *The Moment*, 15, 20, 23, 25, 38, 42, 46, 60, 74, 78, 83–84, 135, 180–82, 197, 213, 290, 311–12, 316, 321, 324, 333, 329–54.
28. Kierkegaard, *Practice in Christianity*, 35–36, 75–83, 94, 119, 102–3, 121.

> stringency in contrast to a given Christian leniency. Certainly not. I am neither leniency nor stringency—I am human honesty.[29]

> This must be said; I place no one under obligation to act accordingly—for that I do not have authority. But having heard it you are made responsible and must now act on your own responsibility as you think you can justify it before God.[30]

To make this position very clear, we will consider the indirect nature of *The Moment* and other late writings first as a corrective, second as the making aware of responsibility; and finally, as reduplication below.

The *Attack upon "Christendom"* as Corrective

The Moment reaches the conclusion that not only is Christianity qualitatively different from the world, it is also, by necessity, actively opposed to it.[31] In terms of indirect communication, this development can be seen in the attack as a corrective polemic. Although it may seem at first that a polemic can only be direct, in line with the strictures set by the pseudonyms, it is possible to speak forthrightly without thereby also communicating directly. Here, *Moment*-as-corrective assumes a role along lines Anti-Climacus has already sketched in *Practice in Christianity*:

> If the communication by a communicator is to be direct, then not only the communication must be direct, but the communicator himself must be directly defined. *If not, then even the most direct statement by such a communicator still does not—because of the communicator, because of what the communicator is—become direct communication.*[32]

A corrective is an unbalanced response to an unbalanced situation. It is not known apart from the malign context in which it operates. Hence it is not directly defined. It is a straightforward statement which nonetheless remains *indirect*.

This is the case for this stage in Kierkegaard's career, which is not an exercise in didactic preaching, but rather dialectic engagement. The extreme of his side of the message is set against the extreme of Christendom's message, and Kierkegaard does not wish his polemic to be taken as anything other than a corrective. "Take an emetic!" he cries, offering for his part a picture emphasizing the suffering of true Christianity in order to wake people from their comfortable delusions.[33] Kierkegaard is not

---

29. Kierkegaard, *The Moment*, 46.
30. Ibid., 73.
31. Ibid., 17, 20, 39, 109, 143, 149, 162, 168–69, 170, 188, 206, 222, 226, 257, 321, 332. 334.
32. Kierkegaard, *Practice in Christianity*, 134, emphasis added. See also 134–36.
33. Kierkegaard, *The Moment*, 99–100, also 211.

a waiter,[34] but a surgeon,[35] a fireman,[36] and a detective,[37] all of whom must deal with what is harmful or unsavory in the service of the greater good. Of the inevitable fallout from his attack on Christendom, Kierkegaard says that "everything must burst so that in this nightmare individuals who are able to bear New Testament Christianity might come again into existence."[38]

Christendom, writes Kierkegaard, has stopped Christianity from being a necessary corrective at any given time and place.[39] With his polemic, Kierkegaard is redressing the balance of what has been lost. In his attack, Kierkegaard purposely steers clear of even-handed arguments. At one point, he sarcastically alludes to the academic ideal of being able to talk objectively about Christianity without actually having to live by it.[40] The assistant professors look down on people who are so "one-sided" that they actually practice what they teach. In opposition to these professors, Kierkegaard says that this sort of one-sidedness is exactly what is needed.[41] It is only by being one-sided that Christianity will attain its dialectical purpose as a corrective to *Christendom's* one-sidedness, which Kierkegaard identifies as its claims of sophisticated superiority over every other previous culture.[42] "Christian" for Kierkegaard is a "polemical concept" and thus "one can be a Christian only in contradistinction or by way of contrast."[43] As a result, he perceives that his task to communicate Christianity in an ostensibly Christian land must be approached indirectly. In an important section apparently overlooked by those who assume that *The Moment* must be direct as a matter of course, Kierkegaard provides hints toward his own project of one-sided indirect correction:

> When Christianity entered the world, the task was to proclaim Christianity directly. . . . *In Christendom the relation is different.* . . . If Christianity is to be introduced here, then first and foremost the illusion must be removed. . . . [The task] is directed to what can be done to clear up people's concepts, to instruct them, to stir them by means of the ideals, through pathos to bring them into an impassioned state, *to rouse them up with the gadfly sting.*[44]

Ultimately, the purpose of the surgeon's scalpel, or the sting of the gadfly, is to create pain in order to spark a reaction in an otherwise unresponsive person. In a variation

34. Ibid., 106.
35. Ibid., 12, 24.
36. Ibid., 217–20.
37. Ibid., 40, 130, 226.
38. Ibid., 34.
39. Ibid., 41.
40. Ibid., 194.
41. Ibid., 67.
42. Ibid., 335.
43. Ibid., 143.
44. Ibid., 107, emphasis added.

of his "fire-chief" analogy, Kierkegaard claims that strictly speaking he is not the one ringing the alarm, but the one starting the fire.[45] With his drastic and unbalanced attack, Kierkegaard is not directly conveying knowledge that his public can take or leave as if it were a self-contained package of Christian information. The information imparted by direct communication does not rely on individual appropriation, or on extenuating circumstances, for it to be true. The corrective message of *The Moment* however, requires both an extreme state of affairs to which it runs counter, and the cooperative response of its readers, in order to be successful. It is as a corrective that the attack promotes the "coming to awareness" of individual responsibility. It is this "awareness" factor that leads to the second aspect of the attack's indirect communication. Kierkegaard's dialectic serves to make individuals aware of the discrepancy between Christendom and Christianity, and once they *are* aware it is they who are responsible for deciding about what they will do about it.

The *Attack upon "Christendom"* as Making Aware

That Kierkegaard is not leading a reform movement or asking for followers, but is instead foisting the responsibility for change back onto his listeners, is another mark of the attack's indirect communication:

> As for myself, I am not . . . a reformer, in no way, nor am I a profound speculative intellect, a seer, a prophet—no, I have, if you please, to a rare degree I have a definite detective talent.[46]

Unlike the one leading a movement, the detective merely brings the facts to light, leaving it to others to take the necessary action suggested by the uncovered truth.[47] Even when Kierkegaard began to write in *The Moment*, his own self-published magazine, he fought to dissuade followers. Preferring the purity of the "separateness of singleness," Kierkegaard considers it his task to avert popular movements in his name.[48] In a subsequent edition, Kierkegaard urges his readers *not* to subscribe to his magazine, preferring that people think twice instead of acting from a misplaced and hot-headed rebellious zeal.[49] "Do believe me," he implores, "I do not involve myself with you in a finite sense at all, [I] do not seek to draw you to me in order to found a party, etc. No, I am only religiously doing my duty."[50] Although he is obviously concerned with Christianity, Kierkegaard does not identify himself as one,[51] for that would propel him

---

45. Ibid., 51.
46. Ibid., 40, see also 34.
47. Ibid., 40.
48. Ibid., 76.
49. Ibid., 101.
50. Ibid., 197.
51. Ibid., 46–49, 143, 212–13, and esp. 340–43.

into the sphere of the religious reformer or evangelical revivalist. "I do not participate in changing what Christianity is in order thereby to obtain millions of Christians."[52]

What then, does Kierkegaard want? "Very simply—I want honesty [*Redelighed*]."[53] It has been a temptation of some theologically minded readers to paint a picture of Kierkegaard in this final phase as being a champion of Christianity and a declaimer of the Christian message. Besides the aberration that this makes of *The Moment* regarding direct communication, it also deviates from the attitude to Christianity found throughout the pseudonymous works. There, the pseudonyms agree that whatever else Christianity might be, at the very least whatever is authentic about it is not something that needs to be preached, demonstrated or defended. As Anti-Climacus says in *Sickness Unto Death*:

> Therefore it is certain and true that the first one to come up with the idea of defending Christianity in Christendom is *de facto* a Judas No. 2: he too, betrays with a kiss. . . . To defend something is always to disparage it.[54]

To assume that with his attack Kierkegaard takes on the role of apologist *extraordinaire* is to assign to the author a position completely at odds with anything that has come before. Instead, it should always be kept in mind Kierkegaard's insistence that he is promoting "honesty," not "Christianity" as such. "I am not Christian stringency in contrast to a given Christian leniency. Certainly not, I am neither leniency nor stringency—I am human honesty."[55] Thus, Kierkegaard is not a churchman, fighting for one particular Christian denomination or interpretation over another.

> I am not saying that it is for Christianity I venture—suppose, just suppose that I become quite literally a sacrifice. I would still not become a sacrifice for Christianity but because I wanted honesty.[56]

Despite his consistent claims that he is not a Christian, however, it is still appropriate to speak of Kierkegaard as having a Christian direction to his work. With his abandonment of the title "Christian" for polemical reasons, Kierkegaard was not signifying that he was no longer interested in the authentic concerns of the faith. To interpret Kierkegaard as some sort of proto-atheist by treating as direct communication his claims that he was not a Christian, is again to ignore the setting in which this particular jewel of a phrase inheres.[57] Such phrases cannot be read in isolation from the larger body

---

52. Ibid., 212.

53. Ibid., 46.

54. Kierkegaard, *Sickness Unto Death*, 87. See also Kierkegaard, *Philosophical Fragments*, 43; Kierkegaard, *Concluding Unscientific Postscript*, 46–49; and Kierkegaard, *Practice in Christianity*, 26–31, where Anti-Climacus calls the attempt to defend Christianity "blasphemy."

55. Kierkegaard, *The Moment*, 46.

56. Ibid., 49.

57. The idea that Kierkegaard was an aware and active non-believer, or was at least on his way to becoming one, has its roots in Kierkegaard's first biographer. Georg Brandes, friend of Nietzsche

of work that makes up Kierkegaard's task. It is the whole authorship and the ascent through the stages that looms in the background when we read:

> But although I do not dare say that I venture for Christianity, I remain fully and blissfully convinced that this, my venturing, is pleasing to God, has his approval. Indeed I know it; it has his approval that in a world of Christians where millions and millions call themselves Christians—that there one person expresses: I do not dare call myself a Christian; but I want honesty, and to that end I will venture.[58]

As an alternative to the millions of Christians who have not individually faced the possibility of offense, Kierkegaard would rather open and honest rebellion against God than the hypocritical religion of Christendom.[59]

> So let there be light on this matter, let it become clear to people what the New Testament understands by being a Christian, so that everyone can choose whether he wants to be a Christian or whether he honestly, plainly, forthrightly does not want to be that.[60]

The Moment retains as all-important the choice that the individual must make. The events and writings that make up the attack upon Christendom cannot therefore be thought of as an example of direct communication. Direct communication does not rely on the receiver for it to have achieved its aim. The direct communicator can, like a "barker of subjectivity," didactically pronounce his knowledge from a street corner.[61] His message does not change whether anyone is listening or not, because his message is made up of facts and information. If, in his polemic, Kierkegaard were only promoting the existence of a particular factual version of Christianity, then he too would be a street barker. However, unlike water, which remains the same no matter whether it is drawn by tap or by well, honest Christianity is not indifferent to the way that it is obtained.[62] Kierkegaard cries for "honesty," a goal that necessarily requires the cooperation of the listening public. The content of Kierkegaard's attacking message is that Christianity is no more, and that people must face this, *either* continuing in honest and open defiance of God, *or*, in honesty, submitting themselves to the possibility of authentic faith through the possibility of offense.[63] Kierkegaard is not handing down

---

and chronicler of Kierkegaard's life, celebrated the Dane as a potential atheist "free thinker" in his *Danmark*. Two examples of arguments that Kierkegaard was *never* a Christian come from Usher, *Journey* and Zuidema, *Kierkegaard*.

58. Kierkegaard, *The Moment*, 49. In ibid., 33, Kierkegaard says that to some he appears to be an atheist, but he has God on his side. See also Kierkegaard, "My Task," 340–47, in the last issue of *The Moment*, which was fully prepared, but not published in Kierkegaard's lifetime.

59. Kierkegaard, *The Moment*, 48.

60. Ibid., 97.

61. Kierkegaard, *Concluding Unscientific Postscript*, 77.

62. Kierkegaard, *The Moment*, 110; Kierkegaard, *Concluding Unscientific Postscript*, 73–75.

63. Kierkegaard, *The Moment*, 29, 48, 49, 74, 97, 236.

knowledge as a guru to his disciples, but he is instead making his listeners aware of the responsibility that they have toward the faith they claim to own and the society that uses religious language while denying its power.

In keeping with his aversion to followers, or to being cast as a reformer, Kierkegaard repeatedly throws his audience back into their own resources. After alluding to his own authorship in general, and of the unspoken implications of *Practice in Christianity* in particular, Kierkegaard says of the former head of "official" Christianity that "I have not pronounced judgment upon Bishop Mynster, no, but in the hands of Governance I became the occasion for Bishop Mynster to pronounce judgment upon himself."[64]

Kierkegaard extends the onus of the decision onto all who attend to his message:

> This must be said; I place no one under obligation to act accordingly—for that I do not have authority. But by having heard it you are made responsible and must now act on your own responsibility as you think you can justify it before God.[65]

Having been made aware by the fireman, the surgeon, the detective, and the gadfly, Christendom's citizens can no longer remain content with the soporific herd mentality. Kierkegaard makes it personal, presenting to the individual the stark reality of their situation, a choice of submission of defiance. Taken as a whole, the pseudonymous works, the edifying discourses, the unpublished journals and the prayers and comments during his attack provide ample evidence as to Kierkegaard's opinion of which choice was preferred. Nevertheless, Kierkegaard's message is not to choose Christ but simply to *choose*. "You yourself, then, bear and have to bear the responsibility for how you act, but you have been made aware!"[66] It is only with this primary communication clearly in mind that we can turn to Kierkegaard's idea of what the responsibility of living up to the "Christian" moniker implies. Building mostly from work done previously in *Practice in Christianity*, Kierkegaard provides his opinion of what the opposite of honest defiance would look like. Having been made aware, the individual's responsibility for honest obedience follows only one pattern, "the responsibility is this: imitation of Jesus Christ."[67]

The *Attack upon "Christendom"* as Reduplication

How Kierkegaard brings about the *moment* [Øiblikket] at which the individual becomes aware of his responsibility for a decision is wrapped up with Kierkegaard's own particular imitation of Christ. In *PC*, it was seen that the process of reduplication

---

64. Ibid., 13.
65. Ibid., 73.
66. Ibid., 236. See also ibid., 29, 74, 97, 336.
67. Ibid., 337.

occurred when the messenger existed as the message.[68] Anti-Climacus was keen to shift attention away from the possibility of this sort of indirect communication for normal humans, and instead focused on Christ as the unique example of reduplication.[69] Jesus Christ effectively declares that he is God, inviting all men to "Come here . . . and I will give you rest";[70] yet the being saying this is a lowly human. Thus, the contemporaneous individual is faced with the moment of having to choose whether he will accept or reject the invitation as it stands. In the realm of Christian faith, there is no automatic, logically necessary conclusion. Miracles and other "proofs" do not help, as the choice must be made by faith alone—in fact, Anti-Climacus points out that demonstrations of the divine only serve to emphasize the potential offensiveness of having the holy coexist with the human.[71]

By the time of his attack, Kierkegaard personally appropriates the formerly unique Christ-mode of reduplication, making himself stand as a sign of contradiction, a sign that creates the *moment* when individuals become aware of the choice facing them. It is because of reduplication that Kierkegaard can make such direct statements under his own name, and yet the communication of *The Moment* remains indirect. It is argued that like Christ, Kierkegaard draws attention to himself, effectively making the disparity that exists between him and his message *part of* the message.[72] Christ embodied the communication that people must have faith that God has appeared in human form. Kierkegaard's communication is less cosmically drastic, but no less reduplicated—"I am human honesty."[73]

Roger Poole, in his book *Kierkegaard: The Indirect Communication*, makes a similar argument toward seeing Kierkegaard's embodiment as reduplication. Poole chooses to base his arguments on the events surrounding Kierkegaard's death, devoting most of his chapter on the final events of Kierkegaard's life not on the events of the attack but instead on the personal reflections of Kierkegaard's friends who were with him in the end.[74] It is Poole's intention to demonstrate that Kierkegaard imitated Christ to those around him, thanks to the marriage of irascible outspokenness and a personally meek and gentle demeanor. Poole makes much of various eyewitness accounts that Kierkegaard appeared to emanate a sort of glowing, peaceful aura at the end of his life, thus demonstrating his ability to embody contradictory messages.[75] It is curious that Poole veers off into this sort of speculation, indulging in secondary,

---

68. Kierkegaard, *Practice in Christianity*, 123.
69. Compare ibid., 129–31, with 36, 123–24, and 134–35.
70. Matt 11:28.
71. Kierkegaard, *Practice in Christianity*, 96–97.
72. Kierkegaard, *The Moment*, 23, 25, 38, 60, 74, 78, 83, 213, 290, 311–12, 333, 340.
73. Ibid., 46.
74. Poole, *Kierkegaard*, ch. 9.
75. The deathbed accounts of Kierkegaard's nephew Troels Lund and of Lund's niece Henriette are recounted in Poole, *Kierkegaard*, 274–81.

ethereal memoirs to prove his point when there is much better information closer to hand in Kierkegaard's final writing. In a similar vein, Michael Strawser rightly argues that Kierkegaard's "religious" works are not necessarily more direct than his "philosophical" ones,[76] but Strawser too chooses to focus on sources other than *The Moment*. In his case, Strawser argues for a more "indirect" reading of Kierkegaard by successfully demonstrating that aesthetic and philosophical themes run throughout the early non-pseudonymous texts like the *Edifying Discourses*.[77] However, just as it is for Poole, it is a problem for Strawser's argument that he does not deal with *The Moment*, Kierkegaard's most supposedly direct communication. It seems that even for those critics who question much of the received wisdom on Kierkegaard, the tradition of ignoring the attack remains unchallenged.

This is a shame, for a wealth of information can be found in these final texts supporting the claim that Kierkegaard's last public pronouncements were indirect, *not despite their public nature, but because of it*. We begin with Kierkegaard's view that there is only one requirement from Christ and the apostles: imitation.[78] This Kierkegaard explicitly identifies as "suffering," because truth always suffers in this sinful, hypocritical, selfish world: "Christianity is the suffering truth because it is the truth and is in this world."[79] Christ's mode of being is thus extended to his followers, in that their existence is a suffering on the earth: "That one has faith can be demonstrated in only one way: by being willing to suffer for one's faith."[80] The Christ-imitation of suffering makes up one aspect of the final development of "offence."[81]

But suffering also has communicative properties. Christ's followers embody the life of abasement in order to serve the particular needs of proclaiming Christianity in Christendom.[82] According to Kierkegaard, God wants Christianity to be proclaimed unconditionally to everyone, which is why the apostles were simple, ordinary people and why Christ the prototype (*Forbillede*) is in the lowly form of a servant. "All this to indicate that this extraordinary is the ordinary, is open to all."[83] Christendom stopped looking at Christ as the prototype and saw him instead only as the Redeemer. "Instead of looking at him with respect to imitation, they dwelt on his good works and wished to be in the place of those to whom they were shown."[84]

The implication of this for the communication of Christianity in Christendom is that the "suffering servant" *is* the message. A "suffering servant" is political insofar

76. Strawser, *Both/And*, ch. 8.
77. Ibid., 177.
78. Kierkegaard, *The Moment*, 42, 135, 316.
79. Ibid., 321.
80. Ibid., 324.
81. Ibid., 292. See also 31, 42, 135, 148, 182, 321, and 332.
82. Ibid., 20.
83. Ibid., 180.
84. Ibid., 182.

as the suffering is directed from the settled masters to the unsettled subservient. Suffering and servanthood here necessarily presume orders of hierarchy, notions of common good, reward, station and the like. The suffering of the servant does not happen in azure isolation apart from the mores of the society against which he has offended. Christianly, this works itself out in the authentic follower of Christ who, by his or her very existence, provokes in the polity the opportunity to choose *either* faith *or* social offense by presenting the stark difference between Christ and the comfort of culture. It is important for Kierkegaard that it is ordinary, lowly people who imitate Christ, and consequently act, in their very humbleness, as the sign of contradiction and the possibility of offense.[85] Although he himself an active member of Denmark's intellectual and artistic circles, Kierkegaard stressed his connection to ordinary folk, distancing himself from his successful sophisticated peers.

> You common man! I have not segregated my life from yours, you know that; I have lived on the street, am known by all. Furthermore, I have not become somebody. . . . So if I belong to anyone, I must belong to you common man.[86]

In an effort to draw out Kierkegaard's political applicability to a nonreligious readership, commentators such as Bruce Kirmmse and Jørgen Bukdahl make much of these times when Kierkegaard identifies himself with the proletariat.[87] Yet the passages cannot be used to support a separation of Kierkegaard's Christian concerns from his (secular) political ones, for the whole point of Kierkegaard's sociopolitical humility is that it serves as his imitation of Jesus Christ. Kierkegaard, like Christ, draws attention to himself, but also like Christ, his very being acts as a stumbling block to the message that he is proclaiming. Following the development of indirect communication in the pseudonyms, Kierkegaard moves from his previous style, which took the form of double reflection *via* multiple characters, to the point where Kierkegaard does not seek to distance himself from his message. Yet Kierkegaard is not abandoning indirect communication, for consistently throughout his attack, whenever he asks people to look at his life as if he were an example, Kierkegaard at the same time highlights his own inadequacies for the role that has been foisted upon him.[88] The failure of Kierkegaard to live up to the ideal that he himself is communicating acts as an instance of Christ-like reduplication, with the same implications applying to *his* indirect message as those that applied to Christ's. The listener is not asked to believe the message based on outward, quantifiable reasons, but is, in Kierkegaardian terms initially "drawn in" and then "thrust back upon himself," required to make an honest decision not clouded by attractively compelling appearances.

---

85. Ibid., 334.
86. Ibid., 346, also 84.
87. Bukdahl, *Søren Kierkegaard*; Kirmmse, *Kierkegaard*, 481.
88. Kierkegaard, *The Moment*, 23, 25, 38, 60, 74, 78, 83, 213, 290, 311–12, 333, 340.

Over and over again, passages in *The Moment* repeat a similar pattern, with Kierkegaard initially drawing attention to himself, only to quickly emphasize his own failures and inadequacies. Calling specific attention to the "circumstances of my own life"[89] which have made him more aware than others of authentic Christianity, Kierkegaard then immediately backs down from claiming himself as a Christian example.[90] Kierkegaard is reduplicating the message of *awareness*, not of Christianity. This fact is reinforced when he again draws attention to himself as the one who has the honor of setting forth the idea of contemporaneity which results in awareness, and then quickly reminds his readers that he did not invent the idea—the New Testament did.[91] Kierkegaard justifies his qualification to write as he does about Christianity, boasting that by his many years as an author and by his "life as a public personality," he is entitled to join in the discussion about what Christianity is.[92] Kierkegaard then quickly nullifies his own boast by going on to address the fact of his ongoing public mockery, reminding his readers that the name "Søren" was being used by his enemies as a euphemism for Satan.[93] At times, Kierkegaard holds up his reputation as a famous firebrand and poet, and then says that after all he is possibly "entirely superfluous" and "something quite minor,"[94] someone who can write about something without understanding it himself.[95] Elsewhere, Kierkegaard predicts that he will fail to be understood, and that his attack will not prevail.[96] Anyone who knows him, Kierkegaard says, knows that he is not committing himself to his attack out of skill or interest in party politics.[97] As a writer and public figure, the attack is not earning him any money or prestige, a fact that is clearly evident to everyone.[98] Even when claiming for himself the highest accolade of them all—that he was chosen by Governance and slowly brought up for the special task of the attack—still Kierkegaard refers to his powerlessness and impotence.[99]

Significantly, Kierkegaard takes himself out from under the protection of sociopolitical respectability by refusing to call himself a Christian.[100] In terms of indirect communication, Kierkegaard makes himself a stumbling block by applying

---

89. Ibid., 213.
90. Ibid.
91. Ibid., 290.
92. Ibid., 311.
93. Ibid.
94. Ibid., 25.
95. Ibid., 38.
96. Ibid., 23, also 312.
97. Ibid., 60.
98. Ibid., 74. See also esp. 78, which begins a section that reminds readers of Kierkegaard's miserable life during the time of writing.
99. Ibid., 83.
100. Ibid., 46–49, 143, 212–13, and esp. 340–43.

the judgment of his own message to himself.[101] One cannot accuse Kierkegaard of *hypocritically* setting standards that he himself does not abide by, for he is very aware that his one thesis that there are no Christians in Christendom applies equally to him as to anyone else. Kierkegaard is complicit in Christendom, he does not claim to have the passion "that belongs to being involved with God alone in the most complete separation."[102] As a detective, Kierkegaard can see more clearly than others do their shared state of affairs: "What makes me shudder is this . . . it occurs to no one, no one that by being human beings they are indeed subject to the same conditions as I am, that the accounting of eternity awaits them also."[103]

After Kierkegaard's death, the tenth and final volume of *The Moment* was found among his papers, among the last words he ever wrote, completed and ready for publication.[104] This volume is perhaps the most important text for examining the role that reduplication as indirect communication played in Kierkegaard's life because it stresses Kierkegaard's reasons for not calling himself a Christian. In a section entitled "My Task," he writes: "I do not call myself a Christian; I do not speak of myself as a Christian. It is this that I must continually repeat; anyone who wants to understand my very special task must concentrate on being able to hold this firm."[105]

He knows that this seems a strange thing for him to continually repeat, obviously concerned as he is with Christ, yet in the world which has turned this term into blather, a stand such as his must be made.[106] Saying that he is not a Christian takes a certain respectability and power away from Kierkegaard, thus making him into the right kind of vessel for the communication that he has to make. He refers to the omnipotent power who "especially uses my powerlessness" and who would have no use for him if he changed his statement and decided to identify himself as a Christian after all.[107] Kierkegaard says that he wants to "keep the ideal free."[108] For this reason:

> I do not call myself a Christian. That this is very awkward for the sophists I understand very well, and I understand very well that they would much rather see that with kettledrums and trumpets I would proclaim myself to be the only true Christian, and I also understand very well that an attempt is being made to represent my conduct falsely in this way.[109]

---

101. Ibid., 197.
102. Ibid., 332.
103. Ibid.
104. Vol. 10 is printed as an appendix in ibid., 329–54.
105. Ibid., 340.
106. Ibid.
107. Ibid.
108. Ibid., 341.
109. Ibid., 340–41.

Kierkegaard directly calls attention to himself, and he openly speaks his mind, yet his communication remains indirect, because it is intimately concerned with the response of his listeners. By his very being, Kierkegaard stands at odds with the picture of authentic Christianity that he conjures up in *The Moment*, but it is by this discrepancy that Kierkegaard embodies his message calling people to make an honest decision. Kierkegaard is well aware that he is making a public fool of himself,[110] but this would only detract from his message if he were *directly* preaching Christianity. Instead, the circumstances of Kierkegaard's life serve to prevent any listener from making a choice for the wrong reasons. No one can accuse Kierkegaard of making the Christian life look appealing, or of setting himself up as some sort of charismatic popular leader. It is Kierkegaard's task to bring his readers to awareness of their own responsibility for making an honest choice about Christianity in Christendom. "In my books, I have pursued my task, and with *my being and my authorship* I am a continual attack on the whole Mynsterian proclamation of Christianity."[111] Just as Christ's human life acted as the possibility of offense and the catalyst for faith, so too Kierkegaard appropriates the reduplication model, using his own life to provoke a response that can only be *either* a continued life of hypocrisy, *or* an honest appraisal of Christianity. By acting as a polemic corrective in order to make people aware of the choice facing them, and by doing this using his own life as the sign of contradiction, Kierkegaard's attack is not an aberration from his previous work, but instead it represents the final development of Kierkegaard's indirect communication.

Conclusion

It is with his final attack upon Christendom that Kierkegaard extends to himself and others the possibility of becoming a sign of contradiction, an act of reduplication. Because it is a straightforward, non-pseudonymous polemic, the received wisdom of the secondary literature is that the material from this stage marks Kierkegaard's embrace of direct communication. However, in opposition to this assumption, I proposed that the attack and its written material is indirect for three reasons. First, it is a corrective, part of a dialectic whose meaning is not "self-contained."[112] Second, it is not a reformation manifesto, calling for followers, but instead actively repels people in order to make them aware of the honest choice they have to make regarding Christianity in Christendom.[113] Third, it is not direct communication because it is an example of Kierkegaardian reduplication.[114] Although he is forthright in his own name, because

---

110. Ibid., 311, 333.
111. Ibid., 15, emphasis added.
112. Ibid., 12, 24, 34, 40–41, 51, 67, 99–100, 106–7, 130, 143, 211, 217–20, 226, 335.
113. Ibid., 13, 29, 33–34, 40, 46, 48–49, 73–74, 76, 97, 101, 110, 130, 197, 212, 236, 336–37, 340–47.
114. Ibid., 15, 20, 23, 25, 38, 42, 46, 60, 74, 78, 83–84, 135, 180–82, 197, 213, 290, 311–12, 316, 321, 324, 333, 329–54.

of who Kierkegaard *is*, his communication is rendered indirect. Like Jesus Christ, Kierkegaard stands as a sign of offense, embodying his own message and thus his audience is faced with an *either/or* decision. By following the development of the theme through the authorship, it is apparent that the final attack is a natural culmination of Kierkegaard's project, the practical working out of Anti-Climacus's pure vision of reduplication and the fulfillment of authentic Christian communication within Christendom. This communication, although public and polemical, nevertheless remains "indirect" precisely because it involves lived praxis on behalf of the communicator (Kierkegaard) and demands participation from the audience (the Reader). The attack does not contain the truth but instead creates the opportunity for the possibility of offense. It is in the listener's response that the truth will be known. Kierkegaard's attack upon Christendom is an assault on the assumed morals and inherited affections of his readers, an intentionally unbalanced corrective, which, if received, will invariably lead to consequences that are overtly social, economic and political.

Bibliography

Aiken, David. "Kierkegaard's Three Stages: A Pilgrim's Regress?" *Faith and Philosophy* 13 (1996) 352–67.
Arbaugh, George E., and George B. Arbaugh. *Kierkegaard's Authorship*. London: Allen & Unwin, 1968.
Backhouse, Stephen. *Kierkegaard's Critique of Christian Nationalism*. Oxford: Oxford University Press, 2011.
Best, Steven, and Douglas Kellner. "Modernity, Mass Society, and the Media: Reflections on the Corsair Affair." In *International Kierkegaard Commentary: The Corsair Affair*, edited by Robert L. Perkins, 23–62. Macon, GA: Mercer University Press, 1990.
Blanchot, Maurice. *Faux Pas*. Translated by Charlotte Mandel. Stanford: Stanford University Press, 2001.
Brookfield, Christopher. "What Was Kierkegaard's Task? A Frontier to Be Explored." *Union Seminary Quarterly Review* 18 (1962) 23–35.
Bukdahl, Jørgen. *Søren Kierkegaard and the Common Man*. Translated by Bruce H. Kirmmse. Cambridge: Eerdmans, 2001.
Damgaard, Iben. "Biblical Variations: Kierkegaard's Rewritten 'Life of Jesus.'" In *A Companion to Kierkegaard*, edited by Jon Stewart, 269–80. Oxford: Blackwell, 2015.
Dunning, Stephen. "Who Sets the Task? Kierkegaard on Authority." In *Foundations of Kierkegaard's Vision of Community*, edited by George Connell and C. Stephen Evans, 18–32. London: Humanities, 1992.
Elrod, John. *Kierkegaard and Christendom*. Princeton: Princeton University Press, 1981.
Fenger, Henning. *Kierkegaard: The Myths and Their Origins*. Translated by George Schoolfield. London: Yale University Press, 1980.
Garff, Joakim. *Søren Kierkegaard: A Biography*. Translated by Bruce H. Kirmmse. Princeton: Princeton University Press, 2005.
———. "To Produce Was My Life: Problems, Perspectives within the Kierkegaardian Biography." In *Kierkegaard Revisited*, translated by Stacey Elizabeth Axe, edited by Niels Jørgen Cappelørn and Jon Stewart, 75–93. New York: de Gruyter, 1997.

Hannay, Alistair. *Kierkegaard: A Biography*. Cambridge: Cambridge University Press, 2001.

Hartshorne, M. Holmes. *Kierkegaard, Godly Deceiver*. New York: Columbia University Press, 1990.

Kierkegaard, Søren. *Attack upon "Christendom."* Translated by Walter Lowrie. Princeton: Princeton University Press, 1968.

———. *Concluding Unscientific Postscript to Philosophical Fragments*. Edited and translated by Howard V. Hong and Edna H. Hong. Princeton: Princeton University Press, 1985.

———. *Eighteen Upbuilding Discourses*. Edited and translated by Howard V. Hong and Edna H. Hong. Princeton: Princeton University Press, 1992.

———. *Fear and Trembling; Repetition*. Edited and translated by Howard V. Hong and Edna H. Hong. Princeton: Princeton University Press, 1983.

———. *The Moment and Late Writings*. Edited and translated by Howard V. Hong and Edna H. Hong. Princeton: Princeton University Press, 1998.

———. *Philosophical Fragments*. Edited and translated by Howard V. Hong and Edna H. Hong. Princeton: Princeton University Press, 1985.

———. *The Point of View*. Edited and translated by Howard V. Hong and Edna H. Hong. Princeton: Princeton University Press, 2009.

———. *Practice in Christianity*. Edited and translated by Howard V. Hong and Edna H. Hong. Princeton: Princeton University Press, 1991.

———. *The Sickness Unto Death*. Edited and translated by Howard V. Hong and Edna H. Hong. Princeton: Princeton University Press, 1988.

———. *Two Ages*. Edited and translated by Howard V. Hong and Edna H. Hong. Princeton: Princeton University Press, 1978.

Kirmmse, Bruce H. *Kierkegaard in Golden Age Denmark*. Indianapolis: University Press, 1990.

Lowrie, Walter. *Kierkegaard*. Vols. 1 and 2. New York: Harper Torchbooks, 1962.

———. *A Short Life of Kierkegaard*. New York: Anchor, 1961.

Mackey, Louis. *Points of View*. Tallahassee: Florida State University Press, 1986.

McCombs, Richard. *The Paradoxical Rationality of Søren Kierkegaard*. Bloomington: Indiana University Press, 2013.

McCracken, David. *The Scandal of the Gospels*. New York: Oxford University Press, 1994.

Mooney, Edward, F. "Pseudonyms and 'Style.'" In *The Oxford Handbook of Kierkegaard*, edited by John Lippitt and George Pattison, 191–210. Oxford: Oxford University Press, 2013.

Nordentoft, Kresten. "Hvad Siger Brand-Majoren?" Kierkegaards Opgør Med Sin Samtid. Copenhagen: GEC, 1973.

Pojman, Louis P. *The Logic of Subjectivity*. Birmingham: University of Alabama Press, 1984.

Poole, Roger. *Kierkegaard: The Indirect Communication*. Charlottesville: University Press of Virginia, 1993.

Sponheim, Paul. *Kierkegaard on Christ and Christian Coherence*. London: SCM, 1968.

Stocker, Barry. *Kierkegaard on Politics*. London: Palgrave Macmillan, 2013.

Strawser, Michael. *Both/And: Reading Kierkegaard from Irony to Edification*. New York: Fordham University Press, 1997.

Usher, Arland. *Journey Through Dread*. New York: Devon-Adair, 1955.

Westfall, Joseph. *The Kierkegaardian Author*. Berlin: de Gruyter, 2007.

Zuidema, S. U. *Kierkegaard*. Translated by D. F. Freeman. Philadelphia: Presbyterian and Reformed, 1960.

PART 2

Kierkegaard and the Politics of Faith, Hope, and Love

5

Downward Bound

The Knight of Faith and the Politics of Grace

HEATHER C. OHANESON

IN *FEAR AND TREMBLING*, Kierkegaard, by way of Johannes de Silentio, depicts the figures of the knight of faith and the knight of infinite resignation as dancers. In leaping, each undertakes a double movement: the movement of elevation is, quite naturally, followed by the movement of descent. Significantly, the distinguishing feature of the knight of faith lies not in his upward motion but in his downward step. Unlike the knight of infinite resignation who wavers when he makes contact with the ground, the knight of faith proves graceful in his landing. The seamlessness of his return to *terra firma* and his reentry into the crowd signal his healthy, non-estranged relationship to the ordinary world of finitude. The difficulty of authentic subjectivity, it turns out, is not in transcending the world, pushing oneself up to greater and greater heights; rather, the praiseworthy achievement is in how one brings oneself down.

In this chapter, I seek to apply this insight concerning the paradox of faith to civic circumstances, especially cases of political resistance that necessitate the improvisatory skills of readiness and responsiveness. Conjoining recent scholarship from dance studies with examples from the civil rights movement, I will show that the disciplined actions of falling down and going limp constitute admirable practices of power. Achieved through training, they are unexpectedly effective responses to a range of constraints. Thus, the downward-focused illustration of faith found in *Fear and Trembling* may prompt us to overturn discourses of uplift and taut uprightness into flexible strategies of grace. Consider this, then, not an exercise in intellectual history—in no way am I claiming that modern dancers or protestors look(ed) to the knight of faith in *Fear and Trembling* as their model—but something akin to a constructive project in Kierkegaard studies—an illustration of how we might think with Kierkegaard across a range of disciplinary spheres, including the political.

It is intuitive to rank the following two feats differently. The first to be considered is this: to perform something amazing—an athletic move, a gesture of forgiveness, an academic requirement, a videogame maneuver—all the while conveying (perhaps through one's body language or attitude) the difficulty of the difficult task. One senses the strain in the performer's clenched teeth—in her stumbling, in her complaints, in her sweat. The second form of accomplishment is to carry out a demand of equal proportion but in such a way that the performer, instead of revealing the rigor that the act requires, makes it look easy. At no time is the observer's attention diverted to thoughts of the hardness of the agent's task. Rather, when watching her, the possibility of the feat is simply taken for granted. Her apparent ease becomes part of the enjoyment of beholding her as she unleashes her skill, for the audience does not have to worry about whether she will pull off the joke or make the point or finish the piece or remember the notes or clear the jump. Instead, spectators experience the sheer pleasure of seeing her make her movements and do what she is supremely gifted to do. The difference between these two achievements is similar to the difference between the knight of infinite resignation and the knight of faith in *Fear and Trembling*. The concealment of difficulty in the latter knight's action is a mark of grace.[1]

Who is the knight of faith and what is his place in *Fear and Trembling*? *Fear and Trembling* is a sustained reflection on a life of complete faith in which Kierkegaard's pseudonymous writer Johannes de Silentio shares his admiration for the biblical patriarch Abraham, repeatedly declaring wonderment over his greatness. In his meditation, de Silentio looks not only to the story of Abraham, the father of faith, but also to the way of life of the idealized knight of faith figure. The knight of faith is able to find pleasure in everything. He is a "participator," taking part in everything. The invisible mark of who he is, though, his signature characteristic, is his reliance on the strength of the absurd in all he does.[2] The strength of the absurd is the "how" of his faith.[3]

A case for the greatness of this faith is built in part on a contrast with a lesser individual, the knight of infinite resignation, whose life displays the gap between reality and the ideal—if not quite in awkwardness, in difference and recognizability.[4] The knight of infinite resignation is unable to overcome impossibility on earth because he relies on his own limited strength. He exhausts his energies in making the first

---

1. Graceful ease may also be linked to the knight of faith's incognito, degrees of concealment interrelating.

2. Kierkegaard, *Fear and Trembling*, 39–40. References are to the Hongs' translation of *Fear and Trembling*, unless otherwise noted.

3. "For the movement of faith must continually be made by virtue of the absurd" (ibid., 37). Cf. "[the knight of faith] can be saved only by the absurd, and this he grasps by faith" (ibid., 47).

4. Ibid., 38–39. To clarify, there are three camps of people in Kierkegaard's indirect argument. The first group may be thought of as the masses, among whom there is neither striving nor resignation. The second group is made up of knights of infinite resignation. They represent an advance over the masses in that they "make an upward movement," but they are not able to reconcile infinity with finitude (ibid., 41). And so this first class of knights is surpassed by the knights of faith, the third and greatest group. These figures of faith embody the highest calling of existence in living before the Absolute in such a way that cancels yet elevates their everyday being. Parallels may be drawn between these different sets of people (the masses, the knights of infinite resignation, and the knights of faith) and the three stages of existence that Kierkegaard identifies (the aesthetic, the ethical, and the religious).

movement, the movement of renunciation. In order to cope with his loss, the knight of infinite resignation deals in escapism. It is precisely his flight to the realm of infinity that makes him unable to find joy amid finitude or to relate to the finite in sanguine ways. Thus, he distances himself from the world and shows disdain for the rank of the *bourgeois* philistine. By contrast, the knight of faith moves seamlessly between the acts of renunciation and retrieval. Despite his singularity, his status as the single individual who stands in an absolute relation to the Absolute, the knight of faith is not cut off from other people.[5] He fits in with *bourgeois* philistines just fine. In his commensurability, he may even be mistaken for one.[6]

The knight of faith goes beyond resignation by making a second movement. It is in going further that he comes to faith.[7] Precisely because his faith was finitude-directed, Abraham was able to receive Isaac back in this life *immediately and joyfully* after the call to sacrifice him on Mount Moriah.[8] It is worth pausing over this point, because readers of the biblical text might be so overwhelmed by the horror of the call to sacrifice Isaac that we overlook the difficulty of receiving Isaac back. Do you think the time of trial is over once the Angel of the Lord stays Abraham's hand?[9] Is it not, rather, especially in the aftermath of trauma that grace is needed?

If we relate the upward and downward movements of the knight of faith's leap to Abraham's journey up and down Mount Moriah, we will see that what is even more demanding than ascending the mountain where the sacrifice is to be made is retaining equanimity on the descent. Abraham does not miss a beat on the way down. That is what confounds de Silentio—the instantaneousness of Abraham's ability to pick back up with everyday life following the ordeal, "his needing no preparation and no time to rally to finitude and its joy."[10]

Thus, de Silentio claims that the knight of faith makes the movement of faith successfully by returning to the world in a particular way. He belongs to the Absolute but blends in with the everyday. On one level then, that is, in the sense of outwardly fitting

---

5. Ibid., 56.

6. Espen Dahl addresses the ambiguity that surrounds the role of familiarity in "opening . . . the worldhood of the world." In a passage on Cavell, Wittgenstein, and Heidegger with understandably Kierkegaardian resonances, he writes, "such an opening of the world is double edged, for precisely the same means that open the world up tend to level it out. When the equipments are placed into the orbit of all our diverse occupations, they become transparent and then leveled into the average or fallen everyday life. A similar dynamics is operative in social life, where individuals fall into the anonymous life of *das Man*, the 'they.' Under such circumstances, the ordinary sublime tends to be missed" (Dahl, *Stanley Cavell*, 40). Similarly, the very way that the knight of faith relates to—or even *uses*—finitude, opening its possibilities, causes him to blend into the leveled out crowd of subjectively immature aesthetes. Like the incarnated Christ, he is easy to (dis)miss.

7. Kierkegaard, *Fear and Trembling*, 37. De Silentio is highly critical of his age for presuming to go further than faith without ever having reached or accomplished faith. See, e.g., ibid., 7.

8. Ibid., 37.

9. Gen 22:12.

10. Kierkegaard, *Fear and Trembling*, 37.

in with the crowd, he may even be said to go with the flow.¹¹ Most importantly in light of his relation with the infinity of the Absolute, he "does not lose the finite but gains it whole and intact."¹² His gait reflects his readiness; it is the sign of his faith.

While the adjective "graceful" may be applied in innumerable contexts, movement is its special purview. The language of movement holds a significant place in de Silentio's account as his choice for expressing different ways of being in the world. Conceiving of faith as a double movement leads him to employ dance imagery. The knights, representative of the paradigms of effort and ease, metamorphose into ballet dancers of uneven skill in this "leap into life" passage:

> It is supposed to be the most difficult feat for a ballet dancer to leap into a specific posture in such a way that he never once strains for the posture but in the very leap assumes the posture. Perhaps there is no ballet dancer who can do it—but this knight does it. Most people live completely absorbed in worldly joys and sorrows; they are benchwarmers who do not take part in the dance. The knights of infinity are ballet dancers and have elevation. They make the upward movement and come down again, and this, too, is not an unhappy diversion and is not unlovely to see. But every time they come down, they are unable to assume the posture immediately, they waver for a moment, and this wavering shows that they are aliens in the world. It is more or less conspicuous according to their skill, but even the most skillful of these knights cannot hide this wavering. One does not need to see them in the air; one needs only to see them the instant they touch and have touched the earth—and then one recognizes them. But to be able to come down in such a way that instantaneously one seems to stand and to walk, to change the leap into life into walking, absolutely to express the sublime in the pedestrian—only that knight can do it, and this is the one and only marvel.¹³

The difference between the two kinds of knights is reflected in time. Unlike a knight of infinite resignation who wobbles slightly on his way to walking, a knight of faith hits his stride immediately upon landing.¹⁴ It is the gap in time as much as the wavering of motion in his descent that betrays the identity of a knight of infinite resignation. A close reading of this account may yield the surprising realization that the performances of knights of infinite resignation are nevertheless admired as "not unlovely." De Silentio's concession to their skill does not erase the fact of their strain, however. In privileging the pedestrian (walking doubling as ordinariness), de Silentio retrains readers' focus from the beauty of the leap itself to the marvel of the fact that it is a leap not out of but *into life*. That this knight of faith is connected to reality is evinced there-

---

11. On modern, urban crowds in Copenhagen and their gawping, anonymous members, see Pattison, *Kierkegaard, Religion*, 50–71.

12. Kierkegaard, *Fear and Trembling*, 37.

13. Ibid., 41.

14. Cf. King, "Which Way Is Down?," 36.

fore in his touching the ground. There is an inviting ease in finding the sublime within the everyday, which is manifested by the absence of any vacillation in the superior knight's lowering movement.

Espen Dahl addresses the notion of the ordinary sublime in a charming chapter by that name in his study *Stanley Cavell, Religion, and Continental Philosophy*. Two of his points in particular shed light on Abraham's story and de Silentio's imaginative portrayal of the knight of faith. When Dahl writes that "the return after the sublime is therefore never to the same everyday—something is gained," he gestures toward the advantage of an uncanny sense.[15] The dialectical play of the ordinary and the sublime gives the knight of faith second sight. The remarkable figure who is not recognized for what he is by others in the crowd himself sees better for seeing differently. Moreover, Dahl indicates that precious value belongs to the ordinary sublime *in virtue of its ordinariness*. He describes the potential subtlety of the pedestrian sublime thus: "I regard it as a mark of the ordinariness of the ordinary sublime that it is inherently open to such diverging perspectives. No infinity or might imposes itself on the receivers and commands universal agreement in response—the ordinary sublime comes to pass in a vulnerable gesture that is possible to overlook or reject."[16] This insight concerning the out-of-hand declension of vulnerability has incredible relevance for political theology. For those who lack the eyes to see, power may be quickly dismissed as passivity. Quiet strength is still strength, however.

Another interpreter of Kierkegaard's leap into life passage points to how "sublimity, as it walks along the street," is brought low.[17] Why is the knight of faith able to reconcile the sublime in the ordinary but the knight of infinite resignation is not? Aside from the knights' differing relations with the absurd, what accounts for the discrepancy in their landings?

Kierkegaard's Christ-inspired understanding of the nexus of grace, strength, and paradox offers implications for political movements.[18] A brief reference to *training* in a passage on the traits of the knight of faith is particularly revealing. After describing a number of the ways that the knight of faith treads the line between seriousness and levity—he is "carefree as a devil-may-care good-for-nothing, he hasn't a worry in the world, and yet he purchases every moment that he lives, 'redeeming the seasonable time' [Eph 5:16] at the dearest price"—de Silentio explains the basis for the faithful person's ability to live paradoxically. He is able to enjoy living in the finite realm even after the pain of renouncing finitude:

---

15. Dahl, *Stanley Cavell*, 43.

16. Ibid., 38. Compare the above quotation to this one: "The Gandhian paradox: freedom through submission. Civil disobedience, then, is also about learning or creating a different obedience, in uncertain variation between a potential transgression and a necessary limitation." Singh, "Reinhabiting Civil Disobedience," 378.

17. Fenves, "Chatter," 168.

18. The paradox of grace and strength is expressed in 2 Cor 12:9.

> *For his remaining in the finite bore no trace of a stunted, anxious training*, and still he has this sense of being secure to take pleasure in it, as though it were the most certain thing of all. . . . He resigned everything infinitely, and then took everything back on the strength of the absurd. He is continually making the movement of infinity, but *he makes it with such accuracy and poise* that he is continually getting finitude out of it, and not for a second would one suspect anything else.[19]

Carefree and yet going about the business of redeeming time. Drowning in deep sorrow and yet experiencing bliss. Renouncing the earthly and yet remaining peacefully in finitude. How can the person of faith live in a state of simultaneous security and suspension? I posit that de Silentio's claim that there is no hint of stunted, anxious training underlying his movement not only illumines the key to the knight of faith's paradoxical way of life but also shows the source of the faithful knight's poise. De Silentio cannot elaborate on the knight of faith's preparation.[20] Nevertheless, this statement (in which he gestures toward a type of training) offers a significant clue to the knight of faith's superior movement: It implies that stunted preparation leads to awkward performance, which further suggests that if there is no grace going into his groundwork, there is no grace coming out of his play.

The pattern of the knight of faith relates in striking ways to the dynamic of preparation and responsiveness in the art of contact (dance) improvisation, which in turn relates to protest movements through the themes of performance and responsibility. Contact improvisation is a form of dancing traced back to the 1970s in America. In it, physical contact between dance partners provides a certain "communication" that informs choices of movement, leading especially to acts of lowering such as rolling and falling.[21] Grace may be identified in the contexts of the knight of faith's slipping into the public collectivity of a crowd, the improvisatory practice of dancing, and political activism as the twofold presence of the beauty of smooth movement and generosity of spirit.

In addition to the practice of improvisation itself, which is a growing source of expertise for them, improvising dancers rely on a history of strenuous discipline in order to move well together in the course of performing. That affords them the readiness to respond in appropriate and inspiring ways to the shifting constraints that they encounter onstage. In other words, it is how they become prepared to be unprepared. Graceful movement is not possible, therefore, without rigorous training.[22]

---

19. Kierkegaard, *Fear and Trembling* (trans. Hannay), 69–70, emphasis mine.

20. That is why de Silentio continually marvels at this figure; at most, he is able to describe the movements of faith but he can neither perform those movements nor supply a formula for how to make them. See, e.g., the swimming passage on pp. 37–38 in the Hong translation.

21. On the development of contact improvisation and its features, see the documentary *Fall after Newton* and Laine, "Is Contact Improvisation Really Dance?"

22. Cf. Foster, "Choreographies of Protest," 399–401, 410.

As the ability to handle something difficult with poise, grace is also a power, a "practice of freedom." Paradoxically, such graceful power may be displayed in acts of surrender. This holds true in religion and politics as much as in the realm of aesthetic movement. Thus, instead of a protestor or dancer seeking to express control through vertical positions or motions that approximate flying (leaping *out of* life), improvisation might call for willfully falling down.[23] These are among the claims borne out by Danielle Goldman in *I Want to Be Ready: Improvised Dance as a Practice of Freedom*.

A professional dancer and assistant professor of dance at the New School, Goldman shifts easily between philosophical, political, and kinesthetic sources. Announcing the cross-sections of these fields in the introduction to her book, Goldman claims that recognizing—rather than denying—the role of constraints in improvisation allows one to see improvisation's "most significant power as a full-bodied critical engagement with the world, characterized by both flexibility and perpetual readiness."[24] Improvised dance is powerful as a practice that prepares one to make artful choices in response to constraints. Significantly, this includes constraints belonging to spheres apart from *but addressable by* dance, which is what allows Goldman to claim that improvisation is critical engagement with the world. As Bill T. Jones, a black, gay choreographer who introduced contact improvisation to mainstream modern dance with a piece he created for Alvin Ailey, states, "It was in an improvisation class taught by Richard Bull that I discovered that dance wasn't only about pointing my feet or making lines in space. It was about how I could solve problems."[25]

In performances as well as protests, one is likely to face the problems or constraints of self, society, and sin. First, if a player comes to an event with only slight or stunted training, she may not be able to improvise adequately. It is as if having learned fewer rules, she has fewer to break, or that without much practice (experience), she is at a loss for what to practice (enact). This underdeveloped inner state would limit the number of choices available to her during the piece and would affect her ability to be responsible to others. In Kierkegaardian terms, inauthentic subjectivity prevents one from making genuine choices. Indeed, one grows up existentially and becomes a true self in facing the crisis of the crossroads.[26] This achieved selfhood then bears on how one interacts with others. Second, as underscored by the lives of many African American artists and activists, constraints might not be ludic or aesthetic, but political and social. Last, harkening back to the religious and specifically Christian interest in all of Kierkegaard's authorships, it is worth mentioning the debilitating element of

---

23. Cf. King, "Which Way Is Down?," 36; Jones, *Last Night on Earth*, 117.

24. Goldman, *I Want to Be Ready*, 5.

25. Jones, *Last Night on Earth*, 114; cited in Goldman, *I Want to Be Ready*, 114. Concerning the diverse repertory of Alvin Ailey and the way African American versatility was a strategy for survival, see DeFrantz, "Composite Bodies of Dance."

26. Kierkegaard, *Either/Or*, 2:157.

sin—something that estranges one from God and others.[27] A valuable *technê*, then, for remedying constraints of ranging type and consequence is readiness.

Like a solo from Alvin Ailey's signature piece, *Revelations*, Goldman names her work after the black spiritual with the haunting but simple lyrics "I want to be ready, I want to be read-y, Lord, ready to put on my long white robe." It may not be immediately clear to what the readiness in the song refers. Whether for baptism, death, judgment day, heaven, or some other encounter with God or the world, preparation is needed—and life ought to be lived differently in light of this need. One garners a sense of the inspiration that Ailey's dance holds for Goldman in terms of readiness as well as practice and paradoxical descent (or "controlled fall") through her exposition:

> Although *Revelations*' falls are always followed by recovery, [the piece] "I Want to Be Ready" suggests the need to be prepared, not just for salvation but also for a range of social and historical constraints. *In this austere solo, with everything seemingly at stake, dance emerges as a practice of making oneself ready*, Long-limbed and dressed entirely in white, the soloist begins seated in fourth position, hands planted firmly on the floor, gazing upward. A series of stretches and contractions ensues, danced in keeping with the slow cadences of the spiritual, beseeching in deep tones, "I want to be ready / I want to be read-y / Lord, ready to put on my long white robe." Several times, the man in white rises from the floor with arms outstretched, only to find the floor again in a controlled, expressive fall. The dance's final descent ends as the man dramatically reaches his right arm across the floor, head down.[28]

This downward turn is the provisional, not final, end. After all, the dance is meant to ready the soloist for something else. The next and final section of *Revelations* culminates in the starkly celebrative movements of the entire ensemble dancing, clad in bright yellow costumes. Ailey's piece concludes on a triumphant note, suggesting that the preparation undertaken in the second section was worthwhile, successful. The message seems to be that falls can indeed lead to uplift or victory.[29] To translate this into the terms of *Fear and Trembling*, finitude may be restored through downward motions undertaken with an absurd strength.

Such an interpretation of the specific dance piece *Revelations* points to a form of dance more broadly, one that relies on—while further cultivating—the art of perpetual readiness, what I earlier referred to as the preparation for being unprepared. In

27. Kierkegaard, *Sickness Unto Death*, 77–131.

28. Goldman, *I Want to Be Ready*, 104, emphasis mine.

29. Challenges to the tautness and verticality of the classical dance form came from a number of sources, including the modern choreography of the Nietzsche-inspired Doris Humphrey. At the same time, it was recognized that falling could offer safety; laying low might ensure survival. As the transformation in value was taking place, however, falling was still being contrasted with "recovery," the former representative of submission, the latter, control. On safety and survival, see Goldman, *I Want to Be Ready*, 101–6. For thinking about these themes in terms of the knight of faith, and the political consequence of his blending into the crowd, see Bagger, "From the Double Movement," 342.

contact improvisation, dancers exhibit physical pliability and mental agility as they are responsive and responsible. They are responsible in that they owe each other something in the spur of the moment choices they make as they respond to one another. This art of interacting is not unlike Abraham's immediate responsiveness to the voice of the Angel of the Lord, calling him to spare Isaac's life.[30] Furthermore, protestors are beholden to each other as they entrust one another with their lives in the fraught moments of direct action.[31] In their performances, dancers and protestors alike demonstrate mutual accountability. Such answerability is a daunting objective; having no time for protracted reflection during the course of improvisatory moves, dancers and protestors are forced to rely on their intelligence, attentiveness, and reserve of skills to rise to current, unique challenges.[32]

To ascertain what responsiveness in improvisation entails, one may begin by explaining what being prepared is not. According to the widely celebrated musician Vijay Iyer (a jazzy knight of faith, if ever there was one), doing something memorized or pre-planned is a *verboten* move known as "giving a lie."[33] Slightly less offensive but still significantly out of line with the spirit of improvising are the following gestures: thinking of one's next action in the midst of a fellow player's "offering" and waiting for someone to finish solely so one can do what one wanted to do. These false modes of preparation bring about a sort of absence and rudeness, which remove a player from the flow of play in its teeming generosity. Reactivity "falls short," then, of authentic, gracious responsiveness.[34] Ultimately, these strategies hinder the desired spontaneity of improvisation and block the freedom of the kind of exchange being sought.

The preparation that frees one to act from a place of the fresh and unplanned goes hand in hand with proper responsiveness. Such an accomplishment requires attentive listening—listening that is intuitive, bodily, and of an almost total sort. When dancers let this way of listening determine their actions, they not only honor each other, demonstrating dutiful responsibility, they also create an atmosphere of relaxed awareness. "Relaxed awareness" is one translation for the French word *disponibilité*, an invaluable notion for training improvisers.[35] The virtue of *disponibilité* may also be explained in terms of availability, openness, and even trust. Great improvisation arises out of the willingness of the players to test possibilities, to follow each other into and out of risks, and to be comfortable enough to keep the play going after producing phrases in movement or music that do not "work out." The freedom of the improviser is the ability to be agile like Abraham, who did not

---

30. Gen 22:11–12.
31. Cf. Foster, "Choreographies of Protest," 406.
32. Ibid., 412; Ryle, "Improvisation," 73–74.
33. Iyer, "Imagination and Improvisation."
34. This description is somewhat in tension with Gary Peters's origin-focused account of improvisation in *Philosophy of Improvisation*.
35. Wells, *Improvisation*, 80.

miss a beat when he changed directions and started descending the mountain with Isaac.[36] It is the freedom "to change the leap into life into walking" or to be like a clumsy-yet-graceful walker who recovers quickly from tripping. Limber and cool, he incorporates the fall into his walk.[37] Whether in Jesus' incarnation, the journey of faith, dance, jazz, or normal, pedestrian life, successful improvisation depends on a responsiveness that results from awareness and skill.

Note that the difficulty of this demand does not lead to rigidity but relaxation. Where one looks for exceptional excellence, one discovers the ordinary sublime; where one anticipates tension, there is easing up. This ease corresponds to the carefree, graceful manner of the knight of faith, not the awkwardness of the knight of infinite resignation. The ability to replace rigidity with relaxation does not come automatically but is an accomplishment reached through practice. Furthermore, a relaxed physical and psychological state is practically useful, powerful even. Until this point, we have noted the discrepancy between the exterior and the interior—grace disguising grit. Now we are led to see the contradiction of easy outward appearance and hard-edged effect—passivity covering up power. This second level of paradox is evident when the motion of falling takes on political significance, as it does in a range of performative protest movements, including the quest for the realization of African Americans' civil rights.

Thus far, I have examined the leap of the knight of faith, whose movement into and out of the transcendent is a sign of his otherwise invisible ability to find the sublime in the ordinary; alongside his double movement, I have considered the emphasis on tumbling and falling in the modern dance form known as contact improvisation, and the controlled descent in the Alvin Ailey piece "I Want to Be Ready." These downward-focused dance practices highlight the importance of training for improvisation, which itself cultivates and rewards physical—but also psychological—openness, ease, and relaxation (which are marks of grace). The task now is to turn to the power of paradox for politics, that is, to illuminate how forms of "falling" and the attendant values of improvisation were integral to the success of the civil rights movement. This consideration aligns with the work of political theologians such as Corey D. B. Walker, who examines race, the body, and "the conditions of possibility for the inauguration of a new practice of freedom."[38] To be explicit: I am not maintaining that positions of lowliness or limp-

---

36. "Even more difficult than setting out for Moriah to offer Isaac is the capacity, when one has already drawn the knife, in unconditional obedience to be willing to understand: It is not required." Kierkegaard, *Fear and Trembling*, 268.

37. Robert E. Neale lightheartedly suggests that the incarnation—Jesus' tumbling into the world—was a result of God slipping on a banana peel (in Moltmann, *Theology of Play*, 80). To think further on falling, walking, and graceful recoveries, consult: Kierkegaard, *Fear and Trembling*, 41; King, "Which Way Is Down?," 36. On walking and dancing, recall Nietzsche: "Does [Zarathustra] not walk like a dancer?" *Thus Spoke Zarathustra*, 123.

38. Walker, "Race for Theology," 137. Notably, Walker focuses in this chapter on how Howard Thurman's analysis of spirituals opened new ways of thinking about death. A prominent African American theologian, Thurman traveled to India and met with Gandhi in 1935.

ness are the only, best, or most graceful ways to display resistance.[39] Rather, I am drawing attention to the paradoxical power that can attend postures typically deemed weak, and to the association of those postures with faith and freedom.

The struggle for racial integration and justice in the American South in the 1940s, 1950s, and 1960s was marked by organized direct action, including Freedom Rides, sit-ins, boycotts, and marches. Training in theory and practice was needed in order to carry out these acts of civil disobedience in accordance with the principles of nonviolence. The inclination to retaliate against nasty insults and brutish attacks had to be undermined in advance. Thus, protestors studied Mohandas Gandhi's teaching of *satyagraha*, translated as "truth force" and "soul force," in order to overcome feelings of hatred and ill-will toward their aggressors. They also learned and evaluated specific physical techniques of peaceful noncooperation. Famous among those were going limp and staying seated.[40]

Slackness of musculature offered the following practical and personal advantages. A literal expression of noncooperation, it protracted the arrest process and placed a burden on the authorities. Going limp was also a protective strategy, as relaxed bodies were less susceptible to tissue damage than the bodies of the taut and tensed. Bruce Hartford's "Notes from a Nonviolent Training Session (1963)" attest to these ideological and physiological points. In outline form, Hartford writes:

D. Defending Against Physical Attack

  1. What. The "Non-Violent Position." Dropping to ground and protecting self. Squirming to walls & curbs to protect back.

  2. Why. Best Protection. Least threatening. Startles/scares attackers. Clarifies situation to onlookers and press.

F. Arrests

  3. Going limp. Pros and cons. How to do it. Styles:

      – The Buddha style

      – The Flabby-limp style

      – The Walking limp-collapse

      – Going rough

These training materials, with other nonviolent action guides such as Martin Oppenheimer and George Lakey's *Manual for Direct Action*, reveal the systematic preparation

---

39. One of several compelling counterpoints is the image of Ieshia Evans calmly standing up to rushing police officers. Miller, "Graceful in the Lion's Den."

40. My discussion of civil rights activists' preparation to adopt certain postures is informed by Goldman, *I Want to Be Ready*, 97–98. Other pertinent sources include: Chabot, *Transnational Roots*; Gregg, *Power of Nonviolence*, 141–75; Hohle, "Body and Citizenship," esp. 293–95; and Singh, "Reinhabiting Civil Disobedience," esp. 373–75.

that civil rights activists undertook for the sake of peaceful, effective actions. After role-playing a variety of scenarios and experimenting with different responses in the safe setting of a training session, protestors had reasoned strategies on hand that they could employ and adapt in chaotic, charged environments.[41] In short, they knew how and why to improvise falls.[42]

Closely related to protestors' choice of loosening their posture was the adoption of motionless stances, including the powerful and recognizable examples of remaining seated at a lunch counter and Rosa Parks's refusal to give up her seat on the bus. Like dropping to the ground, stillness reads as pacifist behavior and contrasts starkly with the cruel behavior of attackers; thus, it stands to win public approval. Such calm and controlled behavior also disarms the opponents, disrupting the escalating cycle of violence. Despite these strategic advantages, falling, going limp, and sitting motionless might be perceived (even among the protestors themselves) as forms of weakness. Though active and dignified—that is, genuinely civil—modes of resistance, they raised questions of *apparent* passivity and indignity.

In his stirring essay, "Which Way Is Down? Improvisations on Black Mobility," the Canadian cultural critic and music professor Jason King ties claims about black identity together with the paradoxical notion of locating power in "downwardness"— those lowly postures and acts of falling that I have sought in this chapter to connect with the graceful, earthbound step of Kierkegaard's paradox-driven knight of faith. By challenging the associations of verticality and dignity, on the one hand, and lowliness and shame, on the other, King upends traditional thinking while showing the unexpected advantages that black people in North America have found in socially and politically disadvantaged positions. Like improvisers empowered by skill, they have turned their constraints into means of freedom.

After he defines falling in terms of groundlessness, descent, and disorientation,[43] King suggests that "perhaps no group has more to offer the phenomenon of falling than black people."[44] For, under a society dominated by whites, "to be black is to have already fallen."[45] The rootlessness of the Diaspora affords mobility, and black people

---

41. "Performances are composed of 'strips' of 'restored behavior,' learned repertoires that are both symbolic and meaningful and can be creatively arranged and rearranged to express particular ideas and identities through rehearsal, adaptation, and experiment (Schechner 1985)." Juris, "Embodying Protest," 231.

42. On the civility of civil disobedience, see Gandhi, "Civility," 47–49. David Borgo points to the connection between the civil rights movement and free improvisation or free jazz. See Borgo, "Negotiating Freedom," 168.

43. "Slipping, stumbling and tripping are all performances of disorientation, de-anchoring, rootlessness; they precursor the fall or the slide (the gliding fall) or the tumble (the rolling fall) or the flop (the thudding fall)." King, "Which Way Is Down?," 27.

44. Ibid.

45. Ibid., 28. Black political theology is related to lowliness in that the "best of black political theology seeks to follow Jesus of Nazareth: to take up the cause of outcast, despised, and marginalized children, women, and men; to live at the disposal of the cross (Mark 8:34)." Such a step toward the

have capitalized on that ability to move, conjoining the power of grace with the powerlessness of descent. The correct and proper direction of that movement—its orientation—is a matter for debate, though. Not only do people disoriented from falling or rootlessness need to figure out which way is up, they need to consider the value of verticality itself.[46] Are forms of lowliness good in themselves or are they desirable only in relation to recovery and uplift? What if the piece "I Want to Be Ready" were the final act in *Revelations*, unsurpassed by a third movement and its victorious "Rocka My Soul" finale?

King acknowledges the language of uplift that belongs to celebrated works created by black artists, from Maya Angelou's poem "And Still I Rise" to "Lift Every Voice and Sing," the song that served as the "Negro National Anthem" in the civil rights movement.[47] Curtis Mayfield's "Move on Up" and Bob Marley's "Get up, stand up / stand up for your rights" likewise fit into the paradigm that upholds upward mobility, uprightness, and resurrection.[48] Yet King still leaves room for the potential of the Down Low (DL).[49] He does not immediately eschew being on the DL but rethinks shame. Focusing on directionality, he writes, "What is fascinating, and even worthwhile, about DL is that it literally suggests a new direction for black identity, and it does so in the most unique way—through the metaphor of directionality and mobility. No dead-end is really an end. One can find pride crouching low to the ground, moving under the radar, not just up high, in the air."[50] In the end that is not an end, he sides with the paradox of "Black performance [that] moves toward the co-presence of mobility and immobility," claiming that blackness itself is "ambivalent direction."[51] King implies more than the possible coexistence of freedom and control; he gestures toward the fruitfulness of locating freedom in paradox, whether the paradox of simultaneous mobility and stillness or falling-and-ascent. Similarly, the accomplished practitioner of contact improvisation Nancy Stark Smith affirms, "the expression 'fall from grace,' becomes an impossible statement when falling itself is experienced as a state of grace."[52] Today, the nexus of black identity, fallenness, grace, and political power takes on new life through the "die-ins" staged by activists in the Black Lives Matter movement.[53] They, too, show how falling can be an assertive act, a power play.

---

downtrodden accords with James Cone's conviction "that blackness was not so much a matter of skin color as of placing one's heart, soul, mind, and body with the dispossessed." Copeland, "Black Political Theologies," 272, 283.

46. King, "Which Way Is Down?," 32.
47. Ibid., 29–30.
48. Ibid., 32, 34.
49. Ibid., 38–40.
50. Ibid., 40.
51. Ibid., 42; cited in Goldman, *I Want to Be Ready*, 100.
52. Stark Smith, editor's note, 2.
53. Susan Leigh Foster points to the "determined listlessness" of AIDS activists as they utilized die-ins in the 1980s ("Choreographies of Protest," 404). She observes that the die-ins of the AIDS

As in the dance practice of contact improvisation, the upside-down logic of Kierkegaard's knight of faith is recognizable in the arena of politics, which calls for in-the-moment responses to shifting constraints. The glory and grace of the knight of faith's movement do not reside exclusively in his transcendence, as one might expect. It is how he slides into the everyday, finding the sublime within the ordinary, which shows his greatness. Similarly, the impetus to fall—to partner with gravity in moving downward rather than attempt to defy it by propelling oneself up in the air—is at odds with literally-minded interpretations of "standing up for one's rights" as much as the traditional kinesthetic values of classical ballet. Because political constraints call for improvisation too, falling may be a social and spiritual exercise beyond a strategy in contact-driven, combinatorial movement. It may be a creative-yet-trained response to the unpredictable and physically fraught atmosphere of protests. Or, as the liturgical expert Janet Walton believes, falling may count in a particular context as an action but "really it's a stance in life."[54]

In brief, sublimely pedestrian motions, downward-bound movements, and powerful postures of lowliness are united under the umbrella of Kierkegaardian political theology insofar as they open a new way to think and embody grace as a paradoxical political mode.[55]

Bibliography

Bagger, Matthew C. "From the Double Movement to the Double Danger: Kierkegaard and Rebounding Violence." *Harvard Theological Review* 102 (2009) 327–52.

Borgo, David. "Negotiating Freedom: Values and Practices in Contemporary Improvised Music." *Black Music Research Journal* 22 (2002) 165–88.

Chabot, Sean. *Transnational Roots of the Civil Rights Movement: African American Explorations of the Gandhian Repertoire.* New York: Lexington, 2012.

Copeland, M. Shawn. "Black Political Theologies." In *The Blackwell Companion to Political Theology*, edited by Peter Scott and William T. Cavanaugh, 271–87. Malden, MA: Blackwell, 2003.

Dahl, Espen. *Stanley Cavell, Religion, and Continental Philosophy.* Indiana Series in the Philosophy of Religion. Bloomington: Indiana University Press, 2014.

DeFrantz, Thomas F. "Composite Bodies of Dance: The Repertory of the Alvin Ailey American Dance Theater." *Theatre Journal* 57 (2005) 659–78.

Fall After Newton. Play. Performed by Nancy Stark Smith and Steve Paxton. 1972–1983. DVD. East Charleston, VT: Videoda, 2006.

Fenves, Peter. *"Chatter": Language and History in Kierkegaard.* Stanford: Stanford University Press, 1993.

Coalition to Unleash Power (ACT UP) "featured bodies moving from vertical standing to horizontal lying, occasionally exaggerating the fall with flare and angst" (ibid., 403).

54. Walton, "Imagination and Improvisation."

55. For their intellectual generosity, I wish to thank the editors of this volume, Roberto Sirvent and Silas Morgan, my advisors Wayne Proudfoot and Mark C. Taylor, and Dennis Dalton, from whom I first had the privilege of learning about Gandhi, civil disobedience, and the discipline of love.

Foster, Susan Leigh. "Choreographies of Protest." *Theatre Journal* 55 (2003) 395–412.
Gandhi, Mahatma. "Civility." In *Selected Political Writings*, edited by Dennis Dalton, 47–49. Indianapolis: Hackett, 1996.
Goldman, Danielle. *I Want to Be Ready: Improvised Dance as a Practice of Freedom*. Ann Arbor: University of Michigan Press, 2010.
———. "Imagination and Improvisation: The Holy Play of Congregational Worship." Presentation at Union Theological Seminary, New York, March 29, 2011.
Gregg, Richard B. *The Power of Nonviolence*. New York: Schocken, 1959.
Hartford, Bruce. "Notes from a Non-Violent Training Session (1963)." *Civil Rights Movement Veterans*. http://www.crmvet.org/info/nv1.htm.
Hatton, Nigel. "Martin Luther King, Jr.: Kierkegaard's *Works of Love*, King's *Strength to Love*." In *Kierkegaard's Influence on Social-Political Thought*, edited by Jon Stewart, 89–106. Burlington, VT: Ashgate, 2011.
Hohle, Randolph. "The Body and Citizenship in Social Movement Research: Embodied Performances and the Deracialized Self in the Black Civil Rights Movement 1961–1965." *Sociological Quarterly* 50 (2009) 283–307.
Iyer, Vijay. "Imagination and Improvisation: The Holy Play of Congregational Worship." Presentation and performance at Union Theological Seminary, New York, March 22, 2011.
Jones, Bill T. *Last Night on Earth*. With Peggy Gillespie. New York: Pantheon, 1995.
Juris, Jeffrey S. "Embodying Protest: Culture and Performance within Social Movements." In *Conceptualizing Culture in Social Movement Research*, edited by Britta Baumgarten et al., 227–47. New York: Palgrave Macmillan, 2014.
Kierkegaard, Søren. *Either/Or*. Edited and translated by Howard V. Hong and Edna H. Hong. Vol. 2. Princeton: Princeton University Press, 1987.
———. *Fear and Trembling*. Translated by Alastair Hannay. London: Penguin, 1985.
———. *Fear and Trembling*. Edited and translated by Howard V. Hong and Edna H. Hong. Princeton: Princeton University Press, 1983.
———. *The Sickness Unto Death*. Edited and translated by Howard V. Hong and Edna H. Hong. Princeton: Princeton University Press, 1983.
King, Jason. "Which Way Is Down? Improvisation on Black Mobility." *Women and Performance: A Journal of Feminist Theory* 14 (2004) 25–45.
Laine, Barry. "Is Contact Improvisation Really Dance?" *New York Times*, July 3, 1983. http://www.nytimes.com/1983/07/03/arts/is-contact-improvisation-really-dance-by-barry-laine.html.
LaMothe, Kimerer. *Between Dancing and Writing: The Practice of Religious Studies*. New York: Fordham University Press, 2004.
Miller, Michael E. "'Graceful in the Lion's Den': Photo of Young Woman's Arrest in Baton Rouge Becomes Powerful Symbol." *Washington Post*, July 11, 2016. https://www.washingtonpost.com/news/morning-mix/wp/2016/07/11/graceful-in-the-lions-den-photo-of-young-womans-arrest-in-baton-rouge-goes-viral.
Moltmann, Jürgen. *Theology of Play*. Translated by Reinhard Ulrich. New York: Harper & Row, 1972.
Nietzsche, Friedrich. *Thus Spoke Zarathustra*. In *The Portable Nietzsche*, edited and translated by Walter Kaufmann, 121–439. New York: Penguin, 1982.
Oppenheimer, Martin, and George Lakey. *A Manual for Direct Action: Strategy and Tactics for Civil Rights and All Other Nonviolent Protest Movements*. Chicago: Quadrangle, 1965.

Parviainen, Jaana. "Choreographing Resistances: Spatial-Kinaesthetic Intelligence and Bodily Knowledge as Political Tools in Activist Work." *Mobilities* 5 (2010) 311–29.

Pattison, George. *Kierkegaard, Religion, and the Nineteenth-Century Crisis of Culture*. West Nyack, NY: Cambridge University Press, 2002.

Peters, Gary. *The Philosophy of Improvisation*. Chicago: University of Chicago Press, 2009.

Ryle, Gilbert. "Improvisation." *Mind* 85 (1976) 69–83.

Singh, Bhrigupati. "Reinhabiting Civil Disobedience." In *Political Theologies: Public Religions in a Post-Secular World*, edited by Hent de Vries and Lawrence E. Sullivan, 365–81. New York: Fordham University Press, 2006.

Stark Smith, Nancy. Editor's note. *Contact Quarterly* 5 (1979) 2.

Taylor, Mark C. *Kierkegaard's Pseudonymous Authorship: A Study of Time and the Self*. Princeton: Princeton University Press, 1975.

Tilley, J. Michael. "J. L. A. Kolderup-Rosenvinge: Kierkegaard on Walking Away from Politics." In *Kierkegaard and His Danish Contemporaries*, edited by Jon Stewart, 77–84. Burlington, VT: Ashgate, 2009.

Turner, Robert. "Steve Paxton's 'Interior Techniques': Contact Improvisation and Political Power." *Drama Review* 54 (2010) 123–35.

Walker, Corey D. B. "The Race for Theology: Toward a Critical Theology of Freedom." In *Race and Political Theology*, edited by Vincent W. Lloyd, 134–55. Stanford: Stanford University Press, 2012.

Walther, Bo Kampmann. "Web of Shudders: Sublimity in Søren Kierkegaard's 'Fear and Trembling.'" *Modern Language Notes* 112 (1997) 753–85.

Walton, Janet. "Imagination and Improvisation: The Holy Play of Congregational Worship." Course discussion at Union Theological Seminary, New York, March 29, 2011.

———. "Improvisation and Imagination: Holy Play." *Worship* 75 (2001) 290–304.

Wells, Samuel. *Improvisation: The Drama of Christian Ethics*. Grand Rapids: Brazos, 2004.

6

Searching for a Secular God

A Prolegomena to a Political Theory of Love

JAMIE AROOSI

> Justice is what love looks like in public.
> —CORNEL WEST

Introduction: Flirting with Kierkegaard

POLITICAL THINKERS HAVE LONG flirted with the thought of Søren Kierkegaard. From Georg Lukács to Theodor Adorno, and from Jean-Paul Sartre to Jacques Derrida, Kierkegaard has long proven a fascinating subject.[1] Yet, while other unconventional thinkers, like Nietzsche and Freud, have been canonized in the field, Kierkegaard's inclusion in the world of political thought has always been the exception rather than the rule. Reflecting this trend, Alain Badiou, Jürgen Habermas, and Slavoj Žižek, have all turned to Kierkegaard in recent years, albeit in a predictably limited way. Specifically, each fails to engage the substance of Kierkegaard's Christianity. While this latest turn reflects an incipient awareness that Kierkegaard can help resolve some of the fundamental problems facing political thought, such as the difficulty of reconciling an identity politics of inclusion with a substantive conversation about human nature, their limited engagement prevents this possibility from coming to fruition. This engagement therefore reflects the long-standing and unwarranted suspicion of Kierkegaard's thought born out of the difficulty that political thought has in engaging religious thought, and which tends to label Kierkegaard as either a political conservative or an apolitical ascetic. However, by exploring this recent turn toward Kierkegaard, the hidden political promise of Kierkegaard's thought is revealed, as is a way forward in the potentially mutually enriching conversation between Kierkegaard

---

1. Lukács, "Foundering of Form," 13; cf. also Sartre, "Kierkegaard"; Sartre, *Search for a Method*; Adorno, *Kierkegaard*; Derrida, *Gift of Death*.

scholars and political theorists. Specifically, by drawing Kierkegaard's ethics into the social and political world, we will see that latent within them lies an ethical necessity to engage in political action. In this way, we will see that within Kierkegaard's thought exists a prolegomena to a political theory of love.

Alain Badiou

In his recent work, *Logics of Worlds*, itself the follow-up to his earlier work *Being and Event*, Alain Badiou spends a chapter discussing Kierkegaard.[2] Employing Kierkegaard in the most common way that political theorists do, that is, as a theorist of decisionism,[3] Badiou argues that choice helps reveal the activity of choosing to the chooser.[4] In choosing a world of meaning, or, what Badiou calls a topology, the chooser becomes aware of the fact that such worlds depend on their very own transcendental act of choice.[5] In other words, in choosing the world of meaning that we inhabit, we demonstrate that we are not bound by it, but that we necessarily transcend it. Reciprocally, in making a choice and committing to a world, the chooser consecrates themselves in that world, thereby giving meaning to their own existence.[6] In this way, Badiou draws upon Kierkegaard's theory of stages and his idea of self-choice to legitimize positions that are more clearly his own.

While such decisionist readings of Kierkegaard are the most common political readings of Kierkegaard, dating to his German interwar reception, they take Kierkegaard in a direction he would have been loath to follow. In emptying the leap of faith of its substance, these readings borrow formal elements of Kierkegaard's thought, but leave behind the content. For instance, without the substantive content of Martin Luther King's Christianity, it becomes hard to distinguish his call to break the law from Carl Schmitt's similar call, even though the former advanced the civil rights movement and the latter helped justify Nazism.[7] Yet, Badiou nonetheless helps expose some of Kierkegaard's enduring relevance to contemporary political thought. Specifically, Badiou's interest lies in attempting to reconcile the problem of both needing to understand our particular sociopolitical reality, or world of meaning, while simultaneously recognizing that any such reality is necessarily exclusionary. That is, there are always positions outside of any world of meaning, and, from a political point

---

2. Badiou, *Logics of Worlds*, 425–36.

3. This tradition dates back to the political decisionism of Carl Schmitt, and an infamous reference that Schmitt makes to that "nineteenth century" "Protestant theologian"—to Søren Kierkegaard. See Schmitt, *Political Theology*, 15.

4. Badiou, *Logics of Worlds*, 432.

5. Ibid.

6. Ibid., 433.

7. Despite the ease of orchestrating a substantive conversation between King and Kierkegaard, it is actually Schmitt who explicitly draws on Kierkegaard. See King, "Letter from Birmingham Jail"; Schmitt, *Political Theology*, 13.

of view, these positions are likely to be populated with the vulnerable and exploited.[8] So, Badiou's question, a question in which he is hardly alone, is to ask how we might theorize exclusion itself. Or, if this question is duly politicized, we might instead ask how we can imagine sociopolitical communities that are truly inclusive.

In appropriating Kierkegaard, what therefore motivates Badiou is Kierkegaard's ability to address questions of inclusion in an age wary of reason. If Hegel represents a highpoint for attempting to theorize a universally inclusive community from within the confines of a rational framework, and if the past two centuries of thought exhibit a fundamental suspicion of this possibility, Kierkegaard's radical rebellion against Hegel is a natural place from which to draw. Moreover, his proximity to Hegel affords Kierkegaard the ability to appropriate some of the more promising elements of Hegel's thought—such as Hegel's dialectical understanding of subjectivity, and Hegel's radical formulation of freedom—while drawing them out of the confines of Western rationality. However, for Badiou, these substantive insights are of little concern. What is of concern are purely the formal elements of Kierkegaard's thought—what exclusion and exceptionality look like as abstract categories—rather than a deeper engagement with the substantive claims that Kierkegaard makes about human existence, and why human existence, in particular, defies confinement within a rational universal. For Kierkegaard, the exception might prove the rule—but it was a very specific exception that did so.

By emptying Kierkegaard of the substantive content by which he anchors his critique of Western thought, and which also serves as the ground for his own positive philosophical project, Badiou's engagement with Kierkegaard remains both superficial and instrumental. For Kierkegaard, the exception is not an abstract concept demonstrating the limits of all worlds of meaning, the exception is something quite specific: it is God, as well as our own transcendental nature, that defies reason. Without this content, Badiou is essentially attempting to anchor normative judgment—he is attempting to critique forms of exclusion—in the formal description of Kierkegaard's leap of faith, as have other decisionist thinkers, rather than anchoring them in the specific substantive position that Kierkegaard believes allows us to judge. Ironically, without that positive content, Badiou's criticism remains a purely formal, or abstract, critique, and runs the risk of being exactly the type of philosophy that radical critics of Hegel, like Kierkegaard himself, forsook. Put differently, it runs the risk of being a philosophy that fails the test of being able to help change the world, or the individuals within it, because it gives us a purely abstract reason to do so.

---

8. For perhaps the best recent example of this problem, see Spivak, "Can the Subaltern Speak?"

PART 2: KIERKEGAARD AND THE POLITICS OF FAITH, HOPE, AND LOVE

Jürgen Habermas

In contrast to Badiou, Jürgen Habermas moves in the opposite direction in his approach to Kierkegaard. Rather than emptying Kierkegaard of his substantive content in favor of the formal elements of his thought, Habermas's interest primarily lies with the content. Specifically, in his work *The Future of Human Nature*, Habermas offers Kierkegaard as an answer to questions that arise when our understanding of human nature is challenged by developments in biotechnology.[9] Moreover, Habermas can offer Kierkegaard as an answer because he recognizes that Kierkegaard's substantive claims are post-rational, and therefore not subject to the standard critiques of reason.[10] In other words, Kierkegaard offers an answer that is both substantive *and* formal, giving content to our understanding of what it means to be human, while doing so in a way that allows for, what Habermas calls, "a multiplicity of worldviews," or, what we might call, following the discussion of Badiou, the problem of exclusion.[11] Therefore, in focusing on the substantive elements, i.e., questions of human nature, while acknowledging their formal elements, i.e., Kierkegaard's post-rational philosophy, Habermas is much closer to recognizing the importance of Kierkegaard for contemporary political thought.

Habermas therefore contextualizes his discussion of Kierkegaard by situating it within contemporary pluralism, and the challenge that pluralism makes to earlier forms of political and ethical thought. For Habermas, grounding ethical and political thought in foundational claims regarding nature and history had previously offered philosophers the confidence to answer fundamental questions of the "good life."[12] However, Habermas mentions works like John Rawls's *Political Liberalism* as having marked the end to this tradition, an end that occurred in response to the spread of individualism and a greater inclusion of a plurality of worldviews.[13] As a result, the "ought" questions relating to the nature of the good life have become increasingly tied to identity, as these "ought's" relate to an ought "for 'me,' or even, for 'we,' but . . . [they are] never fully universal, but always particular."[14]

And so, Habermas recognizes that contemporary theories of justice tend to focus on formal rather than normative questions, leaving the larger questions to individuals.[15] Therefore, politics has effectively become decoupled from ethics, leaving ethics to individuals, while the political question of justice is answered only formally.[16] As

---

9. Habermas, *Future of Human Nature*, 5.
10. Ibid.
11. Ibid., 6.
12. Ibid., 2.
13. Ibid.
14. Ibid., 3.
15. Ibid.
16. Ibid., 4.

Habermas aptly notes, the reconciliation of ethics and politics is precisely the question that a fuller engagement with Kierkegaard allows us to solve. Moreover, it is interesting to note that while Habermas points to Rawls as an example of formal theories of justice, Badiou's use of Kierkegaard is not that far removed from Habermas's point about Rawls. In using Kierkegaard to demonstrate a form of radical inclusion that is meant to orient our ethical and political lives, but doing so in a purely formal way, Badiou is also attempting to solve normative questions with formal answers.

Therefore, for Habermas, the formalism within ethical and political thought has left an absence at its heart, which Kierkegaard fills with God.[17] Turning to Kierkegaard's work *The Sickness Unto Death*, Habermas argues that one of Kierkegaard's important contemporary contributions is a recognition that we cannot overcome our state of sin on our own. In other words, we ourselves are not the ground for our freedom and its responsible use; what grounds our freedom is an Other.[18] As Habermas tells it, for Kierkegaard, we overcome the despair of our sinful condition by recognizing that we owe everything to an Other, i.e., that our freedom is born in intersubjectivity.[19] Yet, echoing his earlier criticisms of contemporary ethical and political thought, Habermas also claims that the "the linguistic turn" in philosophy has emptied the idea of the Other of its essential content.[20] As a result, the deep existential and communal nature of truly relating to the Other, and recognizing one's dependency on them, is transformed into something lacking the transformative power of Kierkegaard's intersubjective philosophy. Therefore, by reinvesting the Other with rich substantive meaning, we might begin to answer some of our pressing ethical questions with more than formal answers, while simultaneously reinvesting politics with a rich ethical complement.

Last, Habermas concludes by arguing that this Other need not be understood in Kierkegaard's theological terms, but that it can be rendered in secular terms.[21] Only here does Habermas run into trouble. There is certainly an interesting and important conversation to be had about the possibility of interpreting Kierkegaard in an interdenominational fashion, or even, in a secular but spiritual vein, but in leaving behind Kierkegaard's religiosity too quickly, Habermas runs the risk of losing the importance of thinking of the Other as divine. God might only ever be experienced in the Other, but it is precisely this divine nature that allows us to ground ethics and politics in claims that lie beyond convention. The social and political challenge, then, is not to leave this behind, but to account for it in a truly inclusive, and nondenominational, fashion.

17. Ibid., 7.
18. Ibid., 9.
19. Ibid., 9–11.
20. Ibid., 10.
21. Ibid., 9.

PART 2: KIERKEGAARD AND THE POLITICS OF FAITH, HOPE, AND LOVE

Slavoj Žižek

Turning to Žižek, we find the most interesting and penetrating study of Kierkegaard. If Badiou represents an interest in the formal elements of Kierkegaard's thought, and Habermas, a primary interest in Kierkegaard's substantive claims, in Žižek we find an attempt to balance both. This is likely due to Žižek's immersion in the world of Lacan, for Lacan's psychoanalytic approach allows him to approach many of Kierkegaard's religious insights, albeit from a psychoanalytic point of view. Interestingly, Žižek's reading of Kierkegaard does not begin where most do, with Kierkegaard's famous leap of faith, as it instead begins with the less discussed, but equally interesting, leap into sin. In the context of a long conversation about the dialectic of law and transgression, where Žižek argues that this dialectic characterizes a diverse array of modern thought, from Immanuel Kant through to the Marquis de Sade, and more recently, Georges Bataille, Žižek makes a parallel claim about Kierkegaard.[22] Specifically, reading this dialectic via Lacan, Žižek argues that Kierkegaard realizes that it is through the creation of the symbolic medium of the law that a "primordial self-withdrawal" occurs, and that this incipient form of self-collection leads to the birth of agency.[23] In other words, it is through the transgression that the law allows, that our subjectivity is born, as is the agency that flows from it.[24] Even more simply put, until we are self-conscious, we cannot be free.

Žižek is astute in focusing on this dimension of Kierkegaard's thought, as he finds it in *The Concept of Anxiety*. There, Kierkegaard makes the claim that it is through language that sin is born.[25] For Kierkegaard, the childhood development of language reflects the development of our capacity for symbolic thought, and it is symbolic thought that allows us the possibility of exercising our will.[26] And, as a result of this, sin is born. After all, it is not until we are capable of thinking about the world that the possibility of ethical choice emerges, so that, prior to the development of consciousness, we exist in an amoral or pre-moral state, just like Adam in Eden.[27] However, once consciousness is born, and ethical choice becomes possible, we most commonly act according to either the conventional ethics of the society into which we are born, or else, out of selfish willfulness, that is, Kierkegaard's ethical and aesthetic spheres. And these options, for Kierkegaard, are ethically irresponsible; or, in religious vernacular, they are sinful.

Now, the reason Žižek is astute in focusing on the leap to sin, is that this leap foreshadows the leap of faith, which thereby helps him understand the latter leap with

---

22. Žižek, *Parallax View*, 93–96.
23. Ibid., 89.
24. Ibid., 90.
25. Kierkegaard, *Concept of Anxiety*, 47.
26. Ibid., 45–47.
27. Ibid., 37.

greater sophistication than is typical of political thinkers. In focusing on the birth of will that occurs as a result of self-consciousness, Kierkegaard can refocus ethical conversation away from conversations about the substantive content of our ethical beliefs, and toward the question of the subject's very relationship to her will. As a result, we can come to see the ethical ideas that we have as the instruments by which we learn to exercise our freedom, rather than debating the respective merits of these ideas, so that we can instead focus on the question of our will itself. In this context, we can better understand his leap of faith; rather than a decisionist will to power, whereby we arbitrarily leap beyond conventional ethics, it is instead constituted by a responsible appropriation of our will, in which we no longer need the crutch of conventional ethics.[28]

In focusing on the leap of sin, Žižek is the only one of these three to grasp the nature of Kierkegaard's relevance to political thought, at a level that is more than skin deep. Rather than focusing on the formal elements, like Badiou, or the substantive relevance, like Habermas, Žižek offers an example of Kierkegaard in which the developmental nature of his thought is most evident. Kierkegaard's leap of faith into a post-conventional ethics is not a decisionist leap whereby we simply realize the falsity or limitations of conventional ethics; rather, it reflects a process of self-development, whereby we discover a more ethical way of existing, and, as a consequence, we transcend the limitations of our previous ethics. That is, the formal dimensions of Kierkegaard's thought reflect his insight into the substantive process of human self-development, so that his ethics are not tied to a particular objective doctrine, but to an understanding of the process of becoming an ethical individual.

This process, insofar as it speaks to the development of our capacity for a more authentic ethics, is inclusive in a new vein. Rather than *defining* what it means to be human, thereby offering a definition that will almost certainly exclude people, Kierkegaard's sense of inclusion refers to our very ability to *treat* others inclusively. As a result, inclusion does not depend on an appropriately defined social or political constitution, but on the capacity of its constituent members to treat one another inclusively. Moreover, this capacity for inclusion—what we might also call *neighborly love*—is dialectically the very medium by which we achieve it. That is, it is in being loved that we become loving ourselves. For Kierkegaard, therefore, inclusive communities are not formed when we properly define their nature and the ethics by which they should live, but rather, they are formed when we ourselves become open and loving individuals. By definition, this precludes the problem of exclusion that preoccupies Badiou, just as it gives real substance to Habermas's recognition that Kierkegaard's ethics are post-conventional, and that we become free by way of an Other.

On a final note, Žižek hits upon a further point of importance for a political reading of Kierkegaard, and one that neither Badiou nor Habermas note, but which further reveals Kierkegaard's importance for political thought. While all three share

28. Kierkegaard, *Fear and Trembling*, 60, 115.

an appreciation for how Kierkegaard can help solve one of the most pressing problems facing contemporary political thought, i.e., that of inclusion, Žižek is the only one to note that he can also be of great help in solving the other great problem of political thought, that of inequality. Referring to Lacan's insight that theologians are the only true materialists, Žižek is correct in noting that, while Kierkegaard himself never seemed much interested in such questions, the subjective end-position that Kierkegaard describes is the beginning for a materialist politics.[29] Specifically, in overcoming the conventional ideas we have of one another—be they ideas about race, nationality, gender, sexual orientation, or even, the universal idea of bourgeois individuality—we find ourselves in a position to confront the material, rather than ideational, impediments to the manifestation of equality. That is, inequality is not perpetuated by way of ideas of the Other that we have, but as a result of practices in which we engage—Marx's *relations of production*, for instance—so that seeing ourselves and others clearly can help us expose them.[30] While Kierkegaard might not have been sympathetic to this politics—although even this is quite more complex and debatable than it might appear—Kierkegaard's thought can help take us there.[31]

A Prolegomena to a Political Theory of Love

While Žižek hits closer to the mark, insofar as he focuses on the developmental element in Kierkegaard's thought, his study of Kierkegaard also suffers from a major problem. Like many of his predecessors in the world of political thought, dating back to some of Kierkegaard's earliest political appropriators, such as Georg Lukács and Theodor Adorno, Žižek cannot free himself from seeing Kierkegaard's Christianity as fundamentally ascetic.[32] So, whereas he spends a great deal of time exploring Kierkegaard's thought, and whereas the surrounding sections of Žižek's work clearly owe a tremendous debt to Kierkegaard—one that is sometimes acknowledged but at other times is not—Žižek nonetheless manages to label Kierkegaard's Christianity an ultimate renunciation of the human world, rather than seeing Kierkegaard's Christianity as a fundamental embrace of it. Specifically, in writing of Kierkegaard's Christianity, Žižek reads Christ's sacrifice as exactly the type of self-constituting ascetic act that Nietzsche calls the "will to nothingness."[33] That is, in this act of sacrifice, Žižek reads a radical renunciation of the world, and, along with it, a renunciation of

---

29. Žižek, *Parallax View*, 103.

30. For more on Marx's relations of production, see Marx, "Contribution to the Critique of Political Economy," 263.

31. For instance, based on an expansive survey of Kierkegaard's later writing, Eliseo Perez-Alvarez makes a convincing case that inequality, and the Danish Church's role in legitimizing it, were of prime concern to Kierkegaard. See Perez-Alvarez, *Vexing Gadfly*.

32. See, for instance, Adorno, *Kierkegaard*; Lukács, "Foundering of Form against Life."

33. Žižek, *Parallax View*, 83; Nietzsche, "On the Genealogy of Morals," 599.

every last bit of humanity it is possible to renounce.[34] Therefore, as a consequence of this renunciation stands revealed the inalienable core of humanity, i.e., that which we cannot renounce, which is then reified in the transcendent image of Jesus Christ.[35] As a result, Žižek argues that Kierkegaard's Christian insight needs to be overcome in favor of Nietzsche's "human, all too human."[36] Ironically, then, for Žižek, we need to abandon our Nietzschean reading of Kierkegaard in favor of Nietzsche himself.

For scholars of Kierkegaard, it is hard to see much merit in Žižek's condemnation, as a careful reading of *Fear and Trembling* clearly argues against an ascetic reading.[37] Yet, this has not stopped this misreading from persisting, beginning with Kierkegaard's earliest intellectual reception in interwar Germany and carrying on into the present day. In part, this trend reflects a pervasive mistrust of religion that exists in the world of political thought, and which is only compounded by a tendency to read religion through a Nietzschean lens. However, this was also reinforced by the theological reception of Kierkegaard in interwar Germany, some of whose proponents were explicitly fascist in their politics, while others were quietist.[38] So, when Adorno first made his own "ascetic" critique of Kierkegaard in 1933, it was lodged in an intellectual atmosphere in which many prominent advocates of Kierkegaard were avowed Nazis, while others had insufficiently opposed them.[39]

While contemporary scholarship has laid to rest any connection between Kierkegaard's thought and fascist politics, notably, by offering less superficial readings of *Fear and Trembling*, the charges of quietism are harder to dismiss, and Kierkegaard scholars would do well to take them seriously. In fact, this is the charge that truly lies at the core of Adorno's attack, insofar as Adorno thought that Kierkegaard's overwhelming concern for the individual came at the expense of a concern for the world.[40] For instance, in the context of Nazi Germany, an ethics that focuses solely on our treatment of those around us—our neighbors—but that fails to engage the broader political forces at play, leaves itself open to serious critique. Specifically, while it would be easy to argue that a Kierkegaardian ethic might compel individuals to provide sanctuary for their Jewish neighbors—certainly a brave and admirable task—these ethics says less about the possibility that a fuller ethical response

34. Žižek, *Parallax View*, 110.

35. Ibid., 103, 111.

36. Ibid., 103.

37. For instance, Žižek's reading pays no heed to *Fear and Trembling*'s eponym, which warns against a literal reading of the text; it ignores the pseudonymous nature of the work and it ignores passages in which Kierkegaard argues that through "sacrifice" Abraham "receives" Isaac—and not an Isaac purified of all but his essential qualities, but Isaac as he is, in all of his unique complexity.

38. For instance, see Schulz, "Germany and Austria," 334–47.

39. For a brief look at this, see Morgan, "Adorno's Reception of Kierkegaard."

40. For instance, when Adorno criticizes Kierkegaard's philosophy for being bourgeois, he has in mind Kierkegaard's focus on the individual to the detriment of an interest in the world. See Hullot-Kentor, "Critique of the Organic," 84–85.

might require organized political opposition to Nazism. More broadly, we might begin to explore the way in which ethical acts centered on the individual are suspect when confronting social or political injustices that require a collective response. For political thinkers, despite Kierkegaard's tremendous promise as a potential anchor for normativity—the intimations of which are what fascinate Badiou, Habermas, and Žižek—it is upon this question that their embrace falters. For them Kierkegaard is inextricably a political quietist.

While the stark example of Nazi Germany helps reveal this problem, it only becomes more complex if we think about it within the context of contemporary politics. It would be easy to argue that Kierkegaard's ethics require that we respect others regardless of categories like race, gender, or class.[41] However, it is harder to determine what his ethics might say about societies that are systematically organized according to these categories. For instance, in the context of a society that distributes different criminal justice experiences according to race, that pays women a percentage less for their work when compared to men, and that allows tremendous wealth to coexist alongside tremendous poverty, the limitations of Kierkegaard's ethics begin to emerge. Neighbor love might help humanize those around us, but it does not help us identify the systematic forms of dehumanization to which they might be subject, and which become even harder to identify the less dramatic are the examples. That is, the starkness of the example of Nazi Germany makes it easier to argue that Kierkegaard's ethics might lead to an anti-fascist politics like those of Dietrich Bonhoeffer, but the inherent difficulty in identifying the social and political mechanics involved in more subtle forms of racism, sexism, and exploitation, make it harder to make the claim that a Kierkegaardian ethics has anything to say. Moreover, Kierkegaard's polemics against politics often serve to prevent the extension of Kierkegaard's ethics into the world of politics, because Kierkegaard himself seemed to think that many of the social and political ills of his day were best left unaddressed—at least in their political, rather than personal, incarnation.[42]

Interestingly, this problem does not hinge on an ethical argument, but on a methodological one. Specifically, the ease of drawing Kierkegaard's ethics into an opposition with Nazism, and the relative difficulty of doing so when it comes to combatting contemporary forms of injustice, does not speak to any innate quality within Kierkegaard's ethical position. Instead, it speaks to our ability to identify dehumanization as a political problem. For instance, if our "neighbor" is unjustly arrested and subjected to particularly harsh treatment by the criminal justice system, our ethics might require that we aid them. However, if that unjust treatment is disproportionately distributed to certain groups within our society, and not to others, our ethics might then require

---

41. For instance, see Evans, *Kierkegaard's Ethic of Love*, 318–24.

42. For a work detailing the classical conception of Kierkegaard's relation to politics, see Kirmmse, "Kierkegaard and 1848." However, for a refutation of this position, see Aroosi, "Causes of Bourgeois Culture."

that we engage this larger problem. However, our ability to recognize that our neighbor's treatment is symptomatic of larger problems does not depend on our ethical relationship to them, it depends on our ability to situate their particular experience within a broader political whole. And this depends on exactly the type of analysis that Kierkegaard often decried, as it depends on an objective analysis of our social and political reality. That is, it depends on political thought.

The intention of this analysis is not to make an argument against the validity of Kierkegaard's ethics, but to suggest that there is an ethical necessity to engage in politics. Problematically, unlike the immediacy with which an ethics of love might compel us, a recognition of the ethical necessity of political engagement depends on our willingness to critically engage the mediated realms of social and political life, because without this willingness, we remain blind to situations that ought to compel us. Fortunately, there is a tradition of religiously inspired politics that is a natural match for Kierkegaard's religious ethics, and which is built upon precisely such an ethical necessity. Populated by those like Reinhold Niebuhr, Martin Luther King Jr., and more recently, Cornel West (who has been a vocal proponent of both Occupy Wall Street and Black Lives Matter), it is unfortunate that this tradition is not brought to mind when political theorists think of Kierkegaard. If it were, Kierkegaard might find his home within the world of political thought, as both an explanation and a proponent for what has been one of the most transformative political movements of the twentieth century. In this way, he could urge political thinkers to remain as attentive to questions of subjectivity as they are to the objective world, while also provoking Kierkegaard scholars into further developing the critical tools by which to recognize social and political situations to which Kierkegaard's ethics should lead.

Conclusion: God and Politics

As Kierkegaard well knew, philosophers argue about the essence of things, and not their existence;[43] or, put differently, we debate about the nature of signifiers, and not the existence of the signified, and there is perhaps no more hotly contested signifier than that of God. For those in the world of political thought, God is often seen as exactly the type of rationalization that Kierkegaard spent his life attempting to undermine. Therefore, when it comes to political life, rather than seeing God's presence in the Civil Rights movement, they see it in radical branches of evangelicalism. Yet, ironically, one of the tools Kierkegaard used to undermine such conceptions of God—his indirect style of writing—makes it difficult to correct these mistakes, as these corrections require a substantive conversation about Kierkegaard's thought, and one to which his indirect writing does not immediately lend itself. However, as many commentators have noted, one of the essential qualities of Kierkegaard's conception

---

43. Kierkegaard, *Philosophical Fragments*, 41–42.

of God—if not the essential quality—is love.[44] And love carries with it far less intellectual and political baggage than does God.

This is not to suggest that a conversation with the world of political thought requires a radical revision of Kierkegaard's work, but only that a more substantive approach to his work—and one that borrows his own existential methodology—might lead to a more fruitful conversation with the world of political thought. If we were to do so, we might find that even within so-called secular or non-Christian forms of political thought, there are important similarities, and that they are similarities upon which a mutually enriching conversation can occur between Kierkegaard scholars and political thinkers.[45] In this way, we might also find that the important and productive questions to ask do not pertain to God's existence (a question with which Kierkegaard himself seemed little concerned), but that they instead pertain to the nature of love.

Bibliography

Adorno, Theodor W. *Kierkegaard: Construction of the Aesthetic*. Translated by Robert Hullot-Kentor. Theory and History of Literature. Minneapolis: University of Minnesota Press, 1989.

Aroosi, Jamie. "The Causes of Bourgeois Culture: Kierkegaard's Relation to Marx Considered." *Philosophy and Social Criticism* 22 (2015) 71–92.

Badiou, Alain. *Logics of Worlds*. Translated by Alberto Toscano. New York: Continuum, 2009.

Derrida, Jacques. *The Gift of Death*. Translated by David Wills. Edited by Mark C. Taylor. Chicago: University of Chicago Press, 1995.

Evans, C. Stephen. *Kierkegaard's Ethic of Love: Divine Commands and Moral Obligations*. New York: Oxford University Press, 2004.

Habermas, Jürgen. *The Future of Human Nature*. Malden, MA: Polity, 2003.

Hullot-Kentor, Robert. "Critique of the Organic: Kierkegaard and the Construction of the Aesthetic." In *Things Beyond Resemblance: Collected Essays on Theodor W. Adorno*, edited by Robert Hullot-Kentor, 77–93. New York: Columbia University Press, 2006.

Kierkegaard, Søren. *The Concept of Anxiety*. Edited and translated by Howard V. Hong and Reidar Thomte. Princeton: Princeton University Press, 1980.

———. *Fear and Trembling*. Edited and translated by Howard V. Hong and Edna H. Hong. Princeton: Princeton University Press, 1983.

———. *Philosophical Fragments*. Edited and translated by Howard V. Hong and Edna H. Hong. Princeton: Princeton University Press, 1985.

44. For instance, see Evans, *Kierkegaard's Ethic of Love*, 145–49.

45. It is important to note that C. Stephen Evans has taken important steps in this direction, using the categories of "special" and "general" revelation to argue that many of Kierkegaard's ethical insights are available to those who do not fall within the Christian fold. See ibid., 156–64, 318–24. Furthermore, Evans also notes that Kierkegaard's ethics of love are essentially at odds with inequality, and with forms of exclusion, such as sexism and racism. See ibid., 301–2. However, this important study of Kierkegaard's ethics takes place within the framework of arguing that Kierkegaard is a divine-command theorist, and therefore threatens to alienate many political readers before they even begin. This is hardly a fault of Evans's scholarship, as his interest lies in meta-ethical debates, but it does help reveal the foundations for a future debate with the world of politics.

King, Martin Luther, Jr. "Letter from Birmingham Jail." In *A Testament of Hope*, 289–302. New York: HarperCollins, 1986.

Kirmmse, Bruce H. "Kierkegaard and 1848." *History of European Ideas* 20 (1995) 167–75.

Lukács, Georg. "The Foundering of Form against Life: Søren Kierkegaard and Regine Olsen." Translated by Anna Bostock. In *Soul and Form*, edited by John T. Sanders and Katie Terezakis, 28–41. Cambridge: MIT Press, 1980.

Marx, Karl. "A Contribution to the Critique of Political Economy." Translated by S. W. Ryazanskaya. In *Karl Marx, Frederick Engels: Collected Works*, vol. 29, *Karl Marx, Economic Works, 1857–1861*, 257–420. New York: International, 1988.

Morgan, Marcia. "Adorno's Reception of Kierkegaard: 1929–1933." *Søren Kierkegaard Newsletter: A Publication of the Howard and Edna Hong Library* 46 (2003) 8–12.

Nietzsche, Friedrich. "On the Genealogy of Morals." In *Basic Writings of Nietzsche*, edited and translated by Walter Kaufmann, 437–599. New York: Random House, 1992.

Perez-Alvarez, Eliseo. *A Vexing Gadfly: The Late Kierkegaard on Economic Matters*. Princeton Theological Monograph Series. Eugene, OR: Pickwick, 2009.

Sartre, Jean-Paul. "Kierkegaard: The Singular Universal." In *Søren Kierkegaard*, edited by Harold Bloom, 75–98. New York: Chelsea House, 1989.

———. *Search for a Method*. Translated by Hazel E. Barnes. New York: Vintage, 1968.

Schmitt, Carl. *Political Theology: Four Chapters on the Concept of Sovereignty*. Translated by George Schwab. Chicago: University of Chicago Press, 2005.

Schulz, Heiko. "Germany and Austria: A Modest Head Start; The German Reception of Kierkegaard." In *Kierkegaard's International Reception*, vol. 1, *Northern and Western Europe*, edited by Jon Stewart, 307–420. Aldersot: Ashgate, 2009.

Spivak, Gayatri Chakravorty. "Can the Subaltern Speak?" In *Marxism and the Interpretation of Culture*, edited by Cary Nelson and Lawrence Grossberg, 271–313. Urbana: University of Illinois Press, 1988.

7

Equality

A Proposal Rooted in Kierkegaard's Theological Anthropology and Theology of Love

NATALIA MARANDIUC

INTERSECTING THE DESIDERATUM OF equality in modern democracies with the reality of human difference is treacherous both at the level of thought and practice. Theologically speaking, equal regard for all human beings is rooted in God's universal love for all people. Human beings are creatures whose very presence in the world results from an act of divine love. God's fecund love is the source of God's desire to create all that is not God, including humanity, and to orient human beings teleologically to be the kinds of beings who find their well-being in relations of love, both by loving God and by loving fellow humans. Throughout his corpus, Søren Kierkegaard shows that there is a deep coherence between God's action in the world and God's being: God is not only loving, God is actually love itself. Since human beings are also called to be creatures of love in human ways, God gives them the tools to become so. God teaches us how to love because God wants us to flourish.[1]

However, while human beings are in a rapport of equality with one another through God's own love relation to them, we are at the same time creatures of difference: God loves us with equality and similar regard, but our love for one another is marked by particularities and dissimilarities. The wide-ranging differences that characterize our identities have powerful consequences in both our individual lives and in the social structures that envelop our existence. In his recognition of difference as a destructive seed of inequality in social relations, Kierkegaard anticipates realities that have been amply analyzed and theorized much later.

Kierkegaard conceptualizes human differences as not only utterly real but also as interwoven with another dimension of human identity: an irreducible, equal universality of simply being human, on account of which we are called to love and regard others as equals, mirroring God's own way of love in human ways. In this essay I

---

1. Kierkegaard's *Works of Love* is in its entirety a passionate pedagogy of love.

argue for a framework of equality rooted in Kierkegaard's theological anthropology, which holds promise in light of contemporary concerns for recognizing and valuing human differences, which Kierkegaard also upholds. Specifically, I show that Kierkegaard assumes a bi-stratified human subjectivity consisting of a base layer of universal humanness and an additional stratum of particularity or difference, which needs to be recognized without distortion. I subsequently show how Kierkegaard's theological anthropology parallels his theological focus on love relations, as he envisions universal love for all human neighbors as a baseline ground from which preferential loves extend as another layer. I conclude by proposing an account of possible equality on the basis of this relational bi-stratification.

Kierkegaard's theology as a whole is ultimately a theology of love, aiming to transform those who encounter it into agents of love in the world. He builds his understanding of love on a corresponding double-layered image of the human self. On top of a basic layer of identity shared by all human beings, there is another layer of particularities and differences. Neither difference nor the universal dimension is optional or reducible to the other in the structure of our subjectivity. While one might object to Kierkegaard that invoking universality is too easily self-evident and needs no proof, Kierkegaard pushes this base layer of the human self precisely because we tend to only see particularities and differences and little else. Because of this tendency, we neither love nor treat each other with equal, universal regard: at best, we become enslaved to preferential relations that distance us from those who have not made the cut, while at the same time distancing ourselves from the source of sustainable love and relationality—God.

The significance of basic universal humanity notwithstanding, we don't encounter fellow human beings at such a level of generic, "pure humanity."[2] This is not how embodied human existence unfolds. Kierkegaard is acutely aware of the enormously numerous and complex dissimilarities, distinctions, and differences that make each one of us singularly unique. Our lives are characterized by complicated identity markers that make each of us irreducibly particular, which is how we encounter any person, including ourselves.[3] Contemporary analysis of gender, race, ethnicity, sexuality, class, ability and other identity differences matches well with Kierkegaard's prescient observations. Much harm results from failing to recognize particularity in human subjectivity.

Charles Taylor speaks of recognition as an externally generated yet inwardly validating dialogical exchange with other people that confers solidity to one's sense of self in terms of one's concrete particularity and difference. Recognition bears deep significance for a person's subjectivity and well-being. The opposite is also true. Human beings "can suffer real damage, real distortion, if the people or society around them mirror back to them a confining or demeaning or contemptible picture of themselves.

2. Kierkegaard, *Works of Love*, 73.
3. Ibid., 70.

It can be a form of oppression, imprisoning someone in a false, distorted or reduced mode being."[4] Structural misrecognition is even more deeply injurious. People of color, those of nonconformist sexualities or queer gender, undocumented migrants, persons of low economic class, or those with disability often encounter such pervasive malrecognition from the dominant groups that it becomes an internalized part of their self-understanding and therefore a powerful source of oppression, both inwardly and socially. When distorted images of people's particularities spread through society, the oppression and injustice becomes systemic, making equality impossible. Misrecognition of human difference invalidates human identities and forms social supremacies that damage the social space; white supremacy, heteronormative patriarchy, or the oligarchy of the economic elite are prominent examples. While much more than recognition is necessary for social transformation and for undoing such structural harms, empowering people regardless of their different particularities to flourish, and engendering democratic equality, recognition nonetheless plays a significant role. To acknowledge human difference is "not just a courtesy we owe people. It is a vital human need."[5] Political recognition requires the interpersonal and social acknowledgment of particularities and differences that characterize people and groups. Paradoxically, what is needed is the universal recognition of what is *not* universal but unique, particular, and distinctive. Even beyond the political goal of recognizing difference and particularity, which is a *sine qua non* condition for democratic equality, recognition is needed for the human self to be properly shaped, actualized, and fulfilled, which is an integral part of partaking well in love relations.

Yet Kierkegaard warns that our dissimilarities and differences are the reason why we develop desires and preferences for some people at the expense of others. On one hand, particularity is part and parcel of our existence as we experience it and gives us our unique identity and unique beauty, yet on the other hand, our differences are the most fertile ground for inequality, exclusion, and oppression. To be sure, "there is dissimilarity everywhere in temporality," since the very nature of time-infused history is "the different, the multifarious."[6] Kierkegaard adds that our differences are not simply on a par with each other: some are kings, while some are beggars; some are rich, while some are poor; some are male, while some are female—and all of these differences create unjust hierarchies. Thus, particularity is not just a neutral descriptor of human life, let alone an unqualified marker of beauty, but it is also the dangerous territory of rejection. We are powerfully tempted to associate ourselves with people most like us. The problem grows larger when the markers of our identity are those of unacknowledged privilege and we associate ourselves with others who share the privilege, unquestioningly, blind to the rejection, nonrecognition, and resulting oppression of those who do not share our privilege. In Kierkegaard's estimation, the relationships

---

4. Taylor, "Politics of Recognition," 25.
5. Ibid., 26.
6. Ibid., 81.

with people like ourselves are not relations of love but of selfishness. When the other person is like me, she is in a certain sense another "I" and not a genuine other human being to be recognized and loved as other.[7]

The manifold differences that permeate our lives carry with them unequal privileges, powers, wealth, and social capital. Kierkegaard emphasizes this by invoking differences in social class and material wealth. Glossing on Jesus' parable of the wedding banquet,[8] Kierkegaard imagines a lavish party with luxurious decorations, exotic food, and satisfying beverages. Yet the host does not invite his privileged friends to partake in such fine wining and dining. The host instead invites a dubious crowd of homeless, poor, and destitute people. In the story told by Jesus the host initially invites friends and relatives who share the host's social status, but these over-entertained people refuse to come. Only then the host calls the beggars and the lame, the poor and the homeless, and all variety of the nobodies of the day, who are delighted to come. Kierkegaard makes the denouement even more poignant and envisions the nobodies as the only invitees. Subsequently, a host's friend hears about the party and is outraged for not receiving an invitation. But when he learns who the invitees were, his hurt feelings instantly evaporate. He would have never come to such a gathering, nor would he have ever seen it as a true banquet or desirable party. It seems to him that this is more like an eccentric soup kitchen; the poor and the homeless would never be equal either to him or to the host. In Kierkegaard's thought, differences such as the social-economic ones in this story work against imagining the equal humanity of dissimilar neighbors. "The one who feeds the poor—but still has not been victorious over his mind in such a way that he calls this meal a banquet—sees the poor and the lowly only as the poor and the lowly."[9] Kierkegaard is troubled that the differences in social location threaten the possibility of equal relations and equal regard. Indeed, relational equality is unreachable when difference is hierarchical and generates rejection, exclusion, and oppression. In other words, left on its own, the particularity of difference renders equality elusive. On the other hand, human universality theorized on its own would be incompatible with embodied historical human existence as we know it.

Kierkegaard acknowledges the difficulties of understanding human identity either in universal terms or in terms of particular differences if either category is taken alone. His solution is to construct a picture of human identity in which the human self is a synthesis of these two layers which coexist without collapsing into each other at any given time and without any conflict between them. The self is therefore marked by a stratum of universality which makes each of us recognizable as human beings. In that sense, we are similar to one another, and are each other's human neighbors. Yet, we are also marked by multiple differences and unique features without which

---

7. Cf. Aristotle, *Nicomachean Ethics*, 1825–39 (8.1.1154b1–8.14.1164a1).

8. Matt 22:1–14, or the parallel parable of the banquet (without the wedding implication, at least explicitly) in Luke 14:12–24.

9. Kierkegaard, *Works of Love*, 83.

our individual identity would not be conceivable. These differences make us recognizable as the singular, particular people that we are. The proper way to understand the Kierkegaardian relation between the universal and the particular within human subjectivity is a rapport of continuity. There is no contrast between universality and particularity in the constitution of the human self but rather, the particular grows out of and perfects the universal.

Universal similarity and particular uniqueness are both irreducible features of the self, yet in Kierkegaard's thought, these two ingredients of human identity are not on the same plane. Again, they form two different strata of human subjectivity. Kierkegaard envisions the self as a construction in which our universal humanity operates as a base layer, with particularity extending onto another level. Both these layers constitute the self, in different ways. The universal marks us *qua* human; particularity is a second gift which perfects the universal without obliterating it, opposing it, or diminishing it. Kierkegaard illustrates the relation between universality and particularity within the human self by imagining paper sheets that share a common watermark.[10] Each individual sheet of paper has something written on it: a story, a drawing, or an inscription. This writing gives each sheet its own particular, unique, character, while the watermark impressed on all sheets makes them similar. The unique drawing, scribbling or other writing is the most visible feature of each sheet; the watermark infused in the fabric of the paper is much less discernable. Although the watermark is part of the body of the paper, ingrained in it, we need to hold it up to the light and look carefully to notice it. Kierkegaard thinks that human beings are somewhat analogous to these sheets of paper. We are characterized by the common watermark of our universal humanity, yet we also have a unique story and set of particularities that make up our different identities. As the sheets of paper have different inscriptions on each of them, so are we singularly unique and different from one another. As the sheets share a common watermark that is discernable if one holds the paper against the light, and as the unique inscriptions on each page do not erase it, so is our common, universal humanity discernable if one looks attentively. Our universal humanity is not obviated by our equally powerful particularities. This watermark of common human identity is the base layer on which particularity is built and grows. To be sure, it is less visible than the dissimilarities that readily catch the eye in the same way that the inscriptions on the sheets of paper draw our attention first.

The common watermark stands not just for our universal humanity, but also for the human neighbor whom we are called to love and care for. This is a call for equal regard, regardless of the particular identity markers or story the neighbor carries within herself. Kierkegaard reads the story of the good Samaritan to illustrate the universal human neighbor, and not the Samaritan identity of the main character. The wounded traveler could be anyone. The helper could and ought to be anyone as well, even though the helper's identity was most discernable as a citizen of Samaria in the gospel story.

10. Ibid., 89.

This person proved to be the neighbor of the injured voyager on account of his humanity, in spite of his Samaritan ethnicity or the prejudices that such an ethnicity carried with it at that time. Kierkegaard concludes that we can only see the common, universal humanity in our neighbor when we look beyond the more easily discernable particularities of time and history and see the other person's universal humanity in the light of eternity. However, we cannot bypass human differences and dissimilarities. Eternity's light illuminates our common humanity only through the differences inscribed in our existence because our eyes see these differences first.

The categories of the eternal and historical-temporal complicate Kierkegaard's discussion of the universal and the particular. What makes us similar, as well as equal, is that our identities are permeated by our relation to the eternal God, who has marked each one of us with eternity's own presence in us, and who is both the source of our being and our destiny. Conversely, dissimilarity, difference, and particularity are marks of temporality in our existence. We cannot avoid being creatures of difference or being unique selves any more than we can avoid existing. Our lives are both located in eternity, by virtue of being God's creatures, and in history and temporality, by virtue of living in the world. The double marks of eternity and temporality correspond with the two layers of our common universal humanity and particular differences. The rest of my essay shows how both of these dyadic descriptions of our subjectivity contribute to a synthesis that makes the democratic desideratum of equality realistic.

I have argued thus far that Kierkegaard's theological anthropology is a bi-layered construction: the particular is in continuity with and a perfection of the universal. Kierkegaard's theology of love builds on this bi-stratification of subjectivity. I propose that there is a correspondence between, on one hand, the non-oppositional relation of universal humanness to particular difference and on the other hand, the relation of neighbor love to preferential loves. Neighbor love is a universal duty to love all human beings, while preferential loves expand and perfect this duty, since we grow close to particular people whom we know in more depth and nuance. This is a constructive proposal based on Kierkegaard's more direct assertions; I resist the trend of interpretation that reads him as the enemy of preferential, special relations. Although his claims regarding universal neighbor love and preferential loves may seem to oppose each other at times, a more nuanced reading of his texts allows for a parallel between the non-oppositional strata in human subjectivity and a non-conflicting relation between universal love for all and particular loves of preference which give life meaning and joy.

When Kierkegaard invokes neighbor love, he literally means every single person possible. The circle is pan-human and maximally large. This extensive inclusion foreshadows recent feminist and womanist theological anthropologies that conceptualize all human beings as part of a web of relationality and interconnectivity.[11] While Ki-

---

11. Relationality-centered feminist theological anthropologies have been put forth by, among others, Catherine Keller, Elizabeth Johnson, and Mary Grey; however, there are variegated other contexts

erkegaard is not a feminist *avant la lettre*, his strong injunction that we ought to love our neighbors even as the neighbor is indeed every human being *qua* human, shows at least a thought bridge between his concerns for equality and contemporary feminist and womanist arguments for universal interconnectivity.

Such an emphasis on universal neighbor love might appear to support an oppositional rapport between this universal duty and loves of preference, especially since Kierkegaard does indeed say that "Christianity has thrust erotic love and friendship from the throne" and replaced it with the love of neighbor. Yet he also passionately advocates that "erotic love and earthly love are the joy of life," adding that "erotic love is undeniably life's most beautiful happiness and friendship the greatest temporal good."[12] However, I suggest that such statements are not contradictory. Non-preferential and preferential loves are continuous with each other, and this continuity corresponds to Kierkegaard's bi-layered theological anthropology. My proposal is that preferential loves are not just a different category from neighbor love. They perfect neighbor love in the same way that particularity perfects universality in the identity of the self, with differences extending and growing out of the base layer of common humanity shared by all. Neighbor love is, however, distinct from preferential loves in the sense that it focuses on similarity between people or what might be called universally human, transcending particular differences which are not however denied.[13] Kierkegaard recognizes that the dissimilarities inherent in creation and in human life are utterly irreducible. They are unequivocal features of temporality and history. As they augment our universal common humanity, so do preferential special loves add a new profound dimension to neighbor love. Again, they are not simply another type of love, but rather, an expansion and perfection of neighbor love that does not take away from or contradict anything about the neighbor love as such.

Preferential loves are bi-layered relationships in the same way that we are bi-layered subjectivities. Our desires, inclinations, and the whole magnetism of attraction constitute one of the layers. The other layer is the neighbor love relation, which ought to be in place between all human beings, even though all relationships need not be (and we can easily recognize that they are in fact not) limited to this base layer of relating. We form bonds with particular human beings and certainly not with all whom we come across, let alone the entire global community of human beings. We are too finite for that. We become attached to a mere subset of people, even though all people on the planet will remain our neighbors in Kierkegaard's understanding. This view is at least partially consistent with the relational claims of feminist theological anthropologies such as Catherine Keller's proposal: all human life is engaged in a

---

for such thought, from the African *evele* conceptuality of the human being, which entails an inherent communion with others, to the claims of communion in the Eastern Orthodox tradition as evinced by John Zizioulas.

12. Kierkegaard, *Works of Love*, 267.
13. Ibid., 68.

weblike connectivity that permeates the whole universe. In Kierkegaard's thought this would be a universal neighbor connectivity which nonetheless allows for the formation of attachments and preferential loves with a small subset of people. In Keller's thought there is also room for particular relations through which we enter the web of all-life-connectedness. Particular relations allow us to "glimpse [into] the unseen relatedness of all things—and always back again into the particular."[14] She emphasizes the inescapability of particularity, since particular relations are the gateway toward the universal web of connectedness of the whole human community. For Kierkegaard, however, particular relations of preference are well lived when the strand of universal neighbor love is integrated *within* them. Preferential loves are sources of well-being for us, but people with whom we engage in such meaningful relations ought to never cease to be the universal neighbor, even as they are much more than that.

Kierkegaard's injunction that we ought to love all people as our universal neighbors is not what people typically encounter in their daily lives. Much more common is the experience of preferential love based on similar particularities between partners without neighbor love permeating it. Love relations, friendships, or other partnerships across human differences are much less frequent especially when differences are steep. It is unlikely that a global bank's CEO would become a close friend to a homeless adolescent sleeping on the marble steps of the bank's headquarters, or that a highly affluent person would bond with a Walmart worker who earns less in a month than what this rich individual may pay for an outfit to wear to the gym.

What we encounter most often is love rooted in preferences, which in turn is rooted in sameness, not in universal neighbor love which would transcend dissimilarities regardless of their depth and amplitude. Kierkegaard keenly observes that this reality is a fact, but it is precisely what he would never call good. He suggests instead that we need to make neighbor love a universal feature of life and to never let our preferential loves be devoid of it. Paradoxically, the very kind of love for which we yearn most deeply and which we intuit to be the source of our joy and well-being includes at its core the non-preferential element of neighbor love which solidifies preferential loves with a no-matter-what quality.

Kierkegaard only rejects preferential alliances and special loves insofar as they are problematic when they are mono-layered relationships devoid of the element of neighbor love. In such a case, they would appear to stand in opposition to the non-preferential care for the neighbor, who is any human being. Kierkegaard is adamant about the need for neighbor love to form an integral part of preferential relationships. Kierkegaard's ideal is that two human partners would not be engaged in just a dyad of mutual relating, but that a third element would also be present between them: what he calls "the middle term 'neighbor.'"[15]

---

14. Keller, *From a Broken Web*, 158.
15. Kierkegaard, *Works of Love*, 142.

On one hand, this middle term is a universal duty of love owed to all people, which ensures equality between partners and, by extension, among members of a society. We are not to take advantage of, or be abused by those who are close to us—either lovers, or friends, or relations of kinship, or any other partners. While such people are more than the universal neighbor to whom we owe equal regard (while the same is owed to us), people with whom we are in preferential, special relationships are never less than what a neighbor is. Hence the middle term of neighbor love must be part of any preferential relation. On the other hand, Kierkegaard uses the concept of the middle term to indicate a space between human lovers and partners that is a dwelling place for God. The middle term refers, in Kierkegaard's universe, to both the neighbor and to God. This is an intentional parallelism, as the universality of God's love equally given to all of us and the universality of neighbor love, which implies treating each other with equal regard, are analogous. This logic allows him to construct what I read to be a bi-layered image of human love and relating, with the universal thread of equality as part of all properly and justly lived preferential loves and partnerships. The equivalence between the middle term understood as neighbor love and the middle term understood as God shows not only the equality envisioned in all human relating but also the sanctifying function of such a transcendental element within all preferential loves. God's presence within human preferential loves is the source of their transformation, so as to become permeated by the equality that neighbor love entails.

Kierkegaard is realistic about our need for preferential, special relations and unions, as well as about the fulfillment and pleasure that such relationships bring. He, therefore, is being unfairly accused of opposing eros, passionate attachment, or friendships in human life. He does not ask for a disintegration of passionate loves and preferential alliances between people, but rather introduces the element of neighbor love and divine presence as a foundation of equality and justice within every particular love and relational preference.[16] Kierkegaard accepts the fact that human attraction and desires create eros-based relationships which are distinct from relating to all people with universal neighbor love. His vision is not to eliminate preferential close bonds from the human spectrum of relating, but to place them in the right rapport with the non-preferential equality-inducing kind of love which ought to permeate any preferential love. His concern is to create a framework which allows for relational equality both in preferential and non-preferential loves, as well as responsibility toward all human neighbors, not just the preferred ones. "Christianity does not want to make changes in externals; neither does it want to abolish drives or inclination—it only wants to make infinity's change in the inner being."[17]

The change Kierkegaard is talking about involves becoming permeated by the eternal, above and beyond temporality and history. This is equivalent with a

16. Ferreira, *Love's Grateful Striving*, 92.
17. Kierkegaard, *Works of Love*, 139.

transformation whereby universal neighbor love as well as divine presence become an integral part of preferential loves as an equalizer between the partners. Kierkegaard's vision of social equality is a description of relationships that have become infused with the transcendent. In theological terms this means that God's love and the human analogue of neighbor love saturates as well as sanctifies preferential loves. "In loving the beloved we are first to love the neighbor . . . your [partner] must first and foremost be to you the neighbor; that she is your [partner] is then a more precise specification of your particular relationship to each other. But what is the eternal foundation must also be the foundation of every expression of the particular."[18] Kierkegaard's claims regarding the "eternal" as a foundation for every particular, preferential relationship are coherent with his logic of equivalence between God and neighbor love as the middle term that sanctifies human relationships. Read in political terms, this sanctification is a transformation that is conducive to equality across the whole spectrum of human relationality, therefore throughout the societal spectrum.

Thus preferential relationships of partnership, alliance, or love of any kind are in Kierkegaardian terms a "further . . . expression" of the non-preferential relationality that characterizes universal neighbor love. Neighbor love ought to percolate through them, but neighbor love alone is an insufficient description of how we human beings operate relationally, as well as an insufficient condition for our well-being. We thrive when we experience the close bonds of preferential loves, in the variegated forms of erotic loves, kinship relations, friendships, mentorships, and many more. Since it includes the whole of humanity, the neighbor circle is too large and too diffuse to see anyone's face closely. As Levinas points out, seeing the other's face both physically and metaphorically is the true mark of human relating.[19]

Special loves and preferential partnerships are also insufficient for achieving relational (and implicitly social) justice and equality. Neighbor love ought to become the bedrock out of which they grow in order to ensure equality between the partners, and by extension, equality across all social relations. Since neighbor love is an analogue in Kierkegaard's work to the presence of God as a middle term within human relationships, Kierkegaard in effect imagines human loves to be re-circuited through God. This provides an ultimate context in which human relationships unfold alongside the more proximate context[20] which typically characterizes the very nature of preferential loves and partnerships. Yet the ultimate context of divine presence within preferential loves allows for the possibility of the sanctifying transformation of such loves making them conducive to social equality. The relation between neighbor love and preferential loves

18. Ibid., 141.

19. Levinas, *Totality and Infinity*, 194–219; see also Levinas, "Ethics as First Philosophy."

20. Kelsey, *Eccentric Existence*, develops extensively the distinction between the *proximate context* of human existence as our embodied, historical life unfolds in particular environments, communities, and relationships and the *ultimate context* which grounds the former one and which is defined by our relation to God.

is therefore one of expansion and continuity. Neighbor love is a ground which holds firm the root of preferential loves, which are extensions that grow from this fertile soil. Kierkegaard's worry is that when preferential loves are not rooted in neighbor love, they would single out just one or very few people from the whole human community as recipients of attraction and devotion,[21] risking pervasive inequality since all others are rejected. Kierkegaard's solution is to acknowledge that particular attachments are part and parcel of human existence in an indelible way, yet neighbor love as a mode of loving needs to permeate them in order for equality to permeate the human society.

Bibliography

Aristotle. *Nicomachean Ethics*. In *Complete Works of Aristotle*, translated by Jonathan Barnes, vol. 2. Princeton: Princeton University Press, 1984.

Ferreira, M. Jamie. *Love's Grateful Striving: A Commentary on Kierkegaard's Works of Love*. Oxford: Oxford University Press, 2001.

Keller, Catherine. *From a Broken Web: Separation, Sexism, and the Self*. Boston: Beacon, 1986.

Kelsey, David. *Eccentric Existence: A Theological Anthropology*. Louisville: Westminster John Knox, 2009.

Kierkegaard, Søren. *Works of Love*. Translated by Howard V. Hong and Edna H. Hong. Princeton: Princeton University Press, 1995.

Levinas, Emmanuel. "Ethics as First Philosophy." In *The Levinas Reader*, edited by Sean Hand, 76–87. Malden, MA: Blackwell, 2005.

———. *Totality and Infinity: An Essay on Exteriority*. Pittsburgh: Duquesne University Press, 1969.

Taylor, Charles. "Politics of Recognition." In *Multiculturalism: Examining the Politics of Recognition*, edited by Amy Gutman, 25–73. Princeton: Princeton University Press, 1994.

---

21. Kierkegaard, *Works of Love*, 49.

8

Loving the Ones We See

Kierkegaard's Neighbor-Love and the Politics of Pluralism

JENNIFER ELISA VENINGA

> So then, let this work of love be done—and would that it might be well understood.
>
> —SØREN KIERKEGAARD[1]

THE "WORK OF LOVE" which Søren Kierkegaard describes here is of course his own 1847 signed publication, *Works of Love: Some Christian Deliberations in the Form of Discourses*. Penned in his journals but not included in the published edition of *Works of Love*, Kierkegaard's words above are excerpted from a short reflection he entitled "A Self-Defense."[2] Until recently, *Works of Love* was perhaps not so "well understood," in part because of a lack of scholarly attention to it in favor of Kierkegaard's philosophical pseudonymous texts. Though he suggested that "whether the book acquires readers is not our affair," increased attention to *Works of Love* in the last decades confirms that the book has indeed acquired a readership, one which has been engaged in an ongoing effort to see that it is indeed well understood. Perhaps the most comprehensive of these studies is *Love's Grateful Striving* (2001), M. Jamie Ferreira's insightful commentary on *Works of Love*. Other studies include collections of essays on *Works of Love* in the *International Kierkegaard Commentary* (1999) and the *Kierkegaard Studies Yearbook* (1998), and multiple scholars have examined the book in relation to specific themes (such as faith and hope) or to other works in Kierkegaard's corpus (such as *Fear and Trembling* and *Either/Or*, for example).[3]

---

1. Kierkegaard, *Works of Love*, 461.
2. Ibid., 455–61.
3. See, e.g., Evans, *Kierkegaard's Ethic of Love* (2004); Furtak, *Wisdom in Love* (2005); Hall,

PART 2: KIERKEGAARD AND THE POLITICS OF FAITH, HOPE, AND LOVE

As recent commentators on *Works of Love* have noted, constructive engagement with the book (at least in the latter half of the twentieth century) has had to take into account a strand of negative critique, including Adorno's well-known criticism of the book. Describing the deliberations as "sermons" which make for "tiresome and unpleasant reading,"[4] Adorno's central criticism is that Kierkegaard's concept of love is too inwardly focused and has no real concrete object. "Kierkegaard's doctrine of love remains totally abstract,"[5] Adorno maintains, and later argues that "a doctrine of love which calls itself practical cannot be severed from social insight."[6] Yet that is, according to Adorno, just what Kierkegaard does. Danish theologian K. E. Løgstrup leveled similar criticism thirty years later, arguing that Kierkegaard's conception of love does not require a concrete person and is thus empty of any real ethical content.[7]

In recent decades, however, scholars have countered these claims and argued for the social and political relevance of Kierkegaard's thought in general and of *Works of Love* in particular. As theologian Stephen Backhouse writes, "Even amongst those who would not go as far as proclaiming a proto-socialist Kierkegaard, it is now widely accepted that however much Kierkegaard focuses on the individual, he is certainly not a misanthropic, apolitical *individualist*."[8] George B. Connell's recent work, *Kierkegaard and the Paradox of Religious Diversity*, attests to Kierkegaard's social relevance in its treatment of a theme clearly germane to the present chapter. "Can Kierkegaard, that great connoisseur of anxiety, offer insight into an anxiety that pervades the contemporary spiritual landscape—anxiety over religious diversity?"[9] Connell carefully answers his own question in the affirmative, and as I will argue, an exploration of *Works of Love* supports this affirmation.

This chapter, then, seeks to contribute to the ongoing effort to situate *Works of Love* in the context of sociopolitical theological discourse. Specifically, it argues that Kierkegaard's concept of neighbor-love provides a framework for building and maintaining religiously and culturally pluralistic democratic societies. The model of neighbor-love presented in *Works of Love*, I maintain, is particularly applicable to twenty-first-century democracies on both sides of the Atlantic. While the United States has wrestled with cultural and religious diversity since its beginnings and some Western European nations have become more diverse only in recent decades, all are faced with the question of what it might mean to foster a healthy pluralism in

---

Kierkegaard and the Treachery of Love (2002); and Krishek, *Kierkegaard on Faith and Love* (2009).

4. Adorno, "On Kierkegaard's Doctrine of Love," 414.

5. Ibid., 418.

6. Ibid., 421.

7. See Søltoft, "Presence of the Absent Neighbor," 113–15, for a helpful summary of Løgstrup's criticism.

8. Backhouse, *Kierkegaard's Critique*, 169–70.

9. Connell, *Kierkegaard*, 1.

the present age.[10] As recent violent episodes such as the tragedy in Norway (2011), Copenhagen (2015), Paris (2015) and San Bernardino (2015) have shown, Europe and the United States have a great deal of work to do to shift from sheer diversity to engaged pluralism.

In this chapter, then, I point to three aspects of Kierkegaard's concept of neighbor-love as they are presented in *Works of Love* that can offer resources for considering the meaning of pluralism today: Kierkegaard's neighbor-love is inherently active and action-oriented, involves seeing the neighbor in terms of similarity and equality, and also requires seeing the neighbor in terms of difference and distinctiveness. To probe more fully the meaning of pluralism, I then briefly examine relevant issues in regard to the relation between pluralism and multiculturalism before turning to an application of Kierkegaard's neighbor-love for contemporary social and political life. I shall begin, however, by examining the meaning of "pluralism" as it is employed in this context.

Pluralism

The term "pluralism" has been utilized lately in a number of disciplines and in relationship to a variety of frameworks, including politics, culture, society, theology, religion, and beyond. As sociologist of religion Grace Davie notes, "Not only is the term 'pluralism' used to *describe* the very different situations found in modern Europe (and indeed beyond), it is also used to evoke the moral and political values associated with these shifting profiles."[11] There is, as she explains, uncertainty about whether pluralism refers to "what is" or "what ought to be."[12] For the purposes of this present chapter, I make a distinction between "diversity," which refers to the presence of coexisting multiple religions and cultures ("what is"), and "pluralism," which refers to the best moral and political response to that diversity ("what ought to be") in the context of democracy. "Diversity, of course, is not pluralism," explains Diana Eck, scholar of religion and director of the Pluralism Project at Harvard University. "Diversity is simply a fact, but what will we make of that fact, individually and as a culture?"[13]

Eck suggests four points about pluralism, which inform my analysis of Kierkegaard's neighbor-love. First, pluralism is "not diversity alone, but the energetic engagement with diversity." It involves not passive acceptance but actively seeking to understand the other and necessitates that "neighbors" interact with one another in honest and authentic ways, even if these encounters are difficult and uncomfortable. Second, pluralism is "not just tolerance, but the active seeking of understanding

---

10. For helpful reflections on the historical context of pluralism in Europe and the United States, see Banchoff, *Democracy*.

11. Davie, "Managing Pluralism," 613.

12. Ibid.

13. Eck, *Encountering God*, 43.

across lines of difference," which suggests that traditional liberal ways of conceiving tolerance which actually serve hegemonic power structures, need to be deconstructed. Third, Eck corrects a popular notion that pluralism requires a relinquishment of truth and value claims by emphasizing that pluralism is "not relativism, but the encounter of commitments." Finally, she underscores the value of active engagement by maintaining that pluralism is based on dialogue.[14]

Although Eck does not address the distinction at length in her work, I note that just as there is a difference between "diversity" and "pluralism," as I am discussing it here, pluralism should also be distinguished from the related concept of multiculturalism. As will be addressed later in the chapter, both frameworks are informed by a number of the same public discourses (on tolerance, recognition and identity, for example), and both could be described as ways of responding to the fact of diversity. As with pluralism, the concept of multiculturalism is ambiguous. Similar to Grace Davie's claim above regarding pluralism, multiculturalism has been interpreted in both a descriptive sense to note the diversity in a given society, and in a normative sense, as "a moral stance that cultural diversity is a desirable feature of a given society."[15]

Additionally, the meaning of multiculturalism is context-dependent, so it takes different forms in the United States, Europe, Canada, South America, or elsewhere. Emphasizing that while there is no universal definition, political philosopher Will Kymlicka maintains that we can understand multiculturalism as a reaction to models of the nation-state which have traditionally emphasized homogeneity. As part of a larger human-rights revolution in the wake of World War II, multiculturalism provided an alternative to earlier models of the nation-state in three key ways: by maintaining that the nation belongs equally to all citizens, by replacing assimilation and exclusionary practices with recognition and accommodation, and by acknowledging historic injustice to particular minorities and making amends for those injustices.[16]

While multiculturalism as a moral stance and as a set of practices can be utilized by individual members of a community (or by dominant groups within a society) apart from official political institutions, it is usually associated with policies and practices institutionalized by the state to recognize and/or accommodate minority cultures. I would argue that while pluralism can (and perhaps should) address or include official state policies as multiculturalism does, it offers a broader framework for considering not simply how *state actors, policies, and laws* should relate to citizens but also how *members of communities should regard one another and act accordingly* in a diverse context. While it does not exclude state policies and laws from its concern, for example, the work of the Pluralism Project tends to focus on American religious diversity in public life more generally. Research projects sponsored by the Pluralism

---

14. Eck, "What Is Pluralism?" See also Eck, *Encountering God*, 191–98, for an earlier version of these descriptions.

15. Triandafyllidou et al., "Diversity, Integration, Secularism and Multiculturalism," 4.

16. Kymlicka, *Multicultural Odysseys*, 61–65, and Kymlicka, "Multiculturalism," 5.

Project involve a variety of topics related to pluralism in the public square, including mapping religious diversity in major US cities, documenting interfaith initiatives of civic institutions considered to be "promising practices," and exploring the practice and promise of dialogue in religious and civic institutions.[17]

Pluralism, furthermore, as I am conceiving it here, is both a civic and theological concept. In her work Diana Eck distinguishes the two senses, but also maintains "that our increasing engagement with one another in civil society may well provide the context for new and transformative theological thinking."[18] Neighbor-love, as understood by Kierkegaard, provides a theological vision and a civic practice for how we can best respond to diversity in our present age. His vision, as I maintain, provides a model for moving from diversity in a descriptive sense to pluralism in a normative sense. I turn now to elements of Kierkegaard's neighbor-love which deeply resonate with the framework of pluralism which I have described above.

Neighbor-Love as Inherently Active

Action is crucial for Kierkegaard's concept of neighbor-love [*Kjerlighed*], which he distinguishes from preferential love for the friend or the beloved [*Elskov*]. Indeed, the very title of the book, *Works of Love* [*Kjerlighedens Gjerninger*] conveys the centrality of acts and action. The Danish *gjerninger* simply translates to "deeds" or "acts," and as M. Jamie Ferreira points out, the word here doesn't intend to suggest works as "merit" in the way that Luther would have conceived of "works righteousness."[19]

What Kierkegaard is writing about then, are deeds and acts—the *doing* of love. In deliberation 3A in the first series of *Works of Love*, Kierkegaard offers reflections on Romans 13:10: "Love is the fulfillment of the law." To clarify Paul's understanding of fulfilling the Jewish Law, Kierkegaard distinguishes the way in which Paul (and Christ) answer the question, "What is love?" from the way in which Socrates responds. Socrates, "that simple wise man of old,"[20] had an artful way of questioning, but was focused on knowledge, while Paul and Christ go beyond knowledge to action, Kierkegaard explains. "The essentially Christian, which is not related to knowing but to acting, has the singular characteristic of answering and by means of the answer imprisoning everyone in the task."[21] To further illustrate his point, Kierkegaard discusses the Pharisee's famous question to Jesus: "Who is my neighbor?" Jesus responds by telling about the story of the Samaritan who became the neighbor through his

---

17. For the Pluralism Project's mission and research on "Promising Practices," see http://pluralism.org/about.
18. Eck, *Encountering God*, xi.
19. Ferreira, *Love's Grateful Striving*, 11.
20. Ibid., 96.
21. Ibid.

actions.[22] "Christ imprisoned the questioner in the answer that contained the task," Kierkegaard writes.[23] All of Christ's answers contain the task; they all suggest not just ways of thinking or believing, but of *doing*. "Christian love is sheer action, and its every work is holy, because it is the fulfilling of the Law."[24]

Earlier in the book, again with reference to the merciful Samaritan, Kierkegaard maintains that the question "Who is my neighbor?" can only be answered in regard to our dutiful response to the specific individual in need. In other words, to recognize the neighbor, one must *become* a neighbor to the neighbor: "The one to whom I have a duty is my neighbor, and when I fulfill my duty I show that I am a neighbor. Christ does not speak about knowing the neighbor but about becoming a neighbor oneself, about showing oneself to be a neighbor just as the Samaritan showed it by his mercy. By this he did not show that the assaulted man was his neighbor but that he was a neighbor of the one assaulted."[25] In her commentary on *Works of Love*, M. Jamie Ferreira suggests that "in one sense this is perhaps the most concrete moment in the whole of the book" and "should be considered a guiding principle for any interpretation of *Works of Love*."[26] Kierkegaard's clear emphasis on the action-oriented nature of neighbor-love here provides an obvious challenge to those critics like Adorno and Løgstrup who argue that his neighbor-love is too abstract, ethereal and divorced from material concerns.

Neighbor-Love, Similarity, and Equality

As theologian Arne Grøn has discussed, Kierkegaard's claim that love is action should be complicated and complemented by the question of "how" exactly this love should be enacted. As he points out, one can engage in works of love in ways that do not ultimately affirm the other as an equal and loved by God. As is characteristic of Kierkegaard's thought in general, in *Works of Love*, "ethically, 'how' qualifies 'what.'"[27] Yet *how* is one able to recognize genuine neighbor-love? And perhaps even more challenging a question: How is one able to recognize the neighbor herself? For Kierkegaard, recognizing neighbor-love and the neighbor, as well as discerning how we should respond to both, relies upon *sight*. "The critical point is that love itself is a matter of seeing," explains Grøn. The ethics of deciding how we are to act and the recognition of love as it is discovered in the other "re-situate us in a social world of seeing and being seen, as a field of vision already ethically imbued."[28]

22. Luke 10:25–37.
23. Kierkegaard, *Works of Love*, 97.
24. Ibid., 99.
25. Ibid., 22.
26. Ferreira, *Love's Grateful Striving*, 70.
27. Grøn, "Ethics of Vision," 66.
28. Ibid.

This "ethics of vision"[29] is a theme throughout *Works of Love*, but is particularly elucidated in discussions of sight and seeing in the second and fourth deliberations of the first series. The focus of this section of this chapter is on the second set of deliberations (all on variations of "You Shall Love the Neighbor"), which emphasize that seeing the neighbor rightly means seeing her as an *equal* with a common human identity. In deliberation 2A ("You *Shall* Love"), Kierkegaard explains that the word neighbor [*Næste*] is derived from "nearest" [*Nærmeste*] and thus the neighbor is the one who is "nearer to you than anyone else, yet not in the sense of preferential love."[30] Because we usually choose our friends and romantic lovers, in a certain sense our love for them is simply self-love. In a twist, Kierkegaard suggests, however, that "*the neighbor* comes as close to self-love as possible," but in such a way that *tests* the selfishness of self-love.[31] Because the commandment is that "you shall love your neighbor *as yourself*," it requires what Kierkegaard calls a "redoubling" of one's self. To love the neighbor, one must see her in the same way that one should see oneself, as a spiritual being loved by God.[32]

Crucial to recognizing the neighbor as the one who is nearest to us is Kierkegaard's adamant assertion that "the neighbor is the one who is equal."[33] She or he "is neither the beloved, for whom you have passion's preference, nor your friend, for whom you have passion's preference," he writes. "Nor is your neighbor, if you are a cultured person, the cultured individual with whom you have a similarity of culture—since with your neighbor you have the equality of a human being before God."[34] Equality for Kierkegaard involves not making distinctions among people and not making partial and preferential judgments about them; the commandment is that we *shall* love the lowly and distinguished neighbor equally.

The question of *how* to recognize this radical equality with the neighbor returns us to the theme of vision and sight. In the second set of deliberations in the first series, Kierkegaard's suggestion for seeing the other as the equal neighbor is ironically to *close our eyes*. "One sees the neighbor only with closed eyes, or by looking *away from* the dissimilarities," he writes, for "the sensate eyes always see the dissimilarities and look *at* the dissimilarities."[35] Worldly differences of rank, culture, or other social distinctions make us blind to our innate and eternal commonality. "In being king, beggar, rich man, poor man, male, female, etc., we are not like each other—therein we are indeed different. But in being neighbor we are all unconditionally like each other. Dissimilarity is

---

29. Both Arne Grøn and M. Jamie Ferreira describe Kierkegaard's ethics in this way.
30. Kierkegaard, *Works of Love*, 21.
31. Ibid., 21.
32. For a discussion of the meaning of redoubling, see Andic, "Love's Redoubling and the Eternal Like for Like," 16–17.
33. Kierkegaard, *Works of Love*, 60.
34. Ibid.
35. Ibid., 68.

temporality's method of confusing that marks every human being differently, but the neighbor is eternity's mark—on every human being."[36] By closing our eyes, however, we can suspend this temporal state of distinctions, even to the point of seeing the enemy as an equal. To love the neighbor is to love blindly, so that even the enemy appears as one's neighbor whom we are commanded to love as ourselves. "Love for the neighbor makes a person blind in the deepest and noblest and most blessed sense of the word, so that he blindly loves every human being as the lover loves the beloved."[37] Enacting this noble blindness means that we will love the one standing before us here and now; in this way, both friend and enemy are equally our neighbor.

Neighbor-Love, Difference, and Distinctiveness

If Kierkegaard's understanding of the duty to love the neighbor involved only a blindness to distinctions, it would, as critics have noted, suggest a kind of other-worldly and even dangerous denial of human difference. As noted earlier, Adorno criticizes Kierkegaard's neighbor-love for being too abstract and his understanding of equality as divorced from society. "Instead of any real criticism of inequality in society, he has a fictitious, merely inward doctrine of equality," Adorno writes.[38] But in the fourth deliberation of the first series, "Our Duty to Love the People We See," Kierkegaard shifts his focus from a more abstract sense of duty to one that is more explicitly connected to what he calls "actuality." As M. Jamie Ferreira notes, once we arrive at this section of *Works of Love*, "it looks like a new beginning,"[39] as "attention to ethical concreteness begins in earnest precisely in this fourth deliberation."[40]

Kierkegaard begins the deliberation by presenting the well-known words from 1 John 4:20: "If anyone says, 'I love God,' and hates his brother, he is a liar; for how can he who does not love his brother, whom he has seen, love God, whom he has not seen?" One should, Kierkegaard maintains, start by loving what is unseen—God—but the only way to know that one loves the unseen is through loving the brothers and sisters one actually sees. Here Kierkegaard's framework indeed reveals itself more fully to be concerned with the actuality of this-worldly life. "One must become sober, gain actuality and truth by finding and remaining in the world of actuality as the task assigned to one," Kierkegaard writes. "With regard to loving, the most dangerous of all escapes is wanting to love only the unseen or that which one has not seen."[41] Loving the one we see means that we love the one with imperfections—who it turns out, is

---

36. Ibid., 89.
37. Ibid., 69.
38. Adorno, "On Kierkegaard's Doctrine of Love," 421.
39. Ferreira, *Love's Grateful Striving*, 99.
40. Ibid., 100.
41. Kierkegaard, *Works of Love*, 161.

everyone including oneself. If we only love or see the perfections in a person, we do not actually see them or truly love them.

This suggests an important aspect of Kierkegaard's ethics of vision. There are right ways of seeing, which validate and respect an individual in their very humanness, but there are also wrong ways of seeing, which are ultimately a form of *not* seeing. To see the other only in terms of excellences and perfections is to make an error in terms of vision. A person who has a vision of love that seeks after only such perfections will search in vain. Such a person, Kierkegaard says, keeps searching and "has dizzily reeled out—into loving the unseen, a mirage, which one does not see. Does it not amount to the same thing: *to see a mirage*—and: *not to see*?"[42] If we see the other only as we *wish* they were, it is as though we are living only through the power of our imagination. Furthermore, in this phenomenon of seeing but not seeing, we are failing to recognize the neighbor for who they are. Arne Grøn has described this as part of a "dialectics of recognition" in Kierkegaard's *Works of Love*. "To recognize someone is not just to see, but to affirm what you see. It is to see in the emphatic sense of paying attention to or giving significance to. Recognition is seeing the other human being *as* an other self: affirming the other to be an other self."[43] And, we might add, it involves affirming them as an other with imperfections and concrete differences.

How are we to arrive at this truthful, honest, and loving way of seeing? Kierkegaard recommends the same mechanism as he did earlier when discussing the necessity of seeing the neighbor as one's equal: *we must close our eyes*. Love is the "closed eye of forbearance and leniency that does not see defects and imperfections," he writes.[44] "This is the duty, to find actuality in this way with closed eyes."[45] M. Jamie Ferreira suggests that the blindness that Kierkegaard describes here differs from the earlier version, however. While closing one's eyes in order to see the other as equal does allow for concrete seeing, it doesn't necessarily get us to that vision. But in this deliberation, Kierkegaard situates the call to a kind of blindness in the context of actuality, which can foster concrete sight. "Our eyes are closed to what is not actual in order to see things just as they are," Ferreira explains. "The closed eye of forbearance means that love is an honest, inclusive seeing, which is a concrete seeing."[46]

This kind of concrete seeing allows us not only to see the commonality between ourselves and our neighbors, but also the very real differences between those neighbors and ourselves. Kierkegaard's insistence that neighbor-love involves an appreciation for difference and diversity is reflected later in the book, particularly in the fourth deliberation of the second series, "Love Does Not Seek Its Own." In this section, Kierkegaard extols the value of each individual's distinctiveness. "The truly

---

42. Ibid., 162.
43. Grøn, "Dialectic of Recognition," 148.
44. Kierkegaard, *Works of Love*, 162.
45. Ibid., 163.
46. Ferreira, *Love's Grateful Striving*, 110.

loving one does not love his own distinctiveness but, in contrast, loves every human being according to his distinctiveness; but 'his distinctiveness' is what for him is his own; that is, the loving one does not seek his own; quite the opposite, he loves what is the other's own."[47] In contrast, Kierkegaard describes the "domineering person" as one who refuses to recognize the other's distinctiveness, as well as the "small-minded person," who refuses to recognize her own distinctiveness. Both are missing—or rejecting—the greatest beneficence, which is "in love to help someone toward that, to become himself, free, independent, his own master, to help him stand alone."[48] The greatest gift that we can give is to help a neighbor embrace their own unique individuality. In this way, then, Kierkegaard here is calling human beings to both appreciate and foster genuine difference and diversity.

Pluralism, Multiculturalism, and the Politics of Recognition

Thus far, I have highlighted three aspects of Kierkegaard's neighbor-love as presented in *Works of Love*: it is inherently active, involves seeing similarity and equality, and involves seeing distinctiveness and difference. Before bringing Kierkegaard's concept into contemporary social-political questions of how communities can better approach the challenge of diversity, I want to return to the concept of multiculturalism as it bears on issues related to pluralism.

I first turn to a theme within contemporary discourse about pluralism and multiculturalism—the "politics of recognition"—which is particularly relevant here. The question of what it means to "recognize" the other is deeply related to two characteristics of neighbor-love described in this chapter—that it simultaneously requires us to acknowledge similarity and equality on the one hand, and distinctiveness and difference on the other. To consider the relation between the politics of recognition and multiculturalism and pluralism, we can look to Canadian philosopher Charles Taylor's influential essay on the topic. While recognition has always been a human need, Taylor explains that the modern articulation of the need for recognition came about with a historical shift from regarding identity in terms of honor (as defined by social hierarchies) to dignity (in terms of egalitarian human worth). The contemporary demand for recognition by individuals and subaltern groups is informed by the thesis that "our identity is partly shaped by recognition or its absence, often by the *mis*recognition of others, and so a person or group of people can suffer real damage, real distortion, if the people or society around them mirror back to them a confining or demeaning or contemptible picture of themselves."[49]

The question of how to meaningfully recognize the other, however, is complicated by the related and sometimes-conflicting dynamics of what Taylor calls a "politics of

---

47. Kierkegaard, *Works of Love*, 269.
48. Ibid., 274.
49. Taylor, "Politics of Recognition," 25.

equal dignity" and a "politics of difference." Recognition requires that we acknowledge some universal and "difference-blind" principles which are foundational for liberal democracies, chief among them that all humans deserve dignity and are equally worthy of respect. Yet recognition also necessitates that differences between individuals and groups be respected and that the unique identities of each be acknowledged. The former, in turn, means that nondiscrimination will entail granting particular rights and protections to minorities that have traditionally been oppressed or excluded. "We give due acknowledgment only to what is universally present—everyone has an identity—through recognizing what is peculiar to each," Taylor writes. "The universal demand powers an acknowledgment of specificity."[50]

As noted, however, these two modes of politics can conflict in their call simultaneously to recognize what is the same among people and what is different. As Taylor points out, this conflict is made more complicated by the growing awareness that the ostensible "difference-blindness" of liberal Western democracies is actually a mode of seeing shaped by a culture without regard to the ways that power and particular values have formed these lenses. Thus, non-discrimination itself can be biased. Others have suggested that multiculturalist policies which seek to recognize group identities and rights actually have the effect of obscuring internal diversity within a given group. In a recent book entitled *Multiculturalism and Its Discontents*, for example, Kenan Malik argues that "multicultural policies . . . have not responded to the needs of communities but, to a large degree, have helped create those communities by imposing identities on people and by ignoring internal conflicts arising out of class, gender and intra-religious differences."[51]

As Malik and others describe, however, in the 1970s to the mid-1990s, multiculturalism held much promise as states began to end practices of cultural and religious assimilation. Charles Taylor describes the eight most common policies associated with multiculturalism, including the constitutional, legislative or parliamentary affirmation of multiculturalism; the adoption of multiculturalism in school curricula; exemptions from dress code; allowing of dual citizenship; the funding of ethnic group organizations to support cultural activities; the funding of bilingual or mother-tongue language instruction; and affirmative action for immigrant groups.[52] Since the mid-1990s (especially in Western Europe), however, there has been a general retreat from multiculturalism and the kinds of policies that Taylor describes. In 2010, German Chancellor Angela Merkel remarked, "Of course the tendency had been to say, 'Let's adopt the multicultural concept and live happily side by side, and be happy to be living with each other.' But this concept has failed, and failed utterly."[53] At the conclusion of 2015, despite the fact that Germany accepted over one million refugees in that year,

50. Ibid., 39.
51. Malik, *Multiculturalism*, 60.
52. Taylor, "Multiculturalism," 7.
53. Noack, "Multiculturalism."

Merkel made similar comments, maintaining that "multiculturalism leads to parallel societies and therefore remains a 'life lie.'"[54] In 2011, then-British Prime Minister David Cameron declared that multiculturalism had failed, remarking that "under the doctrine of state multiculturalism, we have encouraged different cultures to live separate lives, apart from each other and the mainstream," leading to a weakening of collective identity and the growth of radicalization among Muslims.[55]

Issues related to these sets of politics have arisen in recent years as critiques of multiculturalism have grown louder, particularly in Europe. One strand of this critique claims that the multicultural ideology of the politics of difference has led to the erosion of national identities. Over the last several decades, anti-immigrant rhetoric has increased in a number of Western European countries as Muslim populations have risen. Far-right parties in countries such as France (National Front), Denmark (Danish People's Party), and the Netherlands (Freedom Party), for example, have called for restrictions on immigration and have cultivated fears of an immanent "Eurabia." These fears have been exacerbated by the terrorist attacks of the last decade, many of which were connected to fundamentalists claiming to speak for Islam.[56]

There is, of course, a long list of other recent issues and events which reflect the fears and tensions of societies that wish to reassert national identity, including (but not limited to) the headscarf debates in France in the 1990s–2000s, the banning of minarets in Switzerland in 2009, the Danish cartoon crisis in 2005–2006, and the 2016 Brexit vote, which was made possible by the anti-immigrant Independence party in the UK. The vote came in the wake of the refugee crisis, which peaked in 2015 and continues to ignite fierce debate on restricting immigration. Perhaps the most extreme example is the 2011 tragedy in Norway perpetrated by ethnic Norwegian Anders Breivik, whose rationale for murdering dozens of young Norwegian Labor Party leaders was that the party had supported the Islamization of Europe which would lead to the collapse of Christendom. "Multiculturalism . . . is the root cause of the ongoing Islamisation of Europe which has resulted in the ongoing Islamic colonization of Europe through demographic warfare," Breivik wrote in his 1,500-page manifesto entitled *2083: A European Declaration of Independence*.[57]

The context in the United States is much different for a number of reasons, including its internal indigenous Native American populations, a long tradition of immigration, and the absence of a historical link between church and state. Yet anti-immigrant and Islamophobic attitudes have recently ignited in the United States, particularly over fears that one of the perpetrators of the November 2015 terrorist attack in Paris may have been a Syrian refugee. Shortly after the attack, two dozen American governors expressed their fear that future refugees might threaten national security

54. Ibid.
55. Cameron, speech on radicalisation.
56. See, e.g., Augstein, "After European Strikes."
57. See Funaro, "Norway Shooting."

and announced plans to curtail or refuse future Syrian refugees.[58] Donald J. Trump's initial calls for a "total and complete shutdown of Muslims entering the United States" (December 2015) and for a wall to be built along the US-Mexican border to prevent illegal immigration (October 2015) resembled the anti-multiculturalist attitudes of populist parties in Europe.[59]

Yet other critics of multiculturalism have issued concern not out of far-right nationalist or Islamophobic ideologies, but rather from the political left. Some feminists, for example, have criticized multiculturalist practices on the grounds that political support for the rights of minority cultures often means allowing or even promoting practices which oppress women. In the late 1990s, political scientist Susan Moller Okin raised the question of whether multiculturalism was "bad for women."[60] She answered in a resounding affirmative, noting examples of multiculturalist policies that she argued had harmed women, such as French legislation in the 1980s which permitted polygamy, as well as cultural practices of clitoridectomy and child marriages. Calling into question the defense of multiculturalism by theorists such as Will Kymlicka, Okin maintains that the liberal promotion of group rights can serve to discriminate and oppress women.[61]

Kierkegaard's Neighbor-Love and the Politics of Pluralism

Some of the challenges (or "discontents") of multiculturalism described above are encountered in attempts to cultivate pluralism in contemporary Western societies. The dynamics of a politics of recognition which Charles Taylor describes, for example, complicate the process of dialogue, a key aspect of pluralism. Engaging in authentic and constructive dialogue with the other, after all, necessitates the difficulty of simultaneously recognizing the equal dignity of the other and the unbridgeable differences between people. But because pluralism as it is understood here is a broader civic, political, and theological concept than multiculturalism, both its promises and challenges are different. In this final section, I raise two related questions: First, how can Kierkegaard's neighbor-love, which reflects the three characteristics above, serve to foster pluralism in contemporary Western democracies? Second, does his concept of neighbor-love apply to individuals only, or might it have implications for official policies and practices of the democratic state itself?[62]

---

58. See Troyan, "After Attacks in Paris."

59. See Imbert, "Donald Trump," and Diamond, "Donald Trump."

60. Okin first published her reflections in the *Boston Review* in 1997 under the title "Is Multiculturalism Bad for Women?" and in 1999, the piece was republished in a collection of essays under the same title.

61. Okin, "Is Multiculturalism Bad for Women?," 20–22.

62. I owe thanks to this volume's coeditor, Silas Morgan, for raising this important question.

In addressing the first question, we can turn to one of Kierkegaard's key paradoxes present not just in *Works of Love*, but throughout his corpus: that there is a persistent dialectical relationship between the particular and the universal. The first element—the individual and/or the particular—is undeniably central to Kierkegaard's thought. He consistently addresses his works to *Den Enkelte*, that single existing individual whom he describes in his *Upbuilding Discourses* as the one "I with joy and gratitude call *my* reader, that single individual."[63] While reflecting on the absolute duty to God, Kierkegaard's pseudonym Johannes de Silentio famously says that "the paradox of faith, then, is this: that the single individual is higher than the universal, that the single individual . . . determines his relation to the universal by his relation to the absolute."[64] A human being on its way to becoming a self, Anti-Climacus explains in the first exasperating page of *The Sickness Unto Death*, "is a relation that relates itself to itself."[65] Not only does Kierkegaard—also through Anti-Climacus—stress the particularity of the individual, but he also insists in *Practice in Christianity* that it is the *particularity* of Jesus Christ which makes him the Paradox of faith: Christ, who issues his invitation to all, "is and wants to be the specific historical person he was eighteen hundred years ago."[66] The historical specificity of Christ's individual life is key, for the fact that "God has lived here on earth as an individual human being is infinitely extraordinary."[67]

At the same time, however, Kierkegaard's paradoxical framework suggests that the universal is also necessary for the individual subject. While the Knight of Faith is called to teleologically suspend the "universal" ethical sphere, Kierkegaard's pseudonym Judge William asserts that the three spheres—the esthetic, ethical and religious—are "the three great allies."[68] The healthy self, Anti-Climacus maintains, must always extend beyond its relation to itself to that universal "power that established it."[69] Jesus, furthermore, was an existing and particular human being, but the power of his love is universal, for he will "draw all" to himself.[70] In his insightful discussion of these themes as they relate to the issue of religious diversity, George Connell notes that Kierkegaard "rejects any simple choice in favor of either the universal or the particular dimension of the human condition."[71] This both/and quality of Kierkegaard, he argues throughout his book, speaks to the challenge of contemporary religious diversity,

---

63. Kierkegaard, *Eighteen Upbuilding Discourses*, 5.
64. Kierkegaard, *Fear and Trembling*, 70.
65. Kierkegaard, *Sickness Unto Death*, 13.
66. Kierkegaard, *Practice in Christianity*, 23.
67. Ibid., 31. See Connell, *Kierkegaard*, 5, for commentary on this passage.
68. Kierkegaard, *Either/Or*, 2:147.
69. Kierkegaard, *Sickness Unto Death*, 14.
70. John 12:32: "And I, when I am lifted up from the earth, will draw all to myself." See Kierkegaard's reflections on the verse in Kierkegaard, *Practice in Christianity*, 151–262.
71. Connell, *Kierkegaard*, 11.

which is "at its core, a matter of balancing the demands of our particular identities, especially our particular religious identities, with the demands of our shared humanity, especially our common need to find ways to coexist harmoniously and appreciatively with people different from us."[72]

The concept of neighbor-love present in *Works of Love* brings together the universal and particular in Kierkegaard's thought in a way that offers insight for thinking about the nature of pluralism. In its insistence upon seeing the similarities and equality between oneself and others, Kierkegaard's neighbor-love stresses recognizing the universal worth and dignity of all people. Kierkegaard's ethics of vision demands that we see the neighbor with the lens of equality, and thus to the extent that they are seen through the eyes of love, our enemy is our equal. With closed eyes, Kierkegaard calls us to see the neighbor—who is "every human being, unconditionally every human being"[73]—as one who shares in our common humanity and is worthy of love.

In a society which strives toward pluralism, this ethics of vision requires the majority to recognize minorities as their human equals even in the context of social and economic inequality, and despite differing cultures or religions. As political scientist Thomas Banchoff writes in his introduction to his excellent volume *Democracy and the New Religious Pluralism*, "There are majority religious traditions and majority political cultures—different on both sides of the Atlantic—within which diversity is articulated. Pluralism is about the responses of minorities to majorities and vice versa."[74] Kierkegaard would say that the uneven playing field that is human society creates false divisions and does not reflect our unconditional and eternal equality. "Love for the neighbor has the perfections of eternity," Kierkegaard writes, and "this perhaps is why at times it seems to fit in so little with the relationships of earthly life and with the temporal dissimilarities of the worldly."[75] Despite these temporal distinctions, the Kierkegaardian society is one in which neighbors see one another's commonality and are called to exercise tolerance and respect. This society would have little patience for the kind of anti-immigrant and Islamophobic attitudes expressed by far-right parties in Europe and the United States today. Members of society—both leaders and "lay" people—would strive to look away from the differences that divide people, such as race, ethnicity, religion, or gender.

Yet Kierkegaard's ethics of vision also demands that, paradoxically, we must see the distinctiveness and the particularity of the neighbor even as we see her as an equal. As Arne Grøn, M. Jamie Ferreira, and others have noted, there are times when we see the neighbor but in such a way that we are not really seeing them. We may fail to see them as equals, as was the case above, but we can also fail to see them if we only recognize the ways in which they are similar to us. Honest and concrete seeing must

---

72. Ibid., 8.
73. Kierkegaard, *Works of Love*, 66.
74. Banchoff, *Democracy*, 6.
75. Kierkegaard, *Works of Love*, 69.

be anchored in actuality rather than imagination, which can allow us to see the real and irreducible differences between one another. This necessary aspect of neighbor-love is reminiscent of Emmanuel Levinas's ethics of responsibility and helps us recall the similarities (as well as differences) between Kierkegaard and Levinas.[76] For Levinas, seeing the other means recognizing her alterity—*seeing* her difference—which he explains in terms of the face of the other. "The face is present in its refusal to be contained. In this sense it cannot be comprehended, that is, encompassed," Levinas writes in *Totality and Infinity*. "The Other remains infinitely transcendent, infinitely foreign."[77] This is, of course, not the language that Kierkegaard uses in *Works of Love*, but his insistence on honoring distinctiveness and individuality resonates with Levinas's call to recognize the alterity of the other.

As noted earlier, Kierkegaard describes the "greatest beneficence" as lovingly helping someone to "become himself, free, independent, his own master."[78] To do so requires not just seeing the distinctiveness of the neighbor but actually helping to foster it. Here I highlight two commentators who offer insight into the political function of Kierkegaard's insistence on singularity and individuality. Following Derrida rather than Levinas, philosopher Mark Dooley has argued that Kierkegaard offers an ethics of responsibility that relies on a "politics of exodus" or "politics of the émigré" who "places the needs of the singular over those of the universal, of one who takes up the cause of the outcast and the marginalized, the victims of injustice, the lepers and the lame, as a means of destabilizing the establishment."[79] Dooley argues that a politics of exodus helps to counter totalizing politics of the state that can tend toward exclusion, and is necessary for the emergence of authentic community.

Theologian Stephen Backhouse, in *Kierkegaard's Critique of Christian Nationalism*, follows Dooley's project of gleaning the social and political significance of Kierkegaard. Backhouse, however, specifically focuses on Kierkegaard's challenge to nationalism and elements of patriotism, arguing that Kierkegaard's political relevance is necessarily tied to his Christian identity. Reading *Works of Love* through a social-political lens, Backhouse maintains that "the *neighbour* provides a superior way to identifying persons than those suggested by national models driven by shared preferences."[80] Kierkegaard's concept of neighbor provides an alternative to the problematic categories of "compatriot" or "conational," which unite citizens only in their devotion to the nation. Nationalism relies on preferential love [*Elskov*], which seeks to exclude diversity in favor of shared culture and custom. "By contrast, neighbour love thrives in situations of difference and it is able to include many people under

---

76. For helpful discussions of the relationship between Levinas and Kierkegaard, see Westphal, *Levinas and Kierkegaard in Dialogue*, and Simmons and Wood, *Kierkegaard and Levinas*.
77. Levinas, *Totality and Infinity*, 194.
78. Kierkegaard, *Works of Love*, 274.
79. Dooley, *Politics of Exodus*, xxi.
80. Backhouse, *Kierkegaard's Critique*, 197.

its wing," Backhouse maintains.[81] "The Christian does not have an ethical duty only towards people whose national narratives dovetail with their own—the duty is to love the neighbor simply *because* he is the neighbor."[82]

This requirement to love the neighbor not because she shares my nationality or my love for my nation, but simply because she is my neighbor, the one nearest to me, is part of cultivating a pluralistic society. Pluralism, as we have seen, challenges exclusivist positions and institutions which seek to define the identity of a community in narrow and prejudicial ways. But it also provides an alternative to inclusivist frameworks which seek to assimilate diversity into a melting pot in which the real differences between individuals are obscured or made invisible. As articulated in *Two Ages* and his public attack on Christendom in his late writings, Kierkegaard's critique of mass entities including the nation and the public (including the press) is relevant here. Kierkegaard detested the way in which he believed the Danish nation had become equated with Christianity as well as the way that the "public" had served to curtail the existential religious commitment of individuals. Both of these entities were "imaginary magnitudes" which worked to homogenize individual particularities.[83] As he writes in *The Moment*, "The number decides whether an opinion has physical power, and this is what they care about all the way through: the single individual in the nation—well, there is no individual, every individual is the public."[84]

In the context of twenty-first-century life, a pluralistic society would support the development of individual identities, which would include recognizing and actively seeking to understand the specific religious and cultural elements of those identities. Two of Diana Eck's characteristics of pluralism can be noted in particular here, including the requirements to go beyond tolerance to seek understanding across differences, and to foster the encounter of diverse commitments. In his effort to preserve the distinctiveness of every individual neighbor, Kierkegaard's neighbor-love offers a framework for the possibility of fulfilling these requirements as societies work toward creating authentic pluralism. Rather than simply tolerating those who are different from us, this stance requires that we recognize their distinctiveness and work to understand them in a way that honors both their common humanity and their alterity.[85] Since both pluralism and Kierkegaard's neighbor-love are to be actively practiced rather than simply contemplated in theory, however, we must consider to whom these requirements apply and how. Here I raise the final question of this chapter: Does Kierkegaard's concept of neighbor-love apply to individuals only, or might it have implications for official policies and practices of the democratic state itself?

---

81. Ibid., 210.
82. Ibid., 211.
83. Kierkegaard, *The Moment*, 37.
84. Ibid., 209.
85. For an insightful critique of tolerance as a liberal democratic virtue, see Brown, *Regulating Aversion*.

As discussed earlier, Kierkegaard was wary of groups such as the state and public, which he believed had leveled out differences among individuals. As noted, critics of approaching Kierkegaard from a political perspective point out that while he did criticize the Danish government and state church, Kierkegaard was more concerned with religion than politics (especially in *Works of Love*, the subject of this discussion). This sentiment was ostensibly evident in the last year of his life, as he wrote in a journal that "political service and religious service relate to each other altogether inversely."[86] Should we understand, then, that Kierkegaard's neighbor-love is most appropriate for fostering pluralism through *individual* relationships, attitudes and actions, rather than through institutions, policies or laws of the state?

In one sense, it seems that we should answer in the affirmative. Arguably, the kind of ethics of vision that allows us to recognize the neighbor as the nearest one to us, the one who is similar and equal to us yet simultaneously distinct, is an ethics suited for individual members of a community. From this perspective, enacting pluralistic neighbor-love would mean fostering interpersonal relationships with the "ones we see" who are right in front of us—even if we deeply disagree with them or appear to have nothing in common with them. Practically, therefore, it might mean that I strive every day not to see my neighbor only as a Muslim, a Christian, or a Hindu, but instead as a fellow human being who shares in similar existential struggles. Perhaps it could suggest that I actively participate in community events which bring my neighbors together to discuss common social concerns.

On this individual level, Kierkegaard's paradoxical embrace of both the universal and the particular, similarity and difference, would also call me to recognize my neighbor exactly how she is. Even if I, as a Muslim, disagree with my Christian neighbor, for example, neighbor-love would demand that I encourage her to become her full potential as both a human being and as a Christian. As we have seen, after all, for Kierkegaard the loving person "loves every human being according to his distinctiveness,"[87] and the greatest beneficence is to help someone "become himself."[88] Neighbor-love might call me to participate not only in public events that highlight common concerns, but also in those that provide a space for dialogue about differences. When enacted, Kierkegaard's neighbor-love would reflect all four of Diana Eck's characteristics of pluralism: that it is active; it is not just tolerance but is rather active seeking of understanding; it is not relativism but rather an encounter of commitments; and it is based upon dialogue.

As existential practices, these characteristics may seem to be more appropriate for actions, attitudes and frameworks of individuals in the public square and civil society than for nation-states. Yet it is possible that the call for a Kierkegaardian ethics of vision could at least inform official political bodies and policies. Kierkegaard's

---

86. Kierkegaard, *The Moment*, 537.
87. Kierkegaard, *Works of Love*, 269.
88. Ibid., 274.

dual emphasis on recognizing similarity and equality (the universal) and difference and distinction (the particular) could provide a needed corrective to both harmful assimilationist policies and the kind of multiculturalist programs that actually end up segregating minorities in an attempt to honor them. Perhaps then a French Muslim could more easily be recognized as having both identities, but in a way that is also particular to him as an existing individual. An American Buddhist with ties to China could equally be respected in her actuality as part of all of those communities. At its best, the politics of pluralism does not just tolerate, but rather encourages, these commitments. George Connell poses a version of these statements in the form of a question which he (and I) answer in the affirmative:

> Does Kierkegaard's dialectical sense of counterpoised particularity and university mean that, for Kierkegaard, fidelity to a specific faith should lead toward, not away from, mutual recognition of shared humanity, that delving more profoundly into the deepest sources of that faith should foster peaceful and appreciative coexistence rather than fomenting discord, that faithfulness invites us to attend with equal seriousness to the common convictions that unite as well as to the contrasting beliefs that distinguish one faith from another?[89]

Appreciating the concepts that Connell mentions—the paradox of particular and universal, mutual recognition of shared humanity and a commitment to one's own distinct faith—are crucial aspects of Kierkegaard's neighbor-love and are also at the heart of pluralism. They are also, I would say to Kierkegaard's critics, as *political* as they are *existential* and *theological*. As recent events in Europe and the United States attest, however, these stances and practices are not easy to cultivate in a diverse society. Slavoj Žižek has aptly pointed out that the commandment to "love your neighbor as yourself" should be jarring. Drawing from Freud and Lacan, Žižek has written about the Law as a violent imposition that calls for us to encounter—and *love*—the neighbor who is a "traumatic Thing" completely other to us. From this perspective, "the neighbor (*Nebenmensch*) as the Thing means that, beneath the neighbor as my *semblant*, my mirror image, there always lurks the unfathomable abyss of radical Otherness, of a monstrous Thing that cannot be 'gentrified.'"[90]

As Kierkegaard and Levinas would agree—though for different reasons perhaps—the Otherness of the neighbor should not (and perhaps cannot) be gentrified or annulled, which is clear from Kierkegaard's insistence on the preservation of individual distinctiveness. Yet neither should we forget that the neighbor is our equal and shares in our very humanity. Pluralism would call us to love these ones we see, to actively encounter and dialogue with these others who are all neighbors, the ones nearest to us. This is no small challenge, but it is a task and a goal that we must continue to strive for if we are to foster a working just peace in the twenty-first

---

89. Connell, *Kierkegaard*, 11.
90. Žižek, "Neighbors and Other Monsters," 143.

century and beyond. To use Kierkegaard's language, we can think of pluralism as a possibility of the good for which we must continually hope, for "*lovingly* to hope all things signifies the relation of the loving one to other people, so in relation to them, hoping for them, he continually holds possibility open with infinite partiality for the possibility of the good."[91]

Bibliography

Adorno, Theodor W. "On Kierkegaard's Doctrine of Love." *Studies in Philosophy and Social Science* 8 (1939–1940) 413–29.

Andic, Martin. "Love's Redoubling and the Eternal Like for Like." In *Works of Love*, edited by Robert L. Perkins, 9–38. Macon, GA: Mercer University Press, 1999.

Appadurai, Arjun. *Fear of Small Numbers: An Essay on the Geography of Anger*. Durham: Duke University Press, 2006.

Augstein, Frank. "After European Terror Strikes, 'Eurabia' Fears Soar." CBS, March 6, 2015. http://www.cbsnews.com/news/after-european-terror-strikes-eurabia-fears-soar.

Backhouse, Stephen. *Kierkegaard's Critique of Christian Nationalism*. Oxford: Oxford University Press, 2011.

Banchoff, Thomas, ed. *Democracy and the New Religious Pluralism*. Oxford: Oxford University Press, 2007.

Brown, Wendy. *Regulating Aversion: Tolerance in the Age of Identity and Empire*. Princeton: Princeton University Press, 2006.

Cameron, David. Speech on radicalisation and Islamic extremism. Munich, February 5, 2011. Transcript. http://www.newstatesman.com/blogs/the-staggers/2011/02/terrorism-islam-ideology.

Connell, George B. *Kierkegaard and the Paradox of Religious Diversity*. Grand Rapids: Eerdmans, 2016.

Davie, Grace. "Managing Pluralism: The European Case." *Society* 51 (2014) 613–22.

Diamond, Jeremy. "Donald Trump: Ban All Muslim Travel to U.S." CNN, December 8, 2015. http://www.cnn.com/2015/12/07/politics/donald-trump-muslim-ban-immigration.

Dobkowski, Michael. "Islamophobia and Anti-Semitism: Shared Prejudice or Singular Social Pathologies." *Cross Currents* 65 (2015) 321–33.

Dooley, Mark. *The Politics of Exodus: Kierkegaard's Ethics of Responsibility*. New York: Fordham University Press, 2001.

Eck, Diana. *Encountering God: A Spiritual Journey from Bozeman to Banaras*. Boston: Beacon, 2003.

———. "What Is Pluralism?" Pluralism Project, Harvard University. http://pluralism.org/what-is-pluralism/.

Evans, C. Stephen. *Kierkegaard's Ethic of Love: Divine Commands and Moral Obligations*. Oxford: Oxford University Press, 2004.

Ferreira, M. Jamie. *Love's Grateful Striving: A Commentary on Kierkegaard's Works of Love*. Oxford: Oxford University Press, 2001.

Funaro, Vincent. "Norway Shooting: Anders Behring Breivik Manifesto Reveals Hatred." *Christian Post*, July 25, 2011. http://www.christianpost.com/news/norway-gunmans-

---

91. Kierkegaard, *Works of Love*, 253.

manifesto-reveals-his-hatred-for-european-mutlticultualism-and-resentment-of-his-family-52786.

Furtak, Rick Anthony. *Wisdom in Love: Kierkegaard and the Ancient Quest for Emotional Integrity*. Notre Dame: University of Notre Dame Press, 2005.

Grøn, Arne. "The Dialectic of Recognition in *Works of Love*." In *Kierkegaard Studies Yearbook 1998*, edited by Niels Jørgen Cappelørn et al., 147–57. Berlin: de Gruyter, 1998.

———. "Ethics of Vision: Seeing the Other as Neighbor." In *Dynamics of Difference: Christianity and Alterity*, edited by Ulrich Schmiedel and James M. Matarazzo Jr., 63–70. London: T. & T. Clark, 2015.

Hall, Amy Laura. *Kierkegaard and the Treachery of Love*. Cambridge: Cambridge University Press, 2002.

Imbert, Fred. "Donald Trump: Mexico Going to Pay for Wall." CNBC, October 28, 2015. http://www.cnbc.com/2015/10/28/donald-trump-mexico-going-to-pay-for-wall.html.

Kierkegaard, Søren. *Eighteen Upbuilding Discourses*. Edited and translated by Howard V. Hong and Edna H. Hong. Princeton: Princeton University Press, 1990.

———. *Either/Or*. Vol. 2. Edited and translated by Howard V. Hong and Edna H. Hong. Princeton: Princeton University Press, 1987.

———. *Fear and Trembling; Repetition*. Edited and translated by Howard V. Hong and Edna H. Hong. Princeton: Princeton University Press, 1983.

———. *The Moment and Late Writings*. Edited and translated by Howard V. Hong and Edna H. Hong. Princeton: Princeton University Press, 1985.

———. *Practice in Christianity*. Edited and translated by Howard V. Hong and Edna H. Hong. Princeton: Princeton University Press, 1991.

———. *The Sickness Unto Death*. Edited and translated by Howard V. Hong and Edna H. Hong. Princeton: Princeton University Press, 1988.

———. *Works of Love*. Edited and translated by Howard V. Hong and Edna H. Hong. Princeton: Princeton University Press, 1995.

Krishek, Sharon. *Kierkegaard on Faith and Love*, New York: Cambridge University Press, 2009.

Kymlicka, Will. *Multicultural Odysseys: Navigating the New International Politics of Diversity*. Oxford: Oxford University Press, 2007.

———. "Multiculturalism: Success, Failure and the Future." Washington, DC: Migration Policy Institute, 2012.

Levinas, Emmanuel. *Totality and Infinity: An Essay on Interiority*. Translated by Alphonso Lingis. Pittsburgh: Duquesne University Press, 1969.

Malik, Kenan. *Multiculturalism and Its Discontents: Rethinking Diversity after 9/11*. London: Seagull, 2013.

Noack, Rick. "Multiculturalism Is a Sham, Says Angela Merkel." *Washington Post*, December 14, 2015. https://www.washingtonpost.com/news/worldviews/wp/2015/12/14/angela-merkel-multiculturalism-is-a-sham.

Okin, Susan Moller. "Is Multiculturalism Bad for Women?" *Boston Review*, October 1, 1997. https://bostonreview.net/forum/susan-moller-okin-multiculturalism-bad-women.

———. "Is Multiculturalism Bad for Women?" In *Is Multiculturalism Bad for Women*, edited by Joshua Cohen et al., 9–24. Princeton: Princeton University Press, 1999.

Perkins, Robert L., ed. *Works of Love*. International Kierkegaard Commentary 16. Macon, GA: Mercer University Press, 1999.

Simmons, J. Aaron, and David Wood, eds. *Kierkegaard and Levinas: Ethics, Politics, and Religion*. Bloomington: Indiana University Press, 2008.

Søltoft, Pia. "The Presence of the Absent Neighbor." Translated by M. G. Piety. In *Kierkegaard Studies Yearbook 1998*, edited by Niels Jørgen Cappelørn et al., 113–28. Berlin: de Gruyter, 1998.

Taylor, Charles. "The Politics of Recognition." In *Multiculturalism: Examining the Politics of Recognition*, edited by Amy Gutman, 25–73. Princeton: Princeton University Press, 1994.

Triandafyllidou, Anna, et al. "Diversity, Integration, Secularism and Multiculturalism." Introduction to *European Multiculturalisms: Cultural, Religious and Ethnic Challenges*, edited by Anna Triandafyllidou et al., 1–29. Edinburgh: Edinburgh University Press, 2012.

Troyan, Mary. "After Attacks in Paris, Governors Refuse to Accept Syrian Refugees." *USA Today*, November 16, 2015. http://www.usatoday.com/story/news/politics/2015/11/16/alabama-refuses-syrian-refugees-paris-terror-attack/75857924.

Westphal, Merold. *Levinas and Kierkegaard in Dialogue*. Bloomington: Indiana University Press, 2008.

Žižek, Slavoj. "Neighbors and Other Monsters." In *The Neighbor: Three Inquiries in Political Theology*, edited by Slavoj Žižek et al., 134–90. Chicago: University of Chicago Press, 2006.

9

Kierkegaard, Badiou, and Christian Hope

Vincent Lloyd

While academic interest in political theology has exploded in the past decade, relatively little of this interest has attended to the political-theological concept of hope. If political theology explores the relationship between political and theological concepts, and political theology as a critical project unmasks such relationships concealed by secularism, hope would seem to be a prime site for political theological critique. Particularly in the US context, hope is a widely used political concept with clear but largely unacknowledged theological resonances.[1] The Christian tradition considers hope, with faith and love, a theological virtue. But, in secular political contexts, invocations of hope can be difficult to distinguish from optimism, and the political rhetoric of hope often sounds vacuous.[2] To speak politically of hope often seems to add as much to political discourse as a smile. For this reason, perhaps, hope does not frequently attract interest of political theologians, ceding the office of the critic to the likes of Sarah Palin, who famously dismissed Barack Obama's "hopey, changey thing." Yet there is an important role for political theologians to play with respect to hope. We can ask what form hope takes: Feeling? Desire? Virtue? We can ask about the object of hope: Is it merely appealing or is it genuinely good? Is the ultimate object of hope God? When we ask these questions, we challenge the secularist presumptions of politics, not only exposing the hollowness of political discourse (Palin does that), but holding political discourse accountable to what it implicitly acknowledges but officially disclaims: theological tradition.[3] Critique is not an end in itself. It is an opportunity to evangelize, to speak to the world about what a robust and vibrant tradition is Christianity. It is an opportunity to transform the titillation offered by religious language spoken in public into embrace of a loving God.

1. See, e.g., Delbanco, *Real American Dream*.
2. On the conflation of hope and optimism, see esp. Lasch, *True and Only Heaven*.
3. In other words, if political discourse is accountable to the norms of a community, and the norms of a community are entangled with the norms of a religious tradition, even if that community proclaims itself religion-neutral the norms of that religious community remain relevant when evaluating political discourse.

This admittedly immodest task for political theology is masked by the field's focus on sovereignty.[4] The analogies between sovereign state, sovereign self, and sovereign God which are the cornerstones of modernity are certainly ripe for challenge. But what comes after sovereignty? *Post* criticism *omne animal triste est*. Instead of fixating on the imagined Death Star of modern politics to be shot with the laser guns of critique—such a phallic fixation—why not acknowledge the subtler ways in which Christian theology has a continuing influence on our social and political worlds? From those plural sites in which we are all implicated, we can reconstruct the community we want and need, whether or not Luke Skywalker makes his shot. Indeed, this is the way that the fantasy of sovereignty will come to an end: our desires will be directed elsewhere, in community, in divine and human complexity, and our libidinal investment in the fantasy will fade. Yet wallowing in complexity or imagined community clearly has limited political potential. The challenge for political theology is to rigorously examine, and politicize, the plural aspects of our lives alone and together. To think critically in this careful, expansive sense, Alain Badiou and Søren Kierkegaard lend assistance. They both refuse the fantasy of sovereignty and instead allow for the irreducible complexity of self and community—opening questions of hope. Badiou is attuned to questions of politics while Kierkegaard is attuned to questions of the self. Both take theology seriously. By placing them in dialogue, we can begin to construct a framework for approaching the political theology of hope.

Why hope and not faith? Both are theological virtues, dispositions oriented toward the divine. But faith, considered politically, lends itself to the same sort of binary, ultimately phallic reasoning that contaminates discussions of sovereignty. Too quickly questions of faith become questions of faith in God or faith in state or faith in self. This is not a defect in the virtue itself; faith has been overdetermined by modernity, affected by the gravitational pull of sovereignty, and so faith is difficult to retrieve.[5] At its best, faith is oppositional: not faith in this or that, but faith in what cannot be seen, in what escapes the hegemony of the visible. This is faith that discourse, or ideology, or the symbolic is not all there is, faith in the unrepresentable. This is faith as critique of ideology (for Badiou), or idolatry (for Kierkegaard). Such faith is quite clearly twinned with hope. If the invisible will never become visible, faith is delusion. There would be no difference between idol and God. To have faith, there must be some expectation that the hegemony of the visible will, in the future, be broken—that God will be revealed. The question of hope, as a theological virtue, is the question of

---

4. In contrast, hope was central to the development of political theology in the German theological context, most notably in the work of Jürgen Moltmann. The term "political theology" names both a secular, political theory conversation and a specifically Christian theological conversation; the latter often remains in dialogue with the work of Moltmann whereas the former is largely unaware of Moltmann, instead focusing on the concept of sovereignty. In this chapter, I am writing of political theology as a critical method employed in the best work of both those participating in the secular and the Christian theological conversations.

5. This point has been made, for example, by Asad in *Genealogies of Religion*.

how such expectation manifests in practice. Kierkegaard and Badiou are known for their reflections on faith, but when we attend to how faith is twinned with hope, and when hope is where the critical potential lies, Kierkegaard and Badiou offer promising resources for a political theology of hope.

This is not an exhaustive or a rigorous account of Kierkegaard and Badiou on hope; I leave that to others. The point here is to construct a framework that advances discussions in political theology and to speak to how Kierkegaard helps us see the role that hope ought to play in that work. To do so, this chapter first suggests how Badiou might politicize Kierkegaard, then it explores how Kierkegaard pushes Badiou on the question of hope's political relevance. While this may seem to take us far from Obama's "hopey, changey" rhetoric, the intellectual task of political theology is to think seriously and carefully at a distance from the tumult of political practice, offering new ways of seeing and understanding that practice—and, hopefully, eventually, authorizing new ways of doing politics.

Badiou's Political Theology

For reasons largely having to do with the oscillations of academic celebrity culture as amplified by American philosophical Francophilia, Alain Badiou is hot. A student of Louis Althusser whose leftist political views became harder as others became softer or disappeared altogether, Badiou has developed an elaborate philosophical project over the past quarter century that supports his Maoist (or post-Maoist) politics.[6] Badiou's writings include both the metaphysical—he is unapologetic about developing a metaphysical "system"—and the political, applying that metaphysical framework to questions of political philosophy and to current events. He wrote, for instance, a pithy book on Nicolas Sarkozy, and he also frequently comments in French newspapers and other public forums. Badiou insists that his metaphysical views result in his political views and not the other way around; furthermore, he contends that his metaphysical views derive from mathematical logic. It is natural to be suspicious of these claims for reasons directly related to his popularity as a philosopher. Academic celebrity is more often awarded for novelty than for genius, and both the specifics of Badiou's system (all the mathematical notation incomprehensible to the vast majority of his "theory" readers) and the very fact that he offers a system (something postmodernism was supposed to have put an end to) certainly have secured his novelty—and his status in certain circles as authority.

From the perspective of political theology, what is most compelling and useful about Badiou is not the technical authorizing apparatus, nor his ever-present rhetorical swagger. It is, rather, his attempt to marry the critique of ideology with the

---

6. Badiou's most significant philosophical works are *Being and Event* and *Logics of Worlds*. His book *Ethics* is an accessible introduction to his work that links philosophical and political themes. *The Meaning of Sarkozy* is a fully political intervention.

promise that we can affect radical transformation. (His *Ethics* is a particularly compelling example of this.) This marriage, when attempted by others, often has gone wrong. Gilles Deleuze tells a story about metaphysical flux concealed by the status quo but ends up commending his readers to wallow in the flux—a politically and ethically impotent conclusion.[7] Michel Foucault uncovers stories about radical transformations, from one arrangement of the world to another, that have been concealed by the status quo, but Foucault is often frustratingly silent on how we ourselves might affect such a dramatic change.[8] In contrast, Badiou persuasively attempts this marriage by enlisting "philosophy," in a rather Platonic sense, to officiate. For Badiou, the project of philosophy is committed to the interrogation of conventional wisdom—in a more Marxist than Platonic idiom, the ideas of the wealthy and powerful masked as common sense—in search of truth. This truth would stand beyond the world, orthogonal to the bodies and languages (Badiou's phrase) that we deal with on a daily basis. We realize our humanity, becoming more than an object, more than an animal, when we relate to truth. And truth can overturn the ways of the world.

To make this account persuasive, Badiou must elaborate what he means by "bodies and languages" and what he means by "truth." This is where Badiou turns to mathematical logic, as explicated in the weighty volumes *Being and Event* (1988) and *Logics of Worlds: Being and Event II* (2006). Among Badiou's innovations is that he understands truth in the plural, and he understands these truths as events. As events, they effectively have no content other than their disruptive potential. That disruptive potential is realized when individuals recognize and commit themselves to a truth, allowing themselves to be pulled in whatever direction the truth may pull. When subject to a truth (and recall that, for Badiou, one is also made a subject by a truth), the old wisdom of the world seems hollow, even absurd. The world is organized in a new way for those committed to a truth, and they act accordingly, making themselves seem irrational or even insane to those around them who ignore the truth. The status quo can only be maintained by rejecting truths, so to be committed to a truth is to be embattled. This commitment Badiou names faith.[9]

Badiou is generalizing the Kuhnian paradigm shift or Foucaultian epistemic shift, but he is also, crucially, adding an agent. Where Kuhn and Foucault's examples of radical transformation are so grand that they seem impersonal, Badiou suggests that we place love, political revolutions, and artistic innovations in the same category as scientific revolutions. In these several cases, it is much easier to see the commitment of the individual (lover, revolutionary, artist) to a cause or "truth" despite the world's rejection of that truth. (Badiou commendably catalogs the techniques those invested

---

7. While Badiou develops a critique in his book *Deleuze*, Hallward's *Out of This World* is more attentive to the theological dimensions implicit and unworked in Deleuze's thought.

8. See Rose, *Dialectic of Nihilism*, ch. 9; Lloyd, *Law and Transcendence*, ch. 2.

9. In these pages, I am summarizing the relevant argumentative themes that occur throughout Badiou's work.

in the status quo will use to discredit or destroy truths as well as the dangers of the misleading appearance of quasi-truths. For this last category, which he labels "evil," Badiou makes Nazism paradigmatic.)

Here we see the political implications of Badiou's metaphysical project. The work of politics is the work of discerning when a genuine event is happening (when a genuine truth is affecting the world and calling for fidelity), preparing oneself for that moment, and embracing that moment when it does occur. This work involves criticizing the status quo (as contingent and ultimately false), cautioning against the appeal of quasi-truths, and coordinating with others who share a commitment to a given truth.

It seems plausible that what Badiou presents as politics might better be labeled political theology, in the sense of a critical method, as described above. There is plenty of circumstantial evidence for the presence of the theological in Badiou's work: he posits truths that exist outside the world, the capacity for faithfulness to these truths as constitutive of our humanity, and of course his privileged example of St. Paul, illustrating how faithfulness works.[10] Badiou, however, vigorously proclaims himself an atheist, and he locates his work within a philosophical, not a theological, tradition (he develops his account of the event through critical engagements with Plato, Spinoza, Hegel, Leibniz, and Descartes, among others). However, political theology concerns implicit, rather than explicit, theological commitments, and it is hard not to read Badiou's views about politics—the patient political subject waiting for unrequested and unexpected revelations of truth to which she will be entirely devoted and so become fully human—as wholly resting on secularized theological concepts.

That Badiou critically engages with the work of Kierkegaard provides an opportunity to further explore how both Badiou and Kierkegaard might be part of a tradition of political theology that is expansive, critical, and that attends to questions of hope. More important than terminology is the framework Badiou helps to sketch of the politicized subject: politicized not in the sense of engaging with particular worldly institutions or networks of power but in precisely the opposite sense, which is a theological sense. The subject is politicized (note that to be a subject, for Badiou, is always to be politicized) to the extent to which she rejects the ways of seeing and acting in the world that are determined by those worldly institutions and networks of power and instead directs her allegiance elsewhere. This elsewhere could be given a name, God, but in the noblest of theological traditions, negative theology, namelessness is the essence of that elsewhere. The pressing question—the question of faith and also of hope—is how such a rejection of worldly ways is lived.

---

10. On the role of religious ideas in Badiou's thought, see, e.g., Phelps, *Alain Badiou*; Depoortere, *Badiou and Theology*. See Belhaj Kacem, *Après Badiou*, for an account of Badiou as "crypto-Catholic."

PART 2: KIERKEGAARD AND THE POLITICS OF FAITH, HOPE, AND LOVE

Badiou's Kierkegaard

Alain Badiou and Søren Kierkegaard are both, essentially, philosophers of faith. They both take faith to mean a commitment to that which is irreducible to worldly terms. Despite the obvious and profound similarities between Badiou's thought and the thought of Kierkegaard, it is only once, and relatively recently, that Badiou has engaged with Kierkegaard in print.[11] This is in stark contrast to, for example, Plato and Leibniz, who Badiou repeatedly discusses and lauds. Badiou's writing on Kierkegaard is found in *Logics of Worlds'* sixth "book," "Theory of Points," in which Badiou is exploring how it is that an individual can be caught up by a truth (Badiou defines a point as "the appearance of the infinite totality of the world . . . before the instance of the decision, that is the duality of the 'yes' and 'no'").[12] In *Being and Event*, it was Pascal who played an analogous role, putting Badiou's metaphysics in contact with the Christian tradition just at the crucial moment, when a truth might be taken up by a human. Now it is Kierkegaard who plays the guide, or who lends authority, as Badiou develops the heart of his metaphysical project—more precisely, the nexus between metaphysics and epistemology in Badiou's philosophy.

Badiou's discussion of Kierkegaard proceeds through broad-stroke explanation of themes strategically chosen so as to complement Badiou's larger project. We learn that "for Kierkegaard, the key to existence is none other than absolute choice"[13] (425); that in this choice "the subject attains the being-there of what Kierkegaard names 'subjective truth' or 'interiority'" (425);[14] "the Christian paradox is . . . a challenge addressed to the existence of each and everyone";[15] "choice—as the guarantor of the connection between subjective time and eternity—localized the subject to the element of truth";[16] and so on. It is clear how these themes help fortify Badiou's own theory: he has an ally in his attempt to show that each individual becomes human (or more precisely a human subject) when she confronts head-on the inadequacies of the world and commits herself, all the way down, to the other-worldly truth that speaks directly to her. Badiou walks the reader through the ethical, the aesthetic, and the religious, bringing us to ultimate choice, to the possibility for "the abiding of subjectivity in the absolute paradox."[17] Badiou notes the benefits, according to Kierkegaard, of choice independent of the objects of choice, that choice brings one near God even if God is everywhere.

---

11. For an overview of Badiou's use of Kierkegaard, see O'Neill Burns, "Alain Badiou," and O'Neill Burns, *Kierkegaard and the Matter of Philosophy*, ch. 5. I regret that I had already completed this essay when O'Neill Burns's book appeared, as we appear to have some similar concerns.

12. Badiou, *Logics of Worlds*, 591.

13. Ibid., 425.

14. Ibid.

15. Ibid., 426.

16. Ibid., 432.

17. Ibid., 430.

After rehearsing themes from Kierkegaard's thought, Badiou offers something of a critique. This is not so much a demonstration of Kierkegaard's faulty argument or inconsistency as it is a critique based on tradition.[18] Badiou situates himself in one philosophical tradition, which he asserts is correct, which a variety of philosophers before him also participated in, and which Badiou sees himself as advancing. Kierkegaard is largely situated in this tradition, but he is not wholly orthodox. Among other characteristics, this tradition is defined by a rejection of Hegel. For his assistance in this philosophical struggle, for developing the critique of Hegel, Badiou at first praises Kierkegaard. What Hegel represents is the location of truth within the world, unfolding through history. Kierkegaard's localizing the eternal in the moment of choice rejects this and, similar to Badiou, offers a way of thinking truth perpendicular to the world, as it were.[19]

Badiou complains that Kierkegaard occasionally moves too close to Hegel and so strays from the center of the philosophical tradition Badiou commends (and of which Badiou himself is the paradigmatic figure). From Badiou's vantage point, Kierkegaard's hierarchy of the ethical, the aesthetic, and the religious is unjustified and compromising. In one sense, this is simply because Badiou is not a Christian and so puts all encounters with truths on equal footing, whether they are scientific, amorous, political, philosophical, or religious.[20] But Badiou offers an additional line of critique. Building on the Kierkegaardian formulation that "aesthetics in a man is that by which he is immediately what he is; ethics is that by which he becomes what he becomes," Badiou suggests we might add "the religious is in a man, when all is said and done, the becoming of what he is at the same time as the being of what he becomes"[21]—a result troublingly close to Hegel. What seems to worry Badiou here is not so much the moment of choice but what happens after that choice: the training, or character development, which occurs to one who has faced that choice. That this post-choice life is in some sense sanctified leads to the alignment of Kierkegaard and Hegel: each acknowledge paradox and each resolve paradox by describing a world educated by paradox—and in doing so each inserts the eternal into the ordinary, transcendence suffusing immanence.

The crux of Badiou's critique, however, has to do with despair. The choice Kierkegaard commends is the choice of despair, and only through that choice can we become ourselves. Who, then, was doing the choosing if the subject only comes into existence after a choice is made? Badiou charges that there is no way to make these

18. To put it more explicitly, I think it may be useful to read Badiou through a lens crafted by Alasdair MacIntyre.

19. John Milbank contrasts Badiou's anti-Hegelian Kierkegaard with Slavoj Žižek's uncomfortably Hegelian Kierkegaard, aligning himself, and his project of political theology, with the former. See Milbank, "Double Glory," 110–233.

20. In fact, Badiou treats the religious as analogous to the four forms of truth rather than as a fifth.

21. Badiou, *Logics of Worlds*, 434.

two subjects one without specifically Christian commitments to God. The Christian God is two at once: eternal and other-worldly but also, in Jesus Christ, historical and human. In order for Kierkegaard's account of choice to hold, for the chooser and the one having chosen to be the same, we must believe that the same God (or the absolute) dwells outside and inside the world. This, again, uncomfortably aligns Kierkegaard with Hegel.[22] Instead of the absolute (or divine) unfolding in the conceptual realm, as it does for Hegel, for Kierkegaard the absolute unfolds in the affective realm, in the dynamics of despair of the subject. Badiou sees apostasy from the philosophical tradition he defends: truth is allowed too great a foothold in the world. Badiou concludes the Kierkegaard chapter, in *Logics of Worlds*, by characterizing Kierkegaard's position thusly: "God, beholding [man's] despair, lets him know that despairing is the true condition of every hope"[23] (435).

Badiou, Kierkegaard, Hope

This is one of the very few places where Badiou substantively addresses hope—and here hope is a symptom of the approach to philosophy that Badiou condemns. Hope is effectively absent from Badiou's two major works of metaphysics, *Being and Event* and *Logics of Worlds*. It is tempting to read his political philosophical (or political theological) project as one commending faith without hope, commitment to struggle without an ultimate object. Indeed, on the purely metaphysical level, Badiou's conceptual maneuver of effectively voiding truth of content would support this reading. Badiou does gesture toward the traditional triptych of theological virtues in his *Saint Paul*, but hope is reduced to "a maxim enjoining us to persevere in this trajectory [of truth]."[24] Here hope is not a virtue at all but rather a rhetoric, a word used to persuade. The apparent work of hope, persevering through hardship, is entailed by the virtue of faith—indeed, this just is the meaning of the virtue of faith.[25]

Badiou could learn some important lessons about hope from Kierkegaard, and staging such an encounter is productive for a political theological engagement with hope. First, though, note the ways in which Badiou politicizes, or at least shows the political potential of Kierkegaard's deep suspicion of idolatry. Badiou finds an ally in Kierkegaard because what Kierkegaard calls idolatry Badiou calls ideology. The ideas of the ruling class, of the wealthy and powerful, that are made to seem natural, obvious, and unavoidable—ideology—is another way of describing the wisdom of the world that is treated as eternal truth, attracting and holding our attention and so distracting us from the divine, i.e., idolatry. For Badiou, Kierkegaard teaches us a lesson in how

---

22. For a recent reevaluation of the relationship between Kierkegaard and Hegel, see O'Neill Burns, *Kierkegaard and the Matter of Philosophy*, 18–22, 71–114.

23. Badiou, *Logics of Worlds*, 435.

24. Badiou, *Saint Paul*, 93.

25. On this all-too-common confusion regarding hope, see Lloyd, *Problem with Grace*, ch. 3.

to strengthen our suspicion of ideology and how to commit ourselves to a life lived in the attempt to construct a new way of seeing the world, a new set of ideas unacknowledged by the world as it currently exists. But Badiou does not offer a particularly robust account of what leading this kind of life looks like. Indeed, faith, as presented by Badiou, is not even really a virtue. It is not a disposition to endure despite hardship; it is a monomaniacal drive to create. How is this sustainable, particularly if there is no God offering assistance along the way? Might there not be shared characteristics of the figures whose lives Badiou extols as truth-directed—St. Paul, Abelard and Heloise, Mao, Picasso—which would fill out what a disposition toward truth might look like?

This is precisely where Kierkegaard may offer assistance.[26] While it is not obvious that hope is a crucial theme for Kierkegaard, despair certainly is, and Kierkegaard defines despair as hopelessness. There are worldly hopes, false hopes, that Kierkegaard rejects. They are cleansed through despair; despair teaches the futility of worldly hopes. Only then can we achieve a genuine and eternal hope: a truly Christian hope. That genuine hope, after despair, is at once a gift of God and essentially human: it comes from that part of the human created in the image of God. This deeper sense of hope, closely tied to love, extends equally to others as to oneself; worldly hope is more closely linked with desire, and more closely tied to self-interest. For Kierkegaard, hope is an expectation of a good; worldly hopes are expectations of worldly goods while hope in the sense Kierkegaard commends is an expectation of an other-worldly good. More precisely, hope is the latter, "authentic" sense is the virtue produced by such an expectation.

Many otherwise perceptive commenters on Kierkegaard have taken faith and hope to be effectively interchangeable concepts for him.[27] I suspect that separating them may be quite fruitful, particularly when our interest is in what happens after the extreme encounter with paradox, back in the ordinary world. There, the relationship to the encounter with the absolute is maintained through hope of the proper sort. Where Badiou reads Kierkegaard as asserting that despair and hope paradoxically coexist, Kierkegaard himself suggests that genuine hope is a stage beyond despair—and that hope signals the receptivity to the absolute that Badiou also commends. Indeed, Badiou does not present a good answer to the question: what disposition is the individual to have before encountering a truth—politically, before the revolution? There is not yet a truth to command allegiance. Kierkegaard suggests an answer: the individual

---

26. Recent scholarship on Kierkegaard's account of hope that I have found helpful includes Bernier, *Task of Hope*; Fremstedal, "Kierkegaard on the Metaphysics of Hope"; and McDonald, "Hope." Bernier sees hope as unifying Kierkegaard's thought, and he defines despair as an unwillingness to hope, and he understands hope as taking up the task of the self, moving toward unity. It remains unclear on Bernier's account how this sense of hope as expectation might be reconciled with the sense of hope as virtue present in the theological tradition. I would suggest that worldly hopes, for Kierkegaard, involve expectation whereas "authentic" hope involves virtue—and it is the latter that has political theological significance.

27. Bernier makes this point in *Task of Hope in Kierkegaard*.

should be hopeful. When God is removed from the story, when truths become plural as they do for Badiou, perhaps we find ourselves in the curious situation of commending hope without faith, or at least before faith. Yet in the Christian story, the story Badiou resists, the two are twinned. A life of commitment to the invisible is also a life oriented toward the future interruption of the visible by the invisible. Crucially, for Kierkegaard but not Badiou this interruption has a moral valence: it is good. Hope is not just expectation, not just orientation to transformation; it is directed at the good. Badiou wants to have this moral valence as well. He names partial transformation evil, and he commends total transformation, but he does not take the next step and say that the proper orientation to transformation would then involve hope.[28]

The political-theological lesson Kierkegaard teaches us about hope, when read with Badiou, is that our view of hope need not focus on hope's object—inevitably an object of fantasy, that ties us to the world, rather than opening us to another worldly possibility.[29] If the virtue of hope is to be commended, what that means in practice is that we must learn how to despair.[30] This is what Kierkegaard teaches so elegantly in *The Sickness Unto Death*. Despair must advance from the simplistic, not getting the object of our desire, to the sophisticated, not knowing the subject who desires—not knowing ourselves. Experience in the world, and reflection on that experience in classrooms, in literature, and in philosophy, can aid us in despairing better. This is not to imply that the better we despair, the better we hope. Rather, we must push the extremes of despair in order to be primed to hope. The ascent of despair requires worldly engagement; without engagement, despair remains in its most primitive form. When this insight is brought to politics, the practical implications of the political theology of hope commended by Badiou are quite different than they seem. Instead of waiting patiently for an encounter with a truth or fixating on a truth, we must engage with the social and political world in ways that are necessarily unsatisfactory. The more we have such deeply unsatisfactory engagements the more we are primed to recognize the possibility of genuine political transformation. We are then better able to recognize the simulacra of truth: to know when we are becoming followers of a Hitler. On this account, the political theology of hope means standing with Sarah Palin as she rejects the rhetoric of hope. Such language is *ejaculatio praecox*, taking away the possibility of genuine satisfaction that hope at its best provides. Hope at its most political, at its most theological, means the results of the frustrating work of an education in despair. That work makes possible hope at its best, hope oriented to its

---

28. While Moltmann, for example, comes close to equating the new (in the proper sense) with the good, he takes this from the Christian theological tradition (see his *Theology of Hope*). How Badiou can make this claim outside of that tradition remains obscure.

29. Hope's object, if it can be put this way, is the highest good, but worldly descriptions of this highest good necessarily describe it wrongly. Theologically, God cannot be reduced to worldly terms.

30. I develop this point in the context of hope for racial justice in my article "For What Are Whites to Hope?"

proper object, consummated in the revolution, in the divine. It is a consummation of which we must not speak, but its mute possibility animates Christian life and ought to animate politics.

Bibliography

Asad, Talal. *Genealogies of Religion: Discipline and Reasons of Power in Christianity and Islam*. Baltimore: Johns Hopkins University Press, 1993.
Badiou, Alain. *Being and Event*. London: Continuum, 2007.
———. *Deleuze: The Clamor of Being*. Minneapolis: University of Minnesota Press, 2000.
———. *Ethics: An Essay on the Understanding of Evil*. London: Verso, 2001.
———. *Logics of Worlds: Being and Event 2*. London: Continuum, 2009.
———. *The Meaning of Sarkozy*. London: Verso, 2008.
———. *Saint Paul: The Foundation of Universalism*. Stanford: Stanford University Press, 2003.
Belhaj Kacem, Mehdi. *Après Badiou*. Paris: Grasset, 2011.
Bernier, Mark C. *The Task of Hope in Kierkegaard*. New York: Oxford University Press, 2015.
Burns, Michael O'Neill. "Alain Badiou: Thinking the Subject after the Death of God." In *Kierkegaard's Influence on Social-Political Thought*, edited by Jon Stewart, 41–51. Kierkegaard Research 14. Farnham, UK: Ashgate, 2011.
———. *Kierkegaard and the Matter of Philosophy: A Fractured Dialectic*. London: Rowman & Littlefield, 2015.
Delbanco, Andrew. *The Real American Dream: A Meditation on Hope*. Cambridge: Harvard University Press, 2000.
Depoortere, Frederiek. *Badiou and Theology*. London: T. & T. Clark, 2009.
Fremstedal, Roe. "Kierkegaard on the Metaphysics of Hope." *Heythrop Journal* 43 (2012) 51–60.
Hallward, Peter. *Out of This World: Deleuze and the Philosophy of Creation*. London: Verso, 2006.
Kierkegaard, Søren. *Sickness Unto Death*. Princeton: Princeton University Press, 1980.
Lasch, Christopher. *The True and Only Heaven: Progress and Its Critics*. New York: Norton, 1991.
Lloyd, Vincent. "For What Are Whites to Hope?" *Political Theology* 17 (2016) 168–81.
———. *Law and Transcendence: On the Unfinished Project of Gillian Rose*. New York: Palgrave Macmillan, 2009.
———. *The Problem with Grace: Reconfiguring Political Theology*. Stanford: Stanford University Press, 2011.
McDonald, William. "Hope." In *Kierkegaard's Concepts*, vol. 3, *Envy to Incognito*, edited by Steven M. Emmanuel et al., 163–68. Kierkegaard Research 15. Farnham: Ashgate, 2014.
Milbank, John. "The Double Glory, or Paradox versus Dialectic." In *The Monstrosity of Christ: Paradox or Dialectic?*, edited by Creston Davis, 110–233. Cambridge: MIT Press, 2009.
Moltmann, Jürgen. *Theology of Hope: On the Ground and the Implications of a Christian Eschatology*. New York: Harper & Row, 1967.
Phelps, Hollis. *Alain Badiou: Between Theology and Anti-Theology*. Durham: Acumen, 2013.
Rose, Gillian. *Dialectic of Nihilism: Post-Structuralism and Law*. Oxford: Blackwell, 1984.

PART 3

Kierkegaard and the Politics of Philosophy

10

The Time Is Out of Joint

*On Social Ontology and Criticism in
Kierkegaard and Heidegger*

JAMES D. REID AND
RICK ANTHONY FURTAK

Introduction

DESPITE SEVERAL AFFINITIES BETWEEN certain aspects of Heidegger's early fundamental ontology of human existence (or Dasein), brought officially to public attention in *Being and Time* (1927), and Kierkegaard's analysis of the present age in *A Literary Review* (1846), there is a widespread and, we think, an unfortunate tendency among commentators to interpret their respective endeavors along categorically discrete lines. This is no doubt due partly to Heidegger's own explicit, and often misleading and self-serving, assessment of Kierkegaard's influence upon his own early work, which involves a (dubiously) sharp contrast between ontic inquiry, on the one hand, and ontological investigation, on the other,[1] combined (on the side of Kierkegaard) with a skeptical attitude, facing the ostensibly systematic ambitions that underwrite *Being and Time*.[2]

Charles Guignon, for instance, in an insightful analysis of Heidegger and Kierkegaard on the topic of death (which plays a central role in their respective efforts

---

1. There are only three references to Kierkegaard in *Being and Time*, none of which is particularly illuminating. The most relevant to the present study comes in a note which reads, in part: "In the nineteenth century, S. Kierkegaard explicitly grasped and thought through the problem of existence as *existentiell* in a penetrating way. But the existential problematic is so foreign to him that in an ontological regard he is completely under the influence of Hegel and his view of ancient philosophy." Heidegger, *Being and Time*, 407. Kierkegaard never figures in Heidegger's later accounts of what he calls "the history of being," and more or less drops out of focus after *Being and Time*. The most extensive later references appear in a course of lectures devoted to the metaphysics of German idealism, held in 1941, and are ancillary to Heidegger's interest in Schelling.

2. For those new to the terminology, the distinction between the ontic and the ontological can be illustrated by the difference between saying something about, say, the blue color of an object, or its specific position in space, and focusing on what it means to *be* colored, or to *be* the sort of thing that takes up space, regardless of the thing's specific color and particular location: the former is an ontic statement, the latter an ontological one.

to illuminate human existence as a whole, and to comment on a chronic failure to be honest about our mortal condition), insists right from the start that "we should take seriously Heidegger's claims that Kierkegaard's reflections were always limited to . . . the domain of inquiry called 'theology,' and that his insights pertained solely to the 'existentiell' and never to the 'existential.'"[3] Assertions of this sort do not always play out in Heidegger's favor, even among those otherwise partial to the self-described fundamental ontologist. At the end of his contribution to *Kierkegaard and Death*, Guignon (himself a prominent Heidegger scholar) concludes that "the power and beauty of Kierkegaard's writings depend in part on his ability to put in question such grandiose projects [as Heidegger's] and to insist on the intensely 'subjective' and personal nature of the truth we are seeking about life-defining matters."[4]

Heidegger's own early work is, in its own way, preoccupied with the problem of individuation and the various forces that stand in the way of the normative task of becoming *eigentlich* (achieving, in Kierkegaard's terms, a life that belongs properly to a particular individual: in Danish, to achieve *Eiendommelighed*), which Heidegger takes to be an essential ingredient in, and perhaps even the aim of, the work of philosophy itself. His ontology, both early and late, is informed *throughout* by concrete ideals of human existence and, especially in the later work, often involves engagement with highly individualized poetic and literary texts (the poetry of Hölderlin, Rilke, and Trakl come readily to mind). On the topic of truth (in opposition to Guignon's tidy contrast), Heidegger is able to write, in a prelude to his first sustained account of primordial truth as ἀλήθεια in its various modes, drawn from Aristotle's ethics but echoing Climacus: "something can indeed be true which is not binding for everyone but only for *the single individual*."[5]

On the other hand, Kierkegaard's various contributions to ontic or existentiell inquiry, often poetic or literary, and animated by questions concerning how to live (or how to become properly *subjective*, perhaps Christian), frequently open onto broader ontological territory. Kierkegaard, like Heidegger, was deeply interested in, for instance, the temporal constitution of human existence *as such* (this concern stands, arguably, at the center of the two works assigned to Johannes Climacus, the *Philosophical Crumbs* and the *Concluding Unscientific Postscript*) and dissatisfied with the philosophical tradition's tendency to privilege abstract conceptions of being that involve the idea of completeness and stasis (i.e., being "finished"), or what Heidegger calls an ontology of the merely "present-at-hand" or a "metaphysics of presence."[6]

3. Guignon, "Heidegger and Kierkegaard," 185.
4. Ibid., 201.
5. Heidegger, *Plato's "Sophist*," 17, emphasis added.
6. It is worth noting, if only in passing, that Heidegger sees in the Aristotelian conception of being an emphasis on being-finished (*Fertigkeit*)—in an important course of lectures held in SS 1924. It would do Climacus no philosophical injustice, we think, to interpret his polemic in ontological terms, as an expression of dissatisfaction with the idea of *finality* at work in the philosophical traditions that come under critical scrutiny in the *Concluding Unscientific Postscript*. See Kierkegaard, *Concluding*

Kierkegaard's various efforts to stress the importance and the difficulty of becoming a Christian in an age of Christendom cannot be readily disentangled from serious engagement with the metaphysical tradition, and often provide *philosophical* alternatives (on truth, agency, decision, subjectivity, being, and the like) to the very tradition he or his pseudonyms call into question.[7] And both thinkers frequently turn to ancient Greek philosophical paradigms as potential correctives to the truncated, anemic, and anxious *epistemological* concerns and ideals of academic philosophy in the modern European era.[8]

Heidegger might appear to have systematic intentions, at least in the period leading up to the publication of *Being and Time*, and Kierkegaard throughout the pseudonymous corpus to oppose The System. But complaints about systematic thought or the absence of systematic concerns are too often offered without much thought about what it means to be systematic, or what form systematic thought should assume. If the systematic impulse is best understood in the light of Spinoza's ambition to advance strictly *more geometrico*, viewing things *aeterno modo*, then neither Kierkegaard nor Heidegger reveals much interest in pursuing systematic philosophy. Some ways of setting up contrasts and oppositions require more careful and detailed explication and defense. And on this score, at least, the controversy between the two thinkers may show itself to be more spurious than real. If "being systematic" means something like "taking an interest in the whole," where by "whole" is meant the "interconnected aspects of a life-view," or the overarching sense of what is meant by being and by being human, then Kierkegaard and Heidegger are both systematic thinkers in this attenuated sense.

Kierkegaard and Heidegger might be said to begin, then, at opposite ends of the philosophical spectrum (although this too may prove debatable): the former taking as his point of departure the failure of individuals to become *individuals*, the latter fundamentally troubled by our contemporary failure to say what being as such means. But their distinctive projects converge in several interesting and, we think, fruitful areas of philosophical concern, organized, for our purposes here, around the idea of social ontology and criticism (or, more accurately, social ontology *as* criticism, and social criticism *as* a form of ontology) and the complex relationship

---

Unscientific Postscript, 91, 103, 160–62.

7. Again, it is worth pointing out, if only to motivate our inquiry on textually faithful grounds, that early Heidegger seems to have interpreted his own philosophical project as part of an effort to detach what he calls "primordial Christianity" from certain metaphysical tendencies derived from the influence of Greek philosophy on early Christian piety.

8. Both thinkers place anxiety at the center of their philosophical, or moral, psychologies, Kierkegaard in *The Concept of Anxiety* and Heidegger in, among other places, §40 of *Being and Time*, where *Angst* is claimed to be a "fundamental attunement" of Dasein and, unlike fear, a mood that reveals a basic and ineradicable aspect of human life, which is unavoidable insecure and *unheimlich*. On Kierkegaard's appeal to classical philosophy, see Furtak, "Kierkegaard and Greek Philosophy." The critique of (modern) philosophy as predominantly epistemology is also echoed by Nietzsche, especially in *Twilight of the Idols*.

between philosophical concept-formation and what early Heidegger calls "facticity" (in an ancient register, the relationship between philosophical speech [*logos*] and concrete way and ongoing shape of life [*bios*]). At the very least, we hope to show that any tidy separation of the ontic and the ontological constitutes a misunderstanding of their respective projects. But more importantly, if ambitiously, we offer here the beginnings of a lengthier argument that the compartmentalization in question represents an egregious *philosophical* error.

It would be another sort of (related) mistake to whitewash important differences between the Danish thinker and his German counterpart. Philosophical work that draws nourishment from both Kierkegaard and Heidegger should not ignore the consequential fact that the former's most influential studies of human existence are themselves literary productions, attributed to a series of pseudonymous authors. This aspect of his authorship makes it notoriously difficult to decide where Kierkegaard's own voice is to be located, where a thought-possibility or literary experiment in the presentation of a "life-view" ends and a serious commitment to a particular way of life begins.[9] Even the critique of the present age offered in the final part of *A Literary Review*, and signed, importantly, in Kierkegaard's own name, is presented as a critical interpretation of a Danish novel (Gyllembourg's *Two Ages* [1845]), which still allows its author to distance himself from the criticism.[10] Similarly, Heidegger's overarching interest in the *Seinsfrage* (the question of being), which is officially claimed in *Being and Time* to motivate the ontic inquiry into specific aspects of human existence, should not be flippantly ignored, even if the Heideggerian question concerning what being means can be shown to have ontic (specifically ethical) origins. The aim of an essay of this sort is not to create superficial harmony among possibly (and productively) dissenting voices. Heidegger was himself interested, for good historical and philosophical reasons, in establishing neglected polemical differences between the extant philosophers whose work he found himself moved to engage with—in opposition to, for instance, neo-Kantian philosophical historians such as Natorp who tried to make Plato over in an image of contemporary epistemology, ethics, and metaphysics. And Kierkegaard's work is clearly moved by polemical intentions, too: most obviously, by an ambition to distinguish between Hegelian reconstructions of Christian belief, which leave uncertainty and the work of salvation in "fear and trembling" behind, and

---

9. The demand for a "life-view," presented by Kierkegaard as early as *From the Papers of One Still Living*, is also prominent in *A Literary Review*. See Kierkegaard, *Literary Review*, 15–16.

10. It is interesting that both Kierkegaard and Heidegger seem interested in dissociating themselves from the moralizing tone of their respective criticisms of human life. Kierkegaard writes, in what reads like an anachronistic echo of Heidegger, that in his account of the present age "there is no question of which age is the better, or the more significant." See Kierkegaard, *Literary Review*, 67–68. Heidegger prefaces his account of the falling of Dasein in *Being and Time* by observing: "Our interpretation has a purely ontological intention and is far removed from any moralizing critique of every Dasein and from the aspirations of a 'philosophy of culture.'" See Heidegger, *Being and Time*, 156 (*SZ*, 167).

the proper concerns of Christian faith and piety, apart from what can be decided in abstract, systematic, and spuriously reassuring terms.

And yet there are, we think, sufficient similarities between the two existential thinkers to avoid the worry, announced playfully by Michael Forster in his study of Hegel and skepticism, that the story we have to tell is of the "Laurel and Hardy" variety, where the combination of characters and voices X and Y has something arbitrary about it.[11] Ultimately, our interest is not so much philological or exegetical but substantive: we mean to draw from both Kierkegaard and Heidegger, where the texts themselves allow the fruitful comparison, and to explore in a *philosophical* spirit the relationship between conceptual universality and the particular concerns of finite human beings that animate philosophic inquiry and the demand for more universal claims in the first place. Both thinkers ask, controversially but usefully, how philosophy itself gets underway in the life of particular philosophizing *individuals*; and what, more generally, it means for *philosophy* to be answerable to its time *and* to the concerns of particular individuals who are moved to think within, and often against, the prevailing tendencies of the age. Although both authors are attentive to the factical circumstances out of which philosophy arises, each attempts to describe the universal conceptual form of a more adequate (or truthful) mode of inhabiting the human world. Both Heidegger and Kierkegaard begin with a religious way of life in view, as one that needs to be renewed in the modern era; and it is in their polemical critique of the modern age that we find most obviously their contributions to what might be called "political theology," as we shall elaborate further.

Philosophy and Facticity

How and where and for whom, then, does philosophy begin? That philosophy gets started, at least as a formal pursuit, in the midst of a (personal) life already underway, seems to be an innocuous statement of fact, and irrelevant to the very nature of philosophy itself. If philosophy could be made over in an image of such hard sciences as mathematics, where the cares and concerns and passions of the thinker can be safely ignored as having no real bearing upon her intellectual orientation and problem-solving competence, it would be unimportant and harmless enough. In the form of a true if obfuscating slogan: The biography of a philosopher is not philosophy. As Heidegger himself was once moved to write, in a lecture course devoted to the basic concepts of Aristotle's philosophy: "The personality of a philosopher has only the following interest: he was born then and there, he worked and died."[12]

---

11. Forster, *Hegel and Skepticism*, 1.

12. Heidegger, *Gesamtausgabe* (hereafter *GA*) Band 18/5. Translations of Heidegger in what follows are our own, unless otherwise noted. The standard edition is published by Vittorio Klostermann, under multiple editors.

There are, to be sure, philosophers, past and present, who maintain that philosophy ought to begin where the personal dimension ends, in light of an ostensibly more objective "view from nowhere." The story of one's becoming interested in the problem of other minds, for instance, or moved to demonstrate the reality of the external world, belongs not to philosophy proper, but to the social and personal psychology of a particular student of philosophy. What matters on this view are the abstract arguments in favor of a certain resolution of the problem and the adequacy of its conceptual foundations. (It isn't often asked what provides foundations for the concepts that lie at the basis of the philosopher's solutions. It is no accident that early Heidegger often poses questions concerning the *Bodenständigkeit* of philosophic concept-formation.) If experience comes into play, it is in any event certainly not supposed to be *personal*. The principles of logical analysis that underwrite the evaluation of philosophical arguments are timelessly, impersonally valid—and various forms of disinterested (usually perceptual) experience can serve as useful points of departure in the philosophical work of generalization, regardless of how we find ourselves disposed or moved, and what sorts of things, broadly construed, we find moving. To define philosophy as an expression of the personal would be to confuse philosophy with the articulation of an individual's *Weltanschauung*. If particular philosophers have their personal views of life (secular, Christian, vaguely religious, and so on), that's their own (non-philosophical) affair.[13] It is the *results*, allegedly, that matter, and the disembodied reasons that buttress our abstract intellectual assent.[14]

Both Kierkegaard and Heidegger, echoing a Socratic conviction, insist by contrast that the sort of philosophy an individual pursues cannot be cleanly divorced from what we might call the "existential situation" of the philosopher in question, where this embraces, *inter alia*, ethical ideals and political and intellectual goals, so-called irrational phenomena (mood, emotion, passion), historically and socially informed experiences of human existence, and obscure background conditions of understanding and interpreting human life and its various worlds that give shape to the philosophical problems that seem relevant and the concepts, judgments, and arguments that appear plausible. The inescapable fact that philosophy begins *in medias res* is itself an important *philosophical* problem. If it is a fact, it is certainly not neutral but comes with crucial normative implications. (This helps to explain why social and moral criticism, beyond the criticism of arguments divorced from life-concerns, belongs for both thinkers to philosophy proper, about which more below; and why the

---

13. Again, Heidegger himself frequently dismisses the idea of philosophy as construction of a worldview. See, for instance, *GA* 56/7, 7–12.

14. Climacus, for instance, praises Lessing for producing no clear-cut *results* in Kierkegaard, *Concluding Unscientific Postscript*, 55; Heidegger dismisses the philosophical ambition to achieve disembodied results throughout his early lecture courses.

phenomenon of history and what early Heidegger calls the "historical I" play a central role in their respective projects.)[15]

But this insistence on the personal in Kierkegaard and what early Heidegger names "facticity," is somewhat elusive and easy to misunderstand and it raises several important questions: What should the philosopher's responsibility be to her own personal life? How should one write, in light of the acknowledged claims of concrete human existence? And what does the interest in facticity mean for philosophy itself?

Critics of Heidegger inspired by Kierkegaard occasionally fault the fundamental ontologist for falling victim to the temptations of systematic philosophy, as if taking an interest in the personal should eschew all forms of philosophic generality and the task were comparable to the writing of a memoir or composing poems. The same readers often fail to acknowledge the highly abstract and generalizing character of the pronouncements on truth, subjectivity, and becoming inward in the *Postscript* and often ignore Climacus's own insistence that those who ask about truth ought to consider "what is meant by 'being.'"[16] Those who approach Heidegger with more conventional systematic ambitions often fail to discern important connections (more evident, to be fair, in the lecture courses) between the fundamental ontology of *Being and Time* and the "ontic" ideals and ways of life that, by Heidegger's own reckoning, enable the more abstract philosophical theses.[17] And some readers of early Heidegger purport to discover good reasons to think that early Heidegger himself is an opponent of philosophy who favors the mysterious play of pre-philosophical life against its conceptual articulation and freezing.[18]

But the work of both thinkers hardly sustains a tidy distinction between the ontic and the ontological, which seems to underwrite and pervade several influential but misleading interpretations of their respective projects. Heidegger's earliest work in Freiburg (1919–1923) and Kierkegaard's entire literary production, beginning officially with the pseudonymous *Either/Or*, move artfully back and forth between the concrete details of a particular form of life-in-the-making and the more general ontological structures embedded in the details. In what scholars of early Heidegger often see as his breakthrough (KNS 1919), Heidegger insists that despite the differences in perception between a university professor, a peasant from the Black Forest, and

---

15. Kierkegaard's dissertation on the concept of irony places the notion of history at the center of his polemic against what he perceives to be the empty conception of the "I" in post-Kantian philosophers such as Fichte; and in lecture courses from the first Freiburg period (1919–1923), Heidegger insists that the self is a historical phenomenon and that philosophy is charged with the task of dismantling inauthentic historical traditions, in order to recover its proper mission to make human life meaningful again. See especially the course of lectures devoted to the phenomenology of intuition and expression held in SS 1920 (*GA* 59).

16. *Concluding Unscientific Postscript*, 159.

17. In *Heidegger's Temporal Idealism*, Blattner attempts to detach Heidegger's ontological theses from Heidegger's own insistence that ontological insights are enabled by authentic ways of existing.

18. This is the gist of John Van Buren's influential *Young Heidegger*.

a native of Senegal, each experiences objects (such as a lectern) under the aspect of significance; and so "universally valid propositions are [nonetheless] possible."[19]

Although the Judge speaks in the second volume of *Either/Or* in the personal mode of epistolary communication and address, and singles out his own married life as an example, his advice to the young man known as "A" amounts to a philosophy of the nature of ethical commitment and its *structural* superiority to the uncommitted, sentimental, and self-absorbed mode of being he associates with his younger friend and interlocutor. It is the aesthete, by the Judge's reckoning, who pays too little attention to the general conditions of becoming a self and who lacks a compelling organizing *idea* of human existence "for which," in Kierkegaard's own words, one ought to be "willing to live and die."[20] The general reflections on chatter, the public, apathy, leveling, and the like that conclude *A Literary Review* are preceded by a series of detailed considerations of a novelistic treatment of two ages (called, respectively, the revolutionary age and the present age), rich in concrete poetic detail: it is, after all, the lives of the characters, as portrayed by the author of *The Two Ages*, that enable the cultural critic's more abstract assessments. And while philosophically inclined readers may ignore the first two parts, Kierkegaard himself insists upon the close connection between abstract philosophical reflection and the more concrete poetic configurations: "It's not a question here of an ethico-philosophical assessment of [the age's] validity, but of the consequences of its special character as this is reflected, and the task is to suggest such consequences only at the level of generality corresponding to the details of the author's novelistic account."[21]

In a similar vein, Heidegger's earliest sustained account of authenticity in the summer semester of 1921 unfolds as a critical appropriation of themes in Augustine's *Confessions*, itself a rich narrative of a particular individual's journey toward the Christian life, but in a way that makes ample room for non-Christian appropriations of the same and serves to justify certain ways of conceptualizing possibilities of concrete human existence in the abstract.[22] A careful reading of the course in question would, we think (if we had space to argue for it here), show that Heidegger's more abstract views on, for instance, temptation and distraction, curiosity, and the pursuit of the good, anchor themselves in concrete readings of a highly individualized narrative of religious concern—and, moreover, that the abstract concepts themselves have purchase only as structural formalizations of a particular ideal of living well, with ways of going astray also clearly in view.

Each of these texts, then, can be seen to embody a particular individual's way of living up to the ideals at stake in the presentation, along with detailed accounts of what the corresponding way of life looks like in the concrete (the Judge, for example, does

19. Heidegger, *GA* 56/7, 72.
20. From the 1835 Gilleleje writings, see Kierkegaard, *Pap.* I A 75.
21. Kierkegaard, *Literary Review*, 53, 60.
22. Heidegger, *GA*, 60.

not only diagnose, in the abstract, his correspondent's failure to treat people in a certain way, but speaks to "A" as a specific person whose existence matters); but they also offer conceptualizations and abstract remarks on what it means to live in those ways. (The aesthete, too, has a philosophy of crop rotation on offer in the first volume of *Either/Or*, as well as general theories of tragedy and modern life and the meaning of music, love, and death.) If the work of each reveals suspicion about the tendency toward generalization, it is the sort of suspicion that comes to voice in Blake's paradoxically generalizing assertion, in his marginal comments on Reynolds's *Discourses*: "To Generalize is to be an Idiot; To Particularize is the Alone Distinction of Merit."

The *Postscript*, which many take to be the canonical formulation of Kierkegaard's hostility to philosophy or philosophical generalization, in the name of the particular individual who falls outside of the system, is dominated by abstract reflections on decision and choice, freedom, the nature of inwardness and appropriation, existential truth and untruth, and what Climacus calls "essential knowing," all in the name of rethinking the general structure of ethical (and religious) life.[23] It would do the work no injustice to read it as a contribution to the philosophical theory of finite subjectivity and what it means, generally speaking, to inhabit a concrete situation of choice with an awareness of ethical urgency. Similarly, when Heidegger brings up the experience of his table in the Black Forest in SS 1923 (a course that makes several passing remarks on Kierkegaard), in contrast to the table as reconfigured in modern epistemological terms, the point is not, or at least not exclusively, to rehearse the meaning of the table *for Heidegger*, but to offer a richer experiential foundation for more general claims about the nature of the contexts of *Bedeutsamkeit* (significance) within which each of us dwells, before certain epistemological theories disfigure the phenomena that are in *philosophical* question. In both cases, the failure is not merely a failure to live up to some parochial tradition of human concern but a failure to own up to the general characteristics of *being* human *as such*.

Heidegger himself addresses the error we have been discussing explicitly in an important course of lectures held in 1921–22 (*GA* 61). He held Kierkegaard clearly in view as an ally. In a lengthy account of the (question-worthy) nature of philosophy, he takes issue with several misunderstandings of the nature, or task, of philosophical concept-formation and definition. On the one hand, we are tempted to overestimate the possibilities of defining our concepts, in ways that detach themselves from the living conditions and existential aims that motivate a philosophical interest in human life. Philosophy, on this view, begins to look (suspiciously) like an attempt to arrive at universally binding definitions that culpably ignore the concrete circumstances of philosophizing individuals, in favor of organizing things away in conceptual cabinets. The universals that emerge here relate indifferently to any possible object of its kind: the best definition of poetry, for instance, need not take into serious consideration questions concerning the *worth* of particular expressions of the poetic impulse, or

23. On this polemic, see Furtak, "Kierkegaardian Ideal."

personal ways of having been moved by the poetic statement. All that matters is whether something can be classified *as a poem*. Once we know what, in general, makes for a poem, we need not trouble ourselves much further.

On the other hand, there are stances toward definition, or refusals to conceptualize, that insist that philosophy (if we can call it that) is entirely a matter of personal experience; that the point is to live intensely or to work concretely, without regard for the *principles* that make life and thought possible. Philosophy, Heidegger insists, is conceptual cognition worked out in a principled fashion. And in case we might be in danger of thinking that adherence to principles is an entirely abstract affair, Heidegger informs his students (while mentioning Kierkegaard by name) that genuine principles of philosophical research are to be acquired "only in the basic experience of passion."[24] The corresponding passage in *A Literary Review* runs: "*Principium*, as the word indicates, is what is primary, that is, the substantial, the idea in the . . . form of feeling and enthusiasm which, in its inner drive, impels the individual forward."[25]

Despite Heidegger's own eventual efforts to distance himself from Kierkegaard—on the grounds that the latter fails to raise the *Seinsfrage*, and so remains confined to the ontic or existentiell—we conclude that both thinkers are engaged in an ontological project, broadly construed; and, just as importantly, that the interest in developing certain general (Heidegger prefers to say "formal") categories of human existence accurately embodies a concern for the particular individuals whose lives (as both thinkers insist) are perennially at issue in philosophy. In the absence of the formalizing ambition—what Heidegger calls "formal indication" and what Climacus names "double reflection"—the particularizing emphasis runs the risk of deflecting the reader's attention away from her own life, in favor of morally irrelevant preoccupation with the particular life of another. The point of reading Heidegger and Kierkegaard is not to become interested in two idiosyncratic authors, but to become genuinely interested *in* what interested *them*. And this interest shows up on a decidedly conceptual plane. There is, to be sure, always some risk inherent in the conceptual enterprise. One could, as Aristotle once complained, get sidetracked in the conceptual tasks, at the expense of the personal work of forming virtuous habits and so fail to form those states or dispositions of character that serious ethical reflection and philosophical theory in its service demand. But it is a risk that both Kierkegaard and Heidegger, following in Aristotle's footsteps, are willing to take.

And so while it is true that both thinkers pay careful and critical attention to the concrete situation out of which philosophy emerges—the factical life from which and back into which philosophical discourse moves—each tries, in his own way, to capture the universal conceptual structures of a more adequate (authentic) mode of inhabiting the human world. Once again, if both begin with a decidedly religious way of life clearly in view, as a form of existence that needs to be renewed in the modern

---

24. Heidegger, *GA*, 61, 24.
25. Kierkegaard, *Literary Review*, 90.

era, their respective criticisms of the present age, their contributions to political theology convey, as we shall see shortly, certain failures in human life.[26] And it is precisely this capacity of their ontological and moral criticisms of modern everyday life to move beyond the Danish Hegelian culture and spurious Christianity of the nineteenth century (Kierkegaard) and the perceived complacency of the Weimer era (Heidegger) which allows their work to shed critical light on the conditions of ethical life in the globalized twenty-first century.

Social Criticism and the Ontology of Sociopolitical Existence

Because of the ways in which Kierkegaard and Heidegger examine both the concrete details of particular forms of life *and* the more general ontological structures of cultural life as such, we ought to look for instances in which what appears to be social criticism aimed at aspects of a particular culture also has a relevance beyond that local context. Even Hannay, one of Kierkegaard's most capable Anglophone translators and a compelling interpreter in his own right, tends to see *A Literary Review* as a largely topical affair, in an important essay that brings Heidegger's more formal analyses into the discussion as well.[27] To begin our more concrete exploration, we can borrow an example from another author—one who (like Kierkegaard) can easily be misread as a *merely* "existentiell" critic, philosophically unconcerned with outlining universal structures of political ontology—to illustrate what we have in mind. The following passage is from Thoreau's *Walden*, and is all the more striking, in light of Heidegger's use of *das Man* (the They) and Kierkegaard's interest in the role of public modes of discourse in shaping or distorting the individual's sense of her tasks and commitments: "When I ask for a garment of a particular form, my tailoress tells me gravely, 'They do not make them so now,' not emphasizing the 'They' at all, as if she quoted an authority as impersonal as the Fates."[28]

As the subsequent elaboration of his dissatisfaction with the seamstress makes clear, Thoreau's criticism is not aimed at the attitudes of a particular individual in Concord (sister to Emerson's neighbor, as it turns out), or if so only proximally and indirectly. His point, rather, is about the *kind* of attitude represented by this seamstress and how typical it is—of his contemporaries, to be sure, but also of human beings

---

26. Paul Kahn, for instance, points out that "political theology understands politics as an organization of everyday life" which is focused upon ways of imagining or experiencing what he calls "the sacred." According to this conception, political theology could be said to concern both Kierkegaard and (early and late) Heidegger conspicuously. See Kahn, *Political Theology*, 22–23.

27. Hannay, "Kierkegaard's Present Age and Ours." As the title of the volume would lead us to expect, Hannay's target is Dreyfus's influential reading of Heidegger and Kierkegaard, coauthored with Jane Rubin and published as an appendix to *Being-in-the-World: A Commentary on Heidegger's Being and Time, Division I*.

28. Thoreau, *Walden*, 23–24.

more generally—to defer to public opinion or "conventional wisdom," to honor Fashion and repeat whatever "They" happen to be saying at the moment. The stance of the tailoress embodies in concrete, exemplary shape a widely shared tendency of human life that needs combatting, in Thoreau's view, throughout the various stations of human existence. The notion of the public, the *concept* of the "They," is of an abstract and impersonal power that takes responsibility away from specific individuals, offering ready-made opinions that are available to be taken up as if they were one's own: what *they* say has the authority granted to whatever people *en masse*, based on hearsay, allegedly think.[29] Despite Thoreau's Kierkegaardian insistence in the opening pages of *Walden* that it is, after all, always only the first person speaking, his work means to address problems that afflict human beings in their mortal condition more generally, as creatures for whom things matter. All three thinkers (we could add Nietzsche here, too, and Emerson also) worry, centrally, about the tendency of human life to be lived by impersonal forces and powers embedded in widely circulating social customs and norms, in the name of an abstract and dubious ideal of conformity. In Heidegger's terse formulation: "Everyone is the other, and no one is himself. The *they* . . . is the *nobody* to whom every Dasein has always surrendered itself."[30]

Kierkegaard—not exclusively, but especially, in *A Literary Review*—develops a set of concepts that, while most clearly exemplified in distinctively modern forms of existence, is meant to capture generic existential tendencies in social life. These include *idle talk* (or "chatter"), *the public* (sometimes "public opinion"), and the all-important *leveling*—which is described as a monstrous, desolating abstraction, "an abstract power [which] is abstraction's victory over individuals."[31] Idle talk, public opinion, and leveling are terms that function much like Thoreau's or Heidegger's *They*. They are put forward in specific shapes, but in the long run as having existential, and not only existentiell, pertinence to the sociopolitical aspects of human life *as such*, and so mean to apply concretely to individuals across various social, political, and economic boundaries.

Likewise, ontological claims about the structure of public life *per se* may originate in, and so be relevant to, an author's parochial situation or her broader yet still "ontic" historical moment. There is an implied comparison between his own time and other actual or possible historical moments underlying Heidegger's Kierkegaardian point in *Being and Time* that "the they" has "various possibilities of concretion" such that "the extent to which its dominance becomes penetrating and explicit may change historically."[32] In texts written at least a decade later, and with his own political situ-

---

29. For more on the relationship between personal interest and philosophical generality in Thoreau, see Reid, "Speaking Extravagantly," 44–47.

30. *SZ*, 128 (§27).

31. Kierkegaard, *Literary Review*, 74–80 and 98.

32. Heidegger, *Being and Time*, 121. *SZ* §27. On "Americanism" and "the American," see for instance "The Age of the World Picture" (in *Holzwege*) and *Hölderlin's Hymn "The Ister"* (*GA* 53) from 1938 and 1942, respectively.

ation more obviously on display, what is pejoratively named "Americanism" or "the American" is a localized manifestation of what Heidegger still seeks to understand as a metaphysical tendency, transcending specific and readily identifiable political and social limits. Similarly, in an earlier course of lectures on Plato's *Sophist*, held in the winter semester of 1924/5, Heidegger sees the problem of *Gerede* (usually translated as "idle talk") as operative not only in the modern era—where the human being, he playfully suggests in the summer term of 1924, should be defined as "the animal who reads newspapers"—but also, and just as importantly, in ancient Greece. On Heidegger's view, idle talk is a permanent possibility of human existence, anchored in the essential, structural (ontological) detachability of words from lives, things, and issues. Again, it would be a mistake to see the critique of *Gerede* as little more than localized moral criticism, representing Heidegger's own dissatisfaction with the political situation in the Weimer era. What prompted Heidegger to make idle talk thematic is, of course, inseparable from his own place and time. But philosophy, in Heidegger's own reckoning, is no merely local affair. In a related vein, Heidegger's own explicit views on why *Destruktion* of the philosophical tradition is important are, to be sure, rooted in culturally specific anxieties about the reception of ancient Greek philosophy in the academic community of German philosophy in the early decades of the twentieth century; but they are just as often tethered to a generic claim about the historical nature of human existence *as such* and what philosophy, throughout the ages, is called upon to do—to think freshly about what *being* might mean.[33]

To dismiss analyses of this kind as examples of warmed-over social critique of parochial historical phenomena, arguably located in certain decades of the nineteenth or twentieth century,[34] is to imply that a philosopher, strictly speaking, should not stoop to attend to the merely contingent—and that, insofar as she does so, she is temporarily leaving aside philosophical tasks in order to dabble in ephemeral political journalism. In fact, if Kierkegaard and Heidegger can both be seen to be offering what Charles Taylor (echoing Nietzsche) might call a "moral ontology" of human existence, then failure to weigh in on the ontological significance of culturally specific ways of failing would be a fatal misstep—one that runs the risk of offering fruitless generalities in a conceptual vacuum, ungrounded in specific worries and animating passions. It ought to matter (to us, today) that idle talk, as a general category of human life, is enabled and encouraged by the modern press and other forms of distinctively modern technologies.

It would be a mistake, then, to assume that what we find in either *The Present Age* or *Being and Time* (see esp. §§25–27 and §§35–38) is only *about* flaws in a particular

---

33. For details on *Destruktion*, ethics, and the project of ontology in early Heidegger, see Reid, "Ethical Criticism."

34. Taylor Carman, e.g., gives some credence to this oft-repeated complaint; then, in seeking to offer a partial defense of Heidegger against it, he seeks to separate the project of *Being and Time* from that of *A Literary Review*, to our mind unconvincingly. See Carman, *Heidegger's Analytic*, 139–42.

culture or era—yet, as we also wish to stress, it would *also* be mistaken, as we have just begun to argue, to assume that these texts must disavow any such ontic applicability in order to earn their credentials as philosophy. Heidegger and Kierkegaard both insist that philosophy, even in its more generic modes and generalizing moods, should not attempt to disburden future generations and individuals of the specific tasks they will face. While they both take issue with Hegel's social and political philosophy, their work can be read as an attempt to think through the present age, with the history of philosophy in the West clearly in mind. There are temporally and historically specific ways in which the problems of philosophy show up that individuals called to philosophical reflection of a certain sort should not avoid, in favor of an easy view of *philosophia perennis* and problems descending from the unchanging heavens. The fact that the perennial temptation of idle talk or chatter shows up for us *today* (see, e.g., Heidegger on *Heute*) in the shape of Internet pressures is all the more reason to think through the specific temptations presented by current media. Demagoguery may be a perennial problem in political life, but there are specific forms of it, enabled by certain phenomena of the so-called digital age, that call for careful *temporally specific* analyses. (Plato's Allegory of the Cave doesn't suffice to illuminate fully the concrete conditions of life with and within the Internet, even if Plato's Socrates can sometimes seem a prescient interpreter of our contemporary pathologies.)

As philosophers, we are always enmeshed in a specific set of factual circumstances: to neglect this in thought would be make a Cartesian mistake (as when, in the Third Meditation, he says that his being as a thinking thing owes nothing to parental upbringing). The philosophical reflection that leads one to conclude that the prevailing habits of thought will always offer ready-made answers to difficult questions, "disburdening" *Dasein* of its existence by making everything easy,[35] or that a crowd *in its very concept* is untruth,[36] ought to begin with and return to a diagnostic evaluation of the distinct failures of one's own age. And a certain dissatisfaction with the present age (of one's own particular life) might prove to be the best way to begin thinking about the more generic failures to live up to the human condition that tempt or afflict philosophizing individuals across time.

Both thinkers have powerful things to say, in culturally specific registers, to be sure, about the general human failure to take seriously the shape and significance of a life of one's own, but also (the two go hand in hand) to own up to the conditions of mortal human life as such. (Heidegger's *Eigentlichkeit* is suggestively ambivalent: it can suggest the personal achievement of becoming an individual, with a life of one's own, led on one's own terms, but also a failure to own up to the human condition *überhaupt*. This comes out most clearly, perhaps, in the moral ontology of death in the second division of *Being and Time*.) The philistine or the inauthentic person, complacently immersed in trivial everydayness, will in each instance appear in a culturally

---

35. Heidegger, *Being and Time*, 120. SZ §27.
36. Kierkegaard, *Point of View*, 106–11.

specific guise, but at the same time will *necessarily* exemplify general features that both Kierkegaard and Heidegger are struggling to conceptualize. They may be wrong to generalize in the way they do; but the generalizing ambition should not be ignored. The fact that few of us are alehouse keepers or prime ministers does not diminish the force, at once moral and ontological, of the following passage from *The Sickness Unto Death*, which centers on a generic failure of the imagination and its constricting sense of the possible (note, too, the "always"):

> Bereft of imagination, as the philistine-bourgeois *always* [our emphasis] is, whether alehouse keeper or prime minister, he lives within a certain trivial compendium of experiences as to how things go, what is possible, what usually happens. . . . The philistine-bourgeois mentality reassures itself with the trite and obvious and is just as much in despair whether things go well or badly.[37]

Similarly, the particular modes of enjoyment and the novels and plays that might attract attention or shock will, of course, vary from time to time, but the structural tendency on display in the following passage from *Being and Time* should be discernible, if with some effort, throughout a variety of empirical instances in distinctive historical climes and individual lives:

> We enjoy ourselves and have fun the way *they* enjoy themselves. We read, see, and judge literature and art the way *they* see and judge. But we also . . . find "shocking" what *they* find shocking. . . . The they [*das Man*, also "the One" or "Anyone"] maintains itself factically in the averageness of what is proper, what is allowed, and what is not.[38]

What is especially problematic in the present age, according to *A Literary Review*, is that individual human beings have no sustaining passions and are somehow stifled into inaction and conformity rather than being moved to act decisively. (Heidegger lodges a similar complaint about indecisiveness in more explicitly ontological terms in *Being and Time*.) But we can conceptually account for what *sort* of tendency is particularly bad, here and now, as Kierkegaard proceeds to do in his book-review-turned-project-in-social-ontology. In the process of comparing an earlier age favorably to the present one, he gains leverage to show that (1) *how things are* is worse than *how things might be*, the latter evidenced, at least in part, by the comparison between the age of revolution and the present age of leveling reflection (again, Heidegger's frequent comparisons between modern philosophical tendencies he finds dubious and more fruitful ancient modes of philosophizing are meant to make a similar point), and (2) although they may be particularly hazardous and pervasive today, phenomena such as idle talk are not uniquely characteristic of the modern era, but represent permanent

---

37. Kierkegaard, *Sickness Unto Death*, 41.

38. Heidegger, *Being and Time*, 118–19. SZ §27. The discussion continues into accounting for these tendencies of *Das Man* in terms of "publicness" and "leveling."

temptations, woven structurally into human existence as *essential* possibilities of what Heidegger calls *Dasein*. The first is an ontic, the second an ontological point. And both perspectives, the ontic and the ontological, are mutually illuminating: our conception of what idle talk *is*, or what it is to *chatter* [at *snakke*] gets enriched by philosophical reflection on, for example, the modern press; and, conversely, an otherwise isolated phenomenon such as the newspaper reveals something like an *essence*, and so takes up residence in a powerful *conceptual* account of human existence, when the ontology of idle talk comes more clearly into view.

In opposition to a mutually exclusive disjunction advanced by Pattison,[39] among others, both perspectives (the ontic and the ontological) are essential to the *ethical* tasks at issue explicitly in Kierkegaard throughout the corpus, and strongly implied by Heidegger's distinctive approach to fundamental ontology in the period culminating in *Being and Time*. The ontic perspective helps rescue us from political apathy, while the ontological standpoint can prevent us from succumbing to utopian fantasies that various undesirable aspects of contemporary life in the *polis* could in principle be eliminated. It makes sense to be critical of what current media (in whatever form they may take) happen to convey, but *also* to recognize that a tendency toward leveling and chatter will be present in any shared life within which people talk—which is to say, in any mode of human existence. General, structural tendencies toward what Heidegger calls *Verfallen* will, presumably, give birth to ever-new occasions to go astray. So, even as *A Literary Review* identifies in contemporary public life some of the abstract, self-forgetting tendencies of "speculation, which is indifferent to existence" as identified in *The Concluding Unscientific Postscript*,[40] it also describes how a specific *culture* can itself express, and thus encourage in each of its members, a tendency toward what in *Either/Or* is named the "aesthetic" mode of life. Aesthetic modes of life do, after all, seem more prevalent in a culture that values the spectator over the participant—a tendency warned about in *A Literary Review*. But Heidegger's readings of ancient Greek philosophy reveal a tendency toward spectatorship, at the expense of uncertain and fallible *praxis*, in premodern societies and philosophies as well. Although "every person [must] work out his own salvation," as Kierkegaard affirms late in *A Literary Review*, the "desolating abstraction of leveling" makes this more difficult for each of

---

39. In Pattison's own words: "What interest could someone persuaded by Johannes Climacus's characterization of the subjective, interested, passionate approach to existence have in developing a universal ontology? . . . If one of the complaints levelled against the system by Climacus was that it had and could have no place for ethics, it is striking that the broad (if not total) consensus of Heidegger commentators is that Heideggerian ontology is similarly lacking in ethical interest in the very precise sense that the philosopher's interest in his own personal ethical choices has no place within the project of fundamental ontology. *Qua* philosopher, [he] is duty-bound to look away from himself—which is just what the Kierkegaardian individual should never do. Which of the two, the fundamental ontologist or the existential thinker, has chosen the better part is, of course, a whole other matter." See Pattison, *Philosophy of Kierkegaard*, 86–87.

40. Kierkegaard, *Concluding Unscientific Postscript*, 211.

us when its dominion is especially penetrating and explicit.[41] If human beings have a natural tendency to avoid social engagement—as Kant observed, ours is an "unsocial sociability"—certain communities and cultures may have specific instruments and institutions in place that aid and abet a more generic tendency to withdraw, thereby making detachment a more pressing problem than it might otherwise be. The problem of anonymity, for instance, is unlikely to show itself prominently in a rural community of farmers and peasants in the early decades of the seventeenth century. In the age of anonymous posting in cyberspace, the difficulty of assigning responsibility to particular individuals is pervasive and chronic. We are not ancient Greeks, to be sure, or medieval peasants, but our world and theirs is sufficiently alike to make fruitful philosophic generalizations possible.

We can and should, then, distinguish gainfully, as Kierkegaard and Heidegger both do, between a form of dissatisfaction with the shortcomings of a particular culture or community, on the one hand, and a refusal to accept *any* concrete limits within a shared life among others, on the other. In *A Literary Review*, Kierkegaard speaks of a mode of life defined by "aesthetic" detachment as one in which "the individual becomes alien to the actual world" by becoming absent from it.[42] In this mode of life, one's estrangement is based not upon an intelligible revolt against surrounding values, but by a refusal to be bound by finite human existence under any conditions. In *Either/Or*, the essay "Rotation of Crops" gives voice to the logical culmination of this attitude. Its author notes that accepting a definite identity means limiting oneself to specific concerns, and concludes that we should refuse to accept this kind of limitation and vulnerability—by avoiding friendship or marriage, or entering a profession.[43] It isn't just the specific examples of commitment but the *kind* of commitment represented in these relationships and institutional practices that the aesthete seems to be rejecting. Or, more generally still, it is the very idea of commitment against which the aesthete rebels.

Yet alienation from surrounding values and practices, if it is not a prejudice against contingent existence as such but a plausible response to one's own political situation, may deserve to be taken seriously. The ability to recoil from what seems unacceptable shows a moral imagination in touch with the possible, beyond the actual conditions of a degraded mode of life, and expecting something better. It prevents a person from complacently accepting the *status quo* just as it is—whether good or evil, significant or utterly vacuous.[44] And the dissatisfaction with political reality as one encounters it, a hesitation to take *any* of the available paths, could be nothing other than the response of an individual who has not yet found a context in which to realize worthy aspirations.[45] The terms used by Kierkegaard in his own voice in *A Present Age*

---

41. Kierkegaard, *Literary Review*, 97–98.
42. Ibid., 17.
43. Kierkegaard, *Either/Or*, 1:295–99.
44. On passion for what is "actually" insignificant, see Kierkegaard, *Christian Discourses*, 124.
45. Kierkegaard, *Literary Review*, 93–94.

echo those employed by the aesthete in the pseudonymous *Either/Or*, when the latter protests that the goals pursued by his contemporaries do not appeal to his need for meaning. Surveying his age, he observes that people are dull, their activities trivial, and their passions lethargic.[46] Thus, seeing no reason to lower himself into a charade of quiet desperation, the aesthete protects his integrity by holding back from social and political engagement. Such a person's hesitancy in coming to terms with public standards of evaluation is, on a charitable reading, based in a refusal to be reconciled to a life of trivial conformity, combined with the concomitant wish for something other than the present state of things. In a culture whose basic orientation is dubious, being a participating citizen does not guarantee attaining moral integrity or personal authenticity—and it seems that this is one way of explaining what's wrong with *any* "passionless and reflecting age," which subtly empties everything of significance and undermines possibilities for meaningful engagement.[47]

If his own sociopolitical situation is, like that of "the present age" as characterized in *A Literary Review*, one of passionlessness, erupting in brief and fleeting enthusiasms, none of which is taken seriously for long,[48] then it is unsurprising to find that *Either/Or*'s aesthete in the same condition of dissatisfaction. It is at least conceivable that the aesthete is hindered not because he is a beautiful soul who categorically rejects the finite world, but by legitimate doubts about the values of a particular civilization. Again and again, the aesthete emotionally revolts against "reality" as represented in his immediate surroundings:

> When I opened my eyes and saw reality, then I began to laugh and since that time I haven't stopped. I saw that the meaning of life was to get an income, its goal to become a counselor-at-law, that the rich desire of love was to catch a well-off girl, that the blessedness of friendship was to help each other in financial difficulties, that wisdom was whatever the majority assumed it to be, that enthusiasm was to make a speech, that courage was to risk losing ten dollars, that kindness was saying "You're welcome" after dinner, and that piety was going to communion once a year. This I saw, and I laughed.[49]

Here, the speaker relies upon a tacit belief that love, friendship, courage, kindness, and so on, *could* be something greater than what they are presently taken to be. And, just as importantly, that there is something about the human condition as such that makes love, friendship, and the like worthwhile for creatures like us. The political situation under analysis in *The Present Age* is to be understood not only for its own sake, but as providing an opportunity to investigate how any "with-world" can accomplish the

---

46. Kierkegaard, *Either/Or*, 1:27–28.
47. Kierkegaard, *Literary Review*, 68–69.
48. Ibid., 60.
49. Kierkegaard, *Either/Or*, 1:34; *SV* 2.36. This is a modified translation, as provided in Furtak, *Wisdom in Love*, 85.

stifling of human possibilities in this manner.[50] At the same time, if *Dasein* must always find itself initially surrounded by inauthentic habits of idle talk, ambiguity, and everydayness, then what appears to be a particularized social critique may have the merit of delineating what it's like to find oneself in *one* of the many historical shapes that a life among others may take. The ontic project has unavoidably ontological implications, and so ought to contribute to any ontology of social existence as such.

Conclusion

As we noted above, it would be a mistake to overlook or deny revealing differences in method between Kierkegaard and Heidegger, differences we have largely ignored in this essay, in order to explore and to stake out possible shared terrain. We did not, for instance, develop an interpretation of the relationship between the first two parts of *A Literary Review* and the third, neglecting thereby an important exegetical task that might have moved us to qualify some of our comparisons between the two thinkers, and to modify our interpretation of what we take to be Kierkegaard's social criticism and ontology. Nor did we present in any detail Heidegger's youthful reading of Augustine's *Confessions*, which, we suggested, prepares the ontic soil, so to speak, out of which emerge several early generalizations on the structure of human existence as such. The present chapter has moved, for the most part, on an *abstract* conceptual plane (even in explaining the need for philosophical attention to concrete life), in a way that runs the risk of overlooking fruitful differences between certain aspects of their respective projects and working methods. These differences help to explain why those of us interested in philosophy in an existential key often seek nourishment in both thinkers, beyond the harmonizing ambition that is more evident above.

It might appear to more careful readers of Heidegger and Kierkegaard that we have tried to make the latter over, suspiciously, in an image of the former. No reader of *A Literary Review* and *Being and Time*, however careless, can fail to perceive at least *formal* differences between the two texts. Nothing in Heidegger's vast philosophical output resembles in form the well-known Seducer's Diary in the first volume of *Either/Or* or the dialogical *Stages on Life's Way* or the (arguably, sometimes philosophical) commentaries on specific passages of Scripture that make up Kierkegaard's *Upbuilding Discourses*.[51]

While it is true, as we have tried to argue above, that any tidy distinction between the ontic and the ontological in Kierkegaard and Heidegger is difficult to sustain—that

---

50. Heidegger, *Being and Time*, 114–15, 162. SZ §§26, 37. Cf. Kierkegaard, *Journals and Papers*, 1541 (*Pap.* I A 340).

51. The closest Heidegger comes to providing commentary on Scripture comes in a course of lecture on the phenomenology of religious life in WS 1920/1 (*GA* 60), which centers on Paul's eschatological letters. But his comments are almost culpably abstract, and far removed from anything Kierkegaard has to offer in the *Discourses*, which are more obviously meant to address human beings in states of affliction and personal concern.

both thinkers are engaged in ontological or existential interpretation of certain ontic (or existentiell) phenomena—it is also worth noting that Heidegger's basic question (What does being as such mean?) is not foundational for Kierkegaard and, conversely, that the task of becoming inward and achieving true selfhood stands more discernibly at the center of Kierkegaard's authorship. This is not to say that questions concerning individuation that engage with the phenomena of a particular world of human concern are foreign to the *Seinsfrage*, or that a preoccupation with the single individual ought to shun ontological reflection. But distinctive accents in their respective projects do make for palpable stylistic differences between them, with noteworthy philosophical implications that ought to matter to those of us who take seriously the pressing problem of *how to speak and write*—as individuals at once profoundly shaken, for example, by the recent death of a close friend and philosophical interlocutor, but also invested in the project of clarifying the general structure of what Heidegger calls "being-toward-death" and looking to *philosophy* to say something, in the more generalizing mood, about the nature of loss and its shadow grief, beyond the painful absence of *this one* here and now. (The question of how to write, and what to keep silent about, troubled both Kierkegaard and Heidegger, and forms another point of contact between them.)

To carry the example further: one might, to be sure, still try to argue that the concrete experience of loss *properly* prompts the more poetic or personal statement, while the latter should be more strictly discursive and impersonal. As grieving individuals, we compose poems, remember the dead in conversation and formal ceremony, and sign our names to sympathy cards addressed to particular individuals; as philosophers we write dispassionate essays on the condition of mortality and our shared responsibilities to the dying, the dead, and to those the deceased leaves behind. But we have already found at least a few formal reasons to suspect that such easy partitioning of intellectual labor—factical, on the one hand, philosophical on the other—will not hold up, at least not for those of us moved to *conceptualize* on the basis of *personal* experience, and in ways that refuse to leave the personal dimension altogether behind.[52] This concern to preserve the personal, or to carry it forward in philosophical speech, does not obviously entail that a grieving response to someone's death in thoughtful poetic lines amounts to a philosophical account of death and dying (cf. Tennyson's *In Memoriam*), but it does prompt us to ask: what forms of discourse are appropriate for creatures like us—always underway and unfinished, chronically afflicted with uncertainty, caring about particular individuals, landscapes, projects, etc., but capable of (and sometimes, perhaps, all too tempted by) the generalizing perspective and the organizing power of universals? If, following Kahn again (who himself follows Arendt), we agree that "the political formation of the experience of the sacred *is* the

---

52. For more on poetry's relation to philosophy, see Rilke, *Sonnets to Orpheus*, and Reid, *Being Here Is Glorious*.

subject of political theology," then political theology like existential philosophy *must* be "a matter of life and death."[53]

To single out several of the more consequential differences between our two philosophical authors on this score would require another essay—to spell them out, in convincing detail, a book-length study in its own right. We conclude by mentioning just one, which bears directly on the themes we've been tracking here, and as a signpost for future investigations.

Heidegger's early ontology reveals far less patience facing what we might call *ontic detail* than Kierkegaard's contributions to existential and ontological inquiry. While Heidegger's early lecture courses are, as we noted in passing, usually more forthcoming about the ontic roots of ontology, *Being and Time* pays scant attention to some of the details embodied in the way of life (the ontic ideal of human existence) that enables the fundamental ontologist's bold generalizations on the ontological constitution of "authentic Dasein." Even the more ontic orientations and starting-points of the early lecture courses (see, in addition to the course on Augustine, the course of lectures held in WS 1919/20) leave something to be desired. This may prove consistent with Heidegger's philosophical desire to leave room for the individual's own work of appropriating the philosophical concepts on display, but may just as readily invite the reader to lose herself in an abstract web of concepts. That contrasts rather sharply with Kierkegaard's approach: his work often lingers over the particular details of, say, an aesthetic or an ethical mode of existing before proceeding to offer formal indications of the general structure of living in a certain way. This is as true of *The Sickness Unto Death* as it is of *Either/Or*, although the latter more clearly is (as its subtitle claims) "a fragment of life." And from this point of view, Guignon might still be right to conclude that Kierkegaard's project has certain advantages over Heidegger's early philosophy: ontic inquiry without ontological generalization may be (philosophically) blind, but ontological concept-formation without detailed ontic investigation runs the risk of appearing empty.[54]

Bibliography

Blattner, William. *Heidegger's Temporal Idealism*. Cambridge: Cambridge University Press, 1999.

Carman, Taylor. *Heidegger's Analytic: Interpretation, Discourse, and Authenticity in "Being and Time."* Cambridge: Cambridge University Press, 2003.

Dreyfus, Hubert. *Being-in-the-World: A Commentary on Heidegger's Being and Time, Division I*. Cambridge: MIT Press, 1991.

Forster, Michael. *Hegel and Skepticism*. Cambridge: Harvard University Press, 1989.

Furtak, Rick Anthony. "Kierkegaard and Greek Philosophy." In *Oxford Handbook on Kierkegaard*, edited by George Pattison and John Lippitt, 129–49. Oxford: Oxford University Press, 2013.

---

53. Kahn, *Political Theology*, 22–23, emphasis added.

54. We dedicate this essay in loving memory, and in friendship, to Matthew W. Geiger (1972–2016).

PART 3: KIERKEGAARD AND THE POLITICS OF PHILOSOPHY

———. "The Kierkegaardian Ideal of 'Essential Knowing' and the Scandal of Modern Philosophy." In *Kierkegaard's "Concluding Unscientific Postscript": A Critical Guide*, edited by Rick Anthony Furtak, 87–110. Cambridge: Cambridge University Press, 2010.

———. *Wisdom in Love: Kierkegaard and the Ancient Quest for Emotional Integrity*. Notre Dame: University of Notre Dame Press, 2005.

Guignon, Charles. "Heidegger and Kierkegaard on Death: The Existentiell and the Existential." In *Kierkegaard and Death*, edited by Patrick Stokes and Adam J. Buben, 184–203. Bloomington: Indiana University Press, 2011.

Hannay, Alastair. "Kierkegaard's Present Age and Ours." *Heidegger, Authenticity, and Modernity*, edited by Mark A. Wrathall and Jeff Malpas, 105–22. Cambridge: MIT Press, 2000.

Heidegger, Martin. *Being and Time*. Translated by Joan Stambaugh. Albany: State University of New York Press, 1996.

———. *Gesamtausgabe*. Frankfurt am Main: Klostermann, 1975–.

———. *Hölderlin's Hymn "The Ister."* Translated by William McNeill and Julia Davis. Bloomington: Indiana University Press, 1996.

———. *Plato's "Sophist."* Translated by Richard Rojcewicz and André Schuwer. Bloomington: Indiana University Press, 1997.

Kahn, Paul W. *Political Theology: Four New Chapters on the Concept of Sovereignty*. New York: Columbia University Press, 2011.

Kierkegaard, Søren. *Christian Discourses*. Edited and translated by Howard V. Hong and Edna H. Hong. Princeton: Princeton University Press, 1997.

———. *Concluding Unscientific Postscript*. Translated by Alastair Hannay. Cambridge: Cambridge University Press, 2009.

———. *Either/Or*. Edited and translated by Howard V. Hong and Edna H. Hong. Princeton: Princeton University Press, 1987.

———. *A Literary Review*. Translated by Alastair Hannay. London: Penguin, 2001.

———. *Papirer*. Edited by P. A. Heiberg et al. Copenhagen: Gyldendal, 1909–1978.

———. *The Point of View*. Edited and translated by Howard V. Hong and Edna H. Hong. Princeton: Princeton University Press, 1998.

———. *The Sickness Unto Death*. Edited and translated by Howard V. Hong and Edna H. Hong. Princeton: Princeton University Press, 1983.

Pattison, George. *The Philosophy of Kierkegaard*. Montreal: McGill-Queen's University Press, 2005.

Reid, James D. *Being Here Is Glorious: On Rilke, Poetry, and Philosophy*. Evanston: Northwestern University Press, 2015.

———. "Ethical Criticism in Early Heidegger's Early Freiburg Lectures." *Review of Metaphysics* 59 (2005) 33–71.

———. "Speaking Extravagantly: Philosophical Territory and Eccentricity in *Walden*." *Thoreau's Importance for Philosophy*, edited by Rick Anthony Furtak et al., 43–67. New York: Fordham University Press, 2012.

Rilke, Rainer Maria. *Sonnets to Orpheus: A New English Version, with a Philosophical Introduction*. Translated by Rick Anthony Furtak. Scranton, PA: University of Scranton Press, 2007.

Thoreau, Henry David. *Walden*. Edited by Jeffrey S. Cramer. New Haven: Yale University Press, 2004.

Van Buren, John. *The Young Heidegger: Rumor of the Hidden King*. Bloomington, IN: Indiana University Press, 1994.

11

Kierkegaard's "Single Individual" and Hardt and Negri's "Multitude"

Theological Resources for a Post-imperial Political Subjectivity

SILAS MORGAN AND KYLE ROBERTS

THE STATUS OF POLITICAL theology is a notoriously open question. It is not altogether clear what political theology *is*, much less what it is *for*, and whether all of this is good news for political subjects in these times of ideological struggle and global conflict. To hazard an answer, we start our exploration of important theoretical texts shaping political theology today, the first of the Hardt and Negri trilogy, *Empire*,[1] and its 2004 sequel, *Multitude*.[2] Our thesis is that Kierkegaard's "single individual" has been incorrectly interpreted in an atomistic, personalistic way, as having to do with a single subject. We argue that it is more accurate to read Kierkegaard's single individual as a style or "form of life" (Wittgenstein) that is as collective as it is individual, even though it is not, as we argue, a form of life that is limited to, only available to, the single hypostasis of an individual person. To help us clarify this further, we link Kierkegaard to Hardt and Negri's theory of the multitude, explored first in *Empire* and then elsewhere in the trilogy. We will not attempt a theological reading of Hardt and Negri through Kierkegaard; rather, we will argue that it is possible to interpret Kierkegaard's "single individual" as a multitudinal "form of life," in a way that Kierkegaard might have not recognized, but that nevertheless allows us to creatively interpret him as a resource for a "multitudinal" political theology.

This links well with discussions of political subjectivity within some threads of political theology, mostly by philosophers and theorists on the left who are interested in the unique ways that Christian theology can be used to shape subjects in distinctly revolutionary ways. This debate has been given a distinctly theological reading by Joerg Rieger and Kwok Pui-lan in their *Occupy Religion*.[3] Bringing Kierkegaard in

---

1. Hardt and Negri, *Empire*.
2. Hardt and Negri, *Multitude*.
3. Rieger and Pui-lan, *Occupy Religion*.

at the most individual and most inward point in his authorship—the single individual—gives us a kind of "parallax view" on what political subjectivity is, what it has to do with authentic human existence, and its theological character. Put differently, Kierkegaard has something to tell us, not only about what political theology is, but also what it is for.

Any attempt to make sense of Kierkegaard's contribution to contemporary political theology must come to terms with his theory of selfhood, or in other words, his theology of faith as the single individual standing in authentic immediacy before God. While this aspect of Kierkegaard's philosophy has long been celebrated, both for its role in shaping existentialism and as exemplary of Kierkegaard's theological voice and his Christian authorship, it has also been blamed for Kierkegaard's antisocial indifference and as such, his unsuitability for contemporary political thought, preoccupied as it is with questions of social identity and belonging. It is clear that the "single individual" looms large in Kierkegaard's apolitical legacy.

This chapter challenges this common narrative and its interpretation of the "single individual." Our position is that Kierkegaard is neither antisocial nor apolitical. We go further in arguing that one need not abandon or overlook the "single individual" to make such an argument about Kierkegaard, but that plenty of evidence for Kierkegaard's suitability as a resource for political thought lies *within* "the single individual." The "single individual" is not simply an existential account of the human person, but an understanding of singularity in relationality akin to how theorists Hardt and Negri describe the "multitude" and its political activity amid Empire. We not only develop corollary themes that link the single individual to the multitude, but rather show how it is that Kierkegaard develops the mode of "single individual" as a form of life in ways that are very multitudinal. Again, the argument is not that Hardt and Negri are saying the same things about the multitude that Kierkegaard did about the single individual, but rather that the latter can—and should—be read as a multitudinal style of life, opening up new ways in which to think of Kierkegaard as a political theologian.

Subjectivity and Political Theology

One of the pressing political questions of our time is the making of the political subject: who will carry out political change? This question has an urgent importance for those who suffer and struggle against the current configuration of neoliberalism, postindustrial capitalism, and globalized finance networks. *How* do we generate the energy for change, and *who* will be the ones to carry out these changes, build the coalitions, and exert force? These questions have preoccupied critical and liberation theory over the last hundred years or so. Furthermore, they have been inherited by theologies eager to lend their hand to this work. In fact, subjectivity has been the topic du jour that has mostly contributed to the new rapprochement between religion and political thought that has been uneasily termed "political theology." Both critical political thought and critical theology has found itself asking the same questions and turning to each other's traditions for answers: what is the role of theology (or religion more broadly) in the formation of the emancipatory political subject?

One notable trend in recent critical theory is the turn to religion—and to Christian theology specifically—for resources to think through the process of remaking a world and forming political subjects. Part of this comes from the post-secular admission, however reluctant it may be, that religion, long expected to disappear as the specializing force of modern rationality took its hold on the social world, has not in fact receded but merely morphed to fit into the postmodern, immanent frame. The appeal, then, of religion is what Jürgen Habermas has called its "semantic value": its ability to successfully bind actors and energies together around widely shared intuitions in ways that are currently unavailable to philosophy, aesthetics, or theory.

As an intellectual—and activist—tradition of thinking, this critical-theoretical form of political theology places subjectivity at its center; that is, it is concerned with the subject of emancipation, the actors who may be called upon to carry out social transformation. Its central practical burden, then, is to generate and form the kind of agents that are needed, and this traditionally called for an alliance with the working class, seen by European leftists, so-called "third-world" theologians, and traditional Marxists alike as the principal hand of historical change. A historical point of origin for this work comes out of the confusion and disappointment of Western Marxists in the early decades of the twentieth century who were devastated by the failure of working class resistance and socialist movements in Europe. The formation of the Frankfurt School as a research program, for example, came as a result of German Marxist intellectuals who wanted to study the social psychology of working class Germans in order to better understand why they were not persuaded or otherwise activated *en masse* by the call of German working class parties to armed resistance and labor strikes in 1918 and 1919. The central question was how to address the motivational deficit that generated disengagement and indifference on the part of political subjects rather than rebellion and resistance in the face of structural alienation and exploitation.[4] The guiding presumption, both then and now, was that ideology prevented the social agents from undergoing what later came to be called the process of conscientization or "critical consciousness" that enabled them to identify authoritative regimes or oppressive systems.[5] It became a question of pedagogy, not in the sense of formal schooling, but of education nonetheless. Workers needed to become critics of their situation, they needed to become aware that what appeared to be natural, universal, and justified was in fact oppressive, exploitative, and alienating. This required a process of becoming subjects and so subjectification became the task of critical philosophy. It was not enough to simply theorize the subject, but rather philosophy had to

---

4. For the decisive account of this history, see Jay, *Dialectical Imagination*.
5. Freire, *Pedagogy of the Oppressed*, 48–86.

work to bring about the conditions for its possibility and in order to do this, it had to reconfigure itself as a critical, and as such negative, project.

The advent of political and liberation theologies (particularly those coming from colonialized and subaltern contexts) in late modernity, many of whom were shaped, at least in part by the intellectual tradition of European left and Western Marxism, brought the political question of the subject to the center of religion as well, particularly as a result of the turn to the post-secular.[6] There is a strong trend among theorists on the political-theological left to identify the unique forces within political theology that galvanize political subjects toward liberative and revolutionary forms of active resistance. This is not unique to the late modern turn (back) to religion within contemporary philosophy and was prefigured in large part by the first generation of critical theorists (to whom the predominance of the subject can be traced), a point which has been decisively made by Mendieta[7] and Brittain[8] and Boer,[9] among others. Adorno and Horkheimer's discussion of subjectivity and religion explores religion as an immanently negative force that can be particularly helpful in critiquing the alienating and dominative effects of reality that generates "damaged human life."[10] Religion is helpful, not because of its metaphysical truth, but because of the critical force of its hope and its ability to identify what is wrong with the present. The uncompromising nature of its eschatological vision of justice, when marshaled toward negative political objectives, can act as glimpses of light, rupturing the social order as it is, reminding subjects that what is need not always be.

As political and constructive theologians whose work is Kierkegaardian in spirit if not in method, we are interested in subjectivity because it is, after all, subjects that compose the sociopolitical body from which all theological belief and expression come. All hope in creating an alternative society, an altogether different future, lies in activating and generating forms of life that speak to and bring back to life the kind of subjectivity capable of resisting on the one hand, and creating on the other. As

---

6. The vast literature on this so-called "post-secular" turn is too complicated to list and organize appropriately here. The most central texts for this conversation are Taylor, *Secular Age*; Habermas, "Religion in the Public Sphere," 114–48, Asad, *Formation of the Secular*, and Mahmood, *Religious Difference in a Post-Secular Age*.

7. Mendieta, introduction to *Frankfurt School on Religion*, 8–16.

8. Brittain, *Adorno and Theology*.

9. Boer, *Criticism of Religion*.

10. Adorno, *Minima Moralia*, 30; Also, see Adorno, *Problems in Moral Philosophy*, 158. The facticity of "damaged human life" limits human ability and capacity to discern the good life, to figure out how best to act in a social world that is thoroughly permuted by the reifying effects of capitalist economy on social and political systems. This is discerned in Adorno's thesis that "wronged life cannot be lived rightly" and it is related to the oft-repeated idea that "there is no good life in false life" or, put differently, "there is no way of living a false life correctly." In a false world, there is no way of doing (or even recognizing or knowing) the morally or politically right thing; it also means that there is no real *living* in a false life. There is only survival and persistence; this is inhumane in that it does violence to the natural freedom and happiness of the human being.

Hardt and Negri point out, this will not come naturally, as an inevitable consequence of reason and/or history, but rather through struggle and failure, insofar as the instability and anarchy of the multitude conspires toward a common social organization unknown to the globalized world of imperial force.

What does Kierkegaard—and more specifically, his theory of the "single individual"—have to contribute to political theology's interest in subjectivity, particularly when subjectivity is understood as a decisively collective and resistant force of creativity and destruction? At first glance, Kierkegaard would seem to offer little more than the foil against this kind of theory, as an existential celebrant of singularity and withdrawal. We think this not only represents a misunderstanding of Kierkegaard and the politics of the single individual, but also of critical subjectivity. To make this case, we turn first to one of the most cited texts in the conversation about politics and subjectivity within political theology today: Michael Hardt and Antonio Negri's *Empire* and their subsequent *Multitude*, wherein they explore their theory of multitude and its importance for anti-imperial political theology today.

Hardt and Negri and the Multitudinal Force

The "multitude" is a central concept in Hardt and Negri's political philosophy, specifically in their theory about the nature of the post-imperialist force of sovereignty amid globalization. In their early work, *Empire*, the world, they argue, is no longer organized around traditional forms of power associated with the nation-state or late advanced capitalist economies. The current political situation can be explained as a crisis of labor and production, whereby a world is no longer being made by subjects, but rather subjects are being made by a world that is itself an excessive surplus of creativity borne of exploitation and alienation. Channeling Foucault, productivity and labor are themselves generated by the disciplinary regimes. These forms of life do not come about by virtue of humanity's natural creativity, but rather are energized by the constitutive ground of Empire: sovereignty.

Who is/are the multitude? Hardt and Negri turn to the "multitude" as the global human collection of actors and energies, forces, and acts that make up the collective resistance to Empire, conditioned by it and yet immanently negative; in short, the multitude is Hardt and Negri's account of political subjects as unbound from sovereignty, and yet emerging from within the conflicting and agnostic forces of empire. It is natural, then, to think of the multitude as a collective, a diasporic gathering of political subjects united in their joint opposition to globalized empire. The intellectual left is littered with appeals to the collectives or coalitions necessary for large-scale, structural, and materialist change, particularly in relation to anti-capitalist struggle. These usually take the form of identity politics (the politics of grievance), working-class struggle (proletarian resistance against bourgeois ideology), the Party (economic interests of working classes linked to state mechanisms), the masses (the *lumpenproletariat* that Marx and Trotsky dismissed and Bakunin and Fanon revered), or "the People." Hardt and Negri's multitude concept is developed in direct contradistinction to these ideas about social subjectivity.

Hardt and Negri argue that the multitude is distinct from "the people," which has always been a "unitary concept," whereby the diversity within "the people" gets reduced to a central unity, a single identity.[11] The problem with "the masses" is that of passivity and indifference, "the essence of the masses is indifference; all differences are submerged and drowned in the masses. All the colours of the people fade to grey."[12] The crowd, or masses "cannot act of their own accord." "These social subjects are fundamentally passive in the sense that they cannot act by themselves but rather must be led."[13] Finally, the multitude is not reduced to simply the working class either, which has too often become an exclusive concept reserved for industrial workers, and so often leaves out those for whom employment and wage status is complicated: migrants, seasonal workers, unpaid domestic laborers, and those who do not receive a wage for labor. This exclusion makes less sense in a globalized economy whereby much of labor within capital is done by the alienating obfuscations of finance.

Finally, the multitude is not the crowd, "the they." This is because of the way Hardt and Negri understand difference: "The different individuals or groups that make up the crowd are incoherent and recognise no common shared elements, their collection of differences remains inert and can easily appear as one indifferent aggregate."[14] The multitude, by contrast, is a political organization whereby "the internal differences of the multitude discover the common that allows them to communicate and act together." One must not choose between multitudinality and singularity, for it is only in multitude that the assemblage of singularity becomes more than a "unified plurality." The multitude is composed in such a way that the difference is enunciated rather than disavowed or sidelined in favor of commonality or generalized interests. Hardt and Negri put it this way: "A multitude is an irreducible multiplicity: the singular social differences that constitute the multitude must always be expressed and can never be flattened into sameness, unity, identity, or indifference."[15]

But the question that most interests Hardt and Negri is not "what is the multitude?" but rather "what can the multitude become?"[16] Their use of the multitude comes out of Hardt and Negri's theoretical distinction between imperialism and the current postmodern Empire, which has "no territorial center of power and does not rely on fixed boundaries and barriers." Rather than sustaining itself through traditional means (military force, policing of borders, economic manipulation, coalitions

---

11. Hardt and Negri, *Multitude*, xiv.
12. Ibid.
13. Ibid., 100.
14. Ibid., 108.
15. Ibid., 105.
16. Ibid.

of power, deal-making), the Empire amid globalization is far more "biopolitical." Borrowing from Foucault the idea that power of the state functions in such a way that it takes control over the body of human being, not just its social agency, Hardt and Negri position "sovereignty" not as a function of the modern nation-state, but as a diffuse mechanism aimed at extending state power through techniques of state discipline that are internalized by, rather that imposed upon, the subject. The subject does not experience these techniques or mechanisms as obligatory or coerced by the forces of empire. This is because they have become the stuff of life, the very structures through which human persons experience themselves as living. Foucault describes biopolitics this way: "the set of mechanisms through which the basic biological features of the human species became the object of a political strategy, of a general strategy of power."[17] This is how postmodern Empire functions, making it very difficult to oppose. It is not always easy to identify the biopolitical forces of empire which are vital to human existence: sex, security, organic food, rights, discipline, good schools, liberty, family, privacy, law, beauty—they all seem to be the same, that is how the empire works.

Hardt and Negri focus so much on the multitude in their analysis because of its potential as a new political subject that benefits from their status as producers; they are the ones involved in social production, the material contributions to social life and attachment, and so are not only victims but powerful agents. In a section titled "The Wealth of the Poors," Hardt and Negri addressed their productivity of their labor in this way:

> It has never been true, of course, that the poor and the unemployed do nothing. The strategies of survival themselves often require extraordinary resourcefulness and creativity. Today, however, to the extent that social production is increasingly defined by immaterial labor such as cooperation or the construction of social relationships and networks of communication, the activity of all in society including the poor becomes more and more directly productive.[18]

In defense of their position that, "in many respects, the poor are actually extraordinarily wealthy and productive," Hardt and Negri argue that the global poor, who are often members of indigenous populations often live in areas of the world with the most biodiversity and so "they know how to live with these plants and animal species, keeping them alive and profiting from their beneficial qualities." They also argue that the migrant poor are "full of knowledges, languages, skills and creative capacities: each migrant brings with him or her an entire world."[19] These experiences energize "their desire for something more, their refusal to accept the ways things are."[20] But Hardt

---

17. Foucault, *Security, Territory, Population*, 1.
18. Hardt and Negri, *Multitude*, 131.
19. Ibid., 133.
20. For those who might object to Hardt and Negri on the grounds that they romanticize poverty,

and Negri are steadfast in their position that as the multitude, "their poverty and their lack of material resources, food, housing, and so forth, the poor do have enormous wealth in their knowledges and powers of creation."[21] They make this point in order to underscore, that "the creativity and inventiveness of the poor, the unemployed, the partially employed, and the migrants are essential to social production," and that "the struggles of the poor against their conditions of poverty are not only powerful protests but also affirmation of biopolitical power—the revelation of a common "being" that is more powerful than their miserable "having, or rather, "not-having."[22]

This common "being" is central to the singularity of the multitude and is the source of their dissident power. Their membership is collective while also singular; they span cultural and social identities, class formations, and economic sectors. They are the "diverse figures of social production"; Hardt and Negri find in their agency potential for subversion and resistance against Empire. One key characteristic of multitudinal existence is how they organize and order themselves through the "creation of new circuits of cooperation and collaboration that stretch across nations and continents and allow an unlimited number of encounters"[23] (communication as what binds singularity and commonality together). In this way, the multitude is a "network," not the people, or an identity, and as such is organized as a relational pattern of communication that constructs a common language that does not reduce singularities but rather communicates them in ways that establish solidarity on the basis of difference.[24] This is the making of multitude.

Formally speaking, we can reconstruct Hardt and Negri's account of the multitude as a political form of existence in the following way: first, the multitude is organized around commonality that does not suppress or otherwise supersede singularity. Within the multitude, there are "innumerable internal differences that can never be reduced to a unity or single identity." "The multitude is a multiplicity of all these singular differences." Second, the point here is that the multitude is a way of political organization "that displaces authority in collaborative relationships" and instead positions itself as a "common labouring substance"[25] "whose difference cannot be reduced to sameness, a difference that remains different."[26] The multitude is not just a discreet set of people, of agents (although it certainly is or can be); it is a strategy of living within empire that mobilizes the excesses, the remainders, and the underside of biopolitical

---

they clarify their position this way: "We do not mean to suggest that the poor or migrants are better off . . . we will present grievances against the enormous and growing forms of poverty and inequality in the global system. These should be combatted in every way possible." Ibid., 134.

21. Ibid.
22. Ibid., 135.
23. Ibid., xiii.
24. Ibid., 57.
25. Ibid., 125.
26. Ibid., 99.

power. Third, multitudinal existence is a position of resistance and opposition. It is a fundamentally antagonist relation that is also productive and is all about positioning human persons in a fecund relationship to being—to becoming.

This multitudinal form of life is not a brand new invention. We find an early-modern expression of it in Kierkegaard's political theology. Some readers will be surprised by this, given that he is often known as an existentialist and is often incorrectly taken to be a proponent of a radical subjectivism or a solipsistic individualism. We argue that it is precisely in his view of the single individual that a productive connection can be made to this "multitudinal existence" as articulated by Hardt and Negri. Not only this, but we argue the theological character of the multitude—the ways in which religion and politics are strewn together throughout Hardt and Negri's account of political subjectivity in the conditions of Empire—is made most clear by examining Kierkegaard's single individual as a theoretical riff on multitudinality.

Kierkegaard and the "Single Individual"

> *The single individual* is the category of spirit, of spiritual awakening, as diametrically opposite to politics as possible.
>
> —Søren Kierkegaard[27]

Kierkegaard's fixation on the "single individual" runs throughout his corpus, as he acknowledges in *Point of View*. In that self-reflective work, he offers two categories for the single individual: (1) the single individual as the remarkable person (defined aesthetically or ethically) and (2) the single individual as the category through which we ought to understand *every person*—and as the way every person ought to understand himself or herself. It is this latter category that most interests Kierkegaard—and us, too.

The pervasiveness and emphasis of the single individual in Kierkegaard has been often noted by scholars, many of whom have found in this concept the source of the flaw of Kierkegaard's excessive individualism and seeming lack of concern for sociality or even recognition of the ways that sociality forms persons and shapes their identities. One energetic modern critic of Kierkegaard, Walter Kaufmann, derided him for his "central category of the individual—as a category that cracks all other categories."[28] For Kaufmann, Kierkegaard was a rampant individualist as well as an extreme authoritarian. He assessed Kierkegaard's concept of inwardness as self-centered preoccupation: "Most religious people are less preoccupied with themselves and their own relationship to themselves; and we may therefore say in the first place that Kierkegaard's religiosity is unusually self-centered."[29] Kaufmann goes so far as to say

---

27. Kierkegaard, *Point of View*, 121.
28. Kaufmann, *From Shakespeare to Existentialism*, 199–200.
29. Ibid., 183.

that Kierkegaard's narcissistic religiosity and his individualistic preoccupations were his "most central faults."[30] Kaufmann's diatribe against Kierkegaard exemplifies in a most visceral way the suspicion that many have held against him: can an individualist-minded theologian really offer something substantive to the problems of political and social life? As Kaufmann starkly puts it, Kierkegaard "is so concerned with his own plight that he is willing to forget that of others."[31] If Kaufmann's Kierkegaard has a political theology, is it not the wrong kind?

This is the "asocial Kierkegaard" that we mentioned earlier; this Kierkegaard would indeed have nothing much to contribute constructively to political theology. If the asocial Kierkegaard were the "real Kierkegaard," then the epigraph above could be taken very much at face value: The category of the "single individual" is "as diametrically opposite to politics as possible."[32]

But to rest content with that interpretation would be to the detriment of a richer, more adequate reading of the single individual and its role in Kierkegaard's thought; it would also miss the central contribution of Kierkegaard to political theologies of the emancipatory subject. In this vein, numerous Kierkegaard scholars have shown that Kierkegaard's thought, even his focus on the single individual, is profoundly more social, more directly political, than even Kierkegaard himself might have acknowledged. The single individual does not lead into an asocial existence or a conservative authoritarianism; rather, the single individual served to counter what Kierkegaard took to be a great flaw of nineteenth-century Denmark: the leveling of distinctive subjectivities through the emergence of the "crowd," or the "public." This leveling was the situation of the passionless, nominalistic, materialistic (consumerist) Christendom against which Kierkegaard wielded his critique of the crowd or the public, via emphasis on the single individual. We argue that it is precisely by drawing attention to the ethico-religious responsibility of the single individual, that social change can be actually effected. Contrary to Kaufmann's reading, Kierkegaard's individual did not reflect a preoccupation with self at the expense of others; rather, by promoting the single individual Kierkegaard sought to challenge the passivity and triumphalism of unjust social and religious structures.

Kierkegaard's "crowd," or "public" (they are synonyms), expresses basically the same idea as Hart and Negri's "the people," or "the masses." For Hardt and Negri, the Empire is largely succeeding, via the seemingly incontrovertible forces of global economics, capitalist consumerism, and expansive technologies, in creating a monochrome, homogenous abstraction to which the throngs of "the people" adhere without difficulty and without noticing. Similarly, the "public" in Kierkegaard's analysis is a "monstrous abstraction,"[33] which has been formed by cultural forces and enabled by

30. Ibid.
31. Ibid., 193.
32. Kierkegaard, *Point of View*, 121.
33. Kierkegaard, *Two Ages*, 90.

"leveling," the sanding down of distinct edges of individual subjectivity. This process is assisted, Kierkegaard emphasizes, with the help of the media (the "press"). The abstraction that is the public becomes the identity-shaper by which the individuals unwittingly define themselves. As a result of being subsumed into the public, individuals lose their will and their power to be and act as responsible selves. The public is not a concrete entity, not a group or collective or coalition, but is something that cannot issue forth in any action and that does not bear responsibility for anything or anyone:

> Contemporaneity with actual persons, each of whom is someone, in the actuality of the moment and the actual situation gives support to the single individual. But the existence of a public creates no situation and no community.[34]

The public "annihilates all the relative concretions of individuality," whereas the single individual in his relationship with God is able to "make up his own mind instead of agreeing with the public."[35] So, for Kierkegaard, the malaise endemic to (nineteenth-century Danish) society is diagnosed in the leveling process undertaken by the public (Hardt and Negri's "the people," as created and conditioned by Empire). The solution to the problem, then, is to be found in a rigorously religious orientation of the self. The sphere of religion, for Kierkegaard, as the culmination of the self's becoming—the apex of subjectivity—offers the antidote to the leveling powers of the public. Only by defining oneself in relation to the eternal, to God, can the individual person regain the possibility and the will to stand apart from the crowd, from the public.

Kierkegaard's singularity was therefore a forceful antidote to the economic, cultural, technological, political, and institutionally religious forces that lowered the bar of responsibility and diluted passion by squeezing all the energy out of what it means to be a human being. The category of Kierkegaard's singularity was filled out via the priority of the religious in Kierkegaard's anthropology: to be an individual in the responsible sense required that a person pursue the task of becoming subjective, a subjective self, which necessitated that God is the criterion for the self's becoming. Through the turn to inwardness that subjectivity involves, the person becomes more than a vacuous, superficial person who is unequipped to live courageously in the world. Through the deepening of subjectivity and inwardness, a person acquires the restlessness of faith that leads to active works of love.

In the *Point of View*, Kierkegaard writes, "*The single individual* is the category through which, in a religious sense, the age, history, the human race must go."[36] The single individual, for Kierkegaard, is a person who has inwardly appropriated the *essentially Christian*, and has thereby shifted from a merely aesthetic or ethical orientation into the deeper life defined by the religious sphere So to be a single individual is

---

34. Ibid., 91.
35. Ibid., 92.
36. Kierkegaard, *Point of View*, 118.

to be an ethically and religiously responsible self: one for whom God and Christ—and the life called for by the New Testament—are the determining factors of one's existence. Conversely, though, to be religious one must be a single individual: as he notes, the "first condition of all religiousness" is "to be an individual human being."[37]

In *Two Ages*, Kierkegaard suggests that an "optimal and normative" situation is "when individuals (each one individually) are essentially and passionately related to an idea and together are essentially related to the same idea." So, while they share the same conviction, religious doctrine, or ideology, they are also distinguished from each other at the same time by "essential inwardness." This inwardness, which is to say a deep religious orientation of each self before God as their ultimate criterion for subjectivity, is what, for Kierkegaard, keeps the individuals distinct and yet sharing their "unanimity to the idea." They are united and yet as individuals they "never come too close to each other in the herd sense." The "herd sense" is yet another expression for the "crowd," or the "public." Individuals, *as single individuals*, can share in the same idea and be unified without collapsing distinctions and being subsumed by the abstract public. For Kierkegaard, what is required is inwardness, or the religious orientation of the self as a responsible self before God and the world. He goes on to say that

> the unanimity of separation is indeed fully orchestrated music. On the other hand, if individuals relate to an idea merely *en masse* (consequently without the individual separation of inwardness), we get violence, anarchy, riotousness, but if there is no idea for the individuals *en masse* and no individually separating essential inwardness, either, then we have crudeness. The harmony of the spheres is the unity of each planet relating to itself and to the whole. Take away the relations, and there will be chaos.[38]

Kierkegaard's single individual is not a solitary loner who is unconcerned with sociality. Rather, he or she is someone who is related to others through agreement or disagreement. Indeed, single individuals might even collectively be unified in agreement with an idea—while still retaining *inward* distinctiveness and the particularly of subjectivity.

This point underscores why Kierkegaard's theory of the single individual, far from being *apolitical*, is actually profoundly constructive for a political theology concerned with the question of political subjectivity. Put differently: contrary to conventional readings of Kierkegaard which contend that his personalistic existentialism troubles any attempts to think of his theology as political, he specifically theorizes existence as a relational dynamism that cannot be overcome by the self; the very excess of the self is that the self-relation is never restricted or contained by the self's inwardness, but also constitutively grounded by that which transcends or even transgresses the self, which is precisely what makes the self so unreliable, so treacherous as a site for truth,

---

37. Ibid., 116–17.
38. Kierkegaard, *Two Ages*, 62–63.

for universality—even for ethics. And so, the religious self is precisely that modality of existence whereby the self recognizes that it must recognize itself as that which is always already "before God"; this cannot be thought of as a leap into metaphysical transcendence, for the "absolute relation to the absolute" is indeed an immanent relation to that which is always the self, but always infinitely other than self. This paradox is precisely the incarnational dynamic that is irrationally confounding and as such, absurd. In this way, the singular individuality of the self is always a multitudinal relation to the other that extends beyond the coordinates of reason or history.

As such, "single individual" presents a significant contribution to questions concerning the role of religion in the formation of revolutionary political subjects, particularly when read in conjunction with Hardt and Negri's understanding of the multitude (as we have done here). Religion is a resource for taking on the pervasive forces of empire today precisely because it introduces a post-imperial way of "thinking otherwise," a point that Hardt and Negri circle around, but never really comment on in an extended way. Not just any kind of religion will do (i.e., institutional religions); it is rather "the religious," as in the orientation of the self as a *self before God*, as an individual who stands before the eternal and recognizes his or her responsibilities and possibilities, as well as the empowerment to turn critically and prophetically against "the crowd": Heidegger's "they," Kierkegaard's "the public," or Hardt and Negri's "the people" of empire.

Admittedly, it is a thin reading to merely suggest that Hardt and Negri's "multitude" (or Kierkegaard's "single individual" for that matter) is marked primarily by its critical and negative posture toward the crowd, the Empire's public. Indeed, our argument here has been that it is wrong to think of Kierkegaard's single individual as adding to the perception of Kierkegaard as having little interest in the political, precisely because it becomes necessary in our view to interpret the "single individual" as a "multitudinal perspective." This means that singularity and multitude are separated by only a "parallax" gap, that position of minimal difference that allows the object of consideration—in this case, the conditions of possibility for the revolutionary political subject—to be indirectly apprehended only by way of a triangulation based on the incommensurability of the positions and the unrepresentable character of the object. By naming—and so thinking and rethinking—political subjectivity in and as this fundamental parallax gap, we are able to perpetuate fundamental tensions and incommensurabilities within our social order, rather than tempering or sublimating them. We have made it clear that the multitude is the subjectivity most capable of thinking and acting from a parallax position, but how about Kierkegaard's "single individual"?

PART 3: KIERKEGAARD AND THE POLITICS OF PHILOSOPHY

A Political Theology of the Neighbor: The Single Individual in Multitudinal Perspective

Kierkegaard's "single individual" speaks of a responsible and responsive agent but cannot be reduced to a discrete person that envisions herself as a *self* apart from others, and as such, can only became that single individual when withdrawn from social relationships and political obligations. Quite the contrary: Kierkegaard suggested that his *Works of Love* was his effort to apply the concept of subjectivity and the single individual to the social sphere.[39] Many critics of Kierkegaard's perceived isolationism and self-centeredness have not attended to *Works of Love* sufficiently or have avoided it altogether. In this work, Kierkegaard articulates a theology of subjectivity as underlined by the duty to love the neighbor as oneself. The centrality of duty toward one's neighbor, not the beloved whom one prefers to love, but the anonymous, little-known, or unloved person whom one *must nonetheless love anyway*, because God commands it, shows that Kierkegaard's political theology has little interest in celebrating the solitary, apolitical individual. He is in fact eager to dispense with it as a symbolic expression of poetic, aesthetic, and preferential love and supplant it with the dutiful, non-preferential, and offensive character of Christian love.

The single individual is thus a political self—not in the strict sense of "politics" as reductively about government, statecraft, or the professional political vocation (what Kierkegaard probably had in view with his aforementioned quip that the single individual is "diametrically opposed to politics").[40] Rather, Kierkegaard's single individual is political in that it is not so much about the individuality or the singularity, but rather about the relation of the subject to God, self, and the world. The individual is a responsible and responding self—with selfhood being defined in relation to others. Single individuals, gathered together around a shared idea or goal and related to a community of others, and motivated by the demands of the eternal as criteria, represent the attainment of a political subjectivity that cannot be but social, and is generated at least in part by what Kierkegaard refers to repeatedly as "being before God," a theological turn of phrase that is not without its own irritating little ironies.

---

39. In a 1847 journal entry, Kierkegaard had this to say about his plan to publish a book with explicitly social application, called *Works of Love*: "Despite everything people ought to have learned about my maieutic carefulness, by proceeding slowly and continually letting it seem as if I knew nothing more, not the next thing—now on the occasion of my new upbuilding discourses they will probably bawl out that I do not know what comes next, that I know nothing about sociality.... Now I have the theme of the next book. It will be called: *Works of Love*." Kierkegaard, *Journals and Papers*, 5:5972 (VIII A 4 5–4 6).

40. Stephen Backhouse draws a distinction between a "strong" and a "weak" meaning of political, the former having to do with "party politics, democratic movements and the machinations of government," and the latter having to do more broadly with "inter-human relationships and organizations." Kierkegaard, in his view, has the strong meaning in mind when he refers to politics. Backhouse, *Kierkegaard's Critique of Christian Nationalism*, 177.

With God, or one's responsibility to eternity, as the "middle term," one relates to the other—to the neighbor—as if one were relating to oneself or to the beloved. There is no room here for self-centered, narcissistic piety; rather, the subjectivity demanded by *Works of Love* is outward (if empowered inwardly), concrete, social, and political. For Kierkegaard, the love of neighbor is empowered by and motivated by the divine command—this cannot be denied. This is also what makes Kierkegaard's political subjectivity *theo*-logical but is also what links singularity with the multitudinal subjectivity of Hardt and Negri: the energetic force of immanent difference that functions in and through singular subjects rather than originating with them. The anti-imperial force of the multitude originates in their "innumerable internal differences" and it is for this reason that it is opposed to both identity politics (i.e., a politics of difference [Iris Marion Young] or recognition [Charles Taylor])[41] and nationalism. This is very important in our global political climate in which tribal populism—whether it be in the form of Brexit, the Dutch *Partij voor de Vrijheid* (PVV, "Party for Freedom"), the Flemish *Interest* (VB, Vlaams Belang)[42] on the far right or homo-nationalism and grievance politics on the left—over determine our political options on an international scale.

In this we agree with Stephen Backhouse, who argues that Kierkegaard's concept of the neighbor constitutes a basis for a political theology that subverts the ideology and idolatry of nationalism:

> Kierkegaard's neighbour is the kind of person who lives in the multivalent, ever-shifting world envisioned by the loosened, established order. . . . Paradoxically the neighbour is a way to articulate undefined "others" insofar as Kierkegaard's "neighbour" is a cipher for "the individual": the "I" who is not oneself. Thus one discusses persons in a way that preserves individuality and avoids collapsing groups of individuals into a gormless herd. As individuals, neighbours are real (not abstract) but their reality includes the fact that their personhood cannot be defined solely by recourse to an exhaustive inventory of cultural influences. They are in this this sense objectively indefinable precisely because they are complex subjects—not simplified units defined primarily by their membership to certain groups such as nations. *Works of Love* demonstrates clearly how neighbour talk can subvert and supplant nation talk.[43]

Our argument builds on Backhouse here in that while he argues that Kierkegaard sets forth a critique of nationalism, we add that his theory of the single individual—insofar as it is read as a political theology—displays a multitudinal character that, when modulated by Hardt and Negri, generates an explicitly post-imperial (rather than simply

---

41. Taylor, "Politics of Recognition," 25–74.
42. Wit, "Politics without Dénouement," 130–32.
43. Backhouse, *Kierkegaard's Critique of Christian Nationalism*, 208. For Backhouse, "the neighbour of *WL* stands as an ethically and socially viable alternative to the person primarily defined as the 'co-national.'"

anti-nationalist) position that helps political theology continue to think through how best to contribute to the formation of emancipatory subjects in the post-secular age.

Conclusion

Our goal in this chapter has been not simply to contend against the asocial interpretation of Kierkegaard's "single individual" that appears to render him unimportant (or worst, not interesting) for the political-theological interest in subjectivity. As we stated earlier, political theology is concerned with the subject primarily due to its early reception of critical theory which, as a form of social philosophy, took its cue from the historical failure of Western Marxism to generate the kind of consciousness required to enact systemic levels of social and political change necessary to free human beings from oppressive and dominative conditions, conditions that not only restrain human creativity, but also their freedom.

It was the freedom of the single individual that motivated Kierkegaard's theory of subjectivity; the freedom to appropriate, to query, to choose, indeed, even to act, without the constrains of a particular form of rationality, of history, of cultured churches, or of the nation-state. Of course, the forces that oppress and dominate human beings only get more sophisticated with time and capital, and as the nineteenth century gave way to the twentieth and into the twenty-first, the challenge facing human freedom was less overtly political and dissipated into the ephemeral symbolics of Empire. Hardt and Negri imagined, in this context, what kind of subject would be necessary to build a post-imperial social world from these forces, and the "multitude" emerged. We have argued that these are not two strains of political thought in the continental tradition—existentialism and Marxist—but rather that they both offer a distinctive contribution to the way political theology is currently working through the subject of subjectivity in the post-secular age: they offer a dialectical way of thinking self and other, multitude and singularity, universality and particularity together in ways that preserve the political energy of resistance produced by conflict and difference, rather than sublimating it in favor of the "common good" or generalized interests.

But this is a book about Kierkegaard and political theology. We have argued that Kierkegaard's single individual is a political theology that is grounded in a deep intersubjectivity that affirms both the importance of the individual as distinctive person, but also as a self in constitutive relation to other selves and to alterity as such. Because the single individual is not defined exclusively by association with a group or collective (such as a nation or an institutional religion), and because the single individual is not defined exclusively by association to an idea (such as a political, economic, or religious ideology), the single individual *as individual self before God* retains the capacity to move in and out of such boundaries and to level criticisms, prophetic analyses, and creative solutions, even while remaining linked within such associations. The single individual is multitudinal in that it is both grounded and fluid, responsible and responsive, socially related and yet distinct in personhood, recognizing both the reality of boundaries and their permeability. And the single individual is both individual and the *multitude*, just as the multitude is both personalist and plural.

Bibliography

Adorno, Theodor. *Minima Moralia*. Translated by Edmund Jephcott. London: Verso, 1978.

———. *Problems in Moral Philosophy*. Edited by Thomas Schröder. Stanford: Stanford University Press, 2000.

Asad, Tala. *Formation of the Secular: Christianity, Islam, Modernity*. Stanford: Stanford University Press, 2003.

Backhouse, Stephen. *Kierkegaard's Critique of Christian Nationalism*. Oxford: Oxford University Press, 2011.

Boer, Roland. *Criticism of Religion: On Marxism and Theology, II*. Leiden: Brill, 2009.

Brittain, Christopher Craig. *Adorno and Theology*. London: T. & T. Clark, 2010.

De Wit, Theo. "Politics without Dénouement, Faith without Guarantee: A Critical Appraisal of the Politics of Religion of the Left and the Right." In *From Political Theory to Political Theology: Religious Challenges and the Prospects of Democracy*, edited by Aakash Singh and Péter Losonczi, 122–38. London: Continuum, 2010.

Foucault, Michel. *Security, Territory, Population: Lectures at the College de France, 1977–1978*. Edited by Michel Senellart. New York: Palgrave MacMillian, 2004.

Freire, Paulo. *Pedagogy of the Oppressed*. New York: Continuum, 1970.

Habermas, Jürgen. *Between Nationalism and Religion*. Cambridge: Polity, 2008.

Hardt, Michael, and Antoni Negri. *Empire*. Cambridge: Harvard University Press, 2000.

———. *Multitude: War and Democracy in the Age of Empire*. New York: Penguin, 2004.

Jay, Martin. *The Dialectical Imagination: A History of the Frankfurt School and the Institute of Social Research, 1923–1950*. Berkeley: University of California Press, 1996.

Kaufmann, Walter. *From Shakespeare to Existentialism: An Original Study*. Princeton: Princeton University Press, 1980.

Kierkegaard, Søren. *Journals and Papers*. Vol. 5. Translated by Howard V. Hong and Edna H. Hong. Bloomington: Indiana University Press, 1978.

———. *Point of View*. Edited and translated by Howard V. Hong and Edna H. Hong. Princeton: Princeton University Press, 2009.

———. *Two Ages*. Edited and translated by Howard V. Hong and Edna H. Hong. Princeton: Princeton University Press, 1978.

Mahmood, Saba. *Religious Difference in a Post-Secular Age: A Minority Report*. Princeton: Princeton University Press, 2015.

Mendieta, Eduardo. Introduction to *The Frankfurt School on Religion: Key Writings by the Major Thinkers*, edited by Eduardo Mendieta, 8–16. New York: Routledge, 2005.

Rieger, Joerg, and Kwok Pui-lan. *Occupy Religion: Theology of the Multitude*. Lanham, MD: Rowman & Littlefield, 2012.

Taylor, Charles. "The Politics of Recognition." In *Multiculturalism: Examining the Politics of Recognition*, edited by Amy Gutmann, 25–74. Princeton: Princeton University Press, 1994.

———. *The Secular Age*. Cambridge: Belknap, of Harvard University Press, 2007.

Young, Iris Marion. *Justice and the Politics of Difference*. Princeton: Princeton University Press, 1990.

12

Tagore and Kierkegaard as Resources for Political Theology

Abraham H. Khan

To pair Rabindranath Tagore (1861–1941) and Søren Kierkegaard (1813–1855) as philosophico-religious thinkers for a conversation on political theology may seem conceptually awkward, at first glance. They are worlds apart on faith tradition, *weltanschauung*, historical sociocultural period, and literary intention. Tagore gained international prominence during his lifetime, and the other, only after his death. Further, one emphasized the community and spoke on behalf of all humanity, while the other took to addressing and emphasizing the single individual. Adding to the seeming asymmetry is whether they have anything relevant to say about a postmodern phenomenon occasioned by a crisis of modern liberal capitalism.

Rabindranath Tagore produced his intellectually mature prose writings mainly in the first few decades of the twentieth century, within a cultural-intellectual revitalizing phase identified as the Bengali Renaissance movement[1] in Indian history. More than a writer, he is a Bengali poet, artist, music-song composer, educator, and social reformer in colonial India. At his best, he is a bard. In 1913, he was awarded the Nobel Prize in Literature for *Gitanjali*, a collection of his poems or song offerings he rendered into English from Bengali. Introducing the collection to Western readers, William Butler Yates described it as "the product of a whole people, a whole civilization immeasurably strange to us."[2] Time and again, Tagore would take as guide in his thinking insights from the *Upanishads*,[3] texts containing core philosophical doctrines

---

1. Denoting a group of nineteenth-century intellectuals in the state of Bengal, the movement is analogous to the Enlightenment in European history, tackling the proliferation of Western ideas under British rule and the impact it was making on the mind-set of Indians with a culture, history, philosophical outlook, and reform strategies of their own for modernizing India. Rationalism tempering free thinking, critical inquiry, atheism, and scientific advancements are some of the hallmarks of that phase.

2. Tagore, *Gitanjali*, xxv.

3. Thirteen principal ones, from among two hundred, are considered to be composed around 500–200 BCE. The texts contain insights of the *rishis* or seers, followed by explanations in the form

or truths about ultimately real and human nature. He was bought up in a culturally rich home that would quote from the Upanishadic collection. Later, his thoughts and criticisms would be of political significance to his intellectual contemporaries—those shaping India into a modern nation or constitutionally secular state with a democratic heritage completely different from that of the West.[4]

In contrast, Kierkegaard is a thinker and religious author of a small Christian kingdom, Denmark, during the middle of the nineteenth century. The period, marked by economic prosperity and romantic nationalism, is considered the last phase of the Danish Golden Age. His literary productions are also at a time of growing political agitations that resulted in a transition from a feudal to a capitalist society in 1849. Politically, the change meant that inhabitants ceased to be subjects of the king to whom the Danish Church belonged. The transition inadvertently left the church without a legal status that later raised for the newly formed parliament questions about its place and significance in the state.[5] Status aside, Kierkegaard argued that the establishment church in the kingdom was preaching a watered-down version of Christianity compared to New Testament teachings. By his observation, many people were living in categories foreign to New Testament teachings but were of the view that belonging to a Christian kingdom was enough to certify them as Christians.[6] That together with the prevailing cultural Christianity forged in the crucible of romanticism and Hegelian philosophy created a frightful illusion, in Kierkegaard's view. He took upon himself the task of offering a corrective, showing what it means to become a Christian. But first the illusion had to be dispelled and his countrymen had to be awakened to the spiritual crisis. This was part of the task he took upon himself, directing his literary talents as an author to be an unsettling and disquieting voice of true, biblical Christianity.

Tagore, on one hand, belonged to a progressive Brahmo sect[7] of neo-Hinduism. Its core teachings include belief in an infinite spirit that is creator and preserver and

---

of a dialogue between guru and student, or of an interactive public argument. Later, a scholar who did his pre-university education at Tagore's school in Shantineketan would note that India has its own tradition of dialogic discussion and argumentation that are that are integral to secularism, public discussion, and democracy. See Sen, *Argumentative Indian*, xi, 12–23, 304–32.

4. Gandhi and Nerhu are among shapers of modern Indian for whom Tagore is political significant. The 42nd amendment to India's constitution in 1976 committed India's future to a secularism understood as being impartial to all religions, a non-alignment with any established religion. That, along with its tradition of freedom and self-determination rooted in Upanishadic thought, instead of the Magna Carta, or the tradition shaped by thinkers such as Hobbes Grotius, Locke, Rousseau, and Tocquville, for example, distinguish its democratic heritage.

5. For more details on church and state, see Kirmmse, *Kierkegaard*, 73–76.

6. Kierkegaard, *Point of View*, 41–54.

7. Known as Adi Dharma or Brahmo, it was founded in 1848 by Rabindranath's father. It considers Hinduism to be corrupt beliefs, and differs by affirming one Supreme Spirit, no salvation (soul is immortal), no revelation or Scripture and no priest or sermon, but affirms dharma as principle (good works of righteousness or through love for Supreme).

worshiped through righteous deeds and love, and in a universal humanism. Tagore blended those beliefs with the spirit of the renaissance movement of which he is the last icon. As such, he was relentless in his opposition to British rule with its aggressive materialism and commercialism that he felt was dealing a deathblow to the spiritual freedom of the individual, and was reducing Indian society to docility. His antipathy to Western imperialism produced his polemical stance against nationalism that morphed into a deification of the nation-state. The state itself was an organized mechanism of power in pursuit of wealth and conquest at the expense of freedom of the individual spirit. For Tagore, the idea of nationalism has no place in the traditions of India transmitted by its saint-poets: Kabir, Guru Nanak, Dadu, Rajjab, Mirabai, and others. While his writings take up modernity as a problem, he strongly advocated for an East-West civilization alliance to benefit all humanity. His literary intention was to that end—to the benefit of humanity.

Kierkegaard, one the other hand, understood himself as an author in Copenhagen, which was then a small market town. He was aware of his literary abilities as a poet of a kind, a dialectician, ironist, polemicist, and social critic. In writing to show the difficulty of becoming a Christian, he implicated himself in the church as well as cultural politics. He refrained from direct involvement in national political agitations for a constitutional monarchy. Instead, he remained focused on a sustained attack leveled at Christendom, making use of his literary talents to reintroduce Christianity to the Danish literary intelligentsia, through mainly communicating aesthetic and ethico-religious possibilities in writing. That is, he sought to describe a possibility such that the reader as a single individual would choose to make it actual in his/her own life. The significance he accorded to the categories of the single individual and human existence made his writings a resource for crisis theology and existentialist thinking in the twentieth century.

Furthermore, neither author was acquainted with political theology. Characteristically, political theology is a Western Christian movement emerging in Europe after World War II and later engaging theologians in a North-South hemispheric dialogue. Its subject matter ranges from liberal democracy, post-colonialism, preferential option for the poor, gender theory to queer theory and even "Indecent Theology," as Marcella Althaus-Reid called her project.[8] Needless to say, questions surround political theology: Is it a discipline, a style of thinking in theology, a discourse about God, a new post-secular version of political theory? It is not entirely clear even whether political theology is possible in the first place. If it is, are there different versions relative to cultural context?[9]

Despite the questions and differences, similarities between Tagore and Kierkegaard emerge to warrant considering them together. Their writings are in the genre of life-philosophy, vis-à-vis modernity as a problematic. Each is focused on the

8. Althaus-Reid, *Indecent Theology*.
9. See Kirwan, *Political Theology*, and Phillips, *Political Theology*.

human condition, seeking to awaken their people from spiritual malaise, the result of something having gone awry within the social-cultural and political context. Their joint concern was to raise a question about the limits of the secular relative to the spiritual. In this, they shared a common mission: to rehabilitate self or personhood by calling attention to how it was compromised by the prevailing social and political institutional arrangements of their own period. They wrote passionately to challenge their audiences or readers to become morally responsible selves as members of society. Moreover, in doing so, each author developed epistemological and metaphysical viewpoints that were similar, while remaining fundamentally oriented to their own religious tradition. Some stark differences at key points in their religious traditions do not prevent similarities and resemblances from arising along the way. But juxtaposing Tagore and Kierkegaard might lead to new or flexible ways of conversing so that they may be seen as a possible resource for political theology or even for interrogating the role of the concept of political theology in theological thinking.

Thus, this study starts a conversation between the two authors with respect to the self or person and political theology. It views the latter broadly as an attempt to understand the proper limits of the secular with respect to the spiritual for each thinker. Limits do get fuzzy, similar to a scrimmage line, when the secular is taken as loosening of the ties between religion and government or when theological reflections lend support to political structures that are just or unjust. Hence, political theology may include calling into question the established order, its sociocultural institutional arrangements, and rule with respect to notions of freedom, justice, and becoming fully human. To assist in starting the conversation I proceed comparatively to answer the question about proper limits of the secular with respect to the spiritual for each thinker. But first, it requires settling on appropriate texts and ideas that have some import for thinking about the primacy of the secular. The argument advanced here is that the positions sketched for Tagore and Kierkegaard on the question from the perspective of the idea of self or person, have a striking affinity to one another.

Preliminary Considerations: The Choice of Texts and Ideas

Pinning down a representative text for each author is difficult. The literary corpus of each is massive, representing different genres and containing a plurality of voices. Tagore, as one scholar notes,[10] has at least three influential voices: that of the bard of Bengal, for he was considered original and powerful as a poet; that of a novelist and storyteller, for he was influential in depicting family and social life, and that of a creative artist, clever satirist, and playwright creating characters and scenarios for his comic plays. There is, I think, a fourth voice, that of the philosophico-religious thinker delivering invited lectures and addresses, at Harvard, Yale, Chicago, Oxford, and other

---

10. Singh, "Desire for Motion," para. 4. Tagore's corpus in Bengali takes up 18,000 pages comprised of 28 volumes of texts which include plays, letters, short stories, etc.

universities aboard, as well as in India. Although hardly a systematic thinker, the voice is rational, engaging in critical inquiry without drawing a distinction between philosophy and religion or poetry as done in the West. He is no philosopher in the academic sense of engaging sophisticated logical techniques as part of argumentation. One of his short comical plays depicts the futility of obsession with analysis to suggest how people can become tied up in knots by such activities.[11] In the *weltanschauung* of this poet-philosopher, philosophy is a kind of seeing reference by the Sanskrit term *darshana*, More specifically, the term refers to a glimpsing of the divine, or in the context that Tagore uses it, a glimpsing of fruitful ways of thinking about humans in relation to one another and the environment.

This thinking or Indian outlook (*darshana*) is exemplified by his first serious English prose writing, *Sadhana* (1915), a collection of spiritual discourses, many of them delivered at Harvard University. It deals with the relation between the self and nature, the realization of selfhood, the dispelling of illusion, and draws on Upanishadic insights to deepen our subjectivity or consciousness. Hence, it might be classified as ethic-religious, referencing an underlying unity between the human and the Infinite or Universal spirit. Ideas from *Sadhana* underlie or are taken up later as discourses and addresses, collected under at least ten different titles. Among well-known ones are *Personality* (1917), *Creative Unity* (1922), and *Religion of Man* (1931). As such, *Sadhana* is one place to look for an answer to our question on limits of the secular with respect to the spiritual.

Kierkegaard is no less problematic in settling on a voice that represents fully his own viewpoint. Many of his best-known works are by pseudonymous authors and editors, strategically deployed to represent different human types or life-orientations. Their literary productions as editor or publisher include even other pseudonymous voices.[12] Kierkegaard's use of pseudonyms may seem confusing, but it allows him to depict in detail different life orientations, putting them into conversation with each other as representing live options. Further, the use of pseudonyms is in keeping with Kierkegaard's theory of indirect communication by directing attention away from the master author—Kierkegaard—so as to engage the reader to choose for him/herself one of the possible lifestyles depicted.

The two-volume *Either/Or* (1843), in his literary corpus of about thirty-four titles, is our choice for this study. The text is representative of Kierkegaard's authorial

---

11. The set is identified as *Riddle Plays* in *Rabindra Rachmanabali*, 6:127–29, according to Gupta, *Philosophy of Rabindranath Tagore*, 7–8. Gupta, calling attention to the particular play *Subtle Analysis*, is one of the handful of scholars taking note of the idea of obsession with analysis, and for that matter the playful, humorous aspect in Tagore's writings. For an instant of the playful humor, see also the opening pages of Tagore, *King of the Dark Chamber*, 2. The guard at the city gate is asked by visitors attending the city festival which path to take. The answer that any path will get you there elicits a derisive remark about the guard.

12. A recent study adds to the perplexity of which voice by referring to a hidden authorship referencing a reduplication of inwardness. Cf. Sawyer, *Hidden Authorship*, 134–35.

intent and thematically comparable to *Sadhana*. It is the earliest and most celebrated of his pseudonymous titles and has ideas that either recur or anticipate others in later texts. Its pseudonymous editor, Victor Eremite, relates that he found accidentally two sets of papers by unknown authors he labeled A and B and has published them respectively as volumes one and two. The A collection reflects the mood of life or outlook of a young person, for whom the highest expression of life is to be found in a heightening of the senses—theater, music, drama, love. The B collection has an underlying principle of duty compared to the depiction of experiencing varieties and moments as in the previous collection. According to the volume editor, the B papers are of a judge named William, responding in earnest to the young person A of volume one. In a friendly letter, the Judge urges him to take responsibility for his life by choosing married life along with all its duties, for it incorporates an aesthetic or pleasurable existence as well. However, as the Judge continues, it becomes clear that either kind of existence (pleasures or duty and pleasure) detracts from realizing oneself as a spiritual individual, and becoming fully a person, even though duty is a move in a forward direction. To underscore the incompleteness of such existential choices (aesthetic and the ethical) the second volume of *Either/Or* closes with a sermon on how in relation to God, people are always in the wrong.

The second volume of *Either/Or*, as with *Sadhana* for Tagore, introduces ideas that are conceptually clarified and even developed by later titles, but from different perspectives. This is so with the closing sermon that indirectly calls into question the Hegelian idea of society as a manifestation of the divine. Kierkegaard did not believe that social institutions such as the church, influenced by Hegelian ideas of civil society and historical progress, could lead troubled people in the right direction to deal with inner difficulties that are suggestive of a relational disharmony or incompleteness as individuals. Only God is in the right and approaching the divine is done through inwardness or faith and not through the social level. For example, the idea of a passionless society as a revolt against the divine is central to the text *Two Ages* (1846). The idea of exception later developed in the 1843 publications *Fear and Trembling* and *Repetition* led the German theorists Carl Schmitt in the twentieth century to formulate what is axiomatic for political theology: political concepts of the modern state are secularized theological ones. The idea of the self is developed by *Sickness Unto Death* (1849). And the polemical *Practice in Christianity* (1850), as well as the *Attack Upon Christendom* (1855), are onslaughts against the deification of the political-social order as contributing to spiritual indifference.

Clearly, *Sadhana* and *Either/Or II*, strike similar notes: political programs and social philosophy of the day are having a leveling effect on the passionate side of the individual. The challenge for their respective authors was to reintroduce those dimensions of selfhood that would enable the individual to regain dignity and become an ethico-religiously responsibly self. What then are the limits of the secular with respect to regaining the spiritual? When does the political-social becoming a hindrance to the spiritual?

The major differences and similarities in their answers depend very much on their intellectual assumptions or what they take as bedrock. One the one hand, each is assuming that his own religious tradition is the proper guide or resource for becoming a full human self and that his own Scripture has the capacity to arouse a human response to meet the ethical-religious deficit of the age. On the other hand, Tagore and Kierkegaard are in accord that nationalist fervor and existing ideologies are hastening the decline already under way as a result of negligence by religious institutions. The range of negligence includes ossifications of the scriptural teachings, and practices, be it the caste system of Orthodox Hinduism, with its mechanical performance of social practices and mindless rituals, or accepting that to be born in Denmark is enough to call oneself a Christian. Central to these concerns, therefore, is the understanding of what it means to be a self. We turn now, to sketch for each author the understanding of self in the selected titles.

Self in *Sadhana*

A view of self is a fruitful starting point for a conversation between our two thinkers relative to political theology. In Tagore's discourses, other terms used to reference the self include individual, soul, and personality. To understand their uses better, it must be recalled that concepts, like individuals, have histories, and so retain a kind of homesickness for their childhood scenes. The backdrop scene for the use of all four terms is a fusion of at least two perspectives: first, in Victorian life, of which Tagore is a child, religious and moral ideals were real to people. There was no argument as to whether they constitute a part of reality. To exist meant the actualizing of ethico-religious ideals. Second, naturalistic assumptions were integral to the twentieth-century scientific culture: only a scientific account gives the full story of reality, and any reference to transcendent reality associated with religion must be imaginary.

Tagore, accepting the importance of the scientific method to determine facts of the objective world to which the self must relate, was aware that the method has its limitation. It could not account for reality of the whole self or individual. The discourse "The Problem of Self" presents the view of the self as having two polarities or aspects, as requiring freedom and as realizing itself through love. It opens with an Upanishadic-like description of the self as a superstructure subtended by two polarities: one relates to the world of objectivity including sociocultural and political norms, in brief the finite world. Tagore strikingly puts it, "At one pole of my being, I am one with stocks [sic] and stones. There I have to acknowledge the rule of universal law. . . . Its strength lies in its being held firm in the class of a comprehensive world and in the fullness of its community with all things."[13] The self, then, has a social dimension implied by it being finite, grounded in time and thus having a history that would include a social relationship with others and in a community, with the world or universe at large. Though necessary, the relations might easily become dysfunctional or take forms that lack the good. It would explain Tagore's disavowal of lifeless social practices connected with institutionalized religion, dogmatic interpretations, scriptural literalism or the seeking to extract oneself from the world through ascetic or contemplative practices. The self stands related to itself, according to this pole, through relating socio-ethically to the community and environment. This means having social and political responsibilities as members of a community. Knowledge, rational inquiry, and freedom of mind or creativity are requisite for relation to the finite.

At the other pole forming its superstructure, the self comes to experience itself through the privacy of subjectivity or consciousness. It wants to touch or reach over the limits of its finiteness but finds expression of the inner urge or surplus through exercising the will in action and love. In its subjective isolation, it is standing alone; separate from the community of social relation or the world of facts. Simply put by the discourse, "at the other pole of my being I am separate from all. There I have broken through the cordon of equality and stand alone as an individual. I am absolutely unique. I am incomparable. The whole weight of the universe cannot crush out this individuality of mine."[14] The relationality or movement that occurs is from the pole or sphere of social-ethical toward the realization of what is deep seated within the self as a gift in its creation.

To arrest that experience of oneself is to demolish individuality; it is to separate the self from what gives it joy. The discourse presents it this way: "If this individuality be demolished, then though no material be lost . . . the creative joy which was crystallized therein is gone . . . this individuality, which is the only thing we can call our own, and which, if lost is also a loss to the whole world."[15] Loss of individuality is not through an act, but by failure to act. Failure is a result of ignorance or *avidya*, a Sanskrit term that Tagore renders as the obstruction of vision, of seeing the truth of the self, realizing it.[16] That is, the self in its total reality is more than its quotidian or phenomenal identity. Not to acknowledge by acting to realize, whether it be by ignorance or defiance, means the demise of individuality or personality.

Not a substance, self is life or activity connected with the idea of freedom. It is born out of a freely willing to relate harmoniously two sets of polar relationships: the social-finite, and the spiritual-Infinite. Tagore understands freedom in a positive sense, not as independence to will as one pleases or in defiance but in taking responsibility for the world, the secular as one might say today. This is what the lines of our cited

13. Tagore, *Sadhana*, 69.
14. Ibid.
15. Ibid., 70.
16. Ibid., 72.

passage above are rendering when it says, that which we call our own (personality or individuality) is, if lost, a loss to the whole world. In speaking about the function of religion he again ties the idea of freedom to becoming a whole or true self: "We gain our freedom when we attain our truest nature. . . . It is the function of religion not to destroy our nature but to fulfil it."[17] Any discussion of the self in relation to freedom for Tagore must take into consideration also the notion of harmony understood from an aesthetic perspective. That is, one's relationship with the world of facts, social and political governance and all sort of civic or social arrangements of the finite world have to be meshed with the spiritual self that is experienced in the privacy of subjectivity. This is precisely what religion helps to accomplish, to take responsibility for political structures and social practices that are unjust or that suppress knowledge, critical inquiry, and freedom of the mind or spirit and set it right, in accord with *dharma*.

For Tagore, religion is not about the sacred or transcendence, about social practices prescribed by Hindu orthodoxy. The Indian tradition has no word for religion as understood in the West. It speaks of *dharma*, which Tagore interprets as a reference to "the innermost nature, the essence, the implicit truth of all things."[18] On his rendition of that Sanskrit term, a human has for dharma realization of the true self or freedom and it may require a sacrifice by which one breaks free from the materialism and worldly advantages of our social-cultural existence. The breaking free is a struggle that may involve making personal sacrifices of worldly benefits and advantage, clashing with the establishment, and opposition to unjust political and instructional structures. That struggle, according to Tagore, will result in experiencing self in its fullness of humanity, freeing itself from the narrowness associated with worldly cares that benefit no other. This is how the discourse explains the two aspects of self: "The self which displays itself, and the self which transcends itself and thereby reveals its own meanings. To display itself it tries to be big, to stand upon the pedestal of its accumulation and to retain everything for itself. To reveal itself it gives up everything it has, thus becoming perfect like a flower that has blossomed out from the bud."[19]

Struggle is a mark characteristic of the integrating activity to gain oneself and hence is dharma action. Voluntary, the struggle stands in contrast to involuntary struggle: disharmony, pain, and suffering occasioned as part of living in the world or engaging in activity that is non-dharmic or not for the good of humanity. A struggle that is integrating may ensue from taking a reflective stance in relation to social and political structures, and whether one is engaged in doing the right thing, doing dharma work. Explaining dharma work, a subsequent discourse, "Realization of Action," references self by the term soul and ties it to the idea of freedom. Accordingly, some may think of "activity being in the material plane" as restricting the free spirit of the

17. Ibid., 74.
18. Ibid.
19. Ibid., 76.

soul.[20] But the discourse continues, "We must remember that as joy expresses itself in law, so the soul finds its freedom in action.... Likewise, it is because the soul cannot find freedom within itself that it wants external action. The soul of man is ever freeing itself from its own soul by its activity.... The more man acts and makes actual what was latent in him, the nearer does he bring the distant Yet-to-be."[21] Elsewhere in the discourse, Tagore mentions that the soul "cannot live in its own internal feelings and imaginings. It is ever in need of external objects; not only to feed its inner consciousness but to apply itself in action, not only to receive but also to give."[22]

Tagore's concept of activity is that which is extending the boundaries of the ego. How? Through engagement with others, building human solidarity and community, allowing room for creative growth by expression of the surplus within the self. This is the activity or work of love that he understands as burning up of acquisitive desires for worldly advantages and power and thus working toward unity or freedom of our self.[23] We have for this understanding of love the emphasis placed on freedom *in* action rather than *from* action. Tagore understands love to be that which an end itself is: "Everything else raises the question 'Why?' in our mind, and we require a reason for it. But when we say, 'I love,' then there is no room for the 'why'; it is the final answer in itself."[24] It is love that makes the struggle against unjust political structures or whatever suffocating the spiritual, not burdensome but a freedom. Love is the surplus expressed, the inner energy or impulse as a gift at creation.

We have culled enough from the discourse on the problem of the self to begin thinking thought what Tagore might say about the limits of the secular relative to the spiritual. Foremost, his understanding of religion as *dharma* does not imply observing a fixed boundary between the secular and the spiritual. Next, self is a rationality concept for it is relating itself simultaneously to finite ends, and Infinite spirit or Universal mind and in accord with *dharma* principle, for the good of all humanity and not for itself. Limits of the secular, with the perspective of the sociopolitical in mind, are conditions that do not impose or favor religious practices of any kind. The flip side is that conditions have to be arranged to avoid stifling the actualizing of moral values or experiencing spiritual disharmony with doing one's *dharma*.

The limits of the secular then are definable in terms of dharma, of holding firmly to the cosmic principle of realizing truth (*satya*) and avoidance of harm (*ahimsa*). A multifaceted concept, dharma may also be unpacked in terms of the upholding of goodness, justice, and truth, at the minimum. Praxis is essential to what dharma action is. As such, limits have to be accommodative of knowledge acquisition, truth

20. Ibid., 120.
21. Ibid.
22. Ibid., 125.
23. Ibid., 78. He is echoing *Bhagavad Gita* 12:10, a core text in the Hindu tradition for the idea of the work of love.
24. Ibid., 77.

seeking and doing, critical inquiry engagement, freewill exercise, and creative impulses. For, how else is one to recognize and have the ego strength to resist unjust political structures or morally stifling social and cultural practices? Limits have to remain porous, but over time may become nonporous or hardened to shut out of daily living the creative urges and surplus defining the self as life.

In Tagore's lifetime, two examples illustrate the limits of the secular becoming nonporous and thus contributing to the spiritual malaise of his time. One is British education in colonial India that in Tagore's view has become narrow, utilitarian, and restrictive with respect to educating the entire self.[25] The other example is nationalism, which he considers an evil, in his drawing of a distinction between society and state or government. Committed to praxis, Tagore as a social and political reformer directed his talents to regenerate his society, to make it truly democratic with porous limits. A question to consider in light of limits becoming nonporous is whether the rule of law that is essential to the modern nation state is ever able to accommodate fully the rule of the people as *dharma*. When law is made universal it can produce tribalism, social indifference, and spiritual emptiness. Tagore's refashioning of the human with respect to *dharma* to which is coupled the question about the rule of law is reminiscent of Carl Schmitt's remark that significant concepts about the modern state are secularized theological concepts. It leaves one pondering whether the concept of sovereignty of law is dharma secularized, in relation to the examples.

Self in *Either/Or II*

As with Tagore, Judge William too takes moral ideals to be real, givens that are simply accepted as defining a form of life. His letter to the young friend A recommends to settle down and take charge of his own life. He declares that what he is urging is not from academic wisdom, but is learned growing up and applicable to anyone.[26] In urging A to make a purposive choice understood as a life commitment the Judge is advancing a position similar to the one that Tagore takes about the self and renders it in terms of activity, freedom, harmony, unity, and joy. In a way, the self for both thinkers is a finite center of experiences, is concretized to make psychically coherent two relational aspects of itself. One is with respect to the external world: the environment including the social-political order. The other is internal to the self, abstract, and experienced only in the isolation of the I, or subjectivity. These twos are integrated by the individual choosing to actualize moral ideals. Hence, the self is the center of experiences. By committing itself, the self acquires consistency and psychic coherency in its doing, hoping, believing, thinking, with respect to setting and realizing life-projects. It has dispositions and capacities that have to be integrated with its wants and desires as a finite and living reality.

25. Ibid.
26. Kierkegaard, *Either/Or*, 2:217.

The young friend is in despair. Writing to him, the Judge renders the idea of self from the perspective of despair but does so introducing other terms such as freedom and personality to demonstrate the how of choosing self. He is clear that in the first place the self is a relationality established through choice (an activity) in the privacy of oneself. How one chooses it is important, for the choice has to be absolute, unconditional, and eternally valid. We are to understand "valid" to mean having applicability or holding true both in the here-now and hereafter, the latter intending to represent beyond the finite and temporal dimensions. Furthermore, that which is to be chosen has to be universally human, accessible to anyone regardless of one's station or condition of life (style). What else can that be other than my reality or self which is such that I cannot rid myself of it?

The Judge puts it to the friend in this way: "But what is it then that I choose—is it this or that? No, I choose absolutely, precisely by having chosen not to choose this or that. I choose the absolute . . . myself in eternal validity. . . . If I choose something else, I choose it as something finite, and consequently."[27] Continuing, he tells that the choice consists of two moments of expression: a first whereby that which is chosen is quite abstract, and a second whereby that which is chosen is "also the most concrete of all—it is freedom."[28] Furthermore, everyone has within themselves that which cannot be erased even by wishing in the harshest situation in life to be somebody else or another. This observation of people in suffering who wish to be other than themselves to escape the situation but not really willing to let go is, according to the Judge, an indication of coming close to the truth, of feeling "the eternal validity of the personality."[29] The Judge draws from his observation, a conclusion that there is "something within him that in relation to everything else is absolute, something whereby he is who he is even if the change he achieved by his wish were the greatest possible."[30]

As such, to choose oneself as the Judge suggests means that the self must dialectically relate two sets of sustainable relationships. One set is finite, is in relation to the social and political world and nature. Every inhabitant in the world does that out of necessity, validating him/herself by acquiring a social identity or social self, acquired simply by being born and socialized. This dimension of self is for Tagore the acquisitive self. The other set follows from what the Judge recommends: to position oneself by a choice that is absolute or by a second dialectical movement whereby the self "is infinitely concrete, for it is he himself, and yet it is absolutely different from his former self, for he has chosen it absolutely. The self has not existed before, because it came into existence through the choice, and yet it has existed for it was indeed 'himself.'"[31]

27. Ibid.
28. Ibid., 214.
29. Ibid.
30. Ibid.
31. Ibid., 215.

The Judge offers a detailed descriptive analysis of what Tagore presupposes in his lectures for a university-level audience. For he notes also that by choosing oneself absolutely, good and evil as categories are posited and come to acquire significance for personal existence: they have an absolute difference between them such that there is no mistake which must recede and which to advance.[32] How does one know with such clarity? According to the Judge, a person in choosing himself freely and absolutely, makes himself absolute; by that choice he declared the validity of the category good for his life, and the good becomes his for it is he himself who willed it: "The good is the being-in-and-for-itself, posited by the being-in-and-for-itself, and this is freedom."[33]

In his meticulous deliberation on choosing absolutely, the Judge is advocating for an ethico-religious form of existence, in contrast to one that is utilitarian or defined by performing dutifully what is expected. The self is ethico-religiously determined, coming to rest in God in the second movement or moment. To choose absolutely takes courage. For that which is chosen in the first instant has an identity or history. It is comprised of a boundless multiplicity of relationships or a relationship to the whole human race through other individuals. Painful moments and events, some deeply buried, are part of the history that has to be acknowledged in choosing oneself finitely, "for he is the person he is only through this history."[34] At the same time, in making the acknowledgment he is fast sinking into isolation, into the "very root by which he is bound up with the whole."[35] However, the uneasy, sinking feeling arouses the passion of freedom, already presupposed in the choice in the first moment and correlates with choosing absolutely himself (the second moment). It struggles in holding to the history despite the most painful memory that surfaces. Why? The history is himself as well, his acquisitive self, and cannot be given up. It is for his sanity or salvation. Repentance is the expression, according to the Judge, for the holding to the history: it is in effect a movement of going "back into himself, back into the family, back into the race, until he finds himself in God. . . . And this is the only condition he wants, for only in this way can he choose himself absolutely."[36]

To underscore my point, struggle correlated with absolute choice does not cancel out responsibility for properly positioning oneself to the surrounding world. This includes obtaining the necessities of life and for that matter relating sociopolitically in the society or community. Though the reward is very small, for it may be barely what is needed to keep going in life, still responsibility for the world and its norms is educative. As the Judge tells it, "Cares about the necessities of life are so ennobling and educative because they do not allow a person to delude himself about himself . . . the struggle is ennobling because it constrains him to see something else in it . . . a

32. Ibid., 69, 223–27.
33. Ibid., 224.
34. Ibid., 216.
35. Ibid.
36. Ibid.

struggle to gain himself."³⁷ And in this context, the Judge follows up by distinguishing an ethical from an aesthetic view of life. The ethical has the advantage in that everyone has a duty to work for a living; further "it is in harmony with actuality, explains something universal in it . . . and conceives of the human being according to his perfection, views him according to his true beauty."³⁸

Having introduced the idea of the self as a finite center of experiences, I am now able to articulate Judge William's views on the limits of the secular with respect to the spiritual. To be sure, the idea of limits is presupposed by his theological anthropology—by his views on what it means to be human. At minimal, limits would refer to whatever situations or conditions, finite relationships, keep one making the second dialectical movement, choosing absolutely. Limits would include obstacles to repenting, to finding oneself in God, or conditions that are snuffing out the passion of freedom, posing a threat to actualizing the universal human in everyone. This would include political structures, ideologies, forms of government, social norms and whatever threatens to deprive the individual or society of the possibility to be in harmony with actualizing moral and spiritual ideals. The choice to make ethico-religious ideals real for one's life is in effect a further step in the direction of becoming fully human, placing oneself before the eternal. The limits are the conditions imposed by human constructs and institutions in social life that rob the individual of the passion for life, that hinder the integration of the two dimensions of relationships, that is capacities including spiritual ones by which we become a coherent personality. The Judge's language for limiting conditions is despair, of which there are multiple forms. As a condition, despair is the shutting out of the spiritual dimension within the self, a failure to choose absolutely a self that is eternally valid. Despair may occur also as a result of either innocently not willing to shut out (aesthetic), or being aware but delaying to will.

Similarities and Differences in the Two Positions on Limits

I am arguing that the positions of the Judge and Tagore on the limits of the secular with respect to the sacred have an affinity to one another. The limits are best understood from the point of view of their religious-philosophical anthropologies. Accordingly, their views of being human are fashioned out of a shared strand or idea that everything finite is related to ultimate reality. In Christian theology, that idea follows from the doctrine of creation. In Indian thought, it comes out of the Upanishadic cognitive account of the nature of ultimate reality, of what lies behind the phenomenal word of experiences, of the unity underling the many and referenced by terms such as Brahman, and Universal Soul. The Judge and Tagore each draws on concepts characteristic of their own faith tradition to fashion their views of what it means to live fully as a

37. Ibid., 285.
38. Ibid., 288.

human being.³⁹ They employ the concepts without bothering about doctrinal loyalty, and as such impart to them fluidity in meaning: repentance in Christianity, *dharma* and *Brahman* or the ultimate in Indian thought. Further, each author correlates experiencing selfhood with struggle and moral ideals that include the following: freedom, unity, harmony, individuality, personality, and joy. When the correlation is interrupted or is not actualized, then the secular has transgressed its limit with respect to the spiritual. In short, the Judge and Tagore see the struggle as that of the personal or ethico-religious self, born of solitude or inwardness and of historicity or contingent life circumstances. That is, he or she is in the first place a social-cultural self that is to be transformed ethico-religiously through deepening of inwardness.

The Judge and Tagore understand the spiritual element within the self to be largely the surplus of emotional energy seeking expression. Both are of the view that humans experience a sense of lack even after their needs are met, and have inwardly a reservoir of emotional energy, a surplus, wanting to express itself to burst through the finite to relate or touch the other side of the finite, the non-finite or infinite and eternal. This is in fact the spiritual dimension seeking freedom and to which the finite dimension or social self must be integrated. God functions linguistically to certify our obligation to attend to the fulfillment of that need through our creative urges for Tagore, and through choosing absolutely for the Judge. From this perspective, the limits of the secular for the Judge and Tagore correlate with situations that tend to dampen the expression of the surplus. This understanding of the surplus or reserve of emotional energy requires neither one to commit to any metaphysical doctrine about reality or creator God. Nor does it require holding that the political and theological are two realities or divisions of the self that are separate. In fact, they both seem to share at the minimal a position that the spiritual is enveloping and that the I or finite self is to become integrated with it.

Different, however, are the backgrounds against which the implied limits of the secular are conceived. They may throw further light on the conditions that tend to threaten our humanness and humanity. Tagore's account is given against a background that differentiates between society and national politics. The nation-state with its politics requires allegiance to principles, ideologies, and conditions that nourish or deify the nation, and that expect citizens to make a sacrifice to the state/political apparatus. The differentiation is evident in Tagore's resistance to nationalism and British rule in India that he saw as reducing humans to utility, machinery in service of the interests of the empire, and thereby stifling the creative urge. He wanted to break out of the limits or confines of the secular by educating the whole person. Hence,

---

39. Gupta makes the point about Tagore not having any dogmatic loyalty to Upanishadic doctrine of ultimate reality. In fact, she points out that what is for the Upanishadic seers a matter of inference from a metaphysical view is for Tagore manifested emotionally and imaginatively as direct personal experience? See Gupta, *Philosophy of Rabindranath Tagore*, 10, 11, 52–55, 78, and 79, that discusses also some themes pertinent to this study such as nationalism, distinguishing it form patriotism, and the notion of self.

he undertook educational and social reforms, and through invited lectures and discussion abroad advocated for an East-West civilizational alliance. He was aware that social practices and political structures have dehumanizing tendencies that he estimated are best countered by reintroducing moral values, and emphasizing rational thinking and human agency. In short, nationalism or political ideology (with its economic interests, territorial sovereignty, and political or military might) could not be an organizing principle that allows for the human spirit to realize those values. It has definite limitations.

When Kierkegaard was composing *Either/Or* (Oct 1841–Nov 1842) the differentiation had not occurred in Denmark. Nationalism was in the air but was not an actuality.[40] Hegel, the bright light of German idealism reaching to Denmark, wanted to make citizenship correlating with a rational state into a personal identity or self. But to Kierkegaard, such correlation blurred the boundary lines between an ethical view and what nationalism called for. In a way, the Judge is making a testimony or deposition that counts against mistaking the limits of the secular (nationalism or state-sanctioned institutions and practices) as the spiritual. Note, however, the Judge's account is incomplete without the sermon by the country priest closing *Either/Or II*. The Judge tells his young friend that the sermon best expresses what he would like to communicate: "the upbuilding that lies in the thought that in relation to God we are always in the wrong." Implicit in what is told is a testimony: the human self does not have the capacity to recognize truth, beauty, and justice. It must reply on God's help to know them and even to discern the limits. This would mean the limits have no fixity, but have to be discerned in fear and trembling.

We may ponder what weight to give to the Judge's deposition that takes the form of letter writing in deriving Kierkegaard's stance on the limits of the secular with respect to the spiritual. But as resource for thinking in terms of political theology, Kierkegaard seems to be more in accord with a radical political theology—a refusal to align the becoming fully a self with any political agenda or stripe. Is Tagore doing that? He offers the option, as a resource for political theology, of a playful dancing or engagement of the spiritual with contemporary culture and politics. In short, Tagore is opting for a twisting free of the self from any religious or political orthodoxy.

Further Conversations

How is the conversation to continue when each of our thinkers has plural voices? A suggestion would be to bring all the pseudonyms and Kierkegaard to sit at the same table with the multitalented, polyphonic Tagore for a conversation. Either the two key authors or a pseudonym might ask also how relevant the concept of political theology is for doing what each sets out to do as an author. Listening to the conversation

---

40. Habermas, *New Conservatism*, 260, holds that nationalism, though a first step toward reflexive appropriation of cultural traditions, does not serve as complement to Kierkegaard's ethical view.

we may come to grasp their significance as resources for dealing with issues characterizing political theology today. That is, it may assist in an astute critical inquiry on how modern liberal democratic structures co-opting religion and religious ideas compromise the limits or how institutionalized religion may unwittingly end up in a dangerous alliance with political structures operating under principles of liberalism, or neo-conservatism in a global world or collective identification instead of being a liberative force for the human spirit. Further still, their discussion may help in drawing a distinction between the personal self and a self that is either social or national and associated with a constitutional patriotism.

Bibliography

Althaus-Reid, Marcella. *Indecent Theology*. Oxford: Taylor & Francis, 2001.
Crockett, Clayton. *Radical Political Theology*. New York: Columbia University Press, 2011.
Easwaran, Eknath, trans. *Bhagvad-Gita*. 2nd ed. Berkeley: Nilgiri, 2007.
Gupta, Kaylan Sen. *The Philosophy of Rabindranath Tagore*. Burlington, VT: Ashgate, 2005.
Habermas, Jürgen. *The New Conservatism*. Cambridge: MIT Press, 1992.
Kierkegaard, Søren. *Either/Or*. Vol. 2. Princeton: Princeton University Press, 1987.
———. *Fear and Trembling; Repetition*. Edited and translated by Howard V. Hong and Edna H. Hong. Princeton: Princeton University Press, 1983.
———. *The Moment and Late Writings*. Edited and translated by Howard V. Hong and Edna H. Hong. Princeton: Princeton University Press, 1998.
———. *The Point of View*. Edited and translated by Howard V. Hong and Edna H. Hong. Princeton: Princeton University Press, 1998.
———. *Practice in Christianity*. Edited and translated by Howard V. Hong and Edna H. Hong. Princeton: Princeton University Press, 1991.
———. *The Sickness Unto Death*. Edited and translated by Howard V. Hong and Edna H. Hong. Princeton: Princeton University Press, 1988.
———. *Two Ages: The Age of Revolution and the Present Age; A Literary Review*. Edited and translated by Howard V. Hong and Edna H. Hong. Princeton: Princeton University Press, 1978.
Kirmmse, Bruce H. *Kierkegaard in Golden Age Denmark*. Bloomington: Indiana University Press, 1990
Kirwan, Michael. *Political Theology*. Minneapolis: Fortress, 2009.
Phillips, Elizabeth. *Political Theology: A Guide to the Perplexed*. Longdon: T. & T. Clark, 2012.
Sawyer, Jacob H. *The Hidden Authorship of Soren Kierkegaard*. Eugene, OR: Wipf & Stock, 2015.
Schmitt, Carl. *Political Theology*. Chicago: University of Chicago Press, 2005.
Sen, Amartya. *The Argumentative Indian*. New York: Farrar, Straus, and Giroux, 2005.
Singh, Amardeep. "'The Desire for Motion': Tagore's Three Voices." *Open Letters Monthly: An Arts and Literature Review*, January 1, 2012. http://www.openlettersmonthly.com/the-desire-for-motion-tagores-three-voices.
Tagore, Rabindranath. *Creative Unity*. London: McMillan, 1922.
———. *Gitanjali (Song Offerings)*. New York: Macmillan, 1920.
———. *King of the Dark Chamber*. Madras: Macmillan, 1970.

———. *Lectures and Addresses*. Madras: Macmillan, 1970.
———. *The Religion of Man*. London: Unwin, 1931.
———. *Riddle Plays*. In *Rabindra Rachmanabali (Collected Works of Tagore)*, 6:127–29. Calcutta: West Bengal Government, 1961.
———. *Sadhana*. Tucson: Omen Communications, 1972.
———. *Towards Universal Man*. New York: Asia, 1961.

13

Theater, Theology, and Empowerment
Kierkegaard and Boal

Helene Russell

Could Kierkegaard be a resource for liberation theology? At first glance, most Kierkegaard readers and scholars might answer this question with a no. While some have explored this question,[1] none have offered a sustained study. I think this is because Kierkegaard is commonly viewed and criticized for not being attentive enough to the world and the importance of material concerns for a Christian theology of ethics.[2] This essay approaches this issue with unusual connection: theater. Theater is usually associated with the secular arts or even a lowbrow entertainment with vaudeville and burlesque. Yet as Carl Hughes's recent book on Kierkegaard, theater, and love argues, Kierkegaard engages theater in a positive and in a spiritually up-building way.[3]

This essay brings Kierkegaard's rhetorical engagement with theater into dialogue with Augusto Boal's theatrical practice of liberating empowerment in *Theater of the Oppressed*.[4] What prompted me to bring these two thinkers into dialogue is that Boal and Kierkegaard both suggest a reversal of roles from the traditional or commonly understood theatrical responsibilities. Usually the actors or speakers move about on stage speaking their lines and inhabiting their characters, while spectators, or listeners, or congregants, sit passively watching and listening, and perhaps empathizing with some characters and rooting against others. There may be prompters or *souffleurs* off-stage whispering lines to the performers in case they forget. Both Boal and Kierkegaard experiment with shuffling these roles by prodding the spectators to be the

---

1. Cf. Hisrich, "Toward a New Theology of Liberation." Also, James Cone's Black Liberation Theology is influenced by existentialism in general and to some degree, Kierkegaard as well. Cf. Cone, *The Cross and the Lynching Tree*, 1–29; also see Walsh, *Living Christianly*, 100–102. Walsh does not write about liberation theology per se, but views Kierkegaard as having a social ethic that is friendly to liberation theology's ultimate goal of liberation for all persons.

2. Ferreira, *Love's Grateful Striving*, 165.

3. Hughes, *Kierkegaard and the Staging of Desire*.

4. Boal, *Theater of the Oppressed*.

ones whose act-ions are important. Both turn upside down the common assumptions about the authority of the persons with power such as the preacher and the director. Instead, they suggest that the liberating function of the preacher, or the director (Boal names this role "Joker"), is to prompt the spectators to elicit their own words, actions, and thoughts. One reason Boal names this role "Joker" is that his approach is a reversal of what is expected. Boal and the "Joker" create a controlled chaos to mix things up. He names this approach to theater as the "joker system" to indicate a use of theater for rehearsing for revolution.[5]

This parallel reversal of roles and the corresponding emphasis upon the agency of the people in the seats got my imagination wondering about the fecund possibilities of a conversation between Boal and Kierkegaard. Boal's analysis reveals the importance of dissolving the division between those who speak and those who listen for the sake of engendering self-awareness and agency in the people, for the sake of empowering those who are oppressed.[6] I will argue that Kierkegaard's emphasis on the believer's active agency in worship coupled with his attention to the subjecthood of those we are called to love, indicate that his work can be a theological and practical resource for a theology of liberation. I conclude by delineating several strengths that this collaboration offers for liberation theology.

Further I note that Boal's analysis of the dangers of theater is in line with Kierkegaard's own "chaos-creating" theological critique of Christendom. Taking both of these notions into account suggests that reformers of Christianity and church life in our own time might benefit from adjusting the divisions between laity and clergy in a way that empowers all believers to take responsibility for their own faith decisions.

At first it might seem as if Kierkegaard's theological explication of the divine command to love each and every neighbor as oneself might lend itself toward a theology that highlights equality between persons. Kierkegaard says in *Works of Love* that Christian love is love of the neighbor without attention to one's own preference. This is in contradistinction to erotic feelings and even friendship. "Erotic love and friendship are . . . the passion of preferential love."[7] Kierkegaard argues that preferential love is opposed to eternal or Christian love. They differ from each other in three significant ways: in the object to which the love is directed, in the purpose of the love, and most importantly, in the source of the love. Preferential love is directed to a particular beloved exclusively. Christian love is directed to the neighbor without reference to one's own preference. It is love expressed equally to each neighbor one sees. Second, preferential love is for the purpose of evoking reciprocal feelings from the beloved, while Christian love is to build up the other in love and a godly relationship. This building up occurs by presuming that love is already present. And last, the source of preferential love is the preference, whereas in Christian love, the source is God's love;

---

5. Ibid., 122.
6. Ibid., x, 120, 141–42.
7. Kierkegaard, *Works of Love*, 52.

the middle term is God. Since God is the middle term, the Christian is called to love each neighbor equally, regardless of their economic and social status or any other distinctive characteristic.

However, even though he formulates Christian love as valuing each neighbor equally,[8] he does not go on to argue that Christians should work to eradicate the earthly inequalities of society. Jamie Ferreira explains that Kierkegaard is not arguing for a "naïve of cavalier dismissal of socioeconomic differences."[9] He writes that "Christianity has not *taken away the dissimilarity*" of earthly life.[10] Rather, he suggests that these dissimilarities "must continue as long as temporality continues and must continue to tempt every human being who comes into the world, inasmuch as by being a Christian he does not become exempt from dissimilarity, but by overcoming the temptations of dissimilarity, he becomes a Christian."[11] In other words, he thinks that the differences between people can be useful for the training of Christians. These differences tempt us to view some persons as more deserving of love than others, revealing how much more inner work needs to be done.[12] The Christian commandment to love one's neighbor as oneself is a commandment to love regardless of the earthly differences; it is a mandate to lift oneself above the earthly differences. The action of changing one's own inner response to these earthly differences is part of the process by which one becomes a Christian. This is one of the primary themes of this book.[13]

One might critique Kierkegaard's position here as being antithetical to the intention of liberation theology or any political liberation. As Jamie Ferreira points out, Kierkegaard is commonly criticized for not being attentive enough to the world and the importance of material concerns for a Christian theology of ethics.[14] Kierkegaard's theology is so focused on an individual's soul that regard for the external conditions of oppression seem insignificant to his goals. He explicitly warns against the attention to creating equality in worldly matters, arguing that it is "a well-intentioned worldliness" that errs not only in attempting the impossible but also in being distracted from the truly Christian notion of equality. That is equality before God, as loved by God.[15] A liberation theologian might argue that if one were called to love the neighbor, including those who are poor or mistreated in society, one would work against economic injustice. Does not loving one's neighbor entail changing the economic structures, or at least, alleviating the suffering in some way, like feeding the poor?

8. In *Works of Love*, Kierkegaard juxtaposes what he calls "preferential love, love based on one's own preference and desire, with Christian love, which entails loving each neighbor equally.

9. Ferreira, *Love's Grateful Striving*, 47.

10. Kierkegaard, *Works of Love*, 70.

11. Ibid.

12. Ibid. These differences also appear to have inherent value, as well, in that he associates their value with the incarnation, and in particular the disciples' presence in the temporal world.

13. Kierkegaard, *Works of Love*, 219.

14. Ferreira, *Love's Grateful Striving*, 165.

15. Kierkegaard, *Works of Love*, 72.

Kierkegaard's answer is affirmative to the last part of the question, but not to the first part. He advocates feeding the poor, but even in this feeding ministry, he remains focused on the individual neighbor and the inner work of Christians to change themselves. This personal and immediate focus is accentuated by his assertion of the manner by which one should feed the poor. Christian love demands not only to feed the poor, but also to give a banquet for those who are poor and lowly. He proclaims "one who feeds the poor—but still has not been victorious over his mind in such a way that he calls this meal a banquet—sees the poor and the lowly only as the poor and the lowly. The one who gives the banquet sees the neighbor in the poor and lowly."[16] Seeing the neighbor is seeing an individual subject who is to be loved and one who can love. Here he makes it clear that the poor ought to be treated with respect and appreciation—as an honored friend. This might be read as suggesting a preferential option for the poor and lowly. Here his thought seems friendlier to liberation theology.

An astute reader might be thinking that giving a banquet does alleviate some of the suffering of economic oppression, but it does not offer anything to ameliorate the oppressive situation in general. The poor continue to be poor, only well-fed and well-celebrated, and even loved. It does not change their basic situation or address the inherent injustice of the system.

Liberation theology seeks a liberation that is double-pronged, including liberation from political and other earthly oppression, as well as liberation from sin for salvation. One could name both of these prongs in terms of sin thusly: Redemption can be viewed as liberation from sin that is committed by others / sinful structures that oppress and harm, and second, liberation from one's own sin and wrongdoings. One wonders if Kierkegaard's interpretation of the command to love by giving a banquet addresses liberation from both of these directions: outer sins of oppression, or one's own inner sin.

This illustration from Kierkegaard explicating Jesus' command in Luke 14 to give a banquet for the poor is only one of the practical examples of his general principles about Christian Love. *Works of Love* as a whole argues that Christians are called to love without preference, for there is infinite equality between human beings. Yet this equality is about the equality before God. The equal worth of each individual as she stands before God. The equal love that God has for each person.[17]

Let me offer what I think Kierkegaard is saying in my interpretation. For Kierkegaard, this Christian work to love each neighbor equally is not done for the purpose of pleasing God, nor in some way to achieve or maintain salvation. It is not even about doing ethics (although as Ferreira points out, many have treated it as a book in Christian ethics).[18] Rather, the Christian loves the neighbor without reference to her own preferences through God. The "work" is to love God and believe that God

16. Ibid., 83.
17. Ferreira, *Love's Grateful Striving*, 47.
18. Ibid.

loves all through one's actions toward the neighbor. We are called to see and treat the neighbor as God does. This seems impossible, but Kierkegaard replies, "with God all things are possible." For it is God's love that is loving the neighbor without preference and with the assured knowledge that love is already present. The Christian's job is to get one's ego out of the way.

To address this critical question from the perspective of liberation theology, let us move to a dialogue partner—a visionary from Brazil with inventive ideas and practices geared toward enabling the liberation of the oppressed through an innovative approach to theater.

Boal's Theater of the Oppressed

Augusto Boal is critical of the way that theater has functioned to reinforce political and moral oppression of the populous through manipulation and indoctrination. Building on Aristotle's analysis of the way that theater manipulates behavior to create virtue in the viewers, Boal believes that the state and ruling classes used drama as a means to reinforce order in society and suppress any tendencies of revolt.[19]

When the ruling classes took over theater, they built walls to separate the performers from the public. This separation enabled them to use the empathy and catharsis of drama to quell the emotions of anger and frustration in the populous. In theater, empathy functions to blend the fictitious character with the real person. The real individual identifies with the character such that she substitutes her own will toward fulfillment for the desire for fulfillment of the character. She surrenders her autonomy and decision-making ability to the emotional situation and impetus of the character. This means that the real person ends up making life decisions according to fabricated situations. Boal says the viewer "accepts as life and reality what is presented to him in the work of art as art."[20] Further, Boal writes, that in empathy, the "spectator assumes a 'passive' attitude and delegates his ability to act."[21] This reinforces the passivity and removes the impetus to act to change one's own situation.

Boal gives examples from television serials and in particular, the genre of Westerns to show how theater can purge unacceptable social behavior. In the Western at first we are directed to empathize with the villain, with his power and his flaws. But then the hero appears and wins, beating the bad guy with his better skills or his virtuousness. Viewers are manipulated into empathizing and identifying with the villain and his vices, and then when he is defeated, they are manipulated into "defeating" the vices within themselves and becoming more socially acceptable in their characteristics and behaviors.

---

19. Boal, *Theater of the Oppressed*, 36, 46.
20. Ibid., 113.
21. Ibid., 102.

Although Boal sees the potential of contemporary theater to coercively manipulate the emotions of the audience, he argues that theater and other narrative arts could be used to resist this oppression. Participation in theater can subvert political power, dominant social norms, and expected roles. *Theater of the Oppressed* generates creative and practical approaches by capitalizing on the activity of performance itself as a means of liberation.

Boal is deeply influenced by fellow countryman Paulo Freire. He utilizes Freire's concept of "*conscientization*," or critical consciousness, in which oppressed persons come to the realization that they do not deserve to be oppressed and throw off their internalized identification with the oppressors' evaluation.[22] According to Freire, it is critical for the oppressed to be awakened from the internal oppression that has been indoctrinated within them through embedded values within the culture. Practicing Freire's theory that true liberation demands that the persons who are oppressed be a part of the solution, Boal's exercises empower those who are oppressed by giving them the means to make changes in their own situation. The ruling class cannot "fix" the oppression without the consent and input of those who are oppressed. In a nutshell, *Theater of the Oppressed* seeks to break down the wall that separates the spectators from the actors and to restore the "protagonist function in theater and society" to the proletariat.[23] This incites oppressed persons to participate in the action of a play or performance, thus reclaiming their agency. Returning the power of agency in play-acting functions as a testing ground and incubator for empowering agency in society.

Viewers participate in the performance as creative and responsible agents becoming what he calls "spect-actors." In breaking down the *fourth wall* (the barrier between the spectators and actors), Boal's theater provides groups faced with oppression an opportunity to create theater that offers a chance for reflection on the problems they face. He encourages people to use theatrical techniques for the artistic expression of their lived experience of oppression. He creates several types of exercises and games such as Image Theatre, which is like depicting a scene with living statues, and Forum Theatre, which utilizes playing out oppressive situations with different scenarios.

For example, in a typical session a group of actors will create, perform, and reflect on scenes that demonstrate instances of oppression. The "spect-actors" will then make changes to the scene until they find a way to deal with the problem that seems acceptable to the group. This activity creates beneficial dialogue among the participants that provides ideas of how to respond to similar occurrences they experience in life. By becoming part of the creative process and having control of the stories and the outcomes, participants are able to have a cathartic experience that purges feelings of helplessness and stagnation in the face of the status quo. Persons are then encouraged to act as agents of resistance and contribute to the transformation of their situation.

---

22. Freire, *Pedagogy of the Oppressed*, 48.
23. Boal, *Theater of the Oppressed*, 119.

The participatory exercises have at least three benefits. First, they can be think/acting tanks in which possible practical solutions to oppressive situations can be generated and tried out. Second, the development of community is a significant benefit. But the third and primary goal is to create agency and *conscientization* in those who are oppressed.

This approach is practical and experiential. It focuses on four goals: (1) empowering oppressed persons toward greater self-confidence, self-assertion, and agency; (2) raising consciousness of problems in the world through dialogue, sharing feelings, and other interactions; (3) inspiring imagination to envision a future with less oppression; and (4) inspiring the passion and energy to change the world toward this future.

Boal's inventive use of theater and performance breaks down barriers in political situations as well. His work instills self-confidence and agency in those who are oppressed and promotes practical solutions for real-life problems faced by many oppressed persons. This creative and effective work has become an international movement with a variety of exercises in the same vein as Boal's original process, and innovations continue to abound. There are trainings for communities that want to practice this use of art for social justice as well as online resources from all over the world.[24]

Given these purposes toward changing social situations, and his methods of empowering the people, Boal's work is clearly a potential resource for liberation theology. While Boal does not engage explicitly religious themes or make religious claims, several authors have developed a link with liberation theology. Charles Gillespie suggests that collaboration between a theology of the oppressed and a theater of the oppressed has several possibilities for bringing about social awareness.[25] Shannon Craigo-Snell offers an excellent constructive work on the problems of apathy among church members. She uses Boal's analysis, insight, and pioneering approach in her quest for an effective renewal of the church.[26] Also Dustin Wright produced an innovative "liturgy of the oppressed" based on Boal's ideas and practices. Wright appropriately points out that liturgy is rightly understood as the "work of the people" and as such, liturgy should explicitly empower the people to be agents of their own faith and as Wright blogs, "develop faith in themselves, their fellow human beings, and most of all, faith in their God."[27]

But what has this to do with Kierkegaard as a resource for liberation theology? No one has yet to bring Kierkegaard to bear in this collaboration between Boal's creative praxis and theology for the church.

---

24. Boal, "Theatre of the Oppressed"; MacDonald and Rachel, "Augusto Boal's Forum Theatre for Teachers"; Philadelphia Theatre of the Oppressed, "Games Classes."

25. Gillespie, "Can Theater Be a Project," 12–31.

26. Craigo-Snell, *Empty Church*, 68–97.

27. Wright, "Liturgy of the Oppressed," para. 6.

Boal to Kierkegaard

The following section applies Boal's critique of the power dynamic that exists between the one who speaks and the ones who listen, to Kierkegaard's famous analogy between theater and sacred dramas, such as in a worship service and inspirational literature to further develop the possibilities in Kierkegaard's critique.

Kierkegaard evokes a similar reversal of the roles of players in his *Upbuilding Discourses in Various Spirits* (*UDVS*). Here he proposes theater as a metaphor for worship and spiritual edification to illustrate his view of difference between the secular and the sacred. In the secular arts of theater, there are three primary roles: *the speaker*, or player who conspicuously draws attention as the center of important activity; *the listeners*, who pay attention to the actor(s); and the *prompter* or "*souffleurs*," who sits off-stage and whispers to the speaker. In applying this metaphor to a religious context, one might think that the preacher would be the actor, the congregation would be the audience, and perhaps the Holy Spirit would be the prompter. However, Kierkegaard rearranges the roles. He says that when one is conscious that God is present and that all of one's actions and thoughts are accomplished before God, then everything is not only intensified, it is changed, even turned upside down. On a religious occasion where God is the ultimate listener, each member of the congregation is the actor. The preacher's role is limited to offering encouragement. The speaker is not like a secular actor drawing attention to him/herself, rather, s/he is merely "the prompter [who] whispers to the actor what to say."[28] Kierkegaard writes that it is the listener who "is present and open before God; he is, if I may put it this way, the actor, who in the true sense is acting before God."[29]

Kierkegaard gives an example of a subdeacon, the church worker who leads the congregation in the Prayers of the People. She is "without *authority*—it is not actually the church worker who is praying. But the listener, who sits in the church and is inwardly before God while he listens to the reading, he is praying."[30] The earnestness of the subdeacon who tells the congregation what to say, is not the key. Rather, the earnestness of the congregant who is speaking to God—this is what is vital.

The lead actor is every individual in the pew; the principal act-ion is what the individual in the pew does in relation to God. The listener is called to look inwardly into himself as the actor standing before God. It is the listener's own "decisive self-activity, upon which everything depends."[31]

And what is this decisive self-activity? I believe there are three dimensions to it. First, Kierkegaard says, "the actor's rendition is the main thing."[32] The speaker, or

---

28. Kierkegaard, *Upbuilding Discourses*, 124.
29. Ibid., 125.
30. Ibid.
31. Ibid., 122.
32. Ibid., 124.

preacher may give direction on *what* is to be said, but *how* the individual says it is the key. The decisive self-activity is enacted in silence inwardly *before God*, where the individual speaks "in himself, with himself, to himself."[33] In other words, the listener should speak internally to God with solemnity and passion. Yet, the earnestness with which the listener says the words in the prayer is only the beginning.

The second and third dimensions require us to remember that this discourse is given on the occasion of confession. Kierkegaard's metaphor is meant to aid the sinner in recognizing her sins/sinfulness so she can confess them, be forgiven, and repent. The sinner must take responsibility decisively for himself, his sins, and his confession. This religious struggle is to remedy what Kierkegaard believes is problematic about Christendom. Christians have become lackadaisical in relation to their own salvation. They pay lip service to the church while letting the pastors and bishops decide religious matters. His reversal of the roles speaks to this problem. He is pointing believers back toward themselves to actively engage themselves as sinners. So when the speaker directs the listener to confess sins, the listener should not merely speak the empty words, but search herself for her sins.

This brings us to what I think is the third dimension of the decisive self-activity. Passionately rendering the call to repentance toward oneself and taking responsibility for one's sins requires becoming conscious of oneself as a single individual before God. The follow-through of decisive self-activity is living a conscious life, conscious that the one should "as a single individual make an accounting of how he has lived as a single individual."[34] This concluding proclamation is the main theme of the discourse. Instead of remaining like a passive spectator in a secular theater, Kierkegaard bids the listener to take the active role of a conscious individual. Here he calls for something akin to what Boal calls a "spect-actor"—one who grasps her own agency. Kierkegaard addresses the one sitting in the pew listening, or on the desk chair, reading this edifying discourse, breaking his own version of a "fourth wall" (the invisible boundary between author and reader). You there, don't rest on your laurels or the pastor's laurels, rather you yourself should speak and act, "in earnestness" and "before God" who is the true audience of your living. You should be the actual actors in the great drama of salvation and liturgy. In other words, it is the listener (or congregant) herself that should be the actor on the stage of the worship and salvation, since she is the one who must decide and engage in her own spiritual drama as an individual.

It might seem that this is but a fancy little analogy to dramatize Kierkegaard's call for serious confession of sins, but Boal's critical analysis of the dangers of theater applies to any convention in which there is a barrier between those who speak and those who listen. The division lulls the observers into becoming passive receivers of the information and diminishes their self-awareness and agency.

33. Ibid.
34. Ibid., 151.

Kierkegaard as Resource for Liberation Theology

Now that we have examined both Boal's radical enactment of reversing the roles of the spectators and actors, and Kierkegaard's similar suggestion of reversing the roles of authority in the church, let us return to the question of Kierkegaard and liberation theology. Above I described liberation theology as seeking a two-pronged liberation—liberation from the sin of the oppressors and the harm this causes, and liberation from one's own sin that inhibits the deepening consciousness of oneself before God.

I suggest that Kierkegaard's interpretation of the command to love the neighbor without reference to one's own preference coupled with his insistence that Christians are enabled to love the neighbor this way by presuming that love is already present offer resources for liberation theology. Kierkegaard's goal may not appear to be consistent with liberation theology's primary focus on alleviating the external political and social forces of oppression, but this does not mean that his theology is without implications for making changes in the world. The changes he sees as consistent with the purpose of Christianity occur from inside out. Changing the way that individuals are treated and appreciated has implications for changing the world. But the essential changes that Kierkegaard's authorship are after are those within the one loving, not the object of the love. He writes, "The one who loves does something to himself—he presupposes that love is present in the other person—which certainly is the opposite of doing something to the other person."[35] The lover is transformed and yet, one wonders if persons are treated as if love is already present in them, as if they are subjects capable of love, then I cannot imagine that this would not change the external political and social world. As Sylvia Walsh sees it, "serious external consequences will surely result from the attempt to mediate one's temporal relationships with Christian love."[36]

Staying focused on the particular example that I highlighted above, giving a banquet, for example, does offer liberation from both of these directions. First, most directly from Kierkegaard's own perspective, giving a banquet for the neighbor who is poor addresses liberation from one's own sin. If I am the one fulfilling the command to love the neighbor, the theological work being done is my internal transformation. The one who loves as a Christian, loves without reference to one's own preference and one's own needs, is changed. The fundamental *work* of love for Kierkegaard is not limited to what the lover can do for the one being loved, but rather, what God's love does for the lover—transforming her into a Christian. I am fulfilling the command to love the neighbor by seeing them as neighbor, not as poor and needy. This shift in perspective is the way that Christian love is effective inwardly.

Second, the one being loved, the neighbor who is hungry, is liberated by being nurtured, both by the food of the banquet and more importantly, by being known as a neighbor, a human being equally loved by God, equally worthy of love, and equally

---

35. Kierkegaard, *Works of Love*, 219.
36. Walsh, *Living Christianly*, 101.

capable of loving. It is this last point that I argue is the most helpful for liberation theology—the neighbor is loved by presuming that she is already a subject herself. And it is the direct implication of Kierkegaard's interpretation of Paul's claim that "love builds up" (1 Cor 8:1) as meaning that Christian love presumes that love is already present and that the neighbor is already worthy and capable of love.[37]

Seeing a person as a "neighbor" suggests three important characteristics. First, a neighbor is a person I see regularly, who is near to me. Thus her well-being impacts my well-being. Second, as a Christian I am called to love my neighbor. Seeing the poor person as my neighbor means that I am called to love her. This leads to the third point, which is based on Kierkegaard's view of love. Kierkegaard develops Paul's claim that Christian love builds up (1 Cor 8). Love does not build in the way that new construction builds a house where there was no foundation already present. Rather, the Christian "love builds up by presuming that love is already present."[38] It builds upon the foundation of love, a foundation upon which the neighbor is seen as one who is already loveable and capable of loving. She is to be seen and treated as a subject who is capable, capable of love and capable of God. I contend when a person is treated as a neighbor, she is likely to be empowered toward her own agency. This means that seeing the neighbor in the person who is poor and lowly means seeing him as one who is not only deserving of love, but also capable of love. In other words, he is a subject with his own agency and subjectivity.

And in this way, giving a banquet for the one who is poor is liberation because it resists the oppressive forces that ignore the subjectivity of the poor and lowly. It not only softens the oppression of economic injustice in feeding with celebration the one who is poor (such a banquet may also provide opportunities for the poor to develop practical worldly connections), but more importantly, this work of love is one way to empower and build up subjecthood and agency one person at a time.

Kierkegaard and Boal share commonalities with a few significant differences. Both thinkers have the common strength that their approaches enable others toward becoming participating subjects of their own liberation. Both are careful to avoid imposing their own view of what the oppressed need upon those who are oppressed.

This is an important insight that has become a common corrective to the works of charity *for* those in need. Instead, social justice organizations seek to empower those in need to be able to do work for themselves. This is not new, of course. It is a contemporary practice inspired, in part, by the quote often attributed to Moses Maimonides: "Give a man a fish and you feed him for a day; teach a man to fish and you feed him for a lifetime."[39] Both Kierkegaard and Boal offer approaches that undercut the assumption that those who are not oppressed know what the oppressed need and can simply hand it over to them and then all shall be well. Rather they

---

37. Kierkegaard, *Works of Love*, 209, 219.
38. Ibid., 218.
39. Maimonides, "Gifts for the Poor," 72–76.

both seek to empower the poor and lowly by giving them voice or treating them as a friend with agency.

Boal and Kierkegaard also have different strengths that function as gifts to give each other toward a theology of liberation. Kierkegaard's strength is in his ability to theorize conscious subjectivity (by which I mean subjecthood in relation to God) in individuals. We see this in both his interpretation of the command to love and as well as in his call to the congregant to be the active agent in her becoming conscious of herself before God. Where Kierkegaard is weak is in his theory and theology of community. His focus on the importance of the individual does not provide any adequately explicit direction for communal support or development. However, I would argue that we could imagine a community of self-conscious subjects who love each other by building each other up; such a community would develop naturally out of the focus on love and subjectivity, but how that would happen is not addressed. It would certainly be an asset for church communities and is consistent with theologies of liberation. Further, he does not apply this liberation to ameliorating the external structures of oppression.

Boal's strong suit is his creative, practical, and experiential approaches toward empowering those who are oppressed toward their own agency. His position is also strong in his critical analysis of the oppressive function of the walls that separate those who speak and act from those who watch and listen, and his attention to breaking down these walls. His immediate focus is not on political change, but he hopes that his work will help enable those who are oppressed to contribute to changing the world for the better. Further, his creative exercises intentionally and directly create community and communal support among those who are oppressed as they figure out together practical solutions to problems of oppression and develop *conscientization*. In terms of weaknesses, I wonder about persons who are not performers, who are shy, not confident enough to stand up and take on the role of the actor, or have not yet developed what Freire calls *conscientization*, or a critical consciousness of their own participation in their oppression. These folks might need an additional aid to bolster their confidence and awareness. Further, he does not provide guidelines for how or why persons should relate to each other in helpful or loving ways.

Let me conclude by sketching a few of the resources that a combination of the strengths of these two thinkers provides for a theology of liberation. Kierkegaard's quieter, more individual approach focusing on the subjecthood of each single individual may be more effective for individuals who are not yet able or confident enough to perform in Boal's theatre. Further, his interpretation that love builds up by presuming that love is already present declares the power of Christian love to build up each individual as a subject who is already worthy of love, already loved, and already capable of loving. This stresses the significance of every individual as an agential subject, even and especially those who are poor and lowly. It also provides theology guidance for how persons ought to relate to each other in social and political life.

Further, when Kierkegaard enjoins the Christian to give a banquet for persons who are hungry and needy, he is celebrating the oppressed individual as a person who is seen by God and others as deserving dignity and attention. His proposed metaphorical reversal of roles, in which the key player of a religious discourse is the listener, not the speaker, reinforces this by bringing attention to the individual in the pew. Each listener becomes more conscious of herself and develops a more accurate and full awareness of herself, her sins, and her standing before God. The consciousness of being in the presence of God intensifies one's awareness of being a single individual, a subject responsible for one's own decisions.

Kierkegaard's call to live consciously as an individual before God dovetails nicely with Boal's engendering agency and conscientization in the people. The difference is that for Boal, the goal is about inspiring conscientization and agency to act as subjects politically, while for Kierkegaard, taking responsibility is about the individual's own personal relationship with God and his/her eternal happiness.

Boal's critical analysis of the problematic ways theater operates could be very helpful in critically reevaluating the way churches function. Like theater, the church is an institution that reinforces the separation of those who speak on the one side and those who should listen on the other. His analysis explains how the structure reinforces the passive absorption of the norms of those who construct the drama, and discourages the active agency of the viewers/parishioners.

Further, Boal's experimental theater of the people is an intriguing model for how to practice church. Consider Boal's technique of what he calls "forum theater," in which the "participant[s] must intervene decisively in the dramatic action and change it."[40] Within the context of the church this could lead to a praxis movement toward a "Liturgy of the Oppressed." In such new form of liturgy, the "work of the people," the preacher might play the Joker (a glorified prompter) and suggest an issue, biblical passage, or theme for the gathering of the group and then step back and simply facilitate the process. Certain elements would need to be included, such as breaking bread together, prayer, reading a passage from Scripture, praise, singing, etc. But the community of congregants gathered would co-create how and when they are included. This is akin to a conversational sermon, but even more deep-seated. Boal's exercises also encourage communal support and sharing of ideas for resisting the oppression and becoming capable of contributing to making changes in the world.

Liberation theologians could learn from Kierkegaard's insistence that the individual Christian is the rightful person of interest to God, not the preacher, the speaker, or the leader. He says that it is not so much what the pastor says to the congregation that is important, but the key element is what the congregant says to himself as he becomes aware of himself, as standing before God. Given that the key goal for liberation theology is to break down the walls between those with power and those without, a worship service or theatrical exercise, or social justice meeting that

---

40. Boal, *Theater of the Oppressed*, 139.

facilitates attention to the subjecthood of each and every individual participant offers a practical approach for making sure that each and every person involved is heard and empowered as a subject.

In conclusion, this essay has shown that a dialogue between Kierkegaard's practical theology of worship and spiritual reflection on the one hand and Boal's theater of the oppressed yields fruitful resources for engaging Christian worship and liberation theology. Kierkegaard's encouragement of listeners—whether they are congregants or theater participants—to reclaim the authority and responsibility that is theirs, to claim their roles as starring actors in the liturgy, the prayers, and the process of liberation is a resource for liberation theology.

Bibliography

Boal, Augusto. *Theater of the Oppressed*. Translated by Charles A. and Maria-Odilia Leal McBribe. New York: Theatre Communications, 1985.

———. "Theatre of the Oppressed." Jana Sanskriti International Research and Resource Institute. http://jsirri.org/theatre-of-the-oppressed.

Cone, James H. *The Cross and the Lynching Tree*. Maryknoll: Orbis, 2011.

Craigo-Snell, Shannon. *The Empty Church: Theater, Theology, and Bodily Hope*. New York: Oxford University Press, 2014.

Ferreira, M. Jamie. *Love's Grateful Striving: A Commentary on Kierkegaard's Works of Love*. Oxford: Oxford University Press, 2001.

Freire, Pablo. *Pedagogy of the Oppressed*. New York: Continuum, 1970.

Gillespie, Charles A. "Can Theatre Be a Project of Liberation Theology?": Explorations in the Case of a Collaboration in Tanzania." *Union Seminary Quarterly Review* 64 (2013) 12–31.

Hisrich, Matthew. "Toward a New Theology of Liberation." Unpublished manuscript. 2007. http://www.sorenkierkegaard.nl/artikelen/Engels/203.%20HisrichLiberationessay050307.pdf.

Hughes, Carl. *Kierkegaard and the Staging of Desire*. New York: Fordham University Press, 2014.

Johnson, Todd E., and Dal Savidge. *Performing the Sacred: Theology and Theater in Dialogue*. Grand Rapids: Baker Academic, 2009.

Kierkegaard, Søren. *Upbuilding Discourses in Various Spirits*. Princeton: Princeton University Press, 1993.

———. *Works of Love*. Princeton: Princeton University Press, 1995.

MacDonald, Susie, and Daniel Rachel. "Augusto Boal's Forum Theatre for Teachers." Notes from a workshop at Athens Conference 2000. http://organizingforpower.org/wp-content/uploads/2009/03/games-theater-of-oppressed.pdf.

Maimonides, Moses. "Gifts for the Poor: Moses Maimonides' Treatise on *Tzedakah*." Translated by Joseph B. Meszler. Edited by Marc Lee Raphael. Department of Religion, College of William and Mary, Williamsburg, Virginia, 2003. http://rabbimeszler.com/yahoo_site_admin/assets/docs/Gifts_for_the_Poor.27084324.pdf.

Marshall, Ronald. *Kierkegaard for the Church*. Eugene, OR: Wipf & Stock, 2013.

Pattison, George. *Kierkegaard's Upbuilding Discourses*. London: Routledge, 2002.

Philadelphia Theatre of the Oppressed. "Games Classes: What We Played." http://tophiladelphia.blogspot.com/2011/10/games-for-actors-non-actors.html.

Walsh, Sylvia. *Living Christianly: Kierkegaard's Dialectic of Christian Existence*. University Park: Pennsylvania State University Press, 2005.

Wright, Dustin. "A Liturgy of the Oppressed." *It's Only a Northern Blog*. June 13, 2014. http://www.itsonlyanorthernblog.com/2014/06/a-liturgy-of-oppressed.html.

14

Politicizing Kierkegaardian Repetition
On Schmitt and Kierkegaard

DANA LLOYD

Everything changes. You can make a fresh start with your final breath.
—BERTOLT BRECHT

Introduction

BOTH SØREN KIERKEGAARD AND Carl Schmitt are concerned with what they understand as the progressing secularization of the world around them. Against this background, Kierkegaard defines the self, and Schmitt defines the sovereign, in terms of decision on the exception. While Kierkegaard's definition is not explicitly political, Schmitt challenges us to think politically with Kierkegaard when he cites the Danish philosopher in his book *Political Theology*. How are we to think politically with Kierkegaard? The most obvious places to turn are to Kierkegaard's writings on Abraham and Socrates. In *Fear and Trembling*, Kierkegaard presents Abraham as someone who is making a sovereign decision to suspend ethics when he finds himself in an exceptional situation, and intends to sacrifice his son in order to pass a test of faith. Even though Kierkegaard's reading of the biblical story of the *Akedah* is not explicitly political, we can easily see the political implications of the story if we understand politics as part of ethics, as Barry Stocker proposes.[1] Abraham is a political exemplar because he is a sovereign self who becomes the father of a sovereign people. Kierkegaard also writes extensively about Socrates, whose trial is another significant theopolitical event. But Schmitt mentions neither Abraham nor Socrates in *Political Theology*. Rather, he quotes at length from a book that reads at first as a romance novel with no political implications at all: *Repetition*. In this essay, I explore Kierkegaard's concept of repetition and its relevance to political theology. I read Schmitt's sovereign

---

1. Stocker, *Kierkegaard on Politics*, 11.

"who decides on the exception" as parallel to Kierkegaard's sovereign self, a self that is constituted as sovereign through repetition.[2]

For Kierkegaard, the ultimate meaning of repetition is religious, but in *Repetition* we are presented with a secularized repetition, through three analogies: one metaphysical, one psychological, and one ethical. Schmitt offers a fourth analogy, a political one, when he writes that "the exception in jurisprudence is analogous to the miracle in theology."[3] Would Kierkegaard agree? Kierkegaard opposed what he called "political movement" to what he called "religious movement." Therefore, one might conclude that Kierkegaard would disagree with the parallel drawn by Schmitt between politics and theology, according to which our political concepts are no more than secularized theological concepts.[4] Nevertheless, both thinkers argued that politics desperately needs religion, and I believe that unfolding the rich meaning of Kierkegaardian repetition will help us see what they both mean by this. Let us begin exploring this need by way of reading Schmitt's *Political Theology*.

Repetition and the Political: Schmitt on Sovereignty

Carl Schmitt admired Kierkegaard. Jacob Taubes writes that for Schmitt "everything revolves around this Kierkegaard of the exception."[5] One finds in Schmitt's library many of Kierkegaard's books in the German translation, with Schmitt's notes in the margins, as well as numerous references to Kierkegaard in Schmitt's diaries. Ellen Kennedy writes that Schmitt was particularly interested in Kierkegaard's critique of his generation's "culture of the trivial, destructive of '*geist*' and seriousness."[6] However, in what many consider his most important work, *Political Theology*, Schmitt quotes from Kierkegaard's *Repetition*, rather than from the latter's more explicitly political works, *Fear and Trembling* or *The Present Age*.

The reference to *Repetition* comes at the end of the first chapter of *Political Theology*. Schmitt writes that "in the exception the power of real life breaks through the crust of a mechanism that has become torpid by repetition."[7] Schmitt is glorifying the exception here, and criticizing repetition of the kind that Kierkegaard himself parodies in *Repetition* in the form of secularized analogies of true, religious repetition. True Kierkegaardian repetition is exactly "the power of real life" that Schmitt strives for. True Kierkegaardian repetition is "a religious movement by virtue of the absurd"[8] and

---

2. On the conceptual parallel between the sovereign state and the sovereign self, see Elshtain, *Sovereignty*.
3. Schmitt, *Political Theology*, 36.
4. Ibid.
5. Taubes, *Political Theology of Paul*, 66.
6. Kennedy, *Constitutional Failure*, 205; see also Ryan, *Kierkegaard's Indirect Politics*, 90–91.
7. Schmitt, *Political Theology*, 15.
8. Kierkegaard, *Repetition*, 324 [*Pap.* IV B 120].

would come to mean "a task for freedom,"⁹ "atonement,"¹⁰ and "true happiness."¹¹ This repetition is indeed the exception. The two are not opposed to one another.

In *Repetition*, Kierkegaard does not directly define repetition; instead, he asks whether repetition is possible. This question is significant because, in some sense, our world gains meaning and sense through consistency and predictability. Language would not have been the same had we not repeatedly used the same words to refer to the same objects; science would not have been what it is had experiments and their results not been repeatable. Things gain sense through repetition (or the possibility of repetition). Law has a similar structure: if it is not repeatedly followed, it loses its grounds. In a way, the sovereign's power to suspend law renders law pointless, because if it can be suspended then how can we see it as law? Similarly, atonement—which is the ultimate meaning of repetition, according to Kierkegaard—suspends law (at least moral law, but in the form of pardon it suspends positive law as well), thereby, ostensibly, rendering it pointless. Counterintuitively, both Kierkegaard and Schmitt tell us that it is the exception that *makes* the general meaningful. How could it be? Does it not render the general meaningless? To understand this statement, let us look more closely into Schmitt's theory of the exception and then return to Kierkegaardian repetition itself.

Schmitt refers to Kierkegaard as a "Protestant theologian who demonstrated the vital intensity possible in theological reflection in the nineteenth century."¹² He quotes (and paraphrases) from *Repetition*:

> The exception explains the general and itself. And if one wants to study the general correctly, one only needs to look around for a true exception. It reveals everything more clearly than does the general. Endless talk about the general becomes boring; there are exceptions. If they cannot be explained, then the general also cannot be explained. The difficulty is usually not noticed because the general is not thought about with passion but with a comfortable superficiality. The exception, on the other hand, thinks the general with intense passion.¹³

Passion is exactly what is needed in politics, what is absent from the repetition of mere law-following. It drives decision-making, both in Kierkegaard's "authentic" self and in Schmitt's sovereign "who decides on the exception."¹⁴ Let me proceed by way of

---

9. Ibid.
10. Ibid.
11. Ibid., 330 [*Pap.* IV B 122].
12. Schmitt, *Political Theology*, 15. Schmitt mentions Kierkegaard in other writings, as well. In *Political Romanticism*, Kierkegaard is "the only great figure among the romantics," and in *Roman Catholicism and Political Form*, he is "the most inward of all Christians." (See Ryan, *Kierkegaard's Indirect Politics*, 102; Ryan, "Carl Schmitt," 186.)
13. Schmitt, *Political Theology*, 15.
14. Ibid., 5.

introducing Schmitt's political theology before returning to Kierkegaardian repetition and showing how Schmitt can help us to politicize Kierkegaard in general and repetition in particular.

"All significant concepts of the modern theory of the state are secularized theological concepts," writes Schmitt.[15] In other words, we can understand modern politics only by means of theological structures. The statement is sweeping but in *Political Theology* Schmitt actually focuses on one application only—the question of sovereignty. Sovereignty, according to him, is a borderline concept, and therefore it cannot be associated with routine; it belongs in extreme cases. Schmitt's *Political Theology* is a polemic with legal formalists, such as Max Weber and Hans Kelsen, who argue that we can understand law only in legal terms (an argument similar to the Hegelian notion that Kierkegaard criticized in *Fear and Trembling*, that the ethical is the universal and can only be understood from the point of view of the universal).[16] We do not understand law in political, economic, or religious terms. Law is autonomous, not affected by politics. This is not necessary but a result of secularization. This notion of law assumes that legal action has force by virtue of the authority of law and not of politics ("the rule of law" rather than "the rule of man"). But this view of law as a closed system with its own logic is illusory, according to Schmitt. When we think seriously about the relation between law and politics we discover that "sovereign is he who decides on the exception."[17] The moment of decision is manifest in the state of emergency, but it is, nevertheless, the organizing principal of law as such. Schmitt's point when analyzing the state of emergency is that we cannot deny the moment of decision. If we examine the state of emergency from a simple legal point of view—this is the point of view of the exception. Ordinary law is suspended in favor of emergency powers. Can we understand emergency from the point of view of the rule of law? The legal formalists' answer is positive. Moreover, according to them, we cannot understand the state of emergency from a non-legal point of view. The rule of law is preserved even in the state of emergency (Kierkegaard's Abraham, similarly, would be dismissed by the Hegelian ethical-universal as a sinner, not affecting the universality of ethics through his actions).

Schmitt disagrees. Emergency law does not really subordinate the state of emergency to the rule of law. There is always room for action; there is always freedom to decide. Someone—the sovereign—will be able to declare the state of emergency and decide how to act in this situation. The sovereign is not limited by the rule of law, just as Abraham was not limited by the ethical when he decided to obey God's command and sacrifice his son. The legal sphere is always open, enabling political decision. From a political point of view, the sovereign cannot be subordinate to law in the same way that God—from a theological point of view—cannot be subordinate to the law of

---

15. Ibid., 36.
16. Kierkegaard, *Fear and Trembling*, 54.
17. Schmitt, *Political Theology*, 5.

nature. Politics, from the point of view of the rule of law, has no force, no libido, no vitality. The freedom to decide is the key to allowing politics to be born anew, just as faith is born from the ethical with Abraham's actions.

Why did Schmitt need Kierkegaardian repetition to tell us all that? Scholars tend to focus on the relationship between repetition and the exception when they try to answer this question.[18] I argue that Schmitt's reference to repetition points to an even stronger connection between his theory of the sovereign and Kierkegaard's theory of the self. Schmitt's sovereign state, that is constituted through the exception, is modeled on Kierkegaard's sovereign self, who is constituted through repetition. Let us, then, turn to Kierkegaardian repetition.

Kierkegaard's Concept of Repetition

Let me briefly present here the narrative of *Repetition*. Constantin Constantius, the pseudonymous author of the book, tells us about a young poet who fell in love with a girl but his love was an unhappy love. He was unable to commit to marrying her but neither could he bring himself to break up with her, and so he eventually fled to Stockholm. In his letters from Stockholm, he tells Constantin that he found comfort in the story of Job, inspired by Job's refusal to believe that he suffered because of his sins.[19] His correspondent's account of the failed love affair makes Constantin wonder whether or not repetition is possible, so he takes a trip to Berlin, a city he has visited before, in order to find out if he can relive the pleasures of his previous trip. Alas, the trip is a series of "disasters," such as a disappointing visit to the theatre, proving to Constantin that repetition is impossible. But this search for repetition via tourism is just as superficial as the poet's reading of the book of Job.

To understand the deep meaning of Kierkegaardian repetition, we have to wander through the concept's secularized analogies (from the realms of metaphysics, psychology, and ethics) before we can discover religious repetition. Then we will consider the fourth possible analogy, in the realm of the political. In *Repetition*, Kierkegaard congratulates the Danish language on a philosophical term. The Danish word he uses is *gjentagelsen*, which commonly means repetition, but which carries another meaning, of returning to an original position (*redintegratio in statum pristinum*).[20] These two meanings seem to contradict each other, and this is exactly why Kierkegaard thinks repetition is "a good Danish word."[21] The two meanings are ostensibly contradictory because when we think of repetition we think of sameness and immutability, while

---

18. Little has been written on Kierkegaard and Schmitt. In English, see, e.g., Conrad, "Kierkegaard's Moment"; Gould, "Laws, Exceptions, Norms"; Ryan, *Kierkegaard's Indirect Politics*; Ryan, "Carl Schmitt"; and Smith, *Friendship and the Political*.

19. Kierkegaard, *Repetition*, 207.

20. Croxall, *Kierkegaard Commentary*, 128.

21. Kierkegaard, *Repetition*, 149.

return to an original position assumes that the thing that returned has changed and moved away from its original position (otherwise there would have been nowhere to return to). If the first meaning is related to sameness, the second is related to change. The two meanings are in tension, tells us Kierkegaard, and the Danish term holds both meanings without resolving the tension, thereby explaining the relation between the Eleatics and Heraclitus.[22]

The opening lines of *Repetition* hint to the idea that it is existence itself that proves that metaphysical inquiry is futile (explaining the relation between the Eleatics and Heraclitus): "When the Eleatics denied motion, Diogenes, as everyone knows, came forward as an opponent. He literally did come forward, because he did not say a word but merely paced back and forth a few times, thereby assuming that he had sufficiently refuted them."[23] These two sentences say a lot about the relation between language, metaphysics and existence. The story wants to convince us that action has more force than any philosophical debate, that it can make a difference and express ideas that words cannot. For this reason, Constantin decides to look for repetition in Berlin (through action) rather than in words (through philosophical musings).

Nevertheless, Kierkegaard goes on to tell us that the Danish language actually does have a word that is philosophical and that can resolve the fundamental problem of metaphysics: "repetition is the *interest* of metaphysics and the interest upon which metaphysics comes to grief."[24] In other words, repetition expresses both the fundamental problem of metaphysics (the possibility of motion) and the problem's solution—which puts an end to all metaphysical inquiry. Repetition is what gives things their meaning. Therefore, if repetition is impossible, "all life dissolves into an empty, meaningless noise."[25] If repetition only means sameness, then there is no motion. If the world is a flux, then repetition is impossible. But searching for continuity in a Heraclitic constantly-changing world provides a solution to the problem of repetition, a solution that is itself somewhat of an oxymoron: discovering that life is a repetition, within a Heraclitic worldview, means that what is continuous in life is change and renewal. Thus, *gjentagelsen*—because of its double meaning—provides us with a solution for the problem of continuity within the Heraclitic worldview—it resolves the debate between the Eleatics and Heraclitus, and metaphysics founders: the metaphysical problem of motion is solved, and what remains is an ethical problem.

The opening lines of repetition hinted in this direction when they suggested that action is stronger than words. In Gilles Deleuze's words, Kierkegaardian repetition wants to "put metaphysics in motion, in action."[26] But once metaphysics is put in action, it becomes ethics. To use Schmittian terminology, while the Eleatics denied mo-

22. Ibid.
23. Ibid., 131.
24. Ibid., 149.
25. Ibid.
26. Deleuze, *Difference and Repetition*, 8.

tion (just as legal formalists describe the sphere of law as closed and unchangeable), Diogenes made a sovereign decision on the exception and came forward, thus refuting them. His action takes us from the sphere of metaphysics to that of ethics, and later on, to that of politics. As we learn from Kierkegaard, repetition is "the watchword in every ethical view"[27]—it will become the *interest* of ethics, and the interest upon which ethics comes to grief.

The Interest of Ethics

The ethical problem is also a psychological one, as *Repetition*'s subtitle—*A Venture in Experimenting Psychology*—suggests.[28] The question of repetition becomes a question of personal identity rather than a metaphysical problem: "The most interior problem of the possibility of repetition is expressed externally, as if repetition, if it were possible, were to be found outside the individual when in fact it must be found within the individual."[29] Catherine Pickstock stresses this point. For her, the question of repetition is a question of identity: "While the individual cannot be identically repeated, and if it appears to be so, as in the case of urban modernity, is alienated from herself, nevertheless, like any other *res*, the individual must be repeated in order to be identified as an individual."[30] Clare Carlisle adds that repetition as creation or declaration of identity is "an inward movement. This means that it is a movement of intensification, of deepening, within the 'heart' or the 'soul' of the individual."[31]

The problem is that, since we did not choose to be born, how can we see ourselves as having any agency? *Repetition*'s nameless poet expresses such a worry in one of his letters to Constantin:

> Who tricked me into this whole thing and leaves me standing here? Who am I? How did I get into the world? Why was I not asked about it, why was I not informed of the rules and regulations but just thrust into the ranks . . . ? How did I get involved in this big enterprise called actuality? Why should I be involved? Isn't it a matter of choice? And if I am compelled to be involved, where is the manager—I have something to say about this.[32]

For life to become "a matter of choice" we need repetition, and indeed, Kierkegaard writes in his journal that repetition is possible because in some situations it is

---

27. Ibid., 149.

28. The relationship between Constantin and the poet resembles that between a therapist and a patient in many ways. Exploring this relationship is beyond the scope of this essay. For an analysis of *Repetition* as a critique of nineteenth-century experimental psychology, see Tang, "Repetition and Nineteenth-Century Experimental Psychology."

29. Kierkegaard, *Repetition*, 304 [*Pap.* IV B 117, 283].

30. Pickstock, *Repetition and Identity*, 92.

31. Carlisle, *Kierkegaard's Philosophy of Becoming*, 76.

32. Kierkegaard, *Repetition*, 200.

extremely needed.[33] We often hear statements such as, "If I had known then what I know now, I would have acted differently." We long for a return to a past situation and for the opportunity to act differently than we actually have. It is not longing to relive the past exactly as it has been, but to change the past, to get a chance to correct it, "to make a fresh start," in Brecht's words. We all know the child's frustration when the child is told "you will understand when you are older." Well, sometimes we do understand when we are older, and then we wish we could go back to childhood and *do something* with this understanding. Kierkegaard himself knows this frustration very well, and he expresses it in his journal: "Philosophy is perfectly right in saying that life must be understood backwards. But then one forgets the other clause—that it must be lived forwards."[34]

Repetition—if it is possible—solves this ethical-psychological problem. We understand repetition as return to the origin, to the moment of becoming, or as rebirth. If *Repetition*'s poet can return to the moment of his own constitution, he can become a subject through his own sovereign decision; he can constitute a life of agency—indeed, he can become the manager that he is looking for. Nevertheless, repetition in this sense seems impossible, as Constantin discovers in his failed experiment in Berlin.

> One can only do something for the first time *once*. To do it again may repeat the externals of the act, but its newness cannot be repeated. Doing the same thing for the second time is, paradoxically, its own first time and so on, *ad infinitum*. In this sense there is no repetition.[35]

But in this sense exactly there *is* repetition. Constantin's failure to recreate his previous trip to Berlin is actually a glorified failure. Because the second trip is not identical to the first one, we can see it as a *first* trip. The reduplication of the Berlin trip brings about renewal and change, and thus repetition manages to hold two contradictory meanings at once. In repetition we both create something new and recreate something old. The thing that repeats itself is, paradoxically, the uniqueness of the experience. What we can learn from the failed Berlin experiment is that the meaningful aspect of an experience is the subjective one. Berlin itself has not changed between Constantin's two trips. The hotel, café, and theater that Constantin has visited are still there. What changed is Constantin's subjective position, and this change creates a totally new experience. Since his point of view is so significant, he can actually reconstitute his life and self, return to the past and change it for the future, become an agent albeit the forced first coming to existence.

When repetition as agency turns out to be possible, another ethical problem is revealed: if we can constitute a life of free choice, see ourselves as agents, and if, as

---

33. Ibid. [*Pap.* XI3 B 122].
34. Kierkegaard, *Journals and Papers*, 1:1030.
35. McCarthy, "*Repetition*'s Repetitions," 271n12.

Milan Kundera notes, "there is no means of testing which decision is better, because there is no basis for comparison,"[36] then the ethical burden we carry becomes unbearable. *Repetition*'s young poet finds comfort in the figure of Job for this reason: "What really appeals to him in Job is that Job was right. Now everything revolves around that. Fate has played a trick on him and let him become guilty. If that is the way it is, then he can no longer take himself back again."[37] Kierkegaard describes the paradox of the ethical in various ways. In *The Concept of Anxiety*, he writes:

> Ethics proposes to bring ideality into actuality. On the other hand, it is not the nature of its movement to raise actuality up into ideality. Ethics points to ideality as a task and assumes that every man possesses the requisite conditions. Thus ethics develops a contradiction, inasmuch as it makes clear both the difficulty and the impossibility.[38]

Ethics posits ideals, which man, due to his finite nature, cannot realize. Ethics cannot lower ideality into actuality and cannot raise actuality up to ideality, and so ideality and actuality can never meet. This means that we can never fulfill the ethical ideal, and therefore we (as ethical creatures) always feel guilty. Therefore, we need forgiveness, but the ethical cannot provide it. As Kierkegaard puts it in the context of Abraham, "if it was a sin . . . he could not understand that it could be forgiven"[39]—either Abraham is not a sinner or his sin cannot be forgiven. Abraham's willingness to sacrifice Isaac is a sin from the point of view of the ethical, and the ethical cannot offer Abraham forgiveness. The problem is that it is the sinner who needs forgiveness, and it is the sinner who cannot be forgiven. The ethical ideal can never be realized, and therefore, she who strives to lead an ethical life is always frustrated. She longs for absolute forgiveness, and the ethical only has relative sources for forgiveness: "The forgiveness we need cannot be *required* of any friend or acquaintance or moral judge; hence ethics cannot secure it for us."[40] Therefore, this ethical paradox must lead us to a leap of faith, to repetition by virtue of the absurd, to God, who can offer absolute forgiveness.

> If repetition is not posited, ethics becomes a binding power. No doubt it is for this reason that the author [Constantin] stated that repetition is the solution in every ethical view. If repetition is not posited, dogmatics cannot exist at all, for repetition begins in faith, and faith is the organ for issues of dogma.[41]

---

36. Kundera, *Unbearable Lightness of Being*, 8.
37. Kierkegaard, *Repetition*, 304 [*Papirer* IV B 117, 284].
38. Kierkegaard, *Concept of Anxiety*, 16.
39. Kierkegaard, *Fear and Trembling*, 13.
40. Mooney, "Repetition," 297.
41. Kierkegaard, *Concept of Anxiety*, 18n.

Repetition becomes religious ("the *ondition sine qua non* for every issue of dogmatics")[42] when it "come[s] to mean atonement,"[43] when God forgives Abraham's unforgivable sin and returns Isaac, when the whirlwind restores Job's world, and when Socrates is born anew through Plato's writings. Religious repetition can be thought of as the exception—Abraham, Job, and Socrates become exceptional through forgiveness or atonement. Translating the problem of repetition into political terminology, we could say that the problem is that of the possibility of sovereignty. This is why Schmitt is so interested in Kierkegaardian repetition. Through it, the self becomes sovereign. She can make decisions and become the manager of her own life. But this cannot happen without God, who enables repetition "on the border of the marvelous."[44] For Deleuze, this is the point where Kierkegaardian repetition fails. The same repetition that so successfully provided an alternative to moral law and to the law of nature, to generality itself, now discovers God and the self "once and for all,"[45] foreclosing any possibility for future development. The "fundamental category of the philosophy of the future"[46] comes to a halt with faith. For Schmitt, on the other hand, it is precisely this point where politics can come in.

Epilogue: Kierkegaard on Politics

Kierkegaard, like Schmitt, thought that politics needs religion. But, as Gould points out, while "Schmitt absorbs religion into politics, Kierkegaard absorbs politics into religion."[47] Though he was ambivalent about politics and often confessed his ignorance about it, as J. Michael Tilley notes, one can find sophisticated analyses of political events in Kierkegaard's published works, as well as in his journals and letters.[48] Let us look at his scarce comments about politics and connect them to his theory of repetition. We have seen that the question of repetition is the question of motion. In 1848, in a letter to a Danish law professor, Kierkegaard distinguished between religious movement and political movement, using this distinction to comment on the unstable political situation in Europe and particularly on the French Revolution.

> Most people believe that so long as one has a fixed point *to which* one wants to get, then motion is no vortex. But this is a misunderstanding. It all depends on having a fixed point *from which to set out*. Stopping is not possible at a point *ahead*, but at a point *behind*. . . . And this is the difference between a political and a religious movement. Any purely political movement, which

---

42. Kierkegaard, *Repetition*, 149.
43. Ibid. [*Pap.* IV B 120, 309].
44. Ibid.
45. Deleuze, *Difference and Repetition*, 95.
46. Ibid., 5.
47. Gould, "Laws, Exceptions, Norms," 12.
48. Tilley, "J. L. A. Kolderup-Rosenvinge," 77.

accordingly lacks the religious element or is forsaken by God, is a vortex, cannot be stopped, and is a prey to the illusion of wanting a fixed point ahead, which is wanting to stop by means of a gadfly [*Bremsen*]; for the fixed point, the only fixed point, lies behind.[49]

Secular politics, in Kierkegaard's reading, is unstable because it has no room for a meaningful (sovereign) decision to be made. It needs religion to give it stability. The need for repetition is a need for decision. To use Schmittian terminology, Kierkegaard tells us that we are mistaken to think that the rule of law can bring stability, that it is actually a sovereign decision that is needed. Secular politics looks for a fixed point ahead, as if it can regulate the future, but it is religion that understands that such a point is not to be found. And Kierkegaard's opinion of the unstable political situation in Europe, therefore, is that "it cannot be stopped except by religion, and I am convinced that . . . the movement of our time, which appears to be purely political, will turn out suddenly to be religious or the need for religion.[50]

Religion teaches us that the only stability is to be found in the moment of decision (when to depart, much like Abraham who starts his three-day journey to Mount Moriah, thereby proving his faith in God, not knowing how the journey is going to end, not having a fixed point ahead). Kierkegaard uses Socrates to illustrate this point:

> Socrates had his fixed point *behind*. His point of departure lay in himself and in the god. That is to say, he knew himself, he possessed himself. By this means he stopped Sophistry, which, like politics, always asks whither one should go instead of asking whence one should depart.[51]

Secular politics looks for a fixed point ahead, which it cannot find because fixed points always lie behind (because life "must be lived forward").[52] Religion, on the other hand, looks for a point of departure, letting the future be determined in the future. And so religion can bring freedom back to politics. It brings decision back to politics because the only decision we can make in the present is "when to depart." Socrates, like Abraham and like Schmitt's sovereign, is exceptional because he can make a decision, thereby stopping the flux of Sophistry.

Bibliography

Carlisle, Clare. *Kierkegaard's Philosophy of Becoming: Movements and Positions*. New York: State University of New York Press, 2005.

---

49. Kierkegaard, *Letters and Documents*, 262.
50. Ibid.
51. Ibid., 263.
52. Kierkegaard, *Journals and Papers*, 1030.

Conrad, Burkhard. "Kierkegaard's Moment: Carl Schmitt and His Rhetorical Concept of Decision." In *Redescriptions: Yearbook of Political Thought, Conceptual History and Feminist Theory*, edited by Kari Palonen, 145–71. Berlin: LIT Verlag, 2011.

Croxall, T. H. *Kierkegaard Commentary*. London: Nisbet, 1956.

Deleuze. Gilles. *Difference and Repetition*. Translated by Paul Patton. New York: Columbia University Press, 1994.

Elshtain, Jean Bethke. *Sovereignty: God, State, and Self*. New York: Basic, 2008.

Gould, Rebecca. "Laws, Exceptions, Norms: Kierkegaard, Schmitt, and Benjamin on the Exception." *Telos* 162 (2013) 1–19.

Kennedy, Ellen. *Constitutional Failure: Carl Schmitt in Weimar*. Durham: Duke University Press, 2004.

Kierkegaard, Søren. *The Concept of Anxiety*. Translated by Reidar Thomte. Princeton: Princeton University Press, 1981.

———. *Fear and Trembling; Repetition*. Translated by Howard V. Hong and Edna H. Hong. Princeton: Princeton University Press, 1983.

———. *Journals and Papers*. Vol. 1. Translated by Howard V. Hong and Edna H. Hong. Bloomington: Indiana University Press, 1967.

———. *Letters and Documents*. Translated by Henrik Rosenmeier. Princeton: Princeton University Press, 1978.

Kundera, Milan. *The Unbearable Lightness of Being*. Translated by Michael Henry Heim. New York: HarperCollins, 2009.

Lippitt, John. *The Routledge Philosophy Guidebook to Kierkegaard and Fear and Trembling*. New York: Routledge, 2003.

McCarthy, Vincent A. "*Repetition*'s Repetitions." In *International Kierkegaard Commentary: Fear and Trembling and Repetition*, edited by Robert L. Perkins, 263–82. Macon, GA: Mercer University Press, 1993.

Mooney, Edward F. "*Repetition*: Getting Back the World." In *The Cambridge Companion to Kierkegaard*, edited by Alastair Hannay and Gordon D. Marino, 282–307. Cambridge: Cambridge University Press, 1998.

———. *Søren Kierkegaard: Dialogue, Polemics, Lost Intimacy, and Time*. Burlington, VT: Ashgate, 2007.

Pickstock, Catherine. *Repetition and Identity*. Oxford: Oxford University Press, 2013.

Ryan, Bartholomew. *Kierkegaard's Indirect Politics: Interludes with Lukács, Schmitt, Benjamin and Adorno*. Leiden: Brill, 2014.

———. "Carl Schmitt: Zones of Exception and Appropriation." In *Kierkegaard's Influence on Social-Political Thought*, edited by Jon Stewart, 177–207. Kierkegaard Research 14. Burlington: Ashgate, 2011.

Schmitt, Carl. *Political Theology: Four Chapters on the Concept of Sovereignty*. Translated by George Schwab. Chicago: University of Chicago Press, 2005.

Smith, Graham M. *Friendship and the Political: Kierkegaard, Nietzsche, Schmitt*. Exeter, UK: Imprint Academic, 2011.

Stocker, Barry. *Kierkegaard on Politics*. London: Palgrave Macmillan, 2013.

Tang, Chenxi. "Repetition and Nineteenth-Century Experimental Psychology." In *Kierkegaard Studies: Yearbook 2002*, edited by Niels Jorgen Cappelørn et al., 93–118. Berlin: de Guyer, 2009.

Taubes, Jacob. *The Political Theology of Paul*. Translated by Dana Hollander. Stanford: Stanford University Press, 2004.

Tilley, J. Michael. "J. L. A. Kolderup-Rosenvinge: Kierkegaard on Walking Away from Politics." In *Kierkegaard and His Danish Contemporaries*, vol. 1, *Philosophy, Politics and Social Theory*, edited by Jon Stewart, 77–84. Burlington, VT: Ashgate, 2009.

15

Lost Expectations

On Derrida's Abraham

MARY-JANE RUBENSTEIN

Introduction

THIS CHAPTER UNDERTAKES A critical analysis of Jacques Derrida's reading of *Fear and Trembling* (*Frygt og Bæven*) in *The Gift of Death* (*Donner la mort*). In a gesture that might be called a faithful betrayal, Derrida seeks in this text to "go further" than de Silentio, pushing Abraham's singular near-sacrifice of Isaac into "the most common" experience of decision, his absolute relation to the Absolute into every relation to any other. Composed largely of anonymous fragments, the essay at hand evaluates the theo-ethico-political stakes of this deconstruction, seeking to reread Derrida's *tout autre* in light of the double-movement he perplexingly omits.

Preface

It is with considerable regret that I confess that I am not exactly the author of the essay you are about to read. I had, of course, meant to write something for the volume at hand, but kept putting it off, thinking after all that there was more than enough time, and that when it comes to matters as weighty as the political in Kierkegaard, there is, as Johannes Climacus would remind us, no need to rush[1]—no need to be in such a holy hurry to get down to business. But as the winter holidays dwindled and still nothing had written itself, my ordinarily reliable loafing became an increasing burden. I planned a last-minute weekend excursion to the mountains to impose some bourgeois discipline on myself, and as the airplane lifted off and hit cruising altitude—after a brief nap—I settled in to jot down some leisurely thoughts. Just then, something very strange befell me. I opened the tray-table attached to the seat in front of me, only to

---

1. Kierkegaard, *Philosophical Fragments*, 16; Kierkegaard, *Philosophiske Smuler, Eller, En Smule Philosophi*, 12. Subsequent references will be cited with English page numbers separated from the Danish with a slash (/).

find a jumble of handwritten pages that fluttered out onto my lap and into my neighbor's bowl of take-out soup. A few pages even lodged themselves under the wheels of a passing beverage cart and ripped, in the confusion, into more pieces than one might think a beverage cart capable of producing.

Once I had gathered the fragments together, I discovered them to be part of a manuscript written by a woman who doubtless has a name but who does not reveal it in them, a self-described accountant who simply refers to herself as "B." She claims to have had—she *insists* she has had—no philosophical training, that she is an amateur yet devoted reader of—and at this revelation, I bolted upright in my chair, spilling my club soda onto my increasingly vexed seatmate—an amateur yet devoted reader of the pseudonymous works of Søren Kierkegaard. The text seems to be a single entry from a quasi-philosophical journal she keeps, concerning the theopolitical afterlife of these pseudonymous texts. Why anyone would keep such a journal—audienceless and ineffective a medium as it is—is beyond me.

When I arrived at my lodging in northern New England, I could not help but share this remarkable story with the inn's assistant proprietor, a recent transplant from Denmark whom I had heard tell the patron in front of me that he—the assistant proprietor—had taken a class as an undergraduate in Kierkegaard's pseudonymous works (he might have been stretching the truth to impress the patron, who looked like she might well be a philosopher, or an architect, or maybe a journalist). At any rate, upon hearing about the incident on the airplane, he insisted that I let him read the manuscript, assuring me he would return it as soon as possible. Sure enough, by 6 o'clock the next morning, the fragments had arrived, now patched together and considerably reordered, under my hotel door. The assistant proprietor had even done me the service, I soon learned, of revising those parts of the manuscript he had found unclear, of adding a quotation or example here and there, of writing footnotes corresponding to B's numerous citations, and of assembling the entries into a format roughly following that of *Fear and Trembling*, whose structure he insisted spoke unconsciously throughout the modest *oeuvre* in question.

I was so intrigued that I spent the rest of the trip and journey home reading the collated fragments and following its footnotes—before falling into the mindless routines of daily living back home. And although I had intended to check the final draft before submitting it to the publisher, thinking after all, there is no need to hurry, I was tragically impeded by the despicable mediations of this carnival time—the Facebook and Twitter and newsfeeds and emails—all of them announcing the end of this, the beginning of that, the most, the greatest, the worst, the final—and I was so busy awaiting the consummation of history that I forgot to consummate the manuscript. (I will not tire you with the details of my thwarted efforts vis-à-vis copyediting, page-proofs, or the other earnest productions of paragraph-gobblers seeking to render the message more palatable, digestible, even anti-emetic.)

What lies before you, then, is the partially reconstructed version of B's journal entry, via New England Airways and a Danish hotelier, with the hopefully obvious assurance that whatever I *would* have written, had this bizarre set of circumstances not befallen me, would have been more serious and scholarly than what I now half-heartedly deliver.—*From the journal of "B," 28 June 2018*

Exordium

On the occasion of a good friend's birthday a month ago, twelve of us stood around an unopened bottle of Chartreuse that her father had preserved in his cellars since the year of her birth. For fifty years it had lain on its side in its little wooden box, growing greener and thicker, more herbal and more imponderably expensive so that it might in the fullness of time intoxicate a group of accountants and their partners on a Nantucket beach in 2018. Trying to feel the full weight of those fifty years, one of us addressed the birthday girl solemnly, "This bottle is from 1968. That's the year you were *born*." Caught in the spirit, another ventured, "1968—this liquid is three years older than Stardustä coffee." Unable to control myself, I grabbed the bottle and said, "This label was printed in the same year as Jacques Derrida's '*Différance*' essay!" At which point my companions stared at me strangely before changing the subject. But I don't mind. I've grown accustomed to being misunderstood.

"*Différance*" was, of course, one of the first watchcries of the literary tactic known as "deconstruction," which for the first decade or two seemed to spell the demolition of all epistemological bulwarks: the author, the book, intention, the subject, the origin, the concept, the referent, metaphysics, teleology, and above all, anything having to do with religion. To cite just a few examples, throughout her introduction to Derrida's *Of Grammatology*, Gayatri Spivak insisted that *différance* was inimical to anything like "mysticism" or "theology";[2] in an early edited volume called *Deconstruction and Theology*, Carl Raschke infamously called différance "the death of God put into writing";[3] and the author himself—if one can even speak this way—proclaimed time and again that deconstruction unsettled even "the most negative of negative theologies."[4]

It was therefore surprising to Derrida's followers and critics alike to find a circle of theologians gathering excitedly around him beginning in the early 1980s. The circles widened and multiplied until Derrida's death in 2004: in that last decade in particular, it seemed that every other month produced a conference, edited volume, or journal dedicated to Derrida and religion, Derrida and the Bible, Derrida and ontotheology, Derrida and the messianic, Derrida and Augustine, and of course, Derrida and negative theology. Derrida's own turn to the question of the religious began in earnest with

---

2. See, e.g., Derrida, *Of Grammatology*, xxviii.

3. Raschke, "Deconstruction of God," 3.

4. Derrida, "Différance," 6. For a discussion of this set of disavowals, see Rubenstein, "Dionysius, Derrida," 725–42.

the publication in 1992 of *Donner la mort*, translated into English as *The Gift of Death*. This book performs an extended reflection on *Fear and Trembling*, which Derrida attributes throughout the text to "Kierkegaard." I should qualify that statement: Derrida does treat the issue of pseudonymous authorship in two early paragraphs, which mention Johannes de Silentio once and then focus on the irresponsibility enacted in refusing to sign one's own name to a text ("*De la responsabilité on pense souvent qu'elle consiste à signer* en son nom").[5] After that, Derrida refers to the author one time as "Kierkegaard-de Silentio," before going on simply to call him "Kierkegaard" through the rest of the book.

As is well known, *Fear and Trembling* has a marvelously hard time getting started. There's a preface (*Forord*) and an exordium (*Stemning*) and a eulogy (*Lovtale*) and some preliminary throat-clearing (*Foreløbig Expectoration*) before Silentio finally dives into his central problematic.[6] Similarly, Derrida's reading of *Fear and Trembling* only gets started halfway through *The Gift of Death*. In fact, he only mentions Kierkegaard once in the book's first two chapters, which focus instead on the *Heretical Essays* written by the Czech philosopher Jan Patočka.[7] Patočka, then, becomes for Derrida something like what Socrates is for Johannes Climacus—a way of getting at Kierkegaard the way that Climacus approaches Hegel: not headlong but sideways, all for the sake of writing indirectly about something that defies direct communication.

Derrida centers his reading on what Patočka names the three major epochs of European responsibility: the so-called orgiastic, the Platonic, and finally the Christian. (Although Derrida does not call attention to such resonances, these three epochs can be heard as collective, historical echoes of Kierkegaard's canonical stages: the aesthetic, the ethical, and the religious.) Patočka's orgiastic names an allegedly prehistorical stage of pagan enthusiasm, sexual excess, and an unbroken continuity of animals, vegetables, humans, and gods. At this stage (again, allegedly), there is no real responsibility, because there is no real *subject*—no doer behind the deed, no unsubstitutable substance behind human actions and accidents. And so when humans died in this mythic ur-era, Patočka suggests, they simply returned to the pantheist whole that produced them, perishing unreflectively like woodland creatures or tomato plants ostensibly do.

For Patočka, Derrida reminds us, the responsible subject is finally born with the entrance not of Judaism (as Nietzsche might have it), but of Platonism.[8] Platonism, for Patočka, carves out a coherent, self-identical subject by giving it a new relationship to

---

5. Derrida, *Gift of Death*, 58; Derrida, *Donner La Mort* (Paris: Galilée, 1999), 85. Subsequent references to this text will be cited with the English page numbers followed by the French and separated by a slash (/).

6. Kierkegaard, *Fear and Trembling*; Kierkegaard, *Frygt Og Bæven*. Subsequent references to this text will be cited with the English page numbers followed by the Danish and separated by a slash (/).

7. Patočka, *Heretical Essays in the Philosophy of History*.

8. Derrida, *Gift of Death*, 10–12/26–29. For Nietzsche's account of the emergence of the responsible subject, see Nietzsche, *On the Genealogy of Morals*, 57–96.

death: if orgiastic death simply dissolves the creature into the whole, Platonic death opens the way to personal immortality by positing an everlasting soul. Of course, not everyone attains immortality; it is a gift reserved for those who have learned to separate their souls from their bodies through the practice of philosophy, which the *Phaedo's* Socrates calls a "rehearsal for death," or *melêtê thanatou*.[9] By means of the discipline of philosophy, the young man learns to separate his soul from his body and himself from the crowd, consenting to being dragged up the rocky path from the cave to the light so he can finally see the Good itself. The individual, substantial, immortal self therefore gathers itself together in relation to death. As Derrida suggests, then, the self is the gift of death: death gives the gift of the self and is, in this sense, itself a gift.

Europe's relationship to death changes again with the dawn of Christianity. According to Patočka, the most profound difference between the Christian and Platonic paradigms is the nature of the Good, or God: whereas Platonism figures the *agathon* as external to the human subject, somewhere "out there," Christianity configures God internally as well, so that God in the Christian paradigm God resides *within* the human mind, memory, or heart that God nevertheless exceeds.[10] Ultimately, then, however difficult the journey out of the cave might be, the Platonic good is accessible, visible, and beautiful, whereas the Christian divinity remains stubbornly inaccessible, invisible, and sublime, inducing among human subjects not calm contemplation, but rather fear, and trembling.[11] And finally, in the place of an impassive and impersonal *agathon*, which resides beyond the worldly fray forever, Christianity introduces a good that empties itself, even sacrificing itself, as a *person* for each other person. The Christian Good, which is the Christian God, dies for me—in other words, the god offers his death to me, as a gift.[12]

Those who have ears to hear might pick up echoes in this either/or between Platonism and Christianity of Johannes Climacus's distinction between the Socratic and the artfully unnamed "other" way, in which the moment is decisive, the teacher is singular, and the learner is transformed.[13] Rather than focusing with Climacus on the Christian introduction of sin, however, Derrida-through-Patočka focuses on the Christian transformation of death. Both the Platonic and the Christian selves are assembled in relation to death, but whereas the Platonist calmly gathers himself together

---

9. Derrida, *Gift of Death*, 12/29. See Plato, *Phaedo*.

10. Patočka, *Heretical Essays*, 116: "*Tremendum*, because responsibility resides henceforth not in an essence that is accessible to the human gaze, that of the Good and the One, but in the relation to a supreme, absolute and inaccessible being that holds us in check not by exterior but by interior force."

11. Derrida, *Gift of Death*, 27/48: "The dissymmetry of the gaze, this disproportion that relates me, and whatever concerns me, to a gaze that I don't see and that remains secret from me although it commands me, is, according to Patočka, the frightening, terrifying mystery, the *mysterium tremendum*. Such a terror has no place in the transcendent experience that relates Platonic responsibility to the *agathon*."

12. Ibid., 33/55.

13. Kierkegaard, *Philosophical Fragments*, 12–22/9–18.

in the face of his own death, the Christian anxiously gives herself away in an imitative response to the death of the other, offering her whole life to a perpetually inscrutable god in an endless gesture of self-sacrifice.[14]

As Derrida reminds us, Patočka offers this tripartite genealogy of the orgiastic, Platonic, and Christian in response to what he perceives to be a resurgence of prehistorical fanaticism in twentieth-century politics. In particular, Patočka attributes the cults of personality, totalitarian regimes, and enthusiastic revolutions of fascism, national socialism, and the French Revolution before them to a resurgence of the orgiastic, which he also calls the demonic, at the forgotten roots of European society.[15] His genealogy is therefore as prescriptive as it is descriptive: through it, Patočka maintains that Europe must *become* what it is by excising the pagan and even Platonic remnants of its history. In this way Europe will finally become truly responsible, self-sacrificing, Christian.

It is at this point that Derrida begins to read Patočka against himself, pointing out that insofar as European responsibility is *constructed* upon a Platonic repression of the orgiastic, the history of responsibility contains irresponsibility within it, as its condition of possibility. There is no such thing, then, as pure responsibility: responsibility "never becomes what it is."[16] Moreover, Derrida maintains, Platonism can never quite give way to Christianity thus construed—there is, rather, an irreducible undecidability between these two (admittedly reductive) paradigms. Christian and Platonic ethics are incompatible, unmediable, and yet we adhere to both of them: "this *aporia of responsibility* would thus define the relation between the Platonic and Christian paradigms throughout the history of morality and politics."[17]

It is rather like the situation in which a hypothetical modern woman, living in an overdeveloped nation under the sway of late capitalism, might find herself whenever she goes to the grocery store. Attempting to buy food responsibly, she will most likely find herself under the equally weighty injunctions of two incompatible ethical frameworks. One tells her she should buy locally sourced, organic food, which is far more expensive than its conventionally-grown counterparts but better for the earth, for laborers, and for the animal and vegetal life involved in its production and consumption. The other set of principles tells her she should save as much money as possible for her family, the homeless shelter she supports, and maybe even her retirement

---

14. Derrida, *Gift of Death*, 48/73: "It institutes responsibility as a *putting-oneself-to-death* or *offering-one's-death*, that is, *one's life*, in the ethical dimension of sacrifice."

15. Ibid., 21/40: "Patočka encourages us to learn a political lesson from this, one for today and tomorrow, by reminding us that every revolution, whether atheistic or religious, bears witness to a return of the sacred in the form of an enthusiasm or fervor, otherwise known as the presence of the gods within us."

16. Ibid., 20/37–38: "If the orgiastic remains enveloped, if the demonic persists, incorporated and dominated, in a new experience of responsible freedom, then the latter never becomes what it is. It will never become pure and authentic, or absolutely new."

17. Ibid., 24/43.

account. And so, she makes both choices, without being able to reconcile them, so that her shopping cart is absurdly half-filled with local, organic groceries and half-filled with whatever is being sold at a discount that day.

Similarly, Derrida explains, the Western tradition has two ways of thinking about responsibility, which operate incompatibly yet with equal force upon our imaginations. What Patočka calls the Platonic paradigm values knowledge over action; I must know before I can do. By contrast, what he calls the Christian paradigm values action over knowledge; I must respond before I know; I must say, "here I am" before I ascertain what is being asked of me.[18] For Derrida, this duality also amounts to an undecidability between Heidegger and Levinas—between ontology and ethics, between singularizing the self and coring it out, between being-toward-death and perpetual self-immolation.[19] Somewhat surprisingly, then, Heidegger maps onto Platonism in this scheme and Levinas onto Christianity. And again, this tension can never be resolved: on the one hand, I have to know what I am getting myself into before I respond; on the other hand, if I wait until I understand, my response will inevitably be too late. This, then, is the "aporia of responsibility": I must know before I respond, and I must respond before I know. Derrida concludes, "in debates concerning responsibility one must always take into account this original and irreducible complexity that links theoretical consciousness (*la conscence theoretique*) . . . to 'practical' conscience (*la conscience 'practique'*) . . . if only to avoid the arrogance of so many 'clean consciences' ('*bonnes consciences*')."[20]

This, then, is what Derrida takes with him on his journey up Mount Moriah: irresponsibility as constitutive of responsibility, an undecidability between knowing and doing, and the ethical importance of a bad conscience.

Problemata

Much as he did with Patočka's *Heretical Essays*, Derrida approaches *Fear and Trembling* on its own terms—except, of course, for his stubborn attribution of the text to Kierkegaard; our friend Johannes de Silentio is escorted off the stage nearly as soon as he is summoned onto it. Nevertheless, the *Gift of Death*'s third chapter gets most of Silentio's major concerns into place, beginning with a meditation on trembling, then opening onto secrecy, the radical alterity of God, the incommunicability of Abraham's act, the singularity of the actor, indirect communication, Abraham's obligation to hate what he loves, and above all, the unmediable conflict between Abraham's obligation to

---

18. Ibid., 25/45: "If it is true that the concept of responsibility has, in the most reliable continuity of its history, always implied involvement in action, a doing, a *praxis*, a *decision* that exceeds simple conscience or simple theoretical understanding, it is also true that the same concept requires a decision or responsible action to answer for itself *consciously*, that is, with knowledge of a thematics of what is done, of what action signifies, its causes, ends, etc."

19. Ibid., 46–49/70–73.

20. Ibid., 25/45.

God and his obligation to everyone else.[21] After all, if Abraham fulfills his duty to God and sacrifices Isaac, Derrida reminds us, then he violates as radically as possible his duty to Isaac and to Sarah—not to mention their scores of descendants who include, if the stories can be trusted, many of us who now inhabit this overstrained earth. On the other hand, if Abraham fulfills his duty to Isaac, Sarah, and the rest of us by refusing to kill Isaac, then he neglects his duty to God. There is, in other words, an *aporia* between Abraham's duty in general and his duty to God—or in terms more familiar to Johannes, between the ethical and the religious.[22]

So here we stand again with Abraham, lifted out of the realm of the universal in absolute relation to the absolute, such that the ethical itself becomes a temptation.[23] To say the ethical becomes a temptation is to say that at the moment of the divine command, Abraham is tempted *not* to kill his son, which is to say he is tempted to do the *right* thing. This is how we know he is not below the ethical, but rather above it. This outlandish phenomenon, in which the ethical itself becomes a temptation, is the absurdity Johannes calls the teleological suspension of the ethical (*teleologisk Suspension af det Ethiske*).[24]

Now again, Derrida says most of this—at least indirectly. What he does *not* say, however, is that all of this might just as well not be the case. Throughout *Fear and Trembling* it remains disturbingly possible—Johannes reminds us continually—that the absurd might be *simply absurd*, rather than an apophatic expression of the highest, and that Abraham might be simply a murderer, rather than a knight of faith. In other words, there may not *be* a knight of faith. There may be no such thing as a single individual absolutely related to the absolute, or a teleological suspension of the ethical, or a realm of the religious above and beyond the universal. But in that case, as Johannes intones throughout the text, "Abraham is lost" (*Abraham er tabt*).[25]

Insofar as Abraham is not lost, however, he is as Silentio and now Derrida position him: singular, beyond the universal, and related absolutely to his absolutely singular God. Hence the silence, the secrecy, the incommunicability—for what on earth could he say? So the terrifying scene freezes on just God and Abraham, lifted above the universal, in one singular and unrepeatable moment. Terrifying. Sleep-destroying. Unthinkable.

And then Derrida decides to go further. "But isn't this the most common thing? (*la chose la plus commune*)," he asks, shattering the scene.[26] He is troubled, it seems,

---

21. Ibid., 53–81/79–113.

22. Ibid., 66/95. "The two duties must contradict one another, one must subordinate (incorporate, repress) the other. Abraham must assume absolute responsibility for sacrificing his son by sacrificing ethics, but in order for there to be a sacrifice, the ethical must retain all its value; the love for his son must remain intact, and the order of human duty must continue to insist on its rights."

23. Kierkegaard, *Fear and Trembling*, 60/68.

24. Ibid., 54/61.

25. Ibid., 120/137.

26. Derrida, *Gift of Death*, 67/97.

by the singularity, the exceptional quality we tend to confer upon Abraham—as if ordinary ethics works just fine under ordinary conditions, and only breaks down every few millennia when God demands something outlandish of an unsuspecting patriarch. Cordoning Abraham off from the ethical, we can assuage our own consciences, relieved that nothing so dreadful will ever be asked of us. But, Derrida cautions,

> what the knights of good conscience don't realize (*Ce que méconnaissent les chevaliers de la bonne conscience*), is that the "sacrifice of Isaac" illustrates—if that is the word in the case of such a nocturnal mystery [notice Derrida is stalling here, throwing us off before throwing us in] the most common and everyday experience of responsibility (*le "sacrifice d'Isaac" illustre . . . l'expérience la plus quotidienne et la plus commune de la responsabilité*).²⁷

"Pardon me?" we might respond. "How can it possibly be the case that the sacrifice of Isaac—extraordinary, vicious, unassimilable—illustrates the most *common* and *everyday* experience of responsibility?" And as if he could hear us, Derrida continues:

> The story is no doubt monstrous, outrageous, barely conceivable (*monstreuse, inouïe, à peine pensable*): a father is ready to put to death his beloved son, his irreplaceable loved one, and that because the Other, the great Other asks him or orders him without giving the slightest explanation (*raison*). . . . But isn't this the most common thing?²⁸

The most common thing? The purported founder of three major monotheisms nearly murders his son in obedience to an unseen God, without reason and without explanation; foundational filicide on a mountain before God; an act that will seal the fate of generations as numerous as the stars . . . and this is the most common thing?

"Let us not look for examples," Derrida implores, before providing to give numerous examples.

> By preferring my work, simply by giving it my time and attention, by preferring my activity as a citizen or as a professorial and professional philosopher, writing and speaking here in a public language, French in my case, I am perhaps fulfilling my duty (*je fais peut-être mon devoir*). But I am sacrificing and betraying at every moment all my other obligations: my obligations to the other others whom I know or don't know, the billion of my fellows ("*semblables*") . . . who are dying of starvation or sickness. I betray my fidelity or my obligations to other citizens, to those who don't speak my language and to whom I neither speak nor respond . . . thus also to those I love in private, my own, my family, my sons, each of whom is the only son I sacrifice to the other, every one being sacrificed to every one else in this land of Moriah that is our

---

27. Ibid.
28. Ibid.

habitat every second of every day" (*chacun étant sacrifié à chacun sur cette terre de Moriah qui est notre habitat de tous les jours et de chaque seconde*).²⁹

And at this moment I, the secondhand editor of B's manuscript and reluctant signatory of this essay, risk a brief interjection: surely this is an overstatement. Derrida's home is the land of Moriah? Your recycling bin is the land of Moriah? Is this edited volume the land of Moriah? To be sure, by having failed to write a proper chapter—and by rendering it in English rather than French or Danish—I am betraying a number of potential readers, not to mention Derrida and Kierkegaard "themselves"—if one can even speak this way—in my very effort to fulfill my obligation to them. But does this betrayal liken my quasi-authorship of this paper to Abraham's near-sacrifice of Isaac? What right does Derrida have to liken any of this terrain to the land of Moriah?

Back to the manuscript:

Derrida's explanation comes very quickly—all in the same long paragraph that called the *akedah*, or the binding of Isaac, "the most common thing." The *akedah* enacts a scene of absolute responsibility, meaning it *binds* Abraham in his singularity to God in God's singularity. "God," then, is the name of the absolute other to whom Abraham is bound absolutely to respond—to whom *any* of us is bound absolutely to respond. That is what God means. But, Derrida continues, God is not the only other.

> There are also others, an infinite number of them, the innumerable generality of others to whom I *should* be bound by the same responsibility, a general and universal responsibility (what Kierkegaard calls the ethical order). I cannot respond to the call, the request, the obligation, or even the love of another without sacrificing the other other, the other others.... *Tout autre est tout autre*, every one else is completely or wholly other.³⁰

As Derrida goes on to parse carefully, the phrase *tout autre est tout autre* is stubbornly overdetermined. It could mean simply that the wholly other is wholly other—a perfectly orthodox formulation, even redolent of the *Sh'ma* or the *Shahada*—God, it would say in this light, is God. But in another light, *tout autre est tout autre* could mean that *every* other is wholly other, which is to say the otherness of God does not outweigh the otherness of any other other. Each, any, and every other is wholly other.

Ontologically, the phrase does risk collapsing in on itself. The locution "every other is wholly other" comes precariously close to saying that every other is equivalent, which is to say that *nothing* is truly other, because everything is effectively the same. Derrida comes closest to this collapse, I would suggest, when he proclaims that

> what can be said about Abraham's relation to God can be said about my relation without relation to every other as wholly other, in particular my relation to my neighbor or my loved ones who are as inaccessible to me, as secret and

---

29. Ibid., 69/98–99.
30. Ibid., 68/98; emphasis added to "should."

transcendent as Jahweh (*à mon prochain ou aux miens qui me sont aussi inaccessibles, secrets et transcendents que Iahvé*).[31]

We might at this point remember that, as complicated as his relation to the tradition might be, Derrida was raised Jewish and remained a Jewish thinker in addition to all the other kinds of thinker he remained. He knew it was forbidden to say, much less write, that particularly "secret and transcendent" name. And yet there it is, laid bare, not only written but also rendered equivalent to every gopher, slug, and stallion. One might therefore ask, whether this pronouncement of the unpronounceable name, this straightforward statement of the purportedly incommunicable, Derrida might in fact capitulate to exactly that abstracting and systematizing tendency that so disgusts Johannes ("This is not the System; it has not the least thing to do with the System" [*Det er ikke Systemet, det har ikke det Mindste med Systemet at gjøre*]).[32] Is Derrida's globalizing gesture not, in fact, what *all* the pseudonyms feared? A massive neo-Hegelian digestion of difference, a swallowing of singularity, a maceration of mystery?

Perhaps. But in the interest of generosity—insofar as we are dealing here with the gift, with genre, and with generations—one might instead read the *tout autre* as saying, not that every other is equally other, but rather that every other is radically *different* from every other other. Along this reading, each vector of otherness would be radically different from the otherness of every other other, each of which would be wholly other in wholly different modes of otherness. So my neighbor and your dog and this treadmill and that arugula plant may each be "just as secret and transcendent" as God, but insofar as the otherness of God is not a calculable otherness, it could never be possible to call these others equivalent. Rather, each of them would, understood this way, be radically inscrutable, irreducibly other, and each so in its own way—otherwise, we would know the measure of otherness ahead of time and everything would in fact amount to everything else.

Understood this way, *tout autre est tout autre* could be heard as a radicalizing of the Kierkegaardian effort to slip out from under Hegel by preserving particularity. Not only is the single individual particular as distinct from the general run of things, not only is the transcendent God particular as distinct from the general run of things, but the general run of things is itself composed only of irreducible particularities—which is to say *there is no general run of things*. Each thing is singular, and just as singular as God. The ontological implications of this possibility can best be discerned in relation to the work of Gilles Deleuze, Baruch Spinoza, Gottfried Leibniz, and Duns Scotus, whose various constructions of univocity on the one hand and *haecceitas* on the other I shall address momentarily . . .

---

31. Ibid., 78/110.
32. Kierkegaard, *Fear and Trembling*, 8/8.

* * *

. . . and here I insert another second-order editor's note: this part of the manuscript seems unfortunately to have been lost—either to wheels of the airplane's beverage cart or to my seatmate's take-out soup.

* * *

. . . ontologically, then, it is not certain whether we have in *The Gift of Death* a thoroughgoing monism or a pluralistic, anti-relational monadology. Ethically, however, the implications of the *tout autre* are clearer; in fact, one could argue that *The Gift of Death* thwarts ontology in order to become an essay in practical ethics.

Ethically speaking, to say that every other is wholly other is to say that I am as obligated to any other as I am to the divine Other. I am as obligated to your family as I am to mine, to your neighbors as I am to God. This infinite obligation may at first sound odd, but it bears echoes of Levinas, for whom God only appears in the face of a human other, or of Matthew 25, which locates God in the poor, hungry, and orphaned people his disciples either serve or fail to serve.[33] So a messianic Jew or incarnationalist Christian could read Derrida's ethic as radically panenethist: God is *in* every other, and thereby binds us infinitely, in absolute responsibility, to every other.

Perhaps unsurprisingly, however, things are not quite this tidy for Derrida. Not only am I bound to respond unreservedly and without delay to each other, but the moment I undertake such a response, I forsake my duty to each other other. Just as Abraham could only do his duty to God by forsaking his duty to Isaac and Sarah and the rest of us, I can only do my duty to one neighbor by forsaking the other, to one nation by betraying the others, and to this manuscript by neglecting my vegetable garden. And just like Abraham, I have no way of accounting for these decisions. As Derrida asks in what has become an infamous passage, "how would you ever justify the fact that you sacrifice all the cats in the world to the cat you feed at home every morning for years, whereas other cats die of hunger at every instant?"[34] Although we might at this point object that neglecting to feed cats is not the same thing as killing them, Derrida insists that the difference between killing and letting die is a "minor" one; practically speaking, it is negligible.[35]

Similarly, we might object that sacrifice is only sacrifice if you *love* what you are sacrificing, so inasmuch as I do not love every cat other than mine, they are not Isaac and I am not sacrificing them. To this riposte, Derrida responds that even though I may not love those scores of anonymous cats, I *ought* to. I am as obligated to them as I am to my own cat as I am to your roommate's uncle as I am to God,

---

33. See Levinas, "God and Philosophy," 55–78. Cf. Matt 25:31–46.
34. Derrida, *Gift of Death*, 71/101.
35. Ibid., 86/118–19.

and, as in the case of Abraham, a response in any of these directions amounts to a betrayal everywhere else.

The upshot of all this failure and betrayal is that there is no safe separation between "absolute responsibility" and "responsibility in general"—no chasm between my responsibility to God and my responsibility to everyone else. In other words, Derrida performs in *The Gift of Death* the deconstruction of the pseudonyms' and Kierkegaard's most sacred distinction, which is to say the absolute separation—*the infinite qualitative distinction!*—between the ethical and the religious.

To account for this collapse, one could say that Derrida pulls the religious down into the ethical, bringing us back to a Kantian equivalence of religion and ethics. At the same time that he pulls the religious down into the ethical, however, Derrida also opens the ethical "up" or out to the religious, at every turn. It is not just Abraham's decision that is impossible and unspeakable, not just the occasional mythic sacrifice; rather, every decision is impossible and unspeakable. Every decision is a betrayal. And yet, Derrida reminds us, "we also do our duty (*devoir*) by behaving thus."[36] In other words, insofar as responsibility to any one is always irresponsibility to every other, irresponsibility is the necessary condition of our being responsible in the first place. Responsibility relies upon irresponsibility as its monstrous yet inexorable condition of possibility. And this, incidentally, is what Derrida was suggesting with his lengthy analysis of Patočka. Responsibility contains irresponsibility not just historically, not just conceptually, but also practically, within it.

The ethical importance of this realization comes across with unparalleled clarity in the transcript of a roundtable discussion between Derrida and a number of theologians gathered at Villanova University in October of 1999. The British theologian John Milbank raised a series of objections to what he called Derrida's "transcendental betrayal," according to which one is infinitely and universally obligated, and therefore infinitely at fault.[37] As a corrective, Milbank cited Thomas Aquinas as having authorized a hierarchy of preferential love, according to which a person is obligated to his own family and friends and nation above all other families, friends, and nations, so there is no need for the sort of runaway bad conscience that feels infinitely obligated to everything. For Aquinas, Milbank reports, it is acceptable—even an obligation—to

---

36. Ibid., 71/101.

37. Kearney, "On Forgiveness," 68: *Milbank*: "I would like to say something very quickly about betrayal. I was really more talking about transcendental betrayal." *Derrida*: "I am too sensitive to transcendental betrayal." *Milbank*: "I think if one has this model of transcendental betrayal, then one somehow thinks that difference is taken to be the ultimate, that if you have got a sort of transcendental difference, and difference is the ultimate, then there is a sense in which everything is on a level and there is a certain kind of indifference and then transcendental betrayal. So you will end up saying, 'well, I have an equal duty to this person and this person. As you put it very wittily in one of your books, you say, why should I look after this cat and not other cats?' That seems to be a consequence of this transcendentalism about betrayal. You will end up thinking, 'nothing has more weight than anything else.'"

love one's own before loving others.[38] The reason Milbank appealed to this affective hierarchy in conversation with Derrida is that he was concerned about a kind of ethical exhaustion. If we think ourselves equally obligated everywhere and therefore doomed to betrayal everywhere, Milbank reasons, then we are likely not to respond anywhere: "*because* you are being too moralistic," he charges, "you will also end up saying that one cannot do anything moral."[39] Along this line of thinking, then, the *aporia* of responsibility encodes a false piety, prompting us ultimately to capitulate to a moral indifference that mirrors the ontological indifference of the *tout autre*.

Derrida's response:

> You might call this indifference, but if you think that the only moral duty you owe is the duty to the people—or the animals—with whom you have affinity, kinship, friendship, neighborhood, brotherhood, then you can imagine the consequences of that. I, of course, have preferences. I am one of the common people who prefers his cat to his neighbor's cat and my family to others. But I do not have a good conscience about that. I know that if I transform this into a general rule, it would be the ruin of ethics. If I put as a general principle that I will feed first of all my cat, my family, my nation, that would be the ruin of any ethical politics. So, when I give preference to my cat, which I do, that will not prevent me from having some remorse for the cat dying or starving next door or, to change the example, for all the people on earth who are starving and dying today. So you cannot prevent me from having a bad conscience, and *that is the main motivation of my ethics and my politics*.[40]

This, then, is the reason for the deconstruction of Patočka, for the deconstruction of Silentio. Derrida uncovers the irresponsibility at the heart of responsibility in order, as he puts it, "to avoid the arrogance of so many 'clean consciences.'"[41]

* * *

And here another editor's note: at this point in the manuscript, the assistant proprietor of the inn at the mountain inserted a marginal annotation in surprisingly flawless penmanship. I am beginning to wonder whether he might have been some monastic scrivener, hiding from an oppressive abbot in the comparative plainclothes of a hotel employee. At any rate, my unexpected collaborator had apparently traveled from Denmark to New York City in the spring of 2007, by which time the United States had been at war with Iraq for nearly four years and Afghanistan for nearly six.

38. Ibid.: *Milbank*: "Aquinas says that you should love your wife and your family more than other people. It is only later on that people have real problems with that. . . . What you are saying seems to me not to take seriously affinity and the erotic."

39. Ibid., 69.

40. Ibid.

41. Derrida, *Gift of Death*, 25/45.

I read from the assistant proprietor's marginalia: "In mid-April, the season when all Americans are required to render unto Caesar the fruits of the previous year's labor, an image appeared on the cover of the *New Yorker* magazine, showing the requisite tax forms folded into fighter jets, armored tanks, and catapult ships—all presumably headed toward the Middle East."[42]

Although the hotelier did not explain himself any further, I think I can discern his meaning—surely resonant with the little essay at hand—our author B informs us, we might recall, that she is an accountant. As a citizen and civilian, my duty to my country is to pay my taxes. In so doing, however, I am participating in the murder of hundreds of thousands of humans and animals, not to mention the destruction of vegetables and minerals, in the Middle East and wherever else my country decides either to declare war, to wage undeclared war, or to provoke the wars it proceeds to ignore. So, I might decide not to pay my taxes, refusing to participate in this slaughter, but in that case I am refusing to fund the government's few remaining safety nets for the homeless, the poor, the old, and the young; I am refusing to contribute to the roads and bridges I use daily; and I am risking saddling my family and my fellow citizens with the burden of supporting me in prison for the foreseeable future. There is no way to make a decent decision in this land of Mount Moriah.

Back once more to the manuscript.

* * *

Derrida insists that the "whole point of [his] ethics and [his] politics"—which accounts for the theopolitical deconstruction of Silentio—is his bad conscience: his conviction that there is no clean option, no fully responsible way to respond. Just as we will never be able to say, "Europe has become fully ethical, or fully responsible" (which is to say, for Patočka, fully "Christian"), we will never be able to say and *must* never be able to say, "I have done my duty; my hands are clean; my own cat is fed and my own kids are in piano lessons and it is safe on the streets of my little town, so I am, as they say, all square." Just like Abraham, we are always abrogating our duty somewhere at the very moment we respond somewhere else.

It is therefore very puzzling to encounter the next and last major move Derrida makes with respect to Silentio's Abraham in *The Gift of Death*. As he rides out to Mount Moriah, unsaddles the donkey and climbs the rocky path with Isaac and the fire and the knife, Derrida writes that Abraham is "absolutely responsible" to God, and therefore "absolutely irresponsible in the face of men and his family, in the face of the ethical."[43] Yet despite all of this, Derrida continues,

---

42. A publicly accessible image can be found at http://bit.ly/2ybKibM.
43. Derrida, *Gift of Death*, 72/103.

> Abraham considers himself to be all square. He acts as if he were discharged (*délié*) of his duty towards his fellows, his son, and humankind. . . . He must *love* them . . . in order to be able to sacrifice them . . . [but] he nevertheless feels absolved (*absous*) of his duty towards his family, towards the human species, and the generality of the ethical.[44]

Here, then, at the height of the unspeakable deed, we find an Abraham with no conflict, no agony, no trembling at all; Abraham, Derrida says, is "all square." In the original, the sentence reads, "*Abraham se sent quitte.*" He is finished; he has given up, or *quit* the ethical; he is unbound *délié*, from the universal the moment he binds himself to God. At this moment, then, Derrida lets Abraham slip through the very ethical framework he has built around him. Abraham becomes precisely a "knight of good conscience," *un chevalier de la bonne conscience*, undisturbed by any conflict of duties, bound only to the absolute, and ready to give up his son, his wife, humanity, and the whole world for God. In short, by producing such an unbound Abraham, Derrida has divested Abraham of his bad conscience—which is to say, his fear, his trembling, his anxiety. The question is, why? Especially when, as Silentio insists, "without this anxiety Abraham is not who he is (*Abraham ikke den, han er, uden denne Angst*")[45]?

Let us not speculate about motivations, which may have something to do with Derrida's suspicion of *Fear and Trembling*'s Christianizing of Abraham.[46] Let us rather focus on the textual process that produces this all-square Abraham, this unbound quitter—a process that amounts, if I can be so bold, to a rare moment of misreading on Derrida's part. At the same time that he calls Abraham "all square," saying Abraham feels absolved of his duty to Isaac and us and the universal, Derrida begins also to say that Abraham renounces everything when he renounces Isaac, even hope. *Et tu avais même renoncé a l'éspoir*, he says to Abraham in the voice of God. A moment later, he writes that Abraham "responds absolutely . . . disinterestedly and without hoping for a reward" (*sans intérêt ni espoir de recompense.*)[47] We find the same charge, which Derrida seems to consider a compliment, leveled again and again through the rest of the book: Abraham had "renounced all hope," he sacrificed Isaac "without any hope of exchange," he "expects neither response nor reward," and finally, he does it all "expecting nothing that can be *given back* to him, nothing that will *come back* to him" (*n'attendant plus ni réponse ni recompense, rien qui lui soit rendu, rien qui lui revienne.*")[48]

But to state too quickly what ought to be more leisurely communicated—I am already feeling the loss of too many billable hours—this is simply not true of the Abraham of *Fear and Trembling*. Silentio insists throughout the text that what marks Abraham as a knight of faith is not that he is able to sacrifice what he loves—anyone

---

44. Ibid., 73/103–4.
45. Kierkegaard, *Fear and Trembling*, 30/33.
46. Derrida, *Gift of Death*, 96–115/131–57.
47. Ibid., 72/103.
48. Ibid., 95–96/131–32.

can discipline herself to sacrifice what she loves. It is excruciating, but possible. And what marks Abraham as a knight of faith is certainly not that he gives up hope—likewise, anyone can give up hope, especially having given up everything she loves. What marks Abraham as the knight of faith is that he gives up what he loves in the absurd expectation that God will give it all back. This is, in fact, the anti-conceptual lynchpin of the whole book: the knight of faith gives up everything he loves and everything he is, infinitely; he knows it is gone forever; and yet impossibly, he still expects it back. Such expectation, of course, constitutes the difference between the knight of infinite resignation and the knight of faith.

"Infinite resignation," Silentio tells us, is "the last stage before faith" (*Den nendelige Resignation er det sidste Stadium, der gaaer forud for Troen*),[49] and yet it is not faith, is not *yet* faith, is separated from faith by an unimaginable counter-leap back into the finite. Called to give up the woman he loves, even the only woman he will ever love, the knight of infinite resignation is able to renounce her infinitely, reconciling himself to the pain and to a lifetime of unhappiness in the full knowledge that she will never return to him. "Now let us meet the knight of faith on the occasion previously mentioned," Silentio continues.

> He does exactly the same as the other knight did: he infinitely renounces the love that is the substance of his life, he is reconciled in pain. But then the marvel happens; he makes one more movement even more wonderful than all the others, for he says, "Nevertheless I have faith that I will get her—that is, by virtue of the absurd, by virtue of the fact that for God all things are possible" (*jeg troer dog, at jeg faaer hende, i Kraft nemlig af det Absurde, i Kraft af, at for Gud er Alting muligt*).[50]

Johannes makes this distinction even clearer when he contrasts *himself* with Abraham, saying that if he had been ordered up the mountain with Isaac, he would have obeyed absolutely—he might even have arrived early, he says, to get the horror over with sooner. "But I also know what else I would have done," he writes. "The moment I mounted the horse, I would have said to myself: Now all is lost, God demands Isaac, I sacrifice him and along with him all of my joy" (*Nu er Alt tabt, Gud fordrer Isaak, jeg offrer ham, med ham al min Glæde.*)[51] Faced with such a scenario, Silentio admits, some overeager contemporary, hell-bent on "going further" than Abraham, might say that Silentio's resignation is "greater" than Abraham's foolish faith in repetition—"more ideal and poetic than Abraham's small-mindedness. But this is utterly false (*Og dog er dette den største Usandhed*)," Silentio insists, "for my immense resignation would be a substitute for faith" (*thi min uhyre Resignation var Surrogatet for Troen*).[52] What Silentio

49. Kierkegaard, *Fear and Trembling*, 46/51.
50. Ibid., 46/52.
51. Ibid., 35/38.
52. Ibid., 34–35/38.

cannot do—what no one by his own strength can do—is to muster himself into believing that that which he gives up infinitely will return. And yet this is the mark of Silentio's Abraham: not his obedience, not his resignation, but his expectation. His absurd expectation that Isaac would somehow be returned to him.

In saying, therefore, that Abraham is "all square," in saying he has renounced all hope and expects nothing in return, Derrida has collapsed the knight of faith into the knight of infinite resignation. He has—in a book devoted to a close reading of *Fear and Trembling*—somehow managed to leave out *faith*.

The practical question, then, concerns the status of the *tout autre*. Does Derrida's puzzling eclipse of faith as a double-movement invalidate his careful deconstruction? Does it restore the ironclad distinction between the religious and the ethical, the absolute and the general, Abraham and everything else? Or is there a way, not to abandon the *tout autre*, but to reconsider its political ethic of bad conscience in light of the forgotten double-movement of faith?

In the dairy section of my local grocery store, they carry organic milk and they carry local milk, but there is no local organic milk. If I buy the local milk rather than the organic milk, I am participating in the killing of insects and the poisoning of groundwater, but I am also reducing the amount of fuel that transports my food and supporting my neighbors who still run family farms in this era of big agriculture. If I buy the organic milk, then I have saved the insects and the groundwater, but I've forsaken my neighbors, used gallons of extra fuel, and participated in the killing of deer, possums, and raccoons by 18-wheel trucks on the transcontinental highways. And either way, I have condemned the cows to perpetual lactation, confinement, and production for an endlessly exploitative market. I could head for soy milk, instead, but then I would still have the fuel and roadkill problems—and would moreover be contributing to the continued clearing of Latin American rainforests as producers struggle to meet the ever-growing global demand for soy.

There is, it seems, no decent decision here.

The question before us, then, is how we might think Derrida's *tout autre* together with the "faith" it perplexingly occludes. What might it mean to approach such a decision not only with the bad conscience that knows I am infinitely obligated and my hands are never clean, but also with the hope that my abandoned hope might somehow be restored? "Yet Abraham had faith," writes Silentio, "and had faith for this life" (*Dog Abraham troede og troede for dette Liv*).[53] What would it mean to approach every decision, not just with resignation to the murderous order of things, but also with the hope—even the expectation—that things might be different *in this world*, that the mechanics of death might be and must be transformed into life, precisely where transformation would be most impossible? Such faith in the impossible would be too much for me; I am, after all, merely a trifler, an afterthinker, an accountant. I cannot

---

53. Ibid., 20/21.

make the dizzying double-movement of faith, but I can see what it might look like, and this without attempting like poor Heraclitus's overeager disciple to go further.[54]

Unconcluding Editorial Postscrawl

With Silentio's Abraham, we remain with faith. And faith, to be sure, is no political program. It may have the capacity to say "no" to the possible and "yes" to the impossible, but after that, it goes no further. Far from grounding an ethic of decisionism or a politics of the exception, the most Silentio will give us is an ethico-politics of bad conscience and a hope against hope that things might be otherwise. But as he continually reminds us, there may be no such thing as faith at all. The "otherwise" might always be *simply* impossible, rather than possible-as-impossible. Or of course it might be even worse than the this-wise we've got.

Bibliography

Derrida, Jacques. "Différance." In *Deconstruction in Context*, edited by Mark C. Taylor, 396–420. Chicago: University of Chicago Press, 1986.

———. *The Gift of Death*. Translated by David Wills. Chicago: University of Chicago Press, 1995.

———. *Of Grammatology*. Translated by Gayatri Chakravorty Spivak. Baltimore: Johns Hopkins University Press, 1976.

Kearney, Richard. "On Forgiveness: A Roundable Discussion with Jacques Derrida." In *Questioning God*, edited by John Caputo et al., 52–72. Indianapolis: Indiana University Press, 2001.

Kierkegaard, Søren. *Fear and Trembling*. Translated by Howard V. Hong and Edna H. Hong. Princeton: Princeton University Press, 1983.

———. *Philosophical Fragments; or, A Fragment of Philosophy*. Translated by Howard V. Hong and Edna H. Hong. Princeton: Princeton University Press, 1985.

———. *Philosophiske Smuler, Eller, En Smule Philosophi / Af Johannes Climacus; Udg. Af S. Kierkegaard*. Copenhagen: Reitzel, 1865.

Levinas, Emmanuel. "God and Philosophy." Translated by Bettina Bergo. In *Of God Who Comes to Mind*, 55–78. Stanford: Stanford University Press, 1998.

Nietzsche, Friedrich. *On the Genealogy of Morals*. Translated by Walter Kaufmann. New York: Vintage, 1989.

Patočka, Jan. *Heretical Essays in the Philosophy of History*. Translated by Erazim Kohák. Edited by James Dodd. Chicago: Open Court, 1996.

Plato. *Phaedo*. In *Complete Works*, edited by John M. Cooper and D. S. Hutchinson. Indianapolis: Hackett, 1997.

Raschke, Karl. "The Deconstruction of God." In *Deconstruction and Theology*, edited by Thomas J. J. Altizer, 1–33. New York: Crossroad, 1982.

Rubenstein, Mary-Jane. "Dionysius, Derrida, and the Problem of Ontotheology." *Modern Theology* 24 (2008) 725–42.

54. Ibid., 123/140–41.

PART 4

Kierkegaard and the Politics of Theology

16

On Whose Authority?

Søren Kierkegaard and Ada María Isasi-Díaz on Christian Truth-Witnessing

MARIANA ALESSANDRI[1]

> The Upbuilding Discourses are "discourses," not "sermons" because the author does not have authority to preach.
>
> —SØREN KIERKEGAARD[2]

> What is authoritative is the experience of the Hispanic Women's community.
>
> —ADA MARIA ISASI-DÍAZ[3]

SØREN KIERKEGAARD NEVER WANTED to be an assistant professor. An author, yes, and a country pastor, but neither a teacher nor a theologian (despite his degree in theology and philosophy). Twice he tried to quit authoring to become the pastor; twice he failed. The author survived these existential tremors, in part by giving birth to pseudonyms and in part by telling himself he was no authority on Christian matters. In choosing authorship over authority, Kierkegaard wrote and signed "discourses" instead of "sermons" because he believed that he lacked the requisite authority to preach.[4] As a consequence, Kierkegaard left us discourses written by an author without authority instead of sermons by an authoritative pastor.

---

1. Many thanks to Margaret Newton, my research assistant for this project.
2. Kierkegaard, *Eighteen Upbuilding Discourses*, 5.
3. Isasi-Díaz, *Hispanic Women*, xiv.
4. Kierkegaard, *Eighteen Upbuilding Discourses*, 5.

Ada Maria Isasi-Díaz failed, too. She failed at being a nun because she wanted to be ordained a priest. Instead of getting more authority, she got more authorship. Kierkegaard might have declared Isasi-Díaz-the-author blessed to have less authority than Isasi-Díaz-the-priest, but Isasi-Díaz *still* worried about having too much authority out of concern for those without it. Her authorship, along with her position as a professor of ethics and theology at Drew University, threatened to be a single theological voice that would eclipse the whole Hispanic/Latino/a community.[5] But instead of using her authority to exclude already marginalized voices, she used it to authorize theirs. Isasi-Díaz coined the term "mujerista theology" to name a branch of liberation theology that "creates a voice for Latinas" and "captures public spaces for the voices of Latinas."[6] Mujerista theologians are Latina organic intellectuals who often do not hold ThM or MDiv degrees; they are grassroots activists whose lived experience in the Latina/o community makes them authoritative on theological issues. In contrast to Kierkegaard who denied his authority, Isasi-Díaz shared hers with others.

Neither Kierkegaard nor Isasi-Díaz had an official congregation; neither gave regular sermons, but both are read today as theologians. As I will show, even in his signed discourses, Kierkegaard attempted to leave his reader alone with her text; to extricate himself from the reading process. Kierkegaard felt it was important for a person to confront a text as a "single individual," because he believed that only single individuals could become Christians. In an essay from 1846 that he never published, Kierkegaard explained why he prioritized the "single individual" above the "crowd." He complained that "the crowd is untruth,"[7] in contrast to the "single individual," who only by herself stands any chance of developing a relationship to Christ. Since he considered truth inaccessible to a crowd, Kierkegaard dedicated himself to creating situations in which he could isolate reader and text from the crowd. This way, his single individual had an opportunity to develop a relationship with Christ and come into the truth.

Isasi-Díaz's authorship, on the other hand, did not target the single individual but rather put Latinas in community with one another and edified them in front of both academy and church. Despite the chasm that exists between Kierkegaard and Isasi-Díaz on who has greater access to truth: community or single individual (which I comment on in my conclusion), they would at least agree that truth is found in unlikely, though thoroughly Christian, places: among the poor, the oppressed, the suffering. In his articles published in *Fædrelandet* and *The Moment* in 1854 and 1855, Kierkegaard implied that anyone who could possibly count as a

---

5. In her early work, Isasi-Díaz mainly used the term Hispanic, "because it is the one commonly used in this society" (Isasi-Díaz, *Hispanic Women*, x–xi). In later works, she used *Latina* and *Hispanic* interchangeably, sometimes choosing Latina/Hispanic. For examples, see the introductions to *Mujerista Theology* and *En la Lucha*. I use them interchangeably.

6. Isasi-Díaz, *Mujerista Theology*, 2.

7. Kierkegaard, *Point of View*, 101–26.

"truth-witness" must necessarily belong to these groups. For her part, Isasi-Díaz admitted to "hermeneutically privileging" Latinas, since they also tend to belong to these groups.[8] Both reluctant authorities believed that the impoverished and oppressed have special insight into Christianity, and that these suffering souls, not their well-to-do pastors or priests, embody a kind of spiritual authority that goes unacknowledged in our world. Earthly authority, in contrast, has and probably always will be given to pastors, professors, and authors. With differing degrees of candor, Kierkegaard and Isasi-Díaz suggested that people who tend to have the most ecclesiastical authority also tend to be least capable of speaking about Christ's suffering from firsthand experience.[9] This belief led Kierkegaard to regularly remind his readers of two related facts: (1) he is no authority, and (2) he is no "truth-witness."[10] It led Isasi-Díaz to amplify the voices of Latina women who are seldom heard by grounding her theology in *lo cotidiano*—the daily lived experience of Latina women. How they responded to the discomfort they felt at the hands of their authority revealed a solid point of agreement: the best theology is more likely to come out of a kitchen or a reader's heart than from a pulpit or even a book.

Kierkegaard and Isasi-Díaz both believed that the poor and oppressed potentially make the best theologians, and I suggest that reading them together highlights the way in which adopting a liberation theology follows from this position.[11] In the

---

8. Kierkegaard, *The Moment*, 5–6; Isasi-Díaz, *En La Lucha* (2004), 7.

9. In this essay, I draw on Kierkegaard's discourses to highlight his uneasy relationship to his authority, and then I draw on his later "attack on Christendom" to outline what he sees as the relationship between Christian suffering and truth. As for Isasi Diaz, I draw mainly from *Hispanic Women* (written with Yolanda Tarrango, 1988), *En La Lucha* (1993), and *Mujerista Theology* (1996) to show both her prioritization of the poor and oppressed as well as her own discomfort with her authority.

10. Whether or not Kierkegaard actually believed these two "facts" is debatable; his earnestness has often been debated, legitimately in my opinion. In this essay, I treat the "Søren Kierkegaard" who authored the discourses and the journal entries as the same author as the "S. Kierkegaard" who published the 1854–1855 articles and who authored *The Point of View of My Work as an Author*. Despite doing so I will not weigh in on whether I think either of these denominations refers to the "real" Søren Kierkegaard or not, since I believe he cleverly left us no access to his "real" beliefs underneath the polyphony of often dissonant voices. Putting aside the question of his access to earnestness, I argue that the author of the discourses was not as effective at shedding his apparently discomforting authority as Isasi-Díaz was by sharing hers. For a compelling argument about why it is appropriate to approach Kierkegaard's supposed earnestness with suspicion (even by Kierkegaard's own lights), see Garff, "Eyes of Argus."

11. It is my hope that other scholars will pick up on the connection between Kierkegaard and liberation theology. As far as I know, there has been almost no work published on this topic to date. James Cone hints at a connection in the first chapter to *The Cross and the Lynching Tree*. Silas Morgan also hints at a connection between Kierkegaard and liberation theology by way of Harvey Cox and Dietrich Bonhoeffer in Morgan, "Harvey Gallagher Cox," 26–27. Wanda Warren Berry writes that religious existentialism in general "provided the framework for the development of liberation theology." In a footnote, she also writes: "Kierkegaard's authorship 'seduces' not only the secular public from aesthetical into ethical life but also the religious public from the quietist and piously fundamentalist Christendom into a liberation theology and radical praxis" (Berry, "Kierkegaard in Feminism," 117, 260). Finally, Mark Dooley writes: "The type of God that Kierkegaard enjoins his reader to imitate is

first section of this essay I provide a chronological account of Kierkegaard's attempt to shake off his authority, focusing on his publication decisions regarding the discourses. As I will show, in the discourses' prefaces Kierkegaard candidly rejected his authority while promoting the idea that the "single individual" should be valued higher than the "public." Kierkegaard's downplaying his authority vis-à-vis Christianity culminated in his "attack on Christendom," in which he explicitly and repeatedly claimed that the deceased Bishop Mynster was no "truth-witness" since he had not suffered for Christianity. I read Kierkegaard's attack on Christendom to be an extension of his discourses, and his insistence on not being a "truth-witness" to be an extension of his insistence on not being an authority. Casting off his authority was Kierkegaard's primary way of calling himself no truth-witness. In my second section, I contrast Kierkegaard to Isasi-Díaz, who faced her discomfort with her authority more directly, by leveraging it to centralize marginalized voices. She may not have called herself a "truth-witness" but Isasi-Diaz did call herself a "theological technician," someone who witnesses to the truth of a community. In my final section, I suggest that Isasi-Díaz's decision to share her authority with mujerista theologians was a more fruitful solution to the problem of what to do with one's unwanted authority than Kierkegaard's lonely attempt to deny his. Nonetheless, I read both responses to their authority as attempts to legitimate unlikely sources of theological insight: Kierkegaard—the "single individual," and Isasi-Díaz—"lo cotidiano," or the everyday experiences of Latina women. In rejecting their earthly authority, each author implied that common, everyday people and their experiences are actually a better source for theology than clergy or academics. But not just any people. My final suggestion is that if we read Kierkegaard's and Isasi-Díaz's actions in light of their beliefs about the poor, oppressed, and suffering, we can reasonably conclude that, for both authors, all good theology will listen—above all—to the hungry, the homeless, the impoverished, the naked, the sick, the imprisoned; in Christ's words, "to the least of these."[12]

Kierkegaard Renounces His Authority

Kierkegaard dealt with his discomfort over his authority by devising an elaborate system of pseudonyms and disclaimers about his authorship. Kierkegaard's first published work—*Either/Or*—was written pseudonymously by A and Judge William before it was edited and published pseudonymously by Victor Eremita on February 20, 1843. His second published work—*Two Upbuilding Discourses*—was written and published by Søren Kierkegaard himself, and it appeared just three months after *Either/Or* on May 16. Eremita fans were underwhelmed by these signed discourses in comparison

---

one that approximates in no small measure the God of liberation theology" (Dooley, *Politics of Exodus*, 19).

12. Matt 25:40.

to the "monster."[13] Exactly five months later Kierkegaard produced another pair of pseudonymous hits: *Fear and Trembling* by Johannes de Silentio and *Repetition* by Constantin Constantius, this time pairing them with three more under-read discourses.[14] This pattern suggests that Kierkegaard chose to sandwich his first five *Upbuilding Discourses* between four volumes of popular aesthetic works. Over the course of his authorship, Kierkegaard would publish seventy-one more signed discourses, wedging them between pseudonymous successes.

Years later Kierkegaard would tell us why he made this strange publishing choice, and why, more generally, his career as an author consisted of a bifurcation: aesthetic pseudonymous writings on the one hand and religious signed writings on the other. In the 1844 preface to *Two Upbuilding Discourses*, Kierkegaard first suggested his reason, which he would only later explicitly call an act of obedience to God in *On My Work as an Author* (published in 1848) and in *The Point of View of My Work as an Author* (published posthumously). Kierkegaard claimed that his left hand was commanded by God to offer aesthetic ideas to an aesthetic people, while his right hand was commanded to offer them religious writings.[15] Although he admitted that the finer points of God's plan were unknown to him at the time, Kierkegaard's publishing decisions were designed to "make aware," that is, to distinguish authentic Christianity from mere "Christendom." In doing so, he hoped to inspire contemporary Denmark to recognize the superficiality of both the aesthetic and the falsely Christian life.[16]

In the preface to his first *Two Upbuilding Discourses*, Kierkegaard used the phrase partially reproduced in the epigraph, one that he repeated in almost all future prefaces: "This book has 'discourses,' not 'sermons,' because its author does not have authority to preach. They are 'upbuilding discourses,' not 'discourses for upbuilding,' because the speaker by no means claims to be a teacher."[17] Neither a preacher nor a teacher, Kierkegaard claimed to have written the discourses for his own "discipline and education."[18] In other words, instead of preaching from the pulpit or even teaching from the podium, Kierkegaard tried to forego his authority, going as far as to

---

13. Howard Hong reports that only one short review came out for *Two Upbuilding Discourses*, and that it did not sell well. In comparison, *Either/Or* received eight reviews (one of them calling the book a "monster"), sold out by 1847, and was one of few works reprinted before his death. See Kierkegaard, *Eighteen Upbuilding Discourses*, xxi, and Kierkegaard, *Either/Or*, xvi.

14. *Three Upbuilding Discourses* sold 139 copies compared to 321 of *Fear and Trembling* and 272 of *Repetition*.

15. See also Kierkegaard, *Eighteen Upbuilding Discourses*, ix–xi, 179; supplement to *Without Authority*, 237–38, Kierkegaard, *Journals and Papers*, 5:5639, 5648.

16. Again, although we have reason to be suspicious of Kierkegaard's "explanation," I am taking it to be consistent with both the discourses and the "attack on Christendom."

17. See Kierkegaard, *Eighteen Upbuilding Discourses*, 5, 53, 107, 179, 231, 295.

18. Ibid., 5.

renounce the only bit of authority left to him—his authorship—by calling himself merely a *reader* of the works.[19]

The "Single Individual"

Roughly half of the *Upbuilding Discourses* are dedicated to his late father, Michael Pederson Kierkegaard, and the other half are dedicated to the "single individual" [*hiin Enkelte*], who, in contrast to the "public," is seriously concerned about her condition as an existing individual. Here and elsewhere Kierkegaard writes about his disdain for the "crowd," or the "public," praising instead the "single individual," "my reader."[20] In *The Point of View for My Work as an Author*, he explains:

> Here again the movement is: to *arrive at* the simple; the movement is: *from* the public *to* "the single individual." In other words, there is in a *religious sense* no public but only individuals; because the religious is earnestness, and earnestness is: the single individual; yet that every human being, unconditionally every human being—which one indeed is—can be, yes, is supposed to be, the single individual.[21]

Though his message was intended to be universally applicable, it could only be appropriated individually.[22] Unlike the aesthetic works, the discourses do not lend themselves to cocktail party conversation; one must pick up a discourse as one plucks a flower from a forest, to use Kierkegaard's imagery. This person becomes "my reader," from whom Kierkegaard would quickly vanish, leaving reader and text alone together.[23] Kierkegaard the author would consider himself successful only if his reader appropriates the book's message, "gives it a good home," "gives it meaning, and transforms it."[24]

Kierkegaard had published half of his discourses by the time he published *Stages on Life's Way* (1845), which he paired with *Three Discourses on Imagined Occasions*. This time he replaced the feminine image of the discourse as a flower waiting to be plucked with an even more feminine image of a bridesmaid waiting patiently for her bridegroom.[25] Finally in 1846, Kierkegaard published "A First and Last Explanation" at the end of *Concluding Unscientific Postscript*. He meant this to be the end of his

---

19. Ibid.
20. For an explanation, see "Single Individual," in Kierkegaard, *Point of View*, 101–26.
21. Ibid., 10.
22. Kierkegaard explained that the "single individual" can mean "the most unique one of all" or "everyone." Kierkegaard, *Eighteen Upbuilding Discourses*, xx.
23. Ibid., 5.
24. Ibid., 107. In the preface to *Three Upbuilding Discourses* from 1844, Kierkegaard expresses a desire to be "absent" when the reader "bring[s] the cold thoughts to flame again," to transform the discourse into a conversation." Ibid., 231.
25. Kierkegaard, *Three Discourses*, 5.

authorship, the end of his hiding. He was determined to give up being an author to become a country pastor; to finally deal with the religious in a direct way.

But instead of trading his authorship for ecclesiastical authority, just one year later Kierkegaard published not two (or three, or four) but twelve *Upbuilding Discourses in Various Spirits*. In other words, instead of adopting the authority of a pastor, Kierkegaard chose to remain an author without (as much) authority.[26] This time, though, he even more forcefully (although arguably less successfully), renounced all authority he had left as an author. Instead of calling himself a mere reader as he had done previously, Kierkegaard decided to publish critical reviews, which for him didn't count against his authorship.[27] Thus, Kierkegaard's second authorship began with the publication of the *Upbuilding Discourses in Various Spirits*, in whose prefaces he took up the familiar theme of vanishing, of being a "prompter in relation to the reader."[28] In these discourses he introduced another metaphor: he compared the inwardness of appropriation to a person who appropriates needlework done by someone else. The beautiful cloth itself is more important than the woman who made it, and like the needlewoman, Kierkegaard the author is rendered unnecessary by the craft he produced. Only the essential remains: the reader and the book.[29]

Kierkegaard published *Works of Love* in September of the same year, under his own name, followed by *Christian Discourses* in 1848, with no pseudonymous work in between. So far, Kierkegaard was making good on his promise to set down his pseudonymous pen. But three months after *Christian Discourses*, he published *The Crisis and a Crisis in the Life of an Actress*, penned under the name Inter et Inter ("between and between" in Latin). Over the next two years, nine more discourses came out. In the preface to his 1851 *Two Discourses at the Communion on Fridays*, Kierkegaard tried to retire a third time, calling these discourses his authorship's "place of rest."[30] In the preface, Kierkegaard repeated his earlier refrain of being "without authority," this time specifically adding the important detail that he did not consider himself a "truth-witness."[31] These two concepts—being without authority and not being a truth-witness—were related even before his "attack on

---

26. According to Joakim Garff, Kierkegaard's decision to remain a city writer instead of becoming a country pastor was driven by the idea that Copenhagen needed him, presumably to defend Christianity against Christendom. Perhaps he thought he could get further *without* the authority of a clergyman. See Garff, *Søren Kierkegaard*, 412–14.

27. Apparently, Kierkegaard did not consider review-writers authors: "in this way I would still avoid becoming an author." Kierkegaard, *Upbuilding Discourses*, ix, 356; Kierkegaard, *Journals and Papers*, 5:5877.

28. This term comes from a review of the *Upbuilding Discourses in Various Spirits*. See ibid., xiii.

29. *Upbuilding Discourses in Various Spirits* was not reprinted during Kierkegaard's lifetime, and it had a total of three reviews. See Kierkegaard, *Upbuilding Discourses*, xii.

30. Kierkegaard, *Without Authority*, 165.

31. Ibid.

Christendom."[32] Instead of being a truth-witness, the Kierkegaard of these last discourses considered himself to be a "singular kind of poet and thinker who, *without authority*, has nothing new to bring."[33]

Truth-Witnessing

As it turned out, Kierkegaard's second authorship only rested for three years (still a notable gain over the short year of his first authorship's retirement), before restarting his authorship in 1854, with a series of signed articles that are now widely referred to as his "attack on Christendom." The term that energized his authorship was the same one he rejected for himself three years prior: "truth-witness," which Professor-soon-to-be-Bishop Martensen had publicly used to describe the recently deceased Bishop Mynster. In the first of several vitriolic articles, a very angry Kierkegaard attacked Mynster's "dubious proclamation of Christianity."[34] Worried that Mynster would be "represented and canonized in the pulpit" by the established church as a truth-witness, Kierkegaard criticized him over and over again along with Martensen.[35] The truth of Christianity, as Kierkegaard saw it—and as anyone deserving the title of truth-witness would see it—means "suffering for the doctrine."[36] Mynster had plenty of authority but none of the suffering; i.e., none of the truth-witnessing. This is not a coincidence for Kierkegaard, since truth-witnesses must necessarily suffer:

> A truth witness is a person who in poverty witnesses for the truth, in poverty, in lowliness and abasement, is so underappreciated, hated, detested, so mocked, insulted, laughed to scorn—so poor that he perhaps has not always had daily bread, but he received the daily bread of persecution in abundance every day.[37]

From these lines it is clear that neither Mynster nor Martensen nor Kierkegaard himself would qualify to be a truth-witness. They, despite or, more likely, because of their earthly authority, have simply not suffered enough, or suffered in the right ways or for the right things.[38] Perhaps this helps explain Kierkegaard's refusal to increase

32. Ibid.
33. Ibid.
34. Kierkegaard, *The Moment*, 4.
35. Ibid.
36. Ibid., 5.
37. Ibid., 5–6.
38. In these articles from 1854–55, Kierkegaard implies that the true Christian seeks suffering as a kind of cleansing oneself from the world, and that suffering can be material, spiritual, or physical in nature. To what extent the Christian must suffer cannot be pinpointed, but it seems clear that for Kierkegaard, one who has not suffered in ways like Christ did cannot possibly be Christian. Pace Anthony Imbrosciano, I do not think that Kierkegaard's idea of Christian suffering necessarily is limited to suffering *for* the doctrine. Rather, it includes suffering as Christ did (in *poverty*, *lowliness*, and *abasement*), which are the types of suffering that liberation theology has in mind. See Imbrosciano,

his authority by becoming a country pastor; Copenhagen could provide him with the suffering he needed to publish his insights about the truth of Christianity. Thus, if authors and church authorities do not qualify as truth-witnesses, then we would have to look outside the standard channels to find an authentic Christian theology. We would have to look for those in "poverty, "lowliness," and "abasement."[39] My suggestion here is that Kierkegaard might have found what he was looking for in the mujeristas that Isasi-Díaz writes with and about: Hispanic women who unquestionably lack his and Bishop Mynster's authority and as such, stand a good chance of being authentic truth-witnesses.

Isasi-Díaz Shares Her Authority

Unlike Kierkegaard, Isasi-Díaz sought *more* clerical authority—she wanted to become a priest so that she could be part of changing the oppressive structures of the Catholic Church. Whereas Kierkegaard denied himself the priesthood, Isasi-Díaz was denied it by the church, leaving her with only the authority of her authorship.

Isasi-Díaz came to the United States from Cuba in 1961 at eighteen. She immediately entered a convent, but balked at the "restrictions on personal relationships that were part of life in the convent."[40] For three of the eight years of her religious life, Isasi-Díaz worked in Peru, but refused to "maintain a lifestyle in which people talked about poverty while living a privileged life."[41] Finally, she recounts, her refusal to tame her "passion" and "spontaneity" "let [her] to realize that [her] garden could not flourish within the convent walls."[42] In 1975 Isasi-Díaz attended the Women's Ordination Conference to advocate for women joining the priesthood of the Catholic Church. During this conference she committed to fighting sexism forever, including the hierarchy of the church.[43] First she joined the Womanchurch movement, until she realized that being a Hispanic in a European-American Feminist movement would mean facing racial and ethnic oppressions. These experiences gave Isasi-Díaz the idea that, for any movement to be liberative, "power had to be shared," and it was then that she committed to sharing hers in the struggle against multiple oppressions.[44]

Early in her writing, even before coining the term "mujerista theology," Isasi-Díaz insisted that her books were to be the place for Latina voices to come out, and for her own voice to be one among many. She wrote:

"Inevitable Martyrdom," 105–6, and Westphal, "Kierkegaard's Teleological Suspension," 110.

39. Kierkegaard, *The Moment*, 5–6.
40. Isasi-Díaz, *Mujerista Theology*, 16.
41. Ibid.
42. Ibid.
43. Ibid., 17–18.
44. Ibid., 19.

> Hispanic Women's experiences and how they understand those experiences are at the core of Hispanic Women's Liberation Theology. That is why Hispanic Women's voices, their very own words, are at the heart of this book. Therefore, we have purposefully dedicated at least half of this book to recording their words verbatim. The rest—the analytical chapters—are complementary, suggestive, and understandable only in view of the verbatim material.[45]

Each subsequent book by Isasi-Díaz is both polyphonic and polyvocal; she consistently insisted on not hiding from difference/disagreement between Hispanic women.

In his condemnation of Bishop Mynster, Kierkegaard implicitly rejected "theology as usual." Isasi-Díaz explicitly did so in *Mujerista Theology*.[46] The basis of her criticism hinged on a suspicion about *objectivity*: "what passes as objectivity in reality merely names the subjectivity of those who have the authority and/or power to impose their point of view."[47] In addition to their distrust for the "objective" viewpoint, Kierkegaard and Isasi-Díaz also agree that those with the most earthly authority—those who have the power to impose their view and call it objective—tend to know little about the experience of suffering under oppression and injustice. Not only that, but they also tend to dismiss those who have this knowledge rooted in experience. Neither author has much faith in clergymen, but Isasi-Díaz turned to a community of *mujeristas* rather than the earnest attempts of a "single individual." Instead of using pseudonyms or denying her authority as Kierkegaard did, Isasi-Díaz leveraged it to write books that would serve as a platform for underrepresented Latina voices. By "hermeneutically privileging" the Latina community, Isasi-Díaz founded mujerista theology on the experiences of Latina women and their interpretations.[48] These Latina voices sometimes directly respond to ecclesiastical authority, but most often put their theological efforts into developing their subjectivity. Isasi-Díaz writes:

> As a theology rooted in the religious thought and practice of Latinas, mujerista theology has made it possible to give voice to those who so far had not been listened to in any theological elaboration, mainly because they were thought incapable of deep, systematic reflection.[49]

Oppressed communities get little or no respect from clergy, nor do they look like truth-witnesses. But, like Kierkegaard, Isasi-Díaz would undoubtedly consider suffering people spiritually authoritative, and capable of generating meaningful Christian theology. Both authors search the bottom social rungs for truth, where, as a whole, mujerista theologians dwell, facing standard oppressions such as racism and sexism, but also a host of micro- and macro-aggressions including, for example,

---

45. Isasi-Díaz, *Hispanic Women*, xv.
46. Isasi-Díaz, *Mujerista Theology*, 79.
47. Ibid., 77.
48. Isasi-Díaz, *En La Lucha*, 7.
49. Ibid.

being dismissed if they lack formal education, being disrespected for having children and/or being expected to have (too) many children, either actually suffering from domestic violence (or assumed to be), being looked down upon for practicing alternative medicines (or being expected to practice them), being made to feel like foreigners in their own country due to skin color, language, or accent, etc. In his day, Christ faced some of these oppressions. Isasi-Díaz would likely argue that today, Christ would face all of them. Based on his status and position as a Galilean son of a carpenter, today's Christ might be a Central American refugee turned away at the border or detained; she would be told to speak English because we are in America, or she might feel ashamed about not being able to speak to her grandmother in Spanish; she would likely be poor and uneducated, or, like Isasi-Díaz and many others, feel conflicted about being educated and/or middle class. Christ today might be the daughter of a school janitor; she might be dark-skinned or feel shame inhabiting her light skin; she might feel trapped in an abusive relationship with step-father, uncle or husband, one in which she is supposed to be subservient and docile. She might not have the means to leave home. In short, mujerista theology teaches us that if you want to discover some truth about God on earth, one fertile place to look is in the everyday experiences of Hispanic women in the United States.

Lo Cotidiano

"Lo cotidiano" is Isasi-Díaz's term for the everyday experiences out of which mujerista theology grows, and it includes:

> particular forms of speech, the experience of class and gender distinctions, the impact of work and poverty on routines and expectations, relations within families and among friends and neighbors in a community, the experience of authority, and central expressions of faith such as prayer, religious celebrations, and conceptions of key religious figures.[50]

As the source of mujerista theology, lo cotidiano means that Latinas are knowers whose lives are the basis of their theologies. The kind of knowledge they have comes more from experience than from books, since, for Isasi-Díaz, "lo cotidiano refers to the way Latinas know and what we know to be the 'stuff' (la tela, literally, the cloth) out of which our lives as a struggling community within the USA is fabricated."[51] As a result, "mujerista theology is not a disembodied discourse but one that arises from situated subjects, Latina grassroots women."[52] Isasi-Díaz's insistence on personal experiences would resonate with Kierkegaard's insistence on subjectivity in the discourses as well as in his pseudonymous works.

---

50. Isasi-Díaz, *Mujerista Theology*, 66–67. Original passage is from Levine, *Popular Voices*, 317.
51. Isasi-Díaz, *Mujerista Theology*, 71.
52. Ibid., 3.

Though *Concluding Unscientific Postscript* is written by a pseudonym, the concept of subjectivity is key for Kierkegaard, and proves to be quite similar to Isasi-Díaz's "lo cotidiano." Johannes Climacus writes that "becoming subjective" is the "highest task assigned to a human being," and insists that a relationship with God trumps any approximations about him.[53] The Kierkegaard of the discourses would agree with Climacus that faith is not measured by one's knowledge about God or theology but by one's relationship with Christ. Focusing on anything other than the "cloth" of our lives, our existence and relationships, puts us in danger of "slipping into a parenthesis," to use Climacus's metaphor.[54] Kierkegaard and Isasi-Díaz would certainly agree that we can learn more about God from our daily interactions than from the *Summa Theologica*.

Theological Technicians

Whereas Kierkegaard's distrust of earthly authority led him to renounce his authority and denounce Mynster's as no "truth-witness," Isasi-Díaz's distrust of authority led her to adopt the term "theological technicians," a concept that simultaneously gives credit to formal theologians without giving them too much authority. Isasi-Díaz believes that theological technicians, who are responsible for translating, transcribing, and transforming *lo cotidiano* into written words, play an important role in mujerista theology. Isasi-Díaz counts herself as a theological technician, one who has "the gift of gathering what the community is saying, writing it down, and making it known," one who, through her writing "offer[s] leadership to the doing of theology in which the community engages."[55] The term "theological technician" was originally coined by Carlos Abesamis, who described one as being

> in possession of certain technical competences in exegesis, social sciences, languages, archaeology, or history and who offer[s] these findings in these different fields to the real theologians to help them in the act of interpreting reality from . . . [their] perspective.[56]

Isasi-Díaz uses the gift of language and her connections in the academy to provide a space for Latina voices, though she does not believe that this makes her more of an authority than anyone else. Isasi-Díaz admits to being separated from many mujerista theologians by her formal education and economic status, so calling herself a theological technician is a way of validating her struggle for the liberation of Hispanic women, by communicating with and for truth-witnesses.[57]

53. Kierkegaard, *Concluding Unscientific Postscript*, 129.
54. Kierkegaard, *Postscript*, 28–29.
55. Isasi-Díaz, *Hispanic Women*, 105–6; xvii.
56. Ibid., 106. Original quote is from Abesamis, "Faith and Life Reflections," 137.
57. Isasi-Díaz, *Mujerista Theology*, 6.

Conclusion

Kierkegaard renounced his authority, but never successfully. Isasi-Díaz was denied priestly authority, but retained academic authority. This difference might explain why Kierkegaard hid his voice in pseudonyms and Isasi-Díaz blended hers into a chorus of Latina women. Perhaps Kierkegaard's invocation of traditional notions of exercising a personal will and committing to God decisively was a direct consequence of the fact that it was his decision not to be a country pastor; no one forced him into the role of invisible needlewoman. And perhaps Isasi-Díaz's reliance on her community, along with her constantly sharing her authority, was a direct result of having been denied what she wanted by those with authority. In any case, the Kierkegaard who wrote the discourses would have been ripe for someone like Isasi-Díaz to come along; had his authorship been truly polyphonic instead of artificially so, he might have been more convincing. Had he faced the kinds of social oppression Isasi-Díaz did, she might have been able to convince Kierkegaard that "lo cotidiano is not a private, individual category, but rather a social category."[58] He might have been tempted to draw a distinction between the community and the crowd (saving his vitriol for the latter), or at least he might be more open to the idea that truth can be accessed by a community in addition to a single individual.[59] Even despite his individualism, Kierkegaard's belief that having authority was irreconcilable with being a truth-witness, coupled with his insistence that truth-witnesses are found "among the least of these," put him in a prime position to hear about liberation theology generally, and mujerista theology specifically. Without naming it, the un-authoritative Kierkegaard of the discourses who became the non-truth-witness of the attack on Christendom, expressed a "preferential option for the poor,"[60] which is the bedrock of liberation theology, including mujerista theology.

Bibliography

Abesamis, Carlos. "Faith and Life Reflections from the Grassroots in the Phillipines." In *Asia's Struggle for Full Humanity: Towards a Relevant Theology*, edited by Virginia Fabella, 123–39. Maryknoll: Orbis, 1980.

Berry, Wanda Warren. "Kierkegaard in Feminism: Apologetic, Repetition, and Dialogue." In *Kierkegaard in Post/Modernity*, edited by Martin Joseph Matuštík and Merold Westphal, 110–24. Indianapolis: Indiana University Press, 1995.

Dooley, Mark. *The Politics of Exodus*. New York: Fordham University Press, 2001.

---

58. Ibid., 71.

59. When Kierkegaard writes that "the crowd is untruth," for example, I do not believe he has in mind intentional communities like mujerista theologians. What makes the crowd so odious to Kierkegaard is that it is unintentional, unthoughtful, and unreflective. I believe that Isasi-Díaz's account of mujeristas theologians would give him pause. See "The Single Individual," in Kierkegaard, *Point of View*, 101–26.

60. See Gutiérrez, *Theology of Liberation*, and Isasi-Díaz, *Mujeristas*.

PART 4: KIERKEGAARD AND THE POLITICS OF THEOLOGY

Garff, Joakim. "The Eyes of Argus: The Point of View and Points of View on Kierkegaard's Work as an Author." In *Kierkegaard: A Critical Reader*, edited by Jonathan Rée and Jane Chamberlain, 75–102. Oxford: Blackwell 1998.

———. *Søren Kierkegaard: A Biography*. Translated by Bruce H. Kirmmse. Princeton: Princeton University Press, 2005.

Gutierrez, Gustavo. *The Power of the Poor in History*. Maryknoll: Orbis, 1983.

———. *A Theology of Liberation*. Maryknoll: Orbis, 1971.

Imbrosciano, Anthony. "Inevitable Martyrdom: The Connection between Faith and Suffering in Kierkegaard's Later Writings." *International Journal for Philosophy of Religion* 36 (1994) 105–16.

Isasi-Díaz, Ada María. *En La Lucha / In the Struggle: A Hispanic Women's Liberation Theology*. Minneapolis: Fortress, 1993.

———. *En La Lucha / In the Struggle: Elaborating a Mujerista Theology*. Minneapolis: Fortress, 2004.

———. *Mujerista Theology: A Theology for the Twenty-First Century*. Maryknoll: Orbis, 1996.

———. "Mujeristas, a Name of Our Own." In *Yearning to Breathe Free: Liberation Theologies in the United States*, edited by Mar Peter-Raoul et al., 121–28. Maryknoll: Orbis, 1990.

Isasi-Díaz, Ada María, and Yolanda Tarango. *Hispanic Women, Prophetic Voice in the Church*. San Francisco: Harper & Row, 1988.

Kierkegaard, Søren. *Christian Discourses*. Edited by Howard V. Hong and Edna H. Hong. Princeton: Princeton University Press, 1997.

———. *Concluding Unscientific Postscript to Philosophical Fragments*. Edited by Howard V. Hong and Edna H. Hong. Princeton: Princeton University Press, 1992.

———. *Eighteen Upbuilding Discourses*. Edited by Howard V. Hong and Edna H. Hong. Princeton: Princeton University Press, 1992.

———. *Either/Or*. Edited by Howard V. Hong and Edna H. Hong. Princeton: Princeton University Press, 1987.

———. *Kierkegaard's Journals and Papers I–V*. Edited by Howard V. Hong and Edna H. Hong. Bloomington: Indiana University Press, 1967–1978.

———. *The Moment and Late Writings*. Edited by Howard V. Hong and Edna H. Hong. Princeton: Princeton University Press, 2009.

———. *Philosophical Fragments*. Edited by Howard V. Hong and Edna H. Hong. Princeton: Princeton University Press, 1985.

———. *The Point of View*. Edited by Howard V. Hong and Edna H. Hong. Princeton: Princeton University Press, 1998.

———. *Three Discourses on Imagined Occasions*. Edited by Howard V. Hong and Edna H. Hong. Princeton: Princeton University Press, 1993.

———. *Two Ages: "The Age of Revolution" and the "Present Age"; A Literary Review*. Edited by Howard V. Hong and Edna H. Hong. Princeton: Princeton University Press, 2009.

———. *Upbuilding Discourses in Various Spirits*. Edited by Howard V. Hong and Edna H. Hong. Princeton: Princeton University Press, 2009.

———. *Without Authority*. Edited by Howard V. Hong and Edna H. Hong. Princeton: Princeton University Press, 2009.

Levine, Daniel H. *Popular Voices in Latin American Catholicism*. Princeton: Princeton University Press, 1992.

Morgan, Silas. "Harvey Gallagher Cox, Jr.: An Uncomfortable Theologian Wary of Kierkegaard." In *Kierkegaard's Influence on Theology: Anglophpone and Scandanavian Protestants*, edited by Jon Stewart, 25–44. Burlington, VT: Ashgate, 2012.

Westphal, Merold. "Kierkegaard's Teleological Suspension of Religiousness B." In *Foundations of Kierkegaard's Vision of Community*, edited by George Connell and C. Stephen Evans, 110–29. Atlantic Highlands, NJ: Humanities, 1992.

17

Politics of the Church, Hidden and Revealed, in Søren Kierkegaard and John Howard Yoder

Jason A. Mahn

It is almost a banality now in Kierkegaardian circles to suggest that Kierkegaard's final, "direct" attack on the established church is markedly different in style and theme than the writings that preceded it, both early and late, both pseudonymous and signed. While there is a host of ways in which this truism remains true, a single factor complicates it—namely, the fact that these latest, direct, polemical writings aim squarely at that which Kierkegaard has had in his sights at least since *Postscript*: the host of sociopolitically-inscribed and religiously-underwritten assumptions and temperaments that he calls "Christendom." In that sense, the attack literature culminates a major trajectory of his life's work rather than departs from it. Yet this continuity in critique of Christendom seems only to highlight a more subtle but important shift. It is only late that we find that critique redirected from "the Establishment" or acculturated Christianity in general to landing squarely *at the church*, with its paid clergy, infant baptism, and lack of "suffering for the truth." Even if one can and should retrieve a marked sense of "community" and "politics" in Kierkegaard, it is very difficult to reconstruct any positive description of church, at least in light of his final attack. There, Christendom seems equivalent with "the church" and the "established" or "inherited" church nothing more or less than "Christendom."

Yet there are ironies here, too. One notes that the shift from Kierkegaard's earlier indirect critique to his direct polemics largely revolves around the question of whether religious suffering is essentially inward and hidden or outward and recognizable.[1] The earlier Kierkegaard championed the hidden inwardness accompanying "dying to the world," convinced as he was that any bourgeois philistine may in fact be a knight of faith.[2] Kierkegaard eventually becomes concerned that such appeals might mask a spiritless lack of having ventured at all or, worse, that they themselves might become clear evidence that one has achieved the highest. Kierkegaard thus eventually assumes

---

1. Kierkegaard, *For Self Examination*, 168–69.
2. Kierkegaard, *Fear and Trembling*, 38–40.

that New Testament Christianity will manifest itself in willed and noticeable suffering ("denying myself, renouncing the world, dying to the world, etc.").[3] Based on this shift from inward to outward, from invisible to manifest, one might guess that Kierkegaard in the end would portray and fight for a *visible* church rather than merely critique the institutional one. In other words, one would expect him to want, not to do away with church as institution, but to make it more pronounced, identifiable, discrete. Others use the "true church" as a norm by which to critique the chief institution of accommodated and cultured Christendom; Kierkegaard by comparison, seems to throw out one with the other, at least at first glance.

This irony shows up best if we compare Kierkegaard's critiques of nineteenth-century Christendom to one of the twentieth century's most influential critics of Christendom—Mennonite theologian, church historian, and social ethicist John Howard Yoder. Yoder's primary complaint about the established church is its presumption to be invisible, a "spiritual" reality as opposed to having a particular, social, political form.[4] In Yoder's phrasing, we mainline denominations and mainstream American culture have "shut [Jesus] up in the monastery of the heart"[5]—quietly refusing to follow his example in our collective life together. Yoder's corrective to Christendom or Constantinianism is thus for the church to become distinguishable from the world, a *visible* polis with its own *distinctive* politic.[6]

In the rest of this essay, I want to trace Kierkegaard's antiestablishment writings alongside Yoder's anti-Constantinian writings in the hopes that the close convergences and enduring differences between the two can help us think through what a hidden, yet manifest church might look like, especially beside a Christendom that is still very much with us. I will concur with Yoder that any understanding of the true church as a spiritual, invisible reality precludes the kind of countercultural witness that both he and Kierkegaard otherwise sought. At the same time, Kierkegaard offers ways to see the church more christologically, that is, as a corporate body that remains incognito—hidden in its very disclosure. To deny direct recognition with Kierkegaard is not the same as rendering the church invisible, although the church may in fact remain hidden. I will close by suggesting that a *visible* but also perpetually *hidden*

---

3. Kierkegaard, *The Moment and Late Writings*, 36.

4. Among the many places Yoder makes this claim, see "Kingdom as Social Ethic," 98–101, and "Let the Church Be the Church," 107–24.

5. Yoder, *Original Revolution*, 175.

6. Yoder, arguably the most influential critic of Constantinian arrangements (especially of the American church's accommodations to war), has now been shown to have committed egregious sexual violence against numerous women he knew throughout much of his career. See Cramer et al., "Theology and Misconduct," 20–23; Goosen, "Defanging the Beast," 7–80; and Guth, *Christian Ethics*, 21–22n36. That Yoder horrifically failed to live up to the Christian pacifism and communitarian politics he professed is clear. By drawing from his work in this essay, I am neither overlooking nor excusing the violence he perpetrated. In fact, putting him in conversation with Kierkegaard may begin to sketch an understanding of church that includes a more self-critical, penitential attitude, as well as a mandate to protect the most vulnerable inside and outside its borders.

church would include penitential and liberatory practices—that is, a distinctive politic—that are sorely needed in America's new Christendom.[7]

Yoder for Kierkegaard

Yoder wrote his best-known work, *The Politics of Jesus*, at an opportune time. Published in 1972, the book built on and gave voice to discontent with America's involvement in an unpopular war as it reconstructed Jesus not as a spiritual, a-political leader of people's hearts (that he would leave to Princess Diana), but as concerned with issues of power, status, and war—both sanctioned and unsanctioned. On Yoder's reading, Jesus and the early church join the Israelites in exhibiting a distinctive social arrangement—an "ethic" or "culture" or "politic"—that is recognizable and inhabitable and that provides a real alternative to the power-politics, hierarchical structures, and sanctioned violence perpetuated by empires and modern-day nation states. Because the life and death of Jesus provide a pattern of radical service, forgiveness, and nonviolent resistance to the powers of church and state, disciples of the crucified one will necessarily find their community countercultural and politically subversive.[8]

Rather than directly or extensively critique those alternative social arrangements, then, Yoder critiques the ways in which Christianity has become depoliticized in the first place. It is only by losing their "original," sociopolitical form that they are thought to be compatible with an essentially non-Christian politics. This he calls "Constantinianism," a name that overlaps considerably with Kierkegaard's use of "Christendom."[9] The real tragedy (what Yoder calls the *apostasy*) of Constantinian arrangements is not that Christianity becomes dominant or mainstream, but that it ceases to have a *distinctive* ethos and politics. Once soldiers and hangmen are baptized, Christianity becomes not a way of life, but a doctrine to believe. Most disconcerting to Yoder is this: once the church and nation share borders—as with the *Holy* Roman Empire or state-church arrangements, and also according to popular sentiments about a "Christian America"—then a "real church" must be posited above and beyond historically visible churches. In other words, in order to preserve the meaningfulness of "the true church" or "the elect," Constantinian churches need to posit a difference between the

---

7. See my *Becoming a Christian in Christendom*.

8. Yoder, *Politics of Jesus*, 134–61.

9. Yoder typically uses the term "Christendom" to name the medieval ecclesiastical-political synthesis jointly presided over by emperor and pope or as a general term for the "majority consciousness" or assortment of assumptions accompanying the accepted social privilege and power of Christianity in the Western world. Yoder, *Royal Priesthood*, 106. By "Constantinian," Yoder typically means something more precise: either *a particular historical lineage* traceable to the legalization and then institutionalization of Christianity by the Roman Empire in the fourth and fifth century, or (more commonly) *a particular priority given to that history* based on assumptions traceable to—but not limited to—that particular period. Yoder, *Priestly Kingdom*, 210n5.

visible and invisible church. The "real" church becomes invisible to the extent that the "actual" church becomes compromised.

Notice, then, that Yoder's leverage against any given Constantinian arrangement depends on his ability to offer a thick description of "the politics of Jesus" and that of the early church. Only a historian of religion—and perhaps one willing to take the latest modern biblical scholarship into full account—can paint the early followers of Jesus with enough detail to exhibit exactly what is lost when the church is rendered invisible and thus made to accommodate other social forms. Without a visible church, past or present, Yoder has nothing by which to mark its absorption into Christendom and disappearance into the hidden church.[10]

Kierkegaard's portrayal of Christendom is similar to that of Yoder. Both portray Christendom as largely the problem of redundancy and identity. If I am a Christian by virtue of birth, upbringing, and default assumptions of the dominant culture, what in the world could it mean to *become* Christian? Both assume that identity relies on borders (something that I am / we are *not*) and that Christendom obscures or elides essential differences between what is and isn't Christianity. Kierkegaard via Socratic ignorance and Yoder via historical reconstructions beg for *redefining* Christianity or the Christian church in light of that which is necessarily outside. The church polis must, for both, be here and not there, and the difference must be "visible."

It is on this point that important differences between Yoder and Kierkegaard might offer the latter a way out of certain problems inherent in his final attack on the church. I suggested earlier that one might *expect* Kierkegaard to offer distinctive marks of the true, visible church when he also began marking the importance of Christian suffering (which is always chosen, and intrinsically related to discipleship)[11] as distinguished from his earlier depictions of the hidden, inward passions of a Christian.[12] Instead, he largely portrays real Christians in the following images of *individual* suffering, which are repeated mantra-like through his latest newspaper articles and attack essays: True Christians "suffer for the doctrine"; they deny themselves, renounce the world, die to the world; they should be salt, and be willing to be sacrificed; they know "cross and agony and suffering, crucifying the flesh, hating oneself . . . etc." Christianity itself is "the doctrine of renunciation, of suffering, of heterogeneity to this world, the doctrine that issues no checks except on another world."[13]

Such tropes serve Kierkegaard well in distinguishing the Christian ideal from Christendom. But notice that heterogeneity with *the world* and thus suffering at the hands of *the world* offer the most defining marks of that Christian ideal. We are not so much given a thick description of discipleship proper but of the necessary suffering that

---

10. For Yoder on the church's visible marks, see Yoder, *Body Politics*. For the marks contrast with "the world," see Yoder, *Original Revolution*, 110.

11. Kierkegaard, *Practice in Christianity*, 106–20.

12. Kierkegaard, *Fear and Trembling* (with *Repetition*), 37–38.

13. Kierkegaard, *The Moment*, 5, 36, 42, 125.

ensues when Christianity is practiced here and now. While this emphasis on present sufferings and tribulations looks similar to Yoder's commitment to portraying Christianity in terms of concrete social forms, there is an important difference: For Kierkegaard, Christianity is "marked" almost entirely by its inability to get along in the world, its "heterogeneity" with the world; whereas, for Yoder, the "narratability" of the Christian church on its own terms and thus its ability to offer an alternative politic—which is fully inhabitable and practical—provides the very ground of his critique of Christian accommodation. For Kierkegaard, while we might *glimpse* true faith in a heroic individual's passion (meaning both her resolve and her suffering), such glimpses are indirect and fleeting and appear to be socially and politically unsustainable.

Compared to Yoder's substantive display of the political structure, concrete practices, and embodied social ethic of the early Christians (as recapitulated by "restorationist" churches), Kierkegaard's final appeals to "New Testament Christianity" or "authentic Christianity" appear disappointingly nominal and thin. It is this thinness, to the point where they approach mere tropes and foils, that leads interpreters to see Kierkegaard abandoning the church itself as he lampoons Christianity. Kierkegaard underscores martyrdom or suffering at the hands of the world as the primary mark of authentic Christianity. Note, then, that that mark exhibits not essential characteristics of Christianity itself—much less of the true Christian church—but rather its being overtaken by a capacious Christendom.

Kierkegaard for Yoder

We have seen that Yoder helps Kierkegaard by insisting on a concrete social form that is able to hold the "not-Christian" in its place and so gain some resistance against the Constantinian blending. But from this description we can already see a number of ways in which Kierkegaard might help Yoder. Kierkegaard better accounts for Christendom's amorphousness and tenacity. While Yoder tries to make sense of "the ever-new shape of the establishment" by showing how "the basic structural error, the identification of a civil authority as bearer of God's cause,"[14] or how church as chaplaincy can be "transposed" into various keys,[15] he does not portray the problem of Christendom as the problem of redundancy as clearly as does Kierkegaard. Kierkegaard more fully recognizes how even the quest to become distinctive vis-à-vis any dominant culture might get reclaimed and repackaged by, and so reabsorbed within, the dominant culture. What happens when being a countercultural Christian becomes permitted and sanctioned, thus becoming the norm and rather normative? Kierkegaard has his finger on this danger in ways that Yoder does not.

Kierkegaard also helps Yoder break down an overly-stable duality between a visible and invisible church and a too-clean distinction between those who belong to the

---

14. Yoder, *Priestly Kingdom*, 141–44.
15. Ibid., 143; Yoder, *Original Revolution*, 147.

elect ("authentic" Christians) and the nominal "Christians" of Christendom. To get at these differences, one must turn from their explicit ecclesiologies to the Christologies undergirding them.

In *The Heterodox Yoder*, Paul Martens traces the contours of Yoder's corpus to show just how "heterodox" (not quite heretical, but not orthodox, either) Yoder's social ethic becomes, theologically and christologically speaking. To quickly condense a work that resists summary: Martens claims that the political or social shape of the church (i.e., the visible church) becomes so determinative for Yoder and that Jesus' life and death so entirely function to exhibit a *repeatable* pattern of human obedience, that any claims about the divinity of Jesus become not only unnecessary, but also obfuscating. In other words, the shape of the church—as *exhibited* by the human life of Jesus, his disciples, and early Christians—takes precedence over the claim that Jesus is God or an understanding of church as a people or body called to worship the particular God made known in Jesus Christ. In short, the life of Jesus becomes an *instance* of the political pattern of the church.[16] One could say that we get an ecclesial Christology rather than a christological ecclesiology (my terms, not Martens's). Obscured by this is what Kierkegaard calls the Christian witness to the "scandal of particularity," to the non-repeatable presence of God in Christ, which can never "show up" except as hidden under an opposite sign.

There are good reasons while many "orthodox" Christians would get nervous about Yoder's descriptions. For our purposes, though, I want to ask whether critiques of Christendom by way of a directly perceivable church can properly stand on their own, or whether both might not depend on something more theologically foundational—faith in God made fully known in Jesus with the intrinsic possibility of offense (which Christendom so easily skirts). Does Jesus provide the foundation for a countercultural community first and foremost as the *example* of the commitment needed to exhibit an alternative politic, as Yoder seems to suggest? Or is that foundation itself founded on something less controllable: the supra-rational ability to *recognize* God in Christ *despite* his being "the Incognito"?

Anti-Climacus, in *Practice in Christianity*, writes of the "inessential offense" that arises when any single individual (or perhaps collection of individuals, including the church)[17] runs up against the leveling and self-deification of the established order. This collusion between faithful Christians and the established order parallels Yoder's distinction between the faithful church and "the world," theologically understood. While Kierkegaard nowhere minimizes the difference between "authentic" Christians

---

16. Martens, *Heterodox Yoder*, 107–14, 141–47.

17. Anti-Climacus suggests that it is only "single individuals" who are capable of struggling against the established order. Kierkegaard, *Practice in Christianity*, 223. He even claims that a "congregation" proper will not exist until eternity, since a congregation is at rest, whereas the single individual will battle and struggle throughout life (ibid.). But while the individual-collective distinction is important, more important is the distinction between striving and intentionality on the one hand, and complacency and carelessness, on the other.

(with Jesus) and "the crowd," this particular mismatch and the accompanying possibility of offense remains for Kierkegaard "inessential."

Essential offense, by contrast, stems from the incarnation as such, the fact that Jesus as the Christ "speaks or acts as if he were God," or that God self-debasingly "proves to be the lowly, poor, suffering, and finally powerless human being."[18] Anti-Climacus's analyses of essential offense are occasioned by a Christology from below (a human claims to be God) and a Christology from above (God becomes a human being). Unlike Yoder, then, who marks the particularity of the Christian church through its discipleship of Jesus the human being, Kierkegaard patterns discipleship on a kenotic Christology. Christians become *Christ*-like and not simply like Jesus, but must do so always indirectly and by non-identically repeating the One who can never disclose himself directly. There is "heterogeneity" between Christ and Christians, for the latter can only "resemble the prototype as much as it is possible for a human being to resemble him."[19] Their discipleship will include an inessential redoubling of an essential redoubling: "A human being [cannot] come closer and closer to God by lifting up his head higher and higher, but inversely by casting himself down even more deeply in worship."[20] Christ and then Christians perpetually remain hidden under opposite signs.[21]

Certainly, Kierkegaard calls Christians to follow the radical named Jesus no less than does Yoder. In fact, for all Anti-Climacus's focus on essential offense occasioned by God-Man's "composition," that focus is often prefaced and supplemented—even rhetorically supplanted—by passages concerned with the whole life of Jesus and how it might be reduplicated (although never directly) in the lives of Christians. Still, unlike Yoder, for whom Jesus gets reduced to one (albeit the most important) instantiation of the politics of the church, for Kierkegaard, any church politics or discipleship must be non-identically patterned after something that remains *essentially* particular and *essentially* non-repeatable: the scandalous event of God-become-flesh.[22]

Were Kierkegaard to develop such a line of thinking, he might say that the church of this Christ—the very body of this Incognito—is also called not to direct visibility after the humanity of Jesus but to a *revealed hiddenness* or *hidden disclosed-ness*

18. Kierkegaard, *Practice in Christianity*, 94, 102.

19. Ibid., 221, 115.

20. Kierkegaard, *Christian Discourses*, 292.

21. I borrow language of hiding under "opposite signs" and of God remaining "hidden" even as God discloses Godself in Christ and the cross from Martin Luther. In *Becoming a Christian in Christendom* (see n5 above), I argue that Luther's theology of the cross informs the ecclesial politics of both Kierkegaard and Dietrich Bonhoeffer.

22. This non-repeatability of Christ helps explain why Kierkegaard claimed that he, too, was not (yet) a Christian—only that he was trying to become one. Kierkegaard, *The Moment*, 212, 340–43. He adds this: "I am far short of being a Christian to dare to associate myself with anyone who makes such a claim. Even if I am perhaps a little, indeed, even if it were the case, if I were a bit more than a little ahead of the average among us, I am ahead only in the poetic sense—that is, I am more aware of what Christianity is." Kierkegaard, *For Self Examination*, 21.

analogous to the incarnate, scandalous Christ. To my knowledge, Kierkegaard nowhere explicitly links his description of Christ, who as Incognito can only be indirectly disclosed, to a church that is neither wholly visible nor wholly invisible, but rather hides in its very disclosure. There are, however, structural parallels within *Practice in Christianity* that all but beg for this connection.

Near the end of *Practice*, Anti-Climacus paints in broad strokes church history from early Christianity to the present age.[23] In terms familiar to Anti-Constantinians such as Yoder, Anti-Climacus contrasts the "militant church" with the "church triumphant." Early Christianity and the later "official" Christian culture resemble one another no more than a circle resembles a square. The early church can be discerned only inversely (but *directly* so)—by being hated by "the world." In contrast, medieval Christendom's Christians gain favor, honor, and esteem in the world. In fact, Anti-Climacus adds, that "world" is now thought to be identical with Christianity.[24] The church militant and the church triumphant are binary inversions or polar opposites of one another; they establish endpoints of a political-religious spectrum.

But Kierkegaard then introduces a third category, the "church of indifference," which complicates the picture by introducing "another *kind* of opposition."[25] Here, church and world do not blend into one another as they do in the church triumphant. The world as a whole does not necessarily applaud outward demonstrations of religiousness. But neither do the two stand in opposition to one another, as they did in Christianity's earliest years. Rather, in the church of indifference, Christians now face the "peculiar difficulty" of being met with apathetic acquiescence; the world *simply doesn't care* whether someone is earnestly Christian. The problem of maintaining religious identity against indifference is then exacerbated by the fact that this new "established Christendom," as Kierkegaard here calls it, treats all concrete manifestations of faith as shallow and smug. Real Christians, according to this perspective, would never show themselves as such; their piety is too lofty for that.[26] In this era, martyrdom and persecution are just as unimaginable as they were in the church triumphant, since this would presuppose that faith is recognizable, that it might actually do something that mattered, and that anyone would care enough to persecute it. In the age of the church indifferent, the truest sign of one's earnest Christianity is the ability to don the faith loosely, with an air of ironic detachment, and thereby blend into the rest of the (nominally) Christian crowd.

Notice the structural parallels between the church militant, triumphant, and indifferent, on the one hand, and a manifestly visible church, a wholly invisible church, and something like a church that is manifest-but-hidden, a church that can only be glimpsed under opposite signs, on the other hand. Notice, too, how Kierkegaard's

23. Kierkegaard, *Practice in Christianity*, 201–32.
24. Ibid., 212–13.
25. Ibid., 214–15, my emphasis.
26. Ibid., 217.

penetrating descriptions of Christendom's indifference ask for something different—another *kind* of response—than continuous demands for a clearly manifest, visible church. While Kierkegaard never directly or fully articulates what a manifest-but hidden-church would "look" like, his entire analysis suggests that it will be christological in a particular sense. The true faithful church would be hidden among all the tax collectors and bourgeois philistines populating Christendom. And yet one could *find* it there, especially by looking for its particular and peculiar political practices, as I will try to unpack in a final section.

Church Politics

The Christian church becomes Christ-like in its own, analogous kenotic self-emptying. Just as Christ, the Incognito, essentially takes the form of a servant and is thus "expressed" in his very "unrecognizability," so too might the church become visible not as directly noticeable to others looking in (as Yoder assumes), but only insofar as "the world" is able to notice what otherwise remains hidden: the people of God under opposite signs—as servants of the world and those who confess their sin. I conclude with three political forms and practices that would mark a church that is both hidden and revealed.

First, the clearest boundary of the church might just distinguish all political partisanship on the one side—distinctions between conservative and liberal, Democrat and Republican, friend and enemy, right and wrong, white and black, the haves and the have-nots, sinners and saints—and, on the other side, those whose discipleship of Christ and solidarity with out-casted others tears down every other partition. The church might inhabit a politics beyond all partisanship, one that provides a visible alternative to the very self-righteous divisions that otherwise rule our world.

Second and related: a manifest, hidden church would follow Christ in siding and hiding with and among the poor and oppressed. For all of the structural symmetry between Anti-Climacus's high Christology and low Christology, clearly Kierkegaard considers God's kenotic self-emptying into a poor and suffering human being to be determinative for occasioning the possibility of offense and for providing the prototype for Christian emulation. Repeatedly, Anti-Climacus associates triumph and glory with eternity; in this world, disciples have only suffering, humility, and the cross as their models. The church of Christ must therefore be a church of the cross; it must discipline its members to see God in so-called God-forsaken people and in places abandoned by those with conventional political power.

A third way that the church reveals itself as hidden is by publically confessing its sin. Note that theologians who emphasize the invisibility of the church often do so out of a realism about sin. As Karl Rahner has shown, the tendency in Catholicism since Vatican I (and in mainline Protestantism from its inception), has been to be "realistic" about the institutional church's sin by positing purity in an abstract or "spiritual" (invisible) church.[27] But what if the holiness of the church is revealed *as* hidden *in its very repentance for sin*, just as God is made visible in Christ's life of service and suffering?[28] Right up until his final attack on Christendom, Kierkegaard understood that the admission of sin was a legitimate way into authentic Christianity.[29] What if he—or we—were to take such confession of sin not as the narrow entrance into Christianity but as the enduring, visible mark of the true church—that which fully discloses the church of Christ, albeit under an opposite sign, and so remains hidden in its very disclosed-ness?[30]

Confession of sin can sound pretty churchy—hardly the sort of politics befitting of radical discipleship. At full stretch, however, the church's confession of sin provides a way of engaging the world, of acting politically, that resists setting up the very "us versus them" mentality that plagues both partisan politics and sectarian ecclesiologies. Penitential practices might also help Christians more truthfully and effectively engage in what Yoder and other anti-Constantinians designate as the most un-Christian of non-Christian politics: war.

Yoder suggests that the world's legal violence is best diagnosed and held at bay from the alternative, nonviolent, place called church. The difference between the church's original pacifism and the Constantinian recourse to war is as clear as that between visibility and invisibility. Judith Butler, by contrast, assumes that nonviolence itself "denotes the mired and conflicted position of a subject who is injured, rageful, disposed to violent retribution and nevertheless struggles against that action."[31] Or again, she claims that "the struggle against violence accepts that violence is one's own possibility."[32] In other words, only those constantly vigilant of their own inclinations toward violence are capable of offering genuine resistance and subversion. Butler seems to have in mind something like Yoder's all-too-visible church when she warns about the "moralization of the subject that disavows the violence it inflicts."[33] Readers of Ki-

---

27. Rahner, "Sinful Church," 288–89.

28. Incredibly helpful here is Cavanaugh, *Migrations of the Holy*, 141–69.

29. Kierkegaard, *Practice in Christianity*, 67; compare *The Moment*, 69, where Kierkegaard writes that if *Practice* were published during his final attack on Christendom, he would revoke the "lenient" option (the loophole?) of entering into Christianity by confessing one's sin.

30. While these trajectories are broadly Kierkegaardian, it is Dietrich Bonhoeffer who follows them through. According to Bonhoeffer, Christians are formed to be the body of a Christ who has taken on the sin of others, who dies guilty in solidarity with sinners, so that others might live. It follows that the visible form of the true church also hides in the form of those gathered in repentance for their sins and for the sins of others. Bonhoeffer, *Ethics*, 95–98. See also McBride, *Church for the World*, 119–52; compare Harvey, *Whiteness and Morality*. Both McBride and Harvey retrieve the church practices of confession and repentance for addressing white privilege, American imperialism, and other social sins.

31. Butler, *Frames of War*, 171.

32. Ibid.

33. Ibid., 172. That Yoder sexually abused women might exemplify this criticism of his work, but the criticism remains relevant even to those who do not egregiously abrogate their own commitments to nonviolence. See n4 above. I develop this use of Butler a bit more in Mahn, *Becoming a Christian in Christendom*, ch. 8.

erkegaard may seem to have someone like Butler in mind when they link a hidden church to its confession of sin, and confession to political resistance.

Kierkegaard's politics are nowhere as developed or as subversive as Butler's. Having wholly equated the church with Christendom at the end of his life, his ecclesiology also remains undeveloped at best. Still, I have tried to show that Kierkegaard points toward an understanding of church that is both manifest and hidden, and that such a church would have political agency of a particular, subversive sort. Political theologians and radical ecclesiologists can take some cues from Kierkegaard. Countercultural Christians, political protestors, nonviolent activists, and other disciples of Jesus might just do the same.

Bibliography

Bonhoeffer, Dietrich. *Ethics*. Translated by Reinhold Krauss et al. Minneapolis: Fortress, 2005.

Butler, Judith. *Frames of War: When Is Life Grievable?* London: Verso, 2009.

Cavanaugh, William. *Migrations of the Holy: God, State, and the Political Meaning of the Church*. Grand Rapids: Eerdmans, 2011.

Cramer, David, et al. "Theology and Misconduct: The Case of John Howard Yoder." *Christian Century*, August 4, 2014.

Goosen, Rachel Waltner. "'Defanging the Beast': Mennonite Reponses to John Howard Yoder's Sexual Abuse." *Mennonite Quarterly Review* 89 (2015) 7–80.

Guth, Karen V. *Christian Ethics at the Boundary: Feminisms and Theologies of Public Life*. Minneapolis: Fortress, 2015.

Harvey, Jennifer. *Whiteness and Morality: Pursuing Racial Justice through Reparations and Sovereignty*. New York: Palgrave Macmillan, 2007.

Kierkegaard, Søren. *Christian Discourses*. Translated by Howard V. Hong and Edna H. Hong. Princeton: Princeton University Press, 1997.

———. *Fear and Trembling*. Translated by Howard V. Hong and Edna H. Hong. Princeton: Princeton University Press, 1983.

———. *For Self Examination; Judge for Yourself*. Translated by Howard V. Hong and Edna H. Hong. Princeton: Princeton University Press, 1990.

———. *The Moment and Late Writings*. Translated by Howard V. Hong and Edna H. Hong. Princeton: Princeton University Press, 1989.

———. *Practice in Christianity*. Translated by Howard V. Hong and Edna H. Hong. Princeton: Princeton University Press, 1991.

Mahn, Jason. *Becoming a Christian in Christendom: Radical Discipleship and the Way of the Cross in America's "Christian" Culture*. Minneapolis: Fortress, 2016.

Martens, Paul. *The Heterodox Yoder*. Eugene, OR: Cascade, 2012.

McBride, Jennifer M. *The Church for the World: A Theology of Public Witness*. Oxford: Oxford University Press, 2012.

Rahner, Karl. "The Sinful Church in the Decrees of Vatican II." In *Theological Investigations VI: Concerning Vatican Council II*, 288–89. New York: Seabury, 1974.

Yoder, John Howard. *Body Politics: Five Practices of the Christian Community before the Watching World*. Scottdale, PA: Herald, 1992.

———. *The Original Revolution: Essays on Christian Pacifism.* Scottdale, PA: Herald, 2003.

———. *The Politics of Jesus.* 2nd ed. Grand Rapids: Eerdmans, 1994.

———. *The Priestly Kingdom: Social Ethics as Gospel.* Notre Dame: University of Notre Dame Press, 1984.

———. *The Royal Priesthood: Essays Ecclesiastical and Ecumenical.* Scottdale, PA: Herald, 1998.

18

How (Not) to Write a Kierkegaardian Political Theology

*Between Niebuhr and Levinas on
Anxiety, Faith, and Love*

HOWARD PICKETT

BEST KNOWN FOR HIS tireless commentary on the "single individual," Søren Kierkegaard (who once confessed: "No, politics is not for me") seems an unlikely resource for political theology.[1] Critics have long disparaged Kierkegaard's apolitical, antisocial thought.[2] According to Emmanuel Levinas, Kierkegaardian anxiety, in particular, endorses a solitary, unethical "egotism."[3] The concept's afterlife within the pages of Martin Heidegger's *Being and Time* (1927) all but confirms the concept's inadequacy to our ethico-political relations with others; it is hardly a coincidence, Levinas insinuates, that anxiety (an insular self-relation) enjoys pride of place in the work of a former Nazi.[4]

Nevertheless, anxiety's other afterlives include its foundational role in a classic of American political theology, Reinhold Niebuhr's *The Nature and Destiny of Man* (1943). Niebuhr's praise for Kierkegaard's account of anxiety borders on the hyperbolic, if not the idolatrous: "Kierkegaard's analysis of the relation of anxiety to sin is the profoundest in Christian thought."[5] Regarding Kierkegaard's view of the "self, anxious for its life," Niebuhr concludes, "In this, as in other instances, Kierkegaard has interpreted the true meaning of human selfhood more accurately than any modern, and

---

1. "To me . . . this matter of the single individual is the most decisive." Kierkegaard, *Point of View*, 114–15. The disdain for politics appears in a letter from August 1848. Kierkegaard, *Letters and Documents*, 253.

2. Martensen, *Om Tro og Viden, et Lejlighedsskrift*, 133–34; Adorno, "On Kierkegaard's Doctrine of Love," 415; Taylor, *Journeys to Selfhood*, 262.

3. Levinas, *Proper Names*, 68.

4. Levinas, *Entre Nous*, 214.

5. Niebuhr, *Nature and Destiny*, 1:182.

possibly than any previous, Christian theologian."⁶ Insofar as it informs the influential ideas of the twentieth century's most influential political theologian, Kierkegaard's *The Concept of Anxiety* (1844) undergirds Niebuhrian studies and modern political theology alike. Levinas's complaints notwithstanding, then, Kierkegaardian anxiety can, perhaps *must*, figure centrally in political theology.

Rereading Kierkegaard—first and foremost, *The Concept of Anxiety* (1844)—in light of Niebuhr's thought steers a course away from Heidegger's atheistic, apolitical anxiety toward a thoroughly theological, interpersonal anxiety Kierkegaard and Niebuhr share. In pseudonymous and signed works alike, Kierkegaard anticipates (better, formulates) a Niebuhrian train of thought, which advances from (1) *anxiety* with oneself through (2) *faith* in God to (3) *love* of the other. Contrary to Heidegger's case and Levinas's concerns, Kierkegaardian anxiety has always already been relational, another side of love for the (divine and human) other.

Love, however, seems insufficient for politics—and political theology, for that matter. Certainly, love for an *individual* neighbor is insufficient for the complex demands of life in community. As Niebuhr and Levinas remind us, living in the world involves, not just *the* other, but *other* others—minimally, the "one next to the other" or the "third," who interrupts self and neighbor to introduce the demands of justice and politics.⁷ Yet, what that "other other" demands (what justice requires) is what any neighbor needs—namely, love. Thus, it is not just *living*, but *loving* in the world (of countless others) that requires the deliberations and institutions of justice. Rereading Kierkegaard in light of Niebuhr *and Levinas's* thought (their shared dialectic of love and justice, in particular) draws out the final element in a Kierkegaardian political theology: (4) *political agapism*, i.e., the realization that love requires institutional negotiation of the (often) competing demands of multiple neighbors.

Anxiety

So influential has Kierkegaard's account of anxiety become that one can hardly believe pseudonymous author Vigilius Haufniensis's claim that the "concept of anxiety is almost never treated in psychology."⁸ Somewhere between psychology and philosophical anthropology, Haufniensis's *Concept of Anxiety* has as much to do with a *mode* of human being as it does with a *mood*. At the core of this "psychologically orienting deliberation" stands human freedom. Famously, Haufniensis announces, "Anxiety is the dizziness of freedom"; anxiety subjectively reveals (from the inside, as it were) our complicated relationship with our own liberty.⁹ We may be free, but we are not entirely

---

6. Ibid., 171.

7. The need for justice prompted by the "third" person appears in Levinas and Niebuhr. Levinas, *Entre Nous*, 202. Niebuhr, *Nature and Destiny*, 2:248.

8. Kierkegaard, *Concept of Anxiety*, 313.

9. Ibid., 331.

free (i.e., at home) with that freedom. Facing countless possibilities posed by my freedom, I feel dizzy, vacillating between one possibility and another. Furthermore, facing countless limitations to my freedom, I feel dizzier still. The involuntary response of anxiety (the "dizziness" I never freely willed) attests to my unfreedom, even while attesting to my freedom, which stimulated the dizzy feeling. "Dizziness" suits the human subject, who teeters on the fault line, between possibility and actuality, finitude and freedom, "the temporal and the eternal."[10] In short, anxiety discloses the complex, even conflicted, character of the human, "a synthesis of the psychical and the physical . . . united in . . . spirit."[11]

In addition to that synthesis, anxiety also announces the nothingness underlying the self. Unlike fear of "something definite," anxiety highlights a paradoxical relation to "something that is nothing."[12] If "dizziness" evokes the self's multiplicity, "nothingness" evokes its indeterminacy. "The object of anxiety is a nothing"—a nothing *yet*, or no-*thing*.[13] What anxiety concerns is one's possible future self. Hence, nothingness is another aspect of the (free) human, who "is a nothing—the anxious possibility of *being able*."[14] The distinction between fear of *something* and anxiety over *nothing* lives on in the writings of twentieth-century existentialists Martin Heidegger and Jean-Paul Sartre.[15] Both Haufniensis and Heidegger agree that in anxiety one relates to nothing (other than oneself). In Heidegger's words, "Anxiety makes manifest the nothing."[16] Further, "anxiety individualizes"; in other words, my anxiety, alongside my authenticity (another Kierkegaardian-Hedieggerian notion), picks me out from the crowd.[17]

However, the individualistic quality of anxiety disturbs Heidegger's former student Emmanuel Levinas. Having lost most of his family in the Shoah, Levinas sees in Heidegger's picture of the self (free and isolated in its anxiety) evidence of his former teacher's indifference to others and (in retrospect) a premonition of Heidegger's later affiliation with the Nazis.[18] Levinas condemns the isolated self-relation made manifest in the "double intentionality" of anxiety, by which the one "of" whom one has anxiety is the same as the one "for" whom that anxiety is had, namely oneself.[19] Unlike fear, in which I have fear of the gunman for me or my neighbor, anxiety denotes a state in which I have anxiety of myself, for myself. Like Heideggerian "authenticity," anxiety (a navel-gazing self-obsession, in Levinas's view) entails the "dissolution of all relations

10. Ibid., 355.
11. Ibid., 315.
12. Ibid., 313–14.
13. Ibid., 332, 345.
14. Ibid., 315.
15. Heidegger, *Being and Time*, 91; Sartre, *Being and Nothingness*, 65.
16. Heidegger, "What Is Metaphysics?," 88.
17. Heidegger, *Being and Time*, 91.
18. Levinas, *Otherwise than Being*, v.
19. Levinas, *Entre Nous*, 112.

with the other."[20] Because it distracts us from responsibility, "anxiety of the I for itself" is, as Levinas concludes, an unethical "egoism."[21]

Preferable to anxiety's self-involvement is an ethical relation with the other. In opposition to Heidegger's being-towards-(*my*-)death, Levinas emphasizes being-towards-the-*other's*-death: "The excellence of love and sociality, of 'fear for the others' and responsibility for the others . . . is not my anxiety for my death, *mine*."[22] If any anxiety belongs in our lives, it is the un-Heideggerian "anxiety of responsibility," one that is "incumbent on everyone in the death or suffering of the other."[23] In being there for the other, I am not only more ethical; I *am*—i.e., *I am individuated* as the unique, responsible subject I am called to be.[24] By Levinas's account, Heidegger is, not merely *unethical*, but also *inaccurate* in his emphasis on individuating anxiety.

Objections notwithstanding, Kierkegaardian anxiety figures prominently, not only in Heidegger's philosophy, but also in Reinhold Niebuhr's theological anthropology. Like Haufniensis and Heidegger, Niebuhr reads anxiety as revelatory of freedom and the structure of human being. Echoing Haufniensis, Niebuhr defines anxiety as the "dizziness of freedom."[25] Overwhelmed by our freedom—with possibilities good and bad, creative and destructive—we experience anxiety. Furthermore, we try to flee anxiety through self-deception that denies one side or another of the synthetic self. In "sensuality," we pretend to be nothing more than things, lacking freedom and responsibility; in "pride," nothing less than gods, lacking limits and histories.[26] As both Haufniensis and Niebuhr concede, anxiety incites inauthenticity, whether sensuous evasion of the better angels of our nature or proud denial of our kinship with the beasts.[27]

Torn between anxiety's conflicting legacies—between Levinas's rejection and Niebuhr's endorsement—one wonders: Can Niebuhr navigate around, even *through*, the narcissistic tendencies of anxiety to steer a course away from Heideggerian egoism and atheism toward a political theology that combines anxiety, responsibility, and

20. Ibid., 185. To Haufniensis, philosophers of being (Hegelian or Heideggerian) resemble the *omphalopsychoi* ("bellybutton-minds"), detached mystics (hesychasts) who value aesthetic reflection over ethical engagement. Kierkegaard, *Concept of Anxiety*, 350–51; 242n2.

21. Levinas, *Basic Philosophical Writings*, 51; Levinas, *Proper Names*, 68.

22. Levinas, *Basic Philosophical Writings*, 158.

23. Ibid., 164.

24. Levinas, *Otherwise than Being*, 112.

25. Niebuhr, *Nature and Destiny*, 1:252.

26. Ibid., 185. The challenges of that synthesis inspired Niebuhr's Serenity Prayer (1943): "God, give us grace to accept with serenity the things that cannot be changed, courage to change the things that should be changed, and the wisdom to distinguish the one from the other." Niebuhr, *Justice and Mercy*, v. The anxious person must avoid overestimating human freedom (in pride) and underestimating it (in sensuousness).

27. Cf. Haufniensis: "The phenomenon [of anxiety] may appear in connection with the *sensuous* in man (addiction to drink, to opium, or to debauchery, etc.) as well as in connection with the higher (pride, vanity, wrath, hatred, defiance, cunning, envy, etc.)" Kierkegaard, *Concept of Anxiety*, 384.

faith? Furthermore, is that course (which unites the best insights of Niebuhr *and Levinas*) foreshadowed by a Kierkegaardian political theology, in which anxiety coexists with faith, love, and community?

Faith

Although both Niebuhr and Heidegger use Kierkegaardian sources to fashion their anthropologies, anxiety plays a markedly different role in each. Most decisively, Niebuhr subordinates the self-relation of anxiety to a relation with the other—principally, God. The human predicament (the anxiety of our freedom-unfreedom) is "insoluble from the standpoint of man's [sic] own resources and can be solved only from the standpoint of God's resources" and "Providence."[28] Though never fully actualized (due to our inevitable sinfulness), the "ideal possibility is that faith in the ultimate security of God's love would overcome all immediate insecurities of nature and history."[29] Faith overcomes the overwhelming subjective feeling, if not the ontological condition, of anxiety.[30]

A similar relationship between anxiety and faith appears in Kierkegaard's work. Anxiety is "an adventure everyone must go through"; however, one can and should learn "to be anxious in the right way"—specifically, by being "honest about possibility and [having] faith."[31] Thanks to faith, one remains in (ontological) anxiety, though no longer (emotionally) anxious: "Whoever has truly learned how to be anxious will dance when the anxieties of finitude strike up the music."[32] Paradoxically, whoever has "learned how to be anxious" (i.e., in the right way) seems anything but *anxious*; faith in God's grace brings, as it were, the dancer's grace. Anxiety remains, but now in a form we can admire or, at least, use; for the person of faith, "anxiety becomes a serving spirit that . . . leads him where he wishes to go."[33]

What's more, while anxiety depends on faith for its fulfillment, faith also depends on anxiety: "With the help of faith, anxiety brings up the individuality to rest in providence."[34] As that line indicates, faith improves, rather than removes, anxiety. However, as the line also indicates, anxiety gives rise to faith. Insofar as it "brings up" (or educates) "the individuality" to "rest in [God's] providence," anxiety somehow cultivates the very faith that corrects it. By highlighting our liberties and limitations,

---

28. Ibid., 288–89.

29. Ibid., 183.

30. Ibid., 182. Because it is a "concomitant of the paradox of freedom and finiteness in which man is involved" from creation, anxiety is a non-culpable condition of human existence. Even perfect faith is, therefore, faith-with-anxiety.

31. Ibid., 421, 423.

32. Ibid., 427.

33. Ibid., 424.

34. Ibid., 426.

anxiety leads one to faith. By exposing how little a person can do and how much he must do, anxiety "hand[s] him over to faith," Haufniensis says.[35] The idea that anxiety educates one to rest in God's providence anticipates Niebuhr's own remarks.[36] Thrown back on humanity's limited resources, the anxious, sinful person has no way forward, in Niebuhr's view, except by putting her faith in "God's resources"—i.e., God's atoning redemption.[37] Likewise, the one "educated by anxiety will rest," Haufiensis explains, "only in the Atonement."[38] Given their interdependence, Haufniensis speaks, not of *either* anxiety *or* faith, but of "Anxiety as Saving through Faith."[39] For both Kierkegaard and Niebuhr, then, anxiety is the first, but not the final, element in an analysis of the human condition.

For Niebuhr, faith and anxiety are closely bound to one another; for Kierkegaard, the two are virtually synonymous. Both anxiety and faith entail a defining relation to possibility. Anxiety is an inner confrontation with possibility, while "faith is essentially this—to hold fast to possibility."[40] At his most provocative moments, Kierkegaard insinuates that being anxious (in the right way) relates one, not simply to the *infinite possibilities* that anxiety presents, but also to the *Infinite* (full-stop), the God in whom and for whom "all things are possible" (Matt 19:26). After all, one who has learned how to be anxious in the right way "has learned the ultimate"[41]—more suggestively, "the *Ultimate*" (God). In the words of Kierkegaard's other great analyst of anxiety, Anti-Climacus, the pseudonymous author of *The Sickness Unto Death* (1849): "[Since] everything is possible for God, then God is this—that everything is possible."[42] Suffice it to say that, from both Kierkegaardian and Niebuhrian standpoints, anxiety is (pace Heidegger) thoroughly theological.[43] It walks hand and hand with faith.

Love

Yet, faith is not the final word in political theology. Just as anxiety leads to faith, faith leads to love—and love, to justice. By Niebuhr's account, faith not only leads to love; it *is* love. As he says, "Love of God is identical with the two terms in the Pauline triad, 'faith' and 'hope.'"[44] What's more, the love of God we call "faith" also promotes love of

---

35. Ibid., 424.
36. Ibid., 426.
37. Niebuhr, *Nature and Destiny*, 1:288.
38. Kierkegaard, *Concept of Anxiety*, 428.
39. Ibid., 421.
40. Kierkegaard, *Journals and Papers*, 2:1126.
41. Kierkegaard, *Concept of Anxiety*, 421.
42. Kierkegaard, *Sickness Unto Death*, 153.
43. For the linguistic and conceptual challenges posed by Anti-Climacus's line, see Walsh, *Kierkegaard*, 74–76.
44. Niebuhr, *Nature and Destiny*, 1:289.

the neighbor: "The love of the neighbor . . . is . . . a derivative of perfect faith and trust in God."[45] By turning the self outwards, faith creates the possibility of love. "Faith in the wisdom of God is," as Niebuhr observes, "a prerequisite of love because it is the condition without which man is . . . driven by his anxiety into vicious circles of self-sufficiency and pride."[46] In Niebuhr's view, faith in God directs one toward the face of the other: "Without freedom from anxiety man is so enmeshed in the vicious circle of egocentricity, so concerned about himself, that he cannot release himself for the adventure of love."[47] Because anxiety leads to faith, and through faith to neighbor-love, anxiety is doubly relational, connecting us with divine and human other alike.

Admittedly, anxiety's movement through faith to love can be hard to spot in Haufniensis's deliberations. Those looking for a Kierkegaardian understanding of love (and its parallels to Niebuhr's thought) may, therefore, turn (initially, at least) to another of Kierkegaard's writings: not *The Concept of Anxiety*, but *Works of Love* (1847). There, Kierkegaard insists that the "work of love in recollecting one who is dead [i.e., one who cannot reciprocate] is a work of the most unselfish love."[48] Niebuhr makes similar comments about a "sacrificial" love "which seeketh not its own": "But a self which seeks to measure the possible reciprocity which its love towards another may elicit is obviously not sufficiently free of preoccupation with self to lose itself in the life of the other."[49] Notably, this opposition to reciprocity also prefigures what Levinas has to say about "my responsibility for the other, without concern for reciprocity."[50] Following Kierkegaard and Niebuhr (the so-called "modern-day agapists"),[51] Levinas also equates this nonreciprocal responsibility with "love"—what he calls the "grave view of *Agape* ['love'] in terms of responsibility for the other."[52]

Works of Love also shares Niebuhr's view of the close connection between faith and love.[53] Like other Christian theologians, Kierkegaard recognizes that faith (in God's love) leads to the love of others; we love, because God first loved us (1 John 4:10). *Works of Love*'s opening prayer emphasizes the fact that the God in whom one

---

45. Ibid., 293.

46. Ibid., 289.

47. Ibid., 272. Inasmuch as it overcomes anxiety, faith principally overcomes the anxious person's irresponsible tendencies (i.e., pride's will-to-power and sensuality's irresponsibility). Ibid., 178, 186.

48. Kierkegaard, *Works of Love*, 330.

49. Niebuhr, *Nature and Destiny*, 2:72, 82.

50. Levinas, *Entre Nous*, 87. It is this responsibility, Levinas says, that he has "tried to analyze the phenomenon of."

51. According to Nicholas Wolterstorff, Kierkegaard is the initiator of a modern resurgence in agapism. Wolterstorff, *Justice in Love*, 21, 71.

52. Levinas, *Entre Nous*, 113, emphasis added. So important is love to him that Levinas defines philosophy as "the wisdom of love" and "the love of wisdom at the service of love." Levinas, *Otherwise than Being*, 162; cf. ibid., 188n5.

53. Levinas's complicated views on faith (or God) lie outside the scope of this paper. For the similarities between Kierkegaard and Levinas's views of love, see Ferreira, *Love's Grateful Striving*, 127.

has faith is the source of all love (1 John 4:7).[54] Kierkegaard also knows that faith is nothing less than faithful, trusting love in God. More than that, faith is nothing less than love for the God who both *commands* love (Matt 22:39) and *is* love (1 John 4:8). Faithful obedience to the divine command ("You *Shall* Love") is, Kierkegaard thinks, needed to purify all works of love.[55] Without faithful adherence to the divine directive, our good works only appear loving; they are, instead, works of self-interest and personal preference.

Faith is active, in Kierkegaard's view. In words from Kierkegaard's journals, "faith should make striving possible"—including striving to love neighbors.[56] Anything less than effortful striving would make of our faith no faith (no trusting love) at all, but merely "cheap grace" (in the words of another well-known Lutheran theologian).[57] Faith bears fruit; more to the point, it bears *loving* fruit (Luke 6:44).[58] Consequently, if *The Concept of Anxiety* affirms faith (and it does), then it must also affirm love. Seen in the right light, faith and love are inextricably bound together.

More to the point here, seen in the right light (which Haufniensis provides), faith and love are inextricably bound to anxiety. The three denote different dimensions (better, different relationships) within the same moment. In anxiety, the human being faces, not only *possibility*, but also *responsibility*. In anxiety, I stand simultaneously before self, God, and neighbors. Confronted by my own future possibilities, I face a dizzying set of choices: between becoming or denying my true self; between trusting or rejecting the divine will for my life; between addressing or ignoring the needs of neighbors. Too often, I run (whether in pride or sensuousness) from all three relationships: from my anxiety, my vocation, and my responsibility to and for others. Anxiety invites me, however, not only to faith, but also (through faith) to love.

While its closing pages look beyond anxiety toward faith in God, Haufniensis's opening pages look beyond anxiety toward a fundamental responsibility for the other. There, Haufniensis discards what he calls "first ethics," which strives toward the virtuous perfection of the self-sufficient moral individual. In lieu of that "pagan" philosophy, "shipwrecked on the sinfulness of the single individual," Haufniensis endorses a "new" or "second ethics," an anxious, yet faithful ethical outlook that acknowledges our composite position: fallen yet responsible.[59] Like Niebuhr, Haufniensis acknowledges that, through faith in the redemptive work of God, the sinner (partially) overcomes anxiety and self-centeredness to turn outward toward the other.[60]

---

54. Kierkegaard, *Works of Love*, 8.
55. Ibid., 21.
56. Kierkegaard, *Journals and Papers*, 2:1139.
57. Bonhoeffer, *Discipleship*, 43.
58. Kierkegaard, *Works of Love*, 9.
59. Kierkegaard, *Concept of Anxiety*, 293–94.
60. Arguably, the second ethics is worked out (albeit not in name) in *Works of Love*. Grøn, *Concept of Anxiety*, 135.

In contrast, the introverted self ("enmeshed in the vicious circle of egocentricity") is a very different figure, one Haufniensis labels "demonic."[61] The "demonic" self—who succumbs to "anxiety about the good"—"closes itself up within itself" in a state known as the "inclosing reserve."[62] By "inclosing himself"—by closing himself off from God and neighbor alike—the sinner refuses both the "adventure that every human being must go through—to learn to be anxious . . . in the right way,"[63] and also Niebuhr's "adventure of love."[64] Charges of atomistic individualism aside, Kierkegaard (Haufniensis) condemns isolated egoism in preference for a relationship with God (in faith) and neighbors (in love). What's more, by rejecting "inclosing reserve," Haufniensis rejects a satisfied self-relation not unlike Heidegger's anxious, authentic *Dasein*.

Like Heidegger, Niebuhr and Haufniensis see anxiety as a fruitful starting point for an analysis of human being. Like Levinas, however, they admit that that analysis is grossly misleading unless anxiety gives way to love. Perhaps, then, it is not so much anxiety, as *overcoming* anxiety, that takes center stage in a Kierkegaardian-Niebuhrian anthropology. After all, Jesus' injunction to "be *not* anxious" (Matt 6:25) is what, to Niebuhr's ears, "contains the whole genius of the Biblical view of the relation of finiteness to sin in man."[65] In short, one ought to have faith, loving God and others, rather than having anxiety about oneself, a view Kierkegaard anticipates in his many meditations on the carefree "lilies of the field" and "birds of the air" (Matt 6:26–28).[66] Nevertheless, anxiety remains central—and not altogether negative—for both thinkers. Because it is our unavoidable ontological condition—the way God created us—anxiety ought to be, not so much *removed*, as *redeemed*, by and for love. "Be not anxious for your life" is, as Niebuhr explains, the other side to the commandment to "love thy neighbor as thyself."[67] It is, in Haufniensian terms, an injunction to "be anxious in the right way"—in Levinasian terms, to be anxious for the *other's* life, rather than my own.[68]

---

61. Niebuhr, *Nature and Destiny*, 1:272; Kierkegaard, *Concept of Anxiety*, 386.

62. Ibid., 391.

63. Ibid., 421.

64. Niebuhr, *Nature and Destiny*, 1:272.

65. Niebuhr, *Nature and Destiny*, 1:168, emphasis added.

66. Niebuhr's "be not anxious" is also taken from Jesus' discussion of the lilies and the birds. See Pattison and Møller, *Kierkegaard's Pastoral Dialogues*, 91.

67. Reinhold Niebuhr, *Essential Niebuhr*, 108–9.

68. "Be not anxious" is part of Jesus' "Sermon on the Mount" and precedes the charge to seek first the kingdom of God and its justice.

Conclusion: Political Agape

If anxiety leads (through faith) to love, then anxiety also leads to the political in the broad sense (i.e., prosocial behavior within the polis). What remains less clear is whether anxiety can also lead to the political in a narrower sense (i.e., support for state institutions). To be sure, Kierkegaard has his issues with justice, in most cases pitting it against love. According to *Works of Love*, "The one who truly loves ... knows nothing about the claims of strict law or of justice, not even the claims of equity."[69] Instead, the one who loves undergoes the "revolution of love," which purges one of the self-interest that lurks behind calls for reciprocity and justice's distinction between mine and yours: "The more profound the revolution, the more completely the distinction 'mine and yours' disappears, the more perfect is the love ... the more justice shudders."[70] So thoroughgoing is Kierkegaard's animosity toward justice that the final lines of *Works of Love* take one last swing at the human infatuation with a just social order. There, Kierkegaard warns that advocating the principle of justice (i.e., to each her due) threatens to damn us all. Someone interested in salvation, by contrast, "will surely also avoid speaking to God about the wrongs of others against him ... because such a person will prefer to speak to God only about grace, lest this fateful word 'justice' lose everything for him through what he himself evoked, the rigorous like for like."[71]

Reread through a Niebuhrian lens, however, Kierkegaard's commitment to active works of love (his agapism) allows, perhaps *requires*, a turn toward justice (his political agapism). As already indicated, Niebuhr shares Kierkegaard's ideal preference for (self-sacrificial) love over (reciprocal) justice. However, if Niebuhr is right, that ideal love is never fully realizable in a world of sinners. Because of humanity's fallenness, loving-in-the-world requires (institutions of) justice; justice and love are, in effect, two sides of the same coin. In Niebuhr's words, although "without the 'grace' of love, justice always degenerates into something less than justice," without justice, love fails to promote the well-being of actual neighbors.[72] In lieu of a simplistic nonreciprocal agape, Niebuhr adopts what some call "political agapism": the view that the achievement of love's goals in a world of sinners necessitates institutions that strive for justice.[73] In brief, love requires just institutions to promote the well-being of the neighbors we love and also to arbitrate among the competing claims of those neighbors.

Despite a well-known emphasis on nonreciprocal love, Levinas also endorses political agapism. Like Niebuhr, Levinas admits that justice is not an abandonment,

---

69. Kierkegaard, *Works of Love*, 256.
70. Ibid., 254.
71. Ibid., 365.
72. Niebuhr, *Love and Justice*, 28.
73. "Political agapism" means to remind us that Niebuhr's "political realism" is motivated by what Nicholas Wolterstorff labels Niebuhr's "non-classical agapism." Wolterstorff, *Justice in Love*, 65.

but an approximation, of love; in fact, it is derived from love—"born of charity," as he says.⁷⁴ Though an infinite, nonreciprocal responsibility for the other (even to the point of becoming "hostage" to that other)⁷⁵ is Levinas's better-known theme, self-sacrificial responsibility for the other ultimately gives way to calculating, institutional justice and politics as soon as another other enters the scene. The "fact of the multiplicity of men and the presence of someone else next to the Other . . . condition the laws and establish justice."⁷⁶ Furthermore, because there is always "another other" (a "third") on the scene, we always already inhabit the domain of justice and the political.⁷⁷ In effect, Levinas seconds Niebuhr, agreeing that what love needs is the realism of justice, and what justice needs is the idealism of love. In words reminiscent of Niebuhr's own, Levinas declares, "Love must always watch over justice."⁷⁸ Yet, so politically realistic is Levinas (former prisoner of war) that he, like Niebuhr, agrees that justice must also watch over love. Contrary to a common caricature, Levinas defends self-concern and political coercion; a "certain measure of violence is necessary in justice," he says—at least, to stop the violent treatment of the other by another other.⁷⁹ For that reason, and once again echoing Niebuhr, Levinas rejects the idealist's pacifism: "[I] separate myself from the idea of nonresistance to evil."⁸⁰

In essence, I am arguing, not only that Levinas and Niebuhr are political agapists, but that Kierkegaard is (or *ought* to be) one, too. Although underdeveloped in Kierkegaard's writings, justice is the logical extension of love within a Kierkegaardian worldview. If anxiety leads through faith to love, then anxiety also leads *through love* to justice and the political. Put differently, if God commands us to love *all* our neighbors, then God also commands us to navigate the complex dialectic between love and justice. Like both Niebuhr and Levinas, Kierkegaard concedes that we always face multiple (often competing) neighbors: "If there are only two people [i.e., self and other], the other person is the neighbor; if there are millions, everyone of these is the neighbor."⁸¹ Yet, if Niebuhr and Levinas are right, fulfilling the duty to love those millions will require, not only the calculations of justice, but also the efficient institutions of justice (courts, police, armed forces, etc.).⁸²

---

74. Levinas, *Entre Nous*, 91. For a discussion of Niebuhr's and Levinas's overlapping views of love and justice, see Flescher, "Love and Justice," 71, 77.

75. Levinas, *Otherwise than Being*, 112.

76. Levinas, *Ethics and Infinity*, 89.

77. Levinas, *Entre Nous*, 229.

78. Ibid., 92.

79. Ibid., 90; Levinas, *Of God Who Comes to Mind*, 83.

80. Levinas, *Entre Nous*, 90.

81. Kierkegaard, *Works of Love*, 25.

82. Kierkegaard's emphasis on non-preferential, nonreciprocal love need not rule out special relations (e.g., to spouses or children). Likewise, it need not rule out the calculated considerations of justice. We love neighbors by considering their particularities (their relationships with us, their needs in relation to others). See Ferreira, *Love's Grateful Striving*, 91–92.

Justice (as a dialectical accompaniment to love) seems especially necessary given Haufniensis's own recognition of the inevitability of sin, a recognition that informed Niebuhr's own. Like Niebuhr, Haufniensis (the student of the "Doctrine of Hereditary Sin," the purveyor of a "second ethics" for a sinful world) should agree that perfectionist, nonreciprocal love is insufficient for life in our world. Despite his more vocal reservations about justice, Kierkegaard sometimes agrees. Some of us must be "the servant[s] of justice," who "work at discovering guilt and crime."[83] However, from Kierkegaard's perspective, the "the rest of us are called to be neither judges nor servants of justice, but on the contrary, are called by God to love."[84] Justice is not ruled out entirely; Kierkegaard is, after all, neither idealist nor anarchist. However, justice is not his theme; it remains subordinated to the love to which God calls us (e.g., "love your neighbor as yourself"). As Kierkegaard indicates elsewhere, justice is, in the final analysis, God's job; love is ours. Although, by imitating Christ, we "maintain a little justice in Christendom," justice is, first and foremost, not the calculated efforts of human institutions, but the "divine justice" of God.[85]

Despite their overlapping views of anxiety and faith, then, Kierkegaard and Niebuhr ultimately part ways (at least, emphases) at the intersection between love and justice. In the end, Kierkegaard steers a course closer to Levinas than Niebuhr. Like Levinas and unlike Niebuhr, Kierkegaard has greater fear of the evil we do by loving too little (i.e., by relying on impersonal, calculating institutions of justice) than by loving too much (i.e., by relying on idealistic, interpersonal interactions). In short, the Kierkegaardian accent falls squarely on agape before the political. Consequently, anyone interested in writing a Kierkegaardian political theology should remember that anxiety makes room for faith, justice, and love—but the greatest of these is love.

Bibliography

Adorno, Theodor W. "On Kierkegaard's Doctrine of Love." *Studies in Philosophy and Social Science* 8 (1939–40) 413–29.

Bonhoeffer, Dietrich. *Discipleship*. Translated by Barbara Green and Reinhard Krauss. Minneapolis: Fortress, 2003.

Flescher, Andrew. "Love and Justice in Reinhold Niebuhr's Prophetic Christian Realism and Emmanuel Levinas's Ethics of Responsibility: Treading between Pacifism and Just-War Theory." *Journal of Religion* 80 (2000) 61–82.

Grøn, Arne. *The Concept of Anxiety in Søren Kierkegaard*. Translated by Jeanette B. L. Knox. Macon, GA: Mercer University Press, 2008.

Heidegger, Martin. *Being and Time*. Translated by John Macquarrie and Edward Robinson. New York: Harper Perennial Modern Classics, 2008.

---

83. Kierkegaard, *Works of Love*, 279. The distinction between those who further justice (through coercive institutions) and those who uphold love is rarely so clear (especially for those living in a democracy).

84. Ibid., 279.

85. Kierkegaard, *Journals and Papers*, 2:1902; Kierkegaard, *The Moment*, 315.

———. "What Is Metaphysics?" In *Pathmarks*, edited by William McNeill, 82–96. Cambridge: Cambridge University Press, 1998.

Kierkegaard, Søren. *The Concept of Anxiety: A Simple Psychologically Orienting Deliberation on the Dogmatic Issue of Hereditary Sin*. Translated by Reidar Thomte. Princeton: Princeton University Press, 1980.

———. *Journals and Papers*. Vol. 1, *A–E*. Translated by Howard V. Hong and Edna H. Hong. Bloomington: Indiana University Press, 1970.

———. *Journals and Papers*. Vol. 2, *F–K*. Translated by Howard V. Hong and Edna H. Hong. Bloomington: Indiana University Press, 1970.

———. *Letters and Documents*. Translated by Henrik Rosenmeier. Princeton: Princeton University Press, 1978.

———. *"The Moment" and Other Late Writings*. Translated by Howard V. Hong and Edna H. Hong. Princeton: Princeton University Press, 1998.

———. *The Point of View*. Translated by Howard V. and Edna H. Hong. Princeton: Princeton University Press, 1998.

———. *The Sickness Unto Death*. Translated by Howard V. Hong and Edna H. Hong. Princeton: Princeton University Press, 1980.

———. *Works of Love*. Translated by Howard V. Hong and Edna H. Hong. Princeton: Princeton University Press, 1995.

Levinas, Emmanuel. *Basic Philosophical Writings*. Edited by Adriaan T. Peperzak et al. Bloomington: Indiana University Press, 1996.

———. *Entre Nous: Thinking of the Other*. Translated by Michael B. Smith and Barbara Harshav. New York: Columbia University Press, 1998.

———. *Ethics and Infinity*. Translated by Richard A. Cohen. Pittsburgh: Duquesne University Press, 1985.

———. *Of God Who Comes to Mind*. Translated by Bettina Bergo. Stanford: Stanford University Press, 1998.

———. *Otherwise than Being; or, Beyond Essence*. Translated by Alphonso Lingis. Pittsburgh: Duquesne University Press, 2008.

———. *Proper Names*. Translated by Michael B. Smith. Stanford: Stanford University Press, 1996.

Martensen, Hans Lassen. *Om Tro og Viden, et Lejlighedsskrift*. Copenhagen: Reitzel, 1867.

Niebuhr, Reinhold. *The Essential Reinhold Niebuhr: Selected Essays and Addresses*. Edited by Robert McAfee Brown. New Haven: Yale University Press, 1986.

———. *Justice and Mercy*. Edited by Ursula M. Niebuhr. New York: Harper & Row, 1974.

———. *Love and Justice: Selections from the Shorter Writings of Reinhold Niebuhr*. Edited by D. B. Robertson. Louisville: Westminster John Knox, 1957.

———. *The Nature and Destiny of Man: A Christian Interpretation*. Vol. 1, *Human Nature*. New York: Scribner, 1964.

———. *The Nature and Destiny of Man: A Christian Interpretation*. Vol. 2, *Human Destiny*. New York: Scribner, 1964.

Pattison, George, and Helle Møller Jensen. *Kierkegaard's Pastoral Dialogues*. Eugene, OR: Cascade, 2012.

Sartre, Jean-Paul. *Being and Nothingness*. Edited by Hazel E. Barnes. New York: Citadel, 1969.

Taylor, Mark C. *Journeys to Selfhood: Hegel and Kierkegaard*. Berkeley: University of California Press, 1980.

Walsh, Sylvia. *Kierkegaard: Thinking Christianly in an Existential Mode.* Oxford: Oxford University Press, 2009.

Wolterstorff, Nicholas. *Justice in Love.* Grand Rapids: Eerdmans, 2011.

19

The Spotlight and the "Courage to Be an Absolute Nobody"

Toward a Kierkegaardian-Chestertonian Political Theology of Ego

ROBERTO SIRVENT AND DUNCAN REYBURN

> I'm not afraid to compete. It's just the opposite. Don't you see that? I'm afraid I will compete—that's what scares me. . . . Just because I'm so horribly conditioned to accept everybody else's values, and just because I like applause and people to rave about me, doesn't make it right. I'm ashamed of it. I'm sick of it. I'm sick of not having the courage to be an absolute nobody.
>
> —J. D. SALINGER, *FRANNY AND ZOOEY*

Introduction

IN THE ABOVE EPIGRAPH, Salinger highlights a conundrum present in any competitive scenario—the fact that the very act of competing seems to be ethically dubious because of its inherent egotism. True courage, Salinger submits, is located, not in a willingness to compete, but in a decision not to—a decision located in an other-serving self-effacement or self-denial, which operates beyond the dualities produced by egotism. This provocation reflects the many great reversals found in the New Testament; where those who lack spiritual wealth are the blessed,[1] where adamancy disguises uncertainty,[2] where lastness upends the politics of firstness,[3] and where

---

1. Matt 5:3.
2. Matt 9:9–12; 13:13; John 9:41.
3. Matt 19:30.

humility is a sign of true greatness.⁴ To read these great reversals too hastily and unthinkingly, however, is to arrive at a simplistic injunction—*Denounce ego! Deny yourself!*—without necessarily understanding either why or how such an injunction would make sense. It would be important, for instance, to question the way that enforcing humility has become one of the more problematic ideological constructions in the history of Christian theology—a way to ensure a neat distinction between those who have a "predestined" "right" to rule and those who only have the "right" to serve (and thus be abused). In short, a reductionist ethics of self-denial mistakes what is essentially a critique of political ideology as being an affirmation of political norms and abuses. Therefore, in this essay, our aim is to provide a more nuanced theo-political assessment of ego by drawing on the work of two great Christian thinkers, Søren Kierkegaard and G. K. Chesterton, both of whom provide valuable insights on what the desire to "be somebody" or to "be important" or to have the "spotlight" means for Christian ethics and discipleship.⁵ Although we may not be able to arrive at a neat or definitive political theology of ego, this reflection should at least map some important considerations for such a thing.

Egotism: Despair

At the start, it is helpful to note Kierkegaard's concern that egotism is essentially a lie. It is not the truth of the human subject because, among other things, it resists the possibility of self-reflection and self-awareness. If anything, "worldly fame and status are such dangerous traps (dangerous just as wealth tempts one in the direction of losing faith in providential care)," because they set up the coordinates according to which egotism might believe its own misguided hype.⁶ Egotists "do not want to enter God's kingdom as little children but want to be *something*."⁷ This is a problem for Kierkegaard, because it is a forgetting of the essential difference between God and man, and is therefore also a denial of reality.⁸ Simply "being the object of attention by the many, having the fate of all these people in one's hands, can so very easily lead to the erroneous conclusion that [the leader] is more important to God as well."⁹

---

4. Luke 9:48; 14:11.

5. Obviously, Kierkegaard and Chesterton differ in many ways, especially with respect to their personalities, but also with respect to their contexts and aims. Nevertheless, both thinkers share a commitment to their respective Christian traditions, and thus share a predilection for paradox—and this includes a distrust of egotism. Owing to certain constraints, what follows is not a forced or comprehensive synthesis of the work of these two writers, but rather draws from a selection of their ideas.

6. Kierkegaard, *Journals and Papers*, 1:1010.

7. Kierkegaard, *Concluding Unscientific Postscript*, 501, emphasis added.

8. Simpson, *Truth Is the Way*, 34.

9. Kierkegaard, *Journals and Papers*, 2:1010.

Kierkegaard notes that a position of power locks the leader into a (mimetic) relationship with the mindless crowd.[10] Such a relationship is suggested by the apocryphal story about Alexandre Ledru-Rollin who, seeing a crowd pass him by, hurriedly set off to join it while remarking to those in his company, "There go the people. I must follow them, for I am their leader."[11] In Kierkegaard's view, being bound to the crowd in this way—whereby the leader's egotism is a compliant, crowd-pleasing egotism—resists what is essentially ethical; after all, the ethical is something that "can be carried out only by the individual subject"—the subject who does not mimic the untruth of the crowd.[12] Essential to Kierkegaard's conception of the ego is its connection with a lack of self-awareness, inwardness or subjectivity.[13] Consequently, egotism and its alignment with the spotlight and the system that affirms it would be far from desirable. So why, then, would anyone give in to it? Kierkegaard suggests that this attachment is related to the issue of despair.

Tom Miles suggests that "for [Kierkegaard's] Anti-Climacus despair is always an internal problem, a misrelation to one's self, even if it also involves a misrelation to what exists independently of the self. Despair can be called the internal collapse of a way of life in that a self that avoids itself or pretends to be what it is not is internally divided within itself."[14] Attachment to the spotlight or the idea of being "something" is, as Miles intimates, unconscious, and it begets further unconsciousness. Feelings of despair like "frustration, anxiety, and depression" are in fact not despair *per se*. Rather, these are "merely symptoms of the disease of despair."[15]

This distinction between the disease and its symptoms indicates that one may be sick without necessarily experiencing the symptoms of one's sickness: "one could be in despair without feeling despair. . . . This is the case with the person whose immersion in conformity, mediocrity, or pleasure is successful enough to avoid any such unpleasantness."[16] In fact, it is possible to be in despair without experiencing it as despair; it is possible to be in despair while only having a sense of security, peace, and repose.[17]

Ego is its own enemy in this regard: it can provide feelings of loftiness, godlikeness, and power that conceal despair from the despairing subject. Thus, when the subject loses his place in the spotlight, he is likely to experience the loss itself as despair. This, in Kierkegaard's view, is a profound misunderstanding of what is really going on; this

---

10. Kierkegaard, *Essential Kierkegaard*, 471.

11. Quoted in the *New Yorker Magazine* (vol. 80, 2005), 143.

12. Ibid., 217; see Bellinger, "Crowd Is Untruth," 103–19; See Girard, *Violence and the Sacred*, 146–47.

13. Kierkegaard, *Concluding Unscientific Postscript*, 176, 203.

14. Miles, *Kierkegaard and Nietzsche*, 108.

15. Ibid., 109.

16. Ibid.

17. Ibid.

experience of loss is precisely a moment of awakening to the true despair of being in the spotlight. It is the attachment to the spotlight that is the real despair: the source of an "underestimating or overestimating [of] one's self in relation to God."[18] What sustains the lie of the spotlight is that it has become synonymous with truth.

Kierkegaard's (that is, Anti-Climacus's) conception of the "despair of immediacy" further assists in understanding why an attachment to the spotlight can be persisted with despite its unreality. The immediate—experienced in things like financial security, the admiration of others, or the pleasure of power—somehow presents itself as having greater weight than one's spiritual self or true self. Immediacy prevents the recognition of others. This idea is evident in Chesterton's Father Brown story about "The Invisible Man." In that story, the character James Welkin is felt as a presence (a hidden truth, the other) but is somehow never seen in the immediate environment. Therefore, the character Laura Hope relays her strange experience of hearing James Welkin laugh without seeing him when receiving a letter.[19] Later in the story, to dismiss the superstitions around the mystery of James Welkin, the amateur detective Father Brown offers his own explanation for the man's invisibility.

> Have you ever noticed this—that people never answer what you say? They answer what you mean—or what they think you mean. Suppose one lady says to another in a country house, "Is there anybody staying with you?" the lady doesn't answer "Yes; the butler, the three footmen, the parlour-maid, and so on," though the parlour-maid may be in the room, or the butler behind her chair. She says: "There is *nobody* staying with us," meaning *nobody* of the sort you mean.[20]

Father Brown highlights that Laura Hope could not have been "quite alone in a street when she start[ed] reading a letter just received. There must be somebody pretty near; he must be mentally invisible."[21] In the context of Kierkegaard's understanding of despair—here symbolized by the fact that, owing to a spiritual myopia, Laura Hope does not see herself as being equal to the "nobody" James Welkin—this mental invisibility must be dismantled and exposed. And this is precisely what cannot take place under the spotlight of success, fame, power, and political influence. Ironically, the spotlight—a thing that is supposed to reveal—in fact conceals, while humility—symbolized by Father Brown's porous, questioning mind—reveals; the spotlight nurtures egotism, while humility deconstructs it. Moreover, as Chesterton contends, it is humility that brings joy—the redemption of and alternative to despair.[22] What is essential here, especially in relation to what we refer to as a political theology of ego,

---

18. Ibid., 108.
19. Chesterton, *Father Brown*, 93.
20. Ibid., 106.
21. Ibid., 107.
22. Chesterton, *Collected Works*, 234.

is that humility, as Kierkegaard and Chesterton frame it, becomes not only a gateway to understanding but also an essential pathway to ethical action. As Christopher Ben Simpson notes on Kierkegaard's ethics, "the ethical self chooses itself, affirms itself."[23] It is only in this affirmation of the self outside of the illusions framed by the spotlight that one is able to stand as both an individual and as a universal—that is, as one who embodies a concrete truth in the service of others.[24] The egotistical self, on the other hand, chooses against itself, as well as its others.

Incarnation: God's Spotlight-Aversion

The central challenge offered by both Kierkegaard and Chesterton to the cult of ego in politics and social relations is found in their radical presentation of the orthodox Christian idea that God does not want to "be somebody" (in the sense of possessing worldly ambition or being in the spotlight). Rather, in their work, God is the Ground of Being—absolute love hidden within, beneath and beyond the veil of materiality—and therefore escapes the confines of ambitious desire. Desire, after all, requires the possibility of imitation or mimeticism, as the work of René Girard shows, and God—as the Ground of Being—could not possibly imitate anyone; God could not enter the realm of rivalry or competition.[25] Indeed, God even "takes the side of the victim"—one who cannot be envied or viewed as a rival.[26] It follows that God does not experience the despair of the spotlight as human beings do; instead, God models a necessary humility or self-effacement that calls the spotlight and any political-egotistical attachment to that spotlight (and its supporting structures) into question.

Kierkegaard's famous story of the "King and the Maiden" extends this idea in a parable. The story goes that a king with the greatest available political power—a king whose authority caused even other kings to tremble—this king "loved a maiden of lowly station in life."[27] Unfortunately, this love posed a problem, because presenting himself (in his "spotlighted" kingly form) to the humble maiden and declaring his love for her would prevent him from ever knowing whether her reciprocation was genuine; perhaps she would only claim to love him so that she could share in his power or pretend to love him to protect herself from being the target of his wrath. Thus, in the words of Philip Yancey, the king's "kingliness tied his hands."[28]

In Kierkegaard's story, the king's status—a status not real but conjured in the minds of admiring others—was an obstacle to genuine romance primarily because it threatened to crush the freedom of the maiden. The only way for the king to know the

---

23. Simpson, *Truth Is the Way*, 105.
24. Ibid., 105–6.
25. Oughourlian, *Genesis of Desire*, 64.
26. Girard, *I See Satan Fall*, xvii.
27. Kierkegaard, *Philosophical Fragments*, 26.
28. Yancey, *Disappointment with God*, 103.

maiden's love—to be assured that it was authentic—was to degrade himself by taking on the form of a beggar, and thereafter approach the maiden's cottage "with a worn cloak fluttering loose about him."[29] To be truly persuasive, this humble form could not only be a temporary disguise. It had to be "a totally new identity."[30] The king therefore "renounced his throne to declare his love and to win [the love of the maiden]."[31]

One could read this parable through a Hegelian lens and conclude that it represents a process whereby a king takes leave of his position of power, and thereby negates his kingliness. Such a dialectical interpretation, however, would not comply with the essentially paradoxical or nondual stance on the incarnation adopted and proposed by Kierkegaard (and also by Chesterton). It is more likely that Kierkegaard is pointing to the very character of this king, rather than just to his apparent position: subverting the view of others who perceive him as a threatening presence, what the king ends up doing—giving up his throne—provides an insight into who he really is. This king is, ontologically speaking, a self-effacing king, a king who does not take the spotlight of his title "king" too seriously. In this, one cannot help but be reminded of Jacques Lacan's idea that a madman who thinks himself a king may be no more problematic than a king who thinks himself a king.[32] This king's self-effacement is not something that exists only as a result of his abdication of his throne, but is something that precedes it. The king, as we have already noted, does not imitate some other model, but enacts and makes apparent what he really is, which surpasses the title given to him.

Consequently, this is a parable that concerns the king's qualitative difference from the politics of egotism; it signals his essentially humble nature, not just his measurable actions or discernable authority. In other words, it is not that humility is merely the opposite of egotism (and is thus parasitic upon egotism), but is rather something that transcends egotism (and the dialectic of self and other) entirely. Chesterton rearticulates this insight when he presents the image of "something which the scientific critic cannot see." In the incarnation, "the hands that had made the sun and stars were too small to reach the huge heads of the cattle." It is "upon this paradox" or "jest" that "all the literature of our faith is founded."[33]

Chesterton conceives of the incarnation as a joke. It is profoundly incongruous and perhaps even laughable to the ego-obsessed. It undercuts worldly ambition and power by translating the transcendent God into the body of an infant—utterly vulnerable and dependent. This image or jest is more jarring than the one offered by Kierkegaard; in Kierkegaard's parable, we can imagine the king retaining a sense of aura around who he was, but in Chesterton's description, which is in keeping with Kierkegaard's wider vision, we encounter a God who empties himself—Being, the

29. Ibid., 104.
30. Ibid.
31. Ibid.
32. Žižek, *Sublime Object of Ideology*, 21.
33. Chesterton, *Everlasting Man*, 191.

limitless, takes on the form of a finite, limited being.[34] This is most radically evident in the centrality of the crucifixion of Jesus in Christian theology: the entire event may be read as a parody of the spotlight. Jesus is named as king, but crowned with thorns, tortured, and murdered. As Chesterton suggests, through this experience, God-Incarnate even enters into the existential despair of the atheist.[35] This is an event that adds courage to the virtues of the Creator. As the enfleshment of God, Jesus thus represents the surprising necessity of overcoming the spotlight through kenosis. The spotlight is a thing to be challenged, not celebrated; it is to be subverted, not affirmed. In undergoing the cross, Jesus appears as *the* word spoken against the false glory of kingliness.

Incarnation: Indirect Communication

The hypostatic union of the divine and the human in Jesus, and the challenge that this poses to the spotlight, is a communication event. Kierkegaard understands, for instance, that communication is an uneven or imbalanced affair and therefore relies on negotiating meanings through a shared symmetry or point of identification. "Direct communication presupposes that the recipient's ability to receive is entirely in order," but in the relationship between God and humanity, there is a problem of extreme asymmetry.[36] As St. Thomas Aquinas had noticed, our embodiment is precisely how we know things, such that even "if an angel could speak, we would not be able to understand what he said."[37] As a consequence, even the symmetry of shared being—that is, a shared participation in Being that is required for communication to be possible—presupposes asymmetry—that is, the impossibility of direct communication. Simpson writes the following on Kierkegaard's perspective on communication:

> In order to communicate the truth to another where they are it is assumed that the truth, in whole or in part, is what the other is lacking. But to presume to communicate the truth directly to one who is in untruth, who believes falsehood, will likely be met with resistance, rejection, dismissal—for, from the perspective of the other, one is presuming to give them something they already have, something they do not lack, namely the truth.[38]

Every communication of truth therefore assumes the necessity of miscommunication. Even in the gospel story, God appears, communicates himself indirectly to man as a man, and is then so misunderstood that he is mistaken for a political rebel or rival and crucified as such. Nevertheless, this is precisely what seems to be required

---

34. Phil 2.
35. Chesterton, *Everlasting Man*, 243.
36. Kierkegaard, *Point of View*, 54.
37. Eagleton, *Faith, Reason, and Revolution*, 129.
38. Simpson, *Truth Is the Way*, 12.

for truth to stand a chance at being given a hearing. It is better that it is misheard than not heard at all; it is better to communicate something than nothing at all. It is this indirect communication, this asymmetrical event of mutual self-giving, that is the foundation of relationship.

In Kierkegaard's parable, then, there is a sense that the maiden will not see the king for who he is, or perhaps will not see him at all, if he clings to his title and his throne; this implies that the inherent egotism of political power poses a problem to perception itself. It suggests that falsehood will persist if miscommunication is not risked. This is something that Chesterton echoes, albeit differently from Kierkegaard. Chesterton pictures a beggar at the front door of a house being met by the elitist who lives there.[39] The elitist, failing to give himself over to the risk of indirect communication and thus also failing to recognize the humanity of the beggar, simply turns him away and shuts the door. Chesterton points out the significance of this act of shutting the beggar out. It indicates that "from everything that we shut out we are ourselves shut out."[40] Thus, if we shut out those who God is present with, we shut out God himself. Chesterton continues:

> When we shut our door on the wind, it would be equally true to say that the wind shuts its door on us. Whatever virtues a triumphant egoism really leads to, no one can reasonably pretend that it leads to knowledge. Turning a beggar from the door may be right enough, but pretending to know all the stories the beggar might have narrated is pure nonsense; and this is practically the claim of the egoism which thinks that self-assertion can obtain knowledge. A beetle may or may not be inferior to a man—the matter awaits demonstration; but if he were inferior by ten thousand fathoms, the fact remains that there is probably a beetle view of things of which a man is entirely ignorant.[41]

Egotism functions the way that any "philosophy of self-satisfaction" functions: it results in "looking down upon the weak, the cowardly, and the ignorant," and this results in seeing things as if from a great height or distance, with "everything foreshortened or deformed."[42] This foreshortened perspective is further captured in Chesterton's contention that all people are prone to living their lives like a "man who has forgotten his name."[43] He continues:

> The man walks about the streets and can see and appreciate everything; only he cannot remember who he is. Well, every man is that man in the story. Every man has forgotten who he is. One may understand the cosmos, but never the ego; the self is more distant than any star. Thou shalt love the Lord thy God;

---

39. Chesterton, *The Defendant*, 100.
40. Ibid.
41. Ibid., 100–101.
42. Ibid., 101.
43. Chesterton, *Collected Works*, 364.

> but thou shalt not know thyself. We are all under the same mental calamity; we have all forgotten our names. We have all forgotten what we really are. All that we call common sense and rationality and practicality and positivism only means that for certain dead levels of our life we forget that we have forgotten. All that we call spirit and art and ecstasy only means that for one awful instant we remember that we forget.[44]

Here, Chesterton notes that it is in self-forgetting or self-effacement—that is, in being caught up in "spirit" or "art" or any other ecstatic experience—that we remember who we are; it is only in humility that we are able to perceive even ourselves more fairly. It is only in resisting egotism that false perceptions may be properly addressed.

Insofar as Kierkegaard and Chesterton are concerned, the qualitative gap remains between God and humanity even in the incarnation. God as absolute otherness—perhaps more like nothing than like anything else—retains God's otherness, but nevertheless elects to translate this into the failing, fragile, dying body of a human so that (indirect) communication can occur between God and humanity. Kierkegaard writes that "one learns more profoundly and reliably what the highest is by reflecting on suffering than by reflecting on achievements."[45] He thus overcomes duality by noticing that the highest is inside what is lowly, just as Chesterton would say that hierarchy is subverted when he writes that the incarnation offers a "heaven" that "is under the earth"[46] or a home that is discovered only when one is away.[47]

Through Kierkegaard, we find that the lowly cannot see those who are exalted if the exalted do not step down, and through Chesterton, we find that the exalted themselves cannot perceive things clearly without stepping down. Moreover, in the work of both Kierkegaard and Chesterton, we find an image of a God who operates outside of the realm of ambition—a God who does not wish to be associated with the distance and distortion of pure bliss or great stature, and who would rather step into the role of a peasant or a beggar to set up the coordinates according to which love can flourish.

Again, Kierkegaard and Chesterton do not claim the incarnation as a denial or negation of divinity, but instead indicate it as its affirmation, albeit via a redefinition of divinity. If humanity bears the image of God, then there is a congruency in the fact that God would not find that image deplorable or as being in any way beneath Godself. It nevertheless remains to be seen whether humanity will be willing to stoop to the level of bearing God's image, and this is precisely the challenge that a political theology of ego must grapple with. Chesterton suggests in this regard that every human being needs to "enact for itself the gigantic humility of the incarnation. Every man must descend into the flesh to meet mankind."[48] For it is in descending

---

44. Ibid.
45. Kierkegaard, *Upbuilding Discourses*, 100.
46. Chesterton, *Everlasting Man*, 196.
47. Chesterton, *Tremendous Trifles*, 162–63.
48. Chesterton, *What's Wrong with the World*, 70.

into flesh in this way that humanity stands a chance of properly understanding and imitating God's lack of egotism.

This is precisely what many of the early Christians demonstrated in their posture against the violence of the Roman Empire, and especially in their understanding of what it meant to "render to Caesar what is Caesar's."[49] An apparent contradiction existed in the early days of the church in the ideas of (1) "accept[ing] the authority of every human institution"[50] while also (2) "obey[ing] God rather than any human authority."[51] But this contradiction was resolved by many of the early Christians in the following way, as explained by George Kalantzis:

> Unlike the Maccabees who rebelled against Hellenistic domination because of the Seleucid imposition of religious practices antithetical to Judaism (1 Macc. 11:21) and as a sign of Jewish apocalyptic revivalism (1 Macc. 6:16), the apostles neither rebelled against Rome nor sought a particular national identity separate from the eschatological kingdom of Christ (e.g., 2 Thess 2:1–2). Christians *honored the emperor* and the governors as [their] appointed authorities by following the example of Christ in refusing their consent *and* by submitting themselves to the consequences of their rejection, including scourging and death. That is what "rendering to Caesar what is Caesar's" would look like in the new economy; a simultaneous "yes" and "no" that point back to God as supreme. In doing so, they overturned . . . the normative paradigms of the classical traditions and showed how, for the Christians, power is gained through submission.[52]

This was something that "the Romans did not comprehend"—the fact that even martyrdom was not "the fate of the powerless" but was rather "a witness *to* the state of its subordination to the God of heaven."[53] For these martyrs, this was a "repetition" of the ethical posture of Jesus, to borrow Kierkegaard's terms. They did not see themselves as victims of state violence or as confirming the state's death-trade, but as witnesses to a love and a power that does not even fear death. Of course, there is an immediate problem raised by this example, namely the appearance, noted in our introduction, that submission itself might be taken as an inflexible rule. However, such an absolutization of martyrdom would produce a new immorality; it would be to confuse the methodology (dying at the hand of empire) with its ethical aim (to challenge Empire). What is key here is that this martyrdom was a stance *against* victimization, not a confirmation of it. Again, God does not become human to confirm the importance of the "violence of Rome," as certain atonement theories would perhaps have us believe, but precisely to call it into question through a provocative and subversive

---

49. Matt 22:21.
50. 1 Pet 2:13–15.
51. Acts 5:29; 4:19.
52. Kalantzis, *Caesar and the Lamb*, 35.
53. Ibid.

humility. Put differently, the point is not to affirm injustice, but to move more steadily toward real justice and social change.

Incarnation: God Incognito

There is something in Christ that reflects this divine selflessness and a resistance to the spotlight. On this point, Jason Mahn writes about the "incognito" aspect of Christ and his mission.[54] Jaime Ferreira's commentary on *Four Upbuilding Discourses* also carries this idea with reference to giving: the idea that the giver of any gift should become as "'invisible' as possible in the act of gift-giving," "should vanish without waiting for thanks." "The requirement," Ferreira points out "is to give joyfully without calling attention to oneself—i.e., to hide oneself."[55] To put the point more radically in relation to the narratives of the Gospels, it is as if the fame of Christ was an accident, perhaps even a mistake, and not his aim. If Mahn and Ferreira are right in suggesting that we are to view Jesus' life as an "incognito life," then what does this incognito mission have to do with the *imitatio Christi* and *imago Dei*? At the very least, the idea of "Christ incognito" implies that our own embracing of anonymity is likely to bring us into harmony with the incarnate *imago Dei*. To be sure, by embracing anonymity, we will have more in common with the family of God—the "great cloud of witnesses" visible only to the eyes of faith—the vast majority of whom have not been memorialized in any way.

Anonymity can be problematic, of course, as Chesterton was quick to point out. It can mask self-interest; one might even use anonymity to do and say whatever one likes, and thus abandon all forms of accountability.[56] This sort of anonymity would merely be the handmaiden of arrogance. But this is not the anonymity that we find emblematized in the doctrine of the incarnation. Rather, an incarnational anonymity is of a kind that assumes a position for the sake of love: the incarnation represents God's act of stepping down to serve. This fact adds an important facet to understanding humility. Humility is a movement, not just a position. A pauper before a king, for example, is not humble but humiliated; his position has been chosen for him by a larger context and is not a matter of will. But a king who stoops before a pauper demonstrates true humility. Christ can walk the earth *incognito* because he is Christ: he can be nobody because he is not nobody.

We, too, can only choose to lay down ego when we possess an ego. Thus, it needs to be emphasized that for many who have been degraded, victimized and had their self-worth questioned by dominant ideologies and political systems, an absolutist ethics of self-effacement would be deeply damaging and not at all liberating. In the end, it is humility, not humiliation, that we are supporting here, and this is done in a very

---

54. Mahn, *Fortunate Fallibility*, 137.
55. Ferreira, *Kierkegaard*, 64.
56. Chesterton, "Illustrated London News," December 17, 1932.

particular context. We are not speaking only generally about a political theology of ego but are interested in what may be said about the value of self-effacement for those who are caught up in the superficial game of wanting the spotlight.

Of course, one argument used for moving against this self-effacement—that is, against this laying down of ego—is usually one linked to the possibility of the "good" that can be done when one is in the spotlight. Take, for example, the person who wants to be a famous politician, professor, or pastor; or the college graduate who has her mind set on changing the world. This ideological posture is no doubt seductive: *I am the one we have been waiting for!* The problem with this argument is that it offers little more than a concealed narcissism: it presumes that the one who seeks the spotlight should be the "one" to right all wrongs, to address and correct all (or any) social evils. It is also an argument that exaggerates the role of top-down social change. Historically speaking, social change, together with all goods that come from such change, tends to depend far more on those "below," especially those marginalized by political systems, than on those "above." To cite just one example, Lisa Lowe shows how "liberal abolitionist arguments were less important to the passage of the Slave Trade Act and the Slavery Abolition Act than were the dramatic revolts and everyday practices of enslaved peoples themselves."[57] Indeed, there is much to be gained from the spotlight—fame, privilege, applause, praise, and wealth. But at what *epistemic* cost? The problem with wanting that prestigious position, or to break records, or to win the approval of politicians, is that it distorts and blinds us to what is good, true, and right. The crowd and the spotlight corrupt our sense of what justice is. Having the courage to be an absolute nobody does not mean refusing to fight or to speak loudly or to wreak havoc or disruption. It does not mean shutting up. Rather, it means coming to recognize "the epistemic privilege of the oppressed," or the nobodies, and "the way that suffering attunes us to justice."[58]

This brings us, again, to the issue of love suggested in Kierkegaard's parable of the king and the maiden. This is something with vital political implications that is discussed at length by Amy Laura Hall. Hall notes that, following Kierkegaard, "the kind of love we are to choose, will, and cultivate has as its key the self-giving life of Christ, who did not 'seek his own.'"[59] Moreover, "in order to hope in eternity in the way that Kierkegaard commends, we must cease counting up bits of love in a miserable attempt to determine whose love is greater or first or best, but instead 'lose' ourselves in the assumption that the other's love is true."[60] This is love that contests any suggestion that "large, public acts of beneficence, respectable acts of frugality, or reciprocated gestures of generosity" might be thought of as examples of "earnestness." Christian charity has

---

57. Lowe, *Intimacies of Four Continents*, 13; see also Hartman, *Scenes of Subjection*; Scott, *Weapons of the Weak*; Spade, *Normal Life*.

58. Lloyd, *Black Natural Law*, ix.

59. Hall, *Kierkegaard and the Treachery of Love*, 32.

60. Ibid.

mercy, not magnanimity, as its goal. Its "love wins in a quiet way totally foreign to those who seek remarkable signs of achievement."[61]

Chesterton's understanding of love reflects this stance, as well. While egotism is forever expanding—Chesterton coins the word *panegotism* to reflect this perpetual expansion at the expense of the other—love accepts limitations and thus allows the other her place in the world.[62] Love binds itself, not to an ideal or system detached from experience, but to individual others in their concrete specificity.[63] The lover begins to love where she is, not at the level of egotistical goals, but at the level of self-giving mercy. Thus, "loving those who can give back nothing is more akin to Christian love than receiving the approbation of others."[64] Hall follows this reasoning when she argues that Kierkegaard's view on progress points, not "toward our more perfect imitation of Christ," but instead points toward "perfect awareness of our imperfection."[65]

In the end, the final curse of the spotlight, together with its masking of despair and its negation of the indirect communication that makes relationships possible, is in the fact that it opposes the freedom that is able to challenge the politics of the spotlight. This is something already indicated in Kierkegaard's parable of the king and the maiden. The actual metaphor of the spotlight becomes particularly important on this point: a spotlight is a thing that conforms the object or subject of its focus to its own gaze. The spotlight forces the object or subject of its devotion to fit the mold of expectation and power that it represents. Leaders are more often than not forced to follow the mindless crowd. When Kierkegaard and Chesterton talk of love, they are talking about a unique kind of freedom, which elects constraints that benefit not only others, but also the one who has chosen them. To love is to accept that one is already loved, instead of believing love to be the consequence of achieving some sort of greatness. Additionally, these constraints counteract the pull of the spotlight, because they recognize the self as inherently limited. Kierkegaard and Chesterton are pointing to a unique kind of freedom—the kind that David Foster Wallace sums up as follows:

> But of course there are all different kinds of freedom, and the kind that is most precious you will not hear much talk about in the great outside world of wanting and achieving.... The really important kind of freedom involves attention and awareness and discipline, and being able truly to care about other people and to sacrifice for them over and over in myriad petty, unsexy ways every day.[66]

---

61. Ibid., 35.
62. Chesterton, *The Defendant*, 23.
63. Chesterton, *Collected Works*, 1:243–44.
64. Hall, *Kierkegaard and the Treachery of Love*, 35.
65. Ibid., 16–17.
66. Wallace, *This Is Water*, 120.

In the end, it is not difficult to find all the ways that the spotlight has become an idol in various political contexts—an ossified ideological construct that possesses the minds and imaginations of many. However, as we have noted at length, Kierkegaard and Chesterton seem to regard this egotistical construct with a deep suspicion because it is antithetical to the ethical. It does not give rise to love, justice and social change, because it is not ultimately about those things. Rather, it concerns itself with an impotent politics that can only, at best, *pretend* to be powerful or *pretend* to work for the good. It preserves self but does not see that it is self-giving that is at the center of any kind of authentic ethics. In a way, what we have presented here is both a critique of the politics of ego and a kind of manifesto. In short, individuals must have the courage to be an absolute nobody for the sake of the community and for the sake of justice. Moreover, we have argued that this is not just because of what God has done (he has become a nobody), but because of where he is (he is *with* the nobodies, *as* a nobody).

Conclusion

Arguably, it is failure that is the subversive core of the above theo-political assessment of ego, which, to quote Jack Halberstam, "turns on the impossible, the improbable, the unlikely, and the unremarkable."[67] This failure considers the importance of loss for reimagining "other goals for life, for love, for art, and for being." If we take Chesterton and Kierkegaard seriously, then we might start to recognize all the ways that the Christ event reflects this kind of failure. The incarnation shows us the impossible (God becomes a nobody), the irrational and the foolish (God *wants* to become a nobody, enacts a failure of ambition). The incarnation shows us a God who undergoes misrecognition and rejection. When humiliated and laughed at, this embodied God appears as a farce and even as a parody of the divine. And yet, we find a potent political subversion in this joke-God. He helps us to imagine "other goals for life, for love, for art, and for being"—truths located beyond the lie of the spotlight. He gives us another conception of divinity, which does not rely on the hero systems that endorse and create spotlights.

If the field of political theology is frequently about the critique of ideology and idolatry, it must follow a trajectory like the one established by Chesterton and Kierkegaard, who critique many games that people play—games played to seek and arrive at the top; games played to become a "somebody" in the eyes of the crowd; games played to become a "somebody" at the expense of the nobodies; games played to become a "somebody" under the guise of helping the nobodies. This manifests itself in many ways. Success becomes equated with the accumulation of wealth, career advancement, the recognition by the elite members of one's field, and even recognition by systems supported by the state's monopoly on violence. However, to merely critique

---

67. Halberstam, *Queer Art of Failure*, 88.

the ideology and idolatry present in the egotistical games people play is not sufficient. As in Kierkegaard and Chesterton's understanding of the incarnation, political theology must also find a way to "lose quietly" and help people find creative ways to care for, cooperate with, and enjoy one another.

Moving forward, perhaps Kierkegaard and Chesterton's political theology of ego—or, rather, their call for a subversive kind of humility—might best be read as a theology that imagines a preferential treatment for the nobodies—those who are not famous nor want to be famous; those who desire attention and affirmation from their loved ones rather than from a Twitter feed; those who are either outside of or resist capitalistic notions of success; those who never receive nor even desire the applause of the state and its violent institutions. A preferential option for the nobodies calls us to stand alongside the nobodies, to come down from the "top," away from the "center" and into the margins. This would not be a strategy for pulling the nobodies "up" from the bottom, nor would it seek to bring those in the margins to the center. Rather, this would involve a solidarity with the nobodies that could lead us to a place of unique insight—perhaps even a reimagining of the political order. In short, a theological preference for nobodies serves not only as a strategy for social justice, but also as a window into the divine.

Bibliography

Bellinger, Charles. "'The Crowd Is Untruth': A Comparison of Kierkegaard and Girard." *Contagion: Journal of Violence, Mimesis, and Culture* 3 (1996) 103–19.
Chesterton, G. K. *Collected Works*. Vol. 1, *Heretics, Orthodoxy, the Blatchford Controversies*. San Francisco: Ignatius, 1986.
———. *The Defendant*. London: Johnson, 1901.
———. *Everlasting Man*. London: Hodder and Stoughton, 1925.
———. *Father Brown: Selected Stories*. London: Collector's Library, 2003.
———. "Illustrated London News, December 17, 1932." In *Collected Works*, vol. 36, edited by Lawrence J. Clipper., 189–92. San Francisco: Ignatius, 2011.
———. *Tremendous Trifles*. Mineola, NY: Dover, 2007.
———. *What's Wrong with the World*. San Franscisco: Ignatius, 1994.
Eagleton, Terry. *Faith, Reason, and Revolution: Reflections on the God Debate*. New Haven: Yale University, 2009.
Ferreira, M. Jaime. *Kierkegaard*. Oxford: Wiley-Blackwell, 2009.
Girard, René. *I See Satan Fall Like Lightning*. Translated by James G. Williams. New York: Orbis, 2001.
———. *Violence and the Sacred*. Translated by Patrick Gregory. Baltimore: Johns Hopkins University Press, 1977.
Halberstam, Judith. *The Queer Art of Failure*. Durham: Duke University, 2011.
Hall, Amy Laura. *Kierkegaard and the Treachery of Love*. Cambridge: Cambridge University, 2002.
Hartman, Saidiya V. *Scenes of Subjection: Terror, Slavery, and Self-Making in Nineteenth-Century America*. Oxford: Oxford University Press, 1997.

Kalantzis, George. *Caesar and the Lamb: Early Christian Attitudes on War and Military Service*. Eugene: Cascade, 2012.

Kierkegaard, Søren. *Concluding Unscientific Postscript to Philosophical Fragments*. Translated and edited by Howard V. Hong and Edna H. Hong. Cambridge: Cambridge University, 2009.

———. *The Essential Kierkegaard*. Edited by Howard V. Hong and Edna H. Hong. Princeton: Princeton University, 1995.

———. *Journals and Papers*. 7 vols. Translated by Howard V. Hong and Edna H. Hong. Princeton: Princeton University Press, 1967–78.

———. *Philosophical Fragments: Johannes Climacus*. Edited by Howard V. Hong and Edna H. Hong. Princeton: Princeton University Press, 1985.

———. *The Point of View*. Translated and edited by Howard V. Hong and Edna H. Hong. Princeton: Princeton University, 2009.

———. *Upbuilding Discourses in Various Spirits*. Translated by Howard V. Hong and Edna H. Hong. Princeton: Princeton University Press, 1993.

Lloyd, Vincent. *Black Natural Law*. Oxford: Oxford University Press, 2016.

Lowe, Lisa. *The Intimacies of Four Continents*. Durham: Duke University Press, 2015.

Mahn, Jason A. *Fortunate Fallibility: Kierkegaard and the Power of Sin*. Oxford: Oxford University Press, 2011.

Miles, Thomas P. *Kierkegaard and Nietzsche on the Best Way of Life: A New Method of Ethics*. New York: Palgrave Macmillan, 2013.

Oughourlian, Jean-Michel. *The Genesis of Desire*. Translated by Eugene Webb. East Lansing: Michigan State University Press, 2010.

Scott, James C. *Weapons of the Weak: Everyday Forms of Peasant Resistance*. New Haven: Yale University Press, 1987.

Simpson, Christopher Ben. *The Truth Is the Way: Kierkegaard's* Theologia Viatorum. Eugene, OR: Cascade, 2011.

Spade, Dean. *Normal Life: Administrative Violence, Critical Trans Politics, and the Limits of Law*. Durham: Duke University, 2015.

Wallace, David Foster. *This Is Water*. New York: Little, Brown, 2009.

Yancey, Philip. *Disappointment with God*. Grand Rapids: Zondervan, 1997.

Žižek, Slavoj. *The Sublime Object of Ideology*. London: Verso, 2008.

PART 5

Kierkegaard and the Politics of Communication

20

Kierkegaard's *Dagdriver*

Loafing as a Means of Resistance to the Technological, Media, and Consumer System

BARTHOLOMEW RYAN

> Ah, where have they gone, the amblers of yesteryear? Where have they gone, those loafing heroes of folk song, those vagabonds who roam from one mill to another and bed down under the stars? Have they vanished along with footpaths, with grasslands and clearings, with nature?
>
> —MILAN KUNDERA, *SLOWNESS*

> His imagination was so creative that a little went a long way. Outside the one window in the living room grew approximately ten blades of grass. Here he sometimes discovered a little creature running among the stems. These stems became an enormous forest that still had the compactness and darkness the grass had. Instead of the filled space, he now had empty space; he stared again but saw nothing except the enormous expanse.
>
> —JOHANNES CLIMACUS

THIS IS AN ESSAY about Kierkegaard's *Dagdriver* which is the figure of the loafer that may well be one of the last means of resistance to the technological, media and consumer system which shapes the contemporary sociopolitical world. Over the last two decades there has been a surge in the number of articles and books linking Kierkegaard to the political.[1] This is no surprise given that some of the more radical modern thinkers

---

1. See O'Neill Burns, *Kierkegaard and the Matter of Philosophy*; Wennerscheid and Avanessian,

reflecting on and attempting to transform the political sphere have noted Kierkegaard as a vital inspiration and influence—ranging from extreme Right to Left which is most explicit in figures such as Carl Schmitt and Georg Lukács. The recent interest in linking Kierkegaard with the political also becomes easier to understand when, for example, one reads again his literary review of 1846[2] where Kierkegaard brilliantly articulated aspects of what has now become an accepted contemporary global economic, sociopolitical and media landscape, or when one simply delves deeper into his labyrinthine authorship whose primary objective is to unsettle the reader and propel him or her into action.[3] But what has largely gone unnoticed is the motif of the *Dagdriver* or *Lediggænger* that is at the heart of Kierkegaard's polemical and poetic thought. These somewhat archaic terms, translated into English as "loafer" and "idler," offer a way to endure and observe critically the rapidly transforming technologies, the consumer system and vapid information overload of modern society. I will show where and what a loafer is in Kierkegaard's authorship as well as being a motif for the imagination and opening a path to spiritual wisdom.

Elsewhere, I have explored what I called Kierkegaard's "indirect politics."[4] My argument was that indirect politics operated in a twofold way: first, Kierkegaard's task is to unsettle the reader by providing various masks and perspectives and through the quasi-political prototypes of Socrates and Christ—whose engaged lives remain an offense to both ancient and contemporary societies; and, second, it is clear that Kierkegaard's thought, styles and perspectives have been appropriated by twentieth-century radical political thinkers such as Lukács, Schmitt, Benjamin and Adorno. What manifested as explicit political theorizations in those thinkers was already latent in Kierkegaard, and their ideas and political critiques would not have manifested in quite the way they did had they not been exposed to his thought.

Edward Clarke has recently explored the ways in which the act of reading a poem is a return to slowness and indolence that actually increases application to a task by allowing for more imaginative possibilities and inventiveness. He accepts and celebrates this "industrious indolence and indolent industry" as oxymoronic because, at the same time, "slowness does not preclude work, but finds for us our work."[5] Clarke explains: "Like a loafing figure by the roadside, a poem can waylay each of us on the

---

ed. *Kierkegaard and Political Theory*; Ryan, *Kierkegaard's Indirect Politics*; Stocker, *Kierkegaard on Politics*; Boer, "Totality of Ruins," 1–30; Smith, *Friendship and the Political*; Backhouse, *Kierkegaard's Critique of Christian Nationalism*; Assiter, *Kierkegaard, Metaphysics and Political Theory*; Perkins, "Kierkegaard's Anti-Climacus," 274–302; Dooley, *Politics of Exodus*; Nagy, "Abraham the Communist," 196–220.

2. Kierkegaard, *Two Ages*.

3. Halfway through *Concluding Unscientific Postscript*, Kierkegaard's Johannes Climacus states that "the most one person can do for another is to unsettle him." See Kierkegaard, *Concluding Unscientific Postscript*, 387 / SKS7, 352. SKS refers to the Danish edition of the collected works of Kierkegaard (*Søren Kierkegaard Skrifter*, vols. 1–28).

4. See my book *Kierkegaard's Indirect Politics*.

5. Clarke, *Vagabond Spirit of Poetry*, 12.

road to business in town, it can take us out of our worldly concerns for a spell, in order to return us to our path, refreshed to notice new things, to deal differently with others in the world."[6] Analogously, in this essay, I want to rediscover the loafing figure in philosophy which is central to understanding Kierkegaard's polemics and sociopolitical gesture. Kierkegaard wrote that "life is like a poet and thus different from the contemplator, who always comes to a finish; the poet wrenches us out into the middle of life."[7] Through Kierkegaard's *Dagdriver*, the philosopher can again wrench us back out into the middle of life.

Where Is the *Dagdriver*?

Kierkegaard only explicitly uses the actual word *Dagdriver* twice in his entire authorship. The word first appeared when Johannes Climacus is describing Socrates in *Concluding Unscientific Postscript*:

> As is known, Socrates was a loafer [*Dagdriver*] who cared for neither world history nor astronomy (he gave it up, according to Diogenes, and when he later stood still and gazed into space, I cannot simply assume, yet without otherwise deciding what he was doing, that he was stargazing).[8]

And the second time is when Kierkegaard is looking back in his "report to history" (*Point of View*) in describing his pose and performance to the Copenhagen public:

> I was a street-corner loafer [*Dagdriver*], an idler [*Lediggænger*], a flâneur, a frivolous bird, a good, perhaps even brilliant pate [*Hoved*], witty, etc.—but I completely lacked "seriousness" [*Alvor*]. I represented the worldly mentality's irony, the enjoyment of life—the most sophisticated enjoyment of life—but of "seriousness and positivity" there was not a trace; I was, however, tremendously interesting and pungent.[9]

Loafing as a verb (*at dage*) turns up in those crucial semi-autobiographical passages of *Concluding Unscientific Postscript* where the indolent Climacus has to loaf before discovering and laying down his manifesto of "making difficulties everywhere."[10]

> I read a great deal, spent the rest of the day loafing and thinking, or thinking and loafing, but nothing came of it. The productive sprout in me went for everyday use and was consumed in its first greening. An inexplicable power of

---

6. Ibid., 11.
7. Kierkegaard, *Upbuilding Discourses*, 73 / SKS8, 180.
8. Kierkegaard, *Concluding Unscientific Postscript*, 83 / SKS7, 81.
9. Kierkegaard, *Point of View*, 61 / SKS16, 42.
10. Kierkegaard, *Concluding Unscientific Postscript*, 188 / SKS7, 172.

persuasion, both strong and cunning, continually constrained me, captivated by its persuasion. This power was my indolence.[11]

What is essential here is the line that comes after the oft-quoted declaration of "making difficulties everywhere" in that he reveals: "It was especially striking to me that I might actually have my indolence [*Indolents*] to thank that this task became mine."

The other word which is translated as loafer is the *Lediggænger*—another evocative word literally meaning "light walker." Inserted in the preface to *Philosophical Fragments*, Climacus writes: "The accomplishment is, however, in proportion to my talents, for I do not, like that noble Roman, refrain from serving the system *merito magis quam ignavia* [from justifiable motifs rather than from indolence], but I am a loafer [*Lediggænger*] out of indolence *ex animi sententia* [by inclination] and for good reasons."[12] Indolence (*Mageligbed* in Danish above, but Climacus later uses the word *Indolents*), derived from the Latin, is freedom from pain (*In-dolentia*) and is a state of repose for many rambling poets. While Climacus declares himself to be indolent and Kierkegaard masks himself as a *Dagdriver*, they are both ceaselessly working. Their vocation fits well with Clarke's oxymoronic state of "industrious indolence and indolent industry."[13] Kierkegaard and his pseudonyms serve no system, or they serve it by being the indolent "gadfly" [*Bremse*]. As Climacus wickedly declared: "This power was my indolence [*min Indolents*]."[14]

Kierkegaard's art of loafing is in seeing the "insignificant" things or ruins of history, evoked by showing the parallel journeys of the poet and the naturalist in one of Kierkegaard's more impenetrable texts "Guilty / Not Guilty" which lies deep inside *Stages in Life's Way*, and where the narrator in question (Quidam) writes (also revealing the expansiveness of the imagination): "When I was a child, a little pond in a peat excavation was everything to me. The dark tree roots that poked out here and there in the murky darkness were vanished kingdoms and countries, each one a discovery as important to me as antediluvian discoveries to the natural scientist."[15]

And finally, we can find the call to slowness and the *Dagdriver*'s slow reading all over Kierkegaard's authorship, especially made explicit in his prefaces to both the pseudonymous works and upbuilding discourses. One can find examples in many of his prefaces to his books in his approach to attunement [*Stemning*],[16] tuning up [*at stemme*], and hearing the voice [*Stemme*]: in the preface to a book called *Prefaces*, the author states, "The preface is a mood [*Stemning*]. Writing a preface is like sharpening

---

11. Ibid., 187 / SKS7, 172.
12. Kierkegaard, *Philosophical Fragments*, 5 / SKS4, 215.
13. Clarke, *Vagabond Spirit of Poetry*, 12.
14. Kierkegaard, *Concluding Unscientific Postscript*, 186 / SKS7, 171.
15. Kierkegaard, *Stages on Life's Way*, 363 / SKC6, 338.
16. *Stemning* is a word which would later be made famous in philosophy through Heidegger in the German *Stimmung*, in *Being and Time* in his long journey in slow thinking. See Heidegger, *Being and Time*, 172–79 [H. 134–39]; 388–96 [H. 339–46].

a scythe, like tuning [*at stemme*] a guitar, like talking with a child, like spitting out of the window"; or in the note to the reader from any of the prefaces to the *Eighteen Upbuilding Discourses*. Here is one example: Kierkegaard imagines his discourses finding their way to that singular reader:

> I saw how it wended its way down solitary paths or walked solitary on public roads. After a few mistakes, through being deceived by a fleeting resemblance, it finally met that single individual whom I with joy and gratitude call *my* reader, that single individual it is seeking, to whom, so to speak, it stretches out it arms, that single individual who is favourably enough disposed to receive it, whether at the time of the encounter it finds him cheerful and confident or "weary and pensive." . . . It stood there like a humble little flower under the cover of the great forest.[17]

These minor appearances, some of which are more explicit than others but which are all interrelated, are crucial in thinking about Kierkegaard's indirect politics. They encompass this *Dagdriver* under three principal aspects: as polemical stargazer and saunterer; as philosopher of the interlude; and as a call of the incognito in figures such as Don Quixote, Socrates, Christ and "the real poets."[18]

The Polemical Stargazer, Saunterer and Flâneur

Kierkegaard's *Dagdriver* as an indolent, polemical stargazer and saunterer is made quite clear when Climacus defines his hero Socrates as a loafer gazing into space, as well as being well known for walking around the city of Athens prodding its citizens out of their comfort zone. Later in *Christian Discourses*, published in the revolutionary year of 1848, Kierkegaard's single individual, now matured into a Socratic-Christlike citizen, is presented as the apparently absentminded figure without a home who offers discourses to free the reader from the worries or cares [*Bykymringer*] of human existence for "tomorrow." We find the polemical stargazer and saunterer most clearly in his little masterpiece on "The Lily in the Field and the Bird of the Air" published in 1849,[19] which emerges from Kierkegaard's many walks, and which, to overcome the anxiety of temporality—that of the future and of the past, focuses on silence, obedience and joy to exist for today. This discourse brilliantly combines the loafer's vocation which is an acute critique of society as well as offering profound help to living joyfully. As stargazer, Kierkegaard looks to the bird of the air; and as saunterer, he looks to the lily of the field. In a brilliant new introduction to the discourse, Bruce Kirmmse compares Kierkegaard with Henry David Thoreau in their love of walking, and quotes a passage

---

17. Kierkegaard, *Eighteen Upbuilding Discourses*, 5 / SKS5, 13.
18. On this term "the real poet," see Kierkegaard, *Sickness Unto Death*, 72 / SKS11, 186.
19. This discourse is to be found in Kierkegaard's volume *Without Authority*.

from Thoreau on the etymology of the word sauntering.[20] Thoreau playfully imagines it as *sans terre*—without land or home, but at the same time it is the urge to be at home everywhere. This reminds us of Novalis's description of philosophy as being at home everywhere.[21] This combination of stargazer and saunterer encapsulates the figure of the loafer in Socrates and Kierkegaard. It might be hard to believe now that once upon a time Lukács called Kierkegaard a troubadour,[22] but here he understood the loafing aspect of Kierkegaard—that of the restless, mischievous, absentminded poet but also the uncompromising critic of sociopolitical society. Though the journey requires patience, endurance and work, I consider texts such as *Fear and Trembling*, *Concluding Unscientific Postscript*, and *Christian Discourses* as part of Socrates's stargazing and sauntering and giving the reader the polemical tools to prod both the individual and societies out of defeatist complacency.

Kierkegaard's *Dagdriver* continues a tradition that questions a society whose values are skewed in a way that does not value slowness and nonlinear thinking. Of course, the long tradition of the loafer as stargazers, troubadours, and polemical gadflies is mostly evident in the poets and writers, and many of the characters created within texts. The obvious nineteenth-century authors are in the pose of the French urban flâneurs, exemplified most of all in Baudelaire. Here is a city traveler creating a new kind of literature in fusing the sacred and the profane in an interior journey alongside the vision and external presence of the festering rise of the bourgeoisie, metropolis, and modernism. Walter Benjamin's dialectic of the flâneur can be ascribed to Kierkegaard, which is, "on the one side, the man who feels himself viewed by all and sundry as a true suspect and, on the other, the man who is utterly undiscoverable, the hidden man."[23] Baudelaire brings all the monsters and demons down to the ground whether this be in the form of the albatross or Satan, mutating their cracked aspirations into the modern human condition. Baudelaire and Paris (the quintessential city of the flâneur)[24] become the center of Benjamin's obsession in the last decade of his life, as he gathers quotations, sound-bites, images, architectural ideas, Marxist insights and theological fragments into his unfinished *Arcades Project*. After all, the flâneur is in the category of omniscient seeing, the observer of the marketplace, and Copenhagen, as "market harbor" [København-havn], is perfect for Kierkegaard's *Dagdriver*. Baudelaire's poetic experience and Benjamin's projects are a prophetic rebellious act of combating our own contemporary society where everything is entering our own living rooms through the information age. In a memorable passage, Climacus reveals his early education in flâneuring and the flowering of the

20. Kirmmse, "Introduction," xvi.
21. "Philosophie ist eigentlich Heimweh-Trieb überall zu Hause zu sein [Philosophy is really homesickness, an urge to be at home everywhere]." See Novalis, *Philosophical Writings*, 135.
22. Lukács, *Soul and Form*, 35.
23. Benjamin, *Arcades Project*, 420 [M2, 8].
24. Ibid., 417 [M1, 4].

imagination and loafing. His old, strict father takes him on a tour of the city without them ever having to leave the room of the house. It was there where he learned his "father's magic art."[25] After the recollection of his travels with his father around the room, the author in question concludes that Climacus "did not require forests and travels for his adventures but merely what he had: a little room with one window."[26] This is something that does not escape Benjamin who adds it to his section on the "Flâneur" in the sprawling *Arcades Project*.[27]

Across the Atlantic, there are two powerful examples of a more bucolic and cosmic *Dagdriver* from the nineteenth century. As the industrial age takes off, two of America's most celebrated loafers emerge out of the ultimate consumer society. They are Walt Whitman and Herman Melville. Whitman begins the first edition of *Leaves of Grass* (1855) in his opening poem "Song of Myself" with the words "I loafe and invite my soul, / I lean and loafe at my ease observing a spear of summer grass";[28] and Melville starts *Moby Dick* with the enigmatic narrator as an idler wandering the streets that lead him to jump on the doomed boat the Pequod to begin the hunt for that elusive whale. Later, Melville creates a most unsettling and darkly comic loafer in Bartleby, the Scrivener. It is no accident that the literary figure of Bartleby has had an important role in shaping political theology today, most notably in the work of Agamben, Deleuze, Negri, Hardt, and Žižek.[29] Whitman and Melville, as contemporaries of Kierkegaard, are loafers on the epic scale who open up vistas for the wandering spirit, providing a riposte to the busyness of the age, and remind us of the portals of discovery that await us when we learn again to slow down. How far we have fallen in our advanced, sped-up age! The rampant consumerism that figures so prominently in our contemporary societies tends to give little space now to the formative poetic visions of such loafers as Melville or Whitman.

Like these American writers, Kierkegaard's loafer is never at rest, observing society and the human self from various critical perspectives, unsettling the reader in startling books that defy fixed definition. The loafer is never bored; boredom comes from forgetting the power of the imagination. Finding relief from boredom is the great trick of advanced capitalism where we endure a putrid stream of messages demanding that we purchase entertainment.[30] Thus, loafing can be an affirmative defiance of

---

25. Kierkegaard, *Philosophical Fragments*, 120 / SKS15, 19.

26. Ibid., 124 / SKS15, 22.

27. Benjamin, *Arcades Project*, 421 [M2a, 2].

28. Whitman, *Complete Poetry*, 188.

29. See, e.g., Giorgio Agamben's *Homo Sacer: Sovereign Power and Bare Life*, 48; Agamben, "Bartleby, or On Contingency," 243–71; Gilles Deleuze, "Bartleby; Or, the Formula," 68–90; Hardt and Negri, *Empire*, 203–4; and Žižek, *The Parallax View*, 381–85.

30. On analyzing advanced capitalism, consumerism, purchasing entertainment, and what Adorno calls "the culture industry," see, e.g., some formative works such as Veblen's *Theory of the Leisure Class* (1899); Simmel's *Philosophy of Money* (1900); and Adorno's chapter "The Culture Industry: Enlightenment as Mass Deception," in *Dialectic of Enlightenment* (1944).

the encroachments of the technological system and information age that convinces most of us to purchase things we do not need, and keeps us busy and distracted with the "demand of the times,"[31] and throwing us ready-made packages for our time off. Kierkegaard's loafer is of course ironic, humorous and often masked—exemplified in Johannes Climacus. Leisure has fallen into an entertainment industry, and so Kierkegaard, long before Adorno, joins the entertainment industry in his own startling way in the wake of German Idealism and the birth of modern democracy to make difficulties everywhere, creating multiple perspectives, analyzing despair and anxiety as we march toward death, and, while always aiming to write beautiful works, never making life easy for the reader.

More than ever before, in a time where immediacy, connectivity, and all-consuming online communication is now *society* itself, the figure of the loafer, not unlike the work of Benjamin (most brilliantly depicted in *One Way Street*, *The Origin of German Tragic Drama*, and *The Arcades Project*) and Adorno (see especially *Minima Moralia*), looks to the ruins of history and "lesser things."[32] This may provide a clue to why Kierkegaard refers to himself in his journals as being like a bad banknote, having been born in a bad fiscal year;[33] or that Johannes de Silentio begins and ends *Fear and Trembling* with reference to the state of the European economy and comparing it to the poor state of the world of ideas, before beginning on his "lesser" task of trying to understand the story of Abraham, faith, and a teleological suspension of the ethical. And later, when Kierkegaard writes a letter in 1848 that "politics is not for me," he turns this statement around on its head in his trademark ironic and deceptive way by telling us in the same letter what two things do appeal to him that lead us to encounter the same thing—focusing on lesser things and walking: "Politics is too much for me. I love to focus my attention on lesser things, in which one may sometimes encounter exactly the same. . . . I who do not understand politics, do, on the other hand, understand all about walking."[34] As a stargazer and a saunterer, the deceptive loafer does not forget Anti-Climacus's key words that "the condition of man, regarded as 'spirit' . . . is always critical."[35]

Philosopher of the Interlude (*Mellemspil*)

Kierkegaard's place in philosophy is as a philosopher of the interlude, or, as the word is called in Danish, the *Mellemspil*. What indeed is this *Mellemspil*? Another slippery

---

31. This is a sarcastic expression used by Johannes Climacus frequently throughout *Concluding Unscientific Postscript*.

32. For further study linking Kierkegaard and Adorno via the "ruin," see Roland Boer's "A Totality of Ruins: Adorno on Kierkegaard," 1–30.

33. Kierkegaard, *Journals and Papers*, 6:5725 (V A 3 n.d. 1844).

34. Kierkegaard, *Letters and Documents*, 253–55 / SKS28, 392.

35. Kierkegaard, *Sickness Unto Death*, 25 / SKS11, 141.

term, it is, literally, the time and space between the play, that "light entertainment" between the serious stuff. This is the space (on a street corner) and time (slowness) for the *Dagdriver* to exist amid the world of busyness, politics and being encapsulated in a system that bombards us with how we should exist. Of course, this "light entertainment" is actually Kierkegaard's indirect politics and assault on abstracting and alienating the individual from his or herself and the relationship with the world that he or she lives in. Kierkegaard uses a line from Shakespeare for the epigraph of *The Point of View*—"In everything the purpose must be placed on the scale with the folly"[36]—to express the madness with the necessity of his task, in creating an authorship that is the refusal of fixed disciplinary boundaries. Perhaps the whole point of borrowing from various disciplines is not to maintain the integrity of each, but precisely to dissolve the boundaries, and to develop an entirely new framework within which to rethink the act of political praxis. Indirect politics is the interlude, as a set of masks that continually displaces disciplinary identity from one field to the next just as the moment seems clear: theology masks politics, law masks theology, political theory masks philosophy, and psychology masks literary critical approaches. Kierkegaard makes a radical step in confronting the sociopolitical and technological world, for even though the philosopher's primary goal is to meditate on the question of truth, Kierkegaard makes this journey through lies and deception in his typical paradoxical fashion, with his famous pseudonyms or masks as the loafing, incognito philosopher. This is the modern human condition where the self becomes not only a construction but a plurality, and so, as societies are splintered, uniformed, multicultural, conflicting, diffuse; so is the person's selfhood—if there is one to be found—plural, multiplied, dispersed.

The *Dagdriver's Mellemspil* turns up in many key places in Kierkegaard's authorship, most obviously in the prefaces, epigraphs, interrupting quasi-autobiographical stories within the larger works, and the chapter itself called *Mellemspil* between the ultimate and penultimate chapter of *Philosophical Fragments*. I will start with *Fear and Trembling* as an interlude to the system and exercise in street-corner loafing and slowness. One need not go very far at all to see the *Dagdriver's Mellemspil* at work. The book's title is a riddle, paradox, and perfect example of the interlude as a refusal of fixed disciplinary boundaries. It is called *Fear and Trembling*—indicating a religiosity in quoting St. Paul's Letter to the Philippians; its subtitle is *Dialectical Lyric*—expressing both philosophy and poetry; and its author is Johannes de Silentio—indicating secret, mask, other voice, silence. With the book's epigraph, it begins like a fairytale,[37] offering a secret, a message within a message, an incognito, and, of course, the famous indirect communication. The epigraph is borrowed from Johan Georg Hamann, called "the Magus of the North" in his day, who was a minor philosopher of the interlude, whose equally minor text *Socratic Memorabilia* (1759) caused only a tiny ripple in German

---

36. Kierkegaard, *Point of View*, 22 / SKS16, 8.

37. I have developed elsewhere the presence of the fairytale in Kierkegaard's writings: see Ryan, "Kierkegaard's Fairytale," 3–4.

philosophy, and whose linguistic play, use of the fragment, proponent of Socrates and Shakespeare over German philosophy, and advocate of radical Christian existence was an inspiration to Kierkegaard. Then we enter *Fear and Trembling*'s Preface, where the author in question describes himself as the *Extra-Skriver*—literally "extra-writer" (translated as "supplementary clerk" [Hong] and "freelancer" [Hannay])—who "neither writes the system nor gives promises of the system"[38] and whose first sentence of both the preface and epilogue of the book allude to the business world and economics, a world of speed, capital and consumerism. While everyone it seems is encouraging us "to go further"—from philosopher to business man, Johannes de Silentio is calling the reader to slow down for a moment, to meditate, in this particular book, on the madness and impossibility of understanding faith. Christian existence and belief has always been something of a struggle, of difficulty and slowness for Kierkegaard, whether he says it through de Silentio ("Faith was then a task for a whole lifetime")[39] or Climacus: "To pray is just as difficult as to play the role of Hamlet; of which the greatest actor is supposed to have said that only once had he been close to playing it well; nevertheless he would devote all his ability and his entire life to the continued study of this role."[40]

A disruptive strategy of Kierkegaard in the face of political and philosophical expression comes also in the form of his storytelling interludes. The reader experiences this throughout *Fear and Trembling*, beginning with the four different readings of the story of Abraham which begins again with a fairytale opening of "Once upon a time" [*Der var engang*]. It is up to the reader as much as it is to the author which reading may be best, the section is after all called a *Stemning*, an attunement. Johannes de Silentio never really gets started as he keeps faltering before the problem of faith, and, like Beckett after him, would rather "fail again, fail better."[41] The third and final "Problemata" of the book becomes the most complex as the enigmatic author weaves in different stories and subtexts, with the indirect politics rearing its head now and then with incursions such as one startling declaration made that the opening lines from a particular history play from Shakespeare has "more value than all the systems of morality."[42]

The incendiary and symbolic year of 1848 transformed the political landscape forever in Europe. This was the famous year that Marx's *Communist Manifesto* was published and where bourgeois and working-class uprisings occurred all over Europe. It is also the year that Kierkegaard quietly published *Christian Discourses* under his own name, and completed, if not most of each text, *The Point of View*, *Armed Neutrality*, *The Sickness Unto Death*, *Practice in Christianity*, *Two Ethical-Religious Essays*, and

38. Kierkegaard, *Fear and Trembling*, 7 / SKS4, 103.
39. Ibid. / SKS4, 102.
40. Kierkegaard, *Concluding Unscientific Postscript*, 163 / SKS7, 151.
41. Beckett, *Nohow On*, 89.
42. Kierkegaard, *Fear and Trembling*, 105 / SKS4, 194.

parts of *The Book of Adler*. It was also the year of his most jubilant shorter pieces, in which he published the essay "The Crisis and a Crisis in the Life of an Actress" and began the first draft of "The Lily in the Field and the Bird of the Air" discourse. These latter two pieces are good examples of the *Mellemspil* and exercises in slowness and indirect politics in the face of political chatter, mass movements, busyness and the anxiety of the modern human condition. Central to the discourse on the lily and the bird is the emphasis on joy [*Glæde*] and being "present to oneself"[43]—the emphasis on *being* rather than *doing* and on *now, today* rather than tomorrow or yesterday—difficult tasks indeed for the industrious loafer; while in the essay on the actress, the emphasis is on transformative process as the key to the success of the artist. The author of the essay on the actress is the last of Kierkegaard's more aesthetic pseudonyms in the strict sense and is even called "Inter et Inter"—literally "between and between," representing the *Mellemspil* between the publication of *Christian Discourses* and "The Lily in the Field and the Bird of the Air" discourse, and which begins with a critical remark on the demand of the crowd in the "newspaper critics" that "is dreadfully shabby"[44] and "half-witted reviewers."[45] As an explicit interlude, the author follows a certain actress providing an exception to the rule, embodying the beautiful outsider who rises to the top of Danish cultural life, the woman whose name changes, continuing to be a master of her craft, and who conquers time in playing Shakespeare's Juliet a second time in her thirties with greater power, through the transformative process and through repetition (unlike the failed ventures of Constantin Constantius and his more dubious political followers such as Carl Schmitt).[46]

Concluding Unscientific Postscript is the great philosophical text of loafing: dealing with "lesser things," digressions, daydreaming walks in the graveyard, with sharp philosophical acumen and sometimes very self-conscious poetic writing. It is a six-hundred-page "postscript" (*Efterskrift*) to a one-hundred-page thought piece called literally "Philosophical Crumbs" (*Smuler*), a book that rambles on and on as an act of rebellion against academic and conceited philosophy. It is ironic, humorous and passionate, and deceptive and full of masks, and is summed up as "superfluous"[47] long after the declared task in the first half of the book had been to "make difficulties everywhere." And just when the reader thinks that Climacus is getting down to the actual business of philosophy in the well-known section on "Truth Is Subjectivity," he follows

---

43. Kierkegaard, *Without Authority*, 39 / SKS11, 43: "What is joy, or what is it to be joyful? It is truly to be present to oneself, but truly to be present to oneself is this *today*, this *to be* today, truly *to be today*."

44. Kierkegaard, *Christian Discourses*, 303 / SKS14, 93.

45. Ibid., 305 / SKS14, 94.

46. See the concluding paragraph of the first chapter Carl Schmitt's *Political Theology* where he quotes from the end of *Repetition*. Without mentioning the writer by name, Schmitt refers to Kierkegaard as "a Protestant theologian who demonstrated the vital intensity possible in theological reflection in the nineteenth century." Schmitt, *Political Theology*, 15.

47. Kierkegaard, *Concluding Unscientific Postscript*, 618 / SKS7, 561.

it with a great perplexing interlude called "A Glance at a Contemporary Effort in Danish Literature" where he proceeds to analyze and critique all of Kierkegaard's pseudonymous works published up to that point. Critique, however, is not abandonment; rather critique is the possibility of continuing philosophy.[48] Kierkegaard's appendix of sorts which repeats the question throughout the chapter—"What happens?"—is a serious joke indeed, but essential as yet another way to combating and dodging the nets of the all-pervasive political and economic society we live in today by getting in there before the "half-witted reviewers," and opening up the horizon for future philosophers of suspicion such as Nietzsche, Lukács, Adorno, and Derrida. It is a process of self-critique, self-overcoming, and "emptying out" [*at udtømme*],[49] to use Kierkegaard's expression. For Derrida, *Concluding Unscientific Postscript* is a text that is a marvelous performance that literally postfaces, postscripts, or concludes (or all three) a fragment (*Philosophical Fragments*). In this crucial passage by Derrida which attempts to explain dissemination and describing *Concluding Unscientific Postscript*, which is inserted, significantly, as a footnote, Derrida writes: "One is also in fact starting over again, adding an extra text, complicating the scene, opening up within the labyrinth a supplementary digression, which is also a false mirror that pushes the labyrinth's infinity back forever in mimed—that is, endless—speculation."[50] Even in the later, more concise text *The Sickness Unto Death*, Anti-Climacus immediately places it at the *Mellemspil* in the opening sentence, refusing to be caught in the nets of clear definitions and boundaries: "Many may find the form of this 'exposition' strange; it may seem to them too rigorous to be upbuilding and too upbuilding to be rigorously scholarly."[51] Kierkegaard's indirect politics and *Dagdriver* creates a *Mellemspil* within the political sphere that the ruling powers have trouble pinning down or controlling because it is brought forward by the *Dagdriver* who, like de Silentio's Abraham, is an "emigrant from the sphere of the universal,"[52] and remains a thorn to the establishment.

The Incognito: Don Quixote, Socrates, Christ, and "the Real Poets"

Climacus provocatively states in *Concluding Unscientific Postscript*: "Between poetry and religiousness, worldly wisdom about life performs its vaudeville. Every individual who does not live either poetically or religiously is obtuse [*Dum*]." He continues by explaining that those in the "vaudeville" have "lost the poetic illusion" and do not have enough "imagination-passion." I see the prevailing indolent prototypes

---

48. This is something that Adorno and Horkheimer make clear in the preface to the 1969 edition to *Dialectic of Enlightenment*: "As a critique of philosophy it does not seek to abandon philosophy itself." Adorno and Horkheimer, *Dialectic of Enlightenment*, xii.
49. Kierkegaard, *Point of View*, 86 / SKS16, 65.
50. Derrida, *Dissemination*, 27.
51. Kierkegaard, *Sickness Unto Death*, 5 / SKS11, 117.
52. Kierkegaard, *Fear and Trembling*, 115 / SKS4, 204.

for Kierkegaard in four disparate figures: Don Quixote, Socrates, Christ, and Shakespeare. As deranged knight, philosopher, messiah, and poet, respectively, they are all united in having not only the poetic illusion and imagination-passion but revel in the mask, concealment, and the incognito, and disturb the political, social, and economic order of things. As Adorno and Horkheimer's culture industry is "enlightenment as mass deception,"[53] Kierkegaard combats this deception by making space for the *Dagdriver* in his unrecognizables, his incognitos, his spies. Anti-Climacus defines this unrecognizability as "not to be in the character of what one essentially is—for example, when a policeman is in plain clothes."[54] This unrecognizability is "an omnipotently maintained incognito."[55]

Starting with the fictional figure of Don Quixote: the world's most famous knight errant was not really a knight errant at all but rather a Hidalgo whose name was actually Alonso Quixano, an avid reader of books of chivalry and man of mad faith who believed in the impossible, and who quickly was out of sync with his times. Cervantes diagnoses Quixote as "a streaky madness, filled with lucid intervals [*lúcidos intervalos*]."[56] This is a reference to the medieval expression the *lucida intervalla*, which are periods of temporary sanity amid bouts of insanity. Note then that by putting his philosophy at the interlude, the ironic Kierkegaard is mocking thought outside the interlude, and it is not a coincidence that he calls his journal his *lucida intervalla*.[57] It is no wonder that Miguel de Unamuno, greatly inspired by Kierkegaard, uses Don Quixote as the prototype for his tragic philosophy. So enthralled with the character and the story, Kierkegaard even suggested a corrective to Cervantes's masterpiece, revealing also the eternal movement and unfinished wanderings at the heart of Quixote's and Kierkegaard's mad quest:

> It is a sad mistake by Cervantes to make Don Quixote sensible and then to let him die. Cervantes, who himself had the superb idea of having him become a shepherd! It ought to have ended there. That is, Don Quixote should not come to an end; he ought to be presented as going full speed, so that he opens vistas upon an infinite series of new fixed ideas. Don Quixote is endlessly perfectible in madness, but the one thing he cannot become (for otherwise he could become everything and anything) is sensible. Cervantes seems not to have been dialectical enough to bring it to this romantic conclusion (that there is no conclusion).[58]

53. Adorno and Horkheimer, *Dialectic of Enlightenment*, 95–136.

54. Kierkegaard, *Practice in Christianity*, 127 / SKS12, 132.

55. Ibid., 132 / SKS12, 142.

56. Cervantes, *Don Quixote*, second part, ch. 18, 571. For more on the *lucida intervalla* in Kierkegaard and Cervantes, see also Ziolkowski, *Literary Kierkegaard*, 143–45, and Ziolkowski, "Kierkegaard's Subterranean Fluvial Pseudonymity," 288.

57. My thanks to Eric Ziolkowski on notifying me of the medieval usage of this term. For more on reading Kierkegaard's journals as *lucida intervalla*, see Pap. 39 II A 576 / SKS18, 63.

58. Kierkegaard, Pap. VIII I A 59, 1847.

PART 5: KIERKEGAARD AND THE POLITICS OF COMMUNICATION

There is something inconclusive about Kierkegaard's own quixotic quests of *Concluding Unscientific Postscript* and *Fear and Trembling*, in that when it comes to faith, one is never in fact finished, and these books that tackle the elusive issue of faith are forever faltering in the ceaseless, existential journey. It also makes sense that Lukács, soon to make a Kierkegaardian leap into Bolshevism,[59] read Quixote in the following way, while still under the spell of Kierkegaard: "Don Quixote is the first great battle of interiority [*Innerlichkeit*] against the prosaic vulgarity of outward life, and the only battle in which interiority succeeded."[60] Kierkegaard's inwardness would soon become Lukács's expression for revolutionary praxis.

Kierkegaard, as the masked *Dagdriver*, is also forever caught in a *Mellemspil*—in conflict between aesthetic and religious pursuits. Halfway through *The Sickness Unto Death*, there appears a *Mellemspil* in the tightly focused text where Anti-Climacus seems to be exposing Kierkegaard's predicament as the religious poet:

> His conflict is this: has he been called? Does his thorn in the flesh signify that he is to be used for the extraordinary? Before God, is it entirely in order to be the extraordinary he has become? Or is the thorn in the flesh that under which he must humble himself in order to attain the universally human?—But enough of this. With the accent of truth I may ask: to whom am I speaking?[61]

Here we have the issue of "the call," which only the artists and the religious figures seem to hear. But they come in disguise, "deceiving one to the truth." The "real poets" may be Byron, Shelley, or Shakespeare[62]—three Englishmen whom Vigilius Haufniensis names and whose work is haunted by the demonic (and hence their inclusion in *The Concept of Anxiety*); or, as Anti-Climacus later puts it, "the poets, the real ones, who always lend 'demonic' ideality—using the word in its purely Greek sense—to their creations."[63] These poets are potential *Dagdrivers*, living and creating

---

59. There is the excellent essay on the Lukács-Kierkegaard relationship by András Nagy called "Abraham the Communist." See Nagy, "Abraham the Communist," 196–220.

60. Reflecting on his last great work before the turn to Marxism-Leninism, Lukács wrote in the preface (written over forty years after the first publication of *The Theory of the Novel*): "Kierkegaard always played an important role for the author of *The Theory of the Novel*, who, long before Kierkegaard had become fashionable, wrote an essay on the relationship between his life and thought." See Lukács, *Theory of the Novel*, 18–19.

61. Kierkegaard, *Sickness Unto Death*, 78 / SKS11, 192.

62. Kierkegaard, *Concept of Anxiety*, 131 / SKS4, 147.

63. Kierkegaard, *Sickness Unto Death*, 72 / SKS11, 186. There is a passage by Anaïs Nin which describes well the madness and plurality of the real poet: "I have always been tormented by the image of multiplicity of selves. Some days I call it richness, and other days I see it as a disease, a proliferation as dangerous as cancer. My first concept about people around me was that all of them were coordinated as a whole, whereas I was made up of a multitude of selves, of fragments. I know that I was upset as a child to discover that we only had one life. It seems to me that I wanted to compensate for this by multiplying experience. Or perhaps it always seems like this when you follow all your impulses and they take you in different directions. In any case, when I was happy, always at the beginning of a love, euphoric, I felt I was gifted for living many lives fully.... It was only when I was in trouble, lost in a

the space and time of slowness. But Shakespeare is constant throughout Kierkegaard's authorship, as the ultimate poet. We can apply Shakespeare's expression "God's spies" to the *Dagdriver*. This passage, very close to Kierkegaard's heart, is taken from Lear's famous final speech to his daughter Cordelia, and which Kierkegaard famously inserts in his journal under the heading "Twenty-Five Years Old." Strangely, the lines with "God's spies" are omitted, perhaps he wanted to keep them just to himself. The passage captures the vocation of the loafer in the call to live, pray, sing, tell old tales, and laugh[64] in the face of the "age of disintegration"[65] of political busyness, philosophical and religious mediocrity, and crowd lunacy. Kierkegaard concludes his 1848 journal entry on the "age of disintegration" by saying that he is "hiding for the time being in the cautious incognito of a flâneur."[66] As flâneur, incognito, and "God's spy," and calling his authorship a "godly satire,"[67] the religious and the poetic existence (Whitman, Melville, Baudelaire, Christ) coexist. We may add here a certain kind of philosopher, such as Diogenes, Socrates, and Kierkegaard and his various pseudonyms performing the "godly satire." There is a return to the state of indolent repose in the celebration of joy in the discourse on the lily and the bird as a response to the political upheaval of 1848, but this is only a brief interlude among the striving that is demanded upon the industrious indolent *Dagdriver*, who wanders incognito and whose job it is to unsettle everyone. In the twentieth-century novel *The Razor's Edge*, Somerset Maugham knew well the difficult task, the "joy in suffering" ahead for the supposed street-corner loafer: "D'you remember his saying that he was just going to loaf? If what he tells you is true his loafing seems to involve some very strenuous work."[68]

In forging a Socratic-Christlike citizenship,[69] Kierkegaard presents his two prototypes Socrates and Christ as incognito, communicating indirectly or parabolically, and as such living as loafers. But hiding behind this mask of a bum or loafer is the wisest man in Athens and the Messiah for Christianity. Anti-Climacus's two published texts, *The Sickness Unto Death* and *Practice in Christianity*, are polemical works imbued with sociopolitical ideas that combat "the present age." His small, substantial

---

maze, stifled by complications and paradoxes that I was haunted or that I spoke of my 'madness,' but I mean the madness of the poets." Nin, *Journals*, 1:54. Also, there is an excellent book on the demonic which includes chapters on Kierkegaard and Shakespeare. See Fernie, *The Demonic*.

64. Here is the passage from *King Lear* in full: "So we'll live, / And pray, and sing, and tell old tales, and laugh / At gilded butterflies, and hear poor rogues / Talk of court news, and we'll talk with them too— / Who loses and who wins, who's in, who's out— / And take upon 's the mystery of things / As if we were God's spies. And we'll wear out / In a walled prison packs and sects of great ones / That ebb and flow by the moon." See Shakespeare, *King Lear*, act 5, scene 3, in *Complete Works*, 1108–9.

65. "The age of disintegration" is how Kierkegaard describes Europe in 1848. See *Papers and Journals*, 351 [48 IX B 63: 7].

66. Kierkegaard, *Papers and Journals*, 351 [48 IX B 63: 7].

67. Kierkegaard, *Point of View*, 17 / SKS13, 24.

68. Maugham, *Razor's Edge*, 94.

69. I am following in the tradition here of Dana Villa's *Socratic Citizenship* by including the religious-poetic element of the *Dagdriver* (via prototypes such as Christ and Shakespeare).

essay *A Literary Review* is full of descriptions of "leveling," "the public," "superficiality," and "formlessness," and the triumphant society of chatter and obtuseness and the "demand of the times," anticipating Lukács and Adorno's Kierkegaardian-Marxist diagnosis of reification. In *The Sickness Unto Death*, the author in question calls out for a new Socrates[70] rather than what the times demand—which is a new republic. As the follow-up, *Practice in Christianity*, presents us with "the God-man"—that other prototype and loafer in Christ who, in his various guises, Anti-Climacus is at pains to remind his reader, is a "lowly, destitute man,"[71] who "has no doctrine, no system,"[72] and whose companions are "idle and unemployed people, street loafers [*Gadestrygere*] and tramps [*Landløbere*]."[73] These are the incognitos and unrecognizables that deceive the reader into the truth, the truth being the quest for subjectivity or the expression of inwardness, which leads us back to the beginning to the young Kierkegaard's reflection up in Gilleleje where the truth is that which is the truth for you—a passionate, paradoxical quest to be honest.

The danger here is that there is madness in this kind of truth: the lunacy of Don Quixote and Socrates in the worldly sense, the madness of the poets, and the mad paradox of faith in following Christ and the actions of Abraham. Climacus states in *Concluding Unscientific Postscript* that "in a solely subjective definition of truth, lunacy and truth are ultimately indistinguishable, because they may both have inwardness."[74] But of course the playful Climacus puts in a footnote that even this really is not true because this madness lacks the "inwardness of infinity." We find ourselves again in the *Mellemspil* which Anti-Climacus shows in navigating between losing oneself to infinity (mysticism, intoxicated religiosity) and losing oneself to finitude (reductionist materialism).[75]

It can be a disaster to bring Kierkegaard's thought directly into political thinking, and while we can argue that the author cannot be blamed for a future reader's actions, we can at least accept that Kierkegaard's thought contains a dynamic indirect call for sociopolitical action. Climacus repeats the task of the religious discourse to "venture everything,"[76] while always at pains to remain free of being pinned down. Kierkegaard's Climacus is not a religious believer and illustrates why we should always make the distinction between the religious and political discourse. Yet staying true to "making difficulties everywhere," the incendiary essay on the present age is published under his own name in the same year as *Concluding Unscientific Postscript*, showing Kierkegaard, the *Extra-Skriver*, to always be moving between

---

70. Kierkegaard, *Sickness Unto Death*, 92 / SKS11, 205.
71. Kierkegaard, *Practice in Christianity*, 37 / SKS12, 51.
72. Ibid., 48 / SKS12, 61.
73. Ibid., 50 / SKS12, 63.
74. Kierkegaard, *Concluding Unscientific Postscript*, 194 / SKS7, 142.
75. Kierkegaard, *Sickness Unto Death*, 30–35 / SKS11, 146–51.
76. Kierkegaard, *Concluding Unscientific Postscript*, 427 / SKS7, 389.

writing as a journalist, aesthete, philosopher, moralist, and as one writing in the face of God. We can see him anticipating and navigating routes that we can reconstruct now as we look for ways to withstand the clutches of Adorno's "culture industry"[77] and today's information age, ways of life and thought performed in the guise of the ever mischievous, multilayered *Dagdriver*.

Conclusion

As the industrious idler, Kierkegaard sparked revolutionary praxis in Lukács, inspired the theory of the exception in Schmitt, shed light on the repressed aspects and ruins of human history that were later evoked in the life and work of Benjamin, and laid some of the foundations for Adorno's negative dialectic. By the time Lukács finds his system in Bolshevism and Schmitt commits to Nazism, there is no longer any space for "indirect politics" and the *Dagdriver*. In his last years, Kierkegaard may have discarded some of his ambiguity and pseudonyms, yet there remains an abundance of wit, sarcasm, and innuendo within the installments of *The Moment* to disrupt any political theology, and the writings of the loafers in the pseudonymous works and religious discourses continue to haunt the theological, political, and philosophical landscape. Like the increasingly dispersed thought of Benjamin, Adorno and others surviving at the edge of the system, Kierkegaard's authorship is a continuous unpeeling of the self, much like a Peer Gynt who "confesses and yet conceals" [*skrifte, og dog dølge*], thus revealing the infinite enigma of the imaginative self, rather than a finished picture of who Kierkegaard and the plural self is. The *Dagdrivers* are like the real poets who are "idlers, and it is to the principle of idleness that astronomy owed its origin, that is to say, when man, freed from the necessity of earning his bread, turned his eyes upwards and questioned the enigma of the skies."[78] But Kierkegaard, like any self-respecting hardworking *Dagdriver*, never forgets to look down either, exemplified in the 1848 discourse where the call is both to look up at the bird of the air and down to the earth to find the lily hidden amid the long blades of grass.

Bibliography

Adorno, Theodor, and Max Horkheimer. *Dialectic of Enlightenment*. Translated by Edmund Jephcott. Stanford: Stanford University Press, 2002.

Agamben, Giorgio. "Bartleby, or On Contingency." In *Potentialities: Collected Essays in Philosophy*, edited and translated by Daniel Heller-Roazeen, 243–71. Stanford: Stanford University Press, 1999.

———. *Homo Sacer: Sovereign Power and Bare Life*. Stanford: Stanford University Press, 1998.

Assiter, Alison. *Kierkegaard, Metaphysics and Political Theory*. London: Continuum, 2011.

---

77. Adorno and Horkheimer, *Dialectic of Enlightenment*, 94–136.
78. Unamuno, *Our Lord Don Quixote*, xviii.

PART 5: KIERKEGAARD AND THE POLITICS OF COMMUNICATION

Avanessian, Armen, and Sophie Wennersheid, eds. *Kierkegaard and Political Theory: Religion, Aesthetics, Politics, and the Intervention of the Single Individual*. Copenhagen: Museum Tusculanum Press, 2014.

Backhouse, Stephen. *Kierkegaard's Critique of Christian Nationalism*. Oxford: Oxford University Press, 2011.

Beckett, Samuel. *Nohow On: Company, Ill Seen Ill Said, Worstward Ho*. New York: Grove, 1996.

Benjamin, Walter. *The Arcades Project*. Translated by Howard Eiland and Kevin McLaughlin. Cambridge: Belknap, of Harvard University Press, 2004.

Boer, Roland. "A Totality of Ruins: Adorno on Kierkegaard." *Cultural Critique* 83 (2013) 1–30.

Cervantes, Miguel de. *Don Quixote*. Translated by Edith Grossman. New York: Vintage, 2007.

Clarke, Edward. *The Vagabond Spirit of Poetry*. Winchester: iff, 2014.

Deleuze, Gilles. "Bartleby; Or, the Formula." In *Essays Critical and Clinical*, translated by Daniel W. Smith and Michael A. Greco, 68–90. Minneapolis: University of Minnesota Press, 1997.

Derrida, Jacques. *Dissemination*. Translated by Barbara Johnson. London: Athlone, 1993.

Dooley, Mark. *Politics of Exodus: Søren Kierkegaard's Ethics of Responsibility*. New York: Fordham University Press, 2001.

Fernie, Ewan. *The Demonic: Literature and Experience*. London: Routledge, 2013.

Hardt, Michael, and Antoni Negri. *Empire*. Cambridge: Harvard University Press, 2000.

Heidegger, Martin. *Being and Time*. Translated by John MacQuarrie and Edward Robinson. New York: Harper & Row, 1962.

Kierkegaard, Søren. *Christian Discourses / The Crisis and a Crisis in the Life of an Actress*. Translated by Howard V. Hong and Edna H. Hong. Princeton: Princeton University Press, 1997.

———. *The Concept of Anxiety*. Translated by Reidar Tomte. Princeton: Princeton University Press, 1980.

———. *Concluding Unscientific Postscript to the Philosophical Fragments*. Translated by Howard V. Hong and Edna H. Hong. Princeton: Princeton University Press, 1992.

———. *Eighteen Upbuilding Discourses*. Translated by Howard V. Hong and Edna H. Hong. Princeton: Princeton University Press, 1990.

———. *Fear and Trembling / Repetition*. Translated by Howard V. Hong and Edna H. Hong. Princeton: Princeton University Press, 1983.

———. *Journals and Papers*. 7 vols. Edited and translated by Howard V. Hong and Edna H. Hong. Princeton: Princeton University Press, 1967–78.

———. *Letters and Documents*. Translated by Henrik Rosenmeier. Princeton: Princeton University Press, 1978.

———. *Papers and Journals: A Selection*. Translated by Alastair Hannay. London: Penguin Classics, 1996.

———. *Philosophical Fragments / Johannes Climacus*. Edited and translated by Howard V. Hong and Edna H. Hong. Princeton: Princeton University Press, 1985.

———. *The Point of View*. Translated by Howard V. Hong and Edna H. Hong. Princeton: Princeton University Press, 1998.

———. *Practice in Christianity*. Translated by Howard V. Hong and Edna H. Hong. Princeton: Princeton University Press, 1991.

———. *The Sickness Unto Death*. Translated by Howard V. Hong and Edna H. Hong. Princeton: Princeton University Press, 1980.

———. *Søren Kierkegaards Skrifter* [SKS]. 28 text vols. and 28 commentary vols. Edited by Niels Jørgen Cappelørn et al. Copenhagen: Gad, 1997–2013.

———. *Stages on Life's Way*. Translated by Howard V. Hong and Edna H. Hong. Princeton: Princeton University Press, 1988.

———. *Two Ages: The Age of Revolution and the Present Age; A Literary Review*. Edited and translated by Howard V. Hong and Edna H. Hong. Princeton: Princeton University Press, 1978.

———. *Upbuilding Discourses in Various Spirits*. Edited and translated by Howard V. Hong and Edna H. Hong. Princeton: Princeton University Press, 2005.

———. *Without Authority*. Translated by Howard V. Hong and Edna H. Hong. Princeton, New Jersey: Princeton University Press, 1997.

Kirmmse, Bruce H. "Introduction: Letting Nature Point beyond Nature." In *The Lily of the Field and the Bird of the Air*, translated by Bruce H. Kirmmse, vii–xxxv. Princeton: Princeton University Press, 2016.

Kundera, Milan. *Slowness*. Translated by Linda Asher. London: Faber & Faber, 1997.

Lukács, Georg. *Soul and Form*. Translated by Anna Bostock. Cambridge: MIT Press, 1974.

———. *The Theory of the Novel*. Translated by Anna Bostock. Cambridge: MIT Press, 1971.

Maugham, Somerset. *The Razor's Edge*. London: Vintage, 2000.

Nagy, András. "Abraham the Communist." In *Kierkegaard: The Self in Society*, edited by George Pattison and Steven Shakespeare, 196–220. Hampshire: Palgrave Macmillan, 1998.

Nin, Anaïs. *The Journals of Anaïs Nin*. Vol. 1, *1931–1934*. London: Quartet, 1979.

Novalis. *Philosophical Writings*. Translated and edited by Margaret Mahony Stoljar. Albany: State University of New York Press, 1997.

O'Neill Burns, Michael. *Kierkegaard and the Matter of Philosophy: A Fractured Dialectic*. London: Rowman & Littlefield, 2015.

Perkins, Robert L. "Kierkegaard's Anti-Climacus in His Social and Political Environment." In *International Kierkegaard Commentary to Practice in Christianity*, edited by Robert L. Perkins, 274–302. Macon, GA: Mercer University, 2004.

Ryan, Bartholomew. "Kierkegaard's Fairytale." Milan: *Rivista di Filosofia Neo-Scolastica* 3–4 (2014) 945–61.

———. *Kierkegaard's Indirect Politics: Interludes with Lukács, Schmitt, Benjamin and Adorno*. New York: Rodopi, 2014.

Schmitt, Carl. *Political Theology: Four Chapters on the Concept of Sovereignty*. Translated by George Schwab. Chicago: University of Chicago Press, 2005.

Shakespeare, William. *The Complete Works*. Edited by Peter Alexander. London: Collins, 1966.

Smith, Graham M. *Friendship and the Political: Kierkegaard, Nietzsche, Schmitt*. Charlottesville: Imprint Academic, 2011.

Stocker, Barry. *Kierkegaard On Politics*. Basingstoke, UK: Palgrave Macmillan, 2014.

Unamuno, Miguel de. *Our Lord Quixote*. Translated by Anthony Kerrigan. Princeton: Princeton University Press, 1967.

Villa, Dana. *Socratic Citizenship*. Princeton: Princeton University Press, 2001.

Whitman, Walt. *Complete Poetry and Collected Prose*. New York: Library of America, 1982.

PART 5: KIERKEGAARD AND THE POLITICS OF COMMUNICATION

Ziolkowski, Eric. "Kierkegaard's Subterranean Fluvial Pseudonymity." In *Kierkegaard's Literary Figures and Motifs*, vol. 1, *Agamemnon to Guadalquivir*, edited by Katalin Nun and Jon Stewart, 279–95. Kierkegaard Research 16. Surrey, UK: Ashgate, 2014.

———. *The Literary Kierkegaard*. Evanston: Northwestern University Press, 2011.

Žižek, Slavoj. *The Parallax View*. Cambridge: MIT Press, 2006.

21

Søren Kierkegaard, Indirect Communication, and the Strength of Weak Authority

A Reflection on Parliamentary Democracy

Burkhard Conrad, OPL

Introduction

IN THIS ESSAY, I aim to answer the following set of questions: Is it possible to describe parliamentary democracy—somewhat ideal typically—as indirect communication? Is it possible to transfer this concept, which Søren Kierkegaard developed as part of his existential dialectics, to the level of collective decision-making? And is it possible to assign to parliamentary democracy similar Christian qualities which Kierkegaard assigns to the notion of indirect communication?[1]

It may be rightfully assumed that Kierkegaard was skeptical about what Samuel Huntington called the "first wave of democratization"[2] in the modernizing nineteenth century.[3] I claim, however, that Kierkegaard's democratic skepticism did not prevent him from developing concepts which—in a strange dialectic way—are valuable in a twenty-first-century reflection on the idea of parliamentary democracy. In my view, the idea of indirect communication is such a concept. In order to illustrate that the concept of indirect communication correlates with the idea of parliamentary democracy, I will proceed in two steps: First, I will explain some important features of Kierkegaard's understanding of indirect communication. I am not going to deal comprehensively with either Kierkegaard's own writings on the subject nor the extensive secondary literature on Kierkegaard's ideas on communication. Rather, I will be selective, exemplifying only those points which seem valuable for my overall argument. Second, I will relate Kierkegaard's concept of indirect communication to elements of parliamentary

---

1. I am grateful to Stephen Backhouse and the editors for their valuable comments on an earlier version of this chapter.
2. Huntington, "Democracy's Third Wave," 12.
3. On the political and social background of Kierkegaard's work in the context of the nineteenth century, see Kirmmse "Out with It," 15–47, and Nicoletti "Politics and Religion," 183–95.

democracy as described by a group of twentieth- and twenty-first-century European writers as diverse as Carl Schmitt, Jürgen Habermas, and Kari Palonen. My essay aims to move forward the presumptuous systematic claim that the concept of indirect communication describes one of the main features of parliamentary democracy—namely, that its strength lies in its weakness.

Kierkegaard on Indirect Communication

Socrates

According to Marius Timmann Mjaaland, the concept of indirect communication is rooted in Kierkegaard's treatment of Socrates.[4] If we follow Kierkegaard, being "Socratic" means the art of helping others to give birth to the truth in their lives. It means the art of midwifery in the context of ideas, beliefs, cognitive reasoning or, more specifically, in the context of truth claims. According to Kierkegaard, Socrates did not speak plainly of the truth in front of his pupils. The process of "appropriating truth,"[5] as Mjaaland calls it, is more complicated: as a mother needs to give birth to her child herself with the midwife only as her assistance, so each and everyone needs to give birth to the truth him- or herself, with the teacher only as an assistant. Kierkegaard writes in the *Philosophical Fragments*: "Because I can discover my own untruth only by myself, because only when *I* discover it is it discovered, not before, even though the whole world knew it."[6] It is no use when others tell me what I need to know about myself and the world. I have to undergo the labor pains of finding the truth myself.

The art of Socratic midwifery, thus, consists of a dialectic, negative notion. From the teacher's perspective, this means withholding direct, key information in order to enable the other person to gain this information indirectly for him- or herself. From the student's perspective, this means not expecting direct installments of truth from someone else but probing the information before me for its worth and deeper meaning. The relationship between the teacher and the student is not one in which the teacher is the owner of truth and the student is the learner of truth. There is no direct flow of information between the two of them: "There is no direct relation between the teacher and the learner."[7] Kierkegaard refers to this Socratic art of midwifery in the following way: "At most he [Socrates] was capable of artistically, maieutically helping another person negatively to the same view."[8] This willful communicative "ambiguity,"

---

4. Timmann Mjaaland, "Theaetetus," 115–46.
5. Ibid., 117.
6. Kierkegaard, *Philosophical Fragments*, 14.
7. Kierkegaard, *Concluding Unscientific Postscript*, 247.
8. Ibid., 80.

as Turnbull calls it,[9] has nothing to do with conscious lying or malign deception with the aim of hurting other people or gaining a personal advantage. Rather, cognitive midwifery fulfills a didactic purpose, because it is "a very fruitful strategy for removing self-deception," as Aumann writes.[10]

Neither the student, pupil, follower, disciple, etc., nor the teacher, instructor, master, etc., will come into full possession of the gift which is transferred in this midwifery fashion. Kierkegaard stresses on numerous occasions that he is not interested in a static knowledge of the truth in which the process of seeking truth has come to a standstill and the transfer from one to the other has turned into a monotonous stream. Kierkegaard aims for a dynamic process: "One who is existing is continually in the process of becoming; the actually existing subjective thinker, thinking, continually reproduces this in his existence and invests all his thinking in becoming."[11] Midwifery, thus, is not the art of helping others to find and possess truth, but rather it is supporting others in their never-ending story of growth and becoming. The Socratic art, thus, is the appropriate way to grow intellectually and emotionally in an age of open-ended processes, ever more contingent social settings and a human condition marked by fluidity and change: "The perpetual process of becoming is the uncertainty of earthly life, in which everything is uncertain"[12]—so Kierkegaard.

Helping others to grow and to learn entails another dimension. "In order to truly help someone else,"[13] one more element needs to be added. This is the dimension of serving. The hierarchy between the teacher and the student is neither top down nor is it simply bottom up. The roles of teacher and learner are not simply reversed, they are inversed. The hierarchy which exists between the two is inverted.[14] The teacher draws his or her legitimacy as teacher not from the fact that he possesses superior "Herrschaftswissen" or that tradition is on his or her side or that the student admires him or her. Rather, their task as a teacher is to serve their students while still remaining the teacher. The teacher teaches with authority but this authority lasts only so long as it is grounded in an act of true service. In Kierkegaard's own words: "But all true helping begins with a humbling. The helper must first humble himself under the person he wants to help and thereby understand that to help is not to dominate but to serve, that to help is not to be the most dominating but the most patient, that to help is a willingness for the time being to put up with being in the wrong and not understanding what the other understands."[15]

9. Turnbull, "Ambiguity," 13–22.
10. Aumann, "Kierkegaard on Indirect Communication," 324.
11. Kierkegaard, *Concluding Unscientific Postscript*, 86.
12. Ibid.
13. Ibid., 45.
14. Conrad, "Heilige Herrschaft," 4.
15. Kierkegaard, *Point of View*, 45.

The true (religious) teacher goes even so far that he not only humbles himself under the student but that he accepts to be denounced and ridiculed—not necessarily by the student, but by the crowd surrounding both of them. Everyone who communicates truthfully about the truth may become subject to this kind of scorn. Kierkegaard writes about "authentic religious teachers": So long as they live, they are being "insulted, persecuted, laughed to scorn, mocked, spat upon."[16] Thus, true teachers suffer as well as they serve. But in this suffering lies also the victory, as "in this world the truth is victorious only by suffering."[17] Indirect communication, therefore, begins by an act of true service and humility on behalf of the teacher.

Jesus Christ

It should have become clear by now that the Socratic element here has been supplemented by a second element. This is the christological idea of, as Taylor puts it, "God's incarnation in the historical figure of Jesus."[18] Marius Mjaaland states that "Kierkegaard applies the Socratic method to the Christian claim of truth,"[19] thereby also putting a distance between himself and the historical Socrates. "Christ thus becomes the master of maieutics and the final reason for using the maieutic method."[20] In the end, Christ appears to be the true midwife.

This christological dimension may be exemplified through the metaphor of the servant, which for Kierkegaard, exemplifies the religious ethical dimension of the God-human paradox, the rationally absurd idea that God became human in the incarnated body of Jesus Christ. Kierkegaard uses this metaphor regularly when he—directly or indirectly—speaks of Jesus Christ as the kenotic way of God's earthly presence. This means: Christ is characterized not through his wisdom, beauty, power, or purity. According to Kierkegaard, Christ's chief characteristic is his lowliness, his kenosis: a humility and powerlessness which are condensed in the mere fact that he became incarnate as a human being. In *Practice in Christianity* Kierkegaard refers to Christ as "God-man,"[21] both God and human. As such he—Christ—was a person who caused immense "offense"[22] because he refused to be transparent as divine and reveal himself directly as God's son. Indeed, it was precisely his lowliness as a normal human being and his death on the cross coupled with the claim to be God's son which caused "offense": "The possibility of offense, it is easy to see, is in relation to lowliness. Just as being the God-man, that it would mean suffering a criminal's punishment,

16. Ibid., 68.
17. Kierkegaard, *Practice in Christianity*, 193–94.
18. Taylor, "Christology," 194.
19. Timmann Mjaaland, "Theaetetus," 145.
20. Ibid., 143.
21. Kierkegaard, *Practice in Christianity*, 81.
22. Ibid., 82.

is an occasion for offense, so is it also an occasion for offense to be sent out by the Father's only begotten Son, that it will mean being persecuted, cast out from society, and finally put to death—and in such a way that everyone who does it will think he is doing God a service."[23]

In *Philosophical Fragments*, Kierkegaard recalls the (heretic) Docetic teaching in early Christian thought when he writes that "the servant form is not something put on but is actual, not a parastatic but an actual body."[24] God really did become human in Christ and this human being really did live the life of a servant, not of a master. Being a servant meant for God that "he was a lowly human being, a lowly man who did not set himself off from the human throng either by soft raiment or by any other earthly advantage and was not distinguishable to other human beings, not even to the countless legions of angels he left behind when he humbled himself."[25]

All this makes the communicative act between God and humankind something rather complicated. We are not talking about "completely direct paragraph-communication or professor-communication."[26] The God whose son is Jesus Christ also does not use "shock and awe" techniques in order to draw people to his side. God does not reveal Godself directly. More so: God specifically refuses to communicate directly. God's presence is indirect, existential: God's spirit is present in the weakness of a human body. God's divinity is present in a human being. God's magnitude is present in the meekness of one historical individual. Direct communication is refused, thereby a choice has to be made: "There is no direct communication and no direct reception: there is a choice."[27] This is a choice which may or may not lead to faith in the source of this indirect communication, the teacher. Teacher and teaching are one and the same,[28] and the relationship to the student is complicated by the fact that the teacher—Christ—has no exterior features that make him desirable or a superior charismatic gift that turns him into a magnet for possible followers. You have faith in him, the "offense," or you do not.

This has direct consequences for the authority and the power of the one who communicates in the name of God, indirectly. In this context, authority and power can only be framed in terms of a paradox as we saw earlier on.[29] Kierkegaard exemplifies this further in an essay entitled "The Difference between a Genius and an Apostle" in the following way: "Between God and a human being, then, there is and remains an eternal essential qualitative difference. *The paradoxical-religious relation . . . appears when God*

---

23. Ibid., 115–16.
24. Kierkegaard, *Philosophical Fragments*, 55.
25. Ibid., 56.
26. Kierkegaard, *Practice in Christianity*, 123.
27. Ibid., 140.
28. Ibid.
29. Dunning, "Who Sets the Task?," 18–32.

appoints a specific human being to have divine authority."[30] Communicating the truth can never be done with the help of power but only "by means of powerlessness."[31] I agree with Mjaaland when he writes: "The communicator is the powerful one in so far as he has superior knowledge about the almighty God. Such a powerful position implies that the violent (ab)use of spiritual power is a significant problem, a problem Kierkegaard is well aware of. Thus, in order to communicate knowledge to others, he claims that the communicator ought to totally renounce his own power in order to 'suffer' the truth."[32] The archetype of this form of indirect communication is Jesus Christ. As shown above Christ is the indirect communicator per se. His incarnation as the divine becoming mortal flesh sets a pattern for every kind of communication, verbal or nonverbal. This communication needs to be humble, willing to confront the paradoxical, and open to let go of any superficial, overt authority.

Communicating Truth

We have now arrived at the difference between direct and indirect communication. In this context both direct and indirect communication try to communicate truth. One difference between direct and indirect communication, though, lies in the intended effect of the communicative act on the recipient. Is the recipient supposed to be impressed and instantly convinced by the assumed truth? Will he swear imminent allegiance to its power and reject any doubt? In this case, we would speak of direct communication. Indirect communication on the other hand leaves space for doubt and discussion. Indirect communication stresses that the recipient needs time to digest the truth that he has heard. It does not aim for followers.[33] The recipient of the communication needs to venture on a long path of personal becoming by finding the truth for himself: "The essential in this knowledge is the appropriation itself."[34] For not only the communicated truth as such is important. Even more important is one's own personal approach to this truth. Whereas the communicative act—the truth-claim—is, in Kierkegaard's words, the first reflection, the second reflection consists of one's own position in regard to this communicative act or truth-claim.[35] Indirect communication, thereby, entails stringent self-reflection and the willingness to change through a sometimes humiliating process of personal becoming. Knowing the truth, thus, has less to do with direct knowledge but more

---

30. Kierkegaard, *Without Authority*, 100.
31. Kierkegaard, *Point of View*, 50.
32. Timmann Mjaaland: "Theaetetus," 138.
33. Garrett "Essential Secret," 340.
34. Kierkegaard, *Concluding Unscientific Postscript*, 79.
35. Ibid., 76.

with indirect being: "And therefore, Christianly understood, truth is obviously not to know the truth but to be the truth."[36]

Being the truth is obviously far more difficult than knowing a few facts which run under the title of "truth." For every existential being, in Kierkegaard's view, has to deal with the reality of its own contingency, constantly awaiting fulfillment. Herein lies another main difference between direct and indirect communication. Direct communication aims for finality. It cannot deal with unfinished business. Kierkegaard writes in the *Unscientific Postscript*: "Direct communication requires certainty, but certainty is impossible for a person in the process of becoming, and it is indeed a deception."[37] Indirect communication will never be able to present final results and ultimate solutions.

Whereas direct communication equals static finality and existential conclusiveness, indirect communication equals open-ended becoming and willingness to deal with contingency. In Kierkegaard's own words: "One who is existing is continually in the process of becoming; the actually existing subjective thinker, thinking, continually reproduces this in his existence and invests all his thinking in becoming . . . for one continually feels an urge to have something finished, but this urge is of evil and must be renounced. The perpetual process of becoming is the uncertainty of earthly life, in which everything is uncertain."[38] The proper response then to complexity and uncertainty lies not in the radical reduction of complexity and the urge of imminent certainty. Rather it lies in the willingness to accept the ongoing struggle with contingency as a fact of human life and as a sign that truth is at work.

One's communicative style, which is nothing more than the personal inside shown outwards, needs to reflect this openness and willingness to grow, even under resistance. Should I want to serve the truth in my life as a witness, I need to prepare to suffer as Jesus Christ suffered for being a truthful teacher and an offense. In reflection of his own experience as an author, Kierkegaard writes in *The Point of View*: "This is why everyone who in truth wants to serve the truth is *eo ipso* in some way a martyr."[39]

Let me summarize: indirect communication does not dispense with communicating truth. Indirect communication indeed wants to communicate truth. However, it takes into account the inverted role of teacher and student in the communicative process and the need for a critical reflection of the role of power within this process. Thus, it addresses the need for constant, infinite self-reflection and growth. It also considers that the communicated truth is not a static entity, but a living existential reality that is activated by subjective appropriation. And finally, it takes into account the role of humility, powerlessness, and possible suffering for all those who are involved in the act of truth-seeking indirect communication.

36. Kierkegaard, *Practice in Christianity*, 205.
37. Kierkegaard, *Concluding Unscientific Postscript*, 74.
38. Ibid., 86.
39. Kierkegaard, *Point of View*, 109.

PART 5: KIERKEGAARD AND THE POLITICS OF COMMUNICATION

Parliamentary Democracy and the Strength of Weak Authority

As I attempt to transfer Kierkegaard's concept of indirect communication into a reflection on parliamentary democracy, I am certain that I cannot count on the support of the historical Kierkegaard. Also, I need to acknowledge the categorical hurdles which I may encounter by applying Kierkegaard's existential category of indirect communication to the legislative acts of a collective body such as the parliament.

I claim, nonetheless, that parliamentary democracy can ideally be understood as a kind of political indirect communication. I will explain this claim in three steps. First, parliamentary democracy favors so to speak indirect discussions to direct decisions. Second, it conceptualizes the search for truth as a process of infinite becoming. And finally, parliamentary democracy is a form of government in which power relationships are inverted. I understand parliamentary democracy as a representational system or structure of self-government that depends upon the involvement of (theoretically) all adults of any given political unit in the process of collective decision-making, through elections of representatives, on an equal footing and in an environment which guarantees personal freedom.

Discussions vs. Decisions

I mentioned earlier that Kierkegaard's indirect communication evokes a personal response, a choice. The individual needs to learn how to best form a personal opinion and to act out of that in a decisive manner. Within parliamentary democracy, this personal response is usually elicited through and takes place within open, collective discussions rather than solitary decisions.

In parliament, almost every discussion will eventually end in some kind of decision, i.e., a vote. Nevertheless, discussions are not the inferior political prelude for that which is superior, the decision. Discussion and decision belong together. Ideally the course of a parliamentary discussion affects the outcome of the decision. Parliament can only arrive at a sober decision after it has weighed all the alternatives in a proper discussion. Speeches in parliament are in themselves political acts as are parliamentary decisions.[40] Even if they represent the minority opinion, speeches make political alternatives visible and, in the long run, also possible. They are a valuable contribution to a political process which in its very nature is inherently contingent.

This is a thought for which Carl Schmitt caused serious problems. Schmitt's decisionism was based on the assumption that parliamentary discussion do not lead anywhere and are futile exercises. According to him they resemble the romantic notion of an "eternal conversation."[41] Schmitt admits that in theory a discussion "means an exchange of opinion that is governed by the purpose of persuading the opponent

---

40. Palonen, *Rhetorik des Unbeliebten*, 175–81.
41. Schmitt, *Politische Romantik*, 32, my translation.

of the truth and rightness—or be persuaded yourself—with rational arguments."[42] Schmitt, however, thought of real parliaments not as institutions that were seeking truth but as chambers in which mere opinions, conflicting political interests, and ambitions for power collided with each other. For example, Schmitt dismisses parliament as the place "where one deliberates, i.e., where through discourse, the exchange of arguments and counter arguments you find the *relative* truth."[43]

Schmitt is correct in his description of the nature of parliamentary democracy. He is not right, though, with his normative evaluation of parliamentary practices. Schmitt was looking for more than relative, discursive truth. He was looking (or yearning) for definite decisions, brought by a definite, sovereign leader. Famously he regarded sovereignty as the authority to decide about the state of exception.[44] Schmitt wanted sovereign decisions to be free of any normative boundaries. They should be absolute.[45]

The rationale of parliamentary democracy, however, lies exactly in its negation of any absolute, finite decision and in its denial of a nondiscursive sovereignty. Parliamentary politics equals—in Max Weber's famous words—"a strong, slow drilling of hard shelves with passion and a sense of proportion."[46] Not quick direct decisions but long, protracted and thereby indirect discussions are the bread and butter of parliamentary democracy. They are like ongoing self-reflections of a collective body. Whereas the direct communication of quick decisions promises imminent solutions to social problems through the sudden action of either dictatorship or revolution, the indirect communication of parliamentary discussions depends on the hard work of finding compromises which never quite reflect anyone's political views to the full extent. These discussions are also the condition of possibility for forming one's own opinion, one's personal political character.

Truth and Democracy

According to Carl Schmitt, parliament debates relegate the notion of truth to the "mere function of a never-ending competition of opinions."[47] Truth is not allowed to play a substantial role in parliamentary democracy, it is made relative. Eventually, truth is smothered by rivaling opinions and statements. The search for truth is abandoned for the sake of the search for a social equilibrium, an idea abhorrent to Schmitt and, for that matter, also to Kierkegaard.

---

42. Schmitt, *Die geistesgeschichtliche Lage des heutigen Parlamentarismus*, 9, my translation.
43. Ibid., 58, my translation, emphasis added.
44. Schmitt, *Politische Theologie*, 13, my translation.
45. Ibid., 18, my translation.
46. Weber, *Politik*, 82, my translation.
47. Schmitt, *Die geistesgeschichtliche Lage*, 46, my translation.

PART 5: KIERKEGAARD AND THE POLITICS OF COMMUNICATION

The political philosopher of deliberation, Jürgen Habermas, however, does not hesitate to call parliamentary democracy a "wahrheitsempfindliche Regierungsform," a form of government which is sensitive for the truth.[48] Habermas works with a concept of truth—communicative reason—which is far more dynamic than Schmitt's rather static concept of truth. Hauke Brunkhorst comments on this Habermasian notion of truth and says that communicative reason—i.e., truth—consists of an ongoing execution of action.[49] Such a dynamic notion of truth attempts to incorporate the process of truth-finding into the concept of truth itself. In *Unscientific Postscript* Kierkegaard describes truth as a "way," as something that exists only "in the becoming," as a "process of appropriation" and never in a definitive result.[50] I am not sure whether Kierkegaard would agree with a Habermasian deliberative notion of truth, but he would certainly disagree with Schmitt's absolute and finite thinking.

Parliamentary democracy, then, works under the assumption that parliament is not a passive agent of an a priori truth. Parliamentary debates and decisions reflect the common mind of a democratic polity exactly in that they do not formulate metaphysical truth claims but rather provisional convictions of great truthfulness, formed by individual politicians and voters. Democratic truth is preliminary, always in the "becoming." Marie-Christine Kajewski puts it somewhat existentially: "To be in the truth means therefore, to remain in a state of questioning."[51]

Carl Schmitt bemoans the "renunciation of any definitive result"[52] in parliamentary democracy. It is, however, this reluctance to postulate finality which is the essence of any notion of democracy that takes parliamentary debates seriously. In the words of Kierkegaard: "Politics etc. has nothing to do with *eternal truth*. A politics that in the sense of *eternal truth* was in earnest about carrying *eternal* truth into actuality would to the highest degree immediately show itself to be the most 'unpolitical' that can be imagined."[53]

Democracy is open-ended. It deals with problems that call for a solution but these solutions are more often than not temporary. They are certainly not meant to last for eternity. Truth in democracy is therefore not an ontological reality—neither in the sense of Carl Schmitt nor in the postmodern sense of thinkers like Jean Luc Nancy, who has argued that "democracy is first of all a metaphysics and only afterward a politics. But the latter is not founded on the former. On the contrary, it is but the condition whereby it is exercised."[54] But truth in democracy is also more than a mere search for

48. Habermas, *Religion in der Öffentlichkeit*, 150.
49. In German *laufender Vollzug von Praxis*. See Brunkhorst, "Demokratie und Wahrheit," 497–98.
50. Kierkegaard, *Concluding Unscientific Postscript*, 78.
51. Kajewski, *Wahrheit und Demokratie*, 220, author's translation.
52. Schmitt, *Die geistesgeschichtliche Lage*, 46, author's translation.
53. Kierkegaard, *Point of View*, 109–10.
54. Nancy, *Truth in Democracy*, 34.

the best possible outcome. Parliamentary democracy makes truth a reality in that it values the common, yet always also personal search for truth in debate and discussion, in the preliminary "becoming" of a decision, which is more likely to be a compromise than a consensus. Thus parliamentary democracy attains the natural feeling of a form of existence,[55] among politicians and among members of the electorate.

Strength That Lies in Weakness

The German legal philosopher Josef Isensee once called democracy "the humblest form of government in world history."[56] Democracy can be typically described as a form of government that depends less on the political power of a few people over many than on the service rendered of these few representatives to the many members of the electorate. Fixed electoral cycles, the ever-present possibility of not being renominated as candidate or reelected as a member of parliament, the personal accountability throughout the electoral cycle: these aspects contribute to the relative weakness of politicians within a democratic polity. No clan protects them, no armed militia fights for them, no corrupted judge decides in their favor. A politician within parliamentary democracy depends solely on the goodwill of those people he or she represents and his or her personal competence and truthfulness—in theory at least.

Parliamentary, representative democracy thereby inverts typical hierarchies: those who rule, are ruled over by those whom they represent. Power relations are circular and not simply top down or bottom up. These relations reflect a kenotic movement. The throne of power is not really empty—as Claude Lefort once famously called it—but it is brought down in the middle of the electorate and shared—in theory—by all, in that they ask a few to occupy it, at least for the time being. Democratic government means service quite in the sense of the above quoted passage from Kierkegaard's *Point of View* that helping does not mean to rule but to serve and this service is a form of humility. Therefore, democracy should be called a weak form of authority, because it keeps questioning itself and even invites its enemies to do the same.[57]

The forum of this kenotic movement of democracy is parliament. Parliamentary speeches, according to Kari Palonen, are the medium of politics from below.[58] But they are more than that. Parliamentary speeches are a visible or audible sign of the invisible weakness of politicians within democracy. Members of parliament cannot simply decide and act as they wish, they first have to try to persuade and convince. They cannot decide as if they were the only one whose opinion matters, they have to find a compromise and decide as many. The real political influence of

---

55. Lübbe, "Mehrheit statt Wahrheit," 145.

56. In German: *die bescheidenste Staatsform der Weltgeschichte*. See Isensee, "Widerstand und demokratische Normalität," 48.

57. Nolte, *Was ist Demokratie?*, 20.

58. Palonen, *Rhetorik des Unbeliebten*, 176.

the individual parliamentarian is offset by an equally real powerlessness if the odds are against him or her.

The authority that is present in a politician can thereby be called paradoxical.[59] The individual person who is active as a parliamentarian (or as any other politician outside parliament) within a democratic polity has no real direct power. Should he want to initiate change, he must embark on a long, indirect mission of convincing people and proving his point. This relative powerlessness, however, is part of his authority. He or she is both vulnerable and strong at the same time. If he were strong, he would not be a politician within a democratic polity. This is indeed an "offence" to anyone who thinks that political power needs to be straightforward, direct, and omnipotent.

Conclusion

My somewhat presumptuous point here is this: Kierkegaard's concept of indirect communication can be used to describe the nature of democratic politics and thus also the role of democratically elected parliamentarians. In that sense, parliamentary democracy may be understood as, first, an institutionalized form of collective indirect communication. It involves an institutionalized way of finding political compromises through collective debate, collective self-reflection and, finally, also collective decision-making. This ongoing collective debate, reflection, and decision-making points to the second insight that democracy is also an institutionalized search for truth and meaning. This search does not seek authority through a quest for absolute finality, rather its sincerity is rooted in the truthfulness of the politicians involved, both as individuals and as a collective body. Embedded in all this is, third, the essential quality of parliamentary democracy as an institutionalized and ongoing act of political humility of both individuals and collective. No one claims absolute authority, rather all share in the preliminary nature of the political process. This process of democratic decision-making is as important as its outcome.

Should I accept these assumptions, which are indeed hard to accept if I only look at democracy in its empirical form, they will lead me to a second even more presumptuous assumption, namely that parliamentary democracy can claim to possess christological qualities. It would appear therefore that there are "powerful Christian motivations for supporting and engaging with democracy today."[60] These christological qualities are not derived from a traditional direct representational model (i.e., the divine right of a monarch), but are rooted in the indirect

---

59. Kierkegaard uses the concept of paradoxical authority to describe a human agent of godly authority, the apostle, in Kierkegaard, *Without Authority*, 100. I make analogical use of the concept for my purposes. I am sure Kierkegaard would negate the analogy between apostle and politician.

60. Chaplin, "Christian Theories of Democracy," 37.

communication exemplified by Christ's communication of himself.[61] If democracy can be described as a form of indirect communication and at the same time Christ can be depicted as the paradigmatic indirect communicator, then democracy possess indeed christological qualities. In the end, this would mean that anyone true to the Christian faith—as interpreted by Søren Kierkegaard—would have no choice but to favor parliamentary democracy over any other form of political system.

Bibliography

Aumann, Anthony. "Kierkegaard on Indirect Communication, the Crowd, and a Monstrous Illusion." In *International Kierkegaard Commentary: The Point of View*, edited Robert L. Perkins, 295–324. Macon, GA: Mercer University Press, 2010.

Brunkhorst, Hauke. "Demokratie und Wahrheit. Jürgen Habermas zum 80. Geburtstag." *Leviathan* 37 (2000) 491–500.

Chaplin, Jonathan. "Christian Theories of Democracy." In *The Modern State and the Kingdom of God*, edited by Robert Heimburger, 35–42. Oxford: Las Casas Institute: 2012.

Conrad, Burkhard. "Heilige Herrschaft, säkulare Hierarchien." *Wort und Antwort* 50 (2009) 2–5.

Dunning, Stephen N. "Who Sets the Task? Kierkegaard on Authority." In *Foundations of Kierkegaard's Vision of Community: Religion, Ethics, and Politics in Kierkegaard*, edited by George B. Connell and C. Stephen Evans, 18–32. New Jersey: Humanities, 1992.

Garrett, Eric. "The Essential Secret of Indirect Communication." *Review of Communication* 12 (2012) 331–45.

Habermas, Jürgen. "Religion in der Öffentlichkeit. Kognitive Voraussetzungen für den 'öffentlichen Vernunftgebrauch' religiöser und säkularer Bürger." In *Zwischen Naturalismus und Religion: Philosophische Aufsätze*, 119–54. Frankfurt/Main: Suhrkamp, 2005.

Huntington, Samuel. "Democracy's Third Wave." *Journal of Democracy* 2 (1991) 12–34.

Isensee, Josef. "Widerstand und demokratische Normalität." In *Jurist und Staatsbewußtsein*, edited by Peter Eisenmann and Bernd Rill, 41–52. Heidelberg: Decker & Müller, 1987.

Kajewski, Marie-Christine. *Wahrheit und Demokratie: Eine Zeitdiagnose der Postdemokratie*. Baden-Baden: Nomos, 2014.

Kierkegaard, Søren. *Concluding Unscientific Postscript*: Vol. 1. Princeton: Princeton University Press, 1992.

———. *Philosophical Fragments*. Princeton: Princeton University Press, 1985.

———. *The Point of View*. Princeton: Princeton University Press, 2009.

———. *Practice in Christianity*. Princeton: Princeton University Press, 1991.

———. *Without Authority*. Princeton: Princeton University Press, 1997.

Kirmmse, Bruce H. "'Out with It!': The Modern Breakthrough, Kierkegaard, and Denmark." In *The Cambridge Companion to Kierkegaard*, edited By Alastair Hannay and Gordon D. Marino, 15–47. Cambridge: Cambridge University Press, 1998.

Lübbe, Hermann. "Mehrheit statt Wahrheit. Über Demokratisierungszwänge." In *Demokratietheorie und Demokratieentwicklung*, edited by A. Kaiser et al., 141–54. Wiesbaden: VS Verlag, 2004.

---

61. Rahner *Grundkurs des Glaubens*, 123.

Nancy, Jean-Luc. *Truth in Democracy*. New York: Fordham University Press, 2010.

Nicoletti, Michele. "Politics and Religion in Kierkegaard's Thought: Secularization and the Martyr." In *Foundations of Kierkegaard's Vision of Community: Religion, Ethics, and Politics in Kierkegaard*, edited by George B. Connell and C. Stephen Evans, 183–95. Atlantic Highlands, NJ: Humanities, 1992.

Nolte, Paul. *Was ist Demokratie? Geschichte und Gegenwart*. Munich: Beck, 2012.

Palonen, Kari. *Rhetorik des Unbeliebten: Lobreden auf Politiker im Zeitalter der Demokratie*. Baden-Baden: Nomos, 2012.

Rahner, Karl. *Grundkurs des Glaubens* 11th ed. Freiburg: Herder, 1984.

Schmitt, Carl. *Die geistesgeschichtliche Lage des heutigen Parlamentarismus*. 8th ed. Berlin: Duncker & Humblot, 1996.

———. *Politische Romantik*. 6th ed. Berlin: Duncker & Humblot, 1998.

———. *Politische Theologie: Vier Kapitel zur Lehre von der Souveränität*. 7th ed. Berlin: Duncker & Humblot, 1996.

Taylor, Mark C. "Christology." In *Theological Concepts in Kierkegaard*, edited by George Evans Arbaugh et al., 167–206. Bibliotheca Kierkegaardiana 5. Copenhagen: Reitzel, 1980.

Timmann Mjaaland, Marius. "Theaetetus: Giving Birth, or Kierkegaard's Socratic Maieutics." In *Kierkegaard and the Greek World*, vol. 2, pt. 1, *Socrates and Plato*, edited by Jon Stewart and Katalin Nun, 115–46. Farnham: Ashgate, 2010.

Turnbull, Jamie. "Kierkegaard, Indirect Communication, and Ambiguity." *Heythrop Journal* (2009) 13–22.

Weber, Max, *Politik als Beruf*. Stuttgart: Reclam 1992.

22

Sociological Categories and the Journey to Selfhood

From the Crowd to Community

Matthew D. Kirkpatrick

In a supplement to *The Point of View*, Kierkegaard makes clear the essential problem: "In these times, everything is politics."[1] While the political situation in Denmark is firmly in his mind, for Kierkegaard the political sphere is not simply rooted in the inner workings of the state, but rather in a focus on immediacy, on the outward, physical, animal nature of human existence. Politics has no regard for interiority, and therefore no concern for the individual. Throughout his writings, there is clearly no theme greater than that of the "single individual," and Kierkegaard's purpose is resolutely to draw people into isolation before God. Indeed, Kierkegaard argues that God is so uninterested in politics that, in comparison to the internal movement of the individual,[2] he would consider war on a global scale simply "some nonsense we human beings cook up among ourselves,"[3] a "rummaging in the finite world."[4] Where the religious is concerned with the relationship of the individual to God, the political "begins on earth in order to remain on earth."[5]

When one unites such considerations with that most famous of phrases, "truth is subjectivity," it is not surprising that Kierkegaard has been considered by so many to be irrational, acosmic, and somewhat nihilistic toward concrete social relationships.[6] The aim of this chapter is not to argue for Kierkegaard as a "communitarian"

---

1. Kierkegaard, *Point of View*, 104.
2. Kierkegaard, *Journals and Papers*, 2049 (XI1 A 60 n.d., 1854); 2081 (X12 A 135 n.d., 1854); 2570 (X12 A 54 n.d., 1854).
3. Ibid., 2571 (X12 A 55 n.d., 1854).
4. Ibid., 1067 (X12 A 63 n.d., 1854).
5. Kierkegaard, *Point of View*, 103.
6. As indicative of the situation this essay is addressing, in Merold Westphal's analysis of Kierkegaard's sociology the only Kierkegaardian categories discussed are purely negative subsets of "the crowd," and no consideration is given to the possibility of any positive sociological categorization by

per se, but to consider whether Kierkegaard does entertain a notion of "authentic" community in addition to the individual. To establish such "authenticity" is to ask whether, for Kierkegaard, a community can exist here and now within the religious category used by God in the service of the eternal, or whether it remains a political entity that simply exists as a consequence of human life to which the redeemed, single individual is either indifferent or opposed.

To this end, the essay will consider the dynamic relationship we find between the categories of the crowd, individual, and community, and argue that while the individual must be drawn out from the crowd, for the sake of their relationship to the eternal they must make a second movement into the community. Space will not allow this investigation to draw upon Kierkegaard's final attack and its complex relationship with his earlier work.[7] It will rather limit itself predominantly to the pseudonymous writings of Kierkegaard's first authorship, with a particular focus on *A Literary Review* and its description of an authentic "life-view."

From the Crowd to the Single Individual

The single individual is the person who overcomes all manner of evasion, self-deception, and earthly comfort, and stands before God in fearful honesty.[8] It is no surprise, therefore, that one of the central motifs of Kierkegaard's writing is that of confession. For in the silence of confession,[9] the individual recognizes their identity as sinner, and the infinite qualitative difference between themselves and God.[10] Kierkegaard's work clearly emphasizes the proverbial advice that "the fear of the Lord is the beginning of wisdom."[11] However, it is not simply the voice of God that one fears in confession, but rather also one's own insuppressible voice that speaks through the silence. Alone to himself, the individual acts as his own witness, plaintiff, and judge, and holds the keys to his own annihilation.[12] As Kierkegaard makes clear, "There is no one who accuses except one's thoughts."[13]

However, through the silence of confession this "holy fear" is combined with a blessedness that together create both wonder and worship,[14] because in meet-

---

Kierkegaard (Westphal, "Kierkegaard's Sociology").

7. For more on the impact of 1848 and the movement of Kierkegaard's authorship, see Kirkpatrick, *Attacks on Christendom*, 23–47; Elrod, *Kierkegaard and Christendom*, 3–46; Tilley, "Interpersonal Relationships."

8. Kierkegaard, *Eighteen Upbuilding Discourses*, 309.

9. For more on the complexity of silence in Kierkegaard's work see Rocca, "Søren Kierkegaard and Silence," and Strawser, "Gifts of Silence."

10. Kierkegaard, *Upbuilding Discourses*, 22.

11. Prov 9:10.

12. Kierkegaard, *Eighteen Upbuilding Discourses*, 309.

13. Kierkegaard, *Three Discourses*, 10.

14. Ibid., 18.

ing oneself, one meets God. Through this disposition toward one's sinfulness and hopelessness, one comes to a realization of the central anthropological principle: "To need God is a human being's highest perfection."[15] It is only from a recognition of this principle that an individual may come to know itself, God, and enter into authentic relationship with both. As Kierkegaard clarifies,

> Just as knowing oneself in one's own nothingness is the condition for knowing God, so knowing God is the condition for the sanctification of a human being by God's assistance and according to his intention. Wherever God is in truth, there he is always creating.[16]

For this reason, as Anti-Climacus makes clear in *The Sickness Unto Death*, Christianity begins "with making every man [sic] a single individual, an individual sinner."[17]

The Crowd and the Present Age

To become the single individual is a harrowing experience as one is ultimately led to the recognition of oneself as the worst of all sinners.[18] It is perhaps not surprising, therefore, that people should do everything to try and avoid it. And the antidote for individuality is "the crowd." According to Kierkegaard, his suffering at the hands of the Corsair, and the revolution of 1848, were achieved through the creation and use of the crowd, and it is hard to overstate his antagonism toward it. As he makes clear, "The crowd is untruth."[19] For in the crowd, the individual, the sole recipient of God's forgiveness, grace, and mercy, is excluded. It is well known that Kierkegaard desired to have as his epitaph, "The Single Individual."[20] However, Kierkegaard soon extended it to include the surtitle, "The daily press is the state's disaster, the crowd the world's evil."[21] But what are the contours of the crowd according to Kierkegaard?

The Foundation of Fear

No motivation is perhaps greater than a fear of the self. As Kierkegaard describes in *The Sickness Unto Death*, in the face of one's identity as spirit, many people choose to lose themselves in immediacy, away from the prying eyes of eternity and the requirement of confession. The easiest way to do this is to "absorb oneself in secular

---

15. Kierkegaard, *Eighteen Upbuilding Discourses*, 303.
16. Ibid., 325.
17. Kierkegaard, *Sickness Unto Death*, 122.
18. Kierkegaard, *Three Discourses*, 40.
19. Kierkegaard, *Point of View*, 106, 108. In his journals, Kierkegaard originally designated the crowd "evil" (*JP*, 2932 [VIII1 A 656 n.d., 1847–48]).
20. Kierkegaard, *Point of View*, 118; *JP*, 2004 (VIII1 A 482 n.d., 1847).
21. Kierkegaard, *Journals and Papers*, 2154 (IX A 282 n.d., 1848).

matters," surround oneself with "the others," and find security in social homogeneity. Such a person is one who "forgets himself, forgets his name divinely understood."[22] The crowd provides the perfect environment, for here there is neither ultimate responsibility nor conscience.[23] The mob considers its actions to be right because it has the weight of numbers on its side.[24] And even if the crowd were to commit some heinous act, no one feels guilt as no one need take responsibility.[25] A crowd cannot be judged—only individuals.[26] Quite apart from producing internal scrutiny or soul searching, people are allowed to simply "evaporate into the anonymity of the abstract public."[27] Indeed, as Kierkegaard states, the crowd really isn't anything but an abstraction or phantom.[28]

However, it is not just fear of the self that drives someone into the crowd, but also fear of the crowd itself.[29] Kierkegaard offers his most comprehensive description of the crowd in *A Literary Review*, where he defines it as the greatest embodiment of the "present age."[30] In contrast to a truly revolutionary age that can perceive and commit to an idea, the present age exists dialectically. On the one hand it needs to appear to be revolutionary, passionate, bold, and decisive in order to maintain the illusion of seriousness. It therefore needs the *concept* of the extraordinary.[31] However, on the other hand, it must destroy its actual embodiment in order to avoid the disruption and conviction that such a concept would necessarily entail. Consequently, the present age levels everything out to avoid the distinction and contradiction that undermines its essential status quo. The crowd, therefore, rejects and annihilates anything that undermines its homogeneity and mediocrity.

The crowd is therefore like a criminal protection racket. While it may offer some semblance of peace and protection, one cannot walk away without facing the

---

22. Kierkegaard, *Sickness Unto Death*, 33–34.

23. Kierkegaard, *Point of View*, 107; *JP*, 2955 (X3 A 105 n.d., 1851).

24. Howard Johnson comments that in such a period, "statistics will replace ethics." Cf. Johnson, "Kierkegaard and Politics," 76.

25. Kierkegaard, *Point of View*, 106–7.

26. Kierkegaard, *Without Authority*, 76.

27. Cutting, "Levels," 78.

28. Kierkegaard, *Literary Review*, 81–82.

29. A central element of the fear of self and crowd is envy—a topic that is important but cannot be elaborated on here. For more on envy, see Perkins, "Envy"; Elrod, *Kierkegaard and Christendom*, 108–14; Kylliäinen, "Envy."

30. Space does not allow a full engagement with the nuances of the crowd described in *LR*. For a more comprehensive presentation, see Westphal, "Kierkegaard's Sociology."

31. Unlike the revolutionary age, the present age is "*sensible, reflective, dispassionate, eruptive in its fleeting enthusiasms and prudently indolent in its relaxation*" (Kierkegaard, *Literary Review*, 60). It is an age defined not by passionate engagement, but by "eruptive enthusiasm" and "apathetic indolence" (ibid., 65)—what Kierkegaard had previously referred to in 1835 as a "bustling busyness," "a fitful fumbling," and a "restless rambling" (Kierkegaard, *Early Polemical Writings*, 48).

consequences.[32] The journey to becoming the single individual, therefore, does not simply require overcoming a fear of the self, but equally that of the crowd against which one must stand in all distinctiveness. The easiest move, therefore, is to "mortgage oneself to the crowd"[33]—to give in to the age whose gifts include not simply an easy, secure life, free from conscience and existential responsibility[34] and emboldened by anonymity, but also a means through which one's own personal fear can be channeled and distracted.[35] It is not surprising, therefore, that almost everyone chooses the crowd, and one finds the profound "massification of society," to use Westphal's evocative phrase.[36]

From the Individual to Community

Kierkegaard's authorship is clearly committed to drawing the individual out of the sociological category, "the crowd." However, despite this overwhelming emphasis, Kierkegaard does on occasion turn his mind to a further category, "the community."[37] As he describes at the turn of 1849,

> And insofar as there is the religious "community" or "congregation," this is a concept which lies on the other side of "the single individual"; "the single individual" must have intervened with ethical decisiveness as the middle term in order to make sure that "community" and "congregation" are not taken in vain as synonymous with public, the crowd etc.; and the familiar fact must still be kept in mind that it is not the single individual's relationship to the community or congregation which determines his relationship to God, but his relationship to God which determines his relationship to the congregation. Then too, there is—this should be included—the highest relationship of all, in which "the single individual" is absolutely higher than "congregation." . . . Consequently, from a religious point of view, there is only the single individual (in contrast to "public," "crowd," etc., which have their validity politically).[38]

This passage is clearly provocative toward our goal. It makes clear that in some way the congregation or community becomes a viable option after the person has

---

32. Kierkegaard, *Literary Review*, 72; Kierkegaard, *Journals and Papers*, 2986 (XI2 A 88 n.d., 1854).

33. Kierkegaard, *Sickness Unto Death*, 35.

34. Kierkegaard, *Point of View*, 107.

35. Kierkegaard, *Journals and Papers*, 2986 (XI2 A 88 n.d., 1854).

36. Westphal, "Kierkegaard's Sociology," 134.

37. This essay agrees with Michael Plekon's summary that "[Kierkegaard's] affirmative theology was restrained, even submerged, in both published writings and unpublished journals. Yet it was never repudiated, nor was it ever completely concealed. Kierkegaard's strategy of understatement may have worked too well. We have heard only the side he put first and very strongly" (Plekon, "Kierkegaard the Theologian," 12–13).

38. Kierkegaard, *Journals and Papers*, 595 (X5 B 245 n.d., 1849–50).

become the single individual, and in such a way that their identity as the single individual remains intact. However, the above passage also raises two questions. First, what is the precise identity of this authentic community? It is clearly distinguished from the crowd, which is described as having only political validity. And yet in the same sentence Kierkegaard states that it is only the single individual that is perceivable from the religious point of view. Which domain, therefore, does the authentic community fit into—the religious or political? Second, if the community does not simply fall between these sociological cracks, does Kierkegaard do enough to substantiate it as a real community? We are not talking here of anything so grand as the body of Christ, but for this group to be a community it must be *some kind* of body.

In order to address these two points, and so to establish whether Kierkegaard does have a legitimate concept of community, this essay will take the following definition as its measure: a valid community is that which exists between two or more people in the service of the individual and is on some level constitutive of the individual. A community is not established simply through the impact of the individual upon others—the duty to love one's neighbor, for instance, does not do enough in this respect. Rather, it is only when there is mutuality and reciprocity in the service of the eternal that a community may be said to exist—that is, when individuals not only aid others in their identity as individuals, but require the aid of others in their own journey to individuality. This is a base line from which community must be built, as without such a foundation it has neither purpose nor essence, either as a means to an end or an end in itself.[39]

To begin our analysis, we will start with a concept that bookends Kierkegaard's first authorship, and which is sadly often overlooked—the concept of the "life-view." Here we will find not simply the heart of Kierkegaard's theory of aesthetics, but also the importance of the human other as a communicator of the religious.

Life-View and the *Re-spiratio* of Knowledge

One of Kierkegaard's very first forays into the public eye came at the expense of Hans Christian Anderson. Despite his reputation as a master storyteller and satirist, in *From the Papers of One Still Living*, published 1838, Kierkegaard argued that Andersen simply projected his own ideology through his stories and lacked a "life-gymnastic," "world-view," or "life-view." For Kierkegaard, a "life-view" is not a creation of speculation and sagacity. Rather, it is gained through the combining of immediate, sensory experience with the reflection of one's past, to weave a tapestry of understanding

---

[39]. It is noticeable that in some defenses of a Kierkegaardian community, the aim is indeed to find "genuine interpersonal relationships," yet a precise definition of what this must necessarily entail is ignored (cf. Cutting, "Levels"; Tilley, "Role of Others"). When seeking an authentic understanding of community, it is important that it is not simply assumed to exist through the giving actions of the individual, but rather only through a form of reciprocity.

from which "an unshakeable certainty in oneself won from all experience" is gained.[40] As such, for one who

> does not allow his life to fizzle out too much but seeks as far as possible to lead its single expressions back to himself again, there must necessarily come a moment in which a strange light spreads over life without one's therefore even remotely needing to have understood all possible particulars, to the progressive understanding of which, however, one now has the key. There must come a moment, I say, when, as Daub observes, life is understood backward through the idea.[41]

Through surveying one's own growing history, one undergoes a "transubstantiation of experience,"[42] which therefore effects one's perception and engagement with the truth. A certain passivity is implied in allowing that "strange light" to illuminate one's life. In Kierkegaard's journals, this is further established as Kierkegaard comments in several places that "all knowing is like breathing, a *re-spiratio*."[43] However, this passivity simply reveals the profoundly active responsibility of making oneself receptive to knowledge. Just as a farmer prepares a field but has no control over the seed's germinating power, so our task is "to do everything in order that [knowledge] can express itself," through opening one's life to its experiences.[44]

Although each individual will have their own unique life-view drawn through their own experience, it remains a window into the single truth that unites existence. Consequently, when an author writes through their own unique life-view, their work speaks with "an evangelistic tinge,"[45] as it presents something both new and familiar. Such writing reflects something of that universal truth that the reader may already know, and yet reveals it through the writer's own unique perspective.

In *A Literary Review*, Kierkegaard draws together many of these thoughts and offers the highest praises for the author of *Two Ages* (the subject of Kierkegaard's review), who he believes has written through a highly developed life-view. Kierkegaard describes such an individual as having been "twice-matured": first by an investment in life and experience, and second by an ability to let this experience work within them.[46] In this way, each story and section of the book is utterly unified by this life-view, and therefore presents a coherent vision of life that has the capacity to "persuade" its reader.[47] Much like the "evangelistic tinge," such writing effects and develops the

---

40. Kierkegaard, *Early Polemical Writings*, 77.
41. Ibid., 78.
42. Ibid., 77.
43. Kierkegaard, *Journals and Papers*, 2258 (*Pap.* II A 302; *JP*, 2267 / *Pap*, II A 524).
44. Ibid., 2274 (*Pap.*, III A 5).
45. Kierkegaard, *Early Polemical Writings*, 66.
46. Kierkegaard, *Literary Review*, 13.
47. Ibid., 16.

reader's own life-view—not with arguments and conviction, but through a presentation from the shared truth of life.

At the heart of Kierkegaard's epistemology, therefore, is the belief that the authentic disposition of the individual toward existence will lead to that single truth or idea breaking in, uncorrupted or prejudiced by our own sagacious desires and projections. At its highest this idea is God. As Kierkegaard describes in *Three Discourses on Imagined Occasions*, "There are not, as in confusion, different roads and different truths and new truths, but there are many roads leading to the one truth and each person walks his own."[48] Regardless, therefore, of the theological intentions of the individual, God reveals himself to those who authentically open themselves to a *re-spiratio* of knowledge. In *A Literary Review*, therefore, Kierkegaard argues that the author's work is not the product of natural talent, but rather "the reward God has bestowed on the author, since, twice matured, he has gained something eternal in a life-view." Through the disposition of "active-passivity," God has ministered to the author, and developed their life-view such that their work is able to guide others, to act similarly in service to God within other people's experience. The religious overtones are made explicit as Kierkegaard describes the work as "a resting place or, if you like, a place of prayer, for a certain religious tinge is unmistakable simply because the life-view is not just common sense but common sense mitigated and refined by persuasive feeling and imagination."[49]

The religious dimension is further understood when we consider that this active-passivity is the foundation for confessional silence in all its pregnancy. It is through this same disposition that the individual comes to know themselves and therefore God. These thoughts are further elaborated in *Eighteen Upbuilding Discourses* where Kierkegaard comments, "through that gradual joining of experience to experience which constitutes a good understanding with God, man learns to know God."[50]

The Life-View and the Dialectical Resilience of Community

At the start of *A Literary Review*, Kierkegaard therefore uses the concept of the life-view and its notion of epistemological respiration to show that within the aesthetic dynamic, those with authentic life-views should influence each other religiously and draw each other toward a shared truth or idea. Near the end of *A Literary Review*, Kierkegaard elaborates on how this dynamic acts as a foundation for the possibility of genuine interpersonal relationships when he writes,

> When the individuals (severally) relate to the same idea, that relation is perfect and normal. The relation singles out individually (each has himself to

---

48. Kierkegaard, *Three Discourses*, 38.
49. Kierkegaard, *Literary Review*, 18.
50. Kierkegaard, *Edifying Discourses*, 170; Kierkegaard, *Three Discourses*, 18–19.

himself) and unites ideally. In the essential inward directedness there is that modern reticence between man and man that prevents crude assumption.... Thus individuals never come too close to one another in the brute sense, just because they are united at an ideal distance. The unanimity of the singled out is the band playing well-orchestrated music together.[51]

This position is developed and clarified in a journal entry from 1850, bearing the title, "The Difference between 'the Crowd,' 'the Public'—and Community":

> In the "public" and the like the single individual is nothing; there is no individual.... In community, the single individual is; the single individual is dialectically decisive as the presupposition for forming community, and in community the single individual is qualitatively something essential and can at any moment become higher than "community," specifically, as soon as "the others" fall away from the idea. The cohesiveness of community comes from each one's being a single individual, and then the idea; the connectedness of a public or rather its disconnectedness consists of the numerical character of everything. Every single individual in community guarantees the community; the public is a chimera. In community the single individual is a microcosm who qualitatively reproduces the cosmos.... "Community" is certainly more than a sum, but yet it is truly a sum of ones; the public is nonsense—a sum of negative ones, of ones who are not ones, who become ones through the sum instead of the sum becoming a sum of the ones.[52]

For Kierkegaard, the possibility of genuine community begins with the concept of the idea. The idea can be anything. But to be effective it must be able to induce passion and so inwardness, which, at least to some degree, creates individuality. In contrast to the present age, for instance, the revolutionary age may be wild and untamed, but it does at least for Kierkegaard produce those who create themselves existentially through a passionate commitment to political change. Interpersonal relationships, therefore, are created between people who are committed to the same idea. The idea stands as a "middle term" between them. It unites them through mutual appreciation, but equally separates them individually as the idea remains the central subject of their passion. It acts as a mediator such that individuals relate to one another only indirectly. As such, each individual finds their passion fulfilled in the idea and not in each other.

However, the quality of the idea will affect its ability to induce passion, and to preserve this dialectic. In addition to his description of community, therefore, Kierkegaard adds the stern warning that there is always a danger that a relational dialectical will lose its resilience and so simply morph into the crowd.[53] If one considers

---

51. Kierkegaard, *Literary Review*, 55.
52. Kierkegaard, *Journals and Papers*, 2952 (X2 A 390 n.d., 1850).
53. Kierkegaard, *Literary Review*, 69.

revolutionary movements, for instance, they may start with each person committed to the specific cause for which they are fighting, and so bound together only through this middle term. But when the great victory is not readily apparent, or circumstances change, the movement may simply morph into the relationally abusive regime they sought to overthrow in the first place.

However, when the idea is God, passion and inwardness reach their highest potential as there can be no greater pathos for the individual than the eternal, and its identity and our relation to it never changes. Although Kierkegaard believes that other ideas can have varying degrees of resilience, it is clear that when the idea is God, there is a qualitative difference. As Kierkegaard comments at the turn of 1847, "The truth can neither be communicated or received without the help of God, without God as accomplice, the middle term, since he is the truth. Therefore it can be communicated and received only by "the single individual.""[54] But why is this so? Why is the individual required as the means of God's communication? To understand this statement, a further dynamic of the life-view needs elaboration.

If we turn again to the esteemed writer in *A Literary Review*, Kierkegaard argues that when someone, through inwardness, writes as an individual out of an authentic life-view, they themselves fall into the background. What is left with the reader is the communication, not the communicator. When considering an address, Kierkegaard writes,

> If you have listened properly to a sermon brim-full of inwardness, even if your gaze has been fixed on the pastor, you will find it impossible to describe the pastor's appearance. . . . Outwardness, on the other hand, forces itself upon one, making it impossible to forget because there is nothing to *remember*.[55]

As Kierkegaard elaborates, "Where essential passion is present in inwardness, *the surroundings are forgotten*."[56] In *Upbuilding Discourses in Various Spirits*, Kierkegaard uses the image of the theatre where the prompter whispers to the actor to aid their performance before the audience. In the same way, the voice of the individual other is but a whisper to focus the individual on their self-conscious performance before God.[57] Only individuals can communicate God as only individuals will point away from themselves to bring the other into relationship with themselves before God.

In the crowd, the individual is undermined as each person is bound to protect the status quo and so be focused on the crowd itself. In a genuine community, the individual is created as not only is there a resilient and sustainable idea to which each individual is related as a middle term, but each individual is constantly pointing the other back to that idea. In *Upbuilding Discourses in Various Spirits*, Kierkegaard

---

54. Kierkegaard, *Journals and Papers*, 2932 (VIII1 A 656 n.d., 1847–48).
55. Kierkegaard, *Literary Review*, 30.
56. Ibid., 33.
57. Kierkegaard, *Upbuilding Discourses*, 124–25.

continues his discussion in relation to such earthly responsibilities as marriage, parenthood, and profession and argues that the point is not for the individual to withdraw from these offices,[58] but to understand that when they are conducted rightly the individual is aware that "in this relation you are relating yourself to yourself as a single individual with eternal responsibility."[59] Kierkegaard's point is that such responsibilities can be the means through which we lose ourselves, so when done authentically they become the means through which we come to know and express ourselves as individuals. Kierkegaard's question to each individual is, therefore, whether such relationships are "in conformity with your responsibility as a single individual."[60] Quite apart from separating oneself off from life's responsibilities, such an awareness is intended to "penetrate" life's responsibilities such that it will "support and transfigure and illuminate your conduct in the relationships of life."[61]

It should be noticed that the contribution genuine community makes to the individual is not the imparting of knowledge per se. Such relationships do not provide the content of truth or act as a surrogate for a relationship with God. Rather, the community primarily affects the individual's disposition before and to God. If we recall the impact of a mature writer, their work excites, persuades, and evangelizes the reader in the development of their own life-view, not by teaching them something factually new. These ideas are clarified in *Three Discourses on Imagined Occasions* where Kierkegaard comments,

> But one human being cannot teach another true wonder and true fear. Only when they compress and expand your soul—yours, yes yours, yours alone in the whole world, because you have become alone with the Omnipresent One—only then are they in truth for you.[62]

A knowledge of God can only be received through direct relationship with God. However, the imagery of compressing and expanding is clear in describing how, in a form of spiritual resuscitation, the genuine human relationship helps the individual in breathing God in—as described above, a *re-spiratio*. Through this relationship the individual is therefore brought before God. This is what it means to be in true relationship, when the other is "in truth for you."

---

58. As Kierkegaard comments in 1846, "As in the highest form of religion, the individual is primarily related to God and then to the community, but this primary relation is the highest, yet he does not neglect the second" (Kierkegaard, *Journals and Papers*, 4110 [VII1 A 20 n.d., 1846]).

59. Kierkegaard, *Upbuilding Discourses*, 131, cf. 129.

60. Ibid., 130.

61. Ibid., 137.

62. Kierkegaard, *Three Discourses*, 25.

PART 5: KIERKEGAARD AND THE POLITICS OF COMMUNICATION

Community as Human Necessity?

What is striking about Kierkegaard's vision of community is that it affirms the importance of the differences between individuals for their development. This has already been emphasized by the uniqueness of each person's life-view, and the individual road each person walks to the same truth. For when "truth is subjectivity," it is precisely this subjective element that draws individuals out into new ways of seeing and understanding. In a journal article from 1849 Kierkegaard dismisses the traditional understanding of human community as defined by man and woman and states:

> What is the idea "community"? It is not the association of several people of the same age; it is rather a unity which shows various ages in the most intimate interrelation. Thus: the grandparents, man and wife, children of various ages—this is really community. This is "community" and a beautiful unity, too. Each age has its own eccentric possibility—therefore the different ages provide a corrective for each other. For example, how beneficial the child-adult corrective is, restraining a person from becoming pure spirit or from becoming too serious etc.[63]

This "beautiful unity" is again, we may argue, established in how each member draws the other into their relationship before God through what they effect in that individual. In *Works of Love*, Kierkegaard argues for the primacy of neighbor love over and against erotic love. And this is somewhat confirmed in *The Point of View* where Kierkegaard argues that Christianity creates equality by drawing everyone into relationship as neighbors. However, far from the designation "neighbor" destroying all particularity, what the above discussion reveals is that the neighbor must include the particularity of each individual and, therefore, the uniqueness of their relationship to the individual. Our relationships as children, parents, and lovers are not leveled by neighbor love, but are rather transfigured through the mediation of God, and their particularity allowed to develop the individual uniquely. Community is, therefore, *important* for their spiritual development.

Something of the *necessary* element of community has already been suggested in that it is only the single individual that may communicate God. However, Kierkegaard offers a further justification a year later. When discussing the extremity of the relationship of the individual before God, Kierkegaard argues,

> Right at this point the real meaning of religious sociality is to be found—that is, when the ideality of the God-relationship has become too strong for an individual . . . he must now have another person to discuss it with. From this we see that sociality is not the highest but is really a concession to human weakness. Here, also, is the significance of the idea that God relates himself to the whole race. The idea of the race, of sociality, is then a middle term between

---

63. Kierkegaard, *Journals and Papers*, 4161 (X1 A 369 n.d., 1849).

> God and the single individual.... There is alleviation... in making use of sociality. It is not good for man to be alone, it is said, and therefore woman was given to him for community. But it is true that being alone, literally alone with God, is almost unendurable for a man, is too frightfully strenuous—therefore man needs community. God and man are separated by an infinite qualitative difference; when the relationship becomes too strenuous, the category of community must come between as a middle term.[64]

This entry offers us an illuminating window into Kierkegaard's perception of community. To refer to it as a "concession to human weakness" brings to mind Moses' allowance for divorce in the Old Testament, or rather unfortunate interpretations of 1 Corinthians 7 and Paul's supposed admittance of sex to curb lusts.[65] And yet, despite the use of this begrudging phrase, Kierkegaard still recognizes that it is a requirement of human nature and not something that can be easily cast aside.

One should perhaps here reflect upon Kierkegaard's personal experience. Although his demand for the single individual remains clear and forthright throughout his authorship, it is a concept that stands outside his own experience as he considered that he was not a single individual, and that he had perhaps never met one. However, human relationships were something he considered he knew a lot about. And they were rarely a positive experience, and certainly far from simple. Where Kierkegaard's description of the individual remained static as a somewhat ideal concept, therefore, his description of human relationships remains far less stable and is colored by his own experiences from moment to moment.

Attempting to understand whether Kierkegaard believed that authentic community may be theoretically true, requires seeing through statements that may doubt whether it may be practically possible. When considering human relationships, Kierkegaard was concerned with the resilience of the dialectical relationships described above that separate individuals ideally, and whether they would simply collapse back into the crowd.[66] It may be suggested that sometimes he believed the dialectic could be maintained, and sometimes it could not. In *Practice in Christianity*, for instance, he speaks of it as merely an eschatological possibility.[67] And even in 1846 Kierkegaard had declared that it would be best if the individual spoke exclusively to themselves and

---

64. Kierkegaard, *Journals and Papers*, 1377 (IX A 315 n.d., 1848). Space does not permit this passage to be fully unpacked. Further questions are raised here about what Kierkegaard considered humankind's natural state to be, and whether this "human weakness" was from the beginning. Is, for instance, the creation of Eve a matter of perfection or weakness in Adam for Kierkegaard?

65. Matt 19:8 and 1 Cor 7:2.

66. Even where the middle term is God, it is very clear from Kierkegaard's attacks on Christendom that even the divine can be easily converted into an idea that actively collapses the dialectical tension rather than sustains it. It is in this light that Christ as the paradox maintains its profound importance in undermining our human propensity for this kind of theological sagacity.

67. Kierkegaard, *Practice in Christianity*, 223.

to God.⁶⁸ The above journal entry is therefore illuminating in describing something of this internal tension. Kierkegaard reflects a frustration that human beings cannot ultimately escape each other and live in pure, unadulterated relationship with God. And yet, even in the heart of this frustration, he still recognizes that genuine human community is not just important, but also necessary.

Some Concluding Remarks

Kierkegaard cannot be considered a communitarian thinker per se, and the vision we have described was clearly not at the forefront of Kierkegaard's mind and has had to be teased out somewhat. Drawing the individual out of the crowd was Kierkegaard's task and perhaps, should he have encountered a genuine individual, he might then have had to present something more systematically on this second move into community. And yet, as this essay has shown, the second movement is still present in his work as both important and potentially necessary. Kierkegaard understands that single individuals are those who reject sagacity and speculation for knowledge *re-spiratio*, and who allow an authentic life-view to develop within them. It is from this life-view that they are able to communicate God to others, not specifically through preaching and direct communication, but through the simple expression of their life-view that is revealed throughout their writing, speaking, and form of life. And it is precisely the unique subjectivity of this life-view that proves so evocative and persuasive, and which they find so fruitful in receiving from others. These reciprocal engagements are both important and necessary as each individual becomes bound to each other through the content of their life-views, God as the middle term. Thus far we have therefore answered the first of our questions: what is the nature of the community for Kierkegaard? But what about our second: Does it fall within the religious or political sphere?

The community is clearly different from the crowd, and cannot be considered simply a political entity, according to Kierkegaard's definition at the start. While it may have concern for the earth in terms of the individual's concrete existence, it does not seek to maintain the individual's focus on the earth. It rather develops the individual toward eternity.

However, is it a religious entity? If we understand the religious as defined by God's relationship to something, then we have to answer "No." Although God clearly uses individuals to communicate himself to others, he does not appear to relate to the community qua community. In this respect, we have done nothing to undermine Kierkegaard's statement that "from a religious point of view, there is only the single individual."⁶⁹ And yet neither of these above two points does justice to what we have described. More needs to be said.

68. Kierkegaard, *Point of View*, 106.
69. Kierkegaard, *Journals and Papers*, 595 (X5 B 245).

The point for Kierkegaard is that the community has a kenotic quality to it. Authentic community creates, develops, and sustains the individual by always maintaining the relational dialectic that points away from itself to the middle term, God. Consequently, community never stands in the way of the individual's relationship with God, but evaporates in its communication of God. In some sense, therefore, the community is like the crowd in its identity as a phantom. However, where the crowd disappears as a form of evasion of responsibility, the community disappears *as* its responsibility. The community must, therefore, have some relationship to the religious. However, it is also clear that the community has political relevance in terms of meeting the individual's temporal needs. Even if it is by way of grudging acceptance, Kierkegaard understands that human beings are made for each other and cannot simply exist in exclusive relationship to God. So there is a sense in which, alongside this kenotic ability, the community never ultimately disappears and the individual is to recognize the human others and to be in relationship to them.

Considered in this way, the opposition between the religious and political is redefined and recontextualized. In *Fear and Trembling* Johannes presents us with the evocative image of the Knight of Faith receiving the temporal back again through the eternal. Here we might say that the political is suspended in the religious. However, this does not do justice to the dynamic we have elaborated here. For it is equally the eternal that comes through the temporal, the religious through the political. The difficulty in speaking of this dynamic, we may argue, is due to the context of a sinful world. Eschatologically speaking, the religious and the political may be mutually enforcing, sharing perhaps in the same kenotic qualities that permanently, instantaneously drive individuals from one to the other—our human relationships always evaporating to drive us to God, only for God to drive us back again. To use terminology discussed above, it is to suggest that the religious and political not only "penetrate" each other, but "support and transfigure and illuminate" each other.[70] Indeed, this perhaps draws us closer to Anti-Climacus's definition in *The Sickness Unto Death*, of humankind as spirit as a relation which relates to itself between our polarity as eternal and temporal. And yet, in our sinful state, what is in doubt for Kierkegaard is whether such a redeemed political reality may exist—whether our human relationships can ever drive us kenotically back to God. If it doesn't, then the individual must exist purely in the eternal, which never changes. However, without the mediation of human relationships, the individual comes face to face with the terror of that direct relationship with God that Kierkegaard experienced himself so acutely.

It may be said, therefore, that Kierkegaard does have an understanding of authentic community, at least in principle. However, he leaves us with a question as to its practice. Do such relationships actually exist, or are they now simply an eschatological possibility? Kierkegaard may have given a different answer at different times.[71] If our

---

70. Kierkegaard, *Upbuilding Discourses*, 137.

71. One is reminded here of Kierkegaard's own admissions in 1843 that "if I had had faith I

answer is no, then so be it. We may follow Kierkegaard in his "lonely labyrinth," to use Josiah Thompson's provocative phrase.[72] But if our answer is yes, Kierkegaard provides an extraordinary, subversive, demanding corrective of how our political lives here in temporality must kenotically drive us toward the eternal. And if they don't and the relational dialectic collapses, he offers us his most damning critique.

For some, of course, this concept of community does not do enough, and we are far from a Hauerwasian sect or Bonhoefferian ecclesiology. However, the aim of this essay has been more modest. It has sought to show that Kierkegaard does have an understanding of community that is not simply important for the individual but necessary, and one in which the human other is required in all their reality, particularity, and reciprocity.[73] This does not perhaps rescue Kierkegaard from having failed to grant the community a more ontological existence as opposed to function, but it does go far enough to question such accusations as individualism, acosmism, and moral nihilism that are never far from his door.

Bibliography

Clark, Adam C., and Michael Mawson, eds. *Ontology and Ethics: Bonhoeffer and Contemporary Scholarship*. Eugene, OR: Pickwick, 2013.

Connell, George B, and C. Stephen Evans, eds. *Foundations of Kierkegaard's Vision of Community*. New Jersey: Humanities, 1992.

Cutting, Patricia. "The Levels of Interpersonal Relationships in Kierkegaard's *Two Ages*." In *International Kierkegaard Commentary: Two Ages*, edited by Robert L. Perkins, 73–87. Macon, GA: Mercer University Press, 1984.

Elrod, John. *Kierkegaard and Christendom*. Princeton: Princeton University Press, 1981.

Houe, Paul, et al., eds. *Anthropology and Authority: Essays on Søren Kierkegaard*. Atlanta: Rodopi, 2000.

Johnson, Howard A., and Niels Thulstrup. "Kierkegaard and Politics." In *A Kierkegaard Critique*, edited by Howard A. Johnson et al., 74–84. New York: Harper & Brothers, 1962.

———, eds. *A Kierkegaard Critique*. New York: Harper & Brothers, 1962.

Kierkegaard, Søren. *Early Polemical Writings*. Translated by Julia Watkin. Princeton: Princeton University Press, 1990.

———. *Edifying Discourses: A Selection*. Translated by David F. and Lillian Marvin Swenson. New York: Harper Torchbooks, 1958.

———. *Eighteen Upbuilding Discourses*. Edited and translated by Howard V. Hong and Edna H. Hong. Princeton: Princeton University Press, 1990.

---

would have stayed with Regine," which may suggest a fluctuation as to whether authentic human relationships may exist in service to the eternal. Cf. Kierkegaard, *Journals and Papers*, 5664 (IV B 142 n.d., 1843).

72. Thompson, *Lonely Labyrinth*.

73. The human other is not simply an opportunity for internal reflection or the expression of individuality (cf. Mackey, "Loss of the World," 609–11) but must be a concrete, particular other to which we are submitted.

———. *Journals and Papers*. 7 vols. Translated by Howard V. Hong and Edna H. Hong. Princeton: Princeton University Press, 1967–1978.

———. *A Literary Review*. Translated by Alastair Hannay. London: Penguin, 2001.

———. *The Point of View*. Edited and translated by Howard V. Hong and Edna H. Hong. Princeton: Princeton University Press, 2009.

———. *Practice in Christianity*. Edited and translated by Howard V. Hong and Edna H. Hong. Princeton: Princeton University Press, 1991.

———. *The Sickness Unto Death*. Edited and translated by Howard V. Hong and Edna H. Hong. Princeton: Princeton University Press, 1988.

———. *Three Discourses on Imagined Occasions*. Edited and translated by Howard V. Hong and Edna H. Hong. Princeton: Princeton University Press, 1993.

———. *Upbuilding Discourses in Various Spirits*. Edited and translated by Howard V. Hong and Edna H. Hong. Princeton: Princeton University Press, 2005.

———. *Without Authority*. Edited and translated by Howard V. Hong and Edna H. Hong. Princeton: Princeton University Press, 1997.

Kirkpatrick, Matthew D. *Attacks on Christendom in a World Come of Age: Kierkegaard, Bonhoeffer, and the Question of Religionless Christianity*. Eugene, OR: Wipf and Stock, 2011.

———. "Bonhoeffer, Kierkegaard, and the Teleological Suspension of the Ethical: The Beginning or End of Ethics?" In *Ontology and Ethics: Bonhoeffer and Contemporary Scholarship*, edited by Adam C. Clark et al., 86–101. Eugene, OR: Pickwick, 2013.

Kylliäinan, Janne. "Envy." In *Kierkegaard's Concepts: Envy to Incognito*, edited by Steven M. Emmanuel et al., 1–8. Farnham, UK: Ashgate, 2014.

Mackey, Louis. "The Loss of the World in Kierkegaard's Ethics." In *Review of Metaphysics* 15 (1962) 602–20.

Perkins, Robert L. "Envy as Personal Phenomenon and as Politics." In *International Kierkegaard Commentary*, 107–32.

———, ed. *International Kierkegaard Commentary: Two Ages*. Macon, GA: Mercer University Press, 1984.

Plekon, Michael. "Kierkegaard the Theologian: The Roots of His Theology in *Works of Love*." In *Foundations of Kierkegaard's Vision of Community*, edited by George B. Connell et al., 2–17. Atlantic Highlands, NJ: Humanities, 1992.

Rocca, Ettore. "Søren Kierkegaard and Silence." In *Anthropology and Authority: Essays on Søren Kierkegaard*, edited by Paul Houe et al., 77–83. Atlanta: Rodopi, 2000.

Strawser, Michael. "Gifts of Silence from Kierkegaard and Derrida." *Soundings: An Interdisciplinary Journal* 89 (2006) 55–72.

Thompson, Josiah. *The Lonely Labyrinth: Kierkegaard's Pseudonymous Works*. Carbondale: Southern Illinois University Press, 1967.

Tilley, J. Michael. "Interpersonal Relationships and Community in Kierkegaard's Thought." PhD diss., University of Kentucky, 2008.

———. "The Role of Others in 'On the Occasion of a Confession': From *A Literary* Review to *Works of Love*." In *Kierkegaard Studies Yearbook 2007*, edited by Niels Jørgen Cappelørn et al., 160–76. New York: de Gruyter, 2007.

Westphal, Merold. "Kierkegaard's Sociology." In *International Kierkegaard Commentary: Two Ages*, edited by Robert L. Perkins, 133–54. Macon, GA: Mercer University Press, 1984.

23

Kierkegaard and the Politics of Time

KARA N. SLADE

> At this point we leave Africa, not to mention it again. For it is no historical part of the World; it has no movement or development to exhibit. . . . What we properly understand by Africa, is the Unhistorical, Undeveloped Spirit, still involved in the conditions of mere nature, and which had to be presented here only as on the threshold of the World's History.
>
> —G. W. F. HEGEL[1]

> Too bad that Hegel lacked time; but if one is to dispose of all of world history, how does one get time for the little test as to whether the absolute method, which explains everything, is also able to explain the life of a single human being. In ancient times, one would have smiled at a method that can explain all of world history absolutely but cannot explain a single person even mediocrely.
>
> —SØREN KIERKEGAARD[2]

THE NAMELESS BOY'S FACE smiles up from the page. Dressed in overalls, he sits at a rough-hewn kitchen table, eating vegetables and cornbread with a wide-mouthed grin. When I first saw this image from a postwar issue of *National Geographic* in Amy Laura Hall's *Conceiving Parenthood: American Protestantism and the Spirit of Reproduction*, two thoughts came immediately to mind. The first thought was that it strongly evoked family photos from my father's childhood on a Mississippi farm

---

1. Hegel, *Philosophy of History*, 99.
2. Kierkegaard, *Philosophical Fragments*, 206 (Revision of Pap. V B 14).

during the Great Depression. The second was that my grandmother would have never allowed her son to be photographed in such an undignified manner. Unlike those family pictures of my father in overalls, this image was constructed to convey the idea that this boy is clearly *other*. He is construed as qualitatively different than the image's intended or implied viewers, and as such he can safely be understood as little more than a figure of comic relief. The caption that appeared with it in *National Geographic* reinforced the point: "This Tennessee hill boy's traveling days will come later. Now, with food shortages world-wide, he is better off at home. Most ration tickets went unused among hill folk, for they grew nearly all their own food."[3]

The feature article in which this photo appeared was entitled "America on the Move," and its ostensible subject was the opportunity for travel and domestic convenience afforded by postwar technological and economic progress. The image of the hill boy, placed suggestively alongside a clearly racist photo of a black "Deep South Farm Urchin" eating watermelon, was contrasted with pictures of smiling families boarding passenger aircraft, boxcars carrying consumer goods to market, and children vacationing on the Lake Michigan shore. As Hall writes,

> In the middle of the photographic feature, a two-page spread signals the difference between families who are "on the move" and those who are not. . . . In the commerce of limitless horizons, this boy is out of luck. His community, the "hill folk," was outside the realm of ration tickets, and now is outside the realm of an "America on the move." . . . The Americans "on the move" were "on the move" precisely inasmuch as they were able to distinguish and distance themselves and their own progressing children from children like these.[4]

I became keenly aware that my own story, as the daughter of rural parents who rode the tide of New South prosperity from Depression-era uncertainty to postwar optimism and professional careers, was also enmeshed in this narrative of backwardness and progress.

Such was my introduction to the politics of time, specifically to the notion that the rhetoric of progress and backwardness is a political maneuver rather than a description of the natural order of things. At the heart of this political tactic is a tendency to arrange oneself and one's neighbors on a temporal trajectory, distinguishing one's own contemporaneity from the ostensible primitivity of particular neighbors. This brief chapter is an exploration of that theme, as well as of the role that the work of Kierkegaard can play in reorienting not just our thought but our selves toward contemporaneity with Christ and with our neighbors.

This is not merely a matter of theoretical or of historical interest. The politics of temporal separation and distancing that marked the postwar *National Geographic* feature persist into our present day, in venues that range from well-funded projects in

---

3. Hall, *Conceiving Parenthood*, 317.
4. Ibid., 315.

scientific anthropology to the language of popular political discourse. Using the theoretical insights of anthropologist Johannes Fabian among others, I hope to show how the politics of time are, at a fundamental level, a problem of soteriology. The question that lies underneath the impulse to arrange one's neighbors along a temporal continuum is the question: "Who saves, and by what means?" A reading of Kierkegaard, specifically of *Either/Or II* and *Philosophical Fragments*, may be helpful in elucidating these matters of time and salvation. In addition, and perhaps most importantly, it reminds us that underlying all politics is the inconvenient and persistent question of the neighbor who calls into question our own works of love.

Running Out of Time at the End of History

Far from being an unfortunate artifact of history, the tendency to arrange human beings on a temporal trajectory of progress and atavism persists into the present day. An example from the world of biological anthropology may be helpful in understanding the pervasive presence of this intellectual maneuver. In 1991, an article in the journal *Genomics* heralded the beginnings of what would later be called the Human Genome Diversity Project. The original paper, by Anne Bowcock and Luca Cavalli-Sforza, was entitled "The Study of Variation in the Human Genome" and promised that through the genetic study of "isolated" indigenous populations would reveal "our evolutionary history" as human beings.

> A number of populations of considerable interest are rapidly disappearing. Large geographic areas are being exploited and developed, changing rapidly and irreversibly the aboriginal populations that still survive in every continent. The loss of traditional lifestyles destroys established communities, and their diaspora makes it practically impossible to sample them. It is only from the knowledge of the gene pools of these populations that we can hope to reconstruct the history of the human past. Humans are an endangered species from the point of view of genetic history.[5]

Much to the surprise of Cavalli-Sforza and other leaders of the HGDP, the indigenous subjects of this genetic research objected to being treated as a biological repository of human history. As Jenny Reardon describes in her history of the racial politics of the project, indigenous activists first voiced these concerns in an online forum:

> The Project's focus on preservation, and its use of terms like "Isolates of Historical Interest," demonstrated a preoccupation with the past rather than the future. This focus represented indigenous groups as objects of historical interest that were about to go extinct as opposed to "fully human communities with full human rights"—a stance they described as particularly egregious in 1993, the U.N.-decreed year of indigenous peoples. In short, by redescribing

5. Ibid., 495.

indigenous groups as "vanishing," the Project threatened to once again reduce them to objects of mere scientific interest.[6]

Here, the politics of time function to reduce or eliminate the political agency of those who are marked as variously behind the trajectory of human development. The extent to which such communities are marked as belonging to the past rather than the present is also the extent to which their status as "fully human" is called into question.

This project, and the sense of urgency that accompanied it, can perhaps be best understood as at least in part a product of its own location, both in the geographical and the historical sense. The HGDP emerged in the heady days of the early 1990s, two years after the fall of the Berlin Wall. At that time, Francis Fukuyama had declared that the "End of History" foreseen by Hegel had been achieved in the demise of the USSR and the apparent universal triumph of Western liberal democracy. For Fukuyama, the "triumph of the West, of the Western idea" had been proven by the "total exhaustion of viable systematic alternatives to Western liberalism."[7] As he explains,

> What we may be witnessing is not just the end of the Cold War, or the passing of a particular period of postwar history, but the end of history as such: that is, the end point of mankind's ideological evolution and the universalization of Western liberal democracy as the final form of human government. This is not to say that there will no longer be events to fill the pages of Foreign Affairs' yearly summaries of international relations, for the victory of liberalism has occurred primarily in the realm of ideas or consciousness and is as yet incomplete in the real or material world. But there are powerful reasons for believing that it is the ideal that will govern the material world in the long run.[8]

The task of completing the evolutionary history of human biology can perhaps best be understood as a product of the peculiar cultural moment of the post-Cold War period. The HGDP scientists' sense of urgency was intensified by the sense that Western democratic cosmopolitanism would soon engulf even the most isolated of communities and lead to genetic intermingling. If the end of history was indeed upon us, then the story of that history needed to be filled in before it was too late. And this self-assigned task would be carried out in a way that treated indigenous people not as political contemporaries but as biological raw material, ultimately intended for intellectual consumption.

The History of Man and the History of Salvation

How did this intellectual and political maneuver become so prevalent? One particularly helpful guide to the temporal characteristics of modernity is Johannes Fabian's

6. Reardon, *Race to the Finish*, 105.
7. Fukuyama, "End of History?," 3–18.
8. Ibid.

Time and the Other. In this text, which deals primarily with the problem of time within anthropology, Fabian describes a modern shift that entails both temporal and geographic processes that are deeply tied to secularization. Previously, he argues, time was negotiated in terms of a sacred history, and the determinative temporal framework was the history of salvation based in the specificity and particularity of the incarnation. Modernity, for Fabian, enacts a continual process of secularizing time by not just linearizing, but also by generalizing and universalizing it. He also notes the connection of time and space, as time becomes related to travel in a new way:

> In the Christian tradition, the Savior's and the saints' passages on earth had been perceived as constituent events of a sacred history. To be sure, this had occasioned much travel to foreign parts in the form of pilgrimages, crusades, and missions. But for the established bourgeoisie of the eighteenth century, travel was to become (at least potentially) every man's source of philosophical, secular knowledge. Religious travel had been to the centers of religion, or to the souls to be saved; now, secular travel was from the centers of learning and power to the places where man was to find nothing but himself.[9]

In this form of travel, new people were encountered as a way to write the history of "man." As a result, the temporal was tied to the geographical, and in particular to narratives of exploration and discovery. In the words of the eighteenth-century French explorer the Comte de Lapérouse, "The modern navigators only have one objective when they describe the customs of new peoples: to complete the history of man."[10] This "new science of travel" was inextricably intertwined with "natural-historical projects of observation, collection, and classification."[11]

By linking the temporal and the geographical through these secular, scientific voyages of exploration, the stage would be set for the next shift in anthropological thought. Fabian notes that in the nineteenth century, time became "immanent to," and "coextensive with," the material world or with the idea of "nature."[12] At the same time, relationships between parts of the world were understood as temporal relationships, such that "dispersal in space" indicates "sequence in Time."[13] At the same time as these relationships were presented as objective and universal, however, they reintroduced a covert form of specificity. The histories completed through these scientific voyages, and strikingly repeated in the Human Genome Diversity Project, were part of a particular story of salvation through travel, discovery, and progress that posits some human beings as temporally atavistic or primitive, while others are destined to bring salvation to them:

9. Fabian, *Time and the Other*, 6.
10. Ibid., 8.
11. Ibid.
12. Ibid., 11.
13. Ibid., 12.

> The natural histories of evolutionism reintroduced a kind of specificity of time and place—in fact a history of retroactive salvation—that has its closest counterpart in the Christian-medieval vision contested by the Enlightenment. This was politically all the more reactionary because it pretended to rest on strictly scientific hence universally valued principles. In fact little more had been done than to replace faith in salvation by faith in progress and industry, and the Mediterranean as the hub of history by Victorian England.[14]

Living societies and past cultures were arranged on a continuous temporal slope, in which some were located upstream and others downstream, separated by the temporal rhetoric of "then" and the geographies of "there."[15]

The political tactic of temporal distancing described by Fabian is rooted in what he calls the "denial of coevalness." This is defined as "a persistent and systematic tendency to place the referent(s) of anthropology in a Time other than the present of the producer of anthropological discourse."[16] In the context of exploration and colonialism, this distancing results in what Fabian calls "a kind of political physics," in which "it is impossible for two bodies to occupy the same space at the same time."[17] As the history of colonialism and relations with indigenous peoples tragically reveals, it then becomes logical to either (1) "move or remove the other body," or (2) assign the other body to a different time.[18] In this way, the separation between Western man and the Other as the object of anthropological inquiry as well as political subjugation is maintained.

Foreign and Domestic

The theological politics of our existence in time are not only a matter of dislocating ourselves or our neighbors in time or in space. They are also a matter of looking to the wrong agent of salvation to give us our time, and ourselves, back again. And, it is here that Kierkegaard will enter the conversation. Before turning to his texts, however, one further word of theoretical clarification is in order. By focusing on the interactions of temporality with colonial expansion and exploration, it might be assumed that the politics of time are only a matter of the global, or of the foreign, perspective. The question of saving others by forcibly incorporating them into the Western civilizing project would seem to have little or nothing to do with the intimate politics of middle-class homes within the Western metropole. And yet as we consider how Kierkegaard may be a useful interlocutor as we think about these matters of temporal politics, we

14. Ibid., 17.
15. Ibid., 27.
16. Ibid., 31.
17. Ibid., 29.
18. Ibid.

need to bear in mind there is no clean line of demarcation between the "foreign" and the "domestic," in both senses of the latter word.

Indeed, as Amy Kaplan has noted in her seminal essay "Manifest Domesticity," these two spheres are intimately tied to each other. In fact, the notion of the foreign as the stage upon which politics of grand strategy are enacted is dependent on, and produced by, the concept of the domestic. As Kaplan explains,

> This deconstruction of separate spheres, however, leaves another structural opposition intact: the domestic in intimate opposition to the foreign. In this context domestic has a double meaning that not only links the familial household to the nation but also imagines both in opposition to everything outside the geographic and conceptual border of the home. The earliest meaning of foreign, according to the OED, is "out of doors" or "at a distance from home." Contemporary English speakers refer to national concerns as domestic in explicit or implicit contrast with the foreign. The notion of domestic policy makes sense only in opposition to foreign policy, and uncoupled from the foreign, national issues are never labeled domestic. The idea of foreign policy depends on the sense of the nation as a domestic space imbued with a sense of at-homeness, in contrast to an external world perceived as alien and threatening. Reciprocally, a sense of the foreign is necessary to erect the boundaries that enclose the nation as a home.[19]

Specifically, travel into the geographical spaces marked as foreign depends on a sense of the domestic. A well-ordered home and a well-ordered colonial geography depend upon each other, and, indeed, are produced by each other:

> The border between the domestic and the foreign . . . deconstructs when we think of domesticity not as a static condition but as the process of domestication, which entails conquering and taming the wild, the natural, and the alien. Domestic in this sense is related to the imperial project of civilizing, and the conditions of domesticity often become markers that distinguish civilization from savagery. Through the process of domestication, the home contains within itself those wild or foreign elements that must be tamed: domesticity not only monitors the borders between the civilized and the savage but also regulates traces of the savage within itself.[20]

It can be tempting to assume that political theology is only concerned with events on the large scale, whether the global arena of the machinations of nation-states or the common life of cities. But it is a mistake to draw a boundary around the home as an apolitical zone that does not also participate in the interactions between the political, the soteriological, and the temporal.

---

19. Kaplan, "Manifest Domesticity," 581–82.
20. Ibid., 582.

It is here that we turn to Kierkegaard, and in particular to his unmasking of the pathologies that lurk within the image of domestic bliss put forward in *Either/Or II*, where Judge William gives his account of "The Esthetic Validity of Marriage." There, the self-satisfied middle-class husband describes himself as having produced his own salvation and grounded his own existence in time through his "struggles with time"—struggles in which he emerges victorious through his consuming grasp of the domestic tranquility ensured by his wife.[21] As Judge William puts it, only through marriage can one find the unity between time and eternity and the resolution of recollection and hope:

> [The married man] has not fought with lions and trolls but with the most dangerous enemy, which is time. But now eternity does not come forward, as for the knight, but he has eternity in time, has preserved eternity in time. Therefore only he has been victorious over time, for it may be said of the knight that he has killed time, just as one to whom time has no reality always wishes to kill time, but this is never the right victory. Like a true victor, the married man has not killed time but has rescued and preserved it in all eternity.[22]

Marital love, which he describes as the only form of "true love," has "an utterly different value." It "does its work in time" and in fact has "a completely different idea of time and of repetition."[23]

The judge's married life is for him the means of his salvation, and his God is conveniently reduced to "an eyewitness who does not cramp one's style."[24] In particular, he looks to his wife as the mediator who grounds his existence in time, giving it meaning and coherence:

> If, when I am sitting in my study and time is dragging for me, I slip into the living room, I sit down in a corner, I say not a word for fear of disturbing her in her task, for even though it looks like a game, it is done with a dignity and decorum that inspires respect, and she is far from being what you say Mrs. Hansen is, a top that hums and buzzes around and by its humming and buzzing makes matrimonial music in the living room.[25]

For Judge William, then, "the woman" is the key to the existence of "the man" in time. As he explains with an almost ecstatic fervor:

> Is it a perfection in a woman, this secret rapport she has with time; is it an imperfection? Is it because she has a more earthly creature than the man, or because she has more eternity within her? Please do answer; after all, you

21. Kierkegaard, *Either/Or II*, 134.
22. Ibid., 138.
23. Ibid., 141.
24. Ibid., 56.
25. Ibid., 308.

have a philosophic mind. When I am sitting this way, desolate and lost, and then I watch my wife moving lightly and youthfully around the room, always busy—she always has something to take care of—my eyes involuntarily follow her movements. I participate in everything she is doing, and in the end, I find myself within time again, time has meaning for me again, and the moment hurries along again.[26]

Heretically, Judge William also contends that married life has brought him to a state of self-knowledge, such that "through the individual's intercourse with himself the individual is made pregnant by himself and gives birth to himself."[27] In marriage, Judge William escapes the paradox of time in and through himself, but by means of an assimilative and acquisitive consumption of his wife as the salvific "woman." As what may at first seem to be a detour through *Either/Or* reminds us, colonizing voyages of discovery may not save, but neither does what happens within the contours of self-satisfied married life. The problem of misplaced salvation on the global political stage cannot be solved by turning within the boundaries of the home.

In and Out of Time

While Kierkegaard can tell us much about looking to the wrong place and the wrong people to ground our existence in time, he can also reorient us in the right direction. Writing in *Philosophical Fragments*, he playfully turns and returns to the question of time and of contemporaneity with Christ and, in turn, with the neighbors we are given to see and love through Christ. In *Fragments*, Kierkegaard contrasts Christian existence with what he calls "the Socratic," wherein truth lies within the individual and may be extracted through a process of self-knowledge. Again and again, he returns to the refrain, "if the moment is to have decisive significance," arguing that such a moment is not Socratically self-generated but received as sheer, gratuitous gift.[28]

This moment, which occasions the unity between God and humanity, time and eternity, teacher and learner, occurs not by means of a human ascent (even a divinely-assisted ascent) to a pinnacle of exaltation. Rather, it takes place "by means of a descent," in which God takes on "the form of a servant," not just as a divine means of disguise and concealment, but truly and completely. As he writes,

> For this is the boundlessness of love, that in earnestness and truth and not in jest it wills to be the equal of the beloved, and it is the omnipotence of resolving love to be capable of that of which neither the king nor Socrates was capable, which is why their assumed characters were still a kind of deceit.[29]

26. Ibid., 307.
27. Ibid., 259.
28. Kierkegaard, *Philosophical Fragments*, 28.
29. Ibid., 32.

As he continues, Kierkegaard shows Judge William's tactic of do-it-yourself salvation and maritally grounded temporality for the lie that it is:

> The god's love—if he wants to be a teacher—must not only be an assisting love but a procreative love by which he gives birth to the learner, or, as we have called him, one born again, meaning the transition from "not to be" to "to be." The truth, then, is that the learner owes him everything. But that which makes understanding so difficult is precisely this: that he becomes nothing and yet is not annihilated; that he owes him everything and yet becomes boldly confident; that he understands the truth, but the truth makes him free; that he grasps the guilt of untruth, and then again bold confidence triumphs in the truth. Between one human being and another, to be of assistance is supreme, but to beget is reserved for the god, whose love is procreative, but not that procreative love of which Socrates knew how to speak so beautifully on a festive occasion.[30]

To exist in time, in that decisive moment, is to simultaneously exist in debt to the one who has given us everything, and also with the neighbor whom that one commands us with duty's imperative: "You shall love."[31]

And what of those who, as noted earlier in this chapter, would place themselves in what Denise Ferreira da Silva calls the position of transparency, standing outside of time in order to arrange their neighbors on a temporal trajectory?[32] As Amy Laura Hall and I have noted elsewhere, and as Julia Watkin wrote in her commentary on *Concluding Unscientific Postscript*, the one who steps outside of time, away from the "decisive significance" of the "moment" risks losing her neighbor, herself, and indeed the conditions of possibility of ethical thought and action.[33] Watkin explains:

> Loss of contact with ethics occurs firstly through the thinker's make-believe standpoint in which he or she takes some fantastical God's-eye position outside the universe, that is, outside existence. Since objective thinking, in that it concerns description of the world, has no relation to the individual thinker's personal life, daily life becomes an inconvenient appendage to the great work of System-building (CUP, 1:119, 122–23). Secondly, there is a loss of ethics in the Hegelian-style System because it contains ethics and morality as a necessary process. Yet in a necessary process there can be no freedom and hence no ethics.[34]

The rhetorical tactics of temporal distancing and of the denial of coevalness are not merely an unfortunate artifact of scientific hubris or limited to the histories of colonial

---

30. Ibid., 31.
31. Kierkegaard, *Works of Love*, 24.
32. Silva, *Towards a Global Idea of Race*, 20.
33. Hall and Slade, "Single Individual," 66–82.
34. Watkin, "Boom! The Earth Is Round!," 101.

domination. Rather, they are a symptom of a profound political and moral problem, rooted in the past but all too pervasive in the present.

While a reading of Kierkegaard provides a sharp word *otherwise* to those who would distance themselves in time from their neighbors, its political implications extend far beyond the anthropological or the philosophical realms. The problem that Kierkegaard diagnoses is not only a problem of thought or scholarship, but also of political speech on the most mundane of levels. Indeed, the aforementioned temporal maneuvers can also be found in the popular rhetoric that surrounds political debate, especially in some of the lazier pronouncements that emerge from within Western liberalism itself.

One example of this rhetoric could be seen recently in my own home state of North Carolina. Reacting to a nondiscrimination ordinance in the city of Charlotte, in 2106, the state legislature passed House Bill 2, which mandated that "public agencies shall require every multiple occupancy bathroom or changing facility to be designated for and only used by persons based on their biological sex."[35] Ostensibly concerned with the growing visibility of the transgender community both in North Carolina and nationally, HB2 was in reality a law with broad consequences for labor—both in terms of minimum wage laws and protections against many forms of discrimination.

However, much of the opposition to HB2 took on a predictable temporal character. As one popular Internet meme put it, "Welcome to North Carolina. Please set your clocks back 50 years." Rather than argue against HB2 on its merits (or the lack thereof), many political activists focused instead on the perceived temporal reversion that it represented, painting it as a step backward into the past and away from contemporaneity. In this form of liberal rhetoric, the *backwardness* of a political position in and of itself functions as self-evident proof of its *wrongness*. The same habits of speech can be seen in debates on topics ranging from drug policy to energy regulation to religious freedom. One political position is posited as representing contemporaneity (or the future), while the other is cast as a temporally retrograde attempt to pull the social body back down the temporal slope toward the position that its proponents are assumed to occupy. And yet as this chapter has suggested, such temporal distancing makes political discernment and debate difficult, if not impossible to achieve. As a way to describe the contours of human life together, political conversation depends on the relationships that only contemporaneity makes possible. And that contemporaneity, in turn, depends on a recognition that no human project is salvific. Thankfully, that job has already been taken.

Bibliography

Bowcock, Anne, and Luca Cavalli-Sforza. "The Study of Variation in the Human Genome." *Genomics* 11 (1991) 491–98.

---

35. General Assembly of North Carolina, Second Extra Session of 2016, House Bill 2.

Fabian, Johannes. *Time and the Other: How Anthropology Makes Its Object.* New York: Columbia University Press, 2002.

Ferreira da Silva, Denise. *Towards a Global Idea of Race.* Minneapolis: University of Minnesota Press, 2007.

Fukuyama, Francis. "The End of History?" *National Interest,* summer 1989, 3–18.

General Assembly of North Carolina. Second Extra Session of 2016. House Bill 2. http://www.ncleg.net/Sessions/2015E2/Bills/House/PDF/H2v1.pdf.

Hall, Amy Laura. *Conceiving Parenthood: American Protestantism and the Spirit of Reproduction.* Grand Rapids: Eerdmans, 2008.

Hall, Amy Laura, and Kara Slade. "The Single Individual in Ordinary Time: Theological Engagements with Sociobiology." *Studies in Christian Ethics* 26 (2013) 66–82.

Hegel, G. W. F. *The Philosophy of History.* Translated by J. Sibree. New York: Wiley, 1906.

Kaplan, Amy. "Manifest Domesticity." *American Literature* 70 (1998) 581–606.

Kierkegaard, Søren. *Either/Or II.* Translated by Howard V. Hong and Edna H. Hong. Princeton: Princeton University Press, 1987.

———. *Philosophical Fragments.* Translated by Howard V. Hong and Edna H. Hong. Princeton: Princeton University Press, 1985.

———. *Works of Love.* Translated by Howard V. Hong and Edna H. Hong. Princeton: Princeton University Press, 1998.

Reardon, Jenny. *Race to the Finish: Identity and Governance in an Age of Genomics.* Princeton: Princeton University Press, 2005.

Watkin, Julia. "Boom! The Earth Is Round! On the Impossibility of an Existential System." In *Concluding Unscientific Postscript to Philosophical Fragments,* edited by Robert L. Perkins, 95–113. International Kierkegaard Commentary 12. Macon, GA: Mercer University Press, 1997.

www.ingramcontent.com/pod-product-compliance
Lightning Source LLC
Chambersburg PA
CBHW081148290426
44108CB00018B/2477